A Guidebook to Virginia's Historical Markers

THIRD EDITION

A Guidebook to Virginia's Historical Markers THIRD EDITION

Compiled by SCOTT DAVID ARNOLD

Published in association with the
VIRGINIA DEPARTMENT OF HISTORIC RESOURCES *by the*

UNIVERSITY OF VIRGINIA PRESS
CHARLOTTESVILLE AND LONDON

University of Virginia Press

© 2007 by the Virginia Department of Historic Resources

All rights reserved

Printed in the United States of America on acid-free paper

First published 2007

9 8 7 6 5 4 3 2

LIBRARY OF CONGRESS CATALOGING-IN-PUBLICATION DATA

Arnold, Scott David, 1970–

A guidebook to Virginia's historical markers / compiled by Scott David Arnold. — 3rd ed.

p.   cm.

Rev. ed. of: Guidebook to Virginia's historical markers / compiled by John Salmon. Rev. and expanded ed. c1994.

Includes indexes.

ISBN-13: 978-0-8139-2572-1 (pbk. : alk. paper)

1. Historical markers—Virginia—Guidebooks.   2. Virginia—Guidebooks.   3. Virginia—History, Local.   I. Salmon, John S., 1948– Guidebook to Virginia's historical markers. II. Virginia. Dept. of Historic Resources.   III. Title.

F227.A76 2007

917.5504′44—dc22

2006015238

The state and region maps were prepared by and appear courtesy of the Virginia Department of Transportation.

Contents

Foreword

IT HAS BEEN more than a dozen years since the last appearance of a new guidebook to Virginia's historical highway markers. This updated and revised edition coincides with the program's 80th anniversary in 2007—a signal year when Virginia and the nation commemorate the 400th anniversary of the founding of Jamestown. We trust this edition is both timely and that it fills a need, as much as did the first guidebook in 1929.

The marker program is the oldest of many managed by the Department of Historic Resources to foster appreciation of Virginia history and historic places. It stands as well in sharp contrast to today's constantly evolving and increasingly complex preservation and educational tools. The program has changed very little, is the very definition of simplicity, and remains enormously popular. Cost notwithstanding, more than 75 individuals, families, and organizations step forward each year to propose new markers and to offer their generous sponsorships.

That this is so reflects Virginians' commitment to the capacity of history to inform and inspire, to foster pride and understanding, and to guide us into the future by casting light on where we have been, the ideas and ideals that have carried us on our shared and different paths, and on the steps and missteps we have taken along the way. As a means to share history, the marker program's very simplicity may tap into something fundamental and universal: a human need to literally mark places of significance.

If sponsors remain proud to raise roadside markers, what of the modern passersby? Do they still enjoy a reciprocal benefit from the marker program in this hurried day and age? That they do, indeed, was made clear a few years ago when the department sought federal grant funds, and appealed for support letters from, among others, members of the general assembly in order to bolster our prospects. We were swamped with responses. The letters from assemblymen and -women were striking and far from the usual politicians' endorsements. We were touched to read their accounts of treasured memories of learning excursions with parents and grandparents organized around highway markers, and of trips today by the same members, now in the driver's seat, with their own children or grandchildren experiencing the journey.

Thus the Department of Historic Resources is pleased to offer this guide-book in honor of the marker sponsors who enrich our roadsides with the lessons of history, and as a companion to all Virginia travelers.

Kathleen S. Kilpatrick

Director, Department of Historic Resources

Acknowledgments

THIS GUIDEBOOK is a result of the combined efforts of numerous individuals and organizations over several years. They include marker sponsors, state and local officials, historical organizations, members of the Virginia Indian community, members of the Board of Historic Resources past and present, editorial committee members who review historical marker texts prior to board submittal, Sewah Studios (the foundry that has cast the markers since the early 1980s), the Virginia Department of Transportation (VDOT), scholars, and, in some manner, every member of the staff of the Department of Historic Resources (DHR). Preparation of this third edition began almost immediately after the previous edition was published.

A number of people were involved with drafting the third edition, which builds on the work of Margaret T. Peters's first edition in 1985 and John S. Salmon's second edition in 1994.

VDOT's Asset Management Division Land Use Section, which erects and maintains the historical markers, provided great assistance in this project. Staff members helped by confirming the locations of many of the markers and taking photos of several of the signs. This allowed a close examination of each one to ensure the texts and locations are accurately portrayed. Julian Aylor, James R. Barrett, Colleen Bolden, Jerome Bowles, Richard Byrum, Larry Curry, Allen Griffith, Brenda Manning, Janice Miles, C. D. "Buddy" Mullins, Dave Sims, David F. Snead Sr., and Dwaine Ware are just a few of the VDOT employees who greatly assisted in this endeavor. Special thanks is also extended to Bryan Kelley, cartography manager at VDOT's Office of Public Affairs, for drawing the maps for this book. The marker program is indebted to all these employees for their fine work.

This book has been further enhanced by the work of former DHR staff member Trent Park. Trent developed a marker database, into which Charese Young entered texts and other information. Also, numerous current DHR staff members—as well as personnel in other state agencies, scholars, the marker editorial committee, and the University of Virginia Press—greatly aided in the research and preparation of the book. These persons include Ann Andrus, Linda Arrington, Sharon Arrington, Edward Ayres, James Barrett, Deanna Beacham, Zak Billmeier, Robert Carter, Jennifer Cavedo, Pam Doak, Keith Egloff, Joanie Evans, Lyndsay Graham, Renita Henderson,

Warren Hofstra, Patty Hurt, Bob Jolley, John Kern, Tom Klatka, Lauranett Lee, Jamie Lewis, Jean McRae, Ann L. Miller, E. Randolph Turner III, and Marc Wagner. A special thanks goes to David Edwards and David Hazzard of the DHR and their contact persons for spending many hours tracking down and providing information about markers that were thought to be missing; Mary MacNeil and Mark Mones at the University of Virginia Press for going the extra mile in helping me with all of my questions and converting the material to the proper format; all the organizations and people who allowed their illustrations and images to be included in the book; and Randy Jones, the DHR's publications manager, for assisting me with the many aspects of getting the book published. Also, I want to thank DHR director, Kathleen S. Kilpatrick, and deputy director, M. Catherine Slusser, for the opportunity to pursue this project. And I thank my wife, Susan, and my son, Ryan, for their patience as I spent many hours away from home compiling the book.

I also thank former marker editorial committee members M. Karen Berkness, Toni Carter, Kathy Harbury, True Luck, and John G. "Jack" Zehmer, as well as current members James Barrett, John W. Braymer, Bryan Green, Gregg Kimball, Emily Salmon, John S. Salmon, and Addison B. "Tad" Thompson. All of them gave me and the program much support through the years.

Finally, I am especially grateful for the great work of development editor Susan Sheppard. She always seemed to be thinking one or two steps ahead as she went beyond the call of duty in assembling and preparing the book for submission.

Introduction

VIRGINIA DEPARTMENT OF HISTORIC RESOURCES: AN OVERVIEW

Virginia's historic landmarks are unparalleled and irreplaceable resources representing the culture and history of America from prehistoric times to the present. The preservation and commemoration of these reminders of our cultural heritage via highway markers and other means is in the interest of all Virginians. The commonwealth has established policies that encourage the preservation, protection, and proper management of our significant historic resources.

Historic properties provide communities with a sense of identity and stability. Preserving these properties contributes significantly to the vitality of today's communities and ensures that the past will remain viable for future generations. The Department of Historic Resources and its seven-member Board of Historic Resources are responsible for oversight of the state's historic preservation programs, including formally recognizing the most significant properties by listing them in the Virginia Landmarks Register. The department traces its roots to 1966 legislation that created the Virginia Historic Landmarks Commission. That legislation formally began the state's efforts toward the identification and preservation of its historic resources. The department also serves as the State Historic Preservation Office in the federal preservation system, and nominates significant properties to the National Register of Historic Places.

The department's director and its advisory Board of Historic Resources are appointed by the governor. The department's professional staff is made up of architects and architectural historians, archaeologists, historians, and archivists. In addition to offices in Richmond, the department has four regional offices throughout the commonwealth. The department is committed to providing public education in the field of historic preservation and offers technical assistance to local governments, preservation groups, and owners of historic properties. It publishes the *Virginia Landmarks Register* (a compilation of listed sites), *Notes on Virginia* (an annual journal of its activities), and occasional monographs on archaeology, preservation planning, and countywide resource surveys.

The department's Board of Historic Resources is also responsible for authorizing new historical highway markers to commemorate important places, people, and events in Virginia history.

History of Virginia's Historical Highway Marker Program

In 1922, the Virginia General Assembly passed an act to create a board "to place suitable monuments or markers on, at, or in places of historical interest in the Commonwealth." Edith Tunis Sale, a prominent architectural historian, served as chairperson of this board. State records are not clear whether the board developed the specific signage system that now exists on the roadways. Also, Richard C. Wight, an amateur historian who was inspired by his interest in the state's history, contacted Governor E. Lee Trinkle (1922–26) and Governor Harry F. Byrd Sr. (1926–30) about developing a marker program.

The program began after the general assembly created the Conservation and Economic Development Commission in 1926. The original intent of the program was to foster interest nationwide in Virginia's history and to encourage tourism through a uniform system of noting historic events. Dr. H. J. Eckenrode was selected by the commission to direct a program to determine the most prominent historic sites and mark them. Notable Virginia historians such as Douglas Southall Freeman, H. R. McIlwaine, and E. G. Swem served on an advisory committee and assisted Eckenrode in selecting topics and writing the texts for the markers. The first signs were erected along U.S. Route 1 between Fredericksburg and Richmond by the end of 1927.

Markers were placed along major roads to reach the largest number of travelers. Each sign was assigned a letter and number code. Initially, the letter referred to a specific roadway, but now the letter more often refers to the region or nearby road location. The original signs were cast in aluminum. Those signs did not weather well, and some were soon replaced with iron markers. Today's markers are made of a stronger aluminum alloy.

Care was taken to place the markers so motorists could easily read them without impeding safe travel. This could prove tricky, as there were no roadside pull-offs next to the early markers. Soon after the first signs appeared, it became apparent that the increase in automobile speeds and the number of motorists on the roads made a guidebook to the inscriptions on the markers a desirable reference. The commonwealth published the *Key to Inscriptions on Virginia Highway Markers* in 1929. Subsequent editions with updated information appeared periodically through 1948.

By 1934, twelve hundred markers were in place, and during this time pull-offs were created so motorists could stop and read the texts at their leisure. By its tenth anniversary a few years later, the program was widely regarded and had been featured in a number of publications, including the *New York Times*. The Virginia program served as a model for a number of

The historical markers that have long dotted Virginia's roadways have undergone subtle changes to their design, as indicated by this period photograph, taken along Route 60 (Meadow Road) in Henrico County near Seven Pines. The top edges reveal two different styles for the markers, and a separate sign for the alphanumeric code appears below each of two similarly shaped markers. (The Library of Virginia)

other states, including North Carolina. It has continued unabated since 1927, except for a brief suspension during World War II.

After the war the marker program resumed in 1946, despite the views of some politicians and historians who believed that almost all the important historical topics in the state had been covered. Although they discussed eliminating the marker program, public support kept it alive during this period, as it did in the 1960s, when the program was once again threatened with termination.

In 1949, responsibility for the erection and maintenance of markers shifted to the Virginia Department of Highways, and in 1950 the Virginia State Library was tasked with researching and approving new markers.

The library continued to manage the marker program until 1966, when it was transferred to the newly created Virginia Historic Landmarks Commission, the predecessor agency for the current Department of Historic Resources, which still manages the program today. The Virginia Department of Transportation retains primary responsibility for installing new markers and maintaining existing ones (though in a few cases, local jurisdictions handle the maintenance of their markers, since they are responsible for maintaining the roadways in their areas).

In 1976, the commonwealth curtailed the funding of markers. Now, private organizations, local governments, and individuals fund them. Between twenty to forty new markers are erected each year. This number does not include markers that have been replaced through federal funding that the

The sponsors and French officials unveil a state historical marker noting the Washington-Rochambeau route in Alexandria during a ceremony in 1998. Ceremonies organized by local officials and marker sponsors are now routine for the unveiling of new signs. (Virginia Department of Historic Resources)

Department of Historic Resources and the Virginia Department of Transportation receive through the Intermodal Surface Transportation Efficiency Act and Transportation Equity Act for the 21st Century. Since 1996, this funding has paid for the replacement of more than four hundred missing, damaged, and outdated markers.

The earliest markers typically focused on Virginia's "great men," colonial buildings, and events of the American Revolution and Civil War, a pattern that continued through most of the next fifty years. In the past twenty years, however, the program has grown to feature the stories of African Americans, Virginia Indians, women, and events of the twentieth century, as well as many other important but previously neglected subjects. This effort to diversify the coverage and content of the marker program has given it new momentum.

Anyone can submit a proposal for a Virginia historical highway marker. Applicants often work with local government officials and historic organizations to sponsor a marker. Each proposed topic is carefully reviewed to determine if it is eligible, and scholars and other historians verify that proposed accounts have been researched from primary and secondary sources. A marker editorial committee comprised of professional historians, editors, and preservation-minded individuals reviews the texts prior to their submittal for consideration by the Board of Historic Resources.

For information about the marker program criteria and application process, contact the Department of Historic Resources, 2801 Kensington Avenue, Richmond, VA 23221 (http://www.dhr.virginia.gov/hiway_markers/hwmarker_info.htm).

How to Use the Guidebook

THIS THIRD EDITION of the historical highway marker book includes nearly nine hundred new and replacement markers that have been installed along the commonwealth's roadways since the 1994 edition. For this edition, the state has been divided into six geographic-cultural regions: Northern Virginia (Region 1); Northern Piedmont, Valley, and Western Mountains (Region 2); Central Virginia and Central Piedmont (Region 3); Eastern Virginia (Region 4); Southern Piedmont and Blue Ridge (Region 5); and Southwest Virginia (Region 6). Each corresponding section of the book features a map of jurisdictions within the region, along with a short introduction.

Within each of the six sections, the marker text entries are divided according to their locations by county or city and arranged alphanumerically by each marker's letter-number code (for example, A-95, B-12). The title of each entry is given, along with the sign's location, based on records at the Virginia Department of Transportation and the Department of Historic Resources.

This new regional format is designed to help with trip planning and to provide an easier approach for visiting a series of markers in a region.

The traveler should be aware that while there are other historical markers that resemble the state's in shape and design, this book includes only official state historical highway markers. The exception are six signs that discuss the Washington-Rochambeau Route. These signs were a special gift from the French government's Committee of the Bicentennial to the Commonwealth of Virginia in 1976.

A number of localities have developed other marker programs approved by the Board of Historic Resources. Contact the Virginia Department of Historic Resources (see page xviii) to learn more about these programs.

Also, this edition does not include the Z marker texts. Historical markers with a "Z" followed by a number at the top are placed at county and state lines. One side of the marker includes facts about the jurisdiction the traveler is entering, and the other includes information about the place the traveler is leaving. A list of these signs and their locations is included in this book. However, the texts have not been included because they vary from sign to sign. (The 1985 and 1994 editions of this book do include the original standard text in the geographical index sections.)

In most cases, official Virginia historical highway markers measure approximately forty-two by forty inches, although the early signs vary in size. The markers are painted silver and are currently cast in aluminum with black letters. Text usually appears on both sides and ranges from a sentence or two to more than a hundred words. Each sign also includes the marker's title and the letter-number code identifying it; the seal of the commonwealth within an upside-down triangle at the top; and, along the bottom, an attribution indicating what state agency approved the sign and when. While the attributions on recent signs read "Department of Historic Resources," earlier markers name predecessor agencies that managed the program, such as the Department of Conservation and Historic Resources, the Virginia Historic Landmarks Commission, the Virginia State Library, and the Conservation and Development Commission.

When the program was created in the late 1920s, the identification code consisted of a letter that usually referenced a specific road (for example, "E" was given to U.S. Route 1 markers) and a number, usually in sequential order, that related the signs as part of a specific letter series. Markers are now assigned a letter code that matches the primary code used in the jurisdiction where a sign is erected. Each new marker is given the next number in the series. In a few cases during the early years of the program, the same letter-number code was accidentally assigned to multiple signs.

The text of each marker has been reproduced here exactly as it appears on the marker face, including spelling and grammatical errors. For the printed texts herein, corrections have been noted in square brackets. Also, the signs reveal different styles of writing and punctuation, depending on when they were created. For instance, older signs in Clarke County drop the "e" at the end of the county's name. The marker texts reveal something of our history, because they reflect the scholarly and social conventions, avail-

COMMONWEALTH OF VIRGINIA

This state map identifies the guidebook's six geographic–cultural regions; marker texts appear accordingly in the pages that follow.

MILES

0 10 25 50

able documentation, and marker procedures and criteria of the eras in which they were produced.

This book includes only the currently displayed marker texts (with the exception of the Z markers and others mentioned above). Previous editions included old marker inscriptions that had been replaced, as well as signs that were no longer situated on the roadways. A few missing or recently damaged signs that have been taken down are listed in the book. In some cases funding is pending, and the sign is expected to be in place by the time of this book's publication. Some markers listed here may disappear over time for various reasons (repairs, destruction, or relocation due to construction). If you fail to locate a marker, if you discover a damaged sign, or if you have questions about a specific marker text, please contact the Virginia Historical Highway Marker Program.

Several indexes appear in this new edition. One is alphabetical by marker title; another is alphanumeric by marker code; and the third covers various subjects. The latter index allows the reader to refer to all markers relevant to a number of areas of interest and includes new listings for African American

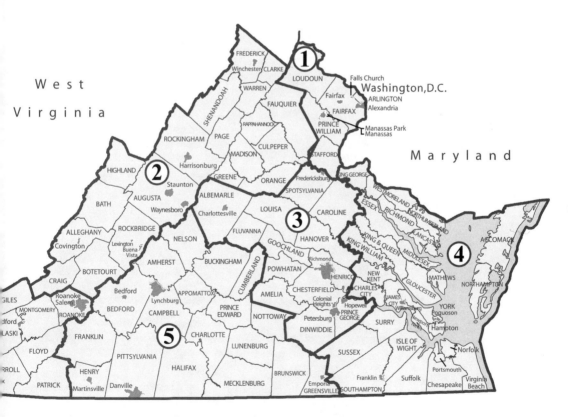

and women's history. Also, the Civil War headings are grouped by the years in which specific events occurred.

For Information

Virginia Department of Historic Resources
Historical Highway Marker Program
2801 Kensington Avenue
Richmond, VA 23221
http://www.dhr.virginia.gov/hiway_markers/hwmarker_info.htm

A Guidebook to Virginia's Historical Markers

THIRD EDITION

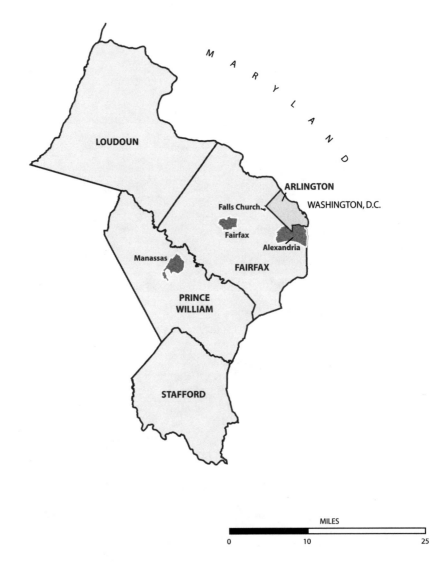

M A R Y L A N D

LOUDOUN

ARLINGTON

Falls Church

WASHINGTON, D.C.

Fairfax

Alexandria

Manassas

FAIRFAX

PRINCE
WILLIAM

STAFFORD

MILES

0   10   25

Northern Virginia

FOR THIS BOOK, northern Virginia comprises the cities of Alexandria, Fairfax, Falls Church, and Manassas, and the counties of Arlington, Fairfax, Loudoun, Prince William, and Stafford. Historical markers attest to the many remarkable events, people, and places that distinguish this region of the commonwealth.

Native Americans, such as the Patawomeck paramount chiefdom, occupied villages and settlements along the Potomac and Occoquan Rivers before the Europeans came. European movement into the area began in the seventeenth century and resulted in intermittent conflicts between the Europeans and Native Americans.

The founding of port towns such as Falmouth in 1727 and Alexandria in 1749 is an example of European development that took place during the eighteenth century. Also during this time, the number of large land holdings in northern Virginia increased, such as the estates of George Washington at Mount Vernon and George Mason at Gunston Hall. Enslaved Africans were used to maintain these properties. Historical markers around the region discuss some of these estates and affiliated communities.

Northern Virginia remained an agriculturally based region well into the nineteenth century. But its pastoral calm was shattered during the Civil War, when it became a major battleground. Roads and rail lines leading from Washington, D.C., to the Shenandoah Valley and other portions of the state made the area strategically significant. Northern Virginia witnessed a number of battles during the war, including those of First and Second Manassas (Bull Run) in 1861 and 1862. Civil War–related markers abound throughout the region, providing brief histories of the people, events, and places involved in that national conflict.

Significant events of the early twentieth century are also documented on markers. Orville Wright, for instance, made the first heavier-than-air flight in Virginia at Fort Myer in Arlington on September 3, 1908. The Wright brothers returned to Fort Myer the following year to showcase their airplane for the U.S. Army, which purchased it. In 1917, women suffragists were imprisoned by the District of Columbia at the Occoquan Workhouse (located at the former Lorton Correctional Complex in Fairfax County) for picketing the White House demanding their right to vote. Their efforts influenced the 1920 ratification of the Nineteenth Amendment to the U.S. Constitution.

Until World War II, northern Virginia remained mostly rural, with a few major cities. However, its proximity to Washington, D.C., and the growth of the federal government spurred development during the postwar years, and today it is a bustling area of sprawling suburbs.

Proximity to the nation's capital also gave northern Virginia a pronounced role during the Cold War. Three historical markers describe the Fairfax, Great Falls, and Lorton Nike antiaircraft missile sites in Fairfax County. These sites and ten other installations in the metropolitan Washington and Baltimore areas were built to protect the capital and the nation against a potential Soviet air attack from the 1950s until the early 1970s.

CITY OF ALEXANDRIA

E-86 HISTORIC ALEXANDRIA

Rte. 7 (King Street), 0.44 miles west of Rte. 1 (Patrick Street). Alexandria was named for the family of John Alexander, a Virginia planter who in 1669 acquired the tract on which the town began. By 1732, the site was known as Hunting Creek Warehouse and in 1749 became Alexandria, thereafter a major 18th-century port. George Washington frequented the town; Robert E. Lee claimed it as his boyhood home. From 1801 to 1847 Alexandria was a part of the District of Columbia, and was later occupied by Federal troops during the Civil War. By the 20th century it had become a major railroad center. In 1946, Alexandria created the third historic district in the United States to protect its 18th-and-19th century buildings.

E-89 ALEXANDRIA ACADEMY

Washington Street (Rte. 400), 0.15 miles south of Rte. 7. On 17 Dec. 1785, George Washington endowed a school here in the recently established Alexandria Academy "for the purpose of educating orphan children." In 1812, an association of free African Americans founded its own school here in space vacated by white students. Young Robert E. Lee attended another school in the Academy from 1818 to 1823, when it closed and the building was sold. During the Civil War the Academy served as a freedman's hospital. Returned to the Alexandria School Board in 1884, the Alexandria Academy was used as a school and administrative facility until 1982. The Historic Alexandria Foundation restored it in 1999.

E-91 LEE'S BOYHOOD HOME

607 Oronoco Street, Rte. 400, 0.48 miles north of Rte. 236 (Duke Street). Robert E. Lee left this home that he loved so well to enter West Point. After Appomattox he returned and climbed the wall to see "if the snowballs were in bloom." George Wash-

ington dined here when it was the home of William Fitzhugh, Lee's kinsman and his wife's grandfather. Lafayette visited here in 1824.

E-92 SITE OF FIRST SYNAGOGUE OF BETH EL HEBREW CONGREGATION

Rte. 400 (Washington Street), 0.72 miles south of Rte. 7. On this site stood Beth El Hebrew Congregation's synagogue, the first structure built as a Jewish house of worship in the Washington metropolitan area. Founded in 1859, Beth El, the first reform Jewish congregation in the Washington area, is northern Virginia's oldest Jewish congregation. Beth El built the synagogue here in 1871 and worshipped in it until 1954. A new synagogue on Seminary Road, Alexandria, was dedicated in 1957.

E-93 LEE-FENDALL HOUSE

614 Oronoco Street, (Route 400), 0.48 miles north of Rte. 236 (Duke Street). "Light Horse Harry" Lee, Revolutionary War officer, owned this land in 1784. The house was built in 1785 by Philip Fendall, a Lee relative. Renovated in 1850 in the Greek Revival style, the house remained in the Lee family until 1903. John L. Lewis, labor leader and president of the United Mine Workers of America and the Congress of Industrial Organizations, was the last resident owner, from 1937 to 1969.

E-106 WASHINGTON-ROCHAMBEAU ROUTE—ALEXANDRIA ENCAMPMENT

Rte. 400 and Oronoco Street, across from 614 Oronoco Street. Most of the American and French armies set sail from three ports in Maryland—Annapolis, Baltimore, and Head of Elk—in mid-Sept. 1781 to besiege the British army in Yorktown. The allied supply-wagon train proceeded overland to Yorktown, its itinerary divided into segments called "Marches." Its "Fourth March" was from Georgetown to Alexandria; the wagons took two days, 24–25

Sept., to cross the Potomac and reunite in Virginia. The Alexandria camp was roughly a half-mile in area, located north of Oronoco Street and bisected by Washington Street. The train left Alexandria on 26 Sept.

E-109 FREEDMEN'S CEMETERY

Rte. 400 (Washington Street), 0.72 miles south of Rte. 7. Federal authorities established a cemetery here for newly freed African Americans during the Civil War. In January 1864, the military governor of Alexandria confiscated for use as a burying ground an abandoned pasture from a family with Confederate sympathies. About 1,700 freed people, including infants and black Union soldiers, were interred here before the last recorded burial in January 1869. Most of the deceased had resided in what is known as Old Town and in nearby rural settlements. Despite mid-twentieth-century construction projects, many burials remain undisturbed. A list of those interred here has also survived.

E-117 JONES POINT

Marker not yet erected. Proposed location to be determined. American Indians first frequented Jones Point to hunt and fish. The point is likely named for an early English settler. By the 1790s, military installations were established at Jones Point due to its strategic location on the Potomac River. The first cornerstone marking the boundary of the District of Columbia was erected on the point in 1791. A ropewalk, a facility for the production of rope, existed here in the 1830s, and a lighthouse was built in 1856 on the peninsula. During World War I the Virginia Shipbuilding Corporation established a shipyard here that employed 7,000 people and built nine freighters.

E-124 ALFRED STREET BAPTIST CHURCH

Rte. 226 (Duke Street) and South Alfred Street, at church. Alfred Street Baptist Church is home to the oldest African American congregation in Alexandria, dating to the early 19th century. It has served as a prominent religious, educational, and cultural institution. In 1818, the congregation, then known as the Colored Baptist Society, began worship services here in the midst of the Bottoms, a free black neighborhood. By 1820 the church created its educational branch, providing religious and secular opportunities for both black children and adults. In 1855, free black craftsmen probably designed and built the brick church. Alterations to the building occurred in the 1880s and in 1994 the church constructed a new sanctuary.

T-44 VIRGINIA THEOLOGICAL SEMINARY—FOUNDED 1823

Rte. 7 (King Street), 0.67 miles east of I-395. Half mile to the southwest. The idea for such an institution was conceived by a group of Alexandria and Washington clergymen in 1818. Among those interested was Francis Scott Key, author of the Star Spangled Banner. Originally at corner of Washington and King Streets in Alexandria, moved to present location in 1827. Closed in 1861 when occupied as a hospital for Union troops. Reopened in 1865.

T-45 EPISCOPAL HIGH SCHOOL

Rte. 7 (King Street), 0.67 miles east of I-395. Episcopal High School, on the hill to the southwest, was founded in 1839 as a boys' preparatory school, one of the first in the South; girls were admitted in 1991. The school was a pioneer in the establishment of student honor codes in preparatory education. In 1861 Union troops occupied the school and used it as a military hospital; the poet Walt Whitman served as a nurse there. Episcopal High School reopened in 1866. The central administration building, now called Hoxton House, was built about 1805 by Elizabeth Parke Custis, a granddaughter of Martha Washington.

ARLINGTON COUNTY

C-1 CLAY AND RANDOLPH DUEL

Rte. 120 (Glebe Road), 0.42 miles east of Rte. 123 (Chain Bridge Road). Although dueling was illegal in Virginia, Secretary of State Henry Clay challenged U.S. Senator John Randolph of Roanoke. Clay called Randolph out to defend his honor after Randolph insulted him in a speech on the Senate floor. Randolph confided to Senator Thomas Hart Benton of Missouri that he had no intention of hurting Clay, who was married and had a child. The duel took place on 8 April 1826 a half mile north at Pimmit Run. Both first shots missed their intended targets. Clay's second shot also missed, and Randolph raised his pistol and fired it in the air. The duel then ended, and the unhurt adversaries met each other halfway and shook hands.

C-2 WORLD'S FIRST PUBLIC PASSENGER FLIGHT

Rte. 50, 1.38 miles east of Rte. 120 (Glebe Road). On September 9, 1908, near this site, Orville Wright carried aloft in public his first passenger, Lt. Frank P. Lahm, for a flight lasting 6 minutes and 24 seconds. Three days later, he took Major George O. Squier on a flight of 9 minutes and 6 seconds duration. From this primitive beginning has evolved an air transportation system that today spans the globe.

C-7 ORVILLE WRIGHT'S FIRST VIRGINIA FLIGHT

Rte. 50, 1.38 miles east of Rte. 120 (Glebe Road). Orville Wright made his first heavier-than-air flight in Virginia at Fort Myer for the U.S. Army on 3 Sept. 1908. He flew the plane slightly more than a minute, reaching a speed of 40 miles per hour. During the next two weeks here, Wright broke world records for speed and time spent in the air for a heavier-than-air craft. On 17 Sept. 1908, however the plane crashed, killing Lt. Thomas Selfridge and injuring Wright. In 1909, the Wright brothers returned to Fort Myer. After additional flight tests, the Army bought their plane for $25,000 on 31 July 1909 for its first military aircraft.

CITY OF FAIRFAX

B-26 MOSBY'S MIDNIGHT RAID

Rte. 123 (Chain Bridge Road), 0.37 miles south of Rte. 236. Col. John Singleton Mosby formed the 43d Battalion Virginia Cavalry "to weaken the armies invading Virginia by harassing their rear." Near midnight on 8 March 1863, he led his horsemen undetected through Union lines to disrupt communications between Dranesville and Alexandria. Without losing a man or firing a shot, Mosby and his Rangers rode into and out of the garrisoned village at Fairfax Court House and captured Union Brig. General Stoughton in his bed, as well as two captains, thirty enlisted men, and fifty-eight horses. It was Mosby's most famous raid.

FAIRFAX COUNTY

B-11 BATTLE OF CHANTILLY (OX HILL)

Rte. 7100, 0.52 miles south of Rte. 50. The Battle of Chantilly (Ox Hill) took place here 1 September, 1862. Union General John Pope's Army, retreating after defeat by Lee at Second Manassas, clashed with Jackson's divisions which were attempting to prevent Pope from reaching Washington. Although Union generals Kearny and Stevens were killed,

Jackson's men were held off by the smaller Union forces. The battle ended the Second Manassas campaign and led to Lee's invasion of Maryland.

B-12 COLONEL JOHN SINGLETON MOSBY

Rte. 50, 0.36 miles west of Rte. 657. This road, along which many of his skirmishes took place, is named for Colonel John Singleton Mosby, commander of the 43rd Battalion of Confederate Partisan Rangers. Their activities in this area helped keep the Confederate cause alive in Northern Virginia toward the end of the Civil War.

B-13 BATTLE OF OX HILL (CHANTILLY)

Rte. 6751, 0.22 miles west of Rte. 608 (West Ox Road). Maj. Gen. Thomas J. "Stonewall" Jackson's wing of the Army of Northern Virginia reached here 1 Sept. 1862. Jackson's march from the battlefield of Second Manassas turned the position of Maj. Gen. John Pope's army at Centreville and threatened the Union line of retreat near Fairfax Court House. Here at Ox Hill, the Confederates encountered Federal troops of the IX and III Corps and a fierce battle was fought amid storm and darkness. Union generals Isaac Stevens and Philip Kearny were killed. Pope retreated to Alexandria and the defenses of Washington. Thus ended the Second Manassas campaign.

B-14 CAMP RUSSELL A. ALGER

Rte. 50, 0.94 miles east of I-495. Named for Secretary of War Russell A. Alger, the camp was established in May 1898 on a 1,400-acre farm called Woodburn Manor. Some 23,500 men trained here for service in the Spanish-American War. The large military population greatly affected the lives of the residents of the small communities of Falls Church and Dunn Loring. The camp was abandoned early in August 1898 after an epidemic of typhoid fever. The War Department began the sale of land in September 1898.

B-29 MARYLAND (ANTIETAM/ SHARPSBURG) CAMPAIGN

Rte. 6751, 0.22 miles west of Rte. 608 (West Ox Road). Following the Battle of Ox Hill (Chantilly) on 1 Sept. 1862, Gen. Robert E. Lee pondered his options and strategy. Encouraged by Confederate victories and Federal disorganization, Lee acted quickly to continue the offensive. On 3 Sept., Lee's Army of Northern Virginia marched north toward Leesburg, from where it could cross into Maryland, flank the Washington fortifications, and draw the Union army out of Virginia. The troops of Maj. Gens. Thomas J. "Stonewall" Jackson and James Longstreet moved north on Ox Road past Frying Pan and Herndon Station to Dranesville. The army concentrated around Leesburg and forded the Potomac into Maryland Sept. 4–7.

BW-2 BURKE'S STATION RAID

Rte. 236, 3.1 miles east of Rtes. 50/29 and 211. Burke's Station, four miles south, was raided by Stuart's cavalry, December, 1862. Stuart telegraphed to Washington complaining of the bad quality of the mules he had captured—a famous joke.

BW-3 BURKE STATION

Rte. 8249, 0.01 miles north of Rte. 652 (Burke Road). Burke Station was raided in December, 1862, by Confederate General J. E. B. Stuart. It was from this site, originally the Burke Station Depot, that he sent his famous telegram to Union Quartermaster General Meigs complaining of the poor quality of the Union mules he had just captured.

BW-4 ORANGE AND ALEXANDRIA RAILROAD

Rte. 1390, 0.35 miles north of Rte. 1155 (Highland Drive), at entrance to Lake Accotink Park. Accotink Park Road lies on the right-of-way of the Orange and Alexandria Railroad, which linked the markets of northern and central Virginia. Construction began in March 1850, and the line was extended to Manassas in 1851 and to Gordonsville in March 1853. The railroad encouraged the growth of Fairfax County and new communities along the way. During the Civil War the line became a strategic prize coveted by both sides, and battles were fought at or near such stops as Manassas Junction, Bristoe Station, and Brandy Station. The Union army seized a large part of the Fairfax section of the railroad and placed it under the control of the U.S. Military Railroad system in 1862.

C-17 MILITARY RAILROAD TERMINUS

Rte. 28, 0.96 miles south of Rte. 29 (Lee Highway). Half a mile west is the terminus of the Centreville Military Railroad, the first railroad in the world constructed exclusively for military purposes. Built by the Confederate army late in 1861 because of impassible roads, it supplied the soldiers in their winter camps at Centreville. Trains from Manassas Junction ran here until March 1862 when Confederate forces withdrew southward. Nearby on 9 Dec. 1862, Privates Michael O'Brien and Dennis Corcoran of Maj. Chatham R. Wheat's "Louisiana Tigers" were court-martialed for mutiny, executed by a firing squad from their own company, and buried. In 1979 their remains were reinterred at St. John's Episcopal Church cemetery in Centreville.

C-18 SULLY PLANTATION

Rte. 28, 0.81 miles north of Rte. 50. The dwelling house at Sully Plantation was built in 1794 by Richard Bland Lee on land that had been patented in 1725. Lee was the first congressman from Northern Virginia and an early member of Phi Beta Kappa. His vote brought the capital city to the banks of the Potomac. Lee was appointed by President Madison as one of three commissioners to superintend the restoration of federal buildings burned by the British in 1814. Born at Leesylvania in Prince William County in 1761, Lee died in Washington in 1827.

C-19 BULL RUN BATTLEFIELDS

Rte. 29 (Lee Highway), 2.97 miles west of Rte. 123. Ten miles west were fought the two battles of Manassas or Bull Run.

C-20 FIRST BATTLE OF MANASSAS

14200 St. Germain Drive, at Fairfax County–Centreville Regional Library. McDowell gathered his forces here, July 18, 1861, to attack Beauregard, who lay west of Bull Run. From here a part of the Union army moved north to cross Bull Run and turn the Confederate left wing, July 21, 1861. This movement brought on the battle.

C-21 CONFEDERATE DEFENSES

14200 St. Germain Drive, at Fairfax County–Centreville Regional Library. Here, while the Confederate army camped at Centreville, Gen. Joseph E. Johnston built strong fortifications in the winter of 1861–1862. In Feb. 1862, President Jefferson Davis ordered Johnston to evacuate them and move his army closer to Richmond, the Confederate capital. Outnumbered by Maj. Gen. George B. McClellan's Army of the Potomac, Johnston complied. On 10 March, McClellan found "Quaker cannon," logs painted black, in the abandoned trenches to deceive his scouts. McClellan, believing that he was outnumbered, already had planned to attack Richmond from the east instead of the north, via the Peninsula between the James and York Rivers.

C-22 SECOND BATTLE OF MANASSAS

14200 St. Germain Drive, at Fairfax County–Centreville Regional Library. Here Pope gathered his forces, August 30–31, 1862. From this point he detached troops to check Jackson at Ox Hill while the Union army retreated to the defenses at Alexandria.

C-23 THE STONE BRIDGE

Rte. 29, 3.61 miles west of Rte. 28. Originally built of native sandstone in 1825, the turnpike bridge over Bull Run became an important landmark in the Civil War battles at Manassas. Union Brig. Gen. Daniel Tyler's division feigned an attack on Col. Nathan G. Evans's brigade guarding the bridge as the First Battle of Manassas began on the morning of 21 July 1861. When the confederates withdrew from the region, they blew up the bridge on 9 Mar. 1862. The rear guard of Maj. Gen. John Pope's retreating army, defeated at the Second Battle of Manassas on 30 Aug. 1862, destroyed a replacement military bridge at the site. Fully reconstructed after the war, it remained in use into the 1920s.

C-25 MOSBY'S ROCK

McNair Farms Road, 0.13 miles north of Rte. 657 (Centreville Road), south of Herndon. This large boulder, located just south of here, served as an important landmark during the Civil War, when Col. John S. Mosby's Partisan Rangers (43d Battalion, Virginia Cavalry) assembled there to raid Union outposts, communications, and supply lines. Laura Ratcliffe, a young woman who lived nearby and spied for Mosby, concealed money and messages for him under the rock. Mosby credited her with saving him from certain capture by Federal cavalry on one occasion. She also was a friend of Maj. Gen. J. E. B. Stuart.

C-40 CAMPAIGN OF SECOND MANASSAS

14200 St. Germain Drive, at Fairfax County–Centreville Regional Library. Seven miles south is Manassas, where Jackson, on his turning movement around Pope, destroyed vast quantities of supplies, August 26–27, 1862. Hill and Ewell of Jackson's force, coming from Manassas, reached Centreville on their way to Jackson's position north of Groveton, August 28, 1862.

C-42 FIRST BATTLE OF MANASSAS— PANIC AT CUB CREEK BRIDGE

Rte. 29 (Lee Highway), 0.91 miles west of I-66. In the afternoon of 21 July 1861, after Gen. Joseph E. Johnston's and Brig. Gen.

P.G.T. Beauregard's Confederates defeated Brig. Gen. Irvin McDowell's Union army, the bridge over Cub Run was jammed with retreating Federal soldiers as well as civilians who had come to watch the battle. Capt. Delaware Kemper's Confederate artillery fired a few parting rounds toward the bridge, and one shell burst directly overhead. The crowd panicked and upset a wagon, thereby blocking the bridge. The mob of civilians and soldiers abandoned carriages, cannons, and caissons, splashed across the stream, and fled on foot to Alexandria.

E-60 BELVOIR

Rte. 1 (Richmond Highway), 3.5 miles south of Rte. 235 (Mt. Vernon Memorial Highway). Belvoir, meaning "beautiful to see," was built about 1741 for William Fairfax, land agent for his cousin Thomas, sixth baron Fairfax of Cameron and Northern Neck proprietor. George Washington was introduced to Belvoir and its gentry culture while in his mid-teens, during stays at Mount Vernon with his half-brother Lawrence, who married William Fairfax's daughter Anne. After the house burned in 1783, Washington wrote to George Fairfax that "the happiest moments of my life had been spent there" at Belvoir. Sept. 1814, British vessels shelled the walls of the house. The U.S. War Department acquired the tract in 1912 for a military camp.

E-61 OCCOQUAN WORKHOUSE

Rte. 123, at county water authority. In the nearby Occoquan Workhouse, from June to December, 1917, scores of women suffragists were imprisoned by the District of Columbia for picketing the White House demanding their right to vote. Their courage and dedication during harsh treatment aroused the nation to hasten the passage and ratification of the 19th Amendment in 1920. The struggle for woman's suffrage had taken 72 years.

E-62 OLD TELEGRAPH LINE

Rte. 1 (Richmond Highway), 1.6 miles south of Rte. 7100 (Fairfax County Parkway). One of the first telegraph lines in the world, a part of the Washington–New Orleans Telegraph Company, was built from Washington to Petersburg in 1847. From this the road took its name.

E-64 FORT BELVOIR

Rte. 1 (Richmond Highway), 3.50 miles south of Rte. 235 (Mt. Vernon Memorial Highway). Fort Belvoir is named for the 18th-century plantation that was owned by William Fairfax. The house burned in 1783. The U.S. War Department acquired much of the Belvoir tract in 1912 as a training center and in 1917 named it Camp A.A. Humphreys for Maj. Gen. Andrew A. Humphreys, a former Chief of Engineers. During World War I the camp was enlarged and the Engineer School moved there. The camp was renamed Fort Humphreys in 1922. In 1935, President Franklin D. Roosevelt changed the name to Fort Belvoir. The Engineer School moved to Fort Leonard Wood, Mo., in 1988.

E-65 GUNSTON HALL

Rte. 242, 0.67 miles east of Rte. 1. Gunston Hall, four miles to the east, is one of the most noted colonial places in Virginia. The land was patented in 1651 by Richard Turney, who was hanged for taking part in Bacon's Rebellion in 1676. In 1696 the second George Mason acquired it. The house was built in 1755–1758 by the fourth George Mason, Revolutionary leader and author of the Virginia Declaration of Rights and the first Constitution of Virginia.

E-66 WOODLAWN

Rte. 235, 0.3 miles south of Rte. 1. Originally part of the Mount Vernon estate, Woodlawn was built in 1800–1805. George Washington gave the plantation, as a wedding gift to Eleanor Parke "Nelly" Curtis and her husband, Lawrence Lewis, respectively Martha Washington's granddaughter and George Washington's nephew. The two were married at Mount Vernon on 22 Feb. 1799, George Washington's last birthday. Designed by Dr. William Thornton, the first architect of the U.S. Capitol, the crisply detailed, beautifully crafted

Women suffragists demanding the right to vote in 1917 were imprisoned at the Occoquan Workhouse (Fairfax County) by District of Columbia police for picketing the White House. (Marker E-61) (Courtesy of the historic National Woman's Party, Sewall-Belmont House and Museum, Washington, D.C.)

George Washington's Mount Vernon is one of the most famous houses in the United States. This illustration shows how the residence looked in the early nineteenth century. (Marker E-68) (Courtesy of the Mount Vernon Ladies' Association)

five-part mansion displays the elegance and refinement so admired in the Federal style. In 1951, Woodlawn became the first historic site of the National Trust for Historic Preservation.

E-67 Doeg Indians

Rte. 235 (Mt. Vernon Memorial Highway), 0.3 miles south of Rte. 1 (Jefferson Davis Highway). A group of Virginia Indians referred to as the Doeg (but also Dogue, Taux, and other names) occupied villages and settlements along the Potomac and Occoquan Rivers by 1607. They included Tauxenent, near the mouth of the Occoquan River, Namasingakent near Mount Vernon and Assaomeck near Alexandria. The Doeg lived a semi-sedentary lifestyle that involved farming and extended hunting and fishing trips. The English forced many of the Doeg out of this region by the late 17th century. Nearby Dogue Creek is named for them.

E-68 Mount Vernon Estate

Rte. 235, 3 miles southeast of Rte. 1. George Washington acquired Mount Vernon in 1754. Over a period of 30 years, he transformed the simple farmhouse into a mansion embellished with rusticated wood siding, a cupola, and a portico overlooking the Potomac River. Every aspect of the estate—its architecture and decoration,

the landscape and the farms—received Washington's careful attention. Despite long absences during the Revolution and his presidency, Washington kept Mount Vernon as his home until his death on 14 December 1799. Since 1858, the Mount Vernon Ladies' Association has maintained and meticulously restored the estate as a true reflection of Washington's character and personality.

E-69 Little Hunting Creek

Parking lot, Riverside Park, George Washington Memorial Parkway. The Washington family land south of here, named Mount Vernon in the 1740s, was part of a grant made in 1677 by the Northern Neck proprietors to Col. Nicholas Spencer and Lt. Col. John Washington, George Washington's great-grandfather. John Washington's son Lawrence Washington, took possession of the eastern half of the grant on Little Hunting Creek. George Washington inherited it in 1761. Across Little Hunting Creek, the Brent family also was granted land in the 17th century. Margaret Brent, secretary to Lord Baltimore, is regarded as the first woman in the British colonies to demand the right to vote.

E-70 Colonial Fort

George Washington Memorial Parkway, 0.1 miles north of Rte. 1322 (Belle Haven Road).

Nearby at John Mathews's land on Hunting Creek, Governor William Berkeley constructed a fort authorized by the Virginia House of Burgesses on 21 Sept. 1674. Militiamen from Lancaster, Middlesex, and Northumberland Counties garrisoned the fort under command of Capt. Peter Knight. The fort defended the northern frontier of the colony against the Susquehannocks and other Indian groups. Berkeley planned for it and other forts to serve as buffers and thereby enable the English and Indians to coexist peacefully. Some colonists, especially those led by Nathaniel Bacon, favored a more aggressive approach. As a result, Bacon's Rebellion erupted in 1675–1676.

E-71 LEWIS CHAPEL/CRANFORD MEMORIAL METHODIST CHURCH

Rte. 242, 0.67 miles east of Rte. 1. This church is a combination of several structures built on the site of the first Pohick Church (1730–1774), making this one of the earliest sites of a religious institution in Fairfax County. Lewis Chapel, named after a Methodist Circuit rider, was built in 1857 and moved from a site nearby in 1952. Cranford Memorial, the main portion of the complex, was constructed in 1900.

E-72 POHICK CHURCH

Rte. 1 (Richmond Highway), 1.6 miles south of Rte. 7100 (Fairfax County Parkway). This building was begun in 1769 and completed by 1774, succeeding an earlier church two miles to the south. It was the lower church of Truro Parish, established in 1732, the parish of Mount Vernon and Gunston Hall. George William Fairfax, George Washington and George Mason, vestrymen, were members of the building committee under which the church was constructed.

E-73 GEORGE WASHINGTON'S GRISTMILL

Rte. 235, 0.3 miles south of Rte. 1 (Richmond Highway). In 1771, George Washington replaced a deteriorated gristmill that his father, Augustine, may have erected as

early as the 1730s. The new mill ground grain from Mount Vernon and neighboring farms, and was outfitted with two pairs of millstones. In 1791, Washington installed improvements that had been recently developed and patented by Oliver Evans, of Delaware. Other structures at the site included a stone whiskey distillery, a malthouse, a cooperage, a miller's cottage, and slave quarters. Washington's mill was razed around 1850, and in 1933 the Commonwealth of Virginia built a reconstruction on the original site.

E-80 INDIAN ATTACK

Rte. 242 (Gunston Highway), 0.67 miles east of Rte. 1 (Richmond Highway). To the east, on Dogue Neck, "Certain Unknown Indians" attacked the house of Thomas Barton about 3:00 P.M. on Sunday, 16 June 1700, killing eight persons with "arrowes & Wooden Tommahawkes." The neighboring Piscataway Indians denied making the attack and blamed the Wittowees. The Indians involved probably were angered by colonial encroachment on their land and may have been encouraged by the French. Lt. Col. George Mason wrote Gov. Francis Nicholson that "this murder was the Horrablest that ever was" in present-day Fairfax Co., then part of Stafford Co. Mason increased the number of militia patrols, but the Indians escaped.

E-81 DEFENSES OF WASHINGTON

Rte. 1 (Richmond Highway), 1.32 miles south of Fairfax County/Alexandria city line. During the Civil War, the U.S. Army constructed a series of forts and artillery batteries around Washington to protect it from Confederate attack. Forts O'Rourke, Weed, Farnsworth, and Lyon stood just to the north, and Fort Willard, which still exists, to the east. These fortifications constituted the extreme southern defense line of the city. By war's end, a line of 163 forts and batteries extended about 37 miles around Washington, but today only a handful survive. A century later, during the Cold War, a ring of Nike missile sites similarly encircled the capital to protect it.

E-94 GUM SPRINGS

Two separate markers, one on Rte. 1, 3.93 miles south of I-95, and the other on Rte. 626 (Sherwood Lane), 0.27 miles east of Rte. 1. Gum Springs, an African-American community, originated here on a 214-acre farm bought in 1833 by West Ford (ca. 1785–1863), a freed man, skilled carpenter, and manager of the Mount Vernon estate. The freedman's school begun here in 1867 at Bethlehem Baptist Church encouraged black settlement. In 1890 the Rev. Samuel K. Taylor, William Belfield, Lovelace Brown, Hamilton Gray, Robert D. King, Henry Randall, and Nathan Webb formed the Joint Stock Company of Gum Springs and sold lots. Gum Springs has remained a vigorous black community.

E-95 SILAS BURKE HOUSE

Rte. 645, 1.36 miles south of Rte. 7100. Here lived Lt. Col. Silas Burke (b. 1796–d. 1854) and his wife, Hannah Coffer. Burke, for whom Burke's Station on the Orange & Alexandria Railroad was named, served as a director of the railroad and the Fairfax Turnpike Company. An innkeeper and farmer, Burke was elected president of the Fairfax Agricultural Society in 1850. He held many county offices with distinction, including road surveyor, commis-sioner of public buildings and schools, county court justice, presiding justice, and sheriff.

E-96 HUNTLEY

Rte. 723 (Harrison Lane), 1.6 miles north of Rte. 1. On the hill above stands Huntley, a Federal-style villa built about 1825 for Thomson F. Mason, a grandson of George Mason of Gunston Hall. Thomson Mason, a prominent Alexandria lawyer, served on the city council, as mayor, and also as president of both the Little River Turnpike and Alexandria Canal companies. The thousand-acre Huntley property stretched across the valley below. Remaining dependencies include a subterranean icehouse with a vaulted ceiling, and a combination privy and storage building. The author of Huntley's unusual design remains unknown, but the house has been attributed to Benjamin H. Latrobe or George Hadfield, two notable early architects.

E-97 LORTON NIKE MISSILE SITE

Rte. 611, 0.47 miles east of Rte. 123 (Ox Road). Located north of here was one of three Nike anti-aircraft missile complexes in Fairfax County operated by the U.S. Army and the Army National Guard between 1954 and 1974. The sites were established during the Cold War to defend Washington from Soviet air attack. This complex, along with those at Great Falls

Nike missile sites such as this one at Lorton in Fairfax County were installed around Washington, D.C., during the Cold War to protect the nation's capital during a potential attack by the former Soviet Union. (Marker E-97) (Washingtoniana Division, DC Public Library)

and Fairfax, was among thirteen Nike sites that surrounded Washington and Baltimore. The ring of Nike sites was reminiscent of the perimeter of forts that had protected the capital during the Civil War. This was the only Nike complex in Fairfax County containing missiles armed with nuclear warheads. It served as a model site for visits by foreign dignitaries.

E-98 FAIRFAX NIKE MISSILE SITE

Rte. 7100, 2.93 miles north of Rte. 123 (Ox Road). During the Cold War a ring of Nike anti-aircraft missile sites defended the nation's capital, reminiscent of the perimeter of forts that protected it during the Civil War. Just east of here was located the launch control equipment for one of the three Nike complexes in Fairfax County. To the west stood the missiles, poised on above-ground launchers. The U.S. Army (1954–1959) and the Army National Guard (1959–1963) operated this battery. Built to oppose Soviet air attack, this complex and those in Great Falls and Lorton were three of thirteen Nike sites that surrounded Washington and Baltimore.

E-101 DEVEREUX STATION

Rte. 645, 3.7 miles south of Rte. 620, Clifton. In 1863, during the Civil War, Pennsylvanian Herman Haupt, a noted bridge designer and the superintendent of Union military railroads, commissioned John Devereux, the railroad superintendent in Alexandria, to build a siding on the Orange & Alexandria R.R. on this site, later known as Devereux Station. When a passenger station was built in 1868, the name was changed to Clifton Station. The station spurred the development of Clifton as a commercial and resort community, with its greatest growth occurring between 1890 and 1920. Although the station was removed in 1958, the town continued to thrive and remains noted for its late-19th-century architecture.

E-102 FORT LYON

Rte. 241 (North Kings Highway), 0.72 miles north of Rte. 1. In this vicinity stood Fort Lyon, the major fortification on the left flank of the Federal defenses guarding the city of Washington during the Civil War. Named in honor of Brig. Gen. Nathaniel Lyon, the fort covered an area of nine acres with its forty gun-emplacements. New York, Massachusetts and Ohio troops garrisoned here controlled the Hunting Creek valley, the Little River Turnpike, and the railroad depot as well as the town of Alexandria. On 10 June 1863, President Lincoln personally inspected the damage caused by the spectacular explosion of the fort's powder magazine.

E-107 COLCHESTER

Rte. 1, 0.38 miles north of Fairfax/Prince William County line. Colchester, founded in 1753 at the location of a ferry crossing, was the second town established in Fairfax County. Located on the main post road from Boston to Charleston, and at the end of the Ox Road leading west to the Blue Ridge, the town prospered as a trading center and tobacco port. In 1781, Gen. Washington and Comte de Rochambeau passed through Colchester en route to Yorktown. The creation of an alternate postal route over a new bridge upstream in 1805; the diversion of grain shipping from the Shenandoah Valley to Georgetown, Alexandria, and Baltimore; and, according to tradition, a great fire in 1815 contributed to the town's decline.

E-112 OLD ROAD TO THE WEST

Rte. 743 (Colvin Run Road), 0.68 miles south of Rte. 7. Colvin Run Road is a remnant of an 18th-century wagon road from the Shenandoah Valley to Alexandria that probably originated as an Indian path. George Washington passed by here in 1753 and 1754 en route to persuade the French on the Ohio River to withdraw from English territory. In 1755, during the French and Indian War, a brigade of Maj. Gen. Edward

Braddock's army traveled the road on its ill-fated march to Fort Duquesne. The road was incorporated into the Middle Turnpike before 1840. A century later, the moving and straightening of the Leesburg Pike reduced Colvin Run Road to a byway.

E-125　BIRTHPLACE OF FITZHUGH LEE

Rte. 644 (Franconia Road), 1.62 miles west of Rte. 611. To the north stood Clermont, the birthplace of Fitzhugh "Fitz" Lee. Born on 19 Nov. 1835, Lee was the nephew of Gen. Robert E. Lee. He graduated from the U.S. Military Academy in 1856. During the Civil War, Fitzhugh Lee was commissioned as a lieutenant in the Confederate army and became a major general in 1863. He served with Maj. Gen. J. E. B. Stuart and commanded cavalry at Sharpsburg, Chancellorsville, and Gettysburg. Lee was the governor of Virginia from 1886 to 1890. He served as Consul General in Havana (1896–1898) and commanded the U.S. Army VII Corps in Cuba during the Spanish-American War. Lee died in Washington, D.C., on 28 Apr. 1905.

T-33　LANGLEY FORK

Rte. 193, 0.27 miles west of Rte. 123. Two 18th-century roads intersect just west of here: Sugarlands Rolling Road (now Georgetown Pike) and Little Falls Road (now Chain Bridge Road). Several historic structures stand near the fork: Langley Toll House (ca. 1820); Langley Ordinary (ca. 1850); Mackall House (ca. 1858); Gunnell's Chapel (ca. 1879); Langley Friends Meeting House (ca. 1893), and Hickory Hill (ca. 1870), at times the home of Supreme Court Justice Robert H. Jackson, then-Senator John F. Kennedy, and his brother Attorney General Robert F. Kennedy. Thomas Lee, of Stratford Hall, acquired Langley in a 1719 land grant and named it for a family estate in England.

T-36　ACTION AT DRANESVILLE

Rte. 7, 2.24 miles east of Fairfax/Loudoun County line. Near here two foraging expeditions came in conflict, December 20, 1861. The Union force was commanded by General Ord, the Confederate by J. E. B. Stuart. Stuart attacked in order to protect his foraging parties, but was forced to retire after a sharp fight. The next day he returned, reinforced, and carried off his wounded.

T-37　SHARPSBURG (ANTIETAM) CAMPAIGN

Rte. 7, 2.24 miles east of Fairfax/Loudoun County line. Here Lee entered this road from Ox Hill, September 3, 1862, and turned west toward Leesburg. Crossing the Potomac at White's Ford, the army entered Maryland, September 5–6, 1862.

T-39　J. E. B. STUART AT MUNSON'S HILL

Rte. 7, 3.03 miles west of I-395. Following the First Battle of Manassas on 21 July 1861, Col. James Ewell Brown Stuart, commander of the 1st Virginia Cavalry, moved his troopers to Fairfax Court House and then here to Munson's Hill, the Confederate position closest to the city of Washington. From his camp Stuart watched Union observers ascend in balloons to study him. Stuart built "Quaker cannons" of logs and marched his men before large campfires to confound the Federals. On 24 September, while still encamped here, he was promoted to the rank of brigadier general.

T-40　LINCOLN REVIEWS TROOPS AT BAILEY'S CROSSROADS

Rte. 7, 2.46 miles west of I-395. After the Union defeat on 21 July 1861 at the First Battle of Manassas, Lincoln appointed Maj. Gen. George B. McClellan as commander of the demoralized army. A superb organizer, McClellan rebuilt the army and on 20 November 1861 staged a formal military review here, between Munson's Hill and Bailey's Crossroads. Lincoln and his entire cabinet attended. Occupying nearly 200 acres, some 50,000 troops, "including seven divisions—seven regiments of cavalry, ninety regiments of infantry, [and] twenty batteries of artillery," took part in the review, at that time the largest ever held in America.

T-41 LITTLE RIVER TURNPIKE

Rte. 236, 1.17 miles west of I-495. The earliest private turnpike charter in Virginia was granted by the General Assembly to the Company of the Fairfax and Loudoun Turnpike Road in 1796. By 1806 the 34-mile-long road connected Alexandria with Aldie on the Little River in Loudoun County. The company placed wooden toll-houses along the road at five-mile intervals, and one stood near here until 1954. The Little River Turnpike became a free road in 1896. In Fairfax County, only this portion of the road in Annandale retains its original name.

T-42 RAVENSWORTH

Rte. 3090, 0.11 miles south of Rte. 620. Near here stood Ravensworth, a Fitzhugh and Lee family home. Built about 1796 by William Fitzhugh, the mansion stood on the largest single land grant in Fairfax County, the 21,966 acres acquired by Fitzhugh's great-grandfather in 1685. During the Civil War the house was not molested by either side. After the war Ravensworth came into the possession of Robert E. Lee's second son, Maj. Gen. W. H. F. ("Rooney") Lee. Ravensworth, a frame Palladian-style mansion, was one of the most imposing residences in Fairfax County until it burned in 1926.

T-43 FRYING PAN MEETING HOUSE

Rte. 657, 1.36 miles south of Rte. 267 (Dulles Toll Road). The Frying Pan Meeting House, constructed by 1791 on land donated by the Carter family in 1783, was used for Baptist services until 1968. Named for nearby Frying Pan Branch, the church is a rare example of 18th-century architecture in western Fairfax County. By 1840 the congregation consisted of 33 whites and 29 blacks; both black and white members are buried in the church cemetery. During the Civil War, Union and Confederate forces each used the meetinghouse several times as a picket post. The last surviving church trustee conveyed the property to the Fairfax County Park Authority in 1984.

T-46 GREAT FALLS NIKE MISSILE SITE

Rte. 674 (Springvale Road), 0.1 miles south of Rte. 193. Just to the southeast were radar and other control equipment that formed a portion of one of three Nike anti-aircraft missile complexes in Fairfax County. The site was operated by the U.S. Army between 1954 and 1962. Established during the Cold War to defend Washington from Soviet air attack, this complex, along with those at Fairfax and Lorton, was among the thirteen sites that encircled Washington and Baltimore. The ring of Nike missile sites was reminiscent of the perimeter of forts that guarded the capital during the Civil War. The missiles, positioned on above-ground launchers, were located near here to the west.

T-48 BAILEY'S CROSSROADS CIVIL WAR ENGAGEMENTS

Rte. 7, 2.33 miles west of I-395, Bailey's Crossroads. After the First Battle of Manassas, Confederate troops led by Col. J. E. B. Stuart occupied nearby Munson's and Mason's Hills from late July until they abandoned their position about 29 Sept. 1861. Confederate troops fought skirmishers of the Union 2d and 3d Michigan Infantry around Bailey's Crossroads for several days starting 28 Aug. 1861. The Federals and Confederates suffered a small number of casualties. Union forces in Maj. Gen. George B. McClellan's Army of the Potomac occupied the Bailey's Crossroads region after the Confederates retired to the Centreville area.

T-49 FORT BUFFALO

Rte. 613 (Sleepy Hollow Road), 0.13 miles south of Rte. 7 (Leesburg Pike). Nearby once stood Fort Buffalo. This earthwork fortification was built by the 21st New York Infantry of the Union army in 1861 and named for the troops' hometown. During the Civil War, a concentration of forts existed in the Seven Corners section of Falls Church. These structures were used in the Federal defense of Washington. First occupied by Brig. Gen. Irvin McDowell's troops during the First Manassas Campaign, the fort was briefly occupied by the Confederates following that Federal defeat in July 1861. In the 1950s, Seven Corners shopping center and the surrounding community was developed on land once part of and surrounding Fort Buffalo.

T-50 MASON'S HILL

Rte. 244 (Columbia Pike), just east of Rte. 236. During the Civil War, Confederate Col. J. E. B. Stuart used Mason's Hill and nearby Munson's Hill as outposts for the First Virginia Cavalry from late July to the end of Sept. 1861. Capt. Edward Porter Alexander of the Signal Corps established a signal station on Mason's Hill. On the Mason residence's observation tower, he installed a six-foot "astronomical glass" to observe Washington, D.C. The telescope could "count the panes of glass in the windows in Washington." Confederate spy E. Pliny Bryan, of Maryland, was to signal messages from his District rooming-house window to the station. Before this scheme could be implemented, however, the Confederates abandoned Mason's Hill.

WASHINGTON-ROCHAMBEAU ROUTE

Rte. 235, 800 feet from entrance to Mount Vernon. General Washington, in 1781, rode 60 miles in one day from Baltimore to Mount Vernon, which he had not visited for over 6 years. General Rochambeau arrived the next day with his and Washington's staff. They spent Sept. 10 and 11 at Mount Vernon before going on to Fredericksburg. *Note:* This is one of five unnumbered signs discussing aspects of the Washington-Rochambeau Route, which were a special gift from the French Government, Committee of the Bicentennial, to the Commonwealth of Virginia in 1976.

CITY OF FALLS CHURCH

C-90 THE FALLS CHURCH

Rte. 29 (Lee Highway), 0.11 miles east of Rte. 7. The first church on this site was built in 1734 and was in Truro Parish. George Washington was elected a vestryman, October 3, 1763. In 1765 the church fell within the newly created Fairfax Parish, of which Washington was chosen a vestryman. The present church was built in 1768. It was used as a recruiting station in the Revolution and as a stable by Union troops, 1862–65.

LOUDOUN COUNTY

B-11 CAMPAIGN OF SECOND MANASSAS

Rte. 50 (Lee Jackson Memorial Highway), 2.3 miles east of Rte. 606 (Old Ox Road). Stonewall Jackson, sent by Lee to move around Pope's retreating army at Centreville and cut it off from Alexandria, reached this place August 31, 1862. Here Jackson turned east toward Fairfax.

B-22 CAVALRY BATTLES

Rte. 50, 2.59 miles west of Rte. 15 (James Monroe Highway). In June 1863, Gen. Robert E. Lee led the Army of Northern Virginia through gaps in the nearby Blue Ridge Mountains and into the Shenandoah Valley to invade the North. Maj. Gen. J. E. B. Stuart's cavalry corps screened the army from Federal observation. The Union cavalry commander, Brig. Gen. Alfred Pleasonton, attempted to break through Stuart's screen, and fought three sharp engagements along this road. They included the Battles of Aldie (17 June), Middleburg (19 June), and Upperville (21 June). Stuart fell back westward under Pleasonton's pressure but kept the Federal cavalry east of the gaps.

B-28 MERCER'S HOME

Rte. 50, 1.18 miles west of Rte. 15. Aldie was the home of Charles Fenton Mercer (born 1778, died 1858), liberal statesman. Mercer was a congressman (1817–1839) and a member of the Virginia constitutional convention of 1829–30, in which he advocated manhood suffrage. His attempt in 1817 to establish a free school system in Virginia nearly succeeded. He was a leading advocate of the colonization of free blacks in Liberia.

B-30 STUART AND BAYARD

Rte. 50, 2.59 miles west of Rte. 15 (James Monroe Highway). After the Battle of Antietam on 17 Sept. 1862, Gen. Robert E. Lee and the Army of Northern Virginia recrossed the Potomac River into Virginia. After President Abraham Lincoln's constant urging, the Union Army of the Potomac, led by Maj. Gen. George B. McClellan, pursued them. Lee ordered part of his army south to Culpeper Court House. To screen Lee's march, Maj. Gen. J. E. B. Stuart's troopers fought a series of engagements against the probing Federal cavalry. On 31 Oct., Stuart attacked Brig. Gen. George D. Bayard's command near Mountville, drove it southeast through Aldie, and discovered the Union army's left flank.

B-32 GETTYSBURG CAMPAIGN

Rte. 50, 2.59 miles west of Rte. 15 (James Monroe Highway). In June 1863, as Gen. Robert E. Lee led the Army of Northern Virginia through Blue Ridge gaps to the Shenandoah Valley, Maj. Gen. J. E. B. Stuart's cavalry screened the army from Federal observation. The Union cavalry chief, Brig. Gen. Alfred Pleasonton, dispatched Brig. Gen. David M. Gregg to penetrate Stuart's screen. On 17 June, Gregg ordered Col. Alfred A. N. Duffié to reconnoiter from Aldie to Middleburg. Duffié drove off Confederate pickets there, alerting Stuart. Duffié withdrew south of Middleburg, but Brig. Gen. Beverly H. Robertson's brigade surrounded and almost wiped out Duffié's command before it escaped the next morning.

B-33 A REVOLUTIONARY WAR HERO

Rte. 50, 2.59 miles west of Rte. 15. Near here stood the home of Sergeant Major John Champe (1752–1798), Continental soldier. Champe faked desertion and enlisted in Benedict Arnold's British command for the purpose of capturing the traitor. Failing in his attempt, Champe rejoined the American army. His meritorious service was attested to by such patriots as General Henry (Light Horse Harry) Lee.

F-1 BATTLE OF BALL'S BLUFF

Rte. 15, 0.2 miles south of Leesburg. One mile east occurred the battle of Ball's Bluff, October 21, 1861. A Union force, which had crossed the river at this point, was driven back over it by the Confederates.

F-2 POTOMAC CROSSINGS

Rte. 15, 5.33 miles north of Leesburg. Here Lee turned east to the Potomac, crossing at White's Ford, September 6, 1862, in his invasion of Maryland. Jubal A. Early, returning from his Washington raid, crossed the river at White's Ford, July 14, 1864.

F-4 PRESIDENT MONROE'S HOME

Rte. 15, 0.18 miles north of Rte. 50 (John Mosby Highway). The house to the north is Oak Hill. Designed by Thomas Jefferson for James Monroe, it was built about 1823. Monroe lived there for some years.

F-5 Wayne's Crossing

Rte. 15 (James Monroe Highway), 4.57 miles south of Rte. 672 (Lovettsville Road). Three miles southeast, at Noland's Ferry, "Mad Anthony" Wayne, on his way to join Lafayette, crossed the Potomac River, May 31, 1781. He passed through Leesburg, June 3, and joined Lafayette near the Rapidan River, June 10.

F-6 Sharpsburg (Antietam) Campaign

Rte. 15, 1.48 miles north of Leesburg. Near here Stonewall Jackson bivouaced [bivouacked] on the march into Maryland, September 4, 1862.

F-7 Goose Creek Chapel

Rte. 15 (James Monroe Highway), 0.87 miles north of Leesburg corporate limits. A short distance west is the site of the "Chapel above Goose Creek", built by the vestry of Truro Parish in 1736. Augustine Washington, father of George Washington, was a member of the vestry at the time. This was the first church on the soil of Loudoun County, erected as a chapel of ease for the benefit of early settlers.

F-15 Mother of Stonewall Jackson

Rte. 15, 0.18 miles north of Rte. 50 (John Mosby Highway). In this vicinity (and according to tradition two miles east at Peach Orchard) was born Julia Beckwith Neale, mother of Stonewall Jackson, February 29, 1798. She married Jonathan Jackson in 1818 and died, October, l831.

F-27 Catoctin Rural Historic District

Rte. 15 (James Monroe Highway), 4.57 miles south of Rte. 672 (Lovettsville Road). The surrounding area of about 25,000 acres has been a cohesive agricultural community since the mid-1700s, when it was settled largely by former Tidewater Virginia planters attracted by its streams and fertile soils. Bordered by Catoctin Mountain (west) and the Potomac River (north and east), the district includes well-preserved farmsteads, historical road networks, and crossroad communities. These resources date from the late 1700s to the early 1900s and enhance the picturesque rural landscape.

F-28 Loudoun County Courthouse

Rte. 15 (North King Street) and Rte. 7 (East Market Street), at courthouse, Leesburg. The Loudoun County Courthouse, first occupied in 1895, is the third on this site, which was designated for that use on the 1759 plat of Leesburg. On 12 Aug. 1776, the Declaration of Independence was read from the doorway of the first courthouse. The second was built of brick in the Federal style about 1811. The Marquis de Lafayette, on his grand tour of the United States, was entertained here on 9 Aug. 1825. President John Quincy Adams and former president James Monroe, who then lived near Leesburg, escorted him. In 1894, the Norris brothers, of Leesburg, built this courthouse, designed by William C. West, of Richmond, in the Classical style.

F-29 Morven Park

Rte. 15 (James Monroe Highway), 0.87 miles north of Leesburg corporate limits. Morven Park was the home of Westmoreland Davis, who as governor of Virginia (1918–1922) created the executive budget system that concentrated state budgeting authority in the governor's hands. Davis bought Morven Park in 1903 and transformed it into a progressive dairy farm. The first owner, Wilson Cary Selden, built a small fieldstone farmhouse in the 1780s. A mid-19th-century owner, Thomas Swann Jr., served as governor of Maryland and United States congressman. In the 1840s, the Baltimore architectural firm of Lind and Murdock enlarged and remodeled the house for Swann in the Greek Revival and Italian Villa styles.

F-31 DODONA MANOR—HOME OF GEN. GEORGE C. MARSHALL

Rte. 7 (East Market Street), 0.28 miles east of Rte. 15 (King Street), Leesburg. This early-19th-century house and its surroundings four acres were purchased in 1941 by Gen. Marshall (1880–1959) and his wife, Katherine Tupper Marshall (1882–1978). A student of the classics, Marshall called the house, in its grove of oaks, "Dodona Manor" after the ancient Greek oracle that spoke through oak leaves. This was their home during the years of Marshall's great achievements as military chief of staff during World War II, presidential emissary to China in 1945, secretary of state (1947–1949), and secretary of defense (1950–1951). The Marshall Plan for restoring war-torn Europe won Marshall the Nobel Prize in 1953.

F-33 OATLANDS

Rte. 15, 5.58 miles north of Rte. 50 (John Mosby Highway). George Carter, a great-grandson of Robert "King" Carter, began this monumental mansion on his 3,408-acre estate in 1804 and embellished it over two decades. In 1827, he graced the facade with fluted Corinthian columns, endowing the Federal-style house with lightness and elegance. He also built terraced gardens, slave quarters, barns, and smokehouses, as well as a greenhouse and gristmill. In 1903, Mr. and Mrs. William Corcoran Eustis purchased Oatlands. They restored the mansion and gardens and held foxhunts on the former farmland. Their daughters donated Oatlands to the National Trust for Historic Preservation in 1965.

G-3 ST. JAMES UNITED CHURCH OF CHRIST

Rte. 673 (East Broad Way), 0.1 miles east of Rte. 287, Lovettsville. Formerly St. James Evangelical and Reformed Church, this is the oldest active congregation of the German Reformed tradition in Virginia. Lovettsville, a German settlement, was founded by settlers of the Reformed faith in 1733. Early records indicate that Elder William Wenner, the first leader of the Lovettsville congregation, arrived in the area as early as 1720.

G-4 TAYLORSTOWN

Rte. 663 (Toll House Road), 4.86 miles north of Rte. 15. Taylorstown, one of Loudoun County's earliest settlements, stands near Catoctin Creek, a Virginia Scenic River, at the junction of the Loyalty and Taylorstown Roads. Among the oldest structures in the village are Hunting Hill (ca. 1737), Foxton Cottage (mid-18th century), and Taylor's Mill (ca. 1800). Two frame Victorian houses and a mid-1930s general store also remain. Located nearby are other log and fieldstone buildings erected by residents of German descent and by Quakers loyal to the Union during the Civil War, thus giving the name Loyalty to this region. The 61-acre Taylorstown Historic District was listed on the National Register of Historic Places in 1976.

T-5 MOTHER OF THE WRIGHT BROTHERS

Business Rte. 7, 0.17 miles north of Rte. 287, Purcellville. Six miles north, at Hillsboro, was born in 1831 Susan Koemer, mother of Wilbur and Orville Wright, inventors of the airplane.

T-22 EARLY'S WASHINGTON CAMPAIGN

Rte. 7 (Leesburg Pike), 0.86 miles east of Rte. 9. Jubal A. Early passed over this road on his return to the Shenandoah Valley, July 16, 1864. After leaving Lee before Richmond, June 13, Early traveled 450 miles, defeating Hunter at Lynchburg and Wallace on the Monocacy River, and threatening the city of Washington. On the approach of large Union forces he withdrew this way.

T-23 OLD STONE CHURCH SITE

Business Rte. 7, 0.1 miles west of Business Rte. 15 (King Street), Leesburg. One block north on Cornwall Street is the site of the first Methodist-owned property in America. Lot 50 was deeded to the Methodist Society in Leesburg on May 11, 1766. In 1778, the Sixth American Conference of Methodists met there, the first such gathering in Virginia. At least two church buildings occupied the site before 1902, when the "Old Stone Church" was demolished. The churchyard is maintained as a national historic shrine of the United Methodist Church.

T-30 BELMONT

Rte. 7 (Leesburg Highway), 4.3 miles east of Leesburg. Belmont was patented early in the eighteenth century by Thomas Lee, of Stratford. About 1800, Ludwell Lee, an officer in the Revolutionary army, built the house and he lived here until his death in 1836. Here he entertained Lafayette in 1825. In 1931, Belmont became the home of Patrick J. Hurley Secretary of War, 1929–1933.

T-38 GETTYSBURG CAMPAIGN

Rte. 637 (Potomac View Road), 0.12 miles north of Rte. 7. J.E. B. Stuart, operating on Lee's right, passed here on his way to the fords of the Potomac north of Dranesville, June 27, 1863. Crossing the river, he became separated from Lee's army and did not rejoin it until July 2, at Gettysburg.

T-47 LOUDOUN COUNTY EMANCIPATION ASSOCIATION GROUNDS

Rte. 611, 0.6 miles south of Rte. 7 (Main Street), Purcellville. The association was organized by African Americans in nearby Hamilton in 1890 to commemorate the preliminary Emancipation Proclamation issued by President Abraham Lincoln on 22 Sept. 1862 and "to cultivate good fellowship, to work for the betterment of the race, educationally, morally and materially." Emancipation Day, or the "Day of Freedom," was celebrated throughout the nation on different days. In 1910, the association incorporated and purchased ten acres of land in Purcellville. More than 1,000 people attended the annual Emancipation Day activities held here until 1967. The site served as a black religious, social, civic, and recreational center. The property was sold in 1971.

T-51 BALL'S BLUFF MASKED BATTERY

Rte. 773 (Edwards Ferry Road), east of Bypass Rte. 15. Nearby is the likely site of the Confederate "masked battery" (concealed artillery) that was an object of Federal concern early in the Civil War. On 21 Oct. 1861, elements of the 13th Mississippi Infantry near there engaged 35 horsemen of the 3rd New York Cavalry sent to draw attention from the Union force upriver at Ball's Bluff and to reconnoiter Confederate positions in the direction of Leesburg. After a brief firefight, the New Yorkers withdrew to Edwards Ferry. The Confederate victor at the Battle of Ball's Bluff, Col. Nathan G. "Shanks" Evans, was later promoted to brigadier general, while the Union commander, Brig. Gen. Charles P. Stone, was imprisoned as the scapegoat for the Federal defeat.

T-52 MAJOR GENERAL BEN H. FULLER

Business Rte. 7 (Colonial Highway), west of Rte. 704, Hamilton. Maj. Gen. Ben H. Fuller was born in Michigan on 27 Feb. 1870. He was graduated from the U.S. Naval Academy in 1889 and was commissioned a second lieutenant in the Marine Corps in 1891. Fuller married Katherine H. Offley on 26 Oct. 1892, and they intermittently lived here at Maplewood, which was owned by her family. Fuller served as the 15th commandant of the Marine Corps from 1930 to 1934. He played a key role in establishing the Fleet Marine Force and influenced the development of the Marine Corps' amphibious doctrine. He died on 8 June 1937 in Washington, D.C., and was buried at the U. S. Naval Academy Cemetery in Annapolis, Maryland.

TA-1 FIRST GERMAN REFORMED CHURCH SITE AND CEMETERY

Rte. 672, 0.67 miles east of Rte. 287, Lovettsville. This is the church site and cemetery of the oldest continuous German Reformed congregation in Virginia. Founded before 1748 by Elder William Wenner, the congregation met in members' houses until the first log meetinghouse was constructed sometime before the American Revolution. About 1819 a brick church was built here; it was demolished in 1901 and its bricks were used to construct the congregation's new church, the St. James United Church of Christ, in Lovettsville.

CITY OF MANASSAS

CL-2 RUFFNER PUBLIC SCHOOL NUMBER 1—JULY 20, 1872

Center Street, 0.1 miles south of Grant Avenue. Named for Wm. H. Ruffner, Virginia's First Superintendent of Public Instruction, and opened as a public school on this site. Before free public schools were established by the Virginia Constitution of 1869, a one room free school was in operation with voluntary gifts.

CL-4 MANASSAS

Rte. 234 (Grant Avenue), 0.14 miles north of Rte. 234 (Sudley Road). According to tradition the name Manassas was derived either from an Indian source or from Manasseh, a Jewish innkeeper at Manassas Gap (35 miles west). The community originated in 1852 at the junction of the Manassas Gap and Orange & Alexandria railroads, which linked northern Virginia and Washington, D. C., with the Shenandoah Valley and central Virginia. During the Civil War the junction's strategic importance led to the battles of First and Second Manassas (Bull Run), both Confederate victories. Manassas was incorporated as a town in 1873 and became a city in 1975.

CL-5 FIFTH PRINCE WILLIAM COUNTY COURTHOUSE

Lee Street, 0.3 miles south of Grant Avenue. The city of Manassas originated in 1852 at the junction of the Manassas Gap and the Orange & Alexandria railroads. During the Civil War the junction's strategic significance led to two important battles nearby. After the war, as the community grew, citizens sought to move the county seat there from Brentsville. In 1872, a year before Manassas was incorporated as a town, and again in 1888, referenda failed. A third referendum in 1892 succeeded. This Romanesque Revival courthouse, designed by James C. Teague and Philip T. Marye, of Norfolk and Newport News, was completed in 1893 and served the county until 1984 when a new courthouse was built nearby.

CL-6 OLD BENNETT SCHOOL

Lee Street, 0.14 miles south of Grant Avenue. In 1908 the General Assembly authorized ten agricultural high schools, one in each congressional district. The first such school was built in Manassas in 1908–1909 and named for Dr. Maitland C. Bennett, who donated the land. During construction, workers discovered the graves of unknown Civil War soldiers. Union veteran George Round, a Manassas school district trustee, and Confederate veteran George Tyler, school superintendent, decided to erect the school over the burials as a monument to the fallen. The school housed teacher training and elementary classes, and students conducted agricultural experiments on the grounds. The building remained a Prince William County public school until 1969.

PRINCE WILLIAM COUNTY

C-26 BATTLE OF GROVETON (BRAWNER FARM)

Rte. 29 (Lee Highway), 4.46 miles east of Rte. 55 (John Marshall Highway). In Aug. 1862, Confederate Gen. Robert E. Lee dispatched Maj. Gen. Thomas J. "Stonewall" Jackson to lure Maj. Gen. John Pope's Union army away from the Rappahannock River. On Aug. 28, Jackson's force concealed itself northeast of here near Groveton atop a wooded ridge on and beyond John Brawner's farm to await the rest of Lee's army. Early in the evening, as Brig. Gen. Rufus King's division of Pope's army marched by in search of Jackson, he attacked, stopping the Federal movement with heavy casualties on both sides. This engagement began the Second Battle of Manassas.

C-27 SECOND BATTLE OF MANASSAS

Rte. 29 (Lee Highway), 3.55 miles west of Rte. 234 (Sudley Road). The center of Lee's army rested here on August 30, 1862; Jackson was to the north of this road, Longstreet to the south. Late in the afternoon, after Jackson had repulsed Pope's assaults, Longstreet moved eastward, driving the Union forces facing him toward Henry Hill. Jackson advanced southward at the same time.

C-28 CAMPAIGN OF SECOND MANASSAS

Rte. 29 (Lee Highway), 3.54 miles west of Rte. 234 (Sudley Road). On 25 Aug. 1862, Maj. Gen. Thomas J. "Stonewall" Jackson with half of the Confederate Army of Northern Virginia began a wide flanking march around Union Maj. Gen. John Pope's Army of Virginia on the Rappahannock River near Warrenton. Jackson first marched west toward the Shenandoah Valley, then turned back east to strike Pope's railroad supply and communication lines. On the afternoon of 26 Aug., Maj. Gen. J. E. B. Stuart joined Jackson near Gainesville to protect his right flank. Jackson next captured Bristoe Station on the Orange and Alexandria Railroad, and then Manassas Junction, in a prelude to the Second Battle of Manassas.

C-31 BULL RUN BATTLEFIELDS

Rte. 29 (Lee Highway), 4.23 miles west of Rte. 234 (Sudley Road). Just to the east were fought the two battles of Manassas or Bull Run.

C-33 ROCK FIGHT

Rte. 29 (Lee Highway), 4.85 miles east of Rte. 55 (John Marshall Highway). In Aug. 1862, during the Second Battle of Manassas, Confederate Maj. Gen. Thomas J. "Stonewall" Jackson's command occupied an unfinished railroad grade northeast of here, including "the Dump," a gap in the grade heaped with construction stone. On 30 Aug., the Federals attacked, the 24th New York Infantry almost broke through. Out of ammunition, Confederates there and at Deep Cut to the west, began hurling rocks. Some startled Federals threw stones back before retreating as Jackson reinforced his line. The Rock Fight became a Southern legend.

C-34 FIRST BATTLE OF MANASSAS

Rte. 29 (Lee Highway), 0.27 miles east of Rte. 234 (Sudley Road). Henry Hill lies just to the south. Here the Confederates repulsed the repeated attacks of the Union army under McDowell, July 21, 1861. Here Jackson won the name "Stonewall," and from here began McDowell's retreat that ended at Washington.

C-44 FIRST BATTLE OF MANASSAS

Rte. 29 (Lee Highway), 0.27 miles east of Rte. 234 (Sudley Road). On the Matthews Hill, just to the north, the Confederates replused [repulsed] the attack of the Unionists, coming from the north, in the forenoon of July 21, 1861. The Union force, reinforced, drove the Confederates to the Henry Hill, just to the south. There the latter reformed under cover of Stonewall Jackson. In the afternoon, McDowell vainly attempted to rally his retreating troops on the Matthews Hill after they had been driven down the Henry Hill.

C-46 SECOND BATTLE OF MANASSAS

Rte. 234 (Sudley Road), 0.71 miles south of Rte. 29 (Lee Highway). On the Henry Hill, Pope's rear guard, in the late afternoon of August 30, 1862, repulsed the attacks of Longstreet coming from the west. If the hill had been taken, Pope's army would have been doomed; but the Unionists held it while the rest of their troops retreated across Bull Run on the way to Centreville.

C-48 CAMPAIGN OF SECOND MANASSAS

Rte. 234 (Sudley Road), 0.71 miles south of Rte. 29 (Lee Highway). Here Taliaferro, of Jackson's force, came into the highway in the late night of August 27, 1862. He was marching from Manassas to the position about a mile and a half to the north held by Jackson in the Second Battle of Manassas.

E-53 REVOLUTIONARY WAR CAMPAIGN OF 1781

Rte. 1 (Fraley Boulevard), 1.62 miles north of Rte. 619 (Joplin Road), Dumfries. The roads through Prince William County were important routes for the Revolutionary War campaign of 1781. In April, the Marquis de Lafayette passed through the county on the King's Highway with a portion of Gen. George Washington's Continental Army. During July, Brig. Gen. Anthony Wayne and his troops marched through the region on the Carolina Road and joined Lafayette at Rapidan. In September, the cavalry and baggage wagons of the French and American armies took the King's Highway to Yorktown. After the Battle of Yorktown, the British troops surrendered to the American and French forces on 19 Oct. 1781.

E-54 ROAD TO THE VALLEY

Marker not erected. Proposed location: Rte. 619, south of Dumfries. By the first quarter of the 1700s, revisions to the road laws in the colony mandated more convenient travel routes over land. In conjunction with new settlement pushing west through the Piedmont region to the Blue Ridge, a series of old Indian trails and new roadways slowly became interconnected and developed into a regional transportation system. Construction began about 1731, and by 1759 this road extended northwest through Prince William County from Dumfries and crossed the Blue Ridge Mountains via Ashby's Gap. Portions of this early route underlie sections of present-day Route 234 (Dumfries Road) and Route 619.

E-58 NEABSCO IRON WORKS

Rte. 1 (Jefferson Davis Highway), at Neabsco Road. Situated along the nearby Neabsco Creek, the Neabsco Iron Works began operation by 1737. Directed by John Tayloe of Richmond County and succeeding family members, the ironworks evolved into a multifaceted antebellum industrial plantation, which included such activities as shipbuilding, milling, smithing, leatherworking, farming, and shoemaking. The complex became an important supplier of raw materials for weaponry during the American Revolution. The Neabsco Iron Works operation ended about 1828, after the death of John Tayloe III, when his sons sold most of the remaining Neabsco lands.

E-59 OCCOQUAN

Rte. 1 (Jefferson Davis Highway), 0.3 miles north of Rte. 123. Captain John Smith explored this region in 1608. The town of Occoquan began with the opening of a tobacco warehouse on the shore of the Occoquan River in 1734. Occoquan grew as the focus of the commercial and manufacturing activities of John Ballendine, who had an iron furnace, forge, and sawmills at the falls of the river before 1759. After the American Revolution, Occoquan emerged as a flour-manufacturing center with one of the nation's first gristmills to use the laborsaving inventions of Oliver Evans. In 1804, Occoquan was established as a town and thrived as a commercial and industrial center into the 1920s.

E-82 DUMFRIES RAID

Rte. 1 (Fraley Boulevard), 1.62 miles north of Rte. 619 (Joplin Road), Dumfries. On 26 December 1862, Maj. Gen. J. E. B. Stuart led 1,800 cavalry out of Fredericksburg on his third and last major raid. Stuart divided his column and on 27 December launched a two-pronged attack on Dumfries, a major Union supply base. The garrison thwarted the Confederate cavalry commanded by Brig. Gen. Fitzhugh Lee and Brig. Gen. W. H. F. ("Rooney") Lee, despite the efforts of Stuart's legendary horse artillery. Stuart continued the raid through Occoquan, Burke's Station, Fairfax Court House, Warrenton, and Culpeper before returning to Fredericksburg on 1 January 1863. During the raid, Stuart seized some 200 prisoners, as many horses and mules, and 20 wagonloads of equipment.

E-83 HISTORY OF DUMFRIES

Rte. 1 (Fraley Boulevard), 1.62 miles north of Rte. 619 (Joplin Road), Dumfries. Dumfries, first settled in the early 18th century, became in 1749 the first town in Prince William County chartered by the House of Burgesses. It soon grew in wealth and importance as a major port, rivaling Alexandria, Baltimore, and New York in tonnage shipped. The town's status as a center for the sale and shipment of tobacco, despite its inland location on a creek, reached its peak in the 1760's. In 1762 the county court moved to Dumfries, where it remained for 60 years. Ironically, the soil erosion caused by tobacco farming resulted in the silting up of Quantico Creek. The prosperity and population of Dumfries declined and the court moved to Brentsville in 1822.

F-14 SIMON KENTON'S BIRTHPLACE

Rte. 15, 6.89 miles south of Rte. 50 (Gilberts Corner). Near Hopewell Gap, five miles west, Simon Kenton was born, 1755. Leaving home in 1771, he became an associate of Daniel Boone and George Rogers Clark in Indian fighting. He won fame as a scout and as one of the founders of Kentucky. Kenton died in Ohio in 1836.

G-15 HENRY HOUSE

Rte. 29 (Lee Highway), 0.27 miles east of Rte. 234 (Sudley Road). These are the grounds of the Henry House, where occurred the main action of the First Battle of Manassas, July 21, 1861, and the closing scene of the Second Battle of Manassas, August 30, 1862.

G-16 JAMES ROBINSON HOUSE

Rte. 29 (Lee Highway), 0.27 miles east of Rte. 234 (Sudley Road). To the south stood the farmhouse of James Robinson, a former slave freed by Landon Carter. There, during the First Battle of Manassas on 21 July 1861, Col. Wade Hampton's Legion covered the Confederates falling back to Henry Hill, where Jackson stood "like a stone wall." The house survived that battle, and during the Second Battle of Manassas in August 1862 served the Union troops as a field hospital. Congress later authorized compensation to Robinson for property damages. The present house stands partially on the foundation of the original.

G-17 SECOND PRINCE WILLIAM COUNTY COURTHOUSE

Rte. 646 (Aden Road), 3.55 miles west of Rte. 234 (Dumfries Road). In 1743, the second Prince William County Courthouse was built near here along Cedar Run, replacing the first county courthouse in Woodbridge. After the creation of Fairfax County, the Cedar Run location, owned by Philemon Waters, became the center of Prince William County. The court remained here only until 1759, when it moved to Dumfries after the creation of Fauquier County. Henry Lee, father of Governor Henry ("Lighthorse-Harry") Lee, and grandfather of General Robert E. Lee, practiced law here. The building, like its predecessor, no longer stands.

G-18 NEABSCO MILLS IRONWORKS

I-95 South, 4.33 miles south of Rte. 123 (Gordon Boulevard), at rest area. The Neabsco Mills Ironworks complex, under the ownership of three generations of the Tayloe family, of Richmond County, operated between 1737 and 1828. Located near this site, it was one of the longest continuously operating ironworks in present-day Northern Virginia. The 5,000-acre iron plantation, which was worked by resident free laborers, indentured servants, and slaves, was a multifaceted operation. The workers produced not only pig and bar iron for sale at home and export to Great Britain, but also engaged in shipbuilding, milling, leatherworking, shoemaking, and farming. The complex was an important supplier of iron for weaponry during the American Revolution and the War of 1812.

G-19 ACTION AT BRISTOE STATION

Rte. 28 (Nokesville Road), 0.6 miles north of Rte. 619. On 26 August 1862 Maj. Gen. Thomas J. "Stonewall" Jackson's command, led by Col. Thomas T. Munford's 2d Virginia Cavalry and Maj. Gen. Richard S. Ewell's division, arrived here at sunset after marching 54 miles in two days around Maj. Gen. John Pope's Union army. They surprised and captured Pope's infantry pickets, derailed two northbound trains, destroyed the Broad Run bridge, and cut telegraph wires to sever the Union lines of supply and communication with Washington. Jackson then captured Pope's supply depot at Manassas Junction (present-day Manassas). Left as a rear guard, Ewell held off Union Maj. Gen. Joseph Hooker's division near Kettle Run the next day, just before the Second Battle of Manassas on 28–30 August.

G-20 BATTLE OF BRISTOE STATION

Rte. 28 (Nokesville Road), 0.59 miles north of Rte. 619. In the autumn of 1863, Gen. Robert E. Lee's Army of Northern Virginia, with Lt. Gen. A. P. Hill's III Corps in the lead, pursued Maj. Gen. George G. Meade's Union army as it withdrew toward Washington. On the afternoon of 14 October, Maj. Gen. Gouverneur K. Warren's II Corps, Meade's rear guard, took a strong defensive position along the railroad embankment to meet an impetuous attack by elements of Hill's corps from the northwest. The Confederates were repulsed with heavy casualties (about 1,300 to Warren's 548), including the loss of an unsupported battery of five guns about 500 yards north. Warren stealthily withdrew after dark to resume his march to Centreville. About 43 Union and 137 Confederate dead were buried on the field.

JQ-1 LEESYLVANIA STATE PARK

Rte. 610 (Neabsco Road), 1.52 miles east of Rte. 1. This 508-acre park was donated to the Commonwealth in 1978 by Daniel K. Ludwig and was opened on June 17, 1989. The park, whose name means "Lee's Woods," is the ancestral home of the famous Lee family of Virginia. The land, which was patented in 1658, was the home of Henry Lee II and Henry "Light Horse Harry" Lee III, father of General Robert E. Lee. Nearby Freestone Point was the site of a Confederate artillery emplacement which successfully blockaded the Potomac River during the Civil War.

STAFFORD COUNTY

E-17 GOLD MINING IN STAFFORD COUNTY

Rte. 17, 6.53 miles north of I-95, 3.89 miles south of Stafford/Fauquier County line. Near here are located ten of the nineteenth-century gold mines of Stafford County. The best-known were the Eagle, Rattlesnake (Horse Pen), Lee, New Hope, and Monroe mines. The Eagle Gold Mining Company, Rappahannock Gold Mine Company of

New York, Rapidan Mining and Milling Company of Pennsylvania, United States Mining Company, and Stafford Mining Company operated here between the 1830s and the early twentieth century. Mining activities gradually ceased because of declining profits.

E-45 FREDERICKSBURG

Rte. 3, east of Rte. 218. Fredericksburg was established in 1728 and named for Frederick Louis, Prince of Wales and eldest son of King George II. It served as the county seat of Spotsylvania County from 1732 to 1778 and was an important port during the colonial era. In his youth, George Washington lived nearby at Ferry Farm. He later spoke of the city's influence on him. The town was devastated by fire in 1807 and again by the First and Second Battles of Fredericksburg that were fought here during the Civil War, yet many 18th- and 19th-century buildings remain and are listed on the Virginia Landmarks Register and the National Register of Historic Places.

E-47 HISTORIC FALMOUTH

Rte. 607, just south of Rte. 1, Falmouth. Founded in 1727 as a trading center for the Northern Neck. Hunter's iron works here were an objective in the Virginia campaign of 1781. The Army of the Potomac camped here from November, 1862 to June, 1863 and moved hence to Chancellorsville and Gettysburg.

E-48 KIDNAPPING OF POCAHONTAS

Rte. 1, 3.8 miles north of Falmouth. Near here, Pocahontas visited friends among the Patawomecks on the Potomac River in April 1613. Capt. Samuel Argall saw an opportunity to capture Pocahontas and exchange her for English prisoners held by her father Chief Powhatan. Argall sought out Iopassus, the chief of the Indian town of Passapatanzy. After Argall made veiled threats, Iopassus obtained permission from his brother the Patawomeck district chief to aid Argall. Iopassus had one of his wives insist that Pocahontas accompany her on a tour of Argall's ship. Once aboard, Pocahontas was detained, the ship departed, and she was held captive elsewhere in the colony. During negotiations for her exchange, Pocahontas married John Rolfe in 1614.

E-49 ACCOKEEK IRON FURNACE

Rte. 630, approximately 2 miles west of I-95, at Colonial Forge High School. The Principio Company constructed the Accokeek Iron Furnace nearby about 1726 on land leased from Augustine Washington (father of George Washington), who became a partner. After Washington's death in 1743, his son Lawrence inherited his interest in the company and the furnace. When he in turn died ten years later, his share descended first to his brother Augustine Washington Jr. and later to William Augustine Washington. The archaeological site is a rare example of an 18th-century Virginia industrial enterprise. It includes the furnace location, the wheel pit and races, a retaining wall made of slag, an extensive slag dump, and mine pits.

E-50 FROM INDIAN PATH TO HIGHWAY

Rte. 1, approximately 0.7 miles north of Rte. 628, north of Fredericksburg. In 1664, a colonial road here probably followed the trace of an old Indian path. Two years later, the road was extended to Aquia Creek. It became a post road in 1750, and in Sept. 1781 Gen. George Washington passed over it on the march to Yorktown. By 1900, a crude dirt road followed this route. The 1914 American Automobile Association Blue Book described it as mostly "very poor and dangerous; should not be attempted except in dry weather." By 1925, auto camps and cabins, the predecessors of auto courts and motels, stood at frequent intervals along present-day U.S. Route 1 between Washington, D. C., and Richmond.

E-75 Marlborough

Rte. 1, 3.8 miles north of Falmouth. Strategically situated at the tip of a peninsula jutting into the Potomac River at Potomac Creek, Marlborough was established under the Town Act of 1691 as a river port town. It served as the county seat of Stafford County from 1691 until about 1718. Marlborough never fully developed. In 1726, noted lawyer John Mercer (1705–1768) moved there and built Marlborough plantation and attempted to revive the town. Mercer had one of the largest private libraries in Virginia, in which the young George Mason received much of his education. Mercer's attempt to revive the town was unsuccessful and it ceased to exist by the end of the 18th century.

E-76 First Roman Catholic Settlement in Virginia

Rte. 1, just north of Rte. 637. The crucifix by sculptor Georg J. Lober, erected in 1930, commemorates the first English Roman Catholic settlement in Virginia. Fleeing political and religious turmoil in Maryland, Giles Brent and his sisters Margaret and Mary established two plantations called Peace and Retirement on the north side of Aquia Creek between 1647 and 1650. Later, they jointly acquired 15,000 acres in Northern Virginia, including the site of present-day Alexandria. Their nephew George Brent, whose plantation Woodstock and family cemetery were located nearby, represented Stafford County in the House of Burgesses in 1688, the only Roman Catholic delegate in the colonial period.

E-79 Peyton's Ordinary

Rte. 1, 1.8 miles north of Stafford. In this vicinity stood Peyton's Ordinary. George Washington, going to Fredericksburg to visit his mother, dined here, March 6, 1769. On his way to attend the House of Burgesses, he spent the night here, October 31, 1769, and stayed here again on September 14, 1772. Rochambeau's army, marching north from Williamsburg in 1782, camped here.

E-85 Civilian Conservation Corps—Company 2363

Rte. 17, south of Rte. 654. Here at Berea, during the Great Depression, was the site of Civilian Conservation Corps Company 2363. This camp, one of many in Virginia, was organized in 1935 and disbanded in 1940. During its existence, the company strung farm fences, planted trees, fought forest fires, and instructed farmers in the practice of soil conservation. The CCC, one of President Franklin D. Roosevelt's New Deal agencies, was created in 1933 to provide public service jobs for unemployed young men. Roosevelt later noted that the recruits "grew with purpose and principle" and predicted that they would serve their communities and country with distinction.

E-90 Aquia Church

Rte. 1, 2.7 miles north of Stafford. Here is Aquia Church, the church of Overwharton Parish, formed before 1680 by the division of Potomac Parish. It was built in 1757, on the site of an earlier church, in the rectorship of Reverend John Moncure, who was the parish minister from 1738 to 1764. The communion silver was given the parish in 1739 and was buried in three successive wars, 1776, 1812 and 1861.

E-116 Hunter's Iron Works

Olde Forge Drive, near Rte. 17. Located south of here on the Rappahannock River, stood Hunter's Iron Works, founded by James Hunter and was in operation by the 1750s. With the outbreak of the American Revolution, the Rappahannock Forge there supplied the Continental army and navy with muskets, swords, and other armaments and camp implements. Due to its wartime significance, Gov. Thomas Jefferson ordered special military protection for the complex. The ironworks contained a blast furnace, forge, slitting, merchant, and other mills, nailery, coopers', carpenters', and wheelwright shops and houses for the managers and workmen. Some of the buildings may have been used for other purposes into the 19th century; none survive today.

E-123 HISTORIC AQUIA CREEK

Rte. 1, just south of Rte. 637, Aquia. The first known permanent English Roman Catholic settlers in Virginia, Giles Brent, his sister Margaret, and other family members, emigrated here from Maryland by 1650. In May 1861, Confederates built artillery batteries on the bluffs overlooking Aquia Landing at the creek's mouth on the Potomac River. An early clash between U.S. Naval vessels and Confederate land batteries took place here, 30 May and 1 June 1861. After the Confederates withdrew in March 1862, the U.S. Army established a huge supply depot there. The Federals burned and abandoned it on 7 June 1863. The landing again served as a Union depot in 1864.

E-126 HARTWOOD PRESBYTERIAN CHURCH

Hartwood Church Road, just off Rte. 17, in front of church, Hartwood. Organized in June 1825 by the Winchester Presbytery as Yellow Chapel Church, the brick church was constructed between 1857 and 1859. It became Hartwood Presbyterian Church in 1868. During the Civil War an engagement took place here on 25 Feb. 1863. Confederate Brig. Gen. Fitzhugh Lee, commanding detachments of the 1st, 2d, and 3d Virginia Cavalry Regiments, defeated a Union force and captured 150 men. The interior wooden elements and furnishings of the church suffered considerable damage during the war, but were replaced. The building was listed on the Virginia Landmarks Register and the National Register of Historic Places in 1989 and it is an American Presbyterian Reformed Historical Site.

J-60 CHATHAM

Rte. 3, 0.2 miles east of Fredericksburg. Here is Chatham, built about 1750 by William Fitzhugh. Here Robert E. Lee came to court his wife. In the battle of Fredericksburg, December 13, 1862, the house was occupied by General Sumner. It was General Hooker's headquarters for a time, 1863.

J-61 GEORGE WASHINGTON'S CHILDHOOD HOME

Rte. 3, east of Rte. 606, east of Fredericksburg. The Washington family moved to a plantation here in 1738 when George Washington was six years old. Along with his three brothers and sister, young Washington spent most of his early life here, where, according to popular fable, he cut down his father's cherry tree and uttered the immortal words, "I cannot tell a lie." His father, Augustine, died here in 1743, leaving the property to him. His mother, Mary Ball Washington, lived here until 1772 when she moved to a house in Fredericksburg that Washington bought for her.

J-92 AQUIA LANDING

Rte. 608, at Rte. 685. The Richmond, Fredericksburg and Potomac Railroad was extended to its terminus here at Aquia Landing in 1846. By steamboat and railroad, travelers from Washington, D.C., to Richmond could complete in 9 hours a journey that took 38 hours by stagecoach. In May–June 1861, Confederate batteries at Aquia Landing exchanged fire with Union gunboats. The first use of nautical mines ("torpedoes") in the war occurred here on 7 July 1861 against the U.S.S. *Pawnee*. After the Confederates abandoned the site in 1862, the Union army built new wharves and storage buildings for supplies. The army burned them in 1863, when it pursued the Confederate army into Pennsylvania. The railroad was extended across Aquia Creek in 1872.

J-93 LITTLE FALLS

Rte. 3, east of Fredericksburg. On 11 December 1862, Union engineers began the construction of pontoon bridges here so the army could cross the Rappahannock River to Fredericksburg. They began in the morning, hidden by fog. Soon the fog lifted, however, and Confederate sharpshooters drove them off. A heavy Union artillery barrage and an amphibious assault finally secured the crossing and the engineers completed the bridges. Two days later, Brig. Gen. William B. Franklin's Left Grand Division, including divisions led by Maj. Gen. George G. Meade and Brig. Gen. Abner Doubleday, crossed over the bridges when the Battle of Fredericksburg began. They were defeated by Confederate Lt. Gen. Thomas J. "Stonewall" Jackson's corps.

N-4 Fredericksburg Campaign

Rte. 17, near Rte. 656, near Berea. Frustrated by the Army of the Potomac's lack of progress, President Abraham Lincoln replaced army commander Maj. Gen. George B. McClellan with Maj. Gen. Ambrose E. Burnside, who assumed command on 9 Nov. 1862. Within a week, he had the army marching from its camps near Warrenton toward Fredericksburg along this road. Burnside hoped to cross the Rappahannock River at Fredericksburg by pontoon bridges and march on Richmond, but a delay in the arrival of the pontoons thwarted his plan. By the time the bridges arrived, Gen. Robert E. Lee's army blocked his path. Burnside forced a crossing of the river on 11 Dec. but was defeated two days later at the Battle of Fredericksburg.

N-5 Cavalry Affairs

Rte. 17, 8 miles northwest of Falmouth. Near here Wade Hampton with a small cavalry force surprised and captured 5 officers and 87 men of the Third Pennsylvania Cavalry, November 28, 1862. At that time Burnside was moving toward Fredericksburg. On February 25, 1863, Fitz Lee, on a reconnaissance, attacked Union cavalry here, driving it back on Falmouth where the Union army was encamped.

N-6 The Mud March

Rte. 17, south of Rte. 654, at Rte. 700. In Jan. 1863, after the Federal defeat at the First Battle of Fredericksburg on 13 Dec., Maj. Gen. Ambrose E. Burnside sought to restore the army's morale by crossing the Rappahannock River at Banks's Ford two miles south and attacking the rear of Gen. Robert E. Lee's army. The march began on 19 Jan.; that night a warm front thawed the frozen roads with 48 hours of pouring rain. Confederates across the river taunted the sodden Federals with large signs: "This Way to Richmond" and "Burnside Stuck in the Mud." Burnside canceled the march on 23 Jan., and two days later President Abraham Lincoln replaced him with Maj. Gen. Joseph Hooker.

N-34 Gen. Hooker's Headquarters

Rte. 218, approximately 0.3 miles south of Rte. 3. Just northeast, Maj. Gen. Joseph Hooker, commander of the Union Army of the Potomac, kept his headquarters, Jan.–June 1863, amid a vast city of tents and camps. It was here he rehabilitated the Union army after its catastrophic defeat in the First Battle of Fredericksburg in Dec. 1862 and its subsequent "Winter of Discontent." From here he designed a campaign to defeat Gen. Robert E. Lee's Army of Northern Virginia at Chancellorsville—a brilliant plan that failed in May 1863 because of his hesitancy and Lee's aggressiveness. President Abraham Lincoln twice visited Hooker, here in April 1863 and again in May, after the defeat.

N-36 Moncure Daniel Conway

Rte. 607, east of Rte. 1003. Nearby to the northwest is the childhood home of renowned abolitionist, writer, and lecturer Moncure Daniel Conway (1832–1907). In 1838 his family moved into this Federal-style house. Conway graduated from Dickinson College in 1849 and Harvard Divinity School in 1854 and became outspoken in the abolitionist movement. During the

Civil War, Conway lived in Cincinnati, Ohio and traveled east in 1862 to lead his family's slaves to freedom in Yellow Springs, Ohio. Conway moved to London in 1863 and spent a number of years abroad, writing for English and American periodicals. He also wrote biographies of Ralph Waldo Emerson, Nathaniel Hawthorne, and Thomas Paine. Conway died in Paris on 15 Nov. 1907.

Northern Piedmont, Valley, and Western Mountains

THIS SECTION COVERS the northern Piedmont and Blue Ridge, the Shenandoah Valley, and the western Alleghenies, all of which comprises the counties of Alleghany, Augusta, Bath, Botetourt, Clarke, Craig, Culpeper, Fauquier, Frederick, Greene, Highland, Madison, Orange, Page, Rappahannock, Rockbridge, Rockingham, Shenandoah, and Warren, and the cities of Buena Vista, Covington, Harrisonburg, Lexington, Staunton, Waynesboro, and Winchester. Numerous tourist destinations, such as Shenandoah National Park, Luray Caverns, and Natural Bridge, showcase the natural beauty of this part of Virginia.

European settlement began in the northern Piedmont in the 1710s. In 1714, Lieutenant Governor Alexander Spotswood founded Germanna in what is now Orange County and settled German immigrants there. The English soon moved into the area. President James Madison was a lifelong resident of Orange County, and President Zachary Taylor was born there. Historical markers note the site of Germanna, as well as Madison's home, Montpelier.

The history of the Valley of Virginia has been influenced by its geography, which features a series of river valleys separated by mountains running generally northeast to southwest. The Valley extends from the Potomac River in the north to the Botetourt/Roanoke County line in the south. The upper half is encompassed by the Shenandoah Valley, drained by the Shenandoah River as it flows north to its confluence with the Potomac. The Allegheny Mountains and West Virginia, a part of the commonwealth until the Civil War, mark the western section of the region.

For thousands of years Native Americans of many nations used the Valley as a trail, and some called it home. The earliest European settlers arrived during the late 1720s and early 1730s, funneling from Pennsylvania south through the corridor. They tended to be German and Scotch-Irish rather than English, and they found rich farmland along the bottoms. By the mid-eighteenth century, the Valley and its Great Wagon Road formed the primary migration and transportation route for those traveling between Pennsylvania and the Carolinas, as well as for settlers heading west through the Cumberland Gap.

Early major cities in the region included Winchester and Staunton. Both began in the mid-eighteenth century as small farming communities and

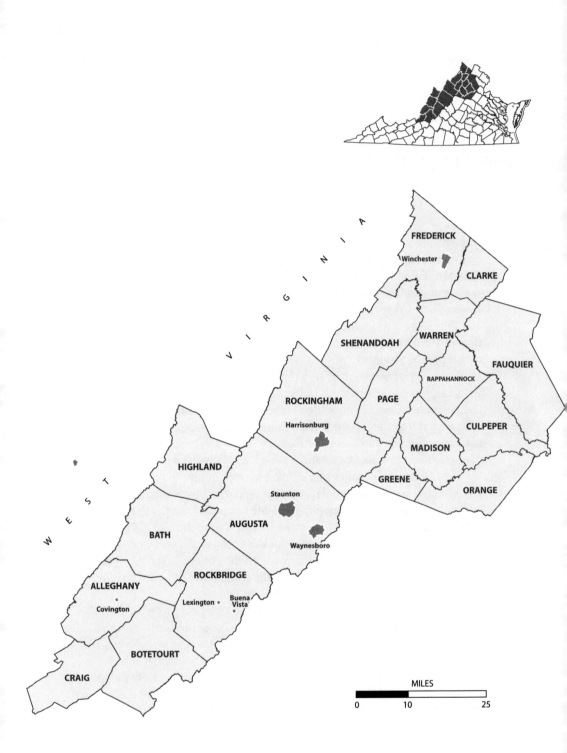

FREDERICK

Winchester

CLARKE

SHENANDOAH

WARREN

FAUQUIER

RAPPAHANNOCK

ROCKINGHAM

PAGE

Harrisonburg

CULPEPER

V I R G I N I A

HIGHLAND

MADISON

GREENE

Staunton

ORANGE

AUGUSTA

BATH

Waynesboro

W E S T

ROCKBRIDGE

ALLEGHANY

Lexington

Buena
Vista

Covington

BOTETOURT

CRAIG

MILES

0   10   25

developed into thriving towns and important trading centers at the junction of several transportation arteries. Winchester served as George Washington's headquarters from 1755 to 1758 while he commanded Virginia troops on the western frontier during the period of the Seven Years' War, and he oversaw the construction of a series of forts there.

During the Civil War, the northern Piedmont and the Shenandoah Valley were of strategic significance—the Piedmont due to its network of roads and rails, and the Valley because of its grain production. Agriculture flourished by the early nineteenth century, leading the Valley to become the principal grain-producing part of the state by the outbreak of the war.

A number of significant military engagements occurred in this area, including the battles of the Wilderness, Brandy Station, and Cedar Mountain; the Shenandoah Valley campaigns of 1862 and 1864–65; and the opening of the Gettysburg campaign of 1863. Markers throughout the region provide information about the Northern and Southern armies and their battles and skirmishes.

Both the northern Piedmont and the Valley recovered rapidly after the war, due in part to the richness of the soil and the renewed exploitation of mineral wealth, particularly in the Valley.

By the early twentieth century, the region had settled back into a predominantly rural existence. In recent decades, rapid growth around Washington, D.C., and the construction of Interstates 81 and 66 have spurred development, and many parts of the area have become suburbs of the nation's capital.

ALLEGHANY COUNTY

D-26 FORT BRECKENRIDGE

Rte. 220, north of Covington. Fort Breckenridge, also called Fort Mann, stood three miles west at the mouth of Falling Spring Creek. It was built by 1756 during the French and Indian War (1754–1763) as one in a series of fortifications to protect Virginia's frontier. Capt. Robert Breckenridge and his militia garrisoned the fort, which was inspected by Col. George Washington on his frontier tour in 1756. In 1763, during Pontiac's War (1763–1764), the Shawnee chief Cornstalk led a force against the fort but was defeated in a hard fought engagement.

D-26 FORT BRECKENRIDGE

Rte. 220, north of Falling Spring Falls. Three miles west at the mouth of Falling Spring Creek was a post garrisoned by militia under Capt. Robert Breckenridge. Washington inspected it in 1756. It survived an attack by Shawnees under Cornstalk during Pontiac's War in 1763.

D-33 LOW MOOR IRON COMPANY COKE OVENS

Rte. 1101, 0.04 miles east of Rte. 696. Here stand the earliest coke ovens of the Low Moor Iron Company (organized 1873). The ovens converted coal into coke to fuel the company's blast furnace. The company built more than a hundred such ovens in 1881. By 1923 the Low Moor Iron Company employed 1,600 workers in Virginia and West Virginia, could produce 75 tons of foundry iron a day, and supported the company town of Low Moor. The last survivor among Alleghany County's once-thriving ironworks, the company closed in 1926.

KH-1 GOVERNOR JOHN FLOYD'S GRAVE

Rte. 311, at the state line. Just over the state line in West Virginia is the grave of physician and politician John Floyd. He was born in Jefferson County, Virginia (now Kentucky), on 24 Apr. 1783. He married Laetitia Preston in 1804 and received his medical degree from the University of Pennsylvania in 1806. After serving in the War of 1812, he was elected to Virginia's General Assembly in 1814. In 1817, he was voted into Congress and remained there until 1829. An advocate of westward expansion, Floyd in 1821 introduced the first bill for organizing the Oregon territory. He served as Virginia's governor from 1830 to 1834. Floyd died in 1837.

L-3 DOUTHAT STATE PARK

Rte. 60, 1.5 miles east of Clifton Forge. This park was developed by the National Park Service, Interior Department, through the Civilian Conservation Corps, in conjunction with the Virginia Conservation Commission. It covers nearly 4500 acres and was opened, June 15, 1936. It lies in a region once extensively devoted to iron smelting.

L-4 OAKLAND GROVE PRESBYTERIAN CHURCH

Rte. 696, west of Selma. First called the Church by the Spring, Oakland Grove Church may have been organized as early as 1834, but it was officially established circa 1847 as a mission of Covington Presbyterian Church. A simple brick house of worship constructed during a religious reawakening among area Presbyterians, Oakland Grove is the oldest-known church building in Alleghany County and is one of the county's chief historic landmarks. During the Civil War, Confederates used the church as a hospital, and its military significance was further enhanced by the proximity of the Jackson River depot on the Virginia Central Railroad just to the east.

L-5 LUCY SELINA FURNACE

Rte. 60, Longdale. This furnace was built in 1827 by Ironmasters John Jordan and John

Irvine and was named for their wives. During the Civil War, iron produced here was used in the manufacture of Confederate Munitions.

AUGUSTA COUNTY

A-31 OLD PROVIDENCE CHURCH

Rte. 11, at Rte. 620, 1.4 miles north of Steeles Tavern. Two and a half miles northwest. As early as 1748, a log meeting house stood there. In 1793 a stone church (still standing) was built. In 1859 it was succeeded by a brick church, which gave way to the present building in 1918. In the graveyard rest ancestors of Cyrus McCormick, inventor of the reaper, and fourteen Revolutionary soldiers.

A-39 NEW PROVIDENCE CHURCH

Rte. 11, Steeles Tavern. This church, seven and a half miles west, was organized by John Blair in 1746. Five successive church buildings have been erected. The first pastor was John Brown. Samuel Brown, second pastor, had as wife Mary Moore, captured in youth by Indians and known as "The Captive of Abb's Valley." The synod of Virginia was organized here, 1788.

A-53 BETHEL CHURCH

Rte. 11, at Rte. 701, 2.1 miles north of Greenville. Two miles west. The first church was built by Colonel Robert Doak in 1779. Captain James Tate, an elder, led in the battles of Cowpens and Guilford Courthouse (1781) a company drawn mainly from this church. In the churchyard 23 Revolutionary soldiers are buried. The present building was erected in 1888.

A-99 WILLOW SPOUT

Rte. 11, at Rte. 742 (Willow Spout Rd), Fort Defiance. Here stood, from the early 19th century until the mid-1900s, the tavern and stagecoach stop first owned by Peter Hanger. In 1848 its second proprietor, Samuel Harnsbarger, planted a willow tree in a spring here, across the newly-constructed Valley Turnpike from the toll-house. Spring water flowed up the trunk and out a spout driven in its side, falling into a wooden trough. For more than a century, three successive "willow spouts" provided water for thirsty travelers, horses, and automobiles.

A-100 AUGUSTA MILITARY ACADEMY

Rte. 11, south of entrance to academy, Fort Defiance. Soon after the Civil War ended in 1865, Confederate veteran Charles S. Roller began teaching at the Old Stone Church nearby at Ft. Defiance. By 1874 he had founded Augusta Male Academy and incorporated military discipline into its classical curriculum by 1880. Roller renamed it Augusta Military Academy in 1890; it was the first military preparatory school in Virginia. In 1919, the Academy was among the first schools in America to adopt a Junior Reserve Officers' Training Corps program. The Academy's international reputation for excellence in secondary-level military education attracted more than 7,000 students from the United States and abroad before it closed in 1984.

A-101 MIDDLEBROOK HISTORIC DISTRICT

Rte. 252, near Rte. 670, Middlebrook. Nestled here in the countryside south of Staunton, along historic Middlebrook Road, is one of the oldest villages in the region. William and Nancy Scott sold the first 27 lots in April 1799 to Scots-Irish and German settlers. In 1851, the stagecoach road through the village became the Middlebrook and Brownsburg Turnpike. By the late 19th century, Middlebrook, the center of a prosperous agricultural community with 274 inhabitants including an African American community, was the county's largest village. Because 20th-century railroads and highways bypassed Middlebrook, the rows of closely spaced dwellings and stores lining the main road retain the picturesque character of the village's heyday in the 1880s.

A-102 SALEM EVANGELICAL LUTHERAN CHURCH

Rte. 804 (Salem Church Road) at Burke's Mill Road, approximately 1 mile west of Rte. 616, at church. Salem Evangelical Lutheran Church traces its existence to 1789 when Shenandoah Valley circuit preacher Paul Henkel held services for the German community in a schoolhouse nearby at Seawright Springs. By 1805, the congregation had built a frame structure on land deeded by Mary and Samuel King. The old Salem cemetery contains several headstones with German inscriptions that date to the early 19th century. In 1859 a new building was constructed. U.S. President Dwight D. Eisenhower's mother, Ida Stover, became a member of the congregation in 1875. The present brick church, dedicated in 1929, stands just north of here.

A-106 MOUNT TABOR LUTHERAN CHURCH

334 Mt. Tabor Road (Rte. 694), approximately 1 mile west of Rte. 252. Shenandoah Valley circuit-riding preacher Paul Henkel formed Mount Tabor Lutheran Church about 1785, several miles to the east. It shared a log building with St. John's, a Lutheran and Reformed union congregation. Under the direction of David Frederick Bittle, the Mount Tabor congregation moved here in 1838 and built a brick church within the current cemetery. In 1842 Bittle and Christopher C. Baughman organized a preparatory school for boys in the church parsonage about a mile west. The school became the Virginia Collegiate Institute in 1845. It moved to Salem in 1847, where it became Roanoke College in 1853. Construction of the present church building was completed in 1889.

D-40 MOSSY CREEK

0.01 miles west of Rtes. 42 and 809. Colonists first settled Mossy Creek in the 1740s. Mossy Creek Iron Works was founded by 1775, when partners Henry Miller and Mark Bird began operating an iron furnace, forge, and mills here. The ironworks became an important industrial enterprise and produced pig iron and finished pieces that were sold throughout western Virginia. Bird sold his interest in the ironworks to Miller in 1779. A community grew up around the ironworks, which likely ceased operation during the Civil War. By 1852 the Mossy Creek Academy was established by Jedediah Hotchkiss, later the cartographer for Confederate Maj. Gen. Thomas J. "Stonewall" Jackson. The school remained in operation until about 1861.

I-11-a ROANOKE COLLEGE

Rte. 11, at Rte. 701, 2.1 miles north of Greenville. Five miles west is the birthplace of Virginia Institute, founded in 1842 by David F. Bittle, assisted by Christopher C. Baughman. Chartered on January 30, 1845, as Virginia Collegiate Institute, the school was moved to Salem, Virginia, in 1847, and was chartered as Roanoke College, March 14, 1853.

I-18 WOODROW WILSON REHABILITATION CENTER

Rte. 250, at Rte. 358, approximately 1 mile west of Fishersville. In 1947 the Woodrow Wilson Rehabilitation Center became the first state comprehensive rehabilitation center in the United States. Operated by the Virginia Department of Rehabilitative Services, this residential facility offers various programs for individuals with a wide range of physical, emotional, and mental disabilities to help them live more independently.

JD-14 JARMAN'S GAP

Rte. 340, south of Rte. 611, 1.2 miles north of Waynesboro. Five miles east, formerly known as Woods' Gap. Michael Woods, his three sons and three Wallace sons-in-law (Andrew, Peter, William), coming from Pennsylvania via Shenandoah Valley, crossed through this pass into Albemarle County in 1734—pioneers in settling this section. In 1780–81 British prisoners taken at Saratoga went through the gap en route to Winchester. In June 1862 part of Jackson's army, moving to join Lee at Richmond, used this passage.

JD-15 JOHN COLTER

Rte. 340, 2.5 miles south of I-64. John Colter, born in Stuart's Draft about 1775, was a member of the northwest expedition led by Meriwether Lewis and William Clark (1804–1806). During his subsequent, solitary explorations of the West, Colter traversed the area now comprising Yellowstone National Park and discovered several passes through the Rocky Mountains suitable for wagon trains. His escape from the Blackfeet Indians following a footrace for his life has become a legend of the West. Colter died in Missouri in 1813.

W-79 LAST INDIAN CLASH

Rte. 250, 4 miles west of Staunton. Near this spot in 1764, Shawnee Indians killed John Tremble (Trimble) in the last such event in Augusta County. During the preceding decade, a series of conflicts between Native Americans and European settlers occurred along the western frontier of the colonies. They included the French and Indian War (1754–1763), Cherokee War (1759–1761), and Pontiac's War (1763–1764). Although Chief Pontiac conducted most of his warfare between Detroit and Pittsburgh, the effects of that conflict rippled up and down the frontier.

W-149 FORT EDWARD JOHNSON

Rte. 250, at Augusta/Highland County line. Confederate troops, the remnant of the Army of the Northwest commanded by Brig. Gen. Edward "Allegheny" Johnson, constructed this fortification about 1 Apr.

1862 to protect the Shenandoah Valley, the "Breadbasket of the Confederacy." Federal troops briefly occupied the fort after he withdrew to West View near Staunton later that month. With Maj. Gen. Thomas J. "Stonewall" Jackson's Army of the Shenandoah, Johnson's command confronted Union forces under Brig. Gen. Robert H. Milroy and Brig. Gen. John C. Frémont at the Battle of McDowell on 8 May. Johnson's ankle was shattered during this first victory in Jackson's famous Valley campaign.

W-155 TINKLING SPRING CHURCH

Rte. 285, at I-64, just north of Fishersville exit. This was first the southern branch of the "Triple Forks of Shenandoah" congregation, which called John Craig as pastor in 1741. A church was completed here about 1748; two other buildings have succeeded it. Beginning with 1777, James Waddel, the noted blind preacher, was supply for some years. R. L. Dabney, of Stonewall Jackson's staff, was the minister here, 1847–1852.

W-156 JAMES EDWARD HANGER

Rte. 250, at Rte. 42 South, Churchville. Born near Churchville on 25 Feb. 1843, Hanger joined the Churchville Cavalry at Phillipi, W.Va., on 2 June 1861, where the next morning he was wounded. The resulting amputation of his leg was probably the first of the Civil War. He convalesced at his parents' house, which stood nearby. Within three months he had invented the first artificial limb modeled on the human leg and hinged at the knee. Hanger constructed factories in Staunton and Richmond, and after WWI he built others in France and England. On 15 June 1919 he died and was buried in Washington, D.C., his home since 1906.

W-159 FIRST SETTLER'S GRAVE

Rte. 250, at eastern entrance to Staunton. One mile north is the grave of John Lewis, first settler in this region, who came here in 1732 and died in 1762. He chose the site of the town of Staunton. His four sons,

Thomas, Andrew, William and Charles, took an important part in the Indian and Revolutionary wars.

W-220 GEORGE CALEB BINGHAM

Rtes. 256 and 668, near Grottoes bridge. George Caleb Bingham, a renowned American genre painter of the 19th century, was born in a frame house just north of here on 20 March 1811. Bingham moved to Missouri in 1819, where he began painting portraits in the 1830s and later specialized in paintings of the American West. He died in July 1879 in Kansas City, Missouri.

W-226 MOUNT PLEASANT

Rte. 732 (Frank's Mill Road), 4 miles north of Rte. 250, west of Staunton, near Mt. Pleasant. Mount Pleasant, a venerable stone dwelling exemplifying traditional Shenandoah Valley domestic architecture, was likely erected after John Archer acquired the property in 1761. Colonel George Moffett (1735–1811), bought the property from Archer's estate and lived here until his death. During the Revolutionary War, Moffett led the Augusta militia. According to local tradition, in June 1781 shelter was provided here to some members of the General Assembly fleeing British troops. Moffett also served as the county lieutenant for Augusta County, a justice of the peace, and a trustee of Liberty Academy, now Washington and Lee University. The Moffett family sold the property in 1826 and the interior was remodeled at that time.

W-227 COLONEL GEORGE MOFFETT

Rte. 732 (Frank's Mill Road), 4 miles north of Rte. 250, west of Staunton, near Mt. Pleasant. George Moffett (1735–1811), a prominent regional military and civic leader, had joined the Augusta County militia by 1758. He participated in the French and Indian War (1756–1763), led a militia company at the Battle of Point Pleasant in 1774, and rose to the rank of colonel by 1778. The Augusta County militia unit he commanded participated in several Revolutionary War battles including Guilford Courthouse in 1781. Moffett served as a justice of the peace, sheriff, and County Lieutenant (the county's highest military officer) for Augusta County (1783–1785). He was also a trustee of Liberty Academy (present-day Washington & Lee University). Moffett lived at Mount Pleasant.

BATH COUNTY

D-24 FORT LEWIS

Rte. 625, 7 miles north of Rte. 39 via Rte. 629, at northwest corner of entrance to Fort Lewis. Col. Charles Lewis, younger brother of Gen. Andrew Lewis, acquired 950 acres of land on the Cowpasture River in June 1750. Nearby, Fort Lewis, a small stockade, initially under the command of then Capt. Charles Lewis, was constructed by 1756 to guard the strategic pass of the Shenandoah Mountain. It was one in a series of forts authorized by the General Assembly to be built on the frontier to protect settlers during the French and Indian War. Fort Lewis existed at least until the end of the war in 1763. The Lewis manor house is located close to where the fort once stood.

D-35 THE COUNTY SEAT OF BATH

Rte. 619, at courthouse, Warm Springs. After 112 years in buildings near the Warm Springs mineral baths a mile northeast, the Bath County Court moved to this site in 1908. The architect, Frank P. Milburn, predicted the new courthouse would be "an honor and ornament to Bath County for generations." It contained a central rotunda with exhibit space, a fireproof vault, and elaborate facilities for jurors including overnight rooms with "nice single iron beds" and toilets. The building burned in 1912, but the county records dating from 1791 onward survived with the loss of only one order book left outside the vault overnight. In 1914 a new, Classical Revival–style courthouse, designed by T. J. Collins and Son, was completed on the same foundation. An addition doubled its size in 1980.

D-36 EARLY BATH COUNTY COURTHOUSES

Rtes. 39 and 220, Warm Springs. Bath County was formed in 1790 from parts of Augusta, Botetourt, and Greenbrier counties. The county court first met here on 10 May 1791 at the house of John Lewis's widow Margaret, who donated two acres opposite the mineral baths for public use. The log jail, built in 1792, and the one-story stone courthouse, constructed in 1796, became inadequate by the 1830s. Citizen petitions to the General Assembly to move the court to nearby Germantown (present-day Warm Springs) or north to Cleek's Mill failed. Instead, the dilapidated buildings were replaced with these brick structures in 1842. The court finally moved to Germantown in 1908 and the old site was advertised for sale as "ideally located for a fine Hotel at this wonderful watering place."

D-37 BACOVA

Rte. 687, 1.2 miles south of Rte. 39, at post office. The Tidewater Hardwood Company built a lumber mill and company town here, 1920–1922, naming it Bacova, a contraction for Bath Co., Va. Narrow-gauge railroads brought the logs to the mill. The company paid workers in scrip redeemable for rent, medical attention, and supplies at the company store. After a decade, mill operations slowed during the Great Depression and stopped altogether in 1936. Salvage metal and railroad engines, rails, and cars were sold to Japan just before World War II. Private investors bought the Bacova tract, and in 1957 the founder of The Bacova Guild, Ltd., a group of artists and craftsmen, purchased the town.

D-38 THE REV. DR. WILLIAM H. SHEPPARD—(28 MAY 1865–25 NOV. 1927)

Rtes. 39 and 220, across from Jefferson Baths, Warm Springs. Born in Waynesboro to former slaves, William H. Sheppard became a Presbyterian missionary to the Belgian colony of Congo Free State in 1890. He and others opposed King Leopold II of Belgium, who encouraged such atrocities as the amputation of children's hands to intimidate Congolese rubber workers. On 21 Aug. 1904, while visiting his mother here, Sheppard spoke out at Warm Springs Presbyterian Church; reportedly, the Belgian ambassador attended. Later, in Africa, Sheppard published his charges, and the Belgian rubber monopoly sued for libel. After a judge dismissed the suit in Sept. 1909, an investigation verified Sheppard's claims and compelled improvements. Sheppard returned permanently to America in 1910.

KB-75 FORT DICKINSON

Rte. 42, 3 miles southeast of Millboro Springs. The site was about one-half mile north of the river. This was one of a chain of frontier forts ordered erected by the Virginia legislature early in 1756. The chain extended from Hampshire County (now West Virginia) to Patrick County on the North Carolina border. These forts were established under the supervision of Colonel George Washington, who made an inspection tour of the chain. This Fort was attacked by Indians at least once in 1756 and again the next year.

Q-5 FORT DINWIDDIE

Rte. 39, 5 miles west of Warm Springs. Known also as Byrd's Fort and Warwick's Fort. Probably built in 1755, it was visited in that year by George Washington.

Q-6 TERRILL HILL

Rtes. 39 and 220, at southeast corner, Warm Springs. Nearby is the site of Terrill Hill, home of the Terrill brothers of Bath County. Brig. Gen. William R. Terrill, a graduate of

West Point, commanded a Union brigade and was killed in the Battle of Perryville, Kentucky, on 8 Oct. 1862. His brother, Brig. Gen. James B. Terrill, a graduate of the Virginia Military Institute, served under A. P. Hill with the 13th Regiment, Virginia Infantry, and died in the Battle of Bethesda Church, on 30 May 1864. The paperwork announcing his promotion to brigadier general arrived just after his death. Legend says their father erected a monument to his sons with the inscription "God alone knows which was right."

Q-13 WINDY COVE PRESBYTERIAN CHURCH

Rte. 39, just west of Rte. 678, at church. Scotch-Irish Presbyterians, seeking freedom of worship and led by the Rev. Alexander Craighead, built a log meetinghouse a mile and a half down the Cowpasture River about 1749. Indians burned it during the French and Indian War. Moving to this site in the cove, named for a nearby limestone "blowing" cave, the congregation erected another log church in 1766. A third log structure, built about 1816, was replaced in 1838 when the prospering community of river planters and upland farmers built the present brick church and session house. A vestibule was added in 1948, and the rear addition in 1959. Windy Cove is the mother church for Presbyterians in Bath and Highland counties.

Q-14 MILLBORO

Rte. 633, 2.5 miles southeast of Rte. 42, Millboro. Millboro began as a settlement around Cady's Tunnel, built by the Central Virginia Railroad. By 1856 the tracks extended from Richmond to Cabin Creek nearby. During the Civil War, Confederate soldiers marched westward down the old Crooked Spur road; army supplies unloaded here were hauled in wagons pulled by confiscated horses. After the war, the town prospered while the railroad brought hundreds of travelers bound for the nearby springs resorts, and while its stockyards shipped large numbers of livestock. When automobile travel and truck-hauling increased, the railroad declined. Stockyards emptied, hotels closed, businesses left, and Millboro settled into a quiet life.

Q-15 MOUNTAIN GROVE

Rte. 39, at Rte. 676, Mountain Grove. The Mountain Grove community grew up around William Gatewood's plantation in the early 19th century. During the Civil War, Brig. Gen. William W. Averell's Federal cavalry attacked from newly created West Virginia late in 1863 and fought with Confederate cavalry in the river valleys and mountain passes of western Bath County. One skirmish occurred while Gen. Robert E. Lee's family vacationed just a few miles east at Warm Springs. Averell sought to halt mining in the caves near Mountain Grove that provided the Confederates with saltpeter, then needed desperately for gunpowder manufacture. He failed, and soon military activity moved to eastern Virginia.

BOTETOURT COUNTY

A-48 AUDLEY PAUL'S FORT

Rte. 11/F-055, 4.5 miles south of Natural Bridge. Nearby stood Capt. Audley Paul's fort, built in 1757 during the French and Indian War (1754–1763) as one in a series of fortifications to protect Virginia's frontier. Paul served as a lieutenant in Maj. Gen. Edward Braddock's ill-fated expedition against the French at Fort Duquesne in 1755. He soon joined Col. William Preston's ranger company as first lieutenant and served in the 1756 expedition against the Shawnee at Sand Creek. In 1761, Paul's fort sheltered settlers fleeing their homesteads in anticipation of Indian attacks. Paul later served in Dunmore's War and fought in the Battle of Point Pleasant, 10 Oct. 1774.

A-58 BUCHANAN

Rte. 11, at Buchanan Presbyterian Church, Buchanan. The town was established in 1811 and named for Colonel John Buchanan, pioneer and soldier. It was incorporated in 1833. Its importance consisted in its being the western terminus of the James River and Kanawha Canal, which reached the town in 1851. Hunter passed here moving to Lynchburg, June, 1864. The town was reincorporated in 1892.

A-80 COMING OF THE RAILROAD

Rte. 11, 4.2 miles north of Troutville. Near here took place the historic meeting of John C. Moomaw and C. M. Thomas that led to the termination of the Shenandoah Valley Railroad at Big Lick (now Roanoke), April, 1881. This was the beginning of the city of Roanoke.

A-81 OLD CAROLINA ROAD

Rte. 11, 8 miles north of Roanoke. This is the old road from Pennsylvania to the Yadkin Valley, over which in early times settlers passed going south. On it were the Black Horse Tavern and the Tinker Creek Presbyterian Church.

A-82 CLOVERDALE FURNACE

Rte. 11, 8.2 miles north of Roanoke. Here was situated Cloverdale Furnace, an early iron industry, developed by Carter Beverly, in 1808.

A-91 LOONEY'S FERRY

Rte. 11, 0.7 miles south of Buchanan. Looney's Ferry, established in 1742, was the first crossing over James River in this region. On the other side of the river was Cherry Tree Bottom, home of Colonel John Buchanan, and above the mouth of this creek stood Fort Fauquier, 1758–1763.

A-92 CARTMILL'S GAP

Rte. 11/F-055, at exit 168. This gap, just west, is named for Henry Cartmill who acquired land nearby on Purgatory Creek. During the French and Indian War (1754–1763), conflicts between Indians and settlers increased in this area. In 1757, Indians laid waste to several nearby farmsteads, including the Robert Renick settlement a few miles north near present-day Natural Bridge. Renick was killed, while his wife and children (William, Robert, Thomas, Joshua, and Betsy) were taken captive. A neighbor, Hannah Dennis, also was made prisoner; Joseph Dennis, her husband, and their child were among those killed. The Indians escaped south through Cartmill's Gap.

D-28 FINCASTLE

Rte. 220, at Rte. 1204, Fincastle. Miller's place here was selected as the county seat of Botetourt in 1770. In 1772 the town of Fincastle was established on land donated by Israel Christian and named for Lord Fincastle, eldest son of Governor Lord Dunmore. It was incorporated in 1828. In 1845 it had a population of 700. The present courthouse was erected about 1850.

D-29 FORT WILLIAM

Rte. 220, at Rte. 670, 3 miles south of Fincastle. Col. William Preston constructed Fort William nearby in 1755 during the French and Indian War (1754–1763) as one in a series of fortifications to protect Virginia's frontier. A group of Indians paid a friendly visit in Oct. 1755, and Col. George Washington inspected the fort during his frontier tour in 1756. Indians attacked the fort in Oct. 1756 but were repulsed. In 1763, during Pontiac's War (1763–1764), nearby settlers flocked to Fort William for protection.

D-30 GREENFIELD

Rte. 220, approximately 5 miles south of Fincastle, just south of entrance to Greenfield

Industrial Park. Half a mile west stood Greenfield, the home of Col. William Preston. According to local tradition, Stephen Rentfroe constructed a fort there in the 1740s. In 1759, Preston bought the property from Rentfroe and soon built a house that evolved into a large log-and-frame, L-shaped dwelling; a portico supported by two-story columns sheltered the front. Preston became a prominent frontier military leader during the French and Indian War (1754–1763) and the Revolutionary War (1775–1783). He also served in the Virginia House of Burgesses (1765–1771). Greenfield, later the home of Gov. James P. Preston, burned in 1959.

D-31 ROANOKE VALLEY BAPTIST ASSOCIATION

Rte. 220, near Rte. 681, north of Fincastle. The (Roanoke) Valley Baptist Association was organized on 7 August 1841 at nearby Zion Hill Baptist Church. Seventeen congregations constituted the original fellowship of churches; during the next century and a half membership grew to more than seventy churches.

D-32 SANTILLANE

Rte. 220, at Rte. 1211, 0.25 miles south of Fincastle. Near here is Santillane, one of Botetourt County's most distinguished properties. The Greek Revival house sits on a tract of land originally owned by Colonel George Hancock, a member of the United States Congress from 1793–1797. In 1808 Hancock's daughter, Judith, married General William Clark. Clark served from 1803 to 1806 as a leader of Thomas Jefferson's famous Lewis and Clark expedition which was instrumental in opening the West for American settlement.

D-33 BRECKINRIDGE MILL

Rte. 600, approximately 1 mile from Rte. 606, Fincastle. Breckinridge Mill is a rare survivor of the grain and milling industry that figured significantly in the economy of antebellum Virginia. The three-and-a-half story brick structure was erected in 1822 for James Breckinridge, and is one of the oldest mills in the region. Breckinridge was a leading Federalist politician and landowner of southwestern Virginia. His mill replaced an 1804 mill also built for Breckinridge, and remained in operation until about 1939.

D-39 BOTETOURT COUNTY COURTHOUSE FIRE

West Main Street, at courthouse, Fincastle. On 15 December 1970, fire gutted the 1848 Greek Revival–style Botetourt County courthouse. Amid the charred wreckage, in a secure vault, the county's historic records fortunately survived almost unharmed. Because of the near-loss of the Botetourt County records, however, the Virginia General Assembly passed the Virginia Public Records Act in 1975. The act mandated that deeds, wills, and other vital records be inventoried and microfilmed and copies of the film stored permanently in the Library of Virginia in Richmond for safekeeping. The Botetourt County courthouse was reconstructed and reoccupied in 1975.

D-41 DALEVILLE COLLEGE

Rte. 220, south of Rte. 674. Daleville College began as a private school that Church of the Brethren educator Isaac N. H. Beahm conducted for the children of Benjamin F. Nininger and George Layman in 1890. The construction of school buildings began the following year. In 1892, the school incorporated as the Botetourt Normal College. It was renamed Daleville College in 1910. Affiliated with the Church of the Brethren, the college merged with Bridgewater College effective in 1924. The campus became Daleville Academy, a secondary school, until it closed in 1933. The surviving academic buildings here are good examples of early-20th-century educational architecture in Virginia.

CITY OF BUENA VISTA

L-11 MOOMAW'S LANDING

Rte. 60 (W. 29th Street), at Culvert Avenue. Here was Moomaw's Landing on the North River Canal. In May 1863 the Packet Marshall passed here bearing the body of General Thomas J. ("Stonewall") Jackson to Lexington. Mrs. Robert E. Lee used the canal in 1865 to join her husband at Washington College (now Washington and Lee University) in Lexington.

CLARKE COUNTY

B-2 THE BRIARS

Rte. 340, at Rte. 620, 3 miles north of Boyce. Two and a half miles to the northwest stands The Briars, a stuccoed stone, two-story, five-bay dwelling that was constructed around 1819 as the home of Dr. Robert Powell Page. His daughter, Mary Francis Page, married John Esten Cooke, noted Virginia novelist, soldier, and historian. They moved to the house in 1869. Cooke lived at The Briars until his death in 1886. Besides being a very successful author, Cooke also served during the Civil War with distinction as the chief ordinance [ordnance] officer for Maj. Gen. J. E. B. Stuart, C.S.A.

B-4 SARATOGA

Rte. 340, at Rte. 723, at volunteer fire company, Boyce. A half-mile east, Revolutionary War hero Daniel Morgan began this limestone Georgian mansion in 1779 while on furlough. He named it for the Battle of Saratoga in which he had recently distinguished himself. The house was probably constructed by Hessian soldiers held prisoner in nearby Winchester. Recalled to duty in 1780, Morgan was made a brigadier general and won a brilliant victory at Cowpens in South Carolina. In the antebellum period Saratoga was the home of Philip Pendleton Cooke, Virginia story writer and poet. It was later occupied by his brother, John Esten Cooke, historical novelist and biographer.

B-7 SIGNAL STATION

Rte. 50/17, 0.7 miles west of Paris. On the hilltop to the south stood an important signal station used by both armies, 1861–1865.

B-23 ASHBY'S GAP

Rte. 50/17, west of Paris. Ashby's Gap was named in honor of John Ashby, a leader among local pioneers and reputedly the first person to haul a hogshead of tobacco through this gap. Part of the house standing just to the south may have been erected in the 1740s by Thomas Ashby or his son, John. Occasionally the house was known as Ashby's Tavern, as was one in Paris, and later another near Ashby's Ferry on the Shenandoah River.

B-37 BLANDY EXPERIMENTAL FARM

Rte. 50/17, at Rte. 780, at entrance to state arboretum. In 1926, Graham F. Blandy bequeathed a 712-acre portion of his estate, The Tuleyries, to the University of Virginia to educate "boys farming in the various branches." Beginning late in the 1920s, the two-story, century-old brick slave quarters was enlarged and converted into laboratories and housing, and 172 acres were developed into an arboretum. Containing one of the most diverse collections of trees and woody shrubs in the eastern United States, Blandy Experimental Farm was designated the State Arboretum of Virginia in 1986. The University of Virginia uses Blandy Farm for environmental research and education.

B-38 GREENWAY HISTORIC DISTRICT

Rte. 50/17, at Rte. 255. This 30-square-mile scenic landscape illustrates the evolution of a unique rural community. Unlike the rest of the Shenandoah Valley, where mostly Scots-Irish and German immigrants settled on small farms, Virginia Tidewater gentry occupied most of this district. These families brought with them their wealth and a slave-based economy, which they employed to build and maintain large plantations. Significant residents included Thomas Lord Fairfax, proprietor of the Northern Neck; Nathaniel Burwell, grandson of Robert "King" Carter; Gen. Daniel Morgan, Revolutionary War hero; and William Meade, third Episcopal Bishop of Virginia.

J-1 BERRYVILLE WAGON TRAIN RAID

Rte. 340, 1 mile north of Berryville. Just after dawn on 13 Aug. 1864, Col. John Singleton Mosby and 300 of his 43d Battalion Partisan Rangers attacked the rear section of Maj. Gen. Philip H. Sheridan's 600-vehicle wagon train here. The train, headed for Winchester, carried supplies for Sheridan's cavalry. Mosby surprised and routed the Federals as they rested, cooked breakfast, and hitched their horses. Mosby's men, losing only one killed and one mortally wounded, captured 200 beef cattle, 500–600 horses, 100 wagons, and 200 soldiers. The raid ended by 6:30 a.m. Berryville's citizens, including many small boys, helped burn the wagons after liberating their contents.

J-1-a BUCK MARSH BAPTIST CHURCH

Rte. 340, 1 mile north of Berryville. Organized near this spot by Wm. and Daniel Fristoe in 1772. Constituted by elders John Marks and John Garrard, the latter serving as its pastor. James Ireland served as pastor from 1778–1806 and is buried here.

J-14 LEE'S BIVOUAC, GETTYSBURG CAMPAIGN

Rte. 340, 1 mile north of Berryville. Gen. Robert E. Lee bivouacked near here on 18–19 June 1863, as he began his invasion of Maryland and Pennsylvania. Part of his Army of Northern Virginia marched north toward Winchester, while Lt. Gen. James Longstreet's corps camped here with Lee. On 13 June, a Union force under Col. Andrew T. McReynolds had evacuated Berryville and marched to Winchester to join Maj. Gen. Robert H. Milroy's division there. Lt. Gen. Richard S. Ewell's corps attacked and defeated Milroy in the Second Battle of Winchester on 13–15 June, thereby clearing the northern Shenandoah Valley in Virginia of Federal forces.

J-18 DOUBLE TOLLGATE

Rte. 340 at Rtes. 522 and 277, Double Tollgate. Early in the 19th century, three important roads crossed here: Nineveh Turnpike leading to Front Royal, Winchester Turnpike leading to the north, and Newtown Turnpike connecting Stephens City and the Shenandoah River via the Winchester and Berrys Ferry Turnpike. Two tollgates served the roads. During the mid-19th century, the intersection was called Highland Corners. A Civil War cavalry engagement occurred here on 11 Aug. 1864 between Confederates led by Brig. Gen. John D. Imboden and Union forces commanded by Brig. Gen. George A. Custer.

J-19 JOSEPHINE CITY

Josephine Street, east of Church Street, Berryville. To improve the lives of former slaves, Ellen McCormick, widow of Edward McCormick, of Clermont, established this African American community of 31 one-acre lots early in the 1870s. The lots, laid out on either side of a 16-foot-wide street that originated near the tollgate on the Berryville Turnpike, sold for $100 each. The community probably was named for Josephine Williams, who owned two lots. By 1900, Josephine City had become an oasis for Clarke County's African American residents and included a school, grocery store, gas station, boarding house, restaurant, cemetery, and two churches.

J-20 LONG MARSH RUN RURAL HISTORIC DISTRICT

Rte. 340, at Rte. 641, north of Berryville. This 16-square-mile scenic landscape illustrates the changing patterns of rural life since the 1730s as shown in its plantations, farms, mills, churches, and African American communities. The first settlers came from various places, including New Jersey, Maryland, and the Virginia Tidewater. English cultural influences, however, shaped the economic, political, and social character of the area into a western outpost of Tidewater society. The district contains many estates associated with pioneer families, including the Washingtons at Fairfield, Audley, and Elmington; the Larues at Bloomfield, Claremont, and Villa La Rue; and the Allens at Clifton and Balclutha.

J-21 TOWN OF BOYCE

Rtes. 340 and 723, Boyce. Boyce was established in 1880 at the intersection of the newly constructed Shenandoah Valley Railroad (now Norfolk Southern) and the road between the Shenandoah River and Winchester (formerly the Winchester and Berry's Ferry Turnpike). First known as Boyceville, the village was named for Col. Upton Boyce (1832–1937), who settled in the area after the Civil War and whose influence secured funding for the railroad. Incorporated as Boyce in 1910, this railroad town retains its handsome 1913 passenger and freight station, 1908 bank, and churches, stores, and residences from that era.

J-30 BATTLE OF BERRYVILLE

Business Rte. 7, at Rte. 636, 0.2 miles west of Berryville. As it maneuvered against Lt. Gen. Jubal A. Early's Army of the Valley, Maj. Gen. Philip H. Sheridan's U.S. Army

of the Shenandoah marched south from Halltown, reaching Berryville on 3 Sept. 1864. Finding part of Brig. Gen. George Crook's corps pitching camp just east of here, Maj. Gen. Joseph B. Kershaw's division attacked with limited results. During the night, Early brought up his entire army but by daylight found the Federal position too strongly entrenched behind its eight miles of earthworks to assault. Early withdrew after dark to Winchester where Sheridan defeated him in the Third Battle of Winchester on 19 Sept 1864.

Q-3 BERRYVILLE

Rte. 340, at southern entrance to Berryville. Before 1798 Berryville was known as Battletown, a name that perhaps originated from a local tavern famous for its fistfights. The General Assembly incorporated the town of Berryville on 15 Jan. 1798. Located at a major crossroads of the Shenandoah Valley and northern Virginia, Berryville saw much military activity during the Civil War. On 13 Aug. 1864 Col. John S. Mosby attacked a Union supply train destined for Maj. Gen. Philip Sheridan's troops at Winchester. Important nearby houses include Audley, the home of Nellie Custis, Washington's stepgranddaughter, and Rosemont, the home of Gov. Harry Flood Byrd, Sr.

Q-3-a BERRYVILLE

Rte. 7, at eastern entrance to Berryville. The town was laid out in 1798 on land of Benjamin Berry and was first known as Battletown. Here at "Audley" lived Nellie Custis, Washington's adopted daughter. Here at "Soldier's Rest" lived General Daniel Morgan, who built "Saratoga." Here Lee's army camped on the way to Gettysburg. Near here many engagements occurred, 1862–64.

Q-3-b BERRYVILLE

Rte. 340, at northern entrance to Berryville. The town was laid out in 1798 on land of Benjamin Berry and was first known as

Battletown. Here at "Audley" lived Nellie Custis, Washington's adopted daughter. Here at "Soldier's Rest" lived General Daniel Morgan, who built "Saratoga." Here Lee's army camped on the way to Gettysburg. Near here many engagements occurred, 1862–64.

Q-3-c BERRYVILLE—CLARKE COUNTY

Rte. 7, at western entrance to Berryville. The town was laid out in 1798 on land of Benjamin Berry and was first known as Battletown. Here at "Audley" lived Nellie Custis, Washington's adopted daughter. Here at "Soldier's Rest" lived General Daniel Morgan, who built "Saratoga." Here Lee's army camped on the way to Gettysburg. Near here many engagements occurred, 1862–64.

T-1 CARTER HALL

Rte. 255, just north of Millwood. The house was completed about 1792 by Nathaniel Burwell. Edmund Randolph, Governor of Virginia and Secretary of State, died here. General Stonewall Jackson had his headquarters here, October, 1862.

T-2 OLD CHAPEL

Rte. 255, at Rte. 340, south of Berryville. Lord Fairfax worshipped here in the "Old Chapel" of Colonial Frederick Parish, established 1738. This stone building dates from 1790 and witnessed the early ministry (1810–1835) of Bishop Meade. Governor Edmund Randolph and Col. Nathaniel Burwell lie in this burying ground with relatives, friends, and neighbors.

T-3 GREENWAY COURT

Rte. 340, at Rte. 50/17, 2 miles northwest of Millwood. Three miles south is Greenway Court, residence of Thomas, sixth Lord Fairfax, proprietor of the vast Northern Neck grant, which he inherited. Born in Leeds Castle, England, in 1693, Fairfax settled in Virginia, in 1747, for the rest of his life. He made Greenway Court his home in 1751. George Washington,

employed as a surveyor on this grant, was there frequently in his youth. Fairfax died there, December 9, 1781.

T-4 AUDLEY

Rte. 7, at Business Rte. 7, east of Berryville. The house to the north is the home of Nellie Parke Custis, George Washington's ward, who married his nephew, Major Lawrence Lewis. After her husband's death in 1839, Nellie Custis Lewis settled here, and here she died in 1852.

T-6 THE BURWELL-MORGAN MILL

Rte. 723/255, Millwood. This grist mill, built in 1782–85 by General Daniel Morgan of Saratoga and Colonel Nathaniel Burwell of Carter Hall, was in continuous operation until 1943. Now owned by the Clarke County Historical Association.

T-7 WHITE POST

Rte. 340, at Rte. 658, in village park, south of Rte. 50/17. The crossroads village of White Post grew up around the white-painted marker that Lord Fairfax had erected in the 1760s to point the way to Greenway Court (south), the nearby estate from which he managed his vast proprietary holdings including Battletown, now Berryville (north), Berry's Ferry (east), and Stephen's City (west). The post that gave the town its name has been replaced several times, but its form has been maintained as a village landmark and symbol of community identity for more than two centuries. Bishop William Meade was born at White Post and later led the remarkable revival of the Episcopal Church in the decades following the War of 1812.

T-8 COLONIAL HIGHWAY

Rte. 7, at Rte. 612, 3.7 miles east of Berryville. This is one of the oldest roads leading from the east to the Shenandoah Valley; it crosses the Blue Ridge at Snicker's Gap. The ferry right over the Shenandoah River was granted, 1766. Washington used this road many times. Some distance to the east the first aerial telegraph signals were sent from the roadside, 1868.

T-9 CASTLEMAN'S FERRY FIGHT

Rte. 7, at Rte. 603. Three miles north in July 1864, General Jubal Early's Army, returning from his raid on Washington, was attacked by Federal units which forced a passage of the river. On July 18, Colonel Joseph Thoburn led his troops against the Confederates but was driven back across the river. Rutherford B. Hayes, 19th President of the United States, commanded a Federal brigade in the action.

T-10 CROOK AND EARLY

Rte. 7, 7.7 miles east of Berryville. Early, while passing through this gap on his return from his Washington raid, was attacked by Crook's cavalry, July 16, 1864. Crook destroyed a few wagons; Early captured a cannon.

T-11 FORERUNNER OF WIRELESS TELEGRAPHY

Rte. 7, 7.7 miles east of Berryville. From nearby Bear's Den Mountain to the Catoctin Ridge, a distance of fourteen miles, Dr. Mahlon Loomis, dentist, sent the first aerial wireless signals, 1866–73, using kites flown by copper wires. Loomis received a patent in 1872 and his company was chartered by Congress in 1873, but lack of capital frustrated his experiments. He died in 1886.

T-12 LONG BRANCH

Rte. 626, 0.2 miles west of Rte. 624. This Classical Revival mansion built for Robert Carter Burwell is one of the few remaining residential works in which B. Henry Latrobe, father of the American architectural profession, played a role in design. Latrobe offered suggestions to Burwell for a staircase and piazza in 1811, a few months after workmen had laid the foundations. Hugh Mortimer Nelson added the porticoes and castellated east wing after 1842,

as well as the Greek Revival-style interior trim based on designs published by the architect Minard Lafever. The late Harry Z. Isaacs renovated the mansion in 1989.

T-13 APPALACHIAN TRAIL AND BEARS DEN

Rte. 7, east of Berryville. This 2,100-mile-long hiking path passes through 14 states from Mount Katahdin, Me., to Springer Mountain, Ga., along the ridges of the Appalachian Mountains. Conceived in 1921 by Benton MacKaye, the trail was completed in 1937. It was designated a National Scenic Trail in 1968. One half mile to the south along the trail is Bears Den, a unique rock formation. The nearby stone mansion of the same name, constructed in 1933, is one of several summerhouses built along the Blue Ridge for wealthy Washingtonians between 1880 and 1940. It has been a hostel and lodge since 1986.

T-14 HARRY F. BYRD SR.

Business Rte. 7, at western entrance to Berryville. Harry Flood Byrd Sr. (1887–1966), governor of Virginia (1926–1930) and U.S. senator from Virginia (1933–1965), was a conservative Democrat who led a political machine that directed state politics for four decades. As governor, he instituted Virginia's "pay as you go" fiscal policy, created the state highway system, and established the state historical marker system. In Congress, he advocated economical government and opposed liberal programs. To the south is Rosemont, his home from 1928 to 1966. George Norris, first sheriff of Clarke Co., lived there from 1811 to 1854.

T-15 CLARKE COUNTY COURTHOUSE

Church Street, Berryville. The year after Clarke County was formed in 1836, construction began on a brick courthouse based on county justice David Meade's design. The courthouse was remodeled in the Neoclassical style about 1850 when the portico and cupola were added. Portraits of locally prominent judges and lawyers from the 1840s to the present are displayed in the courtroom. The 1882 commonwealth's attorney's office, the combination sheriff's office and jail, built about 1895, and the 1977 circuit courthouse are also located on the courthouse grounds. The last public hanging in Clarke County occurred here in 1905.

T-16 MILLWOOD

Rte. 255/723, at post office. This village developed around two late-18th-century gristmills and Nathaniel Burwell's Carter Hall plantation, one of the preeminent estates in the area. The Burwell-Morgan Mill in the center of the village was a commercial gristmill, while the Carter Hall Mill served the plantation. In 1865, Confederate Col. John S. Mosby discussed terms of surrender in the J. H. Clarke house and tavern (1842) located across the road. After the Civil War, Millwood included a community of freed blacks with a school and several churches. The village retains many late-19th- and early-20th-century stores and dwellings.

T-17 THE RETREAT

Rtes. 7 and F-709 (Parker Lane), near Shenandoah River bridge. One and a half miles north is The Retreat, home to three distinguished generations of the Parker family. Thomas Parker, a general in the War of 1812, constructed this imposing Federal-style house in 1799. Richard Parker, his nephew, was a U.S. senator, justice of the state Supreme Court of Appeals, and jury member at the trial of Aaron Burr. His son, Richard Elliot Parker, served in the U.S. House of Representatives and presided as a federal judge at the trial of John Brown. During the Civil War, the Battle of Cool Spring was fought near The Retreat on 18 July 1864.

CITY OF COVINGTON

D-27 FORT YOUNG

Rte. 154 (Durant Road), north of Jackson River. Constructed nearby about 1756 as a wooden palisaded fort, Fort Young, originally known as Dickinson's Fort, stood near the Jackson River. It was one in a series of forts authorized by the Virginia General Assembly to be built on the frontier to protect English settlers during the French and Indian War (1754–1763). Col. George Washington likely inspected this fort during his frontier tour in 1756. The fort was an important post and probably garrisoned until at least the close of the American Revolution. Fort Young had disappeared by the middle of the 19th century.

CRAIG COUNTY

KH-2 GREAT EASTERN DIVIDE— ELEVATION—2704 FEET

Rte. 42, 8.1 miles west of Rte. 311. This point marks a spot along the geographical feature known as the Great Eastern Divide. From here water of Sinking Creek flows southwest into the New River. The New River, probably the oldest stream in eastern North America, becomes the Kanawha before joining the Ohio, the Mississippi, and eventually the Gulf of Mexico. From this spot water of Meadow Creek flows northeast to New Castle where it joins Craigs Creek, which in turn flows into the James River and ultimately into the Atlantic Ocean.

KH-3 WILLIAM ADDISON "ADD" CALDWELL—VIRGINIA TECH'S FIRST STUDENT

Rte. 42, at Rte. 625. Three miles north of here stands the childhood home of William Addison "Add" Caldwell. He walked about 28 miles to Blacksburg on 1 October 1872 and became the first student to register at Virginia Agricultural and Mechanical College, now Virginia Polytechnic Institute and State University. Graduating in 1876, Caldwell was elected secretary of his class alumni association. He worked as a teacher, clerk, and salesman before his death on 29 June 1910. He is buried in Radford, Virginia.

KH-4 NEW CASTLE

Rte. 311, New Castle. This place became the county seat when Craig County was formed in 1851. The courthouse was built in 1851 and remodeled in 1935. General Averell passed through New Castle in his raid of December, 1863, and General Hunter in June, 1864. The town was incorporated in 1890.

KH-5 CAPTAIN

Rte. 632, at Rte. 601. The community of Captain received its unusual name in 1888, when a post office was established in the home of Guy Dingus Huffman, who had served as the captain of Company K, 46th Virginia Infantry Regiment, C.S.A., during the Civil War. Huffman had married Sarah Jane Hutchison, a daughter of Col. Robert Mason Hutchison (a War of 1812 veteran) on 9 Feb. 1853. The couple built their house south of John's Creek on Hutchison's land. Huffman served as postmaster until his death in 1910. The post office closed in 1935.

CULPEPER COUNTY

C-8 STUART'S RIDE AROUND POPE

Rte. 622/613, 6 miles west of Warrenton, at Waterloo-Rappahannock River Bridge. Stuart, starting here with his cavalry on August 22, 1862, rode around Pope's army to Catlett's Station. He destroyed supplies and army material and captured Pope's headquarters wagons.

F-3 GREENWOOD

Business Rte. 15, 0.8 miles south of Culpeper. Home of Judge John Williams Green. Judge Green entertained Lafayette here on August 22, 1825.

F-10 WHERE PELHAM FELL

Rte. 15, Elkwood. Four miles southeast, at Kelly's Ford, Major John Pelham, commanding Stuart's horse artillery, was mortally wounded, March 17, 1863.

F-11 BATTLE OF BRANDY STATION

Rte. 15, 0.7 miles north of Brandy Station. Here on 9 June 1863, the largest cavalry battle in North America occurred when 9,500 of Confederate Maj. Gen. J. E. B. Stuart's troopers fought 8,000 cavalrymen under Union Brig. Gen. Alfred Pleasonton. This daylong battle, the opening engagement of the Gettysburg campaign, erupted when the Federal attack surprised Stuart and his men. The Confederates prevented the Union cavalry from learning the intentions of Gen. Robert E. Lee, who had begun marching his infantry to the Shenandoah Valley to invade the North. For the first time in the Civil War, however, the Federal cavalry proved itself a match for its opponents.

F-12 BETTY WASHINGTON

Business Rte. 15/29, 3 miles north of Culpeper. Two miles south is the grave of Betty Washington Lewis, the younger sister of George Washington. She was born in Westmoreland County in 1733 and married Fielding Lewis in May 1750, becoming his second wife. Her husband purchased land in 1752 and built their house, Kenmore, outside Fredericksburg. They had eleven children together, but only five sons and one daughter lived to adulthood. During the Revolutionary War, Fielding Lewis served in the army as a colonel and supervised a gun factory. Betty Washington died on 31 March 1797 while visiting her daughter Betty Lewis Carter in Culpeper County.

F-13 OPENING OF GETTYSBURG CAMPAIGN

Rte. 762, near Brandy Station. On this plain Lee reviewed his cavalry, June 8, 1863. The next day the cavalry battle of Brandy Station was fought. On June 10, Ewell's Corps, from its camp near here, began the march to Pennsylvania.

F-16 LEE AND POPE

Rte. 15, 2 miles south of Culpeper. To the south is Clark's Mountain, behind which Lee's army was gathered, August 17, 1862. From a signal station on the mountain top Lee looked down on Pope's army, which he wished to attack. Pope, realizing his danger, retired northward.

F-19 BATTLE OF CEDAR MOUNTAIN

Rtes. 15 and 299, south of Culpeper. During the afternoon of 9 Aug. 1862, Confederate Maj. Gen. Thomas "Stonewall" Jackson's division led by Maj. Gen. Richard S. Ewell and Brig. Gen. Charles S. Winder fought Union troops led by Maj. Gen. Nathaniel P. Banks about three miles south. Winder was mortally wounded. Banks attacked Winder's troops, who buckled under the Federal assault until Jackson rallied them. Assisted by the arrival of Maj. Gen. A. P. Hill's Light Division, the Confederates struck back early in the evening and Banks's troops retreated north. Darkness halted the Confederate pursuit here, short of Culpeper. Cedar Mountain was the first clash of the Second Manassas Campaign.

F-20 BATTLE OF CEDAR MOUNTAIN

Rte. 15, 6 miles south of Culpeper. Near here Jackson formed line of battle and received the attack of Banks' Corps of Pope's army. From here he attacked in turn, driving the Union forces northward.

F-21 CROOKED RUN BAPTIST CHURCH

Rte. 15, 9.7 miles south of Culpeper, at church. Crooked Run Baptist Church was organized in 1772 and is named for the stream that flows nearby. James Garnett Sr., one of the early pastors, served the congregation from 1774 until close to his death in 1830. Another member, Thomas Ammon, became a minister and was imprisoned in the Culpeper jail for preaching in the late 1700s. The first meeting of the Orange Baptist Association occurred here in 1789. At first the members met in a meetinghouse, but by 1856 they had built a brick structure. This church was destroyed by a fire in 1910 and rebuilt that same year using the remains of the brick walls.

F-25 MITCHELLS PRESBYTERIAN CHURCH

Rte. 652, 0.28 miles east of Rte. 615, at church. This Gothic Revival church, built in 1879, contains an elaborate example of *trompe-l'oeil* fresco painting done in 1888. Joseph Dominick Phillip Oddenino, an Italian immigrant artist, painted to deceive the eye into believing that his plaster murals of Gothic arches, Renaissance-styled cornices, and embellished Corinthian columns were three dimensional. Oddenino decorated the ceilings at Mitchells Church and Hebron Lutheran Church in Madison with geometric designs.

F-25A MITCHELLS PRESBYTERIAN CHURCH

Rte. 522, at Rte. 615, 0.25 miles south of Winston. Built in 1879, this Gothic Revival church stands two miles south of this location. It contains an elaborate example of *trompe-l'oeil* fresco painting done in 1888. Joseph Dominick Phillip Oddenino, an Italian immigrant artist, painted to deceive the eye into believing that his plaster murals of Gothic arches, Renaissance-styled cornices, and embellished Corinthian columns were three dimensional. The ceiling is decorated with geometric designs.

F-34 MOUNT PONY SIGNAL STATION

Rte. 15, 2 miles south of Culpeper. In Aug. 1862, during the Civil War, Union Maj. Gen. John Pope established a signal station on Mount Pony, just northeast of here. On the summit of the mountain, a high scaffold was constructed out of trees for an observation post and a communication center. Because of the good visibility, "powerful glasses" were used to watch troop movements from this vantage point. Both the Federal and Confederate Signal Corps used this site during the war. Other signal stations were built by the Union army on Stony Mountain, Cedar Mountain, Thoroughfare Mountain, and Clark's Mountain.

F-100 COL. JOHN JAMESON

Oak Lawn Boulevard, off Blue Ridge Avenue, Culpeper. Col. John Jameson (1751–1810) owned land nearby. He served as the Culpeper County court clerk (1772–1810) and a captain in the Culpeper Minute Men battalion during the Revolutionary War. In Sept. 1780, while serving under Gen. Benedict Arnold in New York, Jameson following military protocol initially sent Arnold's co-conspirator, Maj. John André to Arnold and forwarded suspicious documents found on André to Gen. George Washington. Jameson requested André's return after being swayed by Maj. Benjamin Tallmadge. Arnold the traitor escaped, but André was hanged. Jameson's property nearby, during the Civil War, became a burial ground for at least 350 soldiers, mostly Confederates, who died in Culpeper hospitals. In 1881, their remains were re-interred at Citizens' Cemetery (now Fairview Cemetery) in a mass grave marked by an 18-foot obelisk.

G-9 CAMPAIGN OF SECOND MANASSAS

Rtes. 211 and 229, west of Warrenton. Here Lee and Jackson had their headquarters. Here, August 24, 1862, they formed the plan to attack Pope's line of supply and bring him to battle before McClellan could join him.

G-9 LITTLE FORK CHURCH

Rte. 229, 6 miles south of Rte. 211. One-half mile east stands Little Fork Episcopal Church, begun 1753, destroyed by fire in 1773. Present structure completed in 1776.

G-10 GENERAL EDWARD STEVENS

Rte. 229, at northern entrance to Culpeper. Here is buried General Edward Stevens, who served at Brandywine, Camden, Guilford Courthouse and Yorktown. He died on August 17, 1820.

J-5 GEORGE WASHINGTON CARVER REGIONAL HIGH SCHOOL

Rte. 15, 6.5 miles south of Culpeper. George Washington Carver Regional High School was founded in 1948 to serve the educational needs of black students in Culpeper, Madison, Orange, and Rappahannock counties. Secondary schools for blacks in those counties were either nonexistent or inadequate for collegiate preparation. The regional high school was established as an economical solution to these problems. In 1968 the school was renamed the Piedmont Technical Education Center.

J-6 JOHN S. BARBOUR'S BIRTHPLACE

Rte. 522 (Sperryville Pike), at western entrance to Culpeper. Just to the south stood Catalpa, where John Strode Barbour was born on 29 Dec. 1820. In 1849, he was appointed the state's representative on the board of directors of the Orange and Alexandria Railroad. The board elected him president in 1851 and he continued in this capacity until he resigned in 1884. Barbour served in the House of Representatives from 1880 to 1886. He also was the chairman of the state Democratic Party committee from 1883 to 1890, and was appointed to the U.S. Senate in March 1889, representing Virginia and serving until his death on 14 May 1892. He is buried in Prince George's County, Maryland.

J-10 CULPEPER MINUTE MEN

Rte. 522, at western entrance to Culpeper. On the hill to the south the famous Culpeper Minute Men were organized in 1775. John Marshall, later Chief Justice of the Supreme Court, was a lieutenant.

J-15 SIGNAL STATIONS

Rte. 3, between Rte. 522 and Stevensburg. The hilltop northeast of this spot is Cole's Hill. The mountain to the west is Mount Pony. Both were used by Pope as signal stations, 1862.

J-32 SALUBRIA

Rte. 3, 0.5 miles east of Stevensburg. Just south stands Salubria, a rare example of Georgian architecture in Virginia's Piedmont. The house is notable for its elegant proportions, fine Flemish-bond brickwork, and superb interior paneling. Salubria probably was constructed in the mid-eighteenth century for the Reverend John Thompson. According to local tradition, he built Salubria in 1742 when he married his first wife, Ann Butler, the widow of Lieutenant Governor Alexander Spotswood. In 1802 James Hansbrough bought the property and named it Salubria, which means healthful. Salubria was the birthplace and family home of Admiral Cary T. Grayson, personal physician to President Woodrow Wilson.

J-33 OPENING OF THE WILDERNESS CAMPAIGN

Rte. 3, Stevensburg. Near here the Second Corps of Grant's army camped in the winter of 1863–64. To this point came Sheridan's cavalry, the Sixth Corps from Brandy Station, and the Fifth Corps from Culpeper. The Union army moved hence to Germanna and Ely's Fords on the Rapidan River, May 4, 1864, to open the Wilderness Campaign.

J-36 BATTLE OF KELLY'S FORD

Rte. 674/620, 11.5 miles east of Culpeper, east of Elkwood. At dawn on 17 March 1863, Brig. Gen. William W. Averell led 2,100 Union cavalrymen across the Rappahannock River at Kelly's Ford. Brig. Gen. Fitzhugh Lee with about 1,000 Confederate horsemen counterattacked northwest of here about noon. Noted Confederate artillerist Maj. John Pelham accompanied Lee's men and fell mortally wounded while impetuously taking part in a charge. The battle ended in a draw, marking the first time Confederate cavalrymen had not defeated their Union opponents, resulting in new confidence for the Union cavalry. It foreshadowed another Union crossing at Kelly's Ford during the much larger battle of 9 June 1863 at Brandy Station.

J-97 ECKINGTON SCHOOL

21649 Mount Pony Road (Rte. 658), 8 miles south of Culpeper. The Eckington School was built in 1895 as a frame, one-room school for African American students from the nearby communities of Eckington and Poplar Ridge. The school building is typical of the ungraded schools of the 19th century that had all grades housed together in the same room. Such schools were common in rural communities until the mid-20th century. The Eckington School building closed in 1941. This structure stands as a rare example of the nearly vanished one-room schoolhouse type, illustrating the importance of education among the rural black community in the decades after the Civil War.

FAUQUIER COUNTY

B-20 JACKSON'S BIVOUAC

Rte. 50, near Rte. 17, near Paris. After a day's march from Winchester on 19–20 July 1861, Brig. Gen. Thomas J. "Stonewall" Jackson halted his lead brigade of Gen. Joseph E. Johnston's Valley army near here.

At 2:00 A.M. his 2,500 men sank down to rest. When told that no sentries had been posted, Jackson stated, "Let the poor boys sleep. I will guard the camp myself." Relieved of his duty an hour before daybreak, Jackson slept briefly, rising at dawn to march to Piedmont Station (now Delaplane), where railcars waited to transport the 11,000-man army to Manassas Junction. There, nearly 30,000 Confederates faced 35,000 Federals at the First Battle of Manassas.

B-21 DELAPLANE—(FORMERLY PIEDMONT STATION)

Rte. 17, near railroad, Delaplane. On July 19, 1861 Stonewall Jackson's brigade of General Joseph E. Johnston's corps marched to this station from Winchester. They crowded into freight and cattle cars and travelled to the 1st Battle of Manassas. The use of a railroad to carry more than ten thousand troops to the Manassas battlefield gave striking demonstration of the arrival of a new era in military transport and contributed significantly to the Confederate victory there.

B-25 MOSBY'S RANGERS

Rte. 50, near Atoka. Here at Atoka (Rector's Crossroads), on June 10, 1863, Company "A," 43rd Battalion of Partisan Rangers, known as "Mosby's Rangers," was formally organized. James William Foster was elected captain; Thomas Turner, first lieutenant; W. L. Hunter, second lieutenant; and G. H. Whitescarver, third lieutenant. Shortly after, Brawner's company of Prince William cavalry joined the command.

B-31 STUART AND GREGG

Rte. 50, east of Upperville. Near here the Union Cavalry General Gregg attacked Stuart and forced him to retire, June 19, 1863.

B-31a BATTLE OF MIDDLEBURG

Rte. 50, 1 mile west of Middleburg, at Fauquier/Loudoun County line. Here, on 19 June 1863, Maj. Gen. J. E. B. Stuart's

cavalry fought Brig. Gen. David M. Gregg's Union cavalry division. Screening the march of Gen. Robert E. Lee's Army of Northern Virginia through the Shenandoah Valley to invade Pennsylvania, Stuart formed a line along this ridge facing Gregg, who charged down this road from Middleburg. Stuart counterattacked, then fell back to another defensive position a half-mile west. In this action, Maj. Heros von Borcke, a Prussian officer and aide to Stuart, fell wounded with a bullet in his neck; he recovered and was at Stuart's deathbed on 12 May 1864.

B-34 WELBOURNE

Rte. 50, near Atoka. One mile northwest stands Welbourne (ca. 1770), which has housed members of the same family since the 1830s. It is a significant example of a late-18th-century stone farmhouse that evolved into an imposing mansion. Welbourne was the home of Col. Richard H. Dulany, C.S.A., who founded the nation's oldest foxhunting club (Piedmont) in 1840, and the oldest horse show (Upperville) in 1853. Visitors during the Civil War included Stuart and Mosby. In the 1930s F. Scott Fitzgerald and Thomas Wolfe stayed at Welbourne. Each writer published a story using the house as a setting.

B-35 MOSBY'S RAID AT CATLETT'S STATION

Rte. 28, near Rtes. 806/667, Catlett. To halt the flow of supplies to Union forces on the Orange & Alexandria R.R., Maj. John S. Mosby, C.S.A., destroyed a train near here on 30 May 1863. Removing a rail to stop the train, Mosby's Rangers disabled the engine with a recently acquired howitzer, described as "too big to fit in a holster, but too small to be a cannon." Alerted by the firing, nearby Union troops (N.Y., Mich., & Vt.), commanded by Col. William D. Mann, attempted to capture the Confederates. Mosby set fire to the railcars and withdrew, fighting a delaying action with his single artillery piece.

B-36 STUART AND MOSBY

Rte. 28, south of Catlett, Cedar Run. Here on the evening of August 22, 1862, General J. E. B. Stuart raided General Pope's headquarters. Unable to burn the railroad bridge because of a heavy thunderstorm, Stuart withdrew his troops as well as 300 Federal prisoners and Pope's dispatch case.

At nearby Warrenton Junction (Calverton) on May 3, 1863, Colonel John S. Mosby attacked the Federal 1st West Virginia Regiment, but was forced to flee when surprised by 1st Vermont and 5th New York Cavalry.

B-39 ELK RUN ANGLICAN CHURCH SITE

Rte. 806, at Rte. 610, Elk Run. Settlers began moving into this region of Fauquier County in the early 1700s. By the 1740s, a wooden church structure served Anglican communicants in Elk Run. It provided pastoral care as well as secular administration for this active frontier community. The first permanent minister, the Reverend James Keith, grandfather of Chief Justice John Marshall, served this church and the rest of Hamilton Parish from the 1740s until his death in 1752. A brick cruciform structure replaced the first church by the late 1750s. After the Revolutionary War and disestablishment, many churches were abandoned. By 1811 the Elk Run Church had fallen into disuse and ruin.

B-40 DEATH OF 2D LT. JAMES "BIG YANKEE" AMES

Rte. 17, 0.25 miles north of Delaplane. Sergeant James F. Ames of the 5th New York Cavalry deserted the Union army in Feb. 1863 and joined Lt. Col. John S. Mosby's Partisan Rangers (later 43d Cavalry Battalion). Nicknamed "Big Yankee," Ames rose to the rank of 2d lieutenant. On the night of 8 Mar. 1863 he guided Mosby's Rangers on the Fairfax Court House raid in which Mosby captured Union Brig. Gen. Edwin Stoughton. On 9 Oct. 1864 a Federal soldier shot and killed Ames on the road leading to Benjamin "Cook" Shacklett's house. The Union soldier was killed by Ranger Pvt. Ludwell Lake, Jr. Ames was buried nearby in an unmarked grave. Mosby said of Ames, "I never had a more faithful follower."

BX-2 BRENT TOWN

Rte. 806, 5 miles south of Catlett, Bristersburg. In 1687, King James II granted 30,000 acres of land here as a sanctuary for Roman Catholics to George Brent, of Stafford County, and London residents Robert Bristow, Richard Foote, and Nicholas Hayward. Brent established a fortified outpost the next year that overlooked an Indian path later called the Carolina Road; the Indians cut a new path farther west. In 1742, when the Prince William County seat was moved from Woodbridge, Brent Town, as the settlement on the Brent tract was known, was called but rejected as the new site. The exact location of Brent Town is unknown.

BX-7 NEAVIL'S ORDINARY

Rte. 670 and Old Dumfries Road, Auburn. Near here stood George Neavil's Ordinary, built at an early date and existing as late as 1792. George Washington and George William Fairfax on their way to the Shenandoah Valley stopped here in 1748.

C-9 McCLELLAN'S FAREWELL

Rte. 29, near Rte. 605, 2.6 miles northeast of Warrenton. After President Abraham Lincoln relieved Maj. Gen. George B. McClellan of command of the Army of the Potomac on 7 Nov. 1862, the general composed a farewell order. It was read to the army by divisions on 10 Nov. when the new commander, Maj. Gen. Ambrose E. Burnside, held a grand review of the army about half a mile north of here. Both Burnside and McClellan attended, and the three-mile-long line of soldiers cheered McClellan heartily, many weeping. This closed McClellan's military career. He returned home to Trenton, N.J., and ran unsuccessfully against Lincoln on the Democratic Party ticket in 1864.

C-29 COLONIAL ROAD

Rte. 29, at Rte. 605, north of Warrenton. This crossroad is the ancient Dumfries-Winchester highway. Over it William Fairfax accompanied George Washington, then a lad of sixteen, on his first visit to Lord Fairfax at Greenway Court. It was on this occasion that Washington assisted in surveying the Fairfax grant.

C-50 THOROUGHFARE GAP

Rte. 55, at Fauquier/Prince William County line. Just west is Thoroughfare Gap, where Union and Confederate armies clashed during the Civil War. In July 1861, Gen. Joseph E. Johnston marched eastward through the gap to join Brig. Gen. P.G.T. Beauregard

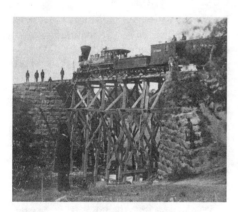

The Orange & Alexandria Railroad (shown here in a photograph by Andrew J. Russell, ca. 1865, entitled "Bridge on the Orange & Alexandria Railroad, as repaired by army engineers under Colonel Herman Haupt") and other rail lines throughout the commonwealth played an important role in shipping farm and mineral products to markets in large cities. The expansion of railroads played a significant role in the state's economic recovery after the Civil War. (Marker C-54) (Library of Congress)

in the First Battle of Manassas. Maj. Gen. Thomas J. "Stonewall" Jackson passed by here on 26 Aug. 1862 to attack the Federal supply depot at Manassas Junction. Two days later, Gen. Robert E. Lee and Maj. Gen. James Longstreet surprised and repelled Union cavalry under Col. Sir Percy Wyndham and an infantry division under Brig. Gen. James Ricketts. Ever after, Union troops occupied the gap whenever Lee's army was near.

C-54 SECOND MANASSAS CAMPAIGN— MANASSAS JUNCTION OPERATIONS

Rte. 29, at Rte. 600, 5.5 miles northeast of Warrenton, New Baltimore. Eight miles southeast, at Bristow (then Bristoe Station), Maj. Gen. Ambrose P. Hill's division of Maj. Gen. Thomas J. "Stonewall" Jackson's corps destroyed the Orange & Alexandria Railroad bridges over Kettle Run and Broad Run on 27 Aug. 1862. The evening before, Jackson had captured Bristoe Station, derailed three trains bound for Manassas Junction, and then, in a rare night attack, seized the huge Federal supply depot at the junction. When Union Maj. Gen. John Pope's army approached from Warrenton the next day, Hill delayed it, burned the bridges, and then marched north with Jackson to the old First Manassas battleground.

C-55 FREDERICKSBURG CAMPAIGN

Rte. 29, at Rte. 605, 2.6 miles northeast of Warrenton. Because he had moved too slowly to attack Gen. Robert E. Lee's Army of Northern Virginia, Maj. Gen. George B. McClellan was relieved of his command of the Army of the Potomac by President Abraham Lincoln. McClellan was replaced by Maj. Gen. Ambrose E. Burnside. Determined to act boldly, Burnside reorganized his army and marched it to Fredericksburg, where he planned to strike south around Lee's right flank toward Richmond. Delays in crossing the Rappahannock River enabled Lee to confront Burnside there, then defeat him in a bloody battle on

13 Dec. 1862—a battle neither general had intended to fight.

C-57 BLACK HORSE CAVALRY

Business Rte. 15, at Rte. 211, Warrenton. The Black Horse Cavalry was conceived at a gathering of Warrenton lawyers in 1858 and was among the local militia companies called to active duty by Governor Henry Wise in 1859. The Black Horse led a successful charge against Union forces at the First Battle of Manassas, winning the special praise of Confederate President Jefferson Davis. Known as Company H of the 4th Virginia Cavalry, the unit served as bodyguard, escort, and scout for generals Joseph E. Johnston and Stonewall Jackson. Following the war, a number of the men of the Black Horse became prominent leaders in the Commonwealth.

C-58 SECOND MANASSAS CAMPAIGN— STUART'S CATLETT STATION RAID

Rte. 211, at Holtzclaw Road, 4 miles west of Warrenton. On 22 Aug. 1862, Maj. Gen. J. E. B. Stuart led his cavalry on a raid behind Union Maj. Gen. John Pope's army. Stuart crossed the Rappahannock River at Waterloo Bridge, two miles west, then rode around Pope's right flank just north of here to attack Catlett Station on the Orange & Alexandria Railroad after dark. The raid did little damage but Stuart captured Pope's colorful dress uniform coat. Stuart, who earlier had lost his plumed hat to Union cavalry, soon wrote Pope suggesting an exchange of "prisoners." Receiving no reply, Stuart sent the coat to Richmond, where Gov. John Letcher displayed it in the Capitol.

C-60 SECOND MANASSAS CAMPAIGN— STRATEGIC RAPPAHANNOCK RIVER CROSSINGS

Rte. 211, 5 miles west of Warrenton, at Rappahannock River bridge, at Fauquier/Culpeper County line. A mile northwest stood Waterloo Bridge, where on 22 Aug. 1862 Maj. Gen. J. E. B. Stuart crossed the Rap-

pahannock River to threaten the rear of Union Maj. Gen. John Pope's army 14 miles southeast at Catlett Station on the Orange & Alexandria Railroad. Pope's men guarded several downstream crossings, including Fauquier White Sulphur Springs (3 miles south), Freeman's Ford, Beverly's Ford, Rappahannock Bridge, Norman's Ford, and Kelly's Ford (16 miles). Gen. Robert E. Lee sent Maj. Gen. Thomas J. "Stonewall" Jackson sweeping north and east around the Federals. The maneuver ended in the Second Battle of Manassas on 29–30 Aug.

CB-1 CAMPAIGN OF SECOND MANASSAS

Rte. 688, 12 miles west of Warrenton, near Orlean. Here Lee and Longstreet, on their way to join Jackson, then at Bristoe Station, camped on August 26, 1862.

CB-2 ASHLAND FARM

Rte. 211, at Rte. 681, 3.5 miles west of Warrenton. The Holtzclaw family acquired Ashland through a grant issued by Lt. Gov. Alexander Spotswood in 1724, and lived on this land until the 1920s. While a portion of the house dates to about 1725, the main residence was completed by 1889, and was remodeled and enlarged by architect William Lawrence Bottomley in 1929. Between 1861 and 1864, the Union army stationed pickets at Ashland, as it was used as a Federal medical dressing station. Legend claims that a Union army payroll, hidden by a paymaster who died in 1862 at nearby Waterloo, Virginia, is still buried here.

CL-3 JOHN MARSHALL'S BIRTHPLACE

Rte. 28, 0.8 miles east of Midland. About one half mile southeast, just across the railroad, a stone marks the site of the birthplace, September 24, 1755. He died at Philadelphia, July 6, 1835. Revolutionary officer, congressman, Secretary of State, he is immortal as Chief Justice of the United States Supreme Court. During his long term of office his wise interpretation of the U.S. Constitution gave it enduring life.

CL-7 German Town

Rte. 643, between Rtes. 28 and 616. About 1719, five years after they immigrated to Germanna in present-day Orange Co., twelve German families moved here as lot owners of 1,805 acres on Licking Run claimed a year earlier by their trustees, John Fishback, John Hoffman, and Jacob Holtzclaw. Melchoir Brumback, Joseph Coons, Harman Fishback, Peter Hitt, John Kemper, John Joseph Martin, John Jacob Rector, John Spilman, and Tilman Weaver headed the other families. With their pastor, the Rev. Henry Hager, they constituted the first German Reformed congregation in the southern colonies. On 22 Aug. 1724, Thomas Fairfax, proprietor of the Northern Neck, issued them a land grant.

CL-8 Stuart's Bivouac

Rte. 667, 1 mile east of Auburn. Reconnoitering on 13 Oct. 1863, Maj. Gen. J. E. B. Stuart found himself and two cavalry brigades cut off from the Army of Northern Virginia by the Union II Corps. The Confederates concealed themselves all night just north of here in a ravine only half a mile from the Federals. The next morning, as Lt. Gen. Richard S. Ewell's infantry corps marched to aid him, with seven pieces of horse artillery Stuart opened fire on Union Brig. Gen. John C. Caldwell's division on a nearby hill and scattered it. Stuart and his men then charged Federal infantry approaching from Auburn and broke through to safety.

CL-9 Battle of Coffee Hill— (Second Battle of Auburn)

Rtes. 670 and 602, east of Warrenton. During the early morning of 14 Oct. 1863, just northwest of here, Maj. Gen. J. E. B. Stuart and two cavalry brigades, cut off from the Army of Northern Virginia by Federal infantry, attacked Union Brig. Gen. John C. Caldwell's forces as they brewed coffee and prepared breakfast on the hill. Confederate Maj. Robert F. Beckham's Horse Artillery fired on Caldwell's troops to begin Stuart's attempted breakout. This surprised Caldwell's men, but the Federals turned their artillery around and responded. During the ensuing conflict, Caldwell's troops repulsed a Confederate cavalry charge. Stuart's actions, however, enabled him to break through the Union lines. Ever since, this hill has been known as Coffee Hill.

F-9 Campaign of Second Manassas

Rte. 55, at Rte. 626, The Plains. Here Jackson, on his march around Pope to Bristoe Station, turned to the southeast, August 26, 1862.

F-18 Goldvein

Rte. 17, at post office, Goldvein. Thomas Jefferson stated in NOTES ON THE STATE OF VIRGINIA (1782) that he found gold bearing rock weighing approximately four pounds near this site. Among the 19 gold mines that have been in operation since then in the area, the Franklin and the Liberty were the most productive with the Franklin producing 6259 ounces of gold as recently as 1936.

FA-1 Campaign of Second Manassas

Rte. 55, at Broad Run, near Fauquier/Prince William County line. Lee and Longstreet, moving eastward to join Jackson at Manassas, found this gap held by a Union force, August 28, 1862. They forced the gap, after some fighting, and moved on toward Manassas, August 29, 1862.

FB-2 Oak Hill—John Marshall's Home

Rte. F-185, between Marshall and Delaplane. Thomas Marshall, the father of future Chief Justice John Marshall, built Oak Hill about 1773 and relocated his family there from The Hollow, their former home nearby. John Marshall resided at Oak Hill for two years until he entered the Continental army in 1775 at the age of twenty. He became the owner of the property in 1785 when his father moved to Kentucky. Although Marshall resided mostly in

Washington, D.C., and Richmond, he improved Oak Hill and used it as a retreat. In 1819 his son Thomas, constructed an attached Classical Revival dwelling.

FB-4 CAMPAIGN OF SECOND MANASSAS

Rte. 55, Marshall. Near here Stonewall Jackson, after a march of twenty-six miles on his way to Bristoe Station, halted for a few hours to rest his men, August 25–26, 1862.

FF-4 LEE'S BIVOUAC, GETTYSBURG CAMPAIGN

Rte. 55, Markham. Gen. Robert E. Lee established his headquarters here on the evening of 17 June 1863 as the Army of Northern Virginia marched north. Lt. Gen. Richard S. Ewell, who had replaced Stonewall Jackson as corps commander after Jackson's death on 10 May, had crossed the Potomac River into Maryland after defeating Union Maj. Gen. Robert H. Milroy on 15 June at Winchester. The way was then clear for Lt. Gen. James Longstreet's corps to enter the Shenandoah Valley at Snicker's Gap and Lt. Gen. A. P. Hill's at Chester Gap. Maj. Gen. J. E. B. Stuart's cavalry screened the army's flank near Aldie as Lee prepared to invade Pennsylvania.

FF-5 LEE'S NARROW ESCAPE

Rte. 55, Marshall. (Six miles southwest of this location), on the morning of 27 Aug. 1862, Gen. Robert E. Lee rested at the head of Lt. Gen. James Longstreet's corps as it marched toward Thoroughfare Gap to join Lt. Gen. Thomas J. "Stonewall" Jackson's corps near Manassas Junction at the Second Battle of Manassas. The 9th New York Cavalry, covering the left flank of Maj. Gen. John Pope's army on its march from Warrenton to Manassas, nearly overran (overtook) Lee's position between Ada and Vernon Mills. His staff mounted quickly and formed a line to protect him. The Federals mistook the horsemen for a Confederate cavalry column and turned away.

FF-6 BIRTHPLACE OF LT. PRESLEY NEVILLE O'BANNON, USMC

Rte. F-185, 1 mile west of Marshall. Just north stood the home of William and Ann (Neville) O'Bannon, where their son, Lt. Presley Neville O'Bannon, was born about 1776. O'Bannon, a Marine, was the first American to command U.S. forces on foreign soil and the first to raise the American flag over a fortress in the Old World. His success at the Battle of Derne, Tripoli (present day Libya), on 27 Apr. 1805, ended a four-year war against the Tripoli pirates, and inspired the phrase "to the shores of Tripoli" in the Marine Corps Hymn. He settled in Kentucky about 1807, served in its legislature, and died in 1850.

FF-7 MOSBY'S RANGERS DISBAND

Rte. 710, 0.1 miles north of Rte. 55, Marshall. Unable to extend a truce with the Union army, Col. John S. Mosby assembled his command, the 43d Battalion Virginia Cavalry, in a field just west of here on 21 Apr. 1865. As Mosby sat astride his horse, his final order was read aloud. It stated in part: "I have summoned you together for the last time. The vision we cherished of a free and independent country has vanished, and that country is now the spoil of a conqueror. I disband your organization in preference to surrendering to our enemies." Strong men wept. This was the end of Mosby's Rangers.

FF-8 McCLELLAN RELIEVED FROM COMMAND

Rte. 55, Marshall. At Rectortown, four miles north, General George B. McClellan received the order relieving him from command of the Army of the Potomac, November 7, 1862. As Burnside, his successor, was present, McClellan immediately turned over the command to him.

FF-9 MANASSAS GAP

Marker missing. Original location: Rte. 55, 0.57 miles east of Linden. The name

Manassas—after Manasseh, a local Jewish innkeeper, according to one tradition published in 1861, or from an unidentified Indian word, according to another—first appeared as "Manasses Run" on a 1737 map. Manassas Gap, at about 950 feet the lowest in the Blue Ridge, initially was named Calmes's Gap for county justice Marquis Calmes, then renamed for Manassas Run. The Manassas Gap Railroad, built through the gap in the 1850s, linked Washington, D.C., with the Shenandoah Valley.

FF-10 BRIG. GEN. TURNER ASHBY, C.S.A.

Rte. 55, 4.40 miles east of Fauquier/Warren County line, Markham. Turner Ashby, Stonewall Jackson's cavalry commander during the brilliant 1862 Shenandoah Valley campaign, was born on 23 Oct. 1828 just north at Rose Bank. From 1853 to 1858, Ashby operated a mercantile business in a large frame building just to the south, at the foot of the hill on which stands his home, Wolf's Crag. An unsuccessful candidate for the House of Delegates in 1858, he left his home in April 1861 to serve the Confederacy as captain of his Mountain Rangers. Ashby was killed in action on 6 June 1862 near Harrisonburg, Virginia, and is buried in Winchester.

FF-11 NUMBER 18 SCHOOL

Marker missing. Original location: Rte. 55, approximately 1 mile east of Marshall. After the Civil War, the constitution of 1869 established a statewide system of free public schools in Virginia. Several new schools in Fauquier were identified by an assigned number; Number 18 was built on land donated by Samuel F. Shackleford. From the time of its construction in 1887 until 1910, this one-room schoolhouse served local white children. When they moved to a newer school in the nearby village of Marshall in 1910, Number 18 then served African American students until it closed in 1964. Number 18 stands today as a rare example of a once-common schoolhouse.

FF-12 THE HOLLOW

Rte. 688, 0.10 miles north of Rte. 55, near I-66 overpass, near Markham. In 1765, John Marshall, then nine, moved with his family from his birthplace 30 miles southeast to a small, newly constructed frame house one-quarter mile east known as The Hollow. The house built by his father, Thomas Marshall, was his home until 1773, when the family moved five miles east to Oak Hill. After the American Revolution began, Thomas Marshall and his sons, John Marshall, James Markham Marshall, and Thomas Marshall Jr. fought in numerous Revolutionary War battles including Great Bridge and Yorktown. John Marshall later served as chief justice of the United States Supreme Court from 1801 to 1835.

G-2 LEETON FOREST

Rte. 802, Warrenton. Half a mile east is the site of Leeton Forest, latter-day home of Charles Lee, Attorney General in Washington's and Adams' cabinets, 1795–1801. The tract was patented by Thomas Lee, of Stratford, in 1718 and descended to his son, Richard Henry Lee, Revolutionary leader. The latter's daughter Anne married Charles Lee, who obtained title to the property in 1803, and who died here in June, 1815.

G-21 GRAPEWOOD FARM ENGAGEMENT

Rte. 602, near old Vint Hill military base. Pursued by Union detachments after raiding a train north of Catlett Station on 30 May 1863, Confederate Col. John S. Mosby and 50 of his Rangers (43d Battalion Virginia Cavalry) made a stand on a hill just to the north. The Rangers used a howitzer to break a charge by the 5th New York Cavalry. The New Yorkers regrouped, however, and with troopers of the 1st Vermont and the 7th Michigan overran Mosby's position. After a hand-to-hand struggle, Mosby and the Rangers fled, abandoning the cannon and losing some 20 men wounded and killed. Among the dead was Capt. Bradford Smith Hoskins, an English professional soldier, who was buried at nearby Greenwich Presbyterian Church. Union losses were 15 killed and 4 wounded.

Q-9 WARRENTON

Business Rte. 15, at Rte. 211, Warrenton. Chosen as county seat in 1759, and first called Fauquier Court House, Warrenton was laid out as a town in 1790. John Marshall began law practice here. In the War Between the States it was the center of operations north of the Rappahannock and many wounded were hospitalized here. Union General Pope headquartered here in the Second Manassas Campaign. Seizing the local press, the Unionists edited the newspaper as "The New York Ninth." Mosby, the ranger, made forays in this vicinity.

FREDERICK COUNTY

A-1 ACTION AT STEPHENSON'S DEPOT

Rte. 11, at Rte. 664, north of Winchester. Near this place on June 15, 1863, Confederate troops of General Edward "Allegheny" Johnson's Division attacked and routed General Robert Milroy's Union Army during its retreat from Winchester. The short, pre-dawn battle resulted in the capture of Milroy's wagon train and more than 2300 Union prisoners. From here, the Confederate Army advanced into Pennsylvania where it suffered defeat two weeks later at Gettysburg.

A-2 ACTION OF RUTHERFORD'S FARM

Rte. 11, 0.1 miles north of I-81, Exit 317, north of Winchester. Near here, the Confederate General Stephen D. Ramseur was attacked by General William W. Averell and pushed back toward Winchester, July 20, 1864.

A-3 CAPTURE OF STAR FORT

Rte. 11, 0.1 miles south of Rte. 1323, north of Winchester. The fort on the hilltop to the southwest, known as Star Fort, was taken by Colonel Schoonmaker of Sheridan's army in the battle of September 19, 1864.

A-4 FORT COLLIER

Rte. 11, at Winchester northern city limits. Just to the east, a redoubt known as Fort Collier was built by Joseph E. Johnston in 1861. Early's left rested here during the Third Battle of Winchester, September 19, 1864.

A-6 FIRST BATTLE OF WINCHESTER

Rte. 11, south of Winchester. On the morning of May 25, 1862, New England troops in Bank's army held this position, facing Jackson, who was advancing from the south.

A-8 SECOND BATTLE OF WINCHESTER

Rte. 11, 0.1 miles south of Rte. 37, south of Winchester. On June 14, 1863, Jubal A. Early moved west from this point to attack Federal fortifications west of Winchester.

A-9 BATTLE OF KERNSTOWN

Rte. 11, 5.3 miles north of Stephens City. On the hill to the west, Stonewall Jackson, late in the afternoon of March 23, 1862, attacked the Union force under Shields holding Winchester. After a fierce action, Jackson, who was greatly outnumbered, withdrew southward, leaving his dead on the field. These were buried next day by citizens of Winchester.

A-10 EARLY AND CROOK

Rte. 11, 1 mile north of Kernstown, south of Winchester. Here Early, just returned from his raid to Washington, attacked a pursuing force under Crook and drove it back, July 24, 1864.

A-11 FIRST BATTLE OF WINCHESTER

Rte. 11, 0.1 miles south of Rte. 37, south of Winchester. The main body of Stonewall

Jackson's army halted here to rest in the early morning of May 25, 1862.

A-12 STEPHENS CITY

Rte. 11, at post office. General David Hunter ordered the burning of this town on May 30, 1864; but Major Joseph Streans [Stearns] of the First New York Cavalry prevented it.

A-12 HOUSE OF FIRST SETTLER

Rte. 11, 1 mile north of Stephens City. Springdale, home of Colonel John Hite, son of Joist Hite, leader of the first settlers in this section, was built in 1753. Just to the south are the ruins of Hite's Fort, built about 1734.

A-14 END OF SHERIDAN'S RIDE

Rte. 11, 3.2 miles south of Stephens City, north of Middletown. This knoll marks the position of the Union Army when Sheridan rejoined it at 10:30 A.M., October 19, 1864, in the battle of Cedar Creek. His arrival, with Wright's efforts, checked the Union retreat.

A-15 BATTLE OF CEDAR CREEK

Rte. 11, 0.2 miles north of Middletown. Near this point General Early, on the morning of October 19, 1864, stopped his advance, and from this position he was driven by Sheridan in the afternoon.

A-16 ENGAGEMENT OF MIDDLETOWN

Rte. 11 (Main Street), north of 1st Street, Middletown. Here Stonewall Jackson, on May 24, 1862, attacked Banks, retreating from Strasburg, and forced him to divide his army.

A-17 TOMB OF AN UNKNOWN SOLDIER

Rte. 11, 1 mile south of Middletown. On the highest mountain top to the southeast is the grave of an unknown soldier. The mountain top was used as a signal station by both armies, 1861–1865.

A-37 OLD STONE FORT

Rte. 11 (Main Street), south of 1st Street, Middletown. One mile west is the Old Stone Fort, built about 1755. The northern end is loopholed for defense against Indians.

A-38 HACKWOOD PARK

Rte. 11, 0.1 miles north of I-81, Exit 317, north of Winchester. One mile east is the site of the Hackwood Estate House, built in 1777 by General John Smith. Documents reveal that the Hackwood House caught fire during the Third Battle of Winchester. Union troops used buildings on the site for a hospital, September 19, 1864.

A-56 BATTLE OF CEDAR CREEK

Rte. 11, 1.3 miles south of Middletown. In early Oct. 1864, portions of Union Maj. Gen. Philip H. Sheridan's army bivouacked here on the hills and rolling farmland just north of Cedar Creek along the Valley Turnpike (present-day U.S. Rte. 11). Just before daybreak on 19 Oct., Confederate Lt. Gen. Jubal A. Early's infantry divisions surprised and attacked the Federals, routing two of Sheridan's three infantry corps. Maj. Gen. Horatio G. Wright, commanding in Sheridan's absence, organized a retreat north. Sheridan arrived on the battlefield from Winchester by midmorning and rode along the front to rally his men. By late afternoon the Federals had counterattacked Early's left front and crushed the Confederate troops, who fled south.

A-67 OLD STONE CHURCH AT GREENSPRING

Rte. 671, at Rte. 676, west of White Hall, Greenspring. One-half mile west at Greenspring stands the Old Stone Church, the second church building on the site, which was built in 1838 for a Lutheran congregation. The first church had been built as a subscription school and as a house of worship. Old Stone Church and its large cemetery both had been long abandoned when, in 1927, Cora Bell Crim led local residents in restoring them and forming the Old Stone Church Memorial Association. The earliest extant Lutheran church in Frederick County, Old Stone Church is a rare example of the simple stone churches once common in the northern Shenandoah Valley.

A-105 MIDDLETOWN

Rte. 627, between I-81 and Rte. 11, Middletown. The Virginia General Assembly established Middletown in 1794. Dr. Peter Senseney laid out the original lots for the village. Surrounded by farms and plantations, including historic Belle Grove, the community grew along the Great Wagon Road, which stretched from Philadelphia to Georgia. Early merchants and businesses included Jacob Danner, clock and instrument maker, James Ridings, a threshing machine designer, and the tavern now known as the Wayside Inn. Shenandoah Valley historian Samuel Kercheval resided here for a number of years and in 1833 published *A History of the Valley of Virginia.* Military activity occurred here throughout the Civil War culminating in the 19 Oct. 1864 Battle of Cedar Creek. Middletown became an incorporated town in 1880.

B-16 COLONEL JOHN SINGLETON MOSBY

Rte. 50/17, at Rte. 723, east of Winchester. This road, along which many of his skirmishes took place, is named for Colonel John Singleton Mosby, commander of the 43rd Battalion of Confederate Partisan Rangers. Their activities in this area helped keep the Confederate cause alive in Northern Virginia toward the end of the Civil War.

B-17 WILLOW SHADE

Rte. 50, 0.2 miles east of Gore. This house, built in 1858, was the childhood home of novelist Willa Cather from 1874 to 1883, when she moved with her family to Nebraska. It was the setting of the final

chapters of her novel SAPPHIRA AND THE SLAVE GIRL. Willa Cather was born December 7, 1873, one mile south in the community of Gore then known as Back Creek Valley.

B-18 WILLA CATHER BIRTHPLACE

Rte. 50, opposite post office, Gore. Here Willa Sibert Cather, the novelist, was born December 7, 1873. This community was her home until 1883 when her family moved to Nebraska. Nearby on Back Creek stands the old mill described in her novel "Sapphira and the Slave Girl."

B-19 SECOND BATTLE OF WINCHESTER

Rte. 50, 0.2 miles west of Rte. 37, south of Winchester. Here Jubal A. Early, detached to attack the rear of Milroy, holding Winchester, crossed this road and moved eastward in the afternoon of June 15, 1863.

J-3 THIRD BATTLE OF WINCHESTER

Rte. 7, at Rte. 656. Here Confederate forces under General Jubal A. Early, facing east, received the attack of Sheridan's army at noon on September 19, 1864. Early repulsed the attack and countercharged, breaking the Union line. Only prompt action by General Emory Upton in changing front saved the Union forces from disaster. At 3 P.M. Sheridan made a second attack, driving Early back to Winchester.

J-13 THIRD BATTLE OF WINCHESTER

Rte. 7, at Rte. 991. On a hill, approximately one-half mile to the west, Philip H. Sheridan established his final position on September 19, 1864. General Jubal A. Early held the ground one-half mile further to the west. At 4 P.M., Sheridan advanced with massed cavalry and infantry and broke Early's line.

J-16 DEFENSES OF WINCHESTER

Rte. 522, 4 miles south of Winchester. The fort on the hilltop to the north is one of a chain of defenses commanding the crossings of the Opequon. It was constructed by Milroy in 1863.

Q-4-b JOST HITE AND WINCHESTER

Rte. 7, at Rte. 656, east of Winchester. German emigrant Jost Hite and about 16 other German and Scots-Irish families from Pennsylvania came to this region in 1732, creating one of the early permanent European settlements. They settled along the Opequon Creek watershed southwest of the present-day city of Winchester. Soon after their arrival, a number of other communities developed regionally, including Fredericktown, present-day Winchester. Winchester was chartered as a town in 1752. It began as a small farming community that developed into a thriving town and important trading center at the junction of several transportation arteries.

Q-4-c GEORGE WASHINGTON IN WINCHESTER

Rte. 11, at Winchester northern city limits. In Mar. 1748, George Washington first visited Winchester, then known as Fredericktown, as a surveyor for Lord Fairfax. Washington purchased property in Winchester in 1753 and was an unsuccessful candidate for a House of Burgesses seat here in 1755. Winchester served as Washington's headquarters from 1755 to 1758 while he commanded Virginia troops on the western frontier during the French and Indian War. He was also involved with the construction of Fort Loudoun here and a series of other frontier forts authorized by the Virginia General Assembly during this period. He represented Frederick County in the Virginia House of Burgesses from 1758 to 1765.

GREENE COUNTY

D-11 RUCKERSVILLE

Rte. 29, at Rte. 33, Ruckersville. A descendant of the Huguenot immigrant Peter Rucker, John Rucker (d. 1794) settled east of here on Rippin's Run, and built Friendly Acres, the first of many Rucker family dwellings in the area. He founded the village of Ruckersville, naming it for his uncle, Captain John Rucker, who was instrumental in selecting the site for St. Mark's Parish Church just west of here in 1732.

D-21 STANARDSVILLE ENGAGEMENT

Rte. 230, near Rte. 619, 2.5 miles north of Stanardsville. Near this site on 1 Mar. 1864, Maj. Gen. J. E. B. Stuart's Confederate cavalry engaged Brig. Gen. George A. Custer's Union cavalry in what is called locally the Battle of Stanardsville. To divert Stuart from Richmond, Custer led his troopers down this road to Charlottesville, destroying the railroad bridge over the Rivanna River there and breaking communications between Gordonsville and Lynchburg. Passing through Stanardsville

again after the raid, taking prisoners and burning Confederate supplies, Custer fought a brief engagement with Stuart, then pressed on toward Orange Court House. Custer's postwar military career ended at the Battle of Little Big Horn in Montana in 1876.

W-217 STANARDSVILLE

Rte. 33, at courthouse, Stanardsville. The village of Stanardsville was founded by William Stanard (died 1807), of Roxbury plantation, on land that was part of his 6,000 acre inheritance from the Octonia Grant of 1729. This grant included most of what is presently northern Greene County and Stanardsville. The Virginia General Assembly incorporated the town on 19 Dec. 1794. Stanardsville became the county seat of Greene County in 1838 when Greene was formed from Orange County. Brig. Gen. George A. Custer skirmished with Confederate cavalry here on 29 Feb. 1864, during his raid enroute to Albemarle County.

CITY OF HARRISONBURG

A-30 WHERE ASHBY FELL

Rte. 11, just south of Port Republic Road. A mile and a half east of this point, Turner Ashby, Stonewall Jackson's cavalry commander, was killed, June 6, 1862, while opposing Fremont's advance.

A-33 HARRISONBURG

Rtes. 11 (Main Street) and 33, Court Square. Here Thomas Harrison and wife deeded land for the Rockingham County public buildings, August 5, 1779. The same act established both Louisville, Ky., and Harrisonburg, May, 1780. Named for its founder, the town was also known as Rocktown. It was incorporated in 1849. In its vicinity battles were fought in 1862 and 1864. The present courthouse was built in 1897. Harrisonburg became a city in 1916.

A-35 END OF THE CAMPAIGN

Rte. 11. Here Stonewall Jackson, retreating up the Valley before the converging columns of Fremont and Shields, turned at bay, June, 1862. A mile southeast Jackson's cavalry commander, Ashby, was killed, June 6. At Cross Keys, six miles southeast, Ewell of Jackson's army defeated Fremont, June 8. Near Port Republic, ten miles southeast, Jackson defeated Shields, June 9. This was the end of Jackson's Valley Campaign.

A-103 JAMES MADISON UNIVERSITY

Rte. 11 (South Main Street), on university campus. The university was founded in 1908, through the efforts of state senator George B. Keezell, of Rockingham County, as the State Normal and Industrial School for Women at Harrisonburg. In 1924 it became the State Teachers College at Harrisonburg, before it was renamed Madison College in 1938 to honor James Madison, the Father of the Constitution and fourth president of the United States. The school admitted men to regular school sessions in 1946 and became fully coeducational in 1966. In 1977 the college was renamed James Madison University and has become a nationally recognized comprehensive public institution.

A-104 JAMES MADISON UNIVERSITY

Rte. 659, at Admissions' Welcome Center, on university campus. The university was founded in 1908, through the efforts of state senator George B. Keezell, of Rockingham County, as the State Normal and Industrial School for Women at Harrisonburg. In 1924 it became the State Teachers College at Harrisonburg, before it was renamed Madison College in 1938 to honor James Madison, the Father of the Constitution and fourth president of the United States. The school admitted men to regular school sessions in 1946 and became fully coeducational in 1966. In 1977 the college was renamed James Madison University and has become a nationally recognized comprehensive public institution.

HIGHLAND COUNTY

W-148 FORT GEORGE ON THE BULLPASTURE RIVER

Rte. 678, 6 miles south of McDowell. Fort George was built in the spring of 1757 by Captain William Preston, acting on orders of Major Andrew Lewis. Local residents assisted in construction of the 80-foot-square log fort located on the land of Wallace Estill. It was never attacked directly by Indians, although arrows were shot at it from a ridge across the Bullpasture River. The fort site is located in the meadow southeast of this marker.

W-150 BATTLE OF McDOWELL

Rte. 250, 1 mile east of McDowell. Stonewall Jackson, to prevent a junction of Fremont and Banks, took position on the hills just to the south and beat off the attacks of Fremont's advance under Milroy, May 8, 1862. Milroy retreated that night.

W-151 FELIX HULL HOUSE

Rte. 250, McDowell. This stately brick house was built about 1855 for Felix Hull (ca. 1823–1861) in the Greek Revival style popular in the late antebellum period.

During the Civil War, his widow, Eliza Mathews Hull, was living here on 7–8 May 1862 when the house was commandeered for headquarters by Union Brig. Gen. Robert H. Milroy and his superior, Brig. Gen. Robert C. Schenck. On 9 May, after the Battle of McDowell on Sitlington's Hill just to the east, the victorious Maj. Gen. Thomas J. "Stonewall" Jackson made his headquarters here. He pursued the Union army westward, then returned here on 14 May for the night before moving toward Staunton.

CITY OF LEXINGTON

A-42 WILLIAM HENRY RUFFNER

Alternate Rte. 11, at Business Rte. 11, at southern city limits. William Henry Ruffner, educational reformer, clergyman, and geologist, was born in Lexington on 11 Feb. 1824. After pursuing careers as a preacher and a geological surveyor, he was appointed in 1870 as Virginia's first superintendent of public instruction by the General Assembly. During Ruffner's tenure, he developed Virginia's free public school system. Resigning from his position in 1882, Ruffner returned to geological surveying and farming before becoming the president of the State Female Normal School, now Longwood College, in 1884. Ruffner retired in 1887 and died in 1908 in Asheville, North Carolina. Nearby stood his house Tribrook.

I-1 VIRGINIA MILITARY INSTITUTE— A NATIONAL HISTORIC LANDMARK

Letcher Avenue, at entrance to college. The nation's first state military college, VMI was founded in 1839 on the concept of the citizen-soldier. The Corps of Cadets fought as a unit in the 1864 Battle of New Market. Confederate General "Stonewall" Jackson and oceanographer Matthew Fontaine Maury were among its faculty. George C. Marshall, a 1901 graduate, served as Army Chief of Staff in W.W. II, and later as Secretary of State, devising the Marshall Plan

to rebuild Europe. He was awarded the Nobel Peace Prize.

I-1 VIRGINIA MILITARY INSTITUTE

Business Rte. 11, on college campus. A state military, engineering and arts college, founded in 1839. Graduates of it have taken a prominent part in every war since the Mexican War, 2,000 of them serving in the World War. The cadets fought as a corps at New Market in 1864. Among the members of the faculty were Stonewall Jackson and the noted scientists, Matthew F. Maury and John M. Brooke.

I-8 WASHINGTON AND LEE UNIVERSITY

Business Rte. 11, at entrance to university. Founded, 1749, as Augusta Academy, near Greenville; reestablished at Timber Ridge, May, 1776, as Liberty Hall Academy; moved to Lexington and chartered as a college, 1782; endowed by George Washington, 1796, and named for him. Under presidency, 1865–1870, of Robert E. Lee (buried in the university chapel), whose name after death was incorporated in the official title.

I-22 LIBERTY HALL ACADEMY RUINS

Nelson Street (Rte. 60), at entrance to Washington and Lee School of Law. Just north stand the ruins of Liberty Hall Academy's stone academic building, which was constructed in 1793. Founded in 1749 near Greenville as Augusta Academy, the school was reestablished in 1776 at Timber Ridge and patriotically renamed Liberty Hall Academy. It moved here to Mulberry Hill in 1782, when the Virginia General Assembly chartered it as a college. In 1796,

in honor of President George Washington's endowment gift of James River (canal) Co. stock, it was renamed Washington Academy. Fire gutted the building in 1803, prompting the college to move to its present location in Lexington, where it is now known as Washington and Lee University.

MADISON COUNTY

F-22 JACKSON'S CROSSING

Rte. 15, 0.2 miles north of Robinson River bridge, 7.6 miles north of Orange. Here at Locust Dale, Stonewall Jackson's army crossed the river moving north to the battle of Cedar Mountain, August 9, 1862. The battle was fought a few hours later.

F-24 WOODBERRY FOREST SCHOOL

Rte. 15, 1 mile north of Rapidan River, at main entrance to school. Two miles northeast is Woodberry Forest School, a college preparatory school for boys, founded in 1889 by Robert Stringfellow Walker, a captain with Mosby's Rangers. The school was named for the estate on which it stands, formerly owned by William Madison, brother of President James Madison.

G-11 CAVALRY ENGAGEMENT AT JACK'S SHOP

Rte. 231, 4.5 miles south of Madison, Rochelle. First known as Jack's Shop for a blacksmith shop that stood nearby, Rochelle was the scene of a cavalry skirmish on 22 September 1863. While Confederate cavalry under Major General J. E. B. Stuart engaged Union Brigadier General John Buford's troops, the cavalry of Brigadier General H. Judson Kilpatrick rode to Buford's support and attacked the rear of Stuart's force. Stuart's horse artillery and his cavalry fired and charged in both directions. They broke through Kilpatrick's lines and escaped.

G-12 JOSEPH EARLY HOME

Rte. 29, 3 miles south of Madison, Oak Hill. One mile west was the home of Joseph

Early, Revolutionary soldier. Washington, in going West and returning, stopped at Early's overnight. His diary for October 2, 1784, shows that he spent the night before at "Widow Early's."

G-13 OAK GROVE BAPTIST CHURCH

Rte. 634, 5 miles southeast of Madison, at church. Joe Thoms, Sr., a slave harnessmaker, founded Oak Grove Baptist Church during the Civil War at his nearby log cabin, which burned in 1869. The congregation then met here, on land owned by John J. Robinson, a white farmer, in a grove of oak they called the "bush arbor." In 1870, Joe Thoms, with Deacons Ambrose Tolliver, Frank Walker, Ed Redd, John Williams, Charles Brock, Spot Mallory, and Ambrose Thoms, built a small frame church here. The third church replaced it in 1894, when Robinson donated the land. A great-great-grandson of Joe Thoms became pastor in 1982.

G-28A ENGAGEMENT AT JAMES CITY

Rte. 29, 1 mile south of Madison/Culpeper County line. On 10 October 1863, Confederate cavalry commanded by Maj. Gen. J. E. B. Stuart engaged Union cavalry and infantry under Brig. Gen. H. Judson Kilpatrick and Maj. Gen. William H. French at James City (present-day Leon). The two forces confronted each other atop the ridges on either side of the village, and an artillery duel ensued. James City virtually disappeared in the smoke. A Confederate detachment captured the Union signal station on Thorofare Mountain, a mile to the south. Late in the day Stuart repulsed a Union cavalry charge, and during the night the Union force withdrew toward Culpeper. This engagement was the only instance during the war when Stuart led a force without a Virginia regiment.

JE-1 Jackson's March to Fredericksburg

Business Rte. 29/231, at northern end of Madison. Stonewall Jackson, on his march from Winchester to Fredericksburg, preceding the battle of Fredericksburg, camped here, November 26, 1862.

JE-2 Knights of the Golden Horseshoe

Rte. 15, 3.3 miles north of Orange, near Rapidan River crossing, near Madison/Orange County line. Near here Governor Alexander Spotswood and his troop of gentlemen, Knights of the Golden Horseshoe, on their way to explore the land beyond the mountains, camped on August 31, 1716.

JE-3 James L. Kemper Residence

Business Rte. 29/231, 2.4 miles north of Madison. This Greek Revival–style house was built about 1852 for state senator Thomas N. Welch. In 1868 James Lawson Kemper (1823–1895) purchased it from his mother-in-law, Mrs. Belfield Cave. Kemper, an attorney, represented Madison County in the House of Delegates (1853–1863), served as

speaker (1861–1863), led a brigade in the Civil War, was wounded in Pickett's Charge at Gettysburg, and served as governor of Virginia (1874–1878). In 1882 he moved from Madison to Walnut Hills in Orange County.

JE-4 Hebron Lutheran Church

Rte. 231, 3 miles northeast of Madison. Nearby stands Hebron Lutheran Church. This cruciform church was built in 1740 and is America's oldest church in continuous use by Lutherans. The congregation was formed by 1725 by German families, some of whom arrived to Virginia in 1717 to work at Germanna, Lieutenant Governor Alexander Spotswood's frontier mining community. The church was enlarged about 1800 and a pipe organ crafted by David Tannenburg of Lititz, Pennsylvania, was installed. The interior of the church has elaborate frescoed ceilings painted by the Italian-born artist Joseph Oddenino. It was listed on the Virginia Landmarks Register and the National Register of Historic Places in 1971.

JE-15 A Camp of Stonewall Jackson's

Rte. 670, 1 mile north of Criglersville. Just to the north, on the night of November 25, 1862, Stonewall Jackson, with his corps, camped. He was on his way to join Lee at Fredericksburg.

ORANGE COUNTY

D-20 Montebello

Rte. 33, between Barboursville and Gordonsville. Here was born Zachary Taylor, twelfth president of the United States, November 24, 1784. Taylor, commanding the American army, won the notable battle of Buena Vista in Mexico, 1847.

D-22 Barboursville

Rte. 33, near Rte. 738, Barboursville. A short distance south are the ruins of Barboursville, built, 1814–1822, by James Barbour

partly after plans made by Jefferson. It was burned, December 25, 1884. James Barbour, buried here, was Governor of Virginia, 1812–1815, United States Senator, Secretary of War, Minister to England.

F-17 Kemper's Grave

Rte. 15, north of Orange, near Rapidan River bridge, near Orange/Madison County line. A mile south is the grave of James Lawson Kemper, who led his brigade of Virginia troops in Pickett's charge at Gettysburg,

July 3, 1863, and fell desperately wounded. He became a major-general in 1864. Kemper was governor of Virginia, 1874–1878.

F-23 CHURCH OF THE BLIND PREACHER

Rte. 15, at northern end of Gordonsville. Near here was the church of James Waddel, the blind Presbyterian preacher. Waddel, who had been a minister in the Northern Neck and elsewhere, came here about 1785 and died here in 1805. William Wirt, stopping in 1803 to hear a sermon, was impressed by Waddel's eloquence. He made it the subject of a classic essay.

F-26 MONTPELIER AND MADISON'S TOMB

Rte. 15 and Business Rte. 20, at courthouse, Orange. Five miles southwest is Montpelier, the home of James Madison, "Father of the American Constitution" and fourth President of the United States, 1809–1817. Near the house is the tomb of Madison, who died at Montpelier on June 28, 1836.

F-30 ORANGE TRAIN STATION

Business Rte. 15, Orange. Beginning in 1749, Orange County's successive courthouses have been located just west of here. In 1854, the Orange & Alexandria Railroad, constructed to link Alexandria with central Virginia, reached Orange and a train station was built near here. The 1804 courthouse was replaced in 1859 by the present Italianate structure a block farther west. The buildings around the train station comprised one of the town's early commercial districts. A 1908 fire destroyed the original train station and the buildings on the north side of this block. The station and the Main Street structures east and west of it were rebuilt in the early 1900s.

F-32 CAMPAIGN OF SECOND MANASSAS

Rte. 15, 3 miles south of Orange. Near here Stonewall Jackson camped, August 13–15, 1862, just after the Cedar Mountain engagement.

J-34 GERMANNA

Rte. 3, near Rapidan River bridge. Here Governor Alexander Spotswood established a colony of Germans in 1714. At that time the Rapidan River was the frontier of Virginia. On August 29, 1716, Spotswood left from this place with his Knights of the Golden Horseshoe on his exploring expedition across the mountains. The German colony later moved to Fauquier County. Spotswood lived for some years at Germanna where he was visited in 1732 by William Byrd who called his house "Spotswood's Enchanted Castle."

J-35 GERMANNA FORD

Rte. 3, near Rapidan River bridge. One of the principal crossings of the Rapidan River from colonial times. Here a part of the Army of the Potomac crossed the river, April 30, 1863, preceding the battle of Chancellorsville. Here a part of Meade's army crossed on the way to Mine Run, November 26, 1863. Here the Fifth and Sixth corps of Grant's army crossed, May 4–5, 1864, to open the Wilderness campaign.

JJ-2 LEE'S HEADQUARTERS

Rte. 20, 1 mile east of Orange. Half a mile west, at the Rogers farm called Middle Hill, Gen. Robert E. Lee kept his headquarters from Dec. 1863 to May 1864. His Army of Northern Virginia, in winter camp, guarded the south side of the Rapidan River from the vicinity of Liberty Mills in Somerset east to Morton's Ford. While Lee strove to reinforce and resupply his depleted ranks, across the river in Culpeper County Lt. Gen. Ulysses S. Grant and Maj. Gen. George G. Meade trained and strengthened the Army of the Potomac for the spring campaign. On 4 May 1864, the Wilderness campaign began anew.

JJ-4 BLOOMSBURY

Rte. 20, 2.5 miles east of Orange, near airport. A mile north is Bloomsbury, estate of the pioneer, James Taylor, ancestor of

Presidents James Madison and Zachary Taylor. He was a member of Spotswood's expedition over the mountains in 1716.

JJ-6 CAMPAIGN OF SECOND MANASSAS

Rte. 20, near Rte. 628, east of Orange. Two miles north, near Pisgah Church, Jackson, Ewell and A. P. Hill camped, August 15–20, 1862, awaiting Longstreet.

JJ-10 MINE RUN CAMPAIGN

Rte. 20, between Locust Grove and Mine Run bridge. Meade, advancing south from the Rapidan River to attack Lee, found him in an entrenched position here on November 28, 1863. Heavy skirmishing went on until December 1. Then Meade, thinking Lee's lines too strong to assault, retired across the Rapidan in time to avoid a counterattack by the Confederates.

JJ-12 STUART'S "VERY NARROW ESCAPE"

Rte. 20, near Rte. 621 (Mine Run Road). At dawn on 18 Aug. 1862, Maj. Gen. J. E. B. Stuart was awakened near here by the clatter of approaching cavalry. Expecting Maj. Gen. Fitzhugh Lee to join him in scouting Maj. Gen. John Pope's Union army, Stuart was surprised by Federal troopers instead. Mounting his horse Skylark, Stuart vaulted a fence and barely escaped, but lost his hat. The next day, he wrote his wife that "I am greeted on all sides with congratulations and 'where's your hat!' I intend to make

the Yankees pay for that hat." On 22 Aug., raiding Catlett Station, Stuart captured Pope's gaudy dress uniform coat and later suggested an exchange of "prisoners" to no avail.

JJ-15 ROBINSON'S TAVERN

Rte. 20, Locust Grove. Near here stood ancient Robinson's Tavern. Here Meade wished to concentrate his army in the Mine Run Campaign, November, 1863, but one corps, coming up late, disarranged his plans. Here Ewell, moving east from Orange in the Wilderness Campaign, camped on May 4, 1864.

JJ-20 BATTLE OF THE WILDERNESS

Rte. 20, 2 miles west of Rte. 3 (Wilderness). Ewell's Corps, the left wing of Lee's army, moving down this road from Orange, came into conflict near here with Warren's Corps of Grant's army, May 5, 1864. The fight moved to and fro until Ewell finally drove Warren back and entrenched here. Late the next afternoon, May 6, Ewell attacked the Unionists. Meanwhile, two miles south, on the Orange Plank Road, the right wing of Lee's army was engaged with Grant's left wing.

JJ-24 CAMPAIGN OF 1781

Old Rte. 20, at Rte. 741, east of Unionville. Lafayette, marching southward from Raccoon Ford, camped here, June 8–9, 1781.

PAGE COUNTY

C-3 CAVALRY ENGAGEMENT

Rte. 340, south of Rte. 211, Luray. In mid-June 1862, after Maj. Gen. Thomas J. "Stonewall" Jackson's Shenandoah Valley campaign, Brig. Gen. Beverly H. Robertson's cavalry screened from Union observation Jackson's movement east to join the Army of Northern Virginia near Richmond. Robertson posted two companies of cavalry here, half a mile north of Luray. On 29 June, a Federal reconnaissance force of Maine,

Michigan, and Vermont cavalry rode south from Front Royal to locate Jackson. About 9:00 A.M. on 30 June, the Union cavalry charged the outnumbered Confederates and dispersed them. Not finding Jackson, who unknown to them, had left the Valley, the Federals returned to Front Royal.

C-30 WHITE HOUSE

Rte. 211/340, 2 miles west of Luray western town limits. The old building just north of the road was built for a fort in 1760. It has long been a landmark in this valley.

C-31 FORT PHILLIP LONG

Rte. 211, 2 miles west of Luray. Six miles south, near Alma, stands Fort Philip Long, a small Germanic stone dwelling with a massive end chimney. Constructed on the edge of a bank, the house is unusual in having two cellar levels, one below the other. A tunnel leads from the lower level to a well located a hundred yards away. The date of construction is not known, but it likely was built late in the 18th century for Philip Long II, grandson of Philip Long who settled the tract in 1737. According to local tradition, the house was built as a fort for protection against Indian attacks.

J-95 EXECUTION OF SUMMERS & KOONTZ

Rte. 340, south of Rte. 651. On 22 May 1865, after the Civil War ended, Capt. George W. Summers, Sgt. I. Newton Koontz, and two other armed veterans of Co. D, 7th Virginia Cavalry, en route to obtain their paroles, robbed six Federal cavalrymen of their horses near Woodstock. The horses were returned the next day to the 192d Ohio Volunteer Infantry at Rude's Hill in Shenandoah County. Despite assurances that all was forgiven, Lt. Col. Cyrus Hussy, temporarily commanding the 192d, later ordered the men arrested at their homes in Page County. The other two escaped, but Summers and Koontz were shot without trial on Rude's Hill on 27 June. They were buried at different locations near here.

RAPPAHANNOCK COUNTY

C-4 CAVALRY ENGAGEMENT

Rte. 211, Sperryville. Near this place an engagement took place between Robertson's brigade and the First Maine Cavalry, July 5, 1862.

C-5 WASHINGTON, VIRGINIA— THE FIRST OF THEM ALL

Old Rte. 211, at northern entrance of Washington. Of the 28 Washingtons in the United States, the "records very conclusively disclose" that this town, "the first Washington of all," was surveyed and platted by George Washington on the 24th of July (old style), 1749. He was assisted by John Lonem and Edward Corder as chainmen. By the General Assembly of Virginia it was officially established as a town in 1796 and incorporated in 1894.

C-6 CAMPAIGN OF SECOND MANASSAS

Rte. 211, at Rte. 643, 0.75 miles west of Amisville. Here Stonewall Jackson, on his march around Pope's army by way of Jeffersonton to Bristoe Station, turned north, August 25, 1862.

C-9a WASHINGTON, VIRGINIA—THE FIRST OF THEM ALL

Bypass Rte. 211/522, near Washington. Of the more than thirty Washingtons in the United States, only this town, "The First Washington of All," was surveyed and platted by George Washington on the 24th day of July (old style) 1749. He was assisted by John Lonem and Edward Corder as chainmen. The General Assembly of Virginia officially established it as a town in 1796 and incorporated in it 1894. Washington has served as the county seat of Rappahannock County since 1833.

C-10 ELLERSLIE

Bypass Rte. 211/522, near Rte. 626, near Washington. One-half mile southeast of this location is Ellerslie, which was built in 1814 by French Huguenot Col. John Jett and his wife Hannah Calvert for their son James Jett, Jr., on a 1,000-acre tract. In 1749, George Washington named Jett Street in the town of Washington, Virginia, for the family. In 1862, some of Union Maj. Gen. John Pope's forces occupied Ellerslie before the Second Battle of Manassas. After the Civil War, Ellerslie fell into disrepair and the property was divided. In 1926, its century-old English boxwoods were moved to the National Cathedral in Washington, D.C., to grace the Bishop's Garden. Ellerslie was destroyed by fire in 1933.

C-56 WILLIAM RANDOLPH BARBEE

Rte. 211, at Skyline Drive, at Panorama at Rappahannock/Page County line. Here stood "Hawburg," birthplace of the eminent Virginia sculptor William R. Barbee (1818–1868). He studied in Florence, Italy, where he carved his famed "Coquette" and "The Fisher Girl." Returning to the United States in 1858 he was at work on a design for the pediment of the U.S. House of Representatives when the outbreak of the war brought his career to an end. He died at "The Bower" which stood not far away.

C-61 CAMPAIGN OF SECOND MANASSAS

Rte. 211, just west of Rappahannock/Culpeper County line. Here J. E. B. Stuart, raiding around Pope's army, turned northeast, August 22, 1862. He passed through Warrenton and went on to Catlett's Station, where he captured some of Pope's wagons, in one of which were found Pope's order book and uniform.

J-25 GETTYSBURG CAMPAIGN

Rte. 522, between Chester Gap and Huntly. Ewell's Corps of Lee's army passed here going north, June 11–12, 1863; Hill's Corps, June 19.

J-26 ALBERT GALLATIN WILLIS

Rte. 522, 3 miles north of Flint Hill. Pvt. Albert G. Willis, Co. C, Col. John S. Mosby's Partisan Rangers (43d Battalion, Virginia Cavalry) and at least one other Ranger were captured about 13 Oct. 1864 near Gaines Crossroads by Union Brig. Gen. William H. Powell's U.S. 2d Cavalry Division. During the Civil War, many Federals considered partisans civilian bushwhackers, not regular soldiers. Powell, in reprisal for what he called the "murder" of a U.S. soldier by alleged partisans, ordered a Ranger executed. According to some postwar sources, Willis, a ministerial student, offered his life in place of a married cohort. He was hanged nearby on 14 Oct. and buried at a Baptist church in Flint Hill.

J-29 POPE'S ARMY OF VIRGINIA

Rte. 522, at Reynolds Baptist Church, Sperryville. On 26 June 1862, President Abraham Lincoln appointed Maj. Gen. John Pope to command the Union army that operated in Virginia. The Corps led by Maj. Gen. Franz Sigel, who had recently replaced Maj. Gen. John C. Frémont, posted around Sperryville, was consolidated with those of Maj. Gens. Nathaniel P. Banks and Irvin McDowell under Pope and named the Army of Virginia. Pope led the army through the Union defeat at the Second Battle of Manassas (Bull Run) on 30 Aug. 1862. He was relieved [of] his command on 2 Sept., and the Army of Virginia was absorbed into Maj. Gen. George B. McClellan's Army of the Potomac.

J-31 SPERRYVILLE

Rte. 211, Sperryville. Laid out by Francis Thornton, Jr., in 1817, Sperryville survives as an upper Piedmont crossroads village. In the early 19th century John Kiger built Conestoga wagons here. By the 1850s two turnpikes (Thornton's Gap and Sperryville & Rappahannock) intersected here. In 1867, the Smoot family, of Alexandria, built a nearby tannery that closed in 1911. By that time, the town boasted four churches, five general stores, one hotel, six mills, numerous shops, a masonic hall, and a population of 350. Sperryville's wooden residences and visual charm have long made it a familiar stop for seasonal tourists to the Blue Ridge Mountains.

J-100 F. T. BAPTIST CHURCH

Rtes. 231 and 707. F. T. Baptist Church was founded nearby as Ragged Mountain Church in 1778. According to tradition the congregation worshipped in a log structure at Sharp Rock until about 1802 before moving to the former F.T. Village by 1804 where it became known as F.T. Baptist Church. F.T. stands for Francis Thornton who received land grants in the region from the 1730s to the early 1750s. In 1816 the congregation moved to the present site and built a new structure. By 1884 the present church was constructed nearby and an addition was added later. F.T. Baptist Church fostered the founding of other churches.

J-101   JOHN JACKSON—TRADITIONAL MUSICIAN

Rte. 522, near Woodville, Millwood. John Jackson, Piedmont guitar master and influential traditional musician, was born near here on 25 Feb. 1924. One of fourteen children of tenant farmers Suddy and Hattie Jackson, Jackson learned songs on the guitar and banjo from his parents, traveling and local musicians, and records. He moved to Fairfax County in 1950, where he worked various jobs and started a grave-digging business. Introduced to the Washington, D.C., folk scene in 1964, Jackson performed on eight records, at clubs, on radio, and at festivals in the U.S. and Europe. He received the prestigious National Heritage Fellowship Award in 1986. Jackson died at home in Fairfax Station on 20 Jan. 2002.

ROCKBRIDGE COUNTY

A-43   McDOWELL'S GRAVE

Rte. 11, 1.1 miles south of Fairfield. Nearby is the cemetery that contains the grave of Capt. John McDowell, who died on 18 Dec. 1742 during a conflict between Iroquois Indians and colonial settlers. Although accounts differ on how the conflict arose, it resulted in the deaths of more than seventeen Indians and settlers including McDowell. To avert a war, Lieutenant Governor George Thomas, of Pennsylvania, mediated the conflict in 1744 with the Treaty of Lancaster. It was decided that Lieutenant Governor William Gooch, of Virginia, would pay the Iroquois a reparation of 100 pounds. Also buried at the cemetery are other members of the McDowell family.

A-44   LIBERTY HALL ACADEMY

Rte. 11, 5.3 miles north of Lexington, at Sam Houston Wayside. This school, which was founded in 1777 and finally grew into Washington and Lee University, stood a short distance to the southwest of this point.

A-45   RED HOUSE AND THE McDOWELL FAMILY

Rte. 11, 1.1 miles south of Fairfield. Nearby once stood a log house painted red, built by the McDowell family. John McDowell received land here for surveying Borden's Grant in the late 1730s. In 1742 McDowell was killed during a conflict between settlers and Indians. Dr. Ephraim McDowell, grandson of John McDowell, was born nearby on 11 November 1771. When he was 13 years old his family moved to Kentucky and he later became a prominent physician. He is referred to as the "father of ovariotomy surgery." A nearby cemetery contains the grave of kinsman James McDowell, governor of Virginia from 1843 to 1845.

A-46   TIMBER RIDGE CHURCH

Rte. 11, 5.3 miles north of Lexington, at Sam Houston Wayside. This Presbyterian Church was built in 1756, nineteen years after the first settlement in Rockbridge County.

A-47   CHERRY GROVE ESTATE

Rte. 11, 0.3 miles south of Fairfield. Here was born James McDowell, Governor of Virginia, 1843–46.

A-49 THORN HILL ESTATE

Rte. 251, 0.6 miles west of Business Rte. 11, south of Lexington. Home of Colonel John Bowyer, an officer in the Revolutionary War, and of General E. F. Paxton, commander of the Stonewall Brigade, killed at Chancellorsville May 3, 1863.

A-51 VIRGINIA INVENTORS

Rte. 11, at Rte. 606 near Augusta County line. A mile and a half northwest, Cyrus H. McCormick perfected, in 1831, the grain reaper. In that vicinity, in 1856, J. A. E. Gibbs devised the chainstitch sewing machine.

A-52 BIRTHPLACE OF SAM HOUSTON

Rte. 11, 5.3 miles north of Lexington, at Sam Houston Wayside. In a cabin on the hilltop to the east Sam Houston was born, March 2, 1793. As commander-in-chief of the Texas army, he won the battle of San Jacinto, which secured Texan independence, April 21, 1836. He was President of Texas, 1836–1838, 1841–1844; United States Senator, 1846–1859; Governor, 1860–1861. He died, July, 1863.

A-70 BROWNSBURG

Rte. 762, Brownsburg. The village of Brownsburg, established on 23 November 1793, is an enduring example of a mid- to late-19th-century Shenandoah Valley community. By 1835 Brownsburg was a thriving commercial hub and was centrally located on the stagecoach line between Staunton and Lexington. Brownsburg Academy, a private Presbyterian high school for young men, was built with funds raised by local residents. The Academy operated as a private institution from 1850 to 1877 and its building was used for classes, religious services, and public meetings. A portion of Brownsburg was listed as a historic district on the Virginia Landmarks Register and National Register of Historic Places in 1973.

This image of Natural Bridge reproduced from a 1930s postcard demonstrates the longstanding popularity of one of the commonwealth's most well-known tourist attractions. The landform has been drawn and photographed by countless people for centuries. (Marker A-72) (Period foldout postcard by Marken & Bielfeld, Inc., of Frederick, Maryland)

A-72 NATURAL BRIDGE

Rte. 11, at Rte. 130, at Natural Bridge. Natural Bridge holds a unique place in American history as one of the natural wonders and first tourist attractions in the New World. Artists and illustrators popularized its image. This natural semielliptical arch is made of limestone carved by nature over millions of years and is approximately 200 feet high. The Monacan Indians held the site sacred and worshiped there. Thomas Jefferson obtained a land grant on 5 July 1774 to preserve it and to ensure the public could visit it. Natural Bridge was listed on the Virginia Landmarks Register in 1997 and was designated a National Historic Landmark in 1998.

L-8 NEW MONMOUTH CHURCH AND MORRISON'S BIRTHPLACE

Rte. 60, at Rte. 669 South, west of Lexington city limits. This is the site of the first church, built 1746. Just northeast was the birthplace of William McCutchan Morrison, born, 1867, died, 1918. A missionary to the Belgian Congo, he translated the Bible into native languages and exposed conditions there. Buried at Luebo, Congo.

L-10 INDIAN AND SETTLER CONFLICT

Rte. 130, at Rte. 501, Glasgow. On 18 Dec. 1742, the first known clash between Indians and colonial settlers in Rockbridge County took place near the mouth of the Maury River. Iroquois en route south from Pennsylvania encountered pioneers led by Capt. John McDowell. Although accounts differ on how the conflict arose, it resulted in the deaths of more than seventeen Indians and settlers including McDowell. To avert a war, Lieutenant Governor George Thomas, of Pennsylvania, mediated the conflict in 1744 with the Treaty of Lancaster. It was decided that Lieutenant Governor William Gooch, of Virginia, would pay the Iroquois a reparation of 100 pounds.

L-63 FRANK PADGET WATER TRAGEDY

Rte. 684 (Blue Ridge Road), Centennial Park, Glasgow. Heavy rains in late Jan. 1854 left the James River and the treacherous Balcony Falls in full flood. On 21 Jan., the canal boat Clinton and its passengers became stranded in the raging waters. Frank Padget, a skilled boatman and slave, led four other men to rescue them. In a heroic attempt to save the last passenger, Padget

drowned, unable to fight the rushing current. Capt. Edward Echols, who witnessed Padget's act, was so moved he commissioned the construction of a granite obelisk monument that was erected beside Lock 16 of the Blue Ridge Canal. It now stands here in Glasgow's Centennial Park.

Q-11-a STONEWALL JACKSON HOUSE

Rte. 60, 1 mile east of Lexington. Future Confederate Lt. Gen. Thomas J. "Stonewall" Jackson and his second wife, Mary Anna Morrison, owned a house on Washington Street from 1859 to 1861, while he taught at the Virginia Military Institute. It is the only house he ever owned. A typical Valley I-house built for Cornelius Dorman in 1801, its facade was altered and a stone addition erected before Jackson bought it. In 1907 the Stonewall Jackson Memorial Hospital opened in the house, and it became a museum in 1954. In the 1970s the Historic Lexington Foundation restored the house to its appearance during Jackson's occupancy. Since 1995 it has been owned by the Stonewall Jackson Foundation.

R-63 FALLING SPRING PRESBYTERIAN CHURCH

Rte. 11, at Rte. 680, approximately 6 miles south of Lexington city limits. The oldest congregation in the Fincastle Presbytery, the Falling Spring Presbyterian Church, was organized before 1748. The Hanover Presbytery met here in October, 1780. The present Gothic Revival church was constructed of slave-made brick during the Civil War. At the time of its dedication in April, 1864, General Thomas L. Rosser's Cavalry Brigade was camped here. The first burial in the present cemetery was that of John Grigsby of Fruit Hill (1720–1794).

ROCKINGHAM COUNTY

A-18 ABRAHAM LINCOLN'S FATHER

Rte. 11, just south of Rte. 808, Lacey Spring. Four miles west, Thomas Lincoln, father

of the President, was born about 1778. He was taken to Kentucky by his father about 1781. Beside the road here was

Lincoln Inn, long kept by a member of the family.

A-29 CAVALRY ENGAGEMENT

Rte. 11, 7.5 miles north of Harrisonburg. Here, at Lacey's Springs, Rosser's Confederate cavalry attacked Custer's camp, December 20, 1864. Rosser and Custer (of Indian fame) had been roommates at West Point.

A-32 SHERIDAN'S LAST RAID

Rte. 11, 0.3 miles south of Mount Crawford. Here was fought the engagement of Mount Crawford, March 1, 1865, in Sheridan's last raid.

A-59 DR. JESSEE BENNETT—1769–1842

Rte. 42, at Rte. 859 (Jessee Bennett Way), Edom. Near Edom, Virginia, on January 14, 1794, in a heroic effort to save his wife, Elizabeth, and child, Dr. Jessee Bennett performed the first successful Caesarian section and oophorectomy to be done in America.

D-1 FORT HARRISON

Business Rte. 42, at Dayton northern corporate limits. Daniel Harrison settled about 1745 at the headwaters of Cook's Creek where it is believed he built the stone portion of the present house. During the decades 1750–1770, when this area was the frontier of the colony, the house served the settlers as a refuge from Indian attacks. Subsequent owners added the brick portion and enlarged the windows and doors. The Harrison family had large land holdings in present Augusta and Rockingham counties.

D-6 BATTLE OF CROSS KEYS

Rte. 33, at Rte. 276, 2.3 miles southeast of Harrisonburg eastern city limits. Three miles south, on Mill Creek, Jackson's rearguard, under Ewell, was attacked by Fremont, June 8, 1862. Trimble, of Ewell's command, counterattacked, driving the Unionists back. Jackson, with the rest of his army, was near Port Republic awaiting the advance of Shields up the east bank of the Shenandoah River.

D-7 FIRST CHURCH IN ROCKINGHAM COUNTY

Rte. 732 (Bowman Road), 0.2 miles west of Rte. 290 (College Street), Dayton. The first church in Rockingham County was built on this site in 1747 on land owned by Captain Daniel Harrison of the colonial militia. Serving as a "Chapel of Ease" for Augusta Parish, the first building is believed to have been built of logs. The chapel was replaced by a larger frame building some 20 years later. Following the Revolutionary War, the church was used by a Methodist congregation; it was sold and functioned as a barn until it was torn down about 1900.

D-10 KNIGHTS OF THE GOLDEN HORSESHOE

Rte. 33, just west of Skyline Drive, Swift Run Gap. On 5 Sept. 1716, in this region, it is believed, Lieutenant Governor Alexander Spotswood and his party of government officials, gentry, Native Americans, soldiers, and servants crossed the Blue Ridge Mountains into the Shenandoah Valley. Their adventure into Virginia's western lands began at Germanna late in Aug. and ended when they returned there on 10 Sept. According to legend, Spotswood gave his companions small golden horseshoes on their return and the group became known as the Knights of the Golden Horseshoe. The journey has been fictionalized and mythologized in literature since the 19th century.

I-13 BRIDGEWATER COLLEGE

Rte. 11, at Rte. 257, Mount Crawford. Located two miles southwest in the town of Bridgewater, this liberal arts college is affiliated with the Church of the Brethren. It grew out of the Spring Creek Normal School and Collegiate Institute, founded in 1880, and became Bridgewater College nine years later. It has been coeducational from the beginning.

I-13-a BRIDGEWATER COLLEGE

Rtes. 613 and 752, Spring Creek. Founded near this site in 1880, the college is now located 4.3 miles east in the town of Bridgewater. This liberal arts college is affiliated with the Church of the Brethren. It grew out of the Spring Creek Normal School and Collegiate Institute and became Bridgewater College nine years later. It has been coeducational from its founding.

JD-8 FIRST SETTLER

Rte. 340, 0.5 miles north of Elkton. "Green Meadows" to the west, was the home of Adam Miller (1703–1783), one of the first Europeans to settle in the Valley. The property remained in the Miller (originally Mueller) family from the 1740s through 1936.

JD-10 BATTLE OF PORT REPUBLIC

Rte. 340, 3 miles north of Grottoes. The cross road here roughly divides the Confederate and Union lines in the battle of June 9, 1862. Jackson attacked Shields, coming southward to join Fremont, but was repulsed. Reinforced by Ewell, Jackson attacked again and drove Shields from the field. At the same time he burned the bridge at Port Republic, preventing Fremont from coming to Shields' aid.

KB-65 LINCOLN'S VIRGINIA ANCESTORS

Rte. 42, 2.5 miles north of Edom. In 1768, John Lincoln moved here with his family from Pennsylvania. His eldest son, Abraham, grandfather of the president, might have remained a Virginian had his friend and distant relative, Daniel Boone not encouraged him to migrate to Kentucky by 1782. Abraham's son, Thomas Lincoln, born in Virginia (ca. in 1778), met and married Nancy Hanks in Kentucky, where the future president was born on 12 February 1809. Nearby stands the Lincoln house built about 1800 by Captain Jacob Lincoln, the President's great-uncle, near the original Lincoln homestead. Five generations of Lincolns and two family slaves are buried on the hill.

SHENANDOAH COUNTY

A-19 TRENCHES ON HUPP'S HILL

Rte. 11, at Stasburg northern limits. These trenches were constructed by Sheridan in the autumn of 1864 while campaigning against Early.

A-20 FRONTIER FORT

Rte. 11 (North Massanutten Street), at Cool Spring Road, Strasburg. This house, built about 1755, is the old Hupp homestead. It was used as a fort in Indian attacks.

A-21 BATTLE OF CEDAR CREEK

Rte. 11, south of Orchard Street, Strasburg. The breaking of this bridge in the evening of October 19, 1864, permitted Sheridan to retake most of the material captured in the morning by Early.

A-22 BATTLE OF FISHER'S HILL

Rte. 11, 1.9 miles south of Strasburg. After his defeat on 19 Sept. 1864 at the Third Battle of Winchester by Maj. Gen. Philip H. Sheridan, Lt. Gen. Jubal A. Early led his 9,500-man army here to Fisher's Hill, a favorite Confederate stronghold. Sheridan pursued, and on 22 Sept. attacked Early with most of his 30,000-man force. Brig. Gen. George Crook, with two divisions, struck Early's left flank about three miles west near Little North Mountain while Sheridan launched a general assault here on Early's center and right. The Confederates fled under the onslaught to Rockfish Gap. Early lost some 1,200 men, Sheridan about 530.

A-23 BATTLE OF FISHER'S HILL

Rte. 11, near Rte. 644, 3.1 miles south of Strasburg. Here Early's Adjutant-General, A. S. Pendleton, while attempting to check Sheridan's attack, was mortally wounded, September 22, 1864.

A-24 BANKS' FORT

Rte. 11 (North Massanutten Street), at Rte. 55 West, Strasburg. The earthworks on the hilltop to the southwest were constructed by General Banks in the campaign of 1862.

A-25 ACTION OF TOMS BROOK

Rte. 11, at Tom's Brook southern town limits. Here Early's cavalry under Rosser and Lomax was driven back by Sheridan's cavalry under Torbert, October 9, 1864.

A-26 CAVALRY ENGAGEMENT

Rte. 11, approximately 2.5 miles south of Mount Jackson. On 15 Nov. 1863, Col. William H. Boyd reconnoitered with a Federal cavalry and artillery detachment south from Charlestown (in present-day W.Va.) toward New Market. The next day, the force encountered Maj. Robert White's cavalry command just north of Mount Jackson. White's Confederates retreated fighting through the town and crossed the Shenandoah River bridge to Rude's Hill. Realizing that White's artillery could sweep the bridge, Boyd withdrew to a bivouac two miles north of Woodstock, pursued by Capt. Thomas S. Davis's cavalry company, and soon returned to Charlestown. Losses from the Mount Jackson engagement were light on both sides.

A-27 RUDE'S HILL ACTION

Rte. 11, approximately 2.5 miles south of Mount Jackson. Rude's Hill was reached by two divisions of Sheridan's Union cavalry following the Confederate General Jubal A. Early, on November 22, 1864. Early promptly took position on the hill to oppose them. The cavalry, charging across the flats, were repulsed in a sharp action and fell back northward.

A-28 BATTLE OF NEW MARKET

Rte. 11, 0.6 miles north of New Market. On the hills to the north took place the battle of New Market, May 15, 1864. The Union Army, under General Franz Sigel, faced southwest. John C. Breckinridge, once Vice-President of the United States, commanded the Confederates. Colonel Scott Shipp commanded the cadet corps of the Virginia Military Institute, which distinguished itself, capturing a battery. The battle ended in Sigel's retreat northward.

A-34 SEVIER'S BIRTHPLACE

Rte. 11, south of New Market, at Shenandoah/Rockingham County line. Near here was born John Sevier, pioneer and soldier, September 23, 1745. He was a leader in the Indian wars and at the battle of King's Mountain, 1780. He was the only governor of the short-lived state of Franklin and the first governor of Tennessee. Sevier died in Georgia, September 24, 1815.

A-36 FAIRFAX LINE

Rte. 11, south of New Market, at Shenandoah/Rockingham County line. Here ran the southwestern boundary of Lord Fairfax's vast land grant, the Northern Neck. It was surveyed by Peter Jefferson, Thomas Jefferson's father, and others in 1746.

A-41 LAST INDIAN-SETTLER CONFLICT

Rte. 11, 1.9 miles south of Woodstock. A series of conflicts between settlers and Native Americans, including the French and Indian War, the Cherokee War, and Pontiac's War, occurred along the western frontier of the colonies. The last documented clash in the Shenandoah Valley took place nearby in 1766. A small band of Indians attacked the Sheetz and Taylor families as they fled for safety to the fort at Woodstock. Mathias Sheetz and Taylor were both killed, but their wives used axes to fight off the Indians and escape with the children.

A-55 FORT BOWMAN

Rte. 11, 1.9 miles north of Strasburg, before Cedar Creek, south of Shenandoah/Warren County line. The stone house to the south is Fort Bowman, or Harmony Hall, built about 1753 for George Bowman who emigrated from Pennsylvania in 1731–1732. The house is an important example of the Pennsylvania German influence on Shenandoah Valley architecture. There was born Maj. Joseph Bowman, second in command in Gen. George Rogers Clark's expedition for the conquest of the Northwest in 1778–1779 during the Revolutionary War. Among those buried in the Bowman family cemetery nearby are Joseph Bowman's brother, Capt. Isaac Bowman, and Samuel Kercheval, the early-19th-century historian of the Valley.

A-65 OUR SOLDIERS' CEMETERY

Rte. 11, at Mount Jackson northern entrance. The Mount Jackson Confederate Hospital's cemetery, now called Our Soldiers' Cemetery, was dedicated on 10 May 1866, the third anniversary of Stonewall Jackson's death. The "Memorial and Decoration Day" organized by the local ladies was one of the first such observances in the South. The service began with an address in the church by Major Henry Kyd Douglas, the youngest of Jackson's staff officers. Afterward, a participant wrote that "ladies, gentlemen and children as well as many ex-Confederates, all carrying wreaths prepared the day before, marched to the cemetery ¾ of a mile north of town to place those wreaths on each of the 400 graves."

A-66 THE CONFEDERATE HOSPITAL

Rte. 11, at Mount Jackson northern entrance. The Confederate hospital was built here under the direction of Dr. Andrew Russell Meem, by order of the Confederate Medical Department in Sept. 1861. The hospital consisted of three two-story buildings, each 150 feet long, accommodating 500 patients. At the end of the war, the 192nd Ohio Volunteer Militia tore down the hospital and used the lumber to construct a large military installation that included a courthouse, guardhouse, gallows, and ballroom on Rude's Hill, three miles south of Mount Jackson. Federal occupation forces used these structures throughout the Reconstruction period. The cemetery, which was established directly across the Valley Pike in 1861, was dedicated in 1866.

A-68 McNEIL'S LAST CHARGE

Rte. 11, 0.1 miles south of Mount Jackson corporate limits. In the predawn darkness of 3 Oct. 1864, Capt. John Hanson McNeill led thirty of his Partisan Rangers, including local resident Joseph I. Triplett, against a hundred-man detachment of the 8th Ohio Cavalry Regiment that was guarding the Meems Bottom bridge on the Valley Turnpike. The attack ended in fifteen minutes with most of the guard captured and McNeill, among the best-known Confederate partisan commanders, mortally wounded. Taken first to the Rev. Anders R. Rude's house a mile south, McNeill was moved on 20 Oct. to Hill's Hotel (Stoneleigh) in Harrisonburg, where he died on 10 Nov. His body was later reinterred in Moorefield, W.Va., his home.

A-69 POST-APPOMATTOX TRAGEDY

Rte. 11, at Rte. 828, approximately 3 miles south of Mount Jackson. On 22 May 1865, after the Civil War ended, Capt. George W. Summers, Sgt. I. Newton Koontz, and two other armed veterans of Co. D, 7th Virginia Cavalry, robbed six Federal cavalrymen of their horses near Woodstock. The horses were returned the next day to the 192d Ohio Volunteer Infantry at Rude's Hill. Despite assurances that all was forgiven, Lt. Col. Cyrus Hussy, temporarily commanding the 192d, later ordered the men arrested. The others escaped, but Summers and Koontz were shot without trial here on 27 June. Thirty years later, Capt. Thomas J.

Adams and friends erected the nearby monument to commemorate their deaths.

AB-1 MEEM'S BOTTOM COVERED BRIDGE

Rte. 11, 0.2 miles south of Rte. 720, south of Mount Jackson. Built in 1892 by Franklin Hiser Wissler to provide access to his apple orchards at Strathmore Farms, this is the longest remaining covered bridge in Virginia. A 200-foot single span located one-half mile northwest, the bridge is a Burr Truss design, a combination of arch with vertical and diagonal supports. All construction materials were obtained locally. Damaged by arsonists in 1976, the bridge was restored and reopened in 1979.

AB-2 CIVIL WAR ACTION IN EDINBURG

Rte. 185 (Stony Creek Boulevard), at Piccadilly Street, Edinburg. During Maj. Gen. Thomas J. "Stonewall" Jackson's 1862 Valley campaign, Confederate Col. Turner Ashby's cavalry and Chew's Battery halted Union Maj. Gen. Nathaniel P. Banks's steady advance southward. Ashby engaged Union forces 28 times in April along Stony Creek and the Valley Pike. Confederate guns located on Cemetery Hill, to the southwest, dueled with Union batteries on Academy Hill directly across the center of Edinburg. In early October 1864, during their burning of the Shenandoah Valley, Maj. Gen. Philip H. Sheridan's troopers set the Edinburg Mill afire but extinguished it after two local girls protested.

CITY OF STAUNTON

A-61 BIRTHPLACE OF WOODROW WILSON—U.S. PRESIDENT 1913–21

Rte. 11, just south of Rte. 275. Three and one half miles south, on Coalter Street in Staunton, is the birthplace of Thomas Woodrow Wilson, 8th Virginia-born president of the U.S. Princeton University president, New Jersey governor, 28th President (World War I), he was chief author and sponsor of the League of Nations. Born Dec. 28, 1856, died in Washington, Feb. 3, 1924. The birthplace is maintained as an historic shrine.

A-62 BIRTHPLACE OF WOODROW WILSON—U.S. PRESIDENT 1913–21

Rte. 11, just north of Rte. 261 (Statler Boulevard), at southern entrance to Staunton. One mile north, on Coalter Street in Staunton, is the birthplace of Thomas Woodrow Wilson, 8th Virginia-born president of the U.S. Princeton University president, New Jersey governor, 28th President (World War I), he was chief author and sponsor of the League of Nations. Born Dec. 28, 1856, died in Washington, Feb. 3, 1924. The birthplace is maintained as an historic shrine.

A-63 DR. ALEXANDER HUMPHREYS

South Augusta Street, at West Johnson Street, downtown Staunton. Dr. Humphreys (1757–1802), an important teacher in 18th-century Virginia, received his M.D. from the University of Edinburgh. He practiced medicine in Augusta County and Staunton from 1783 to 1802 in an office facing the county courthouse. Among Dr. Humphreys' many students were Dr. Ephraim McDowell, the "Founder of Abdominal Surgery;" Dr. Samuel Brown, a pioneer in the use of smallpox vaccination; and President William Henry Harrison. Dr. Humphreys is buried in the churchyard of Trinity Episcopal Church.

A-64 DR. WILLIAM FLEMING

Rte. 250 (New Street), in City of Staunton parking lot. Physician, soldier, and statesman, Dr. William Fleming (1728–1795) studied medicine in his native Scotland before practicing in Staunton from 1763 to 1768. His home stood at the crossing of New Street and Lewis Creek. Dr. Fleming's career included periods as commander of the Botetourt Regiment, Commissioner for Kentucky, member of the Continental Congress, delegate to the Virginia Constitutional Convention, and Acting Governor when the Virginia General Assembly met in Staunton in June, 1781.

I-16 THE VIRGINIA SCHOOL FOR THE DEAF AND THE BLIND, FOUNDED 1839

Bypass Rte. 11 (Commerce Road), just east of school. A State residential school created by an act of the General Assembly of the Commonwealth of Virginia on March 31, 1838 for the purpose of educating the deaf and the blind children of the state.

I-17 MARY BALDWIN COLLEGE

East Frederick and New Streets, at college. The oldest college for women related to the Presbyterian Church, U.S. Founded 1842 by Rufus W. Bailey as Augusta Female Seminary; renamed in 1895 to honor Mary Julia Baldwin, pioneer woman educator and principal, 1863–1897.

I-21 STUART HALL

West Frederick and North St. Clair Streets. Chartered on 13 January 1844 as the

Virginia Female Institute, Stuart Hall is Virginia's oldest college preparatory school for girls. The Rev. Dr. Richard H. Phillips headed the school from 1848 until 1880. Flora Cooke Stuart, "Mrs. General" J. E. B. Stuart, for whom the school was renamed in 1907, was principal from 1880 until 1899. Two of General Robert E. Lee's daughters attended Stuart Hall, and Lee served as president of the school's board of visitors from 1865 until 1870.

QC-1 TRINITY CHURCH

214 West Beverley Street. Known originally as Augusta Parish Church, it was founded in 1746 as the County Parish. The Virginia General Assembly met here in June 1781 to avoid capture by British Raiders. The present church was erected in 1855 and was used by the Virginia Theological Seminary during the War Between the States. The first Bishop of Virginia, James Madison, was a member of this church.

WARREN COUNTY

FF-2 STATE FISH HATCHERY

Rte. 55, at Rte. 678, 5 miles west of Riverton, Waterlick. One mile south. This fish cultural station was established in 1933 for hatching and rearing smallmouth bass and other species of sunfish for the stocking of the public waters of Virginia.

J-7 THE MCKAY HOME

Rte. 340/522, 0.1 miles north of Rte. 627, Cedarville. A short distance west, at Cedarville, stands the old home of the pioneer Robert McKay. Built of walnut logs, it is one of the oldest houses in the Valley. In 1731, Joist Hite, Robert McKay and others received a grant of 100,000 acres. Hite settled on the Opequon and McKay at this place on Crooked Run. These

men opened the Valley to succeeding settlers.

J-8 CAPTURE OF FRONT ROYAL

Rte. 340, at southeast corner of East Main Street and South Royal Avenue, at courthouse, Front Royal. Stonewall Jackson, moving against Banks, captured this town from a Union force under Colonel Kenly, May 23, 1862.

J-9 EXECUTIONS OF MOSBY'S MEN

Rte. 340/522, at Rte. 637, 0.1 miles north of Riverton. On 23 Sept. 1864, in a fight south of town, some of Lt. Col. John S. Mosby's Rangers mortally wounded Lt. Charles McMaster, 2d U.S. Cavalry, after he allegedly surrendered. Union Gen. Alfred T. A.

Torbert's cavalrymen retaliated by executing six captured Rangers nearby. They shot David L. Jones and Lucien Love behind the Methodist church, Thomas E. Anderson beneath an elm tree, and Front Royal resident Henry Rhodes in a field in front of Rose Hill; they hanged William Thomas Overby and a Ranger named Carter at the W. E. Carson house. Mosby, believing Gen. George A. Custer responsible, on 6 Nov. ordered an equal number of his men executed near Berryville.

J-11 GUARD HILL ENGAGEMENT

Rte. 340/522, at Rte. 637, 0.1 miles north of Riverton. In Aug. 1864, part of Confederate Lt. Gen. Richard H. Anderson's corps threatened the left and rear of Union Maj. Gen. Philip H. Sheridan's army. As Brig. Gen. Wesley Merritt's division approached on 15 Aug. to protect the Federal flank, Anderson ordered Brig. Gen. William T. Wofford's infantry brigade and Brig. Gen. Williams C. Wickham's cavalry brigade across the forks of the Shenandoah River to confront Merritt. Wickham was overwhelmed, however, on 16 Aug., and his troopers retreated toward Front Royal, while Union Brig. Gen. George A. Custer's brigade drove Wofford from Guard Hill. Sheridan then retired north to Charles Town, W. Va.

J-12 RECREATIONAL CENTER OF FRONT ROYAL

Rte. 340, 1.1 miles north of Riverton. William E. Carson (1870–1942), the first chairman of the Virginia State Commission on Conservation and Development, a local resident, spearheaded the development of the recreational center for use by the people and visitors of Front Royal and Warren

County. In 1935, the Civilian Conservation Corps (CCC) began designing and developing the center's facilities, including the golf course and a rustic clubhouse that once stood nearby. The park opened to the public in 1938. Carson and his wife, Agnes H. Carson, donated the land for the park and dedicated it to the memory of their only son, William E. Carson, Jr., who died in 1925.

J-17 BROTHER AGAINST BROTHER

Rte. 340 (North Royal Avenue) at Chester Street, Front Royal. The first Maryland Regiment, U.S.A., was a part of the force holding this town when it was attacked by Stonewall Jackson, May 23, 1862. With Jackson was the First Maryland Regiment, C.S.A. The two regiments were arrayed against each other.

JD-1 BELLE BOYD AND JACKSON

Rte. 340, 0.1 miles south of Rte. 619, south of Front Royal. Near here Stonewall Jackson was met by the spy, Belle Boyd, and informed of the position of the Union troops at Front Royal, May 23, 1862. Jackson was advancing northward, attempting to get between Banks' army and Winchester.

JD-2 WILLIAM E. CARSON

Rte. 340, just south of entrance to Shenandoah National Park, south of Front Royal. William E. Carson, of Riverton, was the first chairman of the Virginia Conservation Commission, 1926–34. As such he was a pioneer and leading spirit in the establishment of the Shenandoah National Park and Skyline Drive; the Colonial National Historical Park; the state parks, and the state system of historical markers.

CITY OF WAYNESBORO

JF-15 WALNUT GROVE

Rte. 340, approximately 1 mile south of Rte. 250, at Northgate Avenue. Archibald Stuart—Revolutionary soldier, legislator, and

judge—was born here March 19, 1757, at the home of his grandfather and namesake, an early settler. The property was acquired by William A. Pratt in 1868 and G. Julian Pratt in 1900.

Q-2-a WAYNESBORO

Rte. 250, at eastern entrance of Waynesboro.
Here, on one of the first roads west of the
Blue Ridge, a hamlet stood in colonial
times. The Walker exploring expedition
started from this vicinity in 1748. Here, in
June, 1781, the Augusta militia assembled
to join Lafayette in the East. A town was
founded in 1797. It was established by law
in 1801 and named for General Anthony
Wayne.

Q-2-b WAYNESBORO

*Rte. 250 (West Main Street), at McElroy
Street, Constitution Park.* Settlers began to
arrive to present day Augusta County in
the 1730s and by the Revolutionary War a
small hamlet existed here. By 1797, it was
known as Waynesborough, for Revolutionary War hero Brig. Gen. Anthony Wayne.
It became a town in 1801 and was incorporated in 1834. The last battle fought
in the Shenandoah Valley took place in
Waynesboro on 2 March 1865, near the end
of the Civil War, when Union Maj. Gen.
Philip H. Sheridan defeated Confederate
Lt. Gen. Jubal A. Early. Basic City consolidated with Waynesboro in 1924, and in
1948 the Virginia General Assembly made
Waynesboro a city.

Q-2-c VIRGINIA METALCRAFTERS

Rte. 250, 0.3 miles east of Rte. 340. Virginia
Metalcrafters had its first beginnings with
the founding of the Waynesboro Stove
Company in 1890 by William J. Loth.
The company, which made ornately cast
cookstoves, heaters and all accoutrements
for kitchens of the period, later developed
the electric Hotpoint Range. It merged

with Rife Ram Pump Works, inventors in
1884 of the ram pump widely used to pump
water in rural areas before electrification.
In 1938, the Rife-Loth Corporation began
selling finely crafted brass accessories under the name Virginia Metalcrafters.

Q-19 FISHBURNE MILITARY SCHOOL

*South Wayne and Federal Streets, at school,
downtown Waynesboro.* James Abbott Fishburne, an honor graduate of Washington
College inspired by its president, Robert E.
Lee, opened in 1879 with 24 students what
eventually became Fishburne Military
School. Staunton architectural firm T. J.
Collins & Son designed the 1916–1922
barracks in the castellated Gothic style,
the 1915 library (Virginia's second-oldest
Carnegie library), and the 1940 gymna-
sium-administrative building. In Feb. 1919,
the school adopted one of the nation's
first Army Junior Reserve Officer Training Corps programs. Operated by the
Fishburne-Hudgins Educational Foundation since 1951, the school is listed on
the Virginia Landmarks Register and the
National Register of Historic Places.

W-160 EARLY'S LAST BATTLE

Rte. 250, at Dupont Street. On the ridge west
of Waynesboro occurred the last engagement of Confederate forces commanded
by Lt. Gen. Jubal A. Early. Portions of Maj.
Gen. Philip H. Sheridan's army, including
cavalry led by Maj. Gen. George A. Custer,
attacked and routed Confederate troops under Brig. Gen. Gabriel C. Wharton. Early
and the remnants of his army retreated,
leaving Sheridan in control and ending the
Shenandoah Valley campaigns.

CITY OF WINCHESTER

A-5 FIRST BATTLE OF WINCHESTER

*Rte. 11 (Valley Avenue), 0.1 miles south of
Handley Boulevard.* On May 24, 1862,
Confederate forces under Major General
Thomas J. "Stonewall" Jackson pursued

Major General Nathaniel Banks' Union
Army from Strasburg to Winchester.
Banks made a stand south of Winchester,
posting one of two infantry brigades on
Bower's Hill, now known as Williams-

burg Heights, and the other here in the plain below. In attacks the following day, Jackson routed the Union Army and drove it through the town towards Harper's Ferry.

A-7 FIRST BATTLE OF WINCHESTER

Rte. 11 (Valley Avenue), north of Weems Lane, Winchester. Here Stonewall Jackson, in the early morning of May 25, 1862, halted his advance guard and observed the Union position.

J-4 THIRD BATTLE OF WINCHESTER

National Avenue at Lincoln Steet, at National Cemetery. Near here Early, facing east, took his last position on September 19, 1864. About sundown he was attacked and driven from it, retreating south. Presidents Rutherford B. Hayes and William McKinley served in this engagement on the Union side.

Q-4-a GENERAL DANIEL MORGAN/WINCHESTER

Rte. 50, at eastern city limits. [*Obverse*] Morgan used this road in traveling from his home, "Saratoga," to Winchester. He was a frontiersman, Indian fighter and the commander of Morgan's famous riflemen in the Revolution. He won glory at Quebec and Saratoga, and defeated Tarleton at the Cowpens. He died in 1802 and is buried in Winchester. [*Reverse*] At first called Fredericktown, it was founded in 1744, near a Shawnee Indian village, by Colonel James Wood, a native of the English city of Winchester. The town was situated in Lord Fairfax's proprietary of the Northern Neck. It was chartered in 1752.

Q-4-d LORD FAIRFAX

Rte. 522, 0.3 miles east of Rte. 37. Thomas Fairfax (1693–1781), sixth Baron Fairfax of Cameron, was the proprietor of the

Numerous battles were fought in the northern Piedmont and the Shenandoah Valley during the Civil War. This Currier and Ives illustration, entitled "The Great Victory in the Shenandoah Valley, Va., Sept. 19th, 1864," shows an artist's interpretation of the Third Battle of Winchester. (Marker J-4) (Virginia Historical Society, Richmond, Virginia)

Northern Neck Proprietary, a vast land holding that lay between the Rappahannock and Potomac Rivers, and extended to the Blue Ridge. Born in England, he came to Virginia about 1735 and moved to the Shenandoah Valley about 1747. He eventually lived at Greenway Court in present-day Clarke County, while managing his landholdings. In 1749, he was named a justice of the peace for Frederick County, and also served as one of the justices of the county court of chancery that met in Winchester, and as a county lieutenant for a number of years. He is buried at Christ Episcopal Church in Winchester.

Q-4-e COLONEL JAMES WOOD/WINCHESTER

Rte. 50, just west of Rte. 11, at western entrance to Winchester. [*Obverse*] James Wood, founder of Winchester, named for his native city in England, was the first clerk of Frederick County Court, which was organized in 1743 at the house on his estate, "Glen Burnie." His son, General James Wood, was Governor of Virginia, 1796–1799. [*Reverse*] At first called Freder

icktown it was founded in 1744, near a Shawnee Indian village, by Colonel James Wood, a native of the English city of Winchester. The town was situated in Lord Fairfax's proprietary of the Northern Neck. It was chartered in 1752.

Q-4-f JACKSON'S HEADQUARTERS

415 North Braddock Street. This house was used by Maj. Gen. Thomas J. Jackson, then commanding the valley district, department of Northern Virginia, as his official headquarters from November, 1861, to March, 1862, when he left Winchester to begin his famous valley campaign.

Q-4-g REAR ADMIRAL RICHARD E. BYRD—25 OCTOBER 1888–11 MARCH 1957

Rte. 50 (Amherst Street), at West Boscawen Street. Here was born and reared Richard Evelyn Byrd, aviator and polar explorer. A 1912 U.S. Naval Academy graduate, he received the Medal of Honor for the first flight over the North Pole in 1926, and made the first commercial nonstop transatlantic flight in 1927. In 1928 he organized and led the first of five Antarctic expeditions, and flew over the South Pole in 1929. Byrd spent the winter of 1934 alone a hundred miles from his base at Little America, conducting scientific experiments. Of his several books, the best known is *Alone.* Byrd is regarded as the father of the Antarctic Peace Treaty, which bans the military use of Antarctica. He is buried in Arlington National Cemetery.

Q-4-h GEORGE WASHINGTON'S OUT-LOT

400 block, National Avenue. Here was located George Washington's five-acre out-lot from Thomas Lord Fairfax, Baron of Cameron, by grant of 15 May 1753. Fairfax also granted him a companion in-lot 77 at North Braddock Street and Fairfax Lane. The out-lot was number 16 of 80 in a 439-acre tract located outside Winchester and mostly north of present-day Fairfax Lane and National Avenue. Lord Fairfax had reserved the tract as a "Common for the Use and Benefit of the Inhabitants of the Town." Washington owned both lots until his death in 1799; his executors sold them to Dr. Robert Mackey, a Revolutionary War surgeon, in 1805.

Central Virginia and Central Piedmont

MANY SIGNIFICANT EVENTS in Virginia's history have occurred in the central portion of the state, which comprises the counties of Albemarle, Amelia, Caroline, Chesterfield, Dinwiddie, Fluvanna, Goochland, Hanover, Henrico, Louisa, Powhatan, Prince George, and Spotsylvania, and the cities of Charlottesville, Colonial Heights, Fredericksburg, Petersburg, and Richmond.

Prior to the arrival of the English, a portion of Powhatan's paramount chiefdom stretched into this area. What is believed to be the birthplace of Paramount Chief Powhatan and the village of Powhatan existed just east of present-day Richmond. The English first settled at Henricus Citie in 1611, and a number of European settlements soon followed, including Bermuda Hundred in what is now Chesterfield County and the future city of Petersburg, established in 1645 at the site of an Appamattuck Indian village.

With movement by the English and other Europeans, who followed the navigable rivers, the future cities of Fredericksburg on the Rappahannock and Richmond on the James were established by the middle of the eighteenth century. This period was marked by resistance to British policy, including Patrick Henry's "liberty or death" speech, which was delivered at St. John's Episcopal Church in Richmond and is noted on a historical marker at the site.

In 1780, during the Revolutionary War, the commonwealth's capital moved from Williamsburg to Richmond. Historical markers describe troop movements and conflicts that occurred during the 1781 Virginia campaign, including a number of signs discussing the battle of Petersburg.

Markers focusing on this era also describe places and events associated with Thomas Jefferson, such as Monticello and the University of Virginia. Others mark James Monroe's Ash Lawn–Highland and many other historic homes, courthouses, and towns.

The social and political issues that shaped Virginia and the early republic are also commemorated. Several signs provide details about Gabriel, an enslaved blacksmith from Brookfield plantation in Henrico County, whose unsuccessful attempt to lead an uprising against slavery in 1800 was among the many events that culminated in the Civil War.

That war had a profound impact on this part of the state. Beginning in 1861, Richmond and the surrounding region witnessed numerous battles and

Fredericksburg

SPOTSYLVANIA

Charlottesville

CAROLINE

ALBEMARLE

LOUISA

FLUVANNA

HANOVER

GOOCHLAND

POWHATAN

Richmond

HENRICO

AMELIA

CHESTERFIELD

Colonial
Heights

PRINCE
GEORGE

Petersburg

DINWIDDIE

MILES

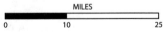

0   10   25

skirmishes, including the Seven Days' campaign and the battle of Fredericksburg in 1862, and the Richmond-Petersburg campaign in 1864 and 1865. Many markers provide information about these events.

With the defeat of the Confederacy and the economic deprivation that followed, a new South emerged by the end of the nineteenth century. In central Virginia, the expansion of cities provided many new job and education opportunities for white Virginians.

Reconstruction also brought such benefits as education, suffrage, and land ownership for African Americans. This progress was brought to a halt, however, by Jim Crow laws and a 1902 state constitution that enforced racial segregation and limited voting rights.

In light of these changes, African Americans established their own churches, corporations, and educational institutions, as well as fraternal and social self-help organizations, several of which are featured on markers throughout the commonwealth. During the civil rights era these groups played an important role in organizing mass efforts to counter segregationist practices.

The early twentieth century also saw continued economic, technological, and population growth in the cities. Markers highlight some of these developments, including the opening of the Broad Street railway station in Richmond and the development of an electric rail line between Richmond and Petersburg.

After World War II, although most of the region remained largely rural, growth continued in and around the major cities, spurred on by automobiles and suburban development. Desegregation brought major changes to the region, as it did to the entire South.

ALBEMARLE COUNTY

FL-8 Ash Lawn–Highland

Rte. 795, off Rte. 53, 4 miles south of Char-lottesville. This estate was the home of James Monroe, fifth president of the United States. In 1793, James and Elizabeth Kortright Monroe purchased 1,000 acres adjoining Jefferson's Monticello. Called Highland, the plantation, eventually total-ing 3,500 acres, was their principal resi-dence from 1799 to 1823. Known in foreign affairs for the Monroe Doctrine, James Monroe also served as governor of Virginia for four one-year terms; U.S. minister to England, France, and Spain; U.S. senator; and secretary of state and war. Enlarged and renamed by subsequent owners, Ash Lawn–Highland is now owned by Monroe's alma mater, the College of William and Mary.

G-22 Proffit Historic District

Rte. 649, 3 miles east of Rte. 29. Ben Brown and other newly freed slaves, who founded the community after the Civil War, first named the settlement Egypt and then Bethel. About 1881, the community be-came known as Proffit when the Virginia Midland Railway placed a stop here, stimu-lating further development between 1890 and 1916 by white landowners who built along Proffit Road. Prominent reminders of Proffit's black heritage are Evergreen Baptist Church, built in 1891, and several houses constructed by the Brown and Flannagan families in the 1880s. The dis-trict was listed on the Virginia Landmarks Register in 1998 and the National Register of Historic Places in 1999.

G-25 General Thomas Sumter

Rte. 231, 2 miles south of Gordonsville. Thomas Sumter was born on 14 Aug. 1734 in this region. Sumter, a member of the Virginia militia during the French and Indian War, moved to South Carolina in 1765. He served as a lieutenant colonel in the Continental Army (1776–1778); in June 1780 he came out of retirement. In Oct.

1780, he became a Brigadier General, and was instrumental in defeating the British in the Carolinas. He served in Congress (1789–1793; 1797–1801) and was an [a] U. S. senator (1801–1810). He died on 1 June 1832. Sumter's name is also asso-ciated with the Civil War, because Fort Sumter is named for him.

G-26 Rio Mills

Rte. 29, 5.75 miles north of Charlottesville. The 19th-century mill village of Rio Mills stood 600 yards west of here, where the former Harrisonburg-Charlottesville Turnpike crossed the South Fork of the Rivanna River. Following the Battle of Rio Hill on 29 February 1864, Union General George Armstrong Custer burned the covered bridge and gristmill at Rio Mills. Immediately rebuilt under the direction of Abraham L. Hildebrand, the gristmill continued to grind wheat and corn for the Confederacy. The milling operation appar-ently closed down soon after 1900.

GA-35 Barclay House and Scottsville Museum

Rte. 6, Scottsville. Here stands the Barclay House, built about 1830, later the home of Dr. James Turner Barclay, inventor for the U.S. Mint and missionary to Jerusalem. He founded the adjacent Disciples Church in 1846 and served as its first preacher. It is now the Scottsville Museum.

GA-36 Historic Scottsville

Rte. 6/20, Scottsville. In 1745 Old Albemarle County was organized at Scott's landing, its first county seat, here on the Great Horseshoe Bend of the James River. In 1818 the town was incorporated as Scottsville. Beginning in 1840 it flourished as the chief port above Richmond for freight and passenger boats on the James River and Kanawha Canal. It played a vital role in the opening up of the west. The 1840s and '50s were its golden era.

GA-37 HATTON FERRY

Rte. 625, 5.75 miles west of Scottsville.
James A. Brown began operating a store
and ferry at this site on rented property
in the late 1870s. In 1881 he bought the
land from S. P. Gantt at which time the
store became a stop on the Richmond and
Alleghany Railroad. Two years later, Brown
was authorized to open a post office in his
store, which was named Hatton for the
young federal postal officer who signed the
authorizing documents. The ferry is one of
only two poled ferries still functioning in
the continental United States.

GA-38 HATTON FERRY

Rte. 6, 0.4 miles west of Scottsville. Five miles
southwest of here is the Hatton Ferry on
the James River which began operating in
the 1870s. James A. Brown established the
ferry and a store on land first rented and
then purchased from S. P. Gantt in 1881.
In 1883 when a post office was approved
for the store, it was named Hatton for the
young federal postal officer who signed the
authorizing documents. The ferry is one of
only two poled ferries still functioning in
the continental United States.

GA-40 STAUNTON AND JAMES RIVER TURNPIKE

Rte. 692, 6 miles west of Rte. 29, Batesville.
The Staunton and James River Turn-
pike ran through here at Batesville and
stretched for 43½ miles from Staunton to
Scottsville. Construction began in 1826
and was completed by 1830. The turnpike
provided a direct route for Shenandoah
Valley farmers to transport agricultural
products to Scottsville, then to Richmond
via the James River and Kanawha Canal.
Because the turnpike became impassable
during wet weather, it was converted to a
plank road (wooden boards laid crosswise
to the road surface) beginning in 1849. The
emergence of the railroad industry and the
high cost of maintenance resulted in its
disuse by the late 1850s and eventual incor-
poration into the country's road system.

GA-41 EARLYSVILLE UNION CHURCH

*Rte. 743, 4 miles west of Charlottesville-
Albemarle Airport, Earlysville.* Earlysville
Union Church is a rare surviving early-
19th-century interdenominational church
constructed in Albemarle County. Built
in 1833, this frame structure served as a
meetinghouse for all Christian denominations on land deeded by John Early, for
whom Earlysville is named. This building
provided an early home for several local
congregations of the Baptist, Methodist,
and Presbyterian faiths. The church is an
excellent example of the 19th-century public architecture of rural Piedmont Virginia.
It was listed on the Virginia Landmarks
Register and the National Register of Historic Places in 1997.

JE-6 MAURY'S SCHOOL

Rte. 231, 4.5 miles southeast of Gordonsville.
Just north was a classical school conducted
by the Rev. James Maury, Rector of Fredericksville Parish from 1754 to 1769. Thomas
Jefferson was one of Maury's students.
Matthew Fontaine Maury, the "Pathfinder
of the Seas," was Maury's grandson.

Q-22 UNION OCCUPATION OF CHARLOTTESVILLE

*Rte. 250, Charlottesville western city lim-
its.* On 3 Mar. 1865, Maj. Gen. Philip H.
Sheridan's Union Army of the Shenandoah
entered Charlottesville to destroy railroad
facilities as the 3rd Cavalry Division led by
Bvt. Maj. Gen. George A. Custer arrived
from Waynesboro. Mayor Christopher H.
Fowler, other local officials, and University
of Virginia professors Socrates Maupin and
John B. Minor and rector Thomas L. Preston met Custer, just east of here. Fowler
surrendered the town, and the professors
asked that the university be protected,
"for it would always be a national asset."
Custer agreed and posted guards during
the three-day occupation. The University
suffered little damage, unlike the Virginia
Military Institute, which had been burned
in June 1864.

W-161 BIRTHPLACE OF MERIWETHER LEWIS

Rte. 250, 5 miles west of Charlottesville. Half a mile north was born, 1774, Meriwether Lewis, of the Lewis and Clark Expedition, sent by Jefferson to explore the Far West, 1804–1806. The expedition reached the mouth of the Columbia River, November 15, 1805.

W-162 JACKSON'S VALLEY CAMPAIGN

Rte. 250, at Mechums River bridge, 2 miles east of Crozet. Late in April 1862, Maj. Gen. Thomas J. "Stonewall" Jackson marched his army out of the Shenandoah Valley through the Blue Ridge Mountains to deceive Union Maj. Gen. John C. Frémont into thinking he was headed for Richmond. On 3 May, Jackson bivouacked at nearby Mechum's Station on the Virginia Central Railroad. The next day, part of the army entrained for the Valley while the rest followed on foot. At the Battle of McDowell on 8 May, Jackson defeated the advance of Frémont's army under Brig. Gen. Robert H. Milroy and Brig. Gen. Robert C. Schenck. Thus began Jackson's 1862 Shenandoah Valley Campaign.

W-163 REVOLUTIONARY SOLDIERS GRAVES

Rte. 250, at Charlottesville western city limits. Jesse Pitman Lewis (d. March 8, 1849), of the Virginia Militia, and Taliaferro Lewis (d. July 12, 1810), of the Continental Line, two of several brothers who fought in the war for independence, are buried in the Lewis family cemetery 100 yards south of this marker.

W-164 MIRADOR

Rte. 250, 3 miles west of Yancey Mills. Nearby stands Mirador, the childhood home of Nancy, Viscountess Astor, the first woman member of Parliament. Born Nancy Witcher Langhorne in 1879, she lived here from 1892 to 1897. In 1906 she married Waldorf Astor and moved to England permanently. Mirador also was home to her sister Irene, wife of Charles Dana Gibson and model for the Gibson Girl of the 1890s. New York architect William Adams Delano remodeled Mirador in the 1920s for Lady Astor's niece, Mrs. Ronald (Nancy Perkins) Tree. Later, as Nancy Lancaster, she greatly influenced interior design by creating the "English country house look."

W-170 CROZET

Rte. 240, Crozet. The town grew around a rail stop established on Wayland's farm in 1876. It was named for Col. B. Claudius Crozet, (1789–1864)—Napoleonic army officer, and the state's engineer and cartographer. He built this pioneer railway through the Blue Ridge. The 4273' tunnel through the rock-solid mountain below Rockfish Gap carried traffic from 1858–1944. His talents were tested in solving safety, drainage and ventilation problems posed by the construction of this tunnel.

W-197 SKIRMISH AT RIO HILL

Rte. 29, 0.2 miles north of Rio Road. On February 29, 1864, General George A. Custer and 1500 cavalrymen made a diversionary raid into Albemarle County. Here, north of Charlottesville, he attacked the Confederate winter camp of four batteries of the Stuart Horse Artillery commanded by Captain Marcellus N. Moorman. Despite the destruction to the camp, 200 Confederates rallied in a counterattack which forced Custer's withdrawal. Few casualties were reported.

W-199 CLARK'S BIRTHPLACE

Rte. 20, 0.1 miles north of Pantops, east of Charlottesville. A mile north was born George Rogers Clark, defender of Kentucky and conqueror of the Northwest, November 19, 1752.

W-201 COLLE

Rte. 53, 1.5 miles southeast of Charlottesville. The house was built about 1770 by workmen engaged in building Monticello. Mazzei, an Italian, lived here for some years adapting grape culture to Virginia. Baron de Riedesel, captured at Saratoga in 1777, lived here with his family, 1779–1780. Scenes in Ford's novel, Janice Meredith, are laid here.

W-202 SHADWELL, BIRTHPLACE OF THOMAS JEFFERSON

Rte. 250, 2.9 miles east of Charlottesville. Thomas Jefferson—author of the Declaration of Independence, third president of the United States, and founder of the University of Virginia—was born near this site on 13 April 1743. His father, Peter Jefferson (1708–1757), a surveyor, planter, and officeholder, began acquiring land in this frontier region in the mid-1730s and had purchased the Shadwell tract by 1741. Peter Jefferson built a house soon after, and the Shadwell plantation became a thriving agricultural estate. Thomas Jefferson spent much of his early life at Shadwell. After the house burned to the ground in 1770, he moved to Monticello, where he had begun constructing a house.

W-203 EDGEHILL

Rte. 250, 5 miles east of Charlottesville, near Shadwell. The land was patented in 1735. The old house was built in 1790; the new in 1828. Here lived Thomas Mann Randolph, Governor of Virginia, 1819–1822, who married Martha, daughter of Thomas Jefferson.

W-204 CASTLE HILL

Rte. 231, 2 miles northwest of Cismont. The original house was built in 1765 by Doctor Thomas Walker, explorer and pioneer. Tarleton, raiding to Charlottesville to capture Jefferson and the legislature, stopped here for breakfast, June 4, 1781. This delay aided the patriots to escape. Castle Hill was long the home of Senator William Cabell Rives, who built the present house.

W-205 REVOLUTIONARY WAR CAMPAIGN OF 1781—MECHUNK CREEK

Rte. 22, 0.57 miles west of Albemarle/Louisa County line. After reinforcements from Brig. Gen. "Mad" Anthony Wayne arrived on 10 June 1781, the Marquis de Lafayette moved south from his camp on the Rapidan River to prevent further raids by Gen. Charles Cornwallis's British troops encamped at Elk Hill. By 13 June, Lafayette had occupied a position along the Mechunk Creek to challenge any British advance toward Charlottesville and Staunton. Lafayette and his troops reached this position by secretly repairing an abandoned road and were able to travel undetected. Cornwallis and his army left Elk Hill on 15 June marching toward Richmond, and Lafayette followed on a parallel course north of the British.

W-225 MILLER SCHOOL

Rte. 635, at main entrance to school. A bequest of Samuel Miller (1792–1869) provided funds to found the Miller School in 1878. Miller, a Lynchburg businessman born in poverty in Albemarle County, envisioned a regional school for children who could not afford an education. The school was a pioneer in combining the value of hands-on labor with a liberal arts education. Coeducational from 1884 until 1928, then all male, the school became coeducational again in 1992. Built on property once owned by Miller, the principal building ("Old Main") was designed by Albert Lybrock and D. Wiley Anderson in the High Victorian Gothic style. Miller School was listed on the Virginia Landmarks Register in 1973 and the National Register of Historic Places in 1974.

AMELIA COUNTY

M-11 LEE'S RETREAT

Business Rte. 360, at western entrance to Amelia. Lee's army, retreating toward Danville, reached this place, April 4–5, 1865, only to find that the supplies ordered here had gone on to Richmond. The famished soldiers were forced to halt to forage. The result was that Lee, when he resumed the march in the afternoon of April 5, found that Sheridan was at Jetersville blocking the way south.

M-12 LEE'S RETREAT

Rte. 360, 4.8 miles southwest of Amelia. Near here Lee, moving south toward Danville, in the afternoon of April 5, 1865 found the road blocked by Sheridan. He then turned westward by way of Amelia Springs, hoping to reach the Southside (Norfolk and Western) Railroad.

M-13 LEE'S RETREAT

Rte. 360, 5.3 miles southwest of Amelia. After evacuating Petersburg and Richmond on 2–3 Apr. 1865, Gen. Robert E. Lee's Army of Northern Virginia retreated west to Amelia Court House to obtain supplies and then turn south to North Carolina. On 6 Apr., however, when Maj. Gen. Philip H. Sheridan's Union cavalry blocked his escape route on the Richmond and Danville R.R., Lee led his army west toward Farmville. Near here Maj. Gen. George G. Meade, commander of the Army of the Potomac, learned of Lee's new course. He ordered his army to pursue on parallel roads and that evening defeated Lee in the Battle of Sayler's Creek.

M-14 LEE'S RETREAT

Rte. 360, 0.7 miles southwest of Jetersville. Sheridan reached here on April 4, 1865 with cavalry and the Fifth Corps, and entrenched. He was thus squarely across Lee's line of retreat to Danville. On April 5, Grant and Meade arrived from the east with the Second Corps and the Sixth Corps.

M-15 LEE'S RETREAT

Rte. 360, Jetersville. From here Union cavalry moved north on April 5, 1865 to ascertain Lee's whereabouts. On the morning of April 6, the Second, Fifth and Sixth corps of Grant's army advanced from Jetersville toward Amelia Courthouse to attack Lee.

M-19 LEE'S RETREAT

Rte. 360, Jetersville. Three miles north is Amelia Springs, once a noted summer resort. There Lee, checked by Sheridan at Jetersville and forced to detour, spent the night of April 5–6, 1865.

M-26 BATTLE OF SAILORS (SAYLER'S) CREEK

Rte. 617, 5 miles northeast of Rice. [*Obverse*] This is the Hillsman House, used by the Unionists as a hospital in the engagement of April 6, 1865. From the west side of the creek the Confederates charged and broke through the Union infantry, but were stopped by the batteries along the hillside here. A mass surrender followed, including a corps commander, Gen. R. S. Ewell, several other generals, many colonels, about 7000 rank and file, and several hundred wagons. It was the largest unstipulated surrender of the war. (over) [*Reverse*] At the same time another engagement took place two miles north, on the main Sailor's (Sayler's) Creek, where Gen. John B. Gordon repulsed pursuing Union Troops. He lost most of his wagons but saved the majority of his men. At this time Gen. Robert E. Lee was retreating from Petersburg toward Danville, closely followed by Gen. Grant. Lee lost half of his troops in these two memorable rearguard actions, which foreshadowed the surrender at Appomattox three days later. (over)

M-28 MARION HARLAND—(12 DEC. 1830–3 JUNE, 1922)

Church and Virginia Streets, behind courthouse, Amelia. Born Mary Virginia Hawes at Dennisville about eight miles south, Harland was a prolific author, producing a syndicated newspaper column for women, many short stories, 25 novels, 25 volumes on domestic life, and 12 books on travel, biography, and Virginia history. Her *Common Sense in the Household* (1871) was the best-selling cookbook in America for more than fifty years, until the *Fannie Farmer Cookbook* and the *Settlement Cookbook* became popular after World War I.

M-31 WILLIAM BRANCH GILES

Church and Virginia Streets, behind courthouse, Amelia. Noted lawyer and statesman William Branch Giles was born 12 Aug. 1762 in Amelia County and educated at Hampden-Sydney College, Princeton, and the College of William and Mary. Giles served Virginia in the United States House of Representatives (1790–1798 and 1801–1803) and in the U.S. Senate (1804–1815), where he was a chief Republican ally of Thomas Jefferson during the Republican and Federalist party debates of that era. Giles was elected governor by the General Assembly in 1827 and served until 1830. He participated in the state constitutional convention of 1829–1830. Giles died 4 Dec. 1830 in Amelia County and is buried near the Wigwam, his house, which stands to the northwest on Rte. 637.

OL-10 LEE'S RETREAT

Rte. 708 at Rte. 622, Namozine Church. Near here Custer, commanding advance guard of the Army of the Potomac, struck and drove back Fitz Lee, left flank guard of Army of Northern Virginia, April 3, 1865.

CAROLINE COUNTY

E-23 LEE AND GRANT

Rte. 1, 2.8 miles south of Carmel Church, at Caroline/Hanover County line. Lee and Grant faced each other on the North Anna, May 23–26, 1864. Union forces crossed here and four miles to the west but found they could not dislodge Lee's center, which rested on the stream. Grant then turned east to Cold Harbor.

E-24 LONG CREEK ACTION

Rte. 1, north of North Anna River, 2.4 miles south of Carmel Church. The earthworks in the angle between this stream and the North Anna River, held by a small Confederate force, were taken by Grant's troops moving southward on May 23, 1864. The Unionists then advanced to the river, on the south side of which was Lee's army.

E-25 GRANT'S OPERATIONS

Rte. 1, Carmel Church. Here, at Mount Carmel Church, on May 23, 1864, Hancock's (Second) Corps turned south to the North Anna River; Warren's (Fifth) Corps and Wright's (Sixth) Corps here turned west to Jericho Mills on the river. Grant had his headquarters in the church on May 24. On May 27, 1864, the four corps of Grant's army, returning from the North Anna, here turned east to Cold Harbor.

E-26 DICKINSON'S MILL

Rte. 1, 2.2 miles south of Ladysmith. Lee camped here, on May 21, 1864, on his way to the North Anna to oppose Grant moving southward. Ewell's and Longstreet's corps rested here that night.

E-27 MANEUVERING TO THE NORTH ANNA RIVER

Rtes. 1 and 639, near Ladysmith. Unable to defeat Gen. Robert E. Lee's Confederates during the Spotsylvania Courthouse battles 8–19 May 1864, Union commander Lt. Gen. Ulysses S. Grant's forces maneuvered east and south, forcing Lee to abandon his entrenched position. The Confederates moved south along Telegraph Road (now U.S. Rte. 1) on 21 May. Union troops, marching along a parallel route, missed a golden opportunity to strike Lee's army. The Federals fell in behind the Confederates near this point and followed them to the North Anna River. On 22 May a portion of Union Maj. Gen. Gouverneur K. Warren's V Corps passed through here and camped nearby that night. During the Battle of the North Anna River 23–26 May, Confederate and Union forces fought to a stalemate.

E-28 NANCY WRIGHT'S

Rte. 1, 5.1 miles north of Ladysmith. A little to the east, at Nancy Wright's, Warren's (Fifth) and Wright's (Sixth) Corps, coming from the east, on May 22, 1864, turned south. Wright camped here on May 22.

E-99 CLARK FAMILY FARM

Rte. 1, at Rte. 639, Ladysmith. In 1754, John and Ann Rogers Clark, with their sons Jonathan and George Rogers, moved from Albemarle County to a farm four miles west. There were born Ann, John, Richard, Edmund, Lucy, Elizabeth, William, and Frances. During the Revolutionary War, George Rogers Clark led troops that captured British outposts at Kaskaskia, Cahokia, and Vincennes in present-day Illinois and Indiana, securing the Old Northwest for the new United States. The Clark family moved to Louisville, Kentucky, in 1784. William Clark and Meriwether Lewis, of Albemarle County, led the 1803–1806 Lewis and Clark Expedition to the Pacific.

E-100 WILLIAM CLARK BIRTHPLACE

Rte. 639, at Rte. 603. William Clark was born to John and Ann Rogers Clark on 1 Aug. 1770 on the family farm about one mile north. The Clark family moved to Louisville, Kentucky, in 1784. William Clark served in the Kentucky militia and in the Indian campaigns in the Old Northwest, including the Battle of Fallen Timbers in 1794. With Meriwether Lewis, he led the 1803–1806 Lewis and Clark Expedition to the Pacific. Clark served as Indian agent for the Louisiana Territory, governor of the Missouri Territory, and superintendent of Indian affairs. He died on 1 Sept. 1838 in St. Louis and is buried there in Bellefontaine Cemetery.

E-110 GOLANSVILLE QUAKER MEETINGHOUSE

Rte. 1, south of Rte. 601, Golansville. Pioneers in asserting the right to religious freedom, the Caroline Friends (Quakers) held their first meeting nearby on 12 March 1739 together with their partner, Cedar Creek Friends Meeting of Hanover County. At a meeting on 9 May 1767, members issued a call to their fellow Quakers to end slaveholding, the first such movement in Virginia. The Friends' testimony against slavery contributed to declining membership as many immigrated west to free states. The Caroline Friends continued to use their meetinghouse and burying ground until 1853. They then joined Cedar Creek and ultimately became Richmond Friends Meeting.

E-115 GABRIEL'S REBELLION

Rtes. 301/2 and 651, at Caroline/Hanover County line. On 24 Aug. 1800, slave Ben Woolfolk met with other slaves at nearby Littlepage's Bridge to recruit individuals for an insurrection planned for 30 Aug. The insurgents led by Gabriel, a slave owned by Thomas Henry Prosser of Henrico County, intended to march into Richmond, capture Governor James Monroe, and force him and other leaders to support political, social, and economic equality. Intense rains delayed the scheme. Mosby Sheppard of Henrico County notified Monroe of the conspiracy after his slaves, Tom and Pharoah, made him aware of the plot. Monroe called out the militia, who captured many of the alleged conspirators. Trials were held in a number of jurisdictions, including Caroline County, resulting in the execution of Gabriel and at least 25 supporters.

EP-20 JOHN WILKES BOOTH

Rte. 301, at Fort A.P. Hill, 9.1 miles northeast of Bowling Green. This is the Garrett place where John Wilkes Booth, assassin of Lincoln, was cornered by Union soldiers and killed, April 26, 1865. The house stood a short distance from this spot.

N-8 THE THIRD LEDERER EXPEDITION

Rte. 17, north of Rappahannock Academy, 6 miles southeast of New Post. In 1669 and 1670, German-born John Lederer led three expeditions to explore Virginia's Piedmont and the Carolinas that encouraged further European exploration. The third expedition began nearby at Robert Talifer's house near the Rappahannock River on 20 Aug. 1670. Col. John Catlett, "nine English horse," and five Indians accompanied Lederer. They reached the junction of the Rappahannock River and the Rapidan River two days later and followed the former inland. At the river's headwaters they approached the Blue Ridge Mountains and reached the summit of one of its peaks on 26 Aug. From there they viewed the Shenandoah Valley, then returned the same way they had come.

N-11 JACKSON'S HEADQUARTERS

Rte. 17, north of Rappahannock Academy, 5.7 miles southeast of New Post. In an outhouse here at Moss Neck, Stonewall Jackson had his headquarters, December, 1862–March, 1863. He was engaged in guarding the line of the Rappahannock with his corps of Lee's army.

N-12 WINDSOR

Rte. 17, north of Rappahannock Academy, 6.9 miles southeast of New Post. This is the ancient Woodford estate. Governor Spotswood and the Knights of the Golden Horseshoe stopped here on their way to the mountains, August, 1716. Here General William Woodford was born, October 6, 1734. He defeated Governor Lord Dunmore at the Great Bridge, December, 1775, and took an important part in the Revolutionary War.

N-13 SKINKER'S NECK

Rte. 17, north of Rappahannock Academy, 6.9 miles southeast of New Post. Two miles north on the Rappahannock River. There Jubal A. Early, in December, 1862, confronted Burnside's army on the other side of the river. His alertness prevented a crossing and battle at this point.

N-14 HAZELWOOD

Rte. 17, 12.7 miles southeast of New Post. Here was the home of John Taylor of Caroline, Jefferson's chief political lieutenant and a leading advocate of States Rights. He died here in 1824.

N-15 RAPPAHANNOCK ACADEMY

Rte. 17, north of Rappahannock Academy, 10 miles southeast of New Post. On this site stood colonial Mount Church, built about 1750. In 1808 the parish glebe was sold and the proceeds were used to establish a school; the church building was turned into Rappahannock Academy, one of the most noted schools in Virginia.

N-16 WHERE BOOTH DIED

Rte. 301, near Rte. 17, near Port Royal. On this road two miles south is the Garrett place. There John Wilkes Booth, Lincoln's assassin, was found by Union cavalry and killed while resisting arrest, April 26, 1865.

N-17 OLD PORT ROYAL

Rte. 1002, off Rte. 301, at town hall, Port Royal. The town was established in 1744 and was one of the principal shipping points on the Rappahannock River in colonial times. In December, 1862, Burnside, commanding the Army of the Potomac, considered crossing the river here but finally moved up to Fredericksburg. Union gunboats, attempting to pass up the river at that time, were driven back by D. H. Hill.

ND-5 Edmund Pendleton's Home

Rte. 301/2, near Rte. 721, 2.5 miles south of Bowling Green. Six miles southeast is the site of Edmundsbury, home of Edmund Pendleton. Pendleton, born September 9, 1721, was in the House of Burgesses; a delegate to the Continental Congress; chairman of the Virginia Committee of Safety, 1775–6; president of the May 1776 convention and the convention that ratified the United States constitution, 1788; president of the Virginia supreme court. He died, October 26, 1803, and was buried there but was later removed to Williamsburg.

ND-7 Campaign of 1781

Rte. 301/2, Bowling Green. Lafayette, marching from Head of Elk, Maryland, to Richmond, camped here the night of April 27, 1781.

ND-10 Meadow Farm—Birthplace of Secretariat

Rte. 30, at Rte. 652, 0.4 miles east of Caroline/Hanover County line. This famous horse-breeding farm was established in 1936 by Christopher T. Chenery and continued under the management of his daughter, Helen "Penny" Chenery until 1979. Secretariat (1970–1989), also known as "Big Red," was born and trained here. A bright chestnut stallion with a white star and narrow stripe, he was a horse of uncommon excellence as he proved when he captured the Triple Crown in 1973. His win at the Belmont Stakes by 31 lengths won him the love and admiration of the nation. Other notable Thoroughbreds such as Riva Ridge, Hill Prince and First Landing also were raised at Meadow Farm.

CITY OF CHARLOTTESVILLE

G-23 James Monroe's First Farm—Site of the University of Virginia

McCormick Road, University of Virginia. In 1788 James Monroe purchased an 800-acre farm here to be close to his friend Thomas Jefferson and to establish a law office. In 1799 the Monroes moved to their new Highland plantation adjacent to Monticello and sold the first farm. In 1817 the Board of Visitors of Central College purchased 43¾ acres of Monroe's old farm, for the Lawn and the Ranges of the "academical village" that Jefferson was planning to build with private contributions. On 6 Oct. President Monroe, with former presidents Jefferson and Madison, laid the cornerstone for its first building, Pavilion VII. On 25 Jan. 1819, Central College was chartered by the General Assembly as the University of Virginia.

G-27 Technical Sergeant Frank D. Peregory

Rte. 29 and University Drive. Born at Esmont on 10 April 1915, Frank D. Peregory enlisted in May 1931 in Charlottesville's Co. K (Monticello Guard), 116th Inf. Regt., 29th Inf. Div. On D-Day, 6 June 1944, T. Sgt. Peregory landed in the assault on Omaha Beach, Normandy, France. At Grandcamp, on 8 June, he single-handedly charged an enemy stronghold with grenades and bayonet, killing 8 soldiers and capturing 35. Six days later he was killed in action near Couvains. For his valor T. Sgt. Peregory was awarded the Medal of Honor. He was the sole Virginian in the 29th Division to be awarded the medal, which was given to only 14 of the 300,000 Virginians who served in the war. Peregory is buried at the American Cemetery in St. Laurent, Normandy, France.

I-3 University of Virginia

University Avenue, at the Rotunda. Thomas Jefferson founded the University of Virginia. The cornerstone of its first building was laid on October 6, 1817, in the presence of three presidents of the United States—Jefferson, James Madison, and James Monroe. In 1825, the university admitted its first scholars, who were educated in what Jefferson called "useful sciences." Following Jefferson's beliefs, the university was nonsectarian and allowed its students to choose their own courses of study. The honor system was established in 1842. In 1987, the United Nations Educational, Scientific, and Cultural Organization (UNESCO) named the original grounds, Thomas Jefferson's "academical village," to its prestigious World Heritage List.

Q-1-a CHARLOTTESVILLE

Rte. 250, at eastern city limits, at Rivanna River. The site was patented by William Taylor in 1737. The town was established by law in 1762, and was named for Queen Charlotte, wife of George III. Burgoyne's army, captured at Saratoga in 1777, was long quartered near here. The legislature was in session here, in June, 1781, but retired westward to escape Tarleton's raid on the town. Jefferson, who lived at Monticello, founded the University of Virginia in 1819.

Q-1-b CHARLOTTESVILLE

Rte. 20, at southern city limits. The site was patented by William Taylor in 1737. The town was established by law in 1762, and was named for Queen Charlotte, wife of George III. Burgoyne's army, captured at Saratoga in 1777, was long quartered near here. The legislature was in session here, in June, 1781, but retired westward to escape Tarleton's raid on the town. Jefferson, who lived at Monticello, founded the University of Virginia in 1819.

Q-1-d CHARLOTTESVILLE

Business Rte. 29, at southern city limits. The site was patented by William Taylor in 1737. The town was established by law in 1762, and was named for Queen Charlotte, wife of George III. Burgoyne's army, captured at Saratoga in 1777, was long quartered near here. The legislature was in session here, in June, 1781, but retired

westward to escape Tarleton's raid on the town. Jefferson, who lived at Monticello, founded the University of Virginia in 1819.

Q-16 FIRST BAPTIST CHURCH WEST MAIN STREET

West Main Street, near Amtrak station. The Charlottesville African Church congregation was organized in 1864. Four years later it bought the Delevan building, built in 1828 by Gen. John H. Cocke, and at one time used as a temperance hotel for University of Virginia students. It became part of the Charlottesville General Hospital and sheltered wounded soldiers during the Civil War. The church members laid the cornerstone for a new building in 1877 on the Delevan site, and the First Baptist Church, West Main Street, was completed in 1883. This building is listed on the National Register of Historic Places.

Q-17 JACK JOUETT'S RIDE

High Street, Courthouse Square, at rear of courthouse. On 4 June 1781, John "Jack" Jouett Jr. arrived at the Albemarle County Courthouse to warn the Virginia legislature of approaching British troops. The state government under Governor Thomas Jefferson had retreated from Richmond to reconvene in Charlottesville because of the threat of British invasion during the Revolutionary War. Jouett had spotted Colonel Banastre Tarleton and his 180 dragoons and 70 cavalrymen 40 miles east at Cuckoo Tavern, and rode through the night to reach here by dawn. Jouett's heroic ride, which allowed Jefferson and all but seven of the legislators to escape, was later recognized by the Virginia General Assembly, which awarded him a sword and a pair of pistols.

Q-20 STONE TAVERN AND CENTRAL HOTEL

South side of Market Street, between 4th and 5th Streets. George Nicholas, Albemarle County's Virginia General Assembly delegate in 1783, built a stone house here in

1784. James Monroe occupied it 1789–1790, while improving the dwelling at his nearby farm, later the site of the University of Virginia. Here on 15 Dec. 1806, while the house was being operated as the Stone Tavern, the return of Meriwether Lewis from his expedition to the Pacific with William Clark was celebrated with a dinner. Thomas Jefferson hosted a reception in the tavern (renamed the Central Hotel), on 12 Nov. 1824, for the Marquis de Lafayette. While serving as a hospital during the Civil War, the building burned with no fatalities in 1862.

Q-21 THREE NOTCH'D ROAD

Main Street, Downtown Mall. Also called Three Chopt Road, this colonial route ran from Richmond to the Shenandoah Valley. It likely took its name from three notches cut into trees to blaze the trail. A major east-west route across central Virginia from the 1730s, it was superseded by Route 250 in the 1930s. Part of Jack Jouett's famous ride and the Marquis de Lafayette's efforts to prevent Gen. Charles Cornwallis from obtaining munitions took place along this road. Today West Main Street and part of University Avenue approximate the Three Notch'd Road's original course through present-day Charlottesville.

Q-23 CHARLOTTESVILLE GENERAL HOSPITAL

Jefferson Park Avenue and West Main Street. During the Civil War, the Rotunda at the University of Virginia, the Charlottesville town hall and the courthouse, as well as nearby homes and hotels were converted into a makeshift hospital complex called the Charlottesville General Hospital. It treated more than 22,000 wounded soldiers between 1861 and 1865. The first of the wounded arrived by train within hours of the First Battle of Manassas (Bull Run) in July 1861. One of the facilities, known as the Mudwall or Delevan Hospital, received wounded soldiers as they arrived at the adjacent railroad depot.

Q-24 CHARLOTTESVILLE WOOLEN MILLS

Merchant and East Market Streets, at Woolen Mills Chapel. As early as 1795, several types of mills operated here. In 1847, Farish, Jones, and Co., opened a cotton and woolen factory. John A. Marchant gained control of it by 1852 and renamed it the Charlottesville Manufacturing Company. His son, Henry Clay Marchant, bought it in 1864. Although the Union army burned the factory in 1865, Marchant reopened it in 1867 as the Charlottesville Woolen Mills, which became Albemarle's largest industry. A community grew up around the mill and Marchant built worker houses and a chapel. By the 1880s the mill specialized in making cloth for uniforms; it remained in operation until 1964.

Q-25 GEN. ALEXANDER ARCHER VANDEGRIFT

Jackson and Park Streets, at courthouse. Gen. Alexander Archer Vandegrift was born in Charlottesville on 13 Mar. 1887. He entered the U.S. Marine Corps in 1909 and served on posts in the Caribbean, Central America, China, and the United States. General Vandegrift led American forces in their first successful major Pacific offensive in World War II at Guadalcanal and was awarded the Navy Cross and the Medal of Honor. He also served as the Commandant of the Marine Corps from 1944 to 1947 and in 1945 became the first active-duty Marine four-star general. He died on 8 May 1973 and is buried at Arlington National Cemetery.

Q-26 GEORGIA O'KEEFFE

Wertland and 12½ Streets. Georgia O'Keeffe was born in Wisconsin in 1887. Her mother moved to Charlottesville in 1909 and rented the house here. Beginning in 1912, O'Keeffe intermittently lived with her mother and sisters. She took a summer drawing class taught by Alon Bement at the University of Virginia. O'Keeffe taught art classes at the university each summer between 1913 and 1916. O'Keeffe used a number of mediums to showcase her artistic talents throughout her long career. In 1916, noted photographer, art impresario, and future husband Alfred Stieglitz began to promote her work. O'Keeffe later became one of America's most renowned artists. She died in New Mexico in 1986.

Q-27 THE FARM

Jefferson Street and Farm Lane. The Farm stands on a 1020-acre tract acquired by Nicholas Meriwether in 1735 and later owned by Col. Nicholas Lewis, uncle of Meriwether Lewis. A building on the property likely served as headquarters for British Col. Banastre Tarleton briefly in June 1781. In 1825, Charlottesville lawyer and later University of Virginia law professor, John A. G. Davis, purchased a portion of the original tract and engaged Thomas Jefferson's workmen to design and build this house. It is considered one of the best surviving examples of Jeffersonian residential architecture. Maj. Gen. George A. Custer occupied the house as his headquarters for a brief time in March 1865.

Q-28 BUCK V. BELL

800 Preston Avenue. In 1924, Virginia, like a majority of states then, enacted eugenic sterilization laws. Virginia's law allowed state institutions to operate on individuals to prevent the conception of what were believed to be "genetically inferior" children. Charlottesville native Carrie Buck (1906–1983), involuntarily committed to a state facility near Lynchburg, was chosen as the first person to be sterilized under the new law. The U.S. Supreme Court, in *Buck v. Bell,* on 2 May 1927, affirmed the Virginia law. After Buck more than 8,000 other Virginians were sterilized before the most relevant parts of the act were repealed in 1974. Later evidence eventually showed that Buck and many others had no

"hereditary defects." She is buried south of here.

Q-29 EDGAR ALLAN POE

McCormick Road, next to West Range. Edgar Allan Poe (1809–1849)—writer, poet, and critic—was born in Boston, Mass. Orphaned at a young age, Poe was raised by John and Frances Allan of Richmond. He attended schools in England and Richmond before enrolling at the University of Virginia on 14 Feb. 1826 for one term, living in No. 13 West Range. He took classes in the Ancient and Modern Languages. While at the university, Poe accumulated debts that John Allan refused to pay. Poe left the university and briefly returned to Richmond, before moving to Boston in Mar. 1827. Some of his best-known writings include the *Raven, Annabel Lee,* and the *Tell-Tale Heart.* He also edited the *Southern Literary Messenger* in Richmond from 1835 to 1837. Poe died in Baltimore, Md.

Q-30 JEFFERSON SCHOOL

Commerce Street, at school. The name Jefferson School has a long association with African American education in Charlottesville. It was first used in the 1860s in a Freedmen's Bureau school and then for a public grade school by 1894. Jefferson High School opened here in 1926 as the city's first high school for blacks, an early accredited black high school in Virginia. The facility became Jefferson Elementary School in 1951. In 1958, some current and former Jefferson students requested transfers to two white schools. The state closed the two white schools. Their reopening in 1959 began the process of desegregation in Charlottesville. Jefferson School housed many different educational programs after integrating in 1965.

Q-31 MONTICELLO WINE COMPANY

McIntire Road and Perry Drive. The Monticello Wine Company's four-story brick building was located on the middle of Perry Drive on the north side. Founded in 1873 using grapes from local vineyards, it operated until about the time Prohibition began in Virginia in Nov. 1916. Spurred by production increases and highest-awards honors from exhibitions in the United States and abroad, the Charlottesville region proclaimed itself the "Capital of the Wine Belt in Virginia." In 1904 its wine was used to christen the USS *Virginia*. The building was last used as a storage facility until fire destroyed it in 1937. The home of the winery's general manager, Adolph Russow, stands nearby at 212 Wine Street.

W-200 MONTICELLO

East Jefferson and Park Streets. Three miles to the southeast. Thomas Jefferson began the house in 1770 and finished it in 1802. He brought his bride to it in 1772. Lafayette visited it in 1825. Jefferson spent his last years there and died there, July 4, 1826. His tomb is there. The place was raided by British cavalry, June 4, 1781.

A few early state markers remain along Virginia's roadways, unchanged from the day they were set in place. This one discussing Thomas Jefferson's Monticello can still be seen in Charlottesville. (Marker W-200) (The Library of Virginia)

CHESTERFIELD COUNTY

K-199 FARRAR'S ISLAND

Rte. 1, between Rte. 288 and Osborne Road, Dutch Gap. In 1611, Farrar's Island was the site of the "Citie of Henrico," one of Virginia's first four primary settlement areas under the Virginia Company of London. Later, it was part of a 2,000-acre land patent issued posthumously to William Farrar in 1637. Farrar, who arrived in Virginia from London in 1618 aboard the *Neptune*, invested in the company under its third charter. In 1626, Governor Sir George Yeardley appointed Farrar to the governor's Council, a position he occupied until 1632. He also served as a justice for two counties. Farrar family members resided on the island until they sold it to Thomas Randolph on 26 Jan. 1727.

K-200 ENON BAPTIST CHURCH

Rte. 746, 0.7 miles north of Rte. 10. Enon Baptist Church was organized on 8 October 1849. The church was built here on a one-acre tract given by the founder, John Alexander Strachan. In May 1864, during the Civil War, Union army troops under Maj. Gen. Benjamin F. Butler dismantled Enon Baptist Church and moved the lumber to nearby Point of Rocks where they used it to build a military hospital. After the war, members of the congregation dismantled the hospital and used the material to rebuild the present Enon Church. Later, the congregation petitioned Congress and was awarded compensation for the army's destruction of the building.

K-201 BATTERY DANTZLER

Rte. 10, east of I-95, Chester. A half-mile northeast stands Battery Dantzler, named for Col. Olin Miller Dantzler, 22d South Carolina Infantry (killed in action nearby on 2 June 1864), and constructed in May–June 1864 to block the Union navy's approach to Richmond. The battery anchored the northern end of the Howlett Line, a series of Confederate earthworks cut across the Bermuda Hundred peninsula from Swift Creek on the south to the James River on the north. Battery Dantzler's artillery included two 7-inch Brooke rifles, two 8-inch smooth-bore Columbiads, and two coastal mortars. The battery operated until 2 April 1865, when it was abandoned and its naval garrison marched with Gen. Robert E. Lee's Army of Northern Virginia westward to Appomattox Court House.

K-202 BERMUDA HUNDRED

Rte. 10, 0.2 miles west of Hopewell. A mile north, on the site of an important Appamatuck Indian village, Sir Thomas Dale established Bermuda Hundred in 1613. The hundred was a traditional English jurisdiction of one hundred families. Dale, the deputy governor and marshal of Virginia, founded an incorporated town and the first system of private land-tenure in English America there between 1611 and 1614. Bermuda Hundred was an official port of entry on the James River in the 1700s, with its own customhouse and inspectors. Benedict Arnold headquartered there briefly during the Revolutionary War. In 1864–1865, during the Civil War, the Federal Army of the James, commanded by Maj. Gen. Benjamin F. Butler, had its base of operations there.

K-203 COLONEL THOMAS LYGON

Rte. 10, 1 mile west of Hopewell. Colonel Thomas Lygon, who came to the Virginia colony in the early 1640s from Worcestershire, England, patented several large parcels of land on the north bank of the Appomattox River in an area known as The Cowpens, near Mount My Lady, which was then part of Henrico County. It is likely that he lived in this area with his wife Mary Harris and their five children. Lygon served in the House of Burgesses from Henrico County in 1656, as a colonel in the county militia, and as surveyor of the county until his death in 1675.

K-204 ETTRICK

Rte. 36, 0.2 miles west of Petersburg. The site of an Appomattox Indian village burned in 1676 in Bacon's Rebellion, the present town of Ettrick stands on land that belonged to "Ettrick Banks" and "Matoax," the boyhood plantation of John Randolph of Roanoke. In 1810 Campbell's Bridge connected Ettrick with Petersburg, hastening the development of mills on the river. Virginia State University, formerly known as the Virginia Normal and Collegiate Institute, was established here in 1882.

K-267 MARY RANDOLPH—(9 AUG. 1762–23 JAN. 1828)

Rte. 10, at Rte. 827 (Allied Road). Mary Randolph, a native of Chesterfield County and author of the first American regional cookbook, lived nearby at Presquile Plantation during the last two decades of the 18th century after her marriage to David Meade Randolph in 1782. The couple then moved to Richmond, where Mary Randolph's reputation as cook, hostess, and entrepreneur flourished. They later moved to Washington, D.C. In 1824, she published *The Virginia Housewife*, an important collection of recipes and advice that has been reprinted many times since. In her book, Mary Randolph revealed not only her own culinary genius, but also the rich and diverse heritage of early American cuisine.

M-5 PINEY GROVE CHURCH MEETING SITE

River Road (Rte. 36), near Jean Machenberg Drive. Late in the 18th century, the Methodist Episcopal Church confronted the possibility of schism. James O'Kelly, a Methodist minister, began challenging Bishop Francis Asbury regarding his appointive powers, his management of church affairs, and other organizational matters late in the 1780s. After several years of intense debate within the church, O'Kelly and his followers broke away in 1792. On 2 Aug. 1793, O'Kelly's and Asbury's adherents met near this site at Piney Grove Church, which no longer stands, in a last attempt at reconciliation. The attempt failed, and O'Kelly and his followers soon formed the Christian Church.

M-6 CLOVER HILL MINING DISTRICT

Off Rte. 360, at Rtes. 621 and 655. Coal mines, including Brighthope, Raccoon, Cox, Hill, Vaden, and others, were located a mile west of here. As early as 1822 coal was sold for local use. By 1845 the Clover Hill Railroad was constructed to transport the coal to the Appomattox River on barges. The Clover Hill (Winterpock) and Midlothian mines were the main coal suppliers to Richmond's Tredegar Iron Works for the manufacture of Confederate munitions. The difficulties of excavation and numerous deaths from gas explosions led to the mines' abandonment. The last mine in operation, owned by the Rudd brothers, closed in the 1920s.

M-7 TRABUE'S TAVERN

Old Buckingham Road (Rte. 677), 0.6 miles west of Huguenot Road (Rte. 147). This was the home of Lt. John Trabue, Revolutionary War soldier and patriot, and of his descendants well into the 20th century. Trabue witnessed the surrender of the British forces at Yorktown in 1781 and later became an original member of the Society of the Cincinnati in Virginia. The Trabues were among the principal coal-mine proprietors in the Midlothian area and here maintained a tavern that was patronized both by travelers and by workers from mines in the vicinity.

M-8 EPPINGTON

Rte. 602, 4.5 miles east of Chesterfield/Amelia County line. Two and one-third miles south stands Eppington, built in the late 1760s by Francis Eppes and his wife Elizabeth Wayles Eppes, half-sister to Martha Wayles Jefferson. Thomas Jefferson frequently visited Eppington. Lucy Jefferson, his daughter, died and was presumably buried at Eppington in 1786. Mary Jefferson, another daughter, was married to John Wayles Eppes, the son of Francis and Elizabeth Wayles Eppes, in 1797, and subsequently resided at Eppington.

M-10 GOODE'S BRIDGE

Rte. 360, just east of Chesterfield/Amelia County line. Here Anthony Wayne took station in July, 1781, to prevent the British from moving southward. Here, April 3, 1865, Longstreet's, Hill's and Gordon's corps of Lee's army, retreating from Petersburg toward Danville, crossed the river.

O-26 MATTOAX

Rte. 36, 1.9 miles west of Ettrick. Mattoax was located to the south on the Appomattox River. John Randolph, Sr., built a house there in the 1770s that burned after 1810; it was the boyhood home of his son, John Randolph of Roanoke. Mattoax also was the residence of St. George Tucker, a noted jurist, and his sons: Henry St. George Tucker, lawyer and legislator, and Nathaniel Beverley Tucker, novelist and law professor. In 1854 Sylvester J. Pearce built a second house on the site that stood until the 1930s.

O-27 BETHLEHEM BAPTIST CHURCH

Rte. 60, east of Moorefield Park Drive. Formerly Spring Creek Church. Organized, July 25, 1790. Benjamin Watkins, founder and first pastor, 1790–1831. Located four miles northwest, 1790–1855. Then four miles southwest, 1855–1897. Moved to this location, 1897. Home church of Nannie Bland David, Missionary to Africa,

1880–1885. Her dying words: "Never give up Africa."

O-28 HUGUENOT SETTLEMENT

Rte. 60, 1.7 miles east of Midlothian. In 1700–1701, Huguenots (French Protestant refugees) settled in this region on land provided to them by the Virginia colony. The Huguenot settlement, known as "Manakin Town" centered at the former site of a Monacan Indian town, located south of the James River. During this period the Monacans and other Indian tribes traded with the settlers. In 1700, the Virginia General Assembly established the King William Parish, which enabled the Huguenots to have their own church, pastor, and set their own parish tithes. Over time the Huguenots obtained individual land grants throughout this region.

O-29 SALISBURY

Rte. 60, Midlothian. Nearby stood Salisbury, built during the middle portion of the 18th century. It was a one-and-a-half-story frame house that had two asymmetrical brick chimneys. Patrick Henry leased Salisbury from Thomas Mann Randolph and lived there while he was governor of Virginia from 1784 to 1786. Randolph sold the farm to Dr. William Turpin, and after Turpin's death his daughter Caroline, married to Dr. Edward Johnson, inherited the property. Their son Confederate Maj. Gen. Edward Johnson inherited the house in 1843 and lived there until his death in 1873. The house burned to the ground in 1923.

O-34 BLACK HEATH

Rte. 60, just west of Huguenot/Courthouse Road, east of Midlothian. Half a mile north stood Black Heath, later owned by Captain John Heth, officer in Continental Army, whose son, Henry Heth, Major-General C.S.A., was born here in 1825. Coal of high quality was mined here.

O-35 MIDLOTHIAN COAL MINES

Rte. 60, Midlothian. South of here are the Midlothian Coal Mines, probably the oldest coal mines in America. Coal was first mined here before 1730, and during the Revolution, coal from these mines supplied the cannon foundry at Westham. The first railroad in Virginia was built from the Midlothian mines to the town of Manchester in 1831. The mines produced coal that was used in casting cannon at the Tredegar Iron Works in Richmond during the Civil War. Mining operations ceased in 1923.

O-37 PROVIDENCE UNITED METHODIST CHURCH

Rte. 678, 0.86 miles south of Rte. 60. Established by 1807, the Providence Church congregation of the Methodist Episcopal Church became one of the first Methodist congregations in Chesterfield County to build a permanent house of worship when it constructed a meetinghouse here before 1813. The congregation included both whites and blacks. During the Civil War, soldiers from both sides used the church for shelter. In 1896 the congregation built a Gothic Revival church here; it was replaced in 1958.

O-40 BELLONA ARSENAL

Rte. 60 (Midlothian Turnpike), at Robious Road. In 1810 Major John Clarke and noted Richmond lawyer, William Wirt, established a weapons factory for the U.S. War Department on the south bank of the James River five miles north of here. Bellona Arsenal, (named for the Roman goddess of war,) was erected in 1816. After five years of disuse, it was leased to Thomas Mann Randolph in 1837 (for use as a silk worm farm.) Junius L. Archer bought the property in 1856, and on January 1, 1863, he leased both the arsenal and foundry to the Confederate government. Bellona Arsenal became one of Virginia's leading producers of arms.

O-47 Union Raid on Coalfield Station

Rte. 60, Midlothian. On the first day of Union Brig. Gen. August V. Kautz's second raid (12–17 May 1864) on Confederate railroads around Richmond, 3,000 cavalrymen rode northwest from Bermuda Hundred and passed Chesterfield Court House at 1:00 P.M. Arriving about midnight at Midlothian's Coalfield Station on the Richmond and Danville Railroad, a quarter-mile north, they cut telegraph lines and burned the depot, woodsheds, and railroad cars. They destroyed the tracks using tools from nearby coal mines. Maj. Samuel P. Wetherill, 11th Pa. Cav., intervened to rescind the orders to set the coal mines afire.

O-50 Bethel Baptist Church

Rte. 607, 0.1 miles north of Rte. 60. In 1799 the local Baptist Society acquired this land and soon built a meetinghouse. The Bethel congregation worshiped in the meetinghouse and was constituted as a church in 1817. About 1820 the members built a brick church here—the first in Chesterfield County. The present sanctuary, which replaced it in 1894, was then the most elaborate rural church in the county, having Gothic buttresses, fine exterior detailing, and a rib-vaulted chancel. In the churchyard are buried soldiers of virtually every war from the Revolution through Vietnam.

O-62 Winfree Memorial Baptist Church—Midlothian Mine Disaster

Rte. 60 (Midlothian Turnpike) and Coalfield Road, at church. Winfree Memorial Baptist Church, constituted in 1852 as Jerusalem Baptist Church, originally stood to the west on Buckingham Pike. In September 1881, to better serve the coal mining community, the frame structure was rolled here on logs. On 3 Feb. 1882, a methane explosion killed 32 miners in the Midlothian Coal Mining Company's

Grove Shaft nearby. David B. Winfree and other members of the congregation raised funds and provided assistance for the individuals who lost family members. The present brick church was dedicated in 1925, and the congregation was renamed in honor of pastors David B. Winfree and his son Robert H. Winfree.

O-64 Chesterfield Railroad

Rte. 60 (Midlothian Turnpike), at Robious Road. In 1829 the Virginia General Assembly chartered the Chesterfield Rail Road Company, which built the first railroad in Virginia. Moncure Robinson (1802–1891), a railroad pioneer, designed the track, which once passed by here. In 1831, the company began hauling coal 13 miles from the Midlothian mines to the Manchester wharves on the James River. Horses and mules towed the loaded cars on some sections. Gravity propelled them on down hill grades and in one area the weight of the cars tugged the empty ones (connected to the full ones by ropes and drums) back toward the mines. This railroad functioned until 1851, when the locomotive-operated Richmond & Danville Railroad provided service to Chesterfield.

O-67 Skinquarter Baptist Church

Moseley Road, 1 mile off Rte. 60. Pastor William Hickman and about 30 people founded Skinquarter Baptist Church in 1778. The first meetinghouse was located east of the church's cemetery. Hickman moved to Kentucky in 1784 and was an early Baptist leader there. Due to anti-missionary sentiment among the members, the congregation left the Middle District Baptist Association and became affiliated with the Zoar Association in 1836. However in 1848 they rejoined the Middle District Baptist Association. During the 19th century, five churches were organized from this congregation. Augustus Barton Rudd, a missionary to Mexico and Puerto Rico in the late 19th and 20th centuries, was a member. After a fire in 1890, the current church was initially built in 1891.

S-2 WARWICK

Rte. 1, just south of Falling Creek bridge, 1.5 miles south of Richmond. Located eight miles downstream from Richmond, Warwick was an important 18th-century James River port and manufacturing center. During the Revolutionary War, Warwick's craftsmen turned out clothing and shoes, and its mills ground flour and meal for the Continental troops stationed at Chesterfield Courthouse. On April 30, 1781, British troops under Benedict Arnold burned the town, destroying ships, warehouses, mills, tannery storehouses, and ropewalks.

S-3 AMPTHILL ESTATE

Off Rte. 1, at entrance to Dupont, 0.7 miles south of Richmond city limits. Built before 1732 by Henry Cary, this was the home of Colonel Archibald Cary, a Revolutionary leader of Virginia. The house was moved, 1929–30, to its present location off Cary Street Road in Richmond's West End.

S-4 FALLING CREEK IRONWORKS

Rte. 1, 1.5 miles south of Richmond, at Falling Creek Wayside. Nearby on Falling Creek is the first ironworks in English North America. It was established by the Virginia Company to supply iron for the colony and for export to England. Construction began in 1619. The works, including a blast furnace, were completed under ironmaster John Berkeley and production began late in 1621 or early in 1622. The facility was destroyed and almost everyone there (twenty-seven people) was killed during the 22 Mar. 1622 Indian attacks coordinated by Chief Opechancanough that struck this and various other English settlements. There were three other unsuccessful 17th-century attempts to restart the ironworks.

S-5 DREWRY'S BLUFF

Rte. 1, south of Falling Creek, 2.5 miles south of Richmond. This bluff on the James River, a mile east, was fortified by Captain A. H. Drewry in 1862. A Union fleet, attempting to pass it, was driven back, May 15, 1862; and thereafter it served as a bar to attacks on Richmond by water. On June 16, 1864, Longstreet's Corps of Lee's army crossed the river there going to the defense of Petersburg.

S-6 THE HOWLETT LINE

Rte. 10, east of I-95 and Chester. Just east of this point running from the James River to the Appomattox River, was the Confederate defense line known as the Howlett line, named for the Howlett House that stood at the north end of the line. Established in May, 1864, by General Beauregard's troops after the Battle of Drewry's Bluff, the line became famous as the "Cork in the Bottle" by keeping General Butler's Army of the James at bay. The Union line was one mile to the east. Parker's Virginia Battery was one-half mile to the south.

S-7 CHESTERFIELD COUNTY COURTHOUSE

Rte. 10, near Rte. 655, Chesterfield. This area, known originally as "Cold Water Run," is the site of the first Chesterfield County courthouse, erected in 1750. In 1917 it was demolished and replaced by a larger Georgian Revival brick building that served the county until the 1960s. The most famous trial here was that of seven Baptist preachers for breach of ecclesiastical law in 1773. In 1780–81, Governor Thomas Jefferson designated the courthouse village as a training post and encampment of all reinforcements for the Continental armies from the southern states.

S-8 BATTLE OF DREWRY'S BLUFF

Rte. 1, south of Bellwood Road, 3.9 miles south of Richmond. From this point the

Confederates, on May 16, 1864, moved to attack the Union Army of the James under Butler advancing northward on Richmond.

S-9 SECOND BATTLE OF DREWRY'S BLUFF

Rte. 1, south of Willis Road (Rte. 613), 4.5 miles south of Richmond. The Second Battle of Drewry's Bluff, or the Proctor's Creek engagement, began on 14 May 1864 when part of Union Maj. Gen. Benjamin F. Butler's Army of the James feigned an attack toward Richmond from Bermuda Hundred. After two days of skirmishing, Federals led by Maj. Gen. William F. Smith and Maj. Gen. Quincy A. Gillmore captured the outer Confederate earthworks here. At dawn on 16 May, however, the Confederates under Maj. Gen. Robert F. Hoke and Maj. Gen. Robert Ransom, Jr., launched several assaults from the inner defenses just north. By midmorning the Federals began retreating south to the Half-Way House.

S-10 HALFWAY HOUSE

10301 Jefferson Davis Highway (Rte. 1), north of Proctors Creek, south of Richmond. This old inn was the headquarters of Major-General B. F. Butler's Union Army of the James during the Battle of Drewery's [Drewry's] Bluff, May 16, 1864. The inn was so named because of its location about midway between Richmond and Petersburg.

S-11 PROCTOR'S CREEK FIGHT

Rte. 1, 0.1 miles north of Rte. 288. To the west of the road here at Proctor's Creek Maj. Gen. Benjamin F. Butler's Union Army of the James attacked the outer line of the Confederates' Drewry Bluff defenses on 13–14 May 1864. On the first day, Union Maj. Gen. Quincy A. Gillmore struck the Confederate right flank, commanded by Maj. Gen. Robert Ransom, Jr. Ransom's troops crumpled under the onslaught, rallied and counterattacked,

and finally fell back to the main lines at Kingsland Creek. On 14 May, Gillmore and Maj. Gen. William F. Smith launched coordinated attacks that drove through the first defensive line but stopped short of the second. The Federals then entrenched.

S-12 INTO THE "BOTTLE"

Rte. 1, 0.1 miles north of Rte. 288. The Union Army of the James, retiring across Proctor's Creek in this vicinity after the battle of Drewry's Bluff, May 16, 1864, turned east into the Peninsula between the James and Appomattox Rivers, where it was "Bottled" by Confederate forces.

S-13 DUTCH GAP

Rte. 1, 6.7 miles south of Richmond. This great bend in the James River lies due east. The town of Henrico was established here in 1611. In August, 1864, B. F. Butler cut a canal through the neck, shortening the river five miles.

S-14 OSBORNES

Rte. 1, between Rte. 288 and Osborne Road, Dutch Gap. The town of Osbornes was named for Captain Thomas Osborne who settled nearby at Coxendale in 1616. During the 17th and 18th centuries, Osborne's plantation wharf was a tobacco inspection station and local shipping center. Thomas Jefferson, grandfather of the President, was born here in 1677. On April 27, 1781, British General Benedict Arnold destroyed nine ships of the American fleet and burned the town's warehouses and stores. George Washington visited Osbornes in 1791 during a national tour designed to afford citizens the opportunity to see their first national hero.

S-15 DREWRY'S BLUFF

Rte. 1, south of Falling Creek, 2.5 miles south of Richmond. A mile east is Drewry's Bluff, James River fortification of Richmond, 1862–1865. Earthworks remain.

S-16 POCAHONTAS STATE PARK

Rte. 655, 4.1 miles west of Chesterfield. This park of 7604 acres was originally known as the Swift Creek Recreational Area. Its purchase in 1934 and subsequent development by the federal government were with the understanding that eventually the State would accept and maintain the property, incorporating it into its Park System. On June 6, 1946 the Virginia Conservation Commission dedicated the park, naming it for the Indian princess Pocahontas.

S-17 CHESTER STATION FIGHT

Rte. 1, just south of Rte. 10. At this station, two miles west, the Union army of the James, turning toward Richmond, fought an action on May 10, 1864 and tore up the railroad.

S-18 THE "BOTTLE"

Rte. 1, 2.8 miles north of Colonial Heights city limits. Here in 1864 on the Bermuda Hundred peninsula between the James and Appomattox Rivers, the Union Army of the James, commanded by Maj. Gen. Benjamin F. Butler, was "bottled up" by Confederate Gen. P. G. T. Beauregard, defender of Petersburg. The cautious Butler had begun constructing earthworks across the peninsula about a mile east in May, shortly after he occupied the peninsula, to protect against attack from the west. The Confederates built parallel earthworks (the Howlett Line) about half a mile east of here to "bottle up" the Federals. In Sept., however, Butler's army easily crossed the James River to attack the Richmond fortifications.

S-19 CONFEDERATE RECONNAISSANCE MISSION

Rte. 1, 3.6 miles north of Colonial Heights city limits. On 2 June 1864, Confederate Gen. P. G. T. Beauregard sent Maj. Gen. Bushrod Johnson's troops toward nearby Federal pickets to reconnoiter their strength. The Confederate troops initially captured the northern portion of the Federal picket line, but by the afternoon Union troops had regained a part of their position. The death of Confederate regimental commander Col. O. M. Dantzler and the arrival of Federal reinforcements prevented the Confederates from taking the southern section of the line. Beauregard determined that it would not be prudent to send Brig. Gen. Matt Ransom's brigade to assist Gen. Robert E. Lee, for fear of losing the rail line. Late the next day Beauregard relented at the order of Lee.

S-20 UNION ARMY RAILROAD RAIDS

Rte. 1, approximately 1 mile north of Colonial Heights. On 5 May 1864, leading elements of Union Maj. Gen. Benjamin F. Butler's Army of the James disembarked off transports at Bermuda Hundred, located to the north of here. The next day this army began severing telegraph lines and nearby portions of the Richmond & Petersburg Railroad, a rail line that carried troops, supplies, and food to Richmond from other junctions. Over the next five days, Butler's troops focused on destroying portions of the railroad and fought a number of skirmishes with Confederate troops. The Confederate army countered the Federal attacks, protected the railroad, and eventually reestablished the rail line.

S-21 BERMUDA HUNDRED

Rte. 1, 7.8 miles south of Richmond. This place, some miles to the east, is on the James at the mouth of the Appomattox. A town was established there in 1613. Phillips and Arnold sailed from there in May, 1781. In May, 1864, it became the base of operations of the Army of the James.

S-22 PORT WALTHALL

Rte. 10, 2.25 miles west of Hopewell, Enon. Port Walthall, which stood on the banks of the Appomattox River several miles to the south, was a major shipping and passenger embarkation point prior to the Civil War. The railroad tracks leading to the port were melted down to manufacture Confederate cannon.

S-23 POINT OF ROCKS

Rte. 10, 2.25 miles west of Hopewell, Enon. Point of Rocks is located two miles south on the Appomattox River. In 1608, Captain John Smith wrote about this high rock cliff which projected out to the channel of the river. Known to all as Point of Rocks, it was severely damaged during a battle between Confederate artillery and Federal gunboats on June 26, 1862. Rock from the point was used to build the wall of the City Point National Cemetery shortly after the Civil War.

S-24 ADVANCE ON PETERSBURG

Rte. 1, approximately 1 mile north of Colonial Heights. Elements of the Union Army of the James, led by Maj. Gen. Benjamin F. Butler, landed at Bermuda Hundred on 5 May 1864 to cut the Confederate rail and supply lines between Richmond and Petersburg. On 9 May, Butler sent divisions to Port Walthall Junction and Chester Station and turned south toward Petersburg. At Swift Creek, they encountered Brig. Gens. Johnson Hagood's and Bushrod R. Johnson's divisions protecting the turnpike and railroad bridges. The Confederates launched a counterattack across the creek, but were overwhelmed by superior Federal numbers. Butler did not follow up this attack, and by 11 May his troops were back at Bermuda Hundred.

S-25 UNION ARMY CHECKED

Rte. 1, south of Harrowgate Road (Rte. 144), 0.1 miles north of Colonial Heights city limits. Here the Army of the James, moving on Petersburg, May 9, 1864, was checked by the Confederate defenses on the creek and turned northward.

S-29 CIVILIAN CONSERVATION CORPS COMPANY 2386

Rte. 655, at entrance to Pocahontas State Park. Located north of this marker is the site of the camp of CCC Company 2386, Beach, Virginia. The camp was organized in 1935 and disbanded in 1942. The company consisted of 2 to 3 military officers, a civilian technical service staff, and approximately 200 enrollees. During its existence, the company built Swift Creek Recreational Area, the forerunner of Pocahontas State Park, and reforested 7,604 acres of land now known as Pocahontas State Forest.

S-29 MAGNOLIA GRANGE

Rte. 10, near Rte. 655, Chesterfield. Built in 1822 by William Winfree, this Federal-style house was named for the large stand of magnolia trees in the front yard. It was originally surrounded by a 600-acre farm. A nearby tavern provided lodging for persons with business at the Courthouse; a grist mill formerly stood on nearby Cold Water Run. From 1881 to 1969 it was the residence of the Cogbill family whose members figured prominently in the political history of Chesterfield County.

S-30 FIRST RAILROAD IN VIRGINIA

Rte. 60, 3.78 miles west of Richmond. Just south of here are the earthen remains and stone culvert of the Chesterfield Railroad. Chartered by the Virginia General Assembly in 1829, the company in 1831 constructed the first railroad in Virginia, one of the earliest in the United States, to haul coal from the Midlothian mines to Manchester's wharves on the James River. Moncure Robinson (1802–1891), a railroad pioneer, designed the track on which the cars were powered by gravity, horses and mules. It remained in operation until the Richmond & Danville Railroad began providing service to the area in 1851.

S-36 REDWATER CREEK ENGAGEMENT

Rte. 1, 0.8 miles north of Colonial Heights city limits. While Union Maj. Gen. Benjamin F. Butler's Army of the James entrenched at Bermuda Hundred on 11 May 1864, Confederate Maj. Gen. Robert F. Hoke led parts of two divisions north from

Petersburg to unite with Maj. Gen. Robert Ransom's division near Drewry's Bluff and Proctor's Creek. Once there, Hoke formed the Confederate left wing with Ransom on the right facing south. At dawn on 12 May, Union Maj. Gen. William F. Smith led his corps through the Federal line to present-day U.S. Rte. 1, then north toward Richmond. After a mile, here at Redwater Creek, a Confederate skirmish line stopped Smith and then fell back to Proctor's Creek.

S-37 Eleazar Clay

Rte. 360, between Genito Road and Rte. 288. Eleazar Clay (1744–1836) led the establishment of the first Baptist church in Chesterfield County, known as Chesterfield (Baptist) Church, Rehoboth Meeting House, or Clay's Church, in 1773. He also supported the Baptist preachers imprisoned for breaching ecclesiastical law in the county jail in 1771. Ordained as a minister in 1775, Clay preached for more than 50 years, organized three other churches, served as a moderator for the Middle District Baptist

Association when it was formed in 1784, and published *Hymns and Spiritual Songs* in 1793. Clay is kinsman of statesman Henry Clay (1777–1852). Eleazar Clay's home site and tomb are located approximately two miles south.

S-38 Lee's Headquarters

Rte. 1, just south of Rte. 10, at John Tyler Community College. To the east, Confederate Gen. Robert E. Lee briefly made his headquarters at Clay's house on 17 June 1864. There he received full details of the Union army's attack on Petersburg that began the evening of 15 June 1864. Lee learned that Lt. Gen. Ulysses S. Grant had committed most of the Union Army of the Potomac to assault the Petersburg fortifications commanded by Confederate Gen. P. G. T. Beauregard. After receiving the reports of the Federal assault on Petersburg, Lee realized that Petersburg stood in immediate danger. He left his nearby headquarters early the next morning and went with most of his army to reinforce the garrison at Petersburg.

CITY OF COLONIAL HEIGHTS

S-26 Lafayette at Petersburg

Rte. 1, at Arlington Avenue. From this hill Lafayette, on May 10, 1781, shelled the British in Petersburg.

S-27 Lee's Headquarters

Arlington Avenue, at Rte. 1. Lee's headquarters from the latter part of June, 1864 to September, 1864 were here.

S-31 "Brave to Madness"

Rte. 1, at northern city limits. Nearby on 9 May 1864, Brig. Gen. Johnson Hagood's South Carolina Brigade attacked advancing elements of the Union X and XVIII Corps. As the 11th S.C. Infantry Regiment engaged the Federals across Swift Creek near Arrowfield Church, the 21st and 25th S.C. crossed the creek and charged up the hill

to attack Brig. Gen. Charles A. Heckman's "Star" Brigade. Repulsed with a loss of 137 casualties, the South Carolinians were praised in an official report as "brave to madness." Their gallant charge succeeded, however, in saving from destruction the turnpike and railroad bridges that crossed Swift Creek and formed vital links in Lee's supply line.

S-32 Ellerslie

Longhorn Street, off Ellerslie Avenue. In 1839, David Dunlop and his wife, Anna Mercer Minge, a niece of President William Henry Harrison, acquired the Ellerslie tract. Robert Young designed the castellated Gothic Revival mansion for Dunlop in 1856, and construction began the next year. Surrounded by elaborately landscaped grounds, Ellerslie was damaged during the Civil War by Union artillery on 9 May 1864. Later, Gen. P. G. T. Beauregard established his headquarters here, and a Confederate rest camp occupied the grounds. In 1910, Carneal and Johnston, of Richmond, remodeled Ellerslie in a fanciful version of the Bungaloid style, but the tower and the basic structure of the house are original.

S-33 Fort Clifton

Conduit Road, at Brockwell Lane. A short distance east on the Appomattox River stands Confederate Fort Clifton, an important fortification that guarded Petersburg against Union naval attack during the Civil War. On 9 May 1864, Federal gunboats commanded by Maj. Gen. Charles K. Graham attacked the fort. During the engagement, Fort Clifton's artillery disabled the army gunboat Samuel L. Brewster, which its crew then scuttled. The fort's garrison, commanded by Capt. S. Taylor Martin, of the Virginia artillery, received a special commendation from Maj. Gen. George E. Pickett, the commander of the Petersburg defenses. Fort Clifton was evacuated on 2 April 1865, one week before Lee's surrender at Appomattox.

S-34 Dunlop's Station

Ellerslie Avenue and Old Town Drive. At the nearby junction of the Richmond and Petersburg Railroad and the Confederate military spur line to Ettrick, stood Dunlop's Station, a Confederate telegraph post and supply depot. During the siege of Petersburg, southbound passengers were detrained here to avoid Federal shells that endangered travel over the Appomattox River railroad bridge to the south. On 2 April 1865, surplus ammunition was moved here as the Confederates prepared to evacuate Petersburg. During the night of 2 April, the ammunition trains were blown up. Despite warnings, civilians climbed aboard the cars in search of food and clothing and many were killed in the ensuing explosions.

S-35 Electric Railway

Ashby Avenue and the Boulevard. Located here was Stop 54 on the electric interurban railway line between Richmond and Petersburg. Opened in 1902 by the Virginia Passenger and Power Co., the line crossed Swift Creek on a steel truss bridge and followed Ashby Avenue to its intersection here with the Richmond-Petersburg Turnpike. Turning south, the line followed the Boulevard to Stop 66 (Chesterfield Ave.) and crossed the Appomattox River on a trestle. Stone and Webster purchased the line in 1925, renamed it the Virginia Electric and Power Company and replaced the trestle with the Appomattox River Bridge. Electric rail operations ceased on 31 Aug. 1936.

DINWIDDIE COUNTY

I-6 Central State Hospital

Rte. 1, 0.4 miles west of Petersburg. Established in 1869 in temporary quarters at Howard's Grove near Richmond. In 1870 it came under control of the State. In 1885 it was moved to the present location, the site of "Mayfield Plantation", which was purchased and donated to the State by the City of Petersburg. The first hospital in America exclusively for the treatment of mental disease in the Negro.

K-303 Butterfield Chapel

Rte. 40, 7.8 miles east of Blackstone. Butterwood Chapel, one of three Anglican chapels constructed in Dinwiddie County in the 18th century, was built by 1763 on or near this site. It probably was the first church built after the creation of Bath Parish in 1742. The Reverend Devereux Jarrett, a father of Methodism in Virginia, ministered to the congregation before the disestablishment of the Church of England in 1786. Capt. Henry D. Dickerson, C.S.A., revived the church after moving his family here to the Darvills community by 1865. William Randolph Atkinson designed and constructed the present frame building about 1866.

K-304 SALLIE JONES ATKINSON—1860–1943

Rte. 40, near Rte. 610 (Old White Oak Road), 2.5 miles west of McKenney. Sallie Jones Atkinson, prominent educator and community leader in Dinwiddie County and her husband, John Pryor Atkinson, gave the land on which Sunnyside High School was built in 1911. By her vision, tireless industry, and determination, the school became the first eight-month rural school accredited in Virginia. Mrs. Atkinson also served on the state committee that worked to secure Governor Montague's approval for women's suffrage.

K-305 ENGAGEMENT AT SUTHERLAND STATION

Rte. 460, east of Rte. 743. On the morning of 2 Apr. 1865, Union forces arrived here by way of Claiborne Road and found Maj. Gen. Henry Heth's Confederate division entrenched on Cox Road. During the day, Maj. Gen. Nelson A. Miles's division made three distinct assaults against the half-mile-long Confederate line, which stretched from Ocran Church to Sutherland's Tavern. The third charge forced Heth's division out of its works and west on the Namozine Road, thereby severing Gen. Robert E. Lee's final supply line, the South Side Railroad. Lee ordered the Army of Northern Virginia to evacuate both Petersburg and Richmond that night.

K-307 BATTLE OF FIVE FORKS

Rte. 751, at Church Road post office. Four miles south is the battlefield of Five Forks. To that point Pickett retired from Dinwiddie Courthouse in the night of March 31, 1865. Sheridan, following, attacked him in the afternoon of April 1, 1865. The

Confederates, outnumbered and surrounded, were overwhelmed. This defeat broke Lee's line of defense around Petersburg and forced him to retreat.

K-308 COLONEL JOHN BANISTER

Rte. 460, at Rte. 623. One mile to the south is the site of Hatcher's Run Plantation and the grave site of Col. John Banister (D. 1787), first mayor of Petersburg and prosperous entrepreneur. Banister represented Dinwiddie County in the House of Burgesses (1765–1775) and the conventions of 1775 and 1776. He was a member of the Continental Congress, a framer and signer of the Articles of Confederation, and a cavalry officer during the Revolution.

K-313 APPOMATTOX CAMPAIGN (SUTHERLAND STATION)

Rte. 460, at Rte. 708. At Sutherland Station, on 2 Apr. 1865, the Confederates made a last attempt to maintain control of the South Side Railroad. Confederate Maj. Gen. Henry Heth organized the defense before returning to the main line in Petersburg. Brig. Gen. John R. Cooke commanded in Heth's absence. Elements of Union Maj. Gen. Nelson's division of the II Corps troops charged the Confederate left flank, commanded by Brig Gen. Samuel McGowan. Overwhelmed, the flank disintegrated and the rest of the line fled as well. The loss severed Gen. Robert E. Lee's supply line.

K-321 BIRTHPLACE OF ROGER ATKINSON PRYOR

Rte. 40, near Rte. 610 (Old White Oak Road), 2.5 miles west of McKenney. Nearby is Montrose, the birthplace of Roger Atkinson Pryor, born 19 July 1828. Pryor practiced law before becoming a journalist and briefly owned newspapers in Richmond and Washington, D.C., in the 1850s. He served his Virginia district in the U.S. House of Representatives (1859–1861). During the Civil War, he served in the Confederate Congress and was a Confederate brigadier general and scout. He moved to New York City after the war and became a prominent lawyer. In 1890 he was appointed to the New York Court of Common Pleas and served as a justice of the New York Supreme Court (1896–1899). Pryor died on 14 Mar. 1919 in New York City.

S-40 SAPONY EPISCOPAL CHURCH

Rte. 40, at Rte. 709. Sapony Episcopal Church stands approximately 1.5 miles to the north. This simple frame building was first constructed in 1725–1726. The Rev. Devereux Jarratt served as rector here and at two other congregations in Dinwiddie County from 1763 until his death in 1801. He was a prominent figure of the Anglican, later Episcopal, Church. During the Great Awakening, he preached to large audiences in Southside Virginia and North Carolina and influenced the Methodist movement. The graves of Jarratt and his wife were moved here in 1869, the same year that part of the building collapsed. It was rebuilt using the original pews, wainscoting, windows, and railings.

S-42 GRAVELLY RUN QUAKER MEETING HOUSE

Rte. 1, at Rte. 660 (Quaker Road), north of Dinwiddie. Quakers began settling the region by the end of the 17th century. Named for nearby Gravelly Run stream, the meetinghouse was built by 1767. It became the religious center for the Quakers in Dinwiddie and surrounding counties. In the early 1800s the yearly meeting for the Upper Monthly Meeting was frequently held at Gravelly Run. Membership began to decline then because the Quakers refused to bear arms and opposed slavery. As a result, several members moved to Ohio, Tennessee, and Indiana, and the meetinghouse was abandoned in the 1830s.

S-45 SCOTT'S LAW OFFICE

Rte. 1, Dinwiddie. Just to the west stands the law office occupied in early life by Lieutenant-General Winfield Scott, commander of the United States Army, 1841–1861. Scott, born near here, June 13, 1786, was admitted to the bar in 1806 and entered the army in 1808. He died, May 29, 1866.

S-46 RACELAND

Rte. 1, at Rte. 660 (Quaker Road), north of Dinwiddie. Nearby stands Raceland, also known as Rice's Tavern, built ca. 1750. The building originally was a simple story-and-a-half dwelling with a hall-and-parlor plan. Subsequent additions transformed it into a two-story Federal-style house. It has been used as a tavern and private home. William "Racer Billy" Wynn, renowned owner of fine horses during the early 19th century, lived here. Wynn had stables and a racetrack on the property and briefly owned Timoleon, considered one of the fastest Thoroughbreds of the 1810s.

S-47 EDGE HILL

Rte. 1, at southern limits of Petersburg. To the north stood William Turnbull's house, Edge Hill, headquarters of Gen. Robert E. Lee from 23 Nov. 1864 to 2 Apr. 1865 during the siege of Petersburg. Here, after dawn on 2 Apr., Lee learned of the Union attack that soon shattered his lines and spoke for the last time with Lt. Gen. A. P. Hill. Nearby, he received word of Hill's death a short time later. When the Federals approached, Lee moved his headquarters to Cottage Farm within the inner Confederate line, and that night he evacuated the Army of Northern Virginia from the city. Union artillery soon destroyed the Turnbull house. The present residence was one of the detached buildings.

S-48 CATTLE (BEEFSTEAK) RAID

Rtes. 1 and 613, 5 miles south of Petersburg. Leaving from a point along the Confederate right flank on Boydton Plank Road on 14 Sept. 1864, Maj. Gen. Wade Hampton took about 3,000 Confederate cavalrymen and rode more than 100 miles around the rear of the Union army. Reaching Coggins' Point on the James River on the

16 Sept., the raiders successfully captured almost 2,500 head of cattle from the Federals and returned to their lines relatively unmolested. The next day the cattle were penned in the field east of the Boydton Plank Road until being slaughtered for the Confederate troops in the Petersburg trenches.

S-49 WHERE HILL FELL

Rte. 1, across from Pamplin Park, 2.8 miles south of Petersburg. In the field a short distance north of this road, the Confederate General A. P. Hill was killed, April 2, 1865. Hill, not knowing that Lee's lines had been broken, rode into a party of Union soldiers advancing on Petersburg.

S-50 HATCHER'S RUN

Rte. 1, at Hatcher's Run, 6.4 miles south of Petersburg. Lee's right wing was defended by earthworks on this stream, here and to the east. These works were unsuccessfully attacked by Union forces, February 5–7, 1865. On the morning of April 2, 1865, they were stormed by Union troops.

S-51 BURGESS MILL

Rte. 1, 6.4 miles south of Petersburg, at Hatcher's Run. An old mill stood here, with earthworks. On October 27, 1864, General Hancock, coming from the south, attempted to cross the run here and reach the Southside Railroad. He was supported on the east by Warren's (Fifth) Corps. The Confederates, crossing the run from the north side, intervened between the two Union forces and drove them back.

S-52 WHITE OAK ROAD

Rte. 1, at Rte. 613 (White Oak Road), 6.8 miles south of Petersburg. The extreme right of Lee's line rested on this road, which was entrenched. General Warren, advancing against Lee's works here, March 31, 1865, was driven back. Reinforced, Warren advanced again, forcing the Confederates to retire to the road. On it, six miles west, the battle of Five Forks was fought next day, April 1, 1865.

S-54 DINWIDDIE COURTHOUSE

Rte. 1, Dinwiddie. Sheridan advanced to this place on March 29, 1865, while Warren was attacking Anderson about three miles north. On March 31 Sheridan moved south but was checked by Pickett and driven back to the courthouse. That night Pickett withdrew to Five Forks.

S-55 VAUGHAN ROAD

Rte. 1, at Rte. 703, Dinwiddie. Hancock moved by it to his defeat at Burgess Mill, October 27, 1864, and in 1865, Grant moved his forces on it from the east to attack Lee's right wing. On March 29, 1865, Sheridan came to Dinwiddie Court House over it in the operations preceeding [preceding] the Battle of Five Forks.

S-56 CHAMBERLAIN'S BED

Rte. 1, at Stony Creek, 1.1 miles south of Dinwiddie. That stream flows into Stony Creek a mile west. On March 31, 1865, Pickett and W. H. F. Lee, coming from Five Forks, forced a passage of Chamberlain's Bed in the face of Sheridan's troops, who were driven back to Dinwiddie Courthouse.

S-62 CAMPAIGN OF 1781

Rte. 1, at Rte. 656, 1.5 miles south of Dinwiddie. The British cavalryman Tarleton, returning to Cornwallis from a raid to Bedford, passed near here, July, 1781.

S-63 BATTLE OF HATCHER'S RUN— 5–7 FEBRUARY 1865

Rte. 613, 2.2 miles east of Rte. 1. Hoping to cut Lee's supply route into Petersburg, in February 1865 Grant ordered two army corps led by Major Generals Gouverneur K. Warren and Andrew A. Humphreys to seize the Boydton Plank Road. The Confederate corps commanded by Maj. Gen. John B. Gordon successfully blocked Warren's attacks at nearby Dabney's Mill on 6–7

February, and Warren's corps withdrew to its previous position. The brief Union campaign enabled Grant to extend his lines, and cost the Confederates the life of Brig. Gen. John Pegram on 6 February.

S-69 DARVILL'S SCHOOL

Rte. 613, almost 2 miles south of Rte. 40. A public school operated here as early as the 1880s. In 1907, three other one-room schools nearby were consolidated here as Darvills Graded School, which was expanded and made a high school in 1913. It was the heart of community activities, notably the annual Darvills Fair, which began in 1916 and continued through the 1930s. Late in 1941, as World War II approached, the U.S. government began condemning 46,000 acres here to establish Camp Pickett. The school closed in 1942 and its buildings were razed except the original graded school, which became a community center. It burned on 5 July 1998.

S-80 QUAKER ROAD ENGAGEMENT— 29 MARCH 1865

Rte. 660 (Quaker Road), 0.8 miles east of Rte. 1, north of Dinwiddie. This was the first in a series of attempts by Grant's army to cut Lee's final supply line—the South Side Railroad—in spring 1865. Here at the Lewis farm, Union forces led by Brig. Gen. Joshua L. Chamberlain engaged Confederates under Maj. Gen. Bushrod R. Johnson. After sharp fighting, the Union troops entrenched nearby along the Boydton Plank Road and Johnson withdrew to his lines at White Oak Road. The Union army cut the rail line four days later, after capturing Five Forks on 1 April.

S-81 WHITE OAK ROAD ENGAGE-MENT—31 MARCH 1865

Rte. 613 (White Oak Road), 1.63 miles west of Rte. 1, at Rte. 631, north of Dinwiddie. Union forces belonging to the V Corps, under Maj. Gen. Gouverneur K. Warren, sought to seize the White Oak Road and sever the Confederate line of communication with Maj. Gen. George E. Pickett's detachment near Five Forks, four miles west. From here Gen. Robert E. Lee personally supervised the counterattack to Gravelly Run by Lt. Gen. Richard H. Anderson's corps. After a brief success, the Confederates were forced back into these entrenchments as Warren's men gained the important roadway.

S-82 CONFEDERATE FORT WHITWORTH

Rte. 1, at Albemarle Street, 0.2 miles north of I-85. Named for the Whitworth family of Mayfield, the farm on which it was built, this outpost (a quarter-mile east) and Fort Gregg, 400 yards to the south, were constructed to protect the western approaches to Petersburg during the 1864–1865 siege. On 2 April 1865, when Gen. U. S. Grant's army attacked the city after turning Gen. R. E. Lee's flank at Five Forks the day before, the forts were the scene of intense fighting. The Union XXIV Corps captured the two positions, suffering 714 casualties. The Confederates lost about 300 men in a stubborn defense that delayed the Union advance for two hours, enabling Lee to withdraw his army safely that night and begin the westward march that ended a week later at Appomattox Court House.

S-83 PRELUDE TO FIVE FORKS

Marker not yet cast. Proposed location: White Oak and Crump (Boisseau) Roads. Here, just before the Battle of Five Forks on 1 Apr. 1865, Federal cavalry overwhelmed a lightly defended section of the Confederate defenses on White Oak Road. Brig. Gen. William P. Roberts's small cavalry brigade (4th N.C. Regt. and 16th N.C. Bn.) formed a thin three-mile-long skirmish line here when Brig. Gen. Ranald S. Mackenzie's Union cavalry division attacked from the direction of Dinwiddie Court House. With Lt. Col. Franklin A. Stratton and the 11th Pa. Cavalry Regt. in the lead, the Federals scattered the North

Carolinians. This action kept the Confederates from reinforcing their position at Five

Forks by way of White Oak Road later that day.

FLUVANNA COUNTY

F-48 S. C. ABRAMS HIGH SCHOOL

Rte. 15, near Rte. 649, in Fork Union. Fluvanna County dedicated its only African American high school on 21 Nov. 1936 and named it the S. C. Abrams High School to honor the Rev. Samuel Christopher Abrams, who served as the county supervisor for the black schools and also as a minister in several Baptist churches. Before 1934 black students had to leave the county to attend high school, but in 1934 a temporary high school opened in a wood-frame building adjacent to New Fork Baptist Church. By 1936 money raised by the black community and the county provided black students with Abrams High School, which became a junior high following the integration of the schools in the 1960s. The Abrams building, located one mile west, has housed administrative offices since 1991.

F-48-a FORK UNION MILITARY ACADEMY

Rte. 15, at academy. Founded in 1898 by Dr. William E. Hatcher with the assistance of Charles G. Snead, Fork Union Academy established military training as part of the curriculum in 1902. It served as a coeducational school until 1909, when the trustees transformed it into an all-male academy. In 1913, it was renamed Fork Union Military Academy and became affiliated with the Baptist General Association of Virginia. From 1919 to 1965, the Academy operated a Junior Reserve Officer Training Candidate program. The Cadet Corps, consisting of an upper and middle school, occupies buildings on 307 acres.

F-49 FLUVANNA COUNTY COURTHOUSE

Rte. 15, at courthouse, Palmyra. The Fluvanna County Courthouse is one of the few

in the state to retain its original configuration. Fluvanna County was formed from part of Albemarle County in 1777 with the county seat located on the southeast side of the Rivanna River. In 1828 Palmyra was selected as the new county seat, and the present courthouse was erected in 1830 by the Reverend Walker Timberlake and John Hartwell Cocke of nearby Bremo. Cocke also prepared the plans for the stone jail, built in 1828, which now houses the Fluvanna County Historical Society's museum.

F-50 POINT OF FORK

Rte. 15, at Rte. 6, Dixie. Four miles southeast is Point of Fork, near which an Indian village stood in 1607. In the Revolution a state arsenal was there. In June, 1781, Simcoe, sent by Cornwallis with a small force to destroy the stores there, succeeded in making Baron Steuben, the American commander, believe the whole British army to be near. Steuben retreated, leaving the stores to be destroyed.

F-51 "TEXAS JACK" OMOHUNDRO BIRTHPLACE

Rte. 15, 1 mile south of Palmyra. J. B. "Texas Jack" Omohundro was born at Pleasure Hill Farm about 1 mile west of here on July 26, 1846. At age 17 he served as a scout under the command of General J. E. B. Stuart. Later he was renowned as a scout and heroic plainsman of the old west. Texas Jack with his friend W. F. "Buffalo Bill" Cody started the first "Wild West" shows in America. He died in Leadville, Colorado, June 28, 1880.

F-52 BREMO

Rte. 15, near James River bridge, 4 miles south of Fork Union. The nearby Bremo properties include three separate houses, all built by planter, soldier, and reformer Gen. John Hartwell Cocke (1780–1866) on his family's 1725 land grant. The three properties—Bremo, Lower Bremo, and Recess—and their associated outbuildings were erected under Cocke's supervision. Bremo, completed in 1820, is an excellent example of Palladian-style architecture. Its design is the result of collaboration between Cocke and master builder John Neilson, who worked for Thomas Jefferson at Monticello and the University of Virginia. Lower Bremo and Recess both are neo-Jacobean-style architecture inspired by Bacon's Castle in Surry County.

F-99 JOHN JASPER

Rte. 15, at Rte. 615, 4.5 miles south of Palmyra, Carysbrook. The Rev. John Jasper, one of the best known black preachers of the 19th century in Virginia, was born a slave in Fluvanna County on 4 July 1812. After working in a tobacco factory, Jasper had a religious awakening in the later 1830s and became a preacher. Self-educated, Jasper was renowned for his fiery oratorical style and for the sermon, "De Sun Do Move," first delivered in 1878 and preached to more than 250 audiences, including the Virginia General Assembly. He organized the Sixth Mount Zion Baptist Church in Richmond in 1867. Jasper died in late March 1901 and is buried in Richmond.

GA-32 POINT OF FORK

Rte. 6, 1 mile west of Columbia. Here was an important supply depot and arsenal of the Virginia government in 1781, and here Baron von Steuben, commanding the American forces, trained recruits for Greene's army in the South. Threatened by Cornwallis's approach, Steuben moved stores across James River. On June 4, 1781, Colonel Simcoe, with his cavalry, made Steuben believe that the whole British army was at hand. Steuben retreated, leaving stores to be destroyed.

GA-33 FORK UNION ACADEMY

Rte. 15, Fork Union. First classes of Fork Union Academy were held here October 15, 1898, in the residence of Susie Payne Cooper. Established as a coeducational English and classical school, it became Fork Union Military Academy for boys in 1903. Organized by ten guarantors who were members of Fork Church, the Academy was sustained mainly by private contributions from the Fork Union community until 1913 when it became affiliated with the Baptist denomination.

GA-34 RASSAWEK

Rte. 6, 0.8 miles west of Columbia. Rassawek, the principal town of the Monacan Indians, stood nearby, according to Capt. John Smith's 1612 map of Virginia. Several smaller satellite villages were located within a few miles of Rassawek. The Monacans, who belonged to the Siouan language group and were enemies of the Powhatans to the east, occupied Virginia's Piedmont until the expanding English colony pushed them to the west and south. A century after the founding of Jamestown in 1607, only remnants of the tribe survived. Monacan descendants live today near Bear Mountain in Amherst County.

GA-39 FORK UNION BAPTIST CHURCH

Rte. 15, near church, Fork Union. Fork Union Baptist Church was constituted in 1798. Presbyterian, Episcopal, Methodist, and Baptist congregations shared as a place of worship the current church, built in 1824 and first known as the Brick Meetinghouse. Gen. John Hartwell Cocke, a local plantation owner who assisted Thomas Jefferson in establishing the University of Virginia, was its architect. It is the oldest Church building in Fluvanna County in continuous use for that purpose. In 1898, ten of its members became the original guarantors of Fork Union Military Academy. The church sanctuary was the site of the first and subsequent academy graduations until 1937.

CITY OF FREDERICKSBURG

E-43 LEE'S POSITION

Business Rte. 1 (Lafayette Boulevard), 0.6 miles south of Rte. 3. From this hill (now called Lee's Hill) a little to the east, Confederate Gen. Robert E. Lee watched the First Battle of Fredericksburg. As the armies prepared for combat, Lee commented that "It is well that war is so terrible—we should grow too fond of it." On 13 Dec. 1862, Union Maj. Gen. Ambrose E. Burnside ordered an assault against the Confederate position. The Confederates withstood the attack, which lasted until dark, and slaughtered the Federals with artillery and small-arms fire. Two days later the defeated Union army retreated across the Rappahannock River.

E-44 BATTLES OF FREDERICKSBURG

Business Rte. 1 (Lafayette Boulevard), 0.1 miles north of Rte. 3. During the First and Second Battles of Fredericksburg, the Confederates occupied Marye's Heights, a defensive position enhanced by a sunken road and stone wall on the eastern slope. On 13 Dec. 1862, during the first battle, Lt. Gen. James Longstreet's Confederate corps withstood attempts by Union Maj. Gen. Joseph Hooker's and Maj. Gen. Edwin V. Sumner's Grand Divisions to take the heights. During the second battle (Chancellorsville campaign), on 3 May 1863, Maj. Gen. John Sedgwick's Union troops repeatedly attempted to capture the ridge from Brig. Gen. William Barksdale's brigade. A bayonet charge finally drove the Confederates off the heights.

E-46-a FREDERICKSBURG

Alternate Rte. 1, south of Armory, 2 miles south of Falmouth. Captain John Smith was here in 1608; Lederer, the explorer, in 1670. In May 1671 John Buckner and Thomas Royster patented the Lease Land Grant. The town was established in 1727 and lots were laid out. It was named for Frederick, Prince of Wales, father of George III. The court for Spotsylvania County was moved here in 1732 and the town was enlarged in 1759 and 1769. Fredericksburg was incorporated as a town in 1781, as a city in 1879, and declared a city of the first class in 1941.

E-49-a "FALL HILL"

Rte. 1, near Fall Hill Avenue, at James Monroe High School. On the heights one mile to the west, the home of the Thorntons from about 1736. Francis Thornton 2nd was a justice, a Burgess 1744–45, and Lieut.-Colonel of his Majesty's militia for Spotsylvania County. He and two of his brothers married three Gregory sisters, first cousins of George Washington. "Fall Hill" is still (1950) owned and occupied by direct Thornton descendants.

E-49-b "FALL HILL"

Rte. 1, at Fall Hill. On the heights one mile to the west, the home of the Thorntons from about 1736. Francis Thornton 2nd was a justice, a Burgess 1744–45, and Lieut.-Colonel of his Majesty's militia for Spotsylvania County. He and two of his brothers married three Gregory sisters, first cousins of George Washington. "Fall Hill" is still (1950) owned and occupied by direct Thornton descendants.

N-7 FREDERICKSBURG GUN MANUFACTORY

Gunnery Road and Dunmore Street. The Fredericksburg Gun Manufactory was established by an ordinance passed by Virginia's third revolutionary convention on 17 July 1775. Built on this site soon thereafter by Fielding Lewis and Charles Dick, it was the first such factory in America. Its workers repaired and manufactured small arms for the regiments of numerous Virginia counties during the Revolutionary War. The factory's principal product was modeled after the British Brown Bess musket, the standard infantry arm of the day.

Only a handful of the Fredericksburg muskets survive. In 1783 the factory closed and the General Assembly transferred the land and buildings to the trustees of the Fredericksburg Academy. The property was sold to a merchant in 1801 and later subdivided.

N-30 CAMP COBB AT GUNNERY SPRINGS

Gunnery Road and Dunmore Street. In 1775, during the Revolutionary War, this "noble spring" was part of a 10½ acre tract purchased for the Fredericksburg Gun Manufactory. On this site in 1898 stood Camp Cobb, a Spanish-American War training camp for the 4th U.S. Volunteer Infantry Regiment. It was named for Confederate Brig. Gen. Thomas R. R. Cobb, killed in the Battle of Fredericksburg, 13 Dec. 1862. Because of the danger yellow fever posed to American troops in Cuba, recruiters sought to fill the regiment with men whose medical backgrounds suggested immunity to tropical diseases. The first company of the "Immunes," as they were called, arrived on 4 June 1898. The Immunes never saw combat, as the fighting ended in July, and the camp was dismantled.

N-31 KENMORE

1200 block, Caroline Street, at Lewis Street. Four blocks west stands Kenmore, built in 1775 by Col. Fielding Lewis for his wife, Betty, sister of George Washington. Near here, between Kenmore and the Rappahannock River, stood Lewis's warehouses and docks. Kenmore's intricate plasterwork is the finest in the country. Among 19th-century owners and occupants were Samuel Gordon, who named it Kenmore, and William Key Howard Jr., who restored

and embellished the mansion's plasterwork. Washington and other Revolutionary leaders often visited, and during the Civil War Union troops used it as a hospital. The Garden Club of Virginia, starting in 1929, rehabilitated Kenmore's gardens as its first restoration project.

N-32 BRIG. GEN. JOHN MINOR

100 block, Princess Anne Street. Hazel Hill, the home of John Minor (13 May 1761– 8 June 1816), a close friend of President James Monroe, once occupied this site. Minor served as a soldier in the American Revolution, as a colonel of the Spotsylvania County militia, and as a brigadier general of militia from 1804 through the War of 1812. Minor also was a member of the Virginia House of Delegates from 1805 to 1807. In 1783, as a private citizen, Minor unsuccessfully urged the General Assembly to pass a bill to emancipate Virginia's slaves.

N-33 FREDERICKSBURG NORMAL AND INDUSTRIAL INSTITUTE

300 block, Tyler Street. Due to the efforts of local blacks, the Fredericksburg Normal and Industrial Institute (FNII) opened in October 1905 at the Shiloh New Site Baptist Church with about 20 students. In 1906 the board of trustees purchased land and a large farmhouse here, named it Mayfield, and opened the school in the autumn. The course of study, modeled after a university curriculum included teacher education classes as well as English, mathematics, history, geography, literature, Greek, and music. By 1938, Mayfield High School had become a part of the segregated city school system.

GOOCHLAND COUNTY

SA-5 ELK HILL

Rte. 6, 1 mile west of Georges Tavern. Two miles south is Elk Hill, once owned by Thomas Jefferson. Lord Cornwallis made

his headquarters there, June 7–15, 1781; this was the western limit of his invasion. On June 15 he turned eastward, leaving the place pillaged and carrying off slaves.

SA-9 GOOCHLAND COUNTY COURTHOUSE

Rte. 6, Goochland. The present courthouse is the fourth to serve the county and the second to occupy this site. The building was erected in 1826 by Valentine Parrish, a Cumberland builder, and Dabney Cosby, a skilled Staunton brickmason who had worked for Thomas Jefferson at the University of Virginia. Jefferson's influence is seen in the Tuscan portico, full Tuscan entablature, temple form, and color scheme of red brick and white trim. The courthouse, together with the clerk's office, old jail, and original wall to exclude wandering cattle, exemplify a rural nineteenth century county seat.

SA-10 GOOCHLAND COURTHOUSE

Rte. 6, Goochland. Near here the ancient trail used by the Iroquois Indians in their raids crossed James River. This trail later became the main north-south road through Virginia. In 1781, Lord Cornwallis, in his invasion of Virginia, marched by this point and his cavalry, under Simcoe, passed here going to Point of Fork. A cavalry skirmish took place here, March 11, 1865.

SA-11 DUNGENESS

Rte. 6, at Rte. 600. Seven miles south once stood Dungeness, built about 1730 by Isham Randolph (1685–1742) who was the grandfather of Thomas Jefferson, President of the United States, and of James Pleasants, Governor of Virginia. Sea captain, merchant and planter, Randolph also served as Virginia's agent in London and Adjutant General of the Colony.

SA-14 DAHLGREN'S RAID

Rte. 6, at Rte. 642, 2.1 miles east of Crozier. Here Colonel Ulric Dahlgren, Union cavalryman, coming from the north, turned east. Dahlgren, who acted in concert with Kilpatrick, left Stevensburg, Culpeper County, on February 28, 1864, and moved toward the James River, tearing up the Virginia Central Railroad near Frederick's Hall. He went on toward Richmond, burning mills and barns.

SA-17 JAMES PLEASANTS

Rte. 6, 0.3 miles west of Crozier. James Pleasants was born on 24 Oct. 1769 at his home, Contention, located two miles south. A Quaker, Pleasants served in the Virginia House of Delegates from 1796 to 1810, and in 1803 was elected its clerk. He sat in the United States House of Representatives from 1811 to 1819, and in the Senate from 1819 to 1822. First elected governor of Virginia by the General Assembly in 1822, he served two consecutive terms until 1825. He last held office in 1829–1830 as a member of the State Constitutional Convention. He died on 9 Nov. 1836, in Goochland County, esteemed for his public service and private virtues.

SA-18 SABOT HILL

Rte. 6, east of Crozier. It was named for Sabot Island, supposed to resemble a wooden shoe. Sabot Hill was the home of James A. Seddon, member of Congress and Confederate Secretary of War, 1862–65, who built the house in 1855. It was visited by Dahlgren in his raid, March 1, 1864.

SA-20 HUGUENOT SETTLEMENT

Rte. 6, 5.9 miles east of Crozier. In 1700–1701, Huguenots (French Protestant refugees) settled in this region on land provided to them by the Virginia colony. The Huguenot settlement, known as "Manakin Town" centered at the former site of a Monacan Indian town, located south of the James River. During this period the Monacans and other Indian tribes traded with the settlers. In 1700, the Virginia General Assembly established the King William Parish, which enabled the Huguenots to have their own church, pastor, and set their own parish tithes. Over time the Huguenots obtained individual land grants on both sides of the James River and throughout this region.

SA-22   WILLIAM WEBBER

Rte. 6, 6 miles east of Crozier, Manakin. Three miles north are the home site and grave of William Webber, pastor of Dover Baptist Church, 1773–1808. As an early Baptist leader before the Revolution, he was imprisoned in the jails of Chesterfield and Middlesex. He aided in organizing the Baptist General Association of Virginia; he was moderator in 1778. He was moderator of the Dover Association, 1783–1806; of the Baptist General Committee and of the General Meeting of Correspondence until his death in 1808.

SA-24   TUCKAHOE

Rte. 650, west of Goochland/Henrico County line. Perhaps the oldest frame residence on James River west of Richmond, Tuckahoe was begun about 1715 by Thomas Randolph. The little schoolhouse still stands here where Thomas Jefferson began his childhood studies. Famous guests here have included William Byrd of Westover, Lord Cornwallis and George Washington. Virginia's Governor Thomas Mann Randolph was born here.

SA-27   DAHLGREN'S CAVALRY RAID

Rte. 650, 0.9 miles west of county line. In February 1864 a young Union officer, Col. Ulric Dahlgren, joined with Brig. Gen. H. Judson Kilpatrick to raid Richmond and free Federal prisoners of war. They planned for Kilpatrick's men to attack the city's northern defenses while Dahlgren would lead his men through Goochland County, cross the James River, and enter the city from the south. A local African American, Martin Robinson escorted the troopers to a nearby ford but the water was too high to cross. Suspecting trickery, Dahlgren hanged him near here on 1 March, and then attacked the city from the west. Defeated, he rode east in search of Kilpatrick and was killed the next day in King and Queen County.

SA-35   BOLLING HALL

Rte. 6, at Rte. 600, west of Goochland. Bolling Hall, to the south, was built in the late 18th century for William Bolling on land patented by his grandfather in 1714. Col. Bolling served as a county justice, militia officer, and legislator, and founded a pioneer school there for the education of deaf children. Remodeled extensively in the mid-19th and mid-20th centuries, Bolling Hall retains its elegant woodwork, its rural setting on the James River, and its historical function as a farm.

SA-36   BOLLING ISLAND

Rte. 6, at Rte. 600, west of Goochland. Bolling Island mansion, overlooking an island of that name, stands at a bend of the James River to the south. John Bolling purchased the land in 1717. Begun about 1771, the house was completed in the late 1830s by Thomas Bolling, son of Col. William Bolling, of Bolling Hall. The principal features of the house are a two-story, Greek Revival-style portico on its south front, and several original outbuildings that stand behind it. Bolling Island remained in the Bolling family until 1870.

SA-51   GEORGE'S TAVERN CROSSROADS

Rte. 6, at Rte. 606, Georges Tavern. In 1792 Captain William George (1760–1827), a veteran of the Revolutionary War, established near this site on River Road an ordinary which stood until about 1900. During the campaign of 1781, General Von Steuben crossed the James River at Cartersville, passing through on his way to meet General Lafayette, who was camped in Louisa County. On 23 February 1782, after visiting Jefferson at Monticello, General Rochambeau passed the future site of George's Tavern on his way to Tuckahoe. Taverns and ordinaries were welcome places for rest and refreshment along stage roads every ten to twelve miles.

SA-55 BYRD PRESBYTERIAN CHURCH

2229 Dogtown Road, Goochland. Byrd Presbyterian Church's congregation is descended from worshipers, organized by theologian and future Princeton University president Samuel Davies at Tucker Woodson's farm in 1748. By 1759 the group had its own building on Byrd Creek. In 1838 descendents of the original congregation began worshiping here when the existing structure was built. Byrd Presbyterian is a notable example of the simple brick churches constructed in Virginia during the 19th century. The building retains some of its original architectural features, including its slate roof and interior window valances, as well as its cemetery.

SA-59 FIRST BAPTIST CHURCH, MANAKIN

214 River Road West, at church, Manakin. Organized as Dover Mines Church about 1863, First Baptist Church, Manakin is one of the oldest African American churches in Goochland County. Its members separated from Dover Baptist Church. Initially conducting their services at different sites, the Dover Mines congregation eventually converted a tool house into a church nearby. In 1891, trustees W. T. Taylor, Scott Houston, and John Christian purchased the Deitrick Hotel lot property here. Church members built this picturesque Italianate church in 1922, using some bricks from the 18th century. According to tradition, the church members hauled the 18th-century bricks from the nearby ruins of Dover Anglican Church.

V-18 REUBEN FORD

Rte. 250, 1.9 miles east of Oilville. A mile north are the home and grave of Reuben Ford, pastor of Goochland Baptist Church, 1771–1823. He was an advocate of equal religious rights for all, a leader in securing separation of church and state in Virginia.

HANOVER COUNTY

E-5 FORK CHURCH

Rte. 738, 4.5 miles west of Rte. 1. Fork Church was first housed in a 1722 frame building near the present church site. It was known as "The Chapel in the Forks" and derived its name from the nearby confluence of the North and South Anna rivers and the Little and Newfound rivers. The present building was erected between 1736 and 1740.

E-11 THE CHICKAHOMINY RIVER & SEVEN DAYS' BATTLES

Rte. 360, at Hanover/Henrico County line. During the Civil War's Seven Days' Battles from 25 June to 1 July 1862, many engagements occurred along and near the Chickahominy River. Union Maj. Gen. George B. McClellan led the Army of the Potomac. His goal was to capture the Confederate capital city of Richmond, defended by Gen. Robert E. Lee. Battles fought near the river include Beaver Dam Creek (Mechanicsville) on 26 June, Gaines's Mill on 27 June, and Savage's Station on 29 June. These and other battles encouraged McClellan to retreat to Harrison's Landing and ended the immediate threat to the capital city.

E-13 LEE'S TURN TO COLD HARBOR

Rte. 1, 4.5 miles south of Ashland. Lee had his headquarters near here, May 27, 1864, while moving south from the North Anna River. Here Longstreet's (Anderson's) and Hill's corps of his army turned east to meet Grant at Cold Harbor, where a great battle was fought, June 3, 1864.

E-14 JACKSON'S MARCH TO MECHANICSVILLE

Rte. 1, north of Ashcake Road, south of Ashland corporate limits. In mid-June 1862, having defeated three Union armies in the

Shenandoah Valley, Maj. Gen. Thomas J. "Stonewall" Jackson and his Valley Army joined Gen. Robert E. Lee to defend Richmond. Jackson and his men marched by here on 26 June to strike the flank of Maj. Gen. George B. McClellan's army near Mechanicsville. Because of Jackson's exhaustion and unfamiliarity with the roads, however, they arrived too late to fight. On 27 June, Jackson and the rest of the Army of Northern Virginia assaulted the Union right flank at Gaines's Mill, Lee's clearest victory in the Seven Days' Campaign.

E-15 HENRY AT HANOVER COURTHOUSE

Rte. 1 (Washington Highway), north of Rte. 54, at Ashland Hanover Shopping Center, Ashland. Six miles east still stands Hanover Courthouse, in which, December, 1763, Patrick Henry delivered his great speech in the "Parsons' Cause," when he denounced the British government for vetoing an act of the Virginia General Assembly.

E-16 ASHLAND

Rte. 1 (Washington Highway), north of Rte. 54, at Ashland Hanover Shopping Center, Ashland. In 1838, the Richmond, Fredericksburg & Potomac Railroad bought 462 acres bordering its tracks twelve miles north of Richmond in Hanover County. The company created a small summer retreat and passenger rest stop there. In 1858, the area was incorporated as the town of Ashland, the name of the Kentucky home of Hanover native son Henry Clay. During the Civil War, Union cavalry attacked the railroad here three times: on 3 May 1863 under Maj. Gen. George Stoneman, on 1 March 1864 under Brig. Gen. H. Judson Kilpatrick, and on 11 May 1864 under Brig. Gen. Henry E. Davies, Jr.

E-17 CONFEDERATE MARCH FROM THE NORTH ANNA RIVER

Rte. 1, south of South Anna River. Following the Union army's departure from the North Anna River on 26 May 1864, Confeder-ate Gen. Robert E. Lee cautiously moved his army south toward Richmond to stay between the Federals and the capital. Lee's wagon trains, using nearby Ellett's Bridge, crossed the South Anna River on 27 May. The Confederate First Corps, led by Lt. Gen. Richard H. Anderson, marched down the tracks of the Richmond, Fredericksburg, and Potomac Railroad and crossed the river on the railroad bridge just north of here. Other Confederate columns pushed south on separate routes, making for Atlee's Station and Totopotomoy Creek.

E-19 LEE'S LEFT WING

Rte. 1, 5.2 miles north of Ashland. On this stream, the Little River, and to the west, Lee's left wing rested while his army faced Grant along the North Anna, May 23–26, 1864.

E-20 LEE'S MOVEMENTS

Rte. 1, 6.2 miles north of Ashland. A short distance east, at Taylorsville, Lee had his headquarters, May 24–26, 1864, as his army moved southeastward to intervene between Grant and Richmond. There Ewell's corps turned to Cold Harbor, May 27, 1864.

E-21 HANOVER JUNCTION

Rte. 1, 7.6 miles north of Ashland. Two 19th-century railroads crossed at grade level just east: the Richmond, Fredericksburg & Potomac and the Virginia Central, which ran west to the Shenandoah Valley, the Confederacy's breadbasket during the Civil War. This junction attained strategic importance in 1864 as the railroads carried supplies to Gen. Robert E. Lee's Army of Northern Virginia. Lt. Gen. Ulysses S. Grant and the Army of the Potomac attempted to disrupt that traffic to hinder Lee and capture Richmond. The Confederates, however, successfully defended the junction during the North Anna River campaign, 21–26 May 1864, and the Union army withdrew east to Cold Harbor.

E-22 LAFAYETTE AND CORNWALLIS

Rte. 1, at Hanover/Caroline County line.
The Marquis de Lafayette and his outnumbered colonial troops abandoned
Richmond on 27 May 1781 to avoid Gen.
Charles Cornwallis's approaching forces.
Lafayette marched north from Richmond through Hanover County and likely
crossed the nearby North Anna River by
31 May. Cornwallis pursued Lafayette to
the North Anna River the next day. There
Cornwallis sent the British troops west in a
two-pronged attack to destroy storehouses
and attempt to capture the governor and
the General Assembly in Charlottesville.
Lafayette continued northward to the Rapidan River to await reinforcements.

E-74 STUART'S RIDE AROUND McCLELLAN

Rte. 1, 1.9 miles north of Ashland. Near here,
on Winston's Farm, J. E. B. Stuart, advancing north, camped on June 12, 1862. Stuart
was scouting to find the position of the
right wing of McClellan's army besieging
Richmond. At this point he turned east to
Hanover Courthouse. Stuart made a complete circuit of the Union army.

E-105 SLASH CHURCH

*Ashcake Road (Rte. 657), at Mt. Herman
Road (Rte. 656).* Erected in 1729–32 as
the Upper Church of Saint Paul's Parish,
Hanover County, Slash Church's location next to swampy woods (a "slash"
in 18th-century terms) gave it its name.
The Reverend Patrick Henry, uncle of the
famous patriot, served as rector from 1737
until 1777. Among its early worshipers the
church claims Patrick Henry, Dolley Madison, and Henry Clay, all once residents
of the area. During the Civil War, Slash
Church was used as a hospital and gave a
nearby battle its name. This white weath-
erboarded structure survives as the oldest
and best-preserved frame colonial church
in Virginia, and the only one to escape
enlargement.

E-111 CHURCH QUARTER

14032 Old Ridge Road (Rte. 738), Doswell.
The two-room log house, a rare survivor
of a once-common house type, was built
about 1843 probably by Sarah Thornton, whose father-in-law John Thornton
acquired the property in 1790. On 16 July
1862, Maj. Gen. Thomas J. "Stonewall"
Jackson and his staff stopped here and requested some water. The woman who lived
here provided him a pitcher from which
to drink. On learning Jackson's identity,
she refused to let anyone else drink from
it, saying that she would give it to her
children as a memento of Jackson's visit.
The Scotchtown Chapter of the Daughters
of the American Revolution purchased and
restored the cabin in 1969.

E-119 EARLY STAGES OF STUART'S RIDE AROUND McCLELLAN

Rte. 660, at Rte. 623. Confederate Brig.
Gen. J. E. B. Stuart with his 1,200 cavalrymen rode past this spot on the morning of
12 June 1862, heading west. On a mission
to gather intelligence about Union Maj.
Gen. George B. McClellan's Army of the
Potomac, Stuart hoped to deceive his foes
into thinking that he was joining Confederate Maj. Gen. Thomas J. "Stonewall"
Jackson in the Shenandoah Valley. His
true objective was northeastern Hanover
County, in the rear of the Union army,
about a dozen miles east of here. The
westward feint and the narrow, tree-lined
country roads, allowed Stuart to conceal
the true nature of his expedition.

E-120 STUART'S RIDE AROUND McCLELLAN BEGINS

Rte. 626, at CSX railway crossing. Here at El-
mont (known as Kilby's Station during the
Civil War), Confederate Brig. Gen. J. E. B.
Stuart assembled the last of his 1,200 cavalrymen and began his ride around Union
Maj. Gen. George B. McClellan's Army of
the Potomac on 12 June 1862. Confederate
Gen. Robert E. Lee had instructed Stuart
to gather intelligence, especially about

the location of the army's flanks, and to disrupt Federal supply and communication lines. The Southern cavalrymen rode about 80 miles in the next 72 hours. Less than two weeks later, Confederate Maj. Gen. Thomas J. "Stonewall" Jackson led his men down many of the same Hanover County roads, benefiting from the information Stuart had collected.

E-121 STUART'S RIDERS SKIRT ASHLAND

Rtes. 54 and 666, west of Ashland. On the afternoon of 12 June 1862, Confederate Brig. Gen. J. E. B. Stuart's column passed here on a mission to gather intelligence about Union Maj. Gen. George B. McClellan's Army of the Potomac. Riding northeast toward the Richmond, Fredericksburg, & Potomac Railroad and bypassing Ashland to avoid discovery, the expedition ended its first day without seeing any Federals. The next day, Stuart surprised Union cavalry near Hanover Court House and encountered the army's rear elements at Old Church and Tunstall's Station. Less than two weeks later, part of Confederate Maj. Gen. Thomas J. "Stonewall" Jackson's army camped here around Independence Church en route to the Seven Days' Battles.

E-122 STUART TURNS NORTH

Rtes. 623 and 666. Late in the morning of 12 June 1862, Confederate Brig. Gen. J. E. B. Stuart and 1,200 cavalrymen reached this intersection on a mission to gather intelligence about Union Maj. Gen. George B. McClellan's Army of the Potomac. Here Stuart's column turned sharply northeast, in the general direction of Ashland. Having put some distance between his force and the Federal army around Mechanicsville, Stuart could move directly toward the upper end of the county. He maneuvered along these roads with confidence, since many of the men in his command, who guided the expedition, were Hanover County natives.

EA-1 NORTH ANNA RIVER CAMPAIGN— 21–26 MAY 1864

Rte. 1, 0.65 miles south of Hanover/Caroline County line. Approaching Richmond from the north after the Wilderness Campaign, Lt. General U. S. Grant sought to cross the North Anna River and capture the critical rail center at Hanover Junction (Doswell). General R. E. Lee ordered the construction of a complex web of earthworks here to defend the river crossing and junction. The Union army probed the defenses and captured some of them but soon abandoned the effort and moved east toward Cold Harbor.

EA-4 ATTACK AT OX FORD— 24 MAY 1864

Rte. 684, 2.43 miles west of Rte. 1, at North Anna Battlefield Park. A half mile north, a brigade of Union infantry commanded by Brig. Gen. James H. Ledlie struck the center of Lee's army, which blocked Grant's approach to Richmond. Formidable earthworks hastily erected by Brig. Gen. William H. Mahone's division anchored the Confederate battle line at Ox Ford on the North Anna River. Although instructed to use "utmost caution," Ledlie, fortified with alcohol, ordered a charge. His men were bloodily repulsed and suffered more than 200 casualties, while Mahone lost about 50. On 27 May Grant withdrew toward Totopotomoy Creek.

I-10-a RANDOLPH-MACON COLLEGE

West Railroad Avenue, at England Street (Rte. 54), Ashland. Chartered in 1830 in Boydton, this institution is the oldest Methodist-affiliated college in continuous operation in the United States. It is named for statesmen John Randolph of Virginia and Nathaniel Macon of North Carolina. The college was moved to Ashland in 1868 due to post–Civil War financial difficulties. Chi Beta Phi, a national honorary science fraternity, was founded here in 1916. In the 1890s, the college's administration founded Randolph-Macon Academy (Front Royal) and Randolph-Macon Woman's College (Lynchburg). The Ashland campus was listed on the National Register of Historic Places and the Virginia Landmarks Register in 1979.

I-10-A RANDOLPH-MACON COLLEGE

Rte. 1 (Washington Highway), north of Rte. 54, at Ashland Hanover Shopping Center, Ashland. Three blocks west is Randolph-Macon College for men, oldest permanent Methodist college in America. Chartered in 1830 and named for John Randolph and Nathaniel Macon. Originally located at Boydton in Mecklenburg County, it was moved here in 1868.

I-10-b RANDOLPH-MACON COLLEGE

Rte. 54, Ashland. Chartered in 1830 in Boydton, this institution is the oldest Methodist-affiliated college in continuous operation in the United States. It is named for statesmen John Randolph of Virginia and Nathaniel Macon of North Carolina. The college was moved to Ashland in 1868 due to post-Civil War financial difficulties. Chi Beta Phi, a national honorary science fraternity, was founded here in 1916. In the 1890s, the college's administration founded Randolph-Macon Academy (Front Royal) and Randolph-Macon Woman's College (Lynchburg). The Ashland campus was listed on the National Register of Historic Places and the Virginia Landmarks Register in 1979.

ND-3 NEWMARKET

Rte. 615, 1.2 miles north of Rte. 606. Newmarket stood on the Little River near Verdon in northern Hanover County until 1987, when to preserve it Robert W. Cabaniss moved it to this site. The seat of the Doswell family for whom the town of Doswell was named, the house is the sole survivor of a large plantation complex that once included a gristmill, tanyard, and cotton factory. James Doswell, a Revolutionary War veteran, probably built Newmarket in the late eighteenth century.

ND-4 PATRICK HENRY'S BIRTHPLACE

Rte. 301/2, at Rte. 638, 8.9 miles south of Hanover. Seven miles east, at Studley, May 29, 1736, was born Patrick Henry, the orator of the Revolution.

ND-6 CLAY'S BIRTHPLACE

Rte. 301/2, at Route 654, 4.5 miles south of Hanover Courthouse. Three miles northwest is Clay Spring, where Henry Clay was born, April 12, 1777. He passed most of his early life in Richmond, removing to Kentucky in 1797. His career as a public man and as a peacemaker between North and South is an important part of American history.

ND-8 THE DEPOT AT BEAVER DAM

Rte. 739, Beaverdam. The first railroad depot at Beaver Dam was built ca. 1840 to serve the farmers of Hanover and Louisa counties. Its strategic location during the Civil War made it the target of many Union raids. The July 20, 1862, raid saw the depot burned and Colonel John S. Mosby, the Gray Ghost, captured as he awaited a train to take him to General Stonewall Jackson. Rebuilt after this raid, the depot was again burned by Union troops on February 29, 1864, and May 9, 1864, the last time by the cavalry of General George A. Custer. The existing depot was rebuilt and rededicated in 1866.

ND-9 CORNWALLIS'S ROUTE

Rte. 301 (Hanover Courthouse Road), 0.1 miles north of Rte. 605 (River Road), south of Hanover Courthouse. Lord Cornwallis, marching northward in pursuit of Lafayette's American force, camped near here, May 30, 1781. He entered this road from the east on his way from Hanover Town to the North Anna at Chesterfield Ford (Telegraph Bridge).

ND-11 LEE'S HEADQUARTERS

Rte. 301, 0.3 miles north of I-295. Just to the east stood the Clarke house (Lockwood), wherein Gen. Robert E. Lee made his field headquarters, 28–31 May 1864. While here, and though ill, Lee deployed troops to key positions in Hanover County, including Haw's Shop, Totopotomoy Creek, and Bethesda Church, and laid plans for his desperately outnumbered army to intercept Lt. Gen. Ulysses S. Grant's advance on Richmond. Lee telegraphed urgent appeals for reinforcements from nearby Atlee's Station on the Virginia Central Railroad. On 29 May President Jefferson Davis and Gen. P. G. T. Beauregard visited the stricken Lee here. Lee's planning culminated in the Battle of Cold Harbor, 31 May-12 June 1864, which stalled the Union offensive. The house was removed in 1990.

ND-12 JANIE PORTER BARRETT— (9 AUG. 1865–27 AUG. 1948)

Rte. 301, at Rtes. 651 and 657. Janie Porter Barrett was born in Athens, Ga. She graduated from Hampton Institute and soon began teaching home-management techniques to other young African American women and girls. In 1915, Barrett founded the Industrial School for Wayward Colored Girls nearby, the third reform school specifically for black girls in the United States. The school long survived its predecessors in Maryland and Missouri, and was also the first—and for several years the only—such state-supported school. Barrett used progressive, humane methods, operating on an honor system and forbidding corporal punishment. In 1950, the school was renamed the Janie Porter School for Girls.

ND-13 JOHN HENRY SMYTH— (14 JULY 1844–5 SEPT. 1908)

Rte. 301 (Hanover Courthouse Road), 0.2 miles south of Courtland Farm Road. Born in Richmond, Va., to a free black mother and enslaved father, John Henry Smyth graduated from Howard University Law School in Washington, D.C., in 1872 and worked variously as a teacher, bank cashier, lawyer, and newspaper editor. He served as minister resident and consul general to Liberia,

1878–1885. His most enduring legacy, however, is the Hanover Juvenile Correctional Center, founded by him in 1897 as the Virginia Manual Labor School, among the first in the United States especially for African American youths. Smyth required his charges to labor on the school's farm to develop a strong work ethic. The center's school is named for him.

O-6 SEVEN DAYS' BATTLES—BATTLE OF BEAVER DAM CREEK

Rte. 156, just east of Mechanicsville, at Bypass Rte. 360. The Civil War battle of Beaver Dam Creek (Mechanicsville) began on the afternoon of 26 June 1862. Confederate Maj. Gen. Ambrose P. Hill's division crossed the Chickahominy upstream at Meadow Bridges and encountered Union skirmishers. The Federals fell back to a strong position east of Beaver Dam Creek at Ellerson's Mill. There the Confederates attacked along a two-mile front, but were repulsed by Maj. Gen. Fitz John Porter's V Corps. That night Union forces abandoned their position and occupied a new defensive line behind Boatswain's Creek, where the Battle of Gaines's Mill took place the next day.

O-8 SHERIDAN'S RAID

Rte. 360, 0.2 miles northeast of Mechanicsville. Union Maj. Gen. Philip H. Sheridan from 9 to 14 May 1864 led three cavalry divisions on a raid around Richmond. His forces severed vital Confederate communication lines, destroyed railroad tracks, and captured stores and supplies. On 11 May Sheridan's troops defeated Confederate Maj. Gen. J. E. B. Stuart's cavalry forces at Yellow Tavern, and mortally wounded Stuart. The next day Sheridan's men fought Confederate forces while crossing the Chickahominy River at the Meadow Bridges, north of here. Once the Federals made it to the Hanover County side of the river, they passed by here to Mechanicsville and bivouacked at Gaines's Mill to the east.

O-9 SEVEN DAYS' BATTLES

Rte. 360, 0.2 miles northeast of Mechanicsville. Here the Confederates attacked the force holding McClellan's fortified position on the east bank of Beaver Dam Creek, June 26, 1862.

O-11 BATTLE OF COLD HARBOR

Rte. 360, 3.6 miles northeast of Mechanicsville. The left of Lee's line at Cold Harbor, June 3, 1864, crossed the road here. The main battle took place to the east, where Grant attacked Lee's trenches without success.

O-12 BATTLE OF BETHESDA CHURCH

Rte. 360, at Rte. 792, east of Mechanicsville. Here stood Bethesda Church, founded about 1830 and used by Baptists and Disciples of Christ until it burned in 1868. In May 1864, during the Civil War, Maj. Gen. Gouverneur K. Warren's V Corps formed the left flank of Lt. Gen. Ulysses S. Grant's Union line here, facing Gen. Robert E. Lee's army. On 30 May, Lt. Gen. Jubal A. Early's attack on Warren's position failed. Early attacked again on 2 June, but was beaten back by Maj. Gen. Ambrose E. Burnside's IX Corps. The next day Grant assaulted the center of Lee's line at Cold Harbor and was defeated with enormous losses.

O-13 CORNWALLIS'S ROUTE

Rte. 360, east of Mechanicsville. Gen. Charles Cornwallis and his British forces left Petersburg on 24 May 1781 to attack the Marquis de Lafayette and his troops stationed in Richmond. Learning of Cornwallis's movements, Lafayette abandoned the city on 27 May and moved north through Hanover County to the North Anna River. After bivouacking at White Oak Swamp on 27 May, Cornwallis pursued Lafayette through Hanover County until 1 June, when the British troops reached the North Anna River. There Cornwallis sent his forces west in a two-pronged attack to destroy colonial storehouses and attempt to capture the governor and the General Assembly in Charlottesville.

O-14 UNION ARMY'S CROSSING OF THE PAMUNKEY RIVER

Rte. 605 (River Road), 3.6 miles west of Rte. 360, 7.6 miles east of Rte. 301. On 26 May 1864, following the engagements along the North Anna River, Union Lt. Gen. Ulysses S. Grant ordered Maj. Gen. Philip H. Sheridan and two cavalry divisions to move southeastward to secure crossings on the Pamunkey River. The next morning Sheridan's troopers had occupied a position near Hanovertown. Engineers built pontoon bridges there and upriver at Nelson's Ferry, allowing the infantry to cross the river. By the end of 28 May Grant's four corps were south of the Pamunkey River and marching toward Richmond. Over the next several days Union and Confederate forces traded attacks along Totopotomoy Creek before the Second Battle of Cold Harbor began on 31 May.

O-15 HENRY'S CALL TO ARMS

Rte. 360, 11.8 miles northeast of Mechanicsville. One mile east on the river was Newcastle. There, on May 2, 1775, Patrick Henry put himself at the head of the Hanover volunteers and marched against the royal governor, Lord Dunmore, who had seized the colony's powder.

O-24 EDMUND RUFFIN'S GRAVE

Rte. 360, 8.9 miles northeast of Mechanicsville. Here at Marlbourne is the grave of Edmund Ruffin (1794–1865), one of the leading American agriculturists of the 19th century. He published and edited the *Farmer's Register*, an agricultural journal, for several years. In 1843, Ruffin moved to Marlbourne, where he performed many experiments to maintain the fertility of the soil using marl (a natural deposit of calcium carbonate) as fertilizer, resulting in increased crop yields. An ardent secessionist, he fired one of the first shots at Fort Sumter on 13 April 1861, and kept detailed journals documenting events during the Civil War. Despondent over the South's defeat, he committed suicide in June 1865.

O-58 STUDLEY

Rte. 615, at Rte. 606. The community of Studley takes its name from the birthplace of Patrick Henry (1736–1799), orator of the American Revolution and first state governor of Virginia. The Henry family resided at Studley until 1750. The house, which burned in 1807, was a two-story brick dwelling with several outbuildings. At the time of the Civil War, the area was called Haw's Shop for a local blacksmith, and a cavalry engagement was fought there on 28 May 1864. The community adopted the name Studley by 1888.

O-63 CAVALRY ACTION AT LINNEY'S

Southard Lane and Rte. 606. During Confederate Brig. Gen. J. E. B. Stuart's intelligence gathering "Ride Around McClellan," a skirmish ensued atop this hill on 13 June 1862 when several companies of the 9th Virginia Cavalry collided with the 5th United States Cavalry. Stuart's men carried the position and continued south into the rear of the Union army, but Capt. William Latané was killed in the brief, close-quarters fight. Latané, the only Confederate killed during the raid, is interred north of here at Summer Hill. William D. Washington memorialized the burial ceremony in his 1864 painting The Burial of Latané, which became a southern icon.

PA-2 SEVEN DAYS BATTLES— MECHANICSVILLE

Business Rte. 360, Mechanicsville. Mechanicsville was held by Union outposts when, in the early afternoon of June 26, 1862, A. P. Hill reached it coming from the north. The Unionists were quickly driven back to their position on Beaver Dam Creek. Then D. H. Hill, followed by Longstreet, crossed the Chickahominy on this road and joined A. P. Hill.

PA-4 SEVEN DAYS BATTLES— MECHANICSVILLE

Rte. 156, at Catlin Road, 0.8 miles southeast of Mechanicsville. Down this slope in the late afternoon of June 26, 1862, A. P. Hill moved to attack the Unionists holding the east side of Beaver Dam Creek. Pender's brigade was on the left, Ripley's on the right. Exposed to a terrible fire from entrenched troops, Pender and Ripley were driven back, though some men reached the stream.

PA-6 SEVEN DAYS BATTLES— MECHANICSVILLE

Rte. 156, 1.2 miles southeast of Mechanicsville. This ridge was occupied by Porter's Corps (facing west), which formed the right wing of McClellan's army, June 26, 1862. The strong position was strengthened by earthworks and by an abatis along the creek. When A. P. Hill attacked late in the afternoon, the Confederates were driven back with severe loss.

PA-8 SEVEN DAYS BATTLES—PORTER'S WITHDRAWAL

Rte. 156, at Brooking Way, 1.7 miles southeast of Mechanicsville. Along this road Fitz-John Porter withdrew from Beaver Dam Creek in the early morning of June 27, 1862. McClellan, having learned that Stonewall Jackson was approaching Porter's rear, late at night ordered the withdrawal to another position. This was on Boatswain Creek, not far from New Cold Harbor.

PA-9 SEVEN DAYS BATTLES—JACKSON'S MARCH TO THE BATTLEFIELD

Rte. 643, just south of Rte. 360. Confederate Gen. Thomas J. "Stonewall" Jackson and his troops passed through this intersection on 27 June 1862, having arrived from the Shenandoah Valley. Jackson's troops united with Gen. Robert E. Lee's forces just south of here at Walnut Grove Church that morning. Later in the day Lee's and Jackson's combined forces and successfully

[*should read:* combined forces successfully]
assaulted the Union V Corps at the Battle
of Gaines's Mill.

PA-10 SEVEN DAYS BATTLES—
GAINES'S MILL

*Rte. 156, across from Walnut Grove Baptist
Church, 2.7 miles southeast of Mechanicsville.*
Here Lee and Stonewall Jackson conferred
in the morning of June 27, 1862. Jackson's
troops halted here until A. P. Hill arrived
from Beaver Dam Creek. Hill then moved
southward by Gaines's Mill and Longstreet along a road near the river; Jackson
turned to the east. All three columns
approached the Union position on Boatswain Creek.

PA-12 SEVEN DAYS' BATTLES—
NEW BRIDGE

*Rte. 156, just east of Rte. 615, southeast of
Mechanicsville.* Leading up to and during
the Seven Days' Battles from 25 June to
1 July 1862, bridges and roads played an important role in the movement of the Union
and Confederate armies. New Bridge on
the Chickahominy River was 1.5 miles
south of here, and was one of the most
important of the many river crossings.
Union army troops marched through this
region to Mechanicsville on 24 May 1862.
Confederate Maj. Gens. James Longstreet's
and Ambrose P. Hill's divisions used the
New Bridge on 29 June 1862 as they moved
south toward Glendale where they fought
elements of Maj. Gen. George B. McClellan's Army of the Potomac the next day.

PA-16 SEVEN DAYS' BATTLES—
GAINES'S MILL

Rte. 156, 5 miles southeast of Mechanicsville.
This is the site of Gaines's Mill, which
gave its name to the battle of June 27,
1862. Here A. P. Hill's advance guard,
following Porter, came in contact with
the Union rear guard. After a short action
the Unionists withdrew to a position on
Boatswain Creek, closely pursued by the
Confederates.

PA-20 SEVEN DAYS' BATTLES—
GAINES'S MILL

*Rtes. 718 and 156, southeast of Mechanics-
ville.* Half a mile south is Boatswain Creek.
The battle that was begun at Gaines's
Mill by A. P. Hill, following Porter's rear
guard, culminated at the Union position
on Boatswain Creek. There A. P. Hill and
Longstreet, moving eastward, and Jackson
coming from the north converged to attack
Unionists.

PA-23 SEVEN DAYS' CAMPAIGN—
GAINES'S MILL

*Rte. 156, near Crown Hill and Rock Hill Roads,
southeast of Mechanicsville.* On 25 June
1862, Gen. Robert E. Lee led his Army
of Northern Virginia in the Seven Days'
Campaign to drive Maj. Gen. George B.
McClellan and his Army of the Potomac
from the gates of Richmond. By 27 June
the Union left flank rested atop Turkey Hill
near Gaines's Mill. At first Lee's piecemeal
assaults failed, as Maj. Gen. A. P. Hill led
his division down this slope and across
Boatswain Swamp, followed on the right by
Maj. Gen. James Longstreet. Finally, Maj.
Gen. Thomas J. "Stonewall" Jackson arrived
late in the afternoon; a coordinated attack
then swept the Federals from the hill.

PA-25 SEVEN DAYS' BATTLES—
GAINES'S MILL

*End of Rte. 718, 0.7 miles from Rte. 156, 6.5
miles southeast of Mechanicsville.* Along the
slopes of Boatswain Creek, facing north
and west, extended Porter's position in the
afternoon of June 27, 1862. The line was
held by Sykes's division facing north, and
Morell's facing west. Later McCall was
thrown in to assist Morell. At dark Lee
broke the Union line, and Porter retreated
across the Chickahominy.

PA-60 SEVEN DAYS BATTLES—
GAINES'S MILL

*Rte. 156, 7.8 miles southeast of Mechanics-
ville.* Stonewall Jackson reached this point

in the afternoon of June 27, 1862, after a circuit of Gaines's Mill. When he learned that A. P. Hill and Longstreet to the west were hard pressed, he moved south to join in the attack.

PA-70 SEVEN DAYS BATTLES— GAINES'S MILL

Rte. 156, 8.2 miles southeast of Mechanicsville. The hill to the south, part of the Union line, was assailed by Stonewall Jackson (with D. H. Hill) in the late afternoon of June 27, 1862, after A. P. Hill's and Longstreet's first assaults on the west had failed. Jackson's men carried the Union position at the bayonet's point, while A. P. Hill and Longstreet were also successful.

PA-80 SEVEN DAYS' BATTLES— GAINES'S MILL

Rte. 156, 8.5 miles southeast of Mechanicsville. On this hill, facing north, Sykes's division was posted in the afternoon of June 27, 1862, holding the eastern end of the Union line. Here Jackson attacked, while to the west A. P. Hill and Longstreet renewed

their assaults. When the Union line was broken on their left, Sykes's regulars fell back to the river still fighting.

W-214 SCOTCHTOWN

Rte. 54, 8 miles northwest of Ashland. A mile north is Scotchtown, Patrick Henry's home, 1771–1777. Dolly Madison, President James Madison's wife, lived here in her girlhood. Lafayette was here in May, 1781, retreating northward before Cornwallis. Cornwallis passed here in June, 1781, moving westward.

WASHINGTON-ROCHAMBEAU ROUTE

Rte. 301, Hanover Courthouse. General Washington and General Rochambeau passed here on Sept. 13, 1781 on their way to victory at Yorktown. One mile south, they turned east on State Route 605. *Note:* This is one of five unnumbered signs discussing aspects of the Washington-Rochambeau Route, which were a special gift from the French Government, Committee of the Bicentennial, to the Commonwealth of Virginia in 1976.

HENRICO COUNTY

E-3 SHERIDAN MANEUVERS EAST

Rte. 1 (Brook Road), 0.1 miles north of Azalea Avenue. In 1864, Brook Road provided the most direct avenue of approach from the north for Union cavalry raids on Richmond. After defeating Maj. Gen. J. E. B. Stuart's Confederate cavalry at Yellow Tavern, four miles north of here, on 11 May 1864, Union cavalry under Maj. Gen. Philip H. Sheridan penetrated Richmond's outer defensive line on the heights above Brook Run, a half mile north. Advancing southward on Brook Road, Sheridan's force encountered Richmond's inner defensive line, near present-day Union Theological Seminary. There he met strong resistance from a combined force of regular infantry and local defense troops. On the morning of 12 May, Sheridan moved his force to the

northeast and retired across the Chickahominy River.

E-4 BROOK ROAD

Rte. 1 (Brook Road), 0.7 miles north of Richmond. According to tradition, the Marquis de Lafayette marched his colonial troops from the north into Richmond on portions of present-day Brook Road late in April 1781. Established in 1812, the Brook Turnpike Company constructed a turnpike along this route from Richmond to Dabney Williamson's tavern in the vicinity of present-day Solomons Store in Henrico County. It was one of the earliest toll roads in Virginia and it improved the transport of goods between Richmond and the northern region of Virginia. Over time portions of Brook Road, now a part of

U.S. Route 1, have shifted to its current local and configuration.

E-6 OUTER FORTIFICATIONS

Rte. 1 (Brook Road), 0.7 miles north of Richmond. Here, east and west, ran the outer line of Richmond defenses, 1862–65. At this point Sheridan's cavalry, raiding to Richmond, broke through the line on May 11, 1864, after the fight at Yellow Tavern.

E-7 YELLOW TAVERN

Rte. 1, at Mountain Road, 2.5 miles north of Richmond. Just south of here on Brook Road (present-day U.S. Route 1) is the site of Yellow Tavern. North of the tavern, on 11 May 1864, Maj. Gen. J. E. B. Stuart deployed his Confederate cavalry to confront Maj. Gen. Philip Sheridan's Union cavalry as it advanced on Richmond. It was during this engagement that Stuart was mortally wounded. Because of the proximity of the engagement to the tavern, it was officially called the Battle of Yellow Tavern.

E-9 STUART'S MORTAL WOUND

Rte. 1, just north of I-295 bridge. One half mile to the east, on the old Telegraph Road, is a monument marking the field where General J. E. B. Stuart was mortally wounded on May 11, 1864. The monument was erected by veterans of Stuart's cavalry in 1888.

E-9 STUART'S MORTAL WOUND

Rte. 1, just north of I-295 bridge. Late in the afternoon of 11 May 1864, Maj. Gen. J. E. B. Stuart, the famous Confederate cavalry commander, was mortally wounded just east of here on Old Telegraph Road while rallying the left of his line during the Battle of Yellow Tavern. As three Michigan regiments of Brig. Gen. George Armstrong Custer's brigade fell back after an unsuccessful frontal charge, Pvt. John A. Huff, 5th Michigan Cavalry, fired the shot that struck Stuart in the abdomen. Maj.

Gen. Fitzhugh Lee assumed command of Stuart's forces, as Stuart was carried by ambulance to Richmond. There, in the home of his brother-in-law, Dr. Charles Brewer, Stuart died on the evening of 12 May.

E-10 GLEN ALLEN

Mountain Road, just west of railroad tracks, Glen Allen. Called Mountain Road Crossing when rail service began in 1836, the settlement which came to be known as Glen Allen took its name from the homestead of a local landowner, Mrs. Benjamin Allen. Its most noted resident was Captain John Cussons, a native Englishman, Confederate scout, author, and entrepreneur. Cussons made his residence here after the Civil War and founded a successful printing company. Later he built a fashionable resort hotel known as Forest Lodge adjacent to the railroad tracks.

E-51 BATTLE OF YELLOW TAVERN

Rte. 1, just north of I-295 bridge. On 11 May 1864, Confederate cavalry commanded by Maj. Gen. J. E. B. Stuart chose ground just east of here to engage Union cavalry under Maj. Gen. Philip H. Sheridan, who was advancing on Richmond by way of Mountain Road. Outnumbered three to one, Stuart's troopers stubbornly resisted until vigorous attacks spearheaded by Brig. Gen. George Armstrong Custer's Michigan brigade broke their line. As the Confederate cavalry retired east toward Telegraph Road, Sheridan's men broke through and continued toward Richmond on Brook Road (present-day U.S. Route 1). The battle received its name from Yellow Tavern, an inn located on Brook Road just south of the battlefield.

E-102 GABRIEL'S REBELLION

Rte. 1 (Brook Road), south of Hilliard Road, 0.5 miles north of Richmond city limits. Gabriel, a slave of Thomas Prosser of nearby Brookfield plantation, planned a slave insurrection against Richmond on 30 Aug. 1800. The slaves intended to kidnap

Governor James Monroe and compel him to support political, social, and economic equality but intense rains delayed the insurgents' scheme. Mosby Sheppard, of Meadow Farm, informed of the plot by family slaves Tom and Pharaoh, dispatched a warning letter to the governor. Monroe called out the militia and Gabriel, his plans foiled, fled to Norfolk. Authorities there captured and returned him to Richmond. Convicted of conspiracy, Gabriel was hanged on 10 Oct. 1800, the last of twenty-six conspirators executed.

E-103 YOUNG'S SPRING

Lakeside Avenue, at Park Street, 0.3 miles north of Richmond city limits. Just one block southwest at Young's Spring on Upham Brook, slaves often congregated on weekends to hold religious services and social gatherings. This is where Gabriel, a slave of William Prosser, planned the slave rebellion scheduled for 30 August 1800. Gabriel and his followers plotted to capture Richmond and to demand their freedom. The attack never took place because a turbulent thunderstorm made roads and bridges to the city impassable. Governor James Monroe, learning of the plot, mustered the militia. Eventually, most of the conspirators were captured and twenty-six slaves were executed.

E-104 EMMANUEL CHURCH AT BROOK HILL EPISCOPAL

Rte. 1 (Brook Road) and Wilmer Avenue. Built directly west by John Stewart of Brook Hill and consecrated by the Right Reverend John Johns on 6 July 1860, Emmanuel Church (Episcopal) is a classic example of late-antebellum Gothic Revival architecture. Considerable military activity took place nearby during the Civil War, when troops from both sides occupied the church. Wounded soldiers were treated there, and many Confederate soldiers lie buried in the cemetery. The Right Reverend Richard Hooker Wilmer, second bishop of Alabama and the only bishop or-dained by the Protestant Episcopal Church in the Confederate States of America, was Emmanuel Church's first rector.

E-108 SAINT JOSEPH'S VILLA

Rte. 1 (8000 Brook Road), south of Parham Road. Saint Joseph's Villa, founded 25 Nov. 1834 and incorporated 3 Oct. 1868, is one of the oldest-operating children's institutions in the United States. For 143 years administered by the Catholic Daughters of Charity as an orphanage and girls' school, it first was located at 4th and Marshall Streets in downtown Richmond. Boys were first admitted in 1919. Railroad magnate Maj. James H. Dooley endowed Saint Joseph's in 1922. The current campus opened in a new facility in 1931 as the first cottage-plan orphanage in the East. The Daughters of Charity withdrew in 1977 and the Villa's mission changed from an orphanage to multiprogram nonsectarian agency.

E-114 OLD DOMINION BUILDING

Laburnum Avenue, at Richmond International Raceway. William Lawrence Bottomley (1883–1951), the well-known architect who planned a number of sophisticated Colonial Revival houses for wealthy Richmond-area clients, also designed this large utilitarian structure. In 1946, Atlantic Rural Exposition, Inc., had it built for the State Fair of Virginia for approximately $116,000 on property then known as Strawberry Hill. The building features a two-story oval exhibition space capped by a hipped roof with twin cupolas, and has been referred to as a cattle barn, shed, covered ring, and Main Exhibit Building. It became a part of the Richmond Raceway Complex in 1999.

EA-1 MEADOW FARM

3400 Mountain Road, at Courtney Road, at entrance to Crump Park. The land comprising Meadow Farm was first patented by William Sheppard in 1713. In 1800, Sheppard family slaves thwarted plans for a well-organized slave uprising known as Gabriel's Insurrection. The farmhouse was built in 1810. Dr. John Mosby Sheppard practiced medicine at Meadow Farm between 1840 and 1877. The last private owner of Meadow Farm, Major General Sheppard Crump, was a founding member of the American Legion and Adjutant General of Virginia from 1956–1960. Until 1960, the Sheppard family farmed the land, growing a variety of grains and tobacco.

EA-2 WALKERTON

Mountain Road, 1.15 miles east of Courtney Road, Glen Allen. Constructed in 1825 for John Walker on Mountain Road, once a major route between Richmond and the western Piedmont of Virginia, Walkerton served as a tavern in 1828 and 1829. Since that time it has been a hotel, store, voting precinct, and private dwelling. It is the largest brick 19th-century tavern still standing in Henrico County. Walkerton is notable for a hinged, swinging, two-segment partition that was used to enlarge an upstairs room to accommodate guests. Members of the Hopkins family lived at Walkerton from 1857 to 1941 and a family cemetery exists here. The building was restored in 1986 and Henrico County purchased it in 1995.

EA-3 LAUREL HISTORIC DISTRICT

Hungary Road, at Old Staples Mill Road. Laurel, first named Hungary Station, was the location of a spur railroad line to the coal fields in western Henrico County. During the Civil War the station here was burned, and Colonel Ulrich Dahlgren's body was secretly buried here in March 1864 and later reinterred in Philadelphia. Nearby stood the first public school in Henrico County. In 1890 the Laurel Industrial School for Boys was established here as an alternative to imprisonment. Several nearby buildings served the institution, later called the Virginia Industrial School; during 1920–1922 the school was moved to Beaumont in Powhatan County.

EA-5 MOUNTAIN ROAD

3024 Mountain Road, across from post office, Glen Allen. Mountain Road was originally an Indian trail. It became the main thoroughfare from Richmond to Charlottesville in the 1700s. During the American Revolution, the Marquis de Lafayette traveled this road on his march to Yorktown. Thomas Jefferson used it on his trips to Richmond and Williamsburg. During the Civil War, on 11 May 1864, Maj. Gen. Philip H. Sheridan encountered Confederate skirmishers as his men destroyed the Richmond, Fredericksburg, and Potomac Railroad tracks here at Glen Allen. Sheridan and Brig. Gen. George A. Custer then rode south into the Battle of Yellow Tavern.

EA-6 WICKHAM'S LINE

Virginia Center Parkway, 0.4 miles west of Rte. 1, at Holliman Drive. In the first phase of the Battle of Yellow Tavern on 11 May 1864, Brig. Gen. Williams C. Wickham and his Confederate cavalry were posted just south of this location below Old Francis Road. Wickham's men fired on Brig. Gen. George A. Custer's Union troopers as they charged Brig. Gen. Lunsford L. Lomax's line on the Federal left flank, preventing Custer's advance. Maj. Gen. Philip H. Sheridan, the Federal commander, then sent Col. George H. Chapman's regiment to attack Wickham's line. This freed Custer to continue up Telegraph Road, where one of his men mortally wounded Maj. Gen. J. E. B. Stuart later that day.

O-5 OUTER FORTIFICATIONS

Rte. 360, 1.4 miles southwest of Mechanicsville. On the hilltops here ran the outer line of Richmond fortifications, 1862–1865.

PA-105 SEVEN DAYS BATTLES— GRAPE VINE BRIDGE

Rte. 156, near Grapevine Road, 11.1 miles south of Mechanicsville, 0.5 miles south of Henrico/Hanover County line. Here Sumner crossed the river to reinforce the part of

McClellan's army fighting at Fair Oaks, May 31, 1862. Here a part of Porter's force crossed in the night of June 27, 1862 after the battle of Gaines's Mill. Here Stonewall Jackson, rebuilding the bridges destroyed by the retreating Unionists, crossed in pursuit, June 29.

PA-125 SEVEN DAYS BATTLES— GOLDING'S FARM

Rte. 156, 12.8 miles south of Mechanicsville. Half a mile northwest occurred the action of Golding's Farm at dusk on June 27, 1862, as the battle of Gaines's Mill, on the other side of the river, was ending. The Confederates, sallying from their defenses, attacked Hancock's brigade holding the right of the Union line south of the river. A severe fight followed that was ended by darkness.

PA-138 HIGHLAND SPRINGS

Rte. 33 (Nine Mile Road), 0.5 miles west of Rte. 156 (North Airport Drive). One of Richmond's earliest streetcar suburbs, Highland Springs was founded in 1890 by Edmund Sewell Read, a wealthy real estate developer from Winthrop, Mass. He named the community for the relatively high altitude and natural springs that suited his ailing wife. Read subdivided 1,000 acres into lots and named the streets alphabetically after his favorite flora, such as Daisy, Elm, and Fern. The Seven Pines Railway Company, chartered in 1888, operated from Church Hill in Richmond east to Seven Pines National Cemetery. One of the stops was located nearby on Oak Avenue.

PA-140 SEVEN DAYS BATTLES— ALLEN'S FARM

Rte. 60/33/156 (Williamsburg Road), east of Whiteside Road, east of Seven Pines. On 26 June 1862, Maj. Gen. George B. McClellan abandoned his plan to besiege Richmond and began his retreat to the James River. Gen. Robert E. Lee pursued, determined to destroy the Army of the Potomac. Just north of here at Allen's Farm, at 9:00 A.M. on 29 June, Maj. Gen. John B.

Magruder's division attacked Brig. Gen. Edwin V. Sumner's corps, which formed the Union rear. The fighting continued for two hours until Sumner retired east to the Federal supply depot at Savage's Station on the Richmond & York River R.R. Another Confederate attack that afternoon ended in a stalemate, and the Union withdrawal continued.

PA-142 SEVEN DAYS BATTLES— SAVAGE'S STATION

Meadow Road, 0.1 miles east of Grapevine Road. Here Magruder's line of battle, facing east, formed in the late afternoon of June 29, 1862. Barksdale's, Semmes's and Kershaw's brigades, extending from south of this road to the railroad, made a desperate effort to prevent the Union withdrawal. After a fierce struggle the Confederates fell back. In this battle they made the first known use of railway artillery.

PA-144 SEVEN DAYS BATTLES— SAVAGE'S STATION

Meadow Road, 0.1 miles east of Grapevine Road. Here, facing west, stretched the Union line in the afternoon of June 29, 1862. Brook's brigade was south of the road with Gorman's and Burn's brigades to the north. In a furious conflict Burn's line was broken but was restored by Sumner in person. Darkness ended the conflict. The Unionists withdrew southward.

PA-148 SEVEN DAYS BATTLES— WHITE OAK SWAMP

Rte. 156, 6.7 miles southeast of Seven Pines. In the hill just to the west Stonewall Jackson placed his artillery about midday on June 30, 1862. An artillery duel then began with Franklin, guarding the south side of White Oak Swamp, that lasted until dark.

PA-152 SEVEN DAYS BATTLES— WHITE OAK SWAMP

Rte. 156, 7.1 miles south of Seven Pines. Here the greater part of McClellan's army and wagon trains crossed the swamp, June

28–30, 1862. Jackson, pursuing, arrived about noon on June 30, to find the bridge destroyed and the Unionists holding the south side. Failing to force a passage that day, Jackson rebuilt the bridge and crossed early on July 1.

PA-153 SECOND BATTLE OF DEEP BOTTOM

Darbytown Road and Fussell's Ridge Drive, 0.3 miles east of Yahley Mill Road. About noon on 16 Aug. 1864, Union Brig. Gen. Alfred H. Terry, with almost 5,000 men in four brigades, attacked the Confederate line over this ground. In a brief yet vicious struggle, Terry's men broke through 400 yards west of here. During the melee, Brig. Gen. Victor J. B. Girardey, leading a Georgia brigade, was shot down; Brig. Gen. John R. Chambliss, a Virginian, was also killed that day. Later in the afternoon, the tide turned when Maj. Gen. Charles W. Field orchestrated a bloody counterattack that forced the Federals to retreat and entrench north of Fussell's Mill Pond on this ridge.

PA-155 SEVEN DAYS BATTLES— WHITE OAK SWAMP

Rte. 156 (Elko Road), south of White Oak Swamp Creek bridge, 0.2 miles north of Hines Road, 7.7 miles south of Seven Pines. Here Franklin, aided by Richardson, held the passage of White Oak Swamp against Jackson while the battle of Glendale raged near by, June 30, 1862. A fierce duel went on all afternoon between the Union batteries here and Jackson's guns on the north side of the swamp.

PA-159 GLENDALE (FRAYSER'S FARM)

Rte. 156, at Charles City and Willis Church Roads, 10.2 miles south of Seven Pines. In this vicinity, the Union Army of the Potomac made a stand on 30 June 1862, during its retreat from the Chickahominy River to-ward the James River. Maj. Gen. George B. McClellan posted several Union divisions facing east and north to protect this inter-section, known locally as Riddell's Shop. In the ensuing battle, Confederate divisions commanded by Major Generals James Long-street and A. P. Hill attacked the Union divisions of Brig. Gen. George A. McCall and Maj. Gen. Philip Kearney. The action became hand-to-hand, the two sides fight-ing with bayonets while they struggled for possession of the Union artillery stationed nearby. Late in the battle, McCall was captured near here by soldiers of the 47th Virginia Infantry. The Union line held, enabling McClellan to continue his retreat.

PA-163 SEVEN DAYS BATTLES— GLENDALE (FRAYSER'S FARM)

Darbytown Road, east of Long Bridge Road, 10.5 miles south of Seven Pines. Here stood the center of Longstreet's line of battle in the afternoon of June 30, 1862. The Con-federates, coming from the west, attacked the Union line just beyond. The battle lasted all afternoon, with varying fortunes and much hand-to-hand fighting. Near nightfall Longstreet sent in A. P. Hill to relieve his exhausted men.

PA-175 SEVEN DAYS BATTLES— GLENDALE (FRAYSER'S FARM)

Rte. 156, 10 miles south of Seven Pines. Willis Church Road runs from here to Malvern Hill. A large part of Union Gen. George B. McClellan's Army of the Potomac followed this road south toward the James River, four miles ahead, near the end of the Seven Days' Battles in 1862. On 30 June, at the Battle of Glendale/Frayser's Farm, seven Union infantry divisions stretched across a wide arc north and west of here to keep this road open. Although Confederate infantrymen pushed to within sight of the critical road, they could not sever it. The Union army retreated on this and parallel roads to Malvern Hill during the night.

PA-180 SEVEN DAYS BATTLES— MALVERN HILL

Rte. 156, 10.6 miles south of Seven Pines. Here Lee met Longstreet and Jackson in the morning of July 1, 1862. D. H. Hill reported the strength of the Union position on Malvern Hill; but Lee, having cause to believe the Unionists were weakening, prepared to attack. Jackson and D. H. Hill moved on this road southward to Malvern Hill.

PA-190 SEVEN DAYS BATTLES— GLENDALE (FRAYSER'S FARM)

Rte. 156, 11.1 miles south of Seven Pines. This was the extreme left of the Union line at Glendale, and was held by Hooker's division. When McCall (just to the north) was broken, Hooker, supported by Burns's brigade, drove the Confederates back. In the night the Union army moved southward.

PA-195 SEVEN DAYS BATTLES— MALVERN HILL

Rte. 156, 12.3 miles south of Seven Pines. Across the road here stretched the Confederate line of battle, facing south, in the afternoon of July 1, 1862. Jackson commanded here, Magruder to the west. Longstreet and A. P. Hill were in reserve. The battle lasted intermittently, from morning to night, reaching its crisis late in the afternoon. The disjointed Confederate attacks were repulsed with heavy loss.

PA-220 SEVEN DAYS BATTLES— MALVERN HILL

Rte. 156, 12.5 miles south of Seven Pines. Here from east to west, Berdan's sharpshooters of Morell's division were strung out in the afternoon of July 1, 1862. Their rapid and accurate fire harassed the Confederates as they emerged from the woods and charged up the hill.

PA-230 SEVEN DAYS BATTLES— MALVERN HILL

Rte. 156, 12.6 miles south of Seven Pines. Across the hill here from east to west the Union artillery was in position in the afternoon of July 1, 1862. The Union batteries overpowered the few cannon the Confed-erates were able to bring up. When the Southern infantry charged from the woods, they were met by a terrible artillery fire but continued to advance until they came under the fire of the Union infantry.

PA-235 SEVEN DAYS BATTLES— MALVERN HILL

Rte. 156, 12.7 miles south of Seven Pines. Across the road here stretched the Union line of battle in the afternoon of July 1, 1862. Couch's, Kearney's and Hooker's divisions were to the east of the road, Morell to the west, with Sykes in reserve. The Confederates made several attacks and, for a time, the battle trembled in the balance; but the assailants were finally repulsed. In the night the Union army withdrew to James River.

PA-240 ENGAGEMENT AT MALVERN CLIFFS

Rte. 5, 2 miles west of Willis Church Road. On 30 June 1862, as Gen. Robert E. Lee concentrated his troops to attack Maj. Gen. George B. McClellan's retreating Union army at Glendale, Maj. Gen. Theophilus H. Holmes's brigade of Confederate troops moved down New Market Road on Lee's right. Union forces on Malvern Hill noticed dust rising above the trees and suspected the movement of the Confederates on New Market Road. As he advanced, Holmes observed the Union troops atop Malvern Hill to the east and deployed his artillery and infantry. When the Confederate artillery opened fire, the massed Union artillery on the hill concentrated its firepower on Holmes's small force. Union gunboats joined in, and Holmes withdrew his force west to the junction of the Long Bridge Road. The Battle of Malvern Hill took place the next day.

PA-251 SAD REUNION

Charles City Road, west of Yahley Mill Road, 0.9 miles east of Turner Road. On 16 August 1864 Confederate Brig. Gen. John R. Chambliss, Jr., was killed near here attempting to evade capture during the Second Battle of Deep Bottom. As troops of the 16th Pennsylvania Cavalry removed his epaulets, sash, and saber, Union Brig. Gen. David M. Gregg rode by and recognized Chambliss, his schoolmate at West Point in the early 1850s. He took charge of the body and sent it through the lines to Chambliss's widow in Hicksford (now Emporia). By his actions, Gregg adhered to the spirit of the West Point hymn, to "grip hands though it be from the shadows."

SA-31 DAHLGREN'S RAID

Horsepen Road, between Three Chopt Road and Patterson Avenue. Col. Ulric Dahlgren's Union cavalry passed through this area late in the evening of 1 March 1864 before defeating the Richmond Armory Battalion at the Battle of Green's Farm, just south on Three Chopt Road. Dahlgren led his command toward Richmond on the Westham Plank Road (now Cary Street Road) for about half a mile. At Hicks's Farm, five miles from Capitol Square, about 420 of his cavalrymen encountered the local defense troops of the Departmental Battalion and the remnants of the Armory Battalion. After a brief skirmish in the darkness during a rain, snow, and sleet storm, Dahlgren retreated and tried to rejoin Brig. Gen. H. Judson Kilpatrick's force on Brook Road. Dahlgren was killed in King and Queen County the next day.

SA-45 VIRGINIA HOME FOR BOYS

8716 West Broad Street (Rte. 250), north of Parham Road, 4.6 miles west of Richmond city limits. The Virginia Home for Boys is the oldest boys' home in continuous service in Virginia and the second oldest in the United States. Founded as the Richmond Male Orphan Society on 30 March 1846 for the "maintenance and instruction" of orphaned boys, it was incorporated by the General Assembly on 9 March 1847. At first located on Church Hill, it moved twice before relocating to this site in 1957. Its name was changed to the Richmond

Home for Boys on 23 June 1969 and to the Virginia Home for Boys on 27 January 1971. Since its founding, the home has served more than 15,000 children ages six and above.

V-1 WILTON

Rte. 5, at Herman Street and New Market Road intersection, 2 miles southeast of Richmond. Five miles southwest. The house was built by William Randolph, son of William Randolph of Turkey Island, early in the eighteenth century. It was Lafayette's headquarters, May 15–20, 1781, just before Cornwallis crossed the James in pursuit of him.

V-2 FORT HARRISON

Rte. 5, 4.5 miles southeast of Richmond. Fort Harrison served as one of the principal works in Richmond's defenses during the Civil War. On 29 Sept. 1864, Maj. Gen. Benjamin F. Butler's Army of the James launched a two-pronged attack against Richmond's defenses as Lt. Gen. Ulysses S. Grant had ordered. While African American regiments assaulted Confederate positions below New Market Heights to the east, Maj. Gen. Edward O. C. Ord led part of XVIII Corps against Fort Harrison, located south of here. Captured after heavy resistance, the fort then became a Union stronghold. The next day, Confederate Gen. Robert E. Lee personally supervised several fierce counterattacks to regain the position, but the Federals held on.

V-3 CURLES NECK AND BREMO

Rte. 5, at Curles Neck Farm, 9.3 miles southeast of Richmond. Curles Neck may take its name from the curls of the river or a family of that name. Richard Cocke, the Immigrant, patented land along the James River on the eastern side of the neck in 1636. There he built Bremo, the seat of the Cocke family for six generations. A descendant, John Hartwell Cock, relocated the family seat to Upper Bremo, in Fluvanna County, early in the 19th century. In 1674 Nathaniel

Bacon, Jr., the Rebel, settled on Curles Neck. In 1676 Bacon led a rebellion against the royal governor, Sir William Berkeley. With the failure of Bacon's Rebellion, some of his land was seized by the Crown to defray the costs of suppressing the rebellion. William Randolph purchased 480 acres of Bacon's land on Curles Neck in 1700.

V-4 MALVERN HILL

Rte. 5, 13.3 miles southeast of Richmond. Nearby stood the Malvern Hill manor house built for Thomas Cocke in the 17th century. The Marquis de Lafayette camped here in July–August 1781, and elements of the Virginia militia encamped nearby during the War of 1812. During the Civil War, 1 July 1862, Gen. Robert E. Lee attacked Maj. Gen. George B. McClellan's Union Army of the Potomac here as it retreated to the James River from the gates of Richmond. Although he dealt Lee a bloody defeat, McClellan continued his withdrawal to Harrison's Landing. The Malvern Hill house survived the battle as a Federal headquarters but burned in 1905.

V-5 TURKEY ISLAND

Rte. 5, 12.3 miles southeast of Richmond. Soon after landing at Jamestown in May 1607, Captain Christopher Newport, while exploring the James River discovered Turkey Island (two miles south). He named it for the large number of wild turkeys there. In 1684, William Randolph purchased Turkey Island; it then became the seat of the Randolph family. His descendants included Thomas Jefferson, John Marshall, and Robert E. Lee. Robert Pickett acquired Turkey Island in 1836. During the Civil War, the large family dwelling was burned by Union troops. Maj. Gen. George E. Pickett and his family lived there in a small cottage after the war.

V-16 CAMPAIGN OF 1781

Rte. 1 (Brook Road), 0.7 miles north of Richmond. The roads through Henrico County were important routes for the Revolutionary War campaign of 1781. To avoid British Gen. Charles Cornwallis's troops advancing from Petersburg, the Marquis de Lafayette left Richmond by 27 May and marched northward through Henrico. Cornwallis bivouacked at White Oak Swamp on the 27th, before continuing the pursuit of Lafayette. In mid June, Cornwallis joined Lt. Gen. Banastre Tarleton near Richmond, where they occupied the city by 16 June. The British troops left the city for Williamsburg on the 20th marching east through Henrico County. Lafayette advanced through Henrico County on 22 June in pursuit of Cornwallis.

V-17 OUTER DEFENSES

Rte. 250, 0.1 miles east of I-64, 1.9 miles west of Richmond city limits. By 1864, a complex series of fortifications north of Richmond and the James River protected the capital of the Confederacy. The outer line of western defenses crossed the road (then called the Deep Run Turnpike) here. The intermediate defensive line stood about three miles southeast and the inner line a mile farther, well within the present-day limits of Richmond. On 1 March 1864, Union Col. Ulric Dahlgren briefly penetrated the outer line to the southwest on Three Chopt Road during his abortive cavalry raid on the city. Dahlgren's force was repulsed at the intermediate line.

V-25 FIRST SUCCESSFUL COLONIAL TOBACCO CROP

Rte. 5, 5 miles east of Richmond. In 1611 John Rolfe became the first Englishman to cultivate tobacco nearby at Varina Farm, on the James River. Rolfe planted seeds bred in Varinas, Spain, and experimented with curing methods to produce a tobacco milder than the native variety. The success of tobacco as a cash crop encouraged the Virginia Company of London and renewed the spirit of confidence among the colonists. It supported a wealthy planter class and enriched shippers and merchants. Tobacco thereby contributed to the economic security and survival of the Virginia colony, and thus the nation.

V-26 BATTLE OF NEW MARKET HEIGHTS

Rte. 5, near I-295, 8.5 miles east of Richmond. On 28 September 1864, elements of Maj. Gen. Benjamin F. Butler's Army of the James crossed the James River to assault the Confederate defenses of Richmond. At dawn on 29 September, 6 regiments of U.S. Colored Troops fought with exceptional valor during their attack along New Market Road. Despite heavy casualties, they carried the earthworks there and succeeded in capturing New Market Heights, north of the road. Of the 20 Medals of Honor awarded to "Negro" soldiers and sailors during the Civil War, 14 were bestowed for this battle. Butler wrote that "the capacity of the negro race for soldiers had then and there been fully settled forever."

V-28 POCAHONTAS

Rte. 5, just east of I-295. Matoaka, nicknamed Pocahontas ("playful one"), the daughter of Powhatan, was born about 1595. At age eleven, she befriended Captain John Smith and later visited the English colonists. In 1613, Samuel Argall kidnapped Pocahontas to use her as a negotiating pawn. According to tradition, she was brought to Henrico Town and cared for by the Rev. Alexander Whitaker. She was baptized and renamed Rebecca, and on 5 April 1614, she married John Rolfe. In 1616, Rolfe and their son, Thomas, accompanied her to England, where King James I and Queen Anne received her. Preparing to return home, she died at Gravesend, England, in March 1617.

V-29 HENRICO TOWN

Rte. 5, 0.3 miles east of I-295. In 1611, Sir Thomas Dale established the second English settlement in Virginia, called Henrico in honor of Henry Frederick, Prince of Wales, son of King James I. The town was located four miles southwest on a peninsula of high land on the James River. A ditch was constructed across the neck of land and a fence surrounded the town. "Henricus Citie" contained "three streets of well-framed houses, a handsome church, store houses, a hospital, and watchtowers." After the Anglo-Powhatan War began in 1622 the town was abandoned. Remaining traces of the land associated with the town comprise Henricus Park in Chesterfield County.

V-30 PROPOSED FIRST UNIVERSITY IN ENGLISH AMERICA

Rte. 5, just east of I-295. A "University and College" was authorized by the Virginia Company charter of 1618 at Henrico Town but never opened. Some 10,000 acres on the James River upstream from the town were to provide agricultural income for the school. The college's mission was to Christianize Indian children and train them in "true Religion moral virtue and Civility." The Anglo-Powhatan War that began in 1622, the revocation of the Virginia Company's charter in 1624, and the lack of royal support for the project delayed the plans for Virginia's first college until 1693 when the College of William and Mary was established.

V-31 JOHN ROLFE—1585–1622

Messer Road, 0.8 miles north of Rte. 5. John Rolfe emigrated from England to Virginia in 1610 and settled in what was to become Henrico County. In 1612 he imported tobacco seeds from Trinidad and cultivated a new strain of mild tobacco. He shipped part of his harvest to England in 1614, and by 1619 tobacco had become Virginia's major money crop. In 1614 Rolfe married Pocahontas, a daughter of Chief Powhatan, and they had one son, Thomas. Rolfe and his family sailed in 1616 to England where Pocahontas died in 1617. Rolfe returned to Virginia, where he died in 1622.

V-32 NATHANIEL BACON

Rte. 5, near Curles Neck Farm, 3.3 miles east of I-295. Bacon was born in 1647 in Suffolk,

England, and was educated at Cambridge University. He came to Virginia in 1673 and settled near here on the north bank of the James River at Curles Neck. In 1676 Bacon led a force of citizen-soldiers against Indians on Virginia's frontier, contrary to the policy of Governor William Berkeley. After Bacon defeated several tribes, he and his followers, branded rebels by Berkeley, captured and burned Jamestown. Bacon's rebellion collapsed after Bacon died of a fever in October 1676.

V-33 VARINA

Rte. 5, just east of I-295. The name derives from the resemblance of the tobacco introduced and grown by John Rolfe in 1614 to a variety grown in Varina, Spain. Varina was established as a town in 1680 and became the civil, judicial, and ecclesiastical center of Henrico County. The town became the county seat and included the first courthouse and jail, dunking stool, tavern, ferry, and racetrack, as well as Henrico Parish's church and glebe. In 1752 the county seat was moved to Richmond. The town of Varina was located on the north bank of the James River just east of the present I-295 bridge.

V-37 HENRICO PARISH CHURCH

Rte. 5, at Mill Road. Sir Thomas Dale established the original Henrico Parish Church at Henricus, 4½ miles southeast of here, in 1611. The first minister, the Reverend Alexander Whitaker, has been credited with converting Pocahontas to Christianity. Other noteworthy ministers included James Blair and William Stith. The parish church was later relocated to Varina, then to Curles, and finally to Saint John's Church in Richmond in 1741. Here, in 1926, the Varina Episcopal Church was constructed and the newly formed Varina Parish was established in this community.

V-40 SURRENDER OF RICHMOND

Rte. 5, at Tree Hill Lane, just west of Osborne Turnpike. At daybreak on 3 April 1865,

Federal troops formed to march into Richmond. A cavalry detachment under Majors Atherton H. Stevens, Jr. and Eugene E. Graves moved up the Osborne Turnpike to its junction with New Market Road. Here they met Richmond mayor Joseph Mayo, who handed Stevens a note of surrender for the city. Stevens accepted the note and had it forwarded to Maj. Gen. Godfrey Weitzel. At 8:15 A.M. at Richmond's city hall, Weitzel formally accepted the terms of surrender. The Union forces assisted in extinguishing the fires, started at around dawn by Confederate soldiers; by mid-afternoon order had begun to be restored to the city.

V-43 PLEASANTS V. PLEASANTS

Rte. 5, at Long Bridge Road. John Pleasants, Sr., nearby landowner and Quaker, requested in his will that his slaves be freed when each became 30 years old. Pleasants died in 1771, but it was not until 1782 that some of his slaves gained freedom when the Virginia General Assembly approved private manumissions. His son, Robert Pleasants, and a few other heirs freed close to 100 slaves in multiple counties. Robert Pleasants attempted to get all of the family to honor the will's stipulations, which culminated in 1798 when the Virginia High Court of Chancery heard it as a legal case. Future U.S. Chief Justice John Marshall and John Warden represented Robert Pleasants on behalf of the slaves. In 1799, the court ruled in favor of freeing the slaves. Some of the freed slaves settled nearby on Robert Pleasants's land to form the Gravely Hill community.

W-1 DARBYTOWN ROAD

Darbytown Road, at Henrico Arms Drive. During the Seven Days' Campaign, Maj. Gen. James Longstreet's and Maj. Gen. A. P. Hill's Confederate divisions moved east along Darbytown Road toward its junction with the Long Bridge Road. This junction is about three miles southwest of Riddell's Shop. Late on the afternoon of

30 June 1862, Longstreet's and Hill's divisions moved up the Long Bridge Road and attacked Maj. Gen. George B. McClellan's retreating Union army at Riddell's Shop (Glendale or Frayser's Farm) on Darbytown Road.

W-2 WILLIAMSBURG ROAD

Rte. 60 (Williamsburg Road) and Charles City Road, east of Richmond city limits. During the Civil War, Union and Confederate armies engaged in battles along major transportation corridors. Union Maj. Gen. George B. McClellan's defensive earthworks blocked Williamsburg Road east of here, for example, during the 1862 Peninsula Campaign. On 31 May, Maj. Gen. D. H. Hill's division marched past here to attack the Federal position. Later that day, part of Maj. Gen. James Longstreet's division joined Hill. During the Seven Days' Battles under Confederate Gen. Robert E. Lee, Brig. Gen. John B. Magruder's three divisions moved east on this road on 29 June to attack McClellan's rear guard at Savage's Station.

W-3 CHARLES CITY ROAD

Rte. 60 (Williamsburg Road) and Charles City Road, east of Richmond city limits. This strategically important road ran from the Williamsburg Road southeast past White's Tavern, across White Oak Swamp, and into the Riddell's Shop intersection with the Long Bridge and Darbytown roads, eight miles distant. As Gen. Robert E. Lee's forces converged on Riddell's Shop on 29–30 June 1862 to cut off Maj. Gen. George B. McClellan's retreating Union army, Maj. Gen. Benjamin Huger's Confederate division moved along the Charles City Road, which had been obstructed by felled trees. After marching to within three miles of Riddell's Shop on 29 June, Huger failed to advance or to take part in the Battle of Glendale on 30 June. He was relieved of command on 12 July.

W-4 MCCLELLAN'S PICKET LINE

Rte. 60, Sandston. The picket line of McClellan's army crossed the road here on the morning of May 31, 1862.

W-5 MCCLELLAN'S FIRST LINE

Rte. 60, west of Finley Drive, Sandston. Union Brig. Gen. Silas Casey held both sides of the road here on 31 May 1862, in Maj. Gen. George B. McClellan's first defensive line at Seven Pines. Confederate Gen. Joseph E. Johnston ordered a dawn attack, but his lieutenants acted slowly. Maj. Gen. D. H. Hill waited with his division about a mile west of here for the sound of gunfire to the south that was his signal to move. Exasperated by the delay, he assaulted on his own at 1 P.M. and smashed through Casey's position to McClellan's second line, but a lack of support combined with the arrival of fresh Union troops halted the attack. That evening, Johnston fell wounded and Gen. Robert E. Lee replaced him the next day.

W-6 MUNITIONS PLANT

Rte. 60, Seven Pines. In 1918, the United States government purchased twelve square miles of land here to construct a powder-packing plant after negotiating a cooperative effort with the Chesapeake and Ohio Railroad and the Du Pont Engineering Company. Within three months, an army of 6,000 workers cleared the land and constructed roads, rail lines, and warehouses to create what the *Richmond Times-Dispatch* called "the mightiest munition-packing plant in all the world." Members of the Women's Munition Reserve worked in the powder bag-loading plant. Formally opened on 12 October, "Liberty Day," the plant was operating for less than a month before the armistice ending World War I was signed. Production was halved on 26 November and the plant closed shortly thereafter.

W-7 FAIR OAKS STATION

Rte. 33 (Nine Mile Road) and Hanover Road. This intersection of the Richmond and

York River Railroad with the Nine Mile Road became one of Henrico County's best-known landmarks during the Civil War. Fair Oaks Station lay on the north side of the junction. As part of Gen. Joseph E. Johnston's Confederate attack at Seven Pines on 31 May 1862, his troops under Brig. Gen. Richard H. Anderson passed here as they assaulted the Union right. On 29 June 1862, an innovative Confederate artillery piece was pushed past the intersection by a locomotive and used during the Battle of Savage's Station. It consisted of a siege gun mounted on a flatcar behind a shield of rails. This was the first use of railroad artillery in warfare.

W-8 MCCLELLAN'S WITHDRAWAL

Meadow Road, 0.1 miles east of Grapevine Road. In this vicinity a part of McClellan's army remained for several weeks after the battle of Seven Pines. The part of his army north of the Chickahominy was attacked by Lee, June 26–27, 1862. McClellan then began to withdraw to the James, June 28–29, 1862.

W-9 MCCLELLAN'S SECOND LINE

400 Williamsburg Road (Rte. 60), Seven Pines. Here, at Seven Pines, was McClellan's second and main line of defense. The Confederates under D. H. Hill, having taken the first line, attacked this position, held by Casey and Couch reinforced by Kearny, May 31, 1862. The battle was bitterly contested until Longstreet sent in fresh troops. The Union line was broken; the Unionists fell back a mile and a half to the east.

W-10 SECOND DAY AT SEVEN PINES

Rte. 33 and Hanover Road. Most of the fighting on the second day of the Battle of Seven Pines (Fair Oaks), occurred near here on 1 June 1862. Confederate Maj. Gen. Gustavus W. Smith, who had assumed command following the wounding of Gen. Joseph E. Johnston the evening before, resumed the attack in the morning. When the Union

defenses proved too strong, the Confederates disengaged and retired to their original lines. Gen. Robert E. Lee, who already had been assigned to command the Confederate troops in front of Richmond early in the day, assumed that command when Smith collapsed from exhaustion during the afternoon.

W-11 MCCLELLAN'S THIRD LINE

Old Rte. 60 (Old Williamsburg Road) and Old Dry Bridge Road, 1.3 miles east of Seven Pines. Here ran McClellan's third line of defense, May 31–June 1, 1862. The Confederates, taking the first and second lines on this road, did not reach the third.

W-12 BATTLE OF SAVAGE'S STATION

Rte. 60, 2 miles east of Seven Pines. On 25 June 1862 began the Seven Days' Battles as Gen. Robert E. Lee engaged Maj. Gen. George B. McClellan's Army of the Potomac, prompting McClellan to withdraw to the James River. Just north of here at 9:00 A.M. on 29 June, Brig. Gen. John B. Magruder's division attacked Brig. Gen. Edwin V. Sumner's corps, which formed the Union rear guard near Savage's Station on the Richmond & York River R.R. Sumner gained the safety of the depot and held his ground until the fighting ended in a draw about 9:00 P.M. The Federals retreated south to Malvern Hill in the night, abandoning some 2,500 wounded at the depot.

W-13 ROUTE TO WHITE OAK SWAMP AND MALVERN HILL

Meadow Road, 0.1 miles east of Grapevine Road. After crossing the Chickahominy River to the north at Grapevine Bridge, portions of Maj. Gen. George B. McClellan's retreating Union army destroyed the bridge and moved southeast along this road on 28 June 1862. After rebuilding the bridge the next day, Maj. Gen. Thomas J. ("Stonewall") Jackson's command (which included his own division and those of Generals Richard S. Ewell, William H. C. Whiting, and Daniel H. Hill) began crossing early in the morning of 30 June. Under orders to clear the enemy from the woods south of the Chickahominy and to follow McClellan's retreating army, Jackson's men captured numerous prisoners as they advanced along this road.

W-15 BOTTOM'S BRIDGE

Rte. 60, at Bottom's Bridge, 15 miles east of Richmond. On 20 May 1862, Maj. Gen. George B. McClellan's Union army crossed the Chickahominy River over Bottom's Bridge into Henrico County. Here Maj. Gen. Erasmus D. Keyes's Federal corps advanced over the bridge unopposed. As McClellan's army advanced on Richmond, the bridge served as a link between units deployed on both sides of the Chickahominy. When McClellan abandoned his supply base at White House on the Pamunkey River on 27–28 June 1862, a herd of cattle as well as some 4,000 wagons loaded with supplies and ammunition moved across Bottom's Bridge in his "change of base" to the James River.

W-72 39TH ILLINOIS VETERAN VOLUNTEERS

Darbytown Road, just east of Yahley Mill Road. On 16 Aug. 1864, Federal infantry stormed Confederate earthworks nearby, in the Second Battle of Deep Bottom. The 39th Illinois helped lead the assault. Pvt. Henry M. Hardenbergh, of Bremen Township, the color bearer, served in Co. G, called the "Preacher's Company" because it was recruited by a minister. Wounded during the charge, Hardenbergh captured the flag of the 10th Alabama Inf. Regt. after mortally wounding its color sergeant. The Confederates soon recaptured the works and drove the Union force back to its bridgehead at Deep Bottom. Hardenbergh was awarded the Medal of Honor and a lieutenant's commission.

W-221 VIRGINIA ESTELLE RANDOLPH

2200 Mountain Road, at Virginia Randolph Education Center. The daughter of parents born in slavery, Virginia Randolph

Virginia Randolph was an important African American educator and in 1908 became the nation's first Jeanes Supervising Industrial Teacher, a position sponsored by the Anna T. Jeanes Fund of Philadelphia for African American Southern education. Randolph, second from left, is shown here visiting an African American school in Henrico County. (Marker W-221) (Jackson Davis Papers [#3072], Special Collections, University of Virginia Library)

(1874–1958) taught in a one-room school-house beginning in 1892. A gifted teacher, she became in 1908 the nation's first Jeanes Supervising Industrial Teacher, a position sponsored by the Anna T. Jeanes Fund of Philadelphia for black Southern education. Randolph developed the Henrico Plan, teaching both traditional subjects and vocational skills. Henrico County named two schools in her honor here in 1915 and 1957. In 1969 the schools were merged to form the Virginia Randolph Education Center; Randolph is buried here.

LOUISA COUNTY

F-40 CAMPAIGN OF 1781

Rte. 15, between Boswells Tavern and Zion Crossroads. Lafayette, moving west to protect stores in Albemarle from Tarleton, passed near here, June, 1781.

V-19 PROVIDENCE CHURCH

Rte. 250, 0.4 miles northwest of Gum Spring. Half a mile northeast stands Providence Presbyterian church, built probably in 1749 and little altered since. John Todd, Senior, a founder of Hampden-Sydney College, was pastor for forty years (1753–1793). Hanover Presbytery met there in October, 1762.

V-20 CAMPAIGN OF 1781

Rte. 250, Ferncliff. Here Lafayette, moving west to protect a supply depot in Albermarle [Albemarle] from Cornwallis, entered this road, June 13, 1781.

W-206 THE MARQUIS ROAD

Rte. 22, near Rte. 15, Boswells Tavern. Lafayette reopened this road in June, 1781, when moving south to intervene between Cornwallis and military stores in Albemarle County. The road has ever since been known as "The Marquis Road. "

W-207 BOSWELL'S TAVERN

Rte. 22, near Rte. 15, Boswells Tavern. At this old tavern Lafayette camped, on June 12, 1781, while moving southward to intervene between Cornwallis and military stores in Albemarle County.

W-208 GREEN SPRINGS

Rte. 33, between Trevilians and Gordonsville. Near here Wade Hampton's Confederate cavalry camped the night of June 10, 1864, just before the battle of Trevilians.

W-209 BATTLE OF TREVILIANS

Rtes. 33 and 22, west of Louisa, Trevilians. Here, on June 12, 1864, Sheridan's cavalry, coming from Trevilians, attacked Wade Hampton, who had taken position across the road. A bloody engagement followed. Fitz Lee joined Hampton, and the Union cavalry was driven back. That night Sheridan retired eastward.

W-210 TREVILIAN STATION BATTLE

Rtes. 33 and 22, 4 miles west of Louisa, Trevilians. In June 1864, Maj. Gen. Philip H. Sheridan led a Union cavalry raid against the Virginia Central Railroad here, which Maj. Gen. Wade Hampton and Maj. Gen. Fitzhugh Lee defended during a two-day battle. On 11 June, the first day, Union Brig. Gen. George A. Custer's brigade got between Lee's division and the rest of Hampton's cavalry and captured Hampton's supply wagons. The Confederates counterattacked and virtually surrounded Custer, who led his troopers in a breakout charge just as Federal reinforcements arrived. Hampton recaptured his wagons, then withdrew two miles west of the station while Lee bivouacked a mile east.

W-211 PATRICK HENRY'S HOME

Rte. 33, at courthouse, Louisa. At Roundabout Plantation, eight miles southwest,

Patrick Henry lived from 1765 to 1768, when he sat for Louisa County in the House of Burgesses. This was the beginning of his political career.

W-212 HISTORIC LOUISA

Rte. 33, Louisa. Here the county seat was established in 1742. The British Cavalryman, Tarleton, stopped here on his raid to Charlottesville, June 3, 1781. Stoneman raided the place and destroyed the railroad, May 2, 1863. Near here Fitz Lee camped, June 10, 1864, just before the Battle of Trevilians.

W-213 JACK JOUETT'S RIDE

Rte. 33, near Rte. 522, Cuckoo. From the tavern that stood here, Jack Jouett rode to Charlottesville, by the Old Mountain Road, in time to warn the members of the Virginia government of the coming of Tarleton's British cavalry, June 3, 1781.

W-215 CIVILIAN CONSERVATION CORPS COMPANY 2347

Rte. 22, Boswells Tavern. Here at Burnley's Farm was the site of Camp Monticello, CCC Company 2347, Boswell's Tavern, Virginia. The camp, originally located near Rocky Mount, Virginia, was moved here in the fall of 1939 and remained until it was dismantled on 18 September 1942, during World War II. It provided work for about two hundred young men from Pennsylvania near the end of the Great Depression. Their responsibilities included clearing forest trails, fighting fires, and stringing and repairing farm fences. They also helped to construct the Skyline Drive.

W-216 CIVILIAN CONSERVATION CORPS COMPANY 2359

Rte. 22, between Louisa and Mineral. This is the site of Camp P-82, CCC Company 2359, Mineral, Virginia. The camp was established in 1934 and provided work for more than two hundred young men during the depths of the Great Depression. Their responsibilities included clearing forest trails, fighting fires, and improving the area's roads. In 1937, Camp 2359 built the 102-foot fire tower on Route 33. The tower was listed in the National Historic Lookout Register in 1994. The camp disbanded in 1942 after World War II began.

W-222 JOHN MERCER LANGSTON BIRTHPLACE

Rte. 33/22, at courthouse, Louisa. John Mercer Langston was born 5.5 miles N.W. of here on 14 Dec. 1829, son of plantation owner Ralph Quarles and his former slave Lucy Langston. A graduate of Oberlin College (1849), in 1855 Langston became township clerk of Brownhelm, Ohio— the first African American popularly elected to office. During the Civil War, he recruited regiments for the Union army. Afterward, he was founder and first dean of the Law Department of Howard University, served as minister resident in Haiti and chargé d'affaires in Santo Domingo, and was first president of what is now Virginia State University. In 1888 he became the first black congressman elected from Virginia. He died on 15 Nov. 1897 in Washington, D.C.

W-223 CUCKOO

Rte. 33, near Rte. 522, Cuckoo. Cuckoo, long a landmark for travelers, was built for Henry Pendleton about 1819. Nearby once stood the Cuckoo Tavern, from which in 1781 Jack Jouett made his famous ride. The Pendletons, a prominent family of physicians whose descendants still own the house, constructed two doctor's offices at Cuckoo that still stand; one was built in the 18th century and one in the 19th. The house retains many Federal-style details as well as an early-20th-century Colonial Revival portico. Cuckoo was listed on the National Register of Historic Places and the Virginia Landmarks Register in 1994.

CITY OF PETERSBURG

QA-1 FOLLY CASTLE

West Washington Street. This house was the town home of Peter Jones, who built it in 1763. It was called "Folly Castle" because it was a large house for a childless man, but Jones later had offspring. Major Erasmus Gill, Revolutionary soldier, also lived here.

QA-2 GOLDEN BALL TAVERN

Old and Market Streets. Here stood a dwelling house, constructed about 1764 by prosperous tobacco merchant, Richard Hanson, who, as a fervent Loyalist, fled Virginia in 1776. During the latter part of the Revolution, the structure became known as the Golden Ball Tavern. According to tradition, British officers serving under Cornwallis were quartered here in 1781. When Petersburg was incorporated as a town in 1784, the town council and the courts used the tavern as their first meeting place. The structure was enlarged by 1820 and utilized as a hotel until after the Civil War when it was used for a number of retail ventures. The building was demolished in 1944.

QA-5 POPLAR LAWN

Filmore and South Sycamore Streets. Poplar Lawn is now known as Central Park. Here the Petersburg Volunteers camped in October 1812, before leaving for the Canadian border. Here Lafayette was greeted with music and speeches in 1824. The place was bought by the city in 1844. Volunteer companies enlisted here, April 19, 1861. In the siege of 1864–65 a hospital stood here.

QA-6 FORT HENRY

West Washington and North South Streets. Four blocks north is the traditional site of Fort Henry, established under the Act of 1645. In 1646 the fort was leased by Abraham Wood. From it, in 1650, Wood and Edmund Bland set out on an exploring expedition; and, in 1671, Batts and Fallam on the first expedition known to have crossed the Appalachian Mountains. The fort was garrsioned [garrisoned] again in 1675, with Peter Jones as commander.

QA-7 GENERAL LEE'S HEADQUARTERS

West Washington and Lafayette Streets. Three blocks north and a half a block west is the Beasley House where General Robert E. Lee had his second headquarters in 1864 during the siege of Petersburg. He moved thence to Edge Hill to be in closer touch with his right wing.

QA-8 BOLLINGBROOK HOTEL

Rte. 1, at Adams Street, at Appomattox River bridge. After a fire destroyed John Niblo's tavern in 1827, Niblo assembled a group of investors who constructed on this site in 1828 the three-story Bollingbrook Hotel, attributed to Otis Manson. The hotel became known as "one of the best taverns in the Atlantic country." In 1857, a fourth story was added to the building and it was restyled to include a bracketed cornice and cast-iron segmental window caps. During the siege of Petersburg in 1864–1865 Confederate officers were housed here. About 1906 the building was renamed the Stratford Hotel and modernized. It was demolished about 1933.

QA-9 BATTERSEA

Rte. 1 (West Washington Street) and Battersea Lane. Battersea was the home of Colonel John Banister, a member of the House of Burgesses, the Revolutionary conventions, and the Continental Congress, as well as a framer of the Articles of Confederation and the first mayor of Petersburg. The elegant but compact house begun in 1768, perhaps best displays the Anglo-Palladian influence on Virginia's colonial plantation homes. Noted travelers, including the Italian Count Castiglioni and the French Marquis de Chastellux visted Battersea: Chastellux observed, "Mr. Banister's handsome country-house is really worth seeing." The elaborate Chinese lattice stair, based on a published design by English architect William Halfpenny, is original and Virginia's finest example.

QA-10 ST. PAUL'S CHURCH

Union Street, near city hall. St. Paul's Church was built in 1856. Here Robert E. Lee and his staff worshipped during the siege of Petersburg, 1864–65. Lee attended the wedding of his son, W. H. F. Lee, in this church in 1867.

QA-11 BLANDFORD CHURCH AND CEMETERY

Crater Road, at Rochelle Lane. The brick church on Well's Hill, now known as Old Blandford Church, was built between 1734 and 1737. The British General Phillips was buried in the churchyard in 1781. In the cemetery is a monument to Captain McRae and the Petersburg volunteers, who at Fort Meigs in 1813 won for Petersburg the name of the "Cockade City of the Union." Soldiers of six wars rest here, among them 30,000 Confederates.

QA-12 BATTLE OF PETERSBURG

Crater Road, at Rochelle Lane. Here was fought the Battle of Petersburg, April 25, 1781. The southside militia, 1000 strong and commanded by Baron Steuben and General Muhlenberg, made a brave resistance to 2500 British regulars under Phillips and Arnold.

QA-13 EAST HILL

East Bank and Fourth Streets. On the hilltop to the south is the site of East Hill, also known as Bollingbrook. There the British General Phillips, Benedict Arnold and Lord Cornwallis stayed in April and May, 1781. The house was bombarded by Lafayette, May 10, 1781. There Phillips died, May 13, 1781.

QA-14 TWO NOTED HOMES

West Washington and South Market Streets. Half a block south is the home of Major

General William Mahone, famed for his gallant conduct at the Battle of the Crater, July 30, 1864. Two blocks south is the Wallace Home, where Abraham Lincoln conferred with General Grant, April 3, 1865, preceding Grant's march to Appomattox.

QA-15 FORMATION OF THE SOUTHERN METHODIST CHURCH

Washington Street, near Sycamore Street, at church. One block west stood the Union Street Methodist Church, completed in 1820. There was held the first general conference of the Methodist Episcopal Church South, May 1–23, 1846. At this meeting the Southern Methodist Church, which had separated from the Northern Church, effected its organization.

QA-16 GRAHAM ROAD

Crater and Graham Roads. On June 9, 1864, Kautz's Union cavalry, 1300 men, after overwhelming Archer's militia, one mile south, moved westward on this road to attack the city. Upon the hillside, one mile west, they were repulsed by the battery of Captain Edward Graham, and later driven to retreat by General James Dearing's cavalry. This attack, in conjunction with an infantry force that did not come up, was the first attempt to capture Petersburg.

QA-17 GRAHAM ROAD

Graham Road and Clinton Street. Upon this site, on June 9, 1864, Captain Edward Graham, commanding two guns of the Petersburg Artillery, repulsed the attack of Kautz's cavalry, 1300 men. And by this gallant defense the city was saved. Later the Union forces were driven to retreat by the supporting cavalry of General James Dearing.

QA-18 THE FIRST METHODIST MEETING HOUSE

Grove Avenue and Fleet Street. The first Methodist Meeting House in Petersburg was a theatre on West Old Street near the river rented by Gressett Davis. Robert Williams, a follower of John Wesley, came to Petersburg to preach in 1773 at the invitation of Davis and Nathaniel Young, local businessmen. From this humble beginning, Methodism became firmly established in Petersburg and spread throughout the surrounding countryside. Petersburg served as Williams' headquarters and later was made part of the Brunswick circuit.

QA-19 GRACE EPISCOPAL CHURCH

High Street, between Cross and Lafayette Streets. The third home of Grace Church, a brick Gothic Revival-style building, stood on this site from 1859 to 1960. The congregation was founded in 1841 by Dr. Churchhill Jones Gibson, rector until 1892. In 1928 a majority of the members, led by the rector, Dr. Edwin Royall Carter, left to form Christ Episcopal Church at 1545 South Sycamore Street. The two congregations reunited in 1953 at the Sycamore Street site as Christ and Grace Episcopal Church.

QA-20 BATTLE OF PETERSBURG, 25 APRIL 1781—ARTILLERY POSITION

Washington and Little Church Streets. On 25 Apr. 1781, Maj. Gen. Friedrich von Steuben's 1,000 Virginia militiamen, driven from the eastern edge of Blandford, established a strong defensive line along the western summit (now Madison Street) above Lieutenant Run valley. Maj. Gen. William Phillips's British force occupied this ridge from here to the Appomattox River. After several unsuccessful infantry attacks, Phillips placed four artillery pieces here and fired on the American line. Facing this threat, and with American ammunition running low, von Steuben decided that any further defense of Petersburg would be futile and ordered a general retreat toward the Pocahontas Bridge to the north.

QA-21 BATTLE OF PETERSBURG, 25 APRIL 1781—BRITISH LINE OF ATTACK

East Washington Street, near Puddledock Road. On 24 Apr. 1781, Maj. Gen. William

Phillips's force of 2,500 British regulars landed at City Point, 12 miles to the east on the James River, as part of a major campaign to disrupt the American force's main line of communication through Virginia. The next morning, Phillips marched his troops along River Road toward Petersburg. Shortly before noon, he and Brig. Gen. Benedict Arnold formed their line of battle in this vicinity and launched their attack on the first line of 500 Virginia militiamen positioned to defend Petersburg one-quarter of a mile west in Blandford.

QA-22 BATTLE OF PETERSBURG, 25 APRIL 1781—EAST HILL

Madison Street, between Washington and Bank Streets. To the west stood East Hill (Bollingbrook), home of the widow Mary Marshall Tabb Bolling. After the 25 Apr. 1781 Battle of Petersburg, British Maj. Gen. William Phillips and Brig. Gen. Benedict Arnold located their headquarters at the house. The British reoccupied it on 9 May, after returning from Richmond. The following day, Maj. Gen. Lafayette shelled Petersburg, from the heights on the north bank of the Appomattox River. After becoming gravely ill, Phillips died there on 13 May. Lieut. Gen. Charles Cornwallis marched into town on 20 May, uniting his force with Arnold's and kept his headquarters at East Hill until he departed on 24 May.

QA-23 BATTLE OF PETERSBURG, 25 APRIL 1781—FIRST LINE OF DEFENSE

Bank and East Streets. On 25 Apr. 1781, American Brig. Gen. Peter Muhlenberg formed his first line of 500 Virginia militia here to meet the British. The line extended along East Street from the Appomattox River to present-day Washington Street and consisted of two infantry regiments. Maj. Gen. William Phillips' 2,500-man army, including one Light Infantry battalion and the 76th and 80th Regiments of Foot, struck the Americans here. After several assaults and the deployment of four British cannon, the militia withdrew westward, through Blandford (then a separate town), across Lieutenant Run, and on to Madison Street in eastern Petersburg.

QA-24 Battle Of Petersburg, 25 April 1781—Flanking Movement

Graham Road, near Southside Virginia Emergency Crew. About midday on 25 April 1781, Maj. Gen. William Phillips discovered that the right flank of the American militia, on the edge of Blandford was vulnerable to attack from the south and rear. He ordered Lt. Col. John Simcoe's Queen's Rangers and a Light Infantry battalion to the south and west on a wide sweep around the flank to attack the Virginians from the rear. Simcoe took this nearby route (now Graham Road) between present-day Crater Road and Sycamore Street, thus moving his large force behind the American line undetected. When Simcoe reached the high ground overlooking Petersburg, the Americans were already retreating.

QA-25 Battle Of Petersburg, 25 April 1781—Second Line Of Defense

Bank and Madison Streets. On 25 Apr. 1781, American Brig. Gen. Peter Muhlenberg's Virginia militia fell back west from Blandford, under heavy British fire, to a prepared line of defense here along the crest of this hill. This second line of Virginia militia, consisting of four regiments of infantry, extended from the Appomattox River on the north and present-day Washington Street to the south of here. The Virginians

repelled several British assaults, but soon their ammunition ran low and, after Maj. Gen. William Phillips unleashed his artillery, Maj. Gen. Friedrich von Steuben, the overall American commander, ordered a retreat west toward the Pocahontas Bridge.

S-43 Cottage Farm

Boydton Plank Road at Fort Lee Road. A little north stood the McIlwaine home, Lee's field headquarters whence on the afternoon of April 2, 1865, the evacuation of Richmond and Petersburg was ordered. Upon issuing the order Lee granted leave to his only staff officer to go to Richmond that evening for his marriage.

S-76 Early English Exploration

North Sycamore and Old Streets. In 1650 Fort Henry, now Petersburg, marked the western and southern extent of English settlement in, and knowledge of, Virginia. On 27 Aug. 1650, Edward Bland, merchant and land speculator, and Abraham Wood, frontier militia commander, left Fort Henry on the first documented English exploration of Southside Virginia. Pyancha, an Appamattuck guide, led Bland, Wood, and four others through the territory of the Nottoway, Meherrin, and Hocomawanck Indians for nine days. They probably reached the falls of the Roanoke River near Weldon, N.C., before returning to Fort Henry. This was the first of a series of explorations that departed from Fort Henry under Abraham Wood's auspices.

POWHATAN COUNTY

O-25 Dunlora Academy

Rte. 60, 5.7 miles west of Powhatan. Two and a half miles north, on Dunlora plantation then owned by Mrs. Ann Hickman, the Virginia Baptist Education Society established, in 1830, a school for ministers. This school, under the principalship of Rev. Edward Baptist, M.A., was known locally as Dunlora Academy. Edward Baptist

resigned in 1832, and the school was removed to Henrico County and then to Richmond. From it developed Richmond College and, later, the University of Richmond.

O-30 Derwent

Rte. 13, 2 miles east of Tobaccoville. Ten miles north is "Derwent" where Robert E. Lee lived in the summer of 1865 as the guest of

Mrs. E. R. Cocke. Lee arrived at "Derwent" early in July. While there he was offered the presidency of Washington College, Lexington, which he accepted on August 24, 1865. On September 15, he left "Derwent" for Lexington.

O-31 GILES'S HOME

Rte. 60, 1.7 miles west of Powhatan. Five miles southwest is the Wigwam, the home of William B. Giles, Jefferson's chief lieutenant; United States Senator, 1804–1815, and Governor of Virginia, 1827–1830, an orator and famous political leader. Giles died there, December 4, 1830.

O-32 POWHATAN COURTHOUSE

Rte. 13, Powhatan. The first courthouse was built here about 1783 and around it grew the village of Scottville. Named for Revolutionary War Gen. Charles Scott, who was born in the area, the town eventually became known as Powhatan Court House. The present courthouse was designed by Alexander Jackson Davis, of New York, and built in 1849. It is a masterpiece of Greek Revival architecture. The oldest building in the court square is the clerk's office built about 1798 and nearby is a late-18th-century double-galleried courthouse tavern. Part of the Confederate army, retreating from Richmond, passed here on 4 Apr. 1865.

O-33 HUGUENOT SETTLEMENT

Rte. 711, 2.55 miles west of Powhatan/Chesterfield County line. Huguenots, the largest single group of French Protestant refugees to come to Virginia, settled near here on the site of a deserted Monacan Indian village during the period 1700–1701. In 1700, the Virginia General Assembly established King William Parish, also known as Huguenot Parish. The Huguenots established a church at this site now known as the Manakin Episcopal Church.

O-36 HUGUENOT SPRINGS CONFEDERATE CEMETERY

Rte. 711, 2.13 miles west of Powhatan/Chesterfield County line. Approximately 250 unidentified Confederate soldiers, who died at nearby Huguenot Springs Confederate Hospital, are buried in unmarked graves about a mile and a half southwest of here. Burial records have never been located. The former Huguenot Springs Hotel Resort/Spa, opened in 1847, was converted to a convalescent hospital during the Civil War. The building was burned about 1890.

OH-10 LEE'S LAST CAMP

Rte. 711, between Rtes. 628 and 616. Here Robert E. Lee, riding from Appomattox to Richmond to join his family, pitched his tent for the last time on April 14, 1865. He stopped here to visit his brother, Charles Carter Lee, who lived nearby at Windsor. Not wishing to incommode his brother, Lee camped by the roadside and the next day ended his journey at Richmond.

PRINCE GEORGE COUNTY

K-205 CITY POINT AND HOPEWELL

Rte. 36, 0.7 miles east of Petersburg. City Point is five miles northeast. There Governor Sir Thomas Dale made a settlement in 1613. In April, 1781, the British General Phillips landed there. Grant had his base of operations there in the siege of Petersburg, 1864–1865. Lincoln was there in April, 1865. In the World War the city of Hopewell grew up near by.

K-206 BAILEY'S CREEK

Off Rte. 106, 2.8 miles east of Prince George. Bailey's Creek is named for Temperance Bailey (ca. 1617–ca. 1652), the daughter of Cicely Bailey and her first husband, whose name is unknown. When he died before Sept. 1620, Temperance inherited 200 acres of land near here at the age of three. Her mother remarried, first Samuel Jordan and then William Farrar, and resided with Temperance at Jordan's Point on the James River. Temperance Bailey married, first, John Browne, and then, by 1632, Richard Cocke, thereby becoming the progenitrix of the Cocke family in Virginia. Late in the twentieth century, archaeologists excavated her childhood home at Jordan's Point.

K-207 HISTORY AT PRINCE GEORGE COURTHOUSE

Rte. 106, Prince George. Lord Cornwallis, going toward the James in pursuit of Lafayette, passed here, May 24, 1781. A part of Grant's army passed here on the way to Petersburg, June, 1864. The place was occupied by Union troops in 1864–65.

K-208 JORDAN'S POINT

Off Rte. 106, 2.8 miles east of Prince George. Weyanoke Indians, part of the Powhatan Chiefdom, occupied Jordan's Point, around two miles north on the James River, when English colonists arrived in 1607. There, about 1620, Samuel Jordan settled; the place was called Jordan's Journey. By 1625, his widow Cicely and more than 50 other people resided there in some 15 households within a fortified compound. More than a century later, Richard Bland (1710–1776), member of the First Continental Congress, lived there. In the late 1980s and early 1990s, excavations at Jordan's Point revealed one of the richest arrays of prehistoric and historic archaeological sites in Virginia.

K-209 MERCHANT'S HOPE CHURCH

Rte. 10, 8.3 miles northwest of Burrowsville. This well-known colonial church's architectural form and detail is typical of early and mid-18th-century Virginia churches. Located half a mile south, the building has Flemish-bond brickwork, modillion cornice, and a gracefully splayed gable roof. Although most of its original interior features were lost during the Civil War, the gallery, stone aisle pavers, and roof framing survived and were repaired by 1870. Historic restoration began in the 1960s and was completed in the 1970s. The original wood trusses were reinforced in 2004. The property was listed on the Virginia Landmarks Register in 1968 and the National Register of Historic Places in 1969.

K-210 COGGINS'S POINT

Marker missing. Original location: Rte. 10, 8.3 miles northwest of Burrowsville. Four miles north on James River. When Benedict Arnold fell back down the James after his raid to Richmond, Baron Steuben, at Coggin's Point, observed his fleet, January 10, 1781. From the bluff General D. H. Hill bombarded McClellan's camp on the north side of the river, July 31, 1862.

K-211 THE CATTLE RAID

Rtes. 609 and 635. Just to the north of the road here, at old Sycamore Church, Wade Hampton, coming from the south, attacked the Union cavalry guarding Grant's beef cattle, September 16, 1864. The Unionists were overpowered; Hampton, rounding up 2,500 beeves, succeeded in escaping with them across the Blackwater and into Lee's lines.

K-212 POWELL'S CREEK

Rte. 10, at Rte. 639 (Flowerdew Hundred Road), 5.3 miles northwest of Burrowsville. The creek nearby was named for Nathaniel Powell, acting governor in 1619. Weyanoke Indian town was here. Nearby is the site of an old mill, known in the Revolution as Bland's, and later, Cocke's Mill. The British General Phillips passed here, May, 1781. Here Grant's army, after crossing the James, turned towards Petersburg, June, 1864.

K-213 MAYCOCK'S PLANTATION

Marker missing. Original location: Rte. 10, 5.3 miles northwest of Burrowsville. Six miles north on James River. The place was patented about 1618 by Samuel Maycock, slain in the massacre of 1622. In 1774, David Meade became the owner. There Cornwallis crossed the river, May 24, 1781. Anthony Wayne crossed there, August 30, 1781.

K-214 FLOWERDEW HUNDRED

Marker missing. Original location: Rte. 10, 5.3 miles northwest of Burrowsville. Four miles north. Governor Sir George Yeardley patented land there in 1619, and in 1621 built at Windmill Point the first windmill in English America. The place was named for Temperance Flowerdew, Yeardley's wife. Near there Grant's army crossed the James in June, 1864.

K-215 HOOD'S

Rte. 10, east of Rte. 614, just west of Burrowsville. Four miles north on James River. There, on January 3, 1781, Benedict Arnold, ascending the river, was fired on by cannon. On January 10, Arnold, returning, sent ashore there a force that was ambushed by George Rogers Clark. Fort Powhatan stood there in the War of 1812.

K-216 WARD'S CREEK

Rte. 10, east of Rte. 614, just west of Burrowsville. Named for John Ward, who patented land here in 1619. The plantation was represented in the first General Assembly, 1619.

K-218 BRANDON

Rte. 10, Burrowsville. This place, five miles northeast, has been owned by the Harrison family for two centuries. John Martin patented the land in 1617; Nathaniel Harrison bought it in 1720. The present house was built about 1770. The British General Phillips landed at Brandon, May 7, 1781. A mile farther is Upper Brandon.

K-323 RICHARD BLAND

Rte. 156, south of entrance of Jordan Parkway. Richard Bland (1710–1776), statesman

and son of Richard and Elizabeth Randolph Bland of Jordan's Point, represented Prince George County in the House of Burgesses from 1742 to 1776. Between the 1750s and 1774, Bland played a leading role through newspaper articles, public letters, and pamphlets in arguing for Virginia control of its internal political and economic affairs. He was a Virginia delegate to the First and Second Continental Congresses and elected to the Virginia House of Delegates in 1776. Bland died in Williamsburg on 26 Oct. 1776. He was buried in a nearby family cemetery at Jordan's Point.

PA-252 SAMUEL JORDAN OF JORDAN'S JOURNEY

Rte. 106/156, 1.4 miles north of Rte. 10, just south of Benjamin Harrison Bridge. Prior to 1619, Native Americans occupied this prominent peninsula along the upper James River, now called Jordan's Point. Arriving in Jamestown by 1610, Samuel Jordan served in July 1619 in Jamestown as a burgess for Charles City in the New World's oldest legislative assembly. A year later, he patented a 450-acre tract here known first as Beggar's Bush and later as Jordan's Journey. He survived the massive Powhatan Indian attack of March 1622 here at his plantation, a palisaded fort that enclosed 11 buildings. He remained at Jordan's Journey with his wife, Cicely, and their daughters until his death in 1623.

UM-20 REAMS STATION

Rte. 301, 12.6 miles south of Petersburg. Three miles north. There, the Union cavalryman, Kautz, in Wilson's raid, destroyed the station, June 22, 1864. Returning from Burkeville, Kautz reached there again June 29, and was joined by Wilson. Attacked by Hampton, Wilson and Kautz hastily retreated to Grant's army. Hancock, while destroying the Weldon railroad, was attacked at Reams Station by A. P. Hill and Hampton, August 25, 1864, and driven back to Grant's army.

CITY OF RICHMOND

E-1 BACON'S QUARTER

Chamberlayne Avenue (Rte. 301), near Bacon Street. Nathaniel Bacon (1647–1676), leader of Bacon's Rebellion, acquired land in 1674 at Curles Neck in Henrico County and property near the falls on the north side of the James River that became known as Bacon's Quarter in what is now present-day Richmond. Bacon's Quarter, located nearby, was run by an overseer and likely contained a trading post. Bacon's Quarter Branch was a small stream that ran through the tract and one time flowed from approximately the Boulevard meandering eastward into Shockoe Creek. Bacon died of dysentery in 1676, while leading a rebellion against the Virginia government and Governor Sir William Berkeley.

E-2 INTERMEDIATE DEFENSES

Chamberlayne (Rte. 301) and Laburnum Avenues. Here ran, east and west, the intermediate line of Richmond defenses during the Civil War. Near this spot on 1 March 1864 Union Brig. Gen. H. Judson Kilpatrick halted his raid that was intended to free Union prisoners and lower morale in the Confederate capital. A detachment led by Col. Ulric Dahlgren was defeated to the west of the city. On 2 March Dahlgren was killed; Southern morale soared.

S-1 BRITISH INVASION OF RICHMOND, JANUARY 1781

Broad Street, between 24th and 25th Streets, at Patrick Henry Park. On 4 Jan. 1781, British troops led by Brig. Gen. Benedict Arnold landed at Westover in Charles City County and began marching to Richmond. Learning of the threat, Governor Thomas Jefferson directed the removal of public records and military stores to safety before evacuating the capital. On 5 Jan., Arnold's troops easily dispersed colonial forces arranged on defensive positions here on Church Hill and Shockoe Hill and occupied Richmond for twenty-four hours.

Before returning the following day to Westover, the British burned some private buildings and public storehouses containing military supplies, and destroyed the foundry and some public records at nearby Westham.

SA-25 FIRST TROLLEY CAR SYSTEM IN RICHMOND

5th Street, between Marshall Street and the Coliseum. In 1888, the world's first successful electric railway, the Richmond Union Passenger Railway, branched at this point to link downtown and Jackson Ward with the suburbs. This system, designed by Frank Julian Sprague (1857–1934), contained 12 miles of track with 40 trolley cars running to Byrd Park in the West End and to 29th and Broad streets in the East End. This model system that revolutionized urban transportation ceased operation in November, 1949.

SA-26 TRINITY METHODIST CHURCH

Broad Street, at 20th Street. Erected in 1860, this building housed Trinity Methodist Church until 1945 when the congregation moved to Henrico County. It was designed by noted Richmond architect Albert West, who was also a leading Methodist. The roots of the Trinity congregation date from 1790 when a small group of converts first met at the foot of Church Hill, marking the founding of organized Methodism in Richmond.

SA-28 WINDSOR

4601 Lilac Lane. Windsor was part of a 600 acre tract that was conveyed to Daniel S. Hylton by Charles Carter, trustee, in the William Byrd lottery of 1776. In the early years of the 19th century Windsor was owned and farmed by William Dandridge, nephew of Martha Washington, who was married to Susan Armistead. Charles F. Gillette, noted landscape architect, worked on the gardens for a period of fifty years beginning in 1919. The present house was built in 1945.

SA-29 WILTON

Cary Street Road and Wilton Road. A short distance south is Wilton, built by William Randolph and completed in 1753. The house, which originally stood on the north side of James River below Richmond, was removed to this place by the Virginia Society of Colonial Dames, 1934.

SA-30 AMPTHILL

Cary Street Road and Ampthill Road. A short distance south is Ampthill House, built by Henry Cary about 1730 on the south side of James River. It was the home of Colonel Archibald Cary, Revolutionary leader, and was removed to its present site by a member of the Cary family.

SA-32 SITE OF J. E. B. STUART'S DEATH

206 West Grace Street. Major General James Ewell Brown Stuart, C.S.A., Commander of the cavalry of the Army of Northern Virginia, died here on May 12, 1864, in the home of his brother-in-law, Dr. Charles Brewer. Cause of his death was a wound received the previous day in the defense of Richmond at the Battle of Yellow Tavern. Dr. Brewer's house was demolished in 1893.

SA-33 VIRGINIA HISTORICAL SOCIETY

Boulevard, at Kensington Avenue. Founded in 1831, the Virginia Historical Society is the oldest such institution in the South. It was located in the Stewart-Lee house in downtown Richmond until 1959, when it moved to its present quarters in Battle Abbey. The Society's extensive collections of Virginiana—manuscripts, rare books, portraits, photographs, and museum objects—form the basis for a research library and museum, as well as publications, lectures, and other public education programs.

SA-34 CRAIG HOUSE

Grace Street, near 19th Street. The Craig House, perhaps Richmond's second oldest structure, was built between 1784 and 1787 by Adam Craig (b. ca. 1760–d. 1808). He was clerk of the Richmond Hustings Court, the Henrico County Court, and the General Court. To save the house, a group of Richmond citizens in 1935 formed the William Byrd Branch of the Association for the Preservation of Virginia Antiquities. The house served Richmond's black community as the Craig House Art Center from 1938 to 1941.

SA-37 SAINT JOHN'S EPISCOPAL CHURCH

Broad Street, near 24th Street. Here on 23 March 1775 Patrick Henry delivered his "Liberty or Death" speech, calling for American independence, during the second Virginia revolutionary convention that included as members George Washington, Thomas Jefferson, Peyton Randolph, and Richard Henry Lee. Saint John's Church was built in 1741 by Richard Randolph on land donated by Richmond's founder, William Byrd II. It continues to serve Henrico Parish (founded 1611). Buried in its churchyard are George Wythe and Elizabeth Arnold Poe, mother of Edgar Allan Poe.

SA-38 MONUMENTAL CHURCH

Broad Street, near College Street. The church is a memorial to the 72 people, including Virginia Governor George W. Smith, who died when the Richmond Theatre burned here in 1811. Several survivors owed their lives to the bravery of Gilbert Hunt, a slave blacksmith. A committee chaired by Supreme Court Chief Justice John Marshall raised funds for the church's construction. Designed by Robert Mills and completed in 1814, the octagonal building served as an Episcopal church until 1965 and later as a chapel for the adjacent Medical College of Virginia.

SA-39 ORIGINS OF RICHMOND

Franklin Street, between 17th and 18th Streets.
There was "no place so strong, so pleasant, and delightful in Virginia, for which we called it None-such." So wrote Captain John Smith about the site he chose in 1609 when he established the first English settlement near the falls of the James River. It stood a few miles south until 1610. William Byrd I founded the second settlement when he patented land here in 1676. He soon built a fortified community, trading post, and warehouses just across the river near the mouth of Goode Creek. In 1737 his son, William Byrd II, laid out Richmond—which he named for Richmond upon Thames, now a borough of London—here in the Shockoe valley.

SA-40 GRANT HOUSE/SHELTERING ARMS HOSPITAL

1008 East Clay Street. William H. Grant, a prominent Richmond tobacconist, built this mansion by 1856 on property acquired from John Wickham's estate. The house, an early example in Richmond of the Italianate style, reflected the wealth and sophistication of late antebellum society. In 1892, after years of mixed use, it was acquired by Sheltering Arms Hospital, founded in 1889 as a "haven of mercy" for impoverished Virginians. The building underwent alterations, including the construction of a connecting wing westward to the Leigh House, before the hospital moved to new quarters in 1965. The Grant House is currently owned by Virginia Commonwealth University.

SA-41 UNION ARMY ENTERS RICHMOND

4400 block, East Main Street (Rte. 5). Here Maj. Gen. Godfrey Weitzel, commander of the Army of the James, entered and took possession of Richmond at 8:15 A.M. on 3 April 1865 after receiving the surrender of the confederate capital from Mayor Joseph Mayo a few miles east. The first units of Weitzel's command to enter the

city were six regiments from Brig. Gen. Edward H. Ripley's 1st Brigade of the XXIVth Army Corps, and U.S. Colored Troops from infantry and cavalry regiments of the XXVth Army Corps. During the next twenty-four hours, the Union troops extinguished the fire that destroyed almost 40 blocks extending along the river and north to Capitol Square, restored order, and occupied Confederate office buildings.

SA-42 RICHMOND EVACUATION FIRE

Main Street, at 9th Street. After midnight on 3 April 1865, Confederate soldiers set fire to several tobacco warehouses nearby on orders from Lt. Gen. Richard S. Ewell, as the army evacuated Richmond and marched west. Two distinct fires spread rapidly throughout the commercial and

Confederate General Robert E. Lee is likely the person most mentioned on state historical highway markers. Here he stands in front of the Stewart-Lee House in Richmond, where he lived briefly following the end of the Civil War. Today, a state marker at the building recalls its history. (Marker SA-44) (Library of Congress)

industrial sections of the capital. The core of the burned-out area, some 35 blocks, extended from the James River in some areas as far north as Capitol Square, and from 4th St. east to 16th St. Frightened citizens huddled in Capitol Square while looters rampaged and firefighters battled the fires. The Union army, which occupied the city early on 3 April, finally brought the fires under control in the afternoon.

SA-43 SIXTH MOUNT ZION BAPTIST CHURCH

14 West Duval Street. The Rev. John Jasper, born a slave in Fluvanna County on 4 July 1812, organized the Sixth Mount Zion Baptist Church congregation in Richmond on 3 Sept. 1867 in a former Confederate stable on Brown's Island. A nationally celebrated preacher, Jasper was best known for his 1878 sermon "De Sun Do Move," which he later delivered by invitation more than 250 times. He died on 30 Mar. 1901 and is buried in Woodlawn Cemetery in Richmond. In 1869, the congregation moved to this site. The present church (built 1887–1890) was remodeled in 1925 in the Gothic Revival style by the noted black architect Charles T. Russell.

SA-44 STEWART-LEE HOUSE

707 East Franklin Street. Built in 1844 for Norman Stewart, a Scottish tobacco merchant, the house was rented from his nephew, John Stewart, by Gen. Robert E. Lee's family during the Civil War. Following Lee's surrender at Appomattox, he lived here for just over two months. In 1893, John Stewart's widow and daughters donated the house to the Virginia Historical Society, which occupied it until 1958. Subsequently, it was used by the Museum of the Confederacy and Historic Richmond Foundation. The building, the sole survivor of Stewart's Row, is one of the finest Greek Revival town houses in the city.

SA-46 BROAD STREET STATION

2500 West Broad Street, at Science Museum of Virginia. Broad Street Station served passengers of the Richmond, Fredericksburg & Potomac Railway and the Atlantic Coast Line Railroad from 6 Jan. 1919 until 15 Nov. 1975. This Neoclassical Revival station was the only commercial building designed by John Russell Pope, who also designed the Branch House in Richmond and the Jefferson Memorial, National Gallery of Art, and National Archives in Washington, D.C. This station is noted architecturally for its Classical details, hundred-foot-high rotunda, and cast-iron and steel butterfly canopies that sheltered travelers from the weather. Listed in the National Register of Historic Places in 1971, the station became the home of the Science Museum of Virginia in 1977.

SA-47 ANNA MARIE LANE—SOLDIER OF THE AMERICAN REVOLUTION

9th Street, at Franklin Street, at Capital Square. Near the Bell Tower in Capitol Square stood the barracks of the Public Guard. There, from 1801 to 1807, lived John Lane and his wife, Anna Maria Lane, the only documented woman veteran of the Revolutionary War to reside in Virginia. She disguised herself and enlisted with her husband in the Connecticut Continental Line. "In the garb, and with the courage of a soldier, (she) performed extraordinary military services," and was wounded at Germantown, Pa., in 1777. She followed Lane through his subsequent service in the Virginia light dragoons, and then, after the war, to the Public Guard. Granted a pension in 1808, she died on 13 June 1810.

SA-48 BARTON HEIGHTS CEMETERIES

St. James Street, between School and Yancey Streets, at cemetery. The Burying Ground Society of the Free People of Color of Richmond established its cemetery (later renamed Cedarwood) here in 1815. African Americans eventually founded five more cemeteries here: Union Burial Ground (later called Union Mechanics), Sons and Daughters of Ham, Ebenezer, Methodist, and Sycamore. The burial societies, fraternal orders, and religious organizations that sustained these cemeteries formed the cultural and economic bedrock of Richmond's nineteenth-century African American community. Here they gathered, especially on Whitmonday, to mourn the loss of revered figures and honor the memory of friends and family members, many of whom experienced the transition from slavery to freedom.

SA-49 VIRGINIA HOUSE

Canterbury Road and Cary Street. Architectural elements of the Priory of Saint Sepulcher (Warwick Priory), originally built more than 900 years ago, were transplanted from England to Richmond in 1925 by American diplomat Alexander Wilbourne Weddell and his wife, Virginia. Reconfigured and renamed Virginia House, with gardens designed by landscape architect Charles F. Gillette, the estate lies a quarter mile south. Virginia House, an expression of the American Country Place movement, and its neighbor, Agecroft Hall, are the only two transplanted English manor houses standing side by side in America. Owned and exhibited by the Virginia Historical Society, Virginia House is on the National Register of Historic Places.

SA-50 WHITE HOUSE OF THE CONFEDERACY

1201 East Clay Street. Built in 1818 as the residence of Dr. John Brockenbrough, this National Historic Landmark is best known as the executive mansion for the Confederate States of America, 1861–1865. President Jefferson Davis and his family lived here until Confederate forces evacuated Richmond on 2 April 1865. After serving five years as the headquarters of Federal occupation troops, the house became one of Richmond's first public schools. In 1890, the Confederate Memorial Literary Society saved the mansion from destruction and

between 1896 and 1976 used it as the Confederate Museum. The Society restored the house to its wartime appearance and reopened it to the public in 1988.

SA-52 CONFEDERATE MEMORIAL CHAPEL

Grove Avenue and Sheppard Street. The chapel was erected in 1887 in memory of the more than 260,000 Confederate war dead and as a place of worship for the veterans who resided here in the Robert E. Lee Camp Confederate Soldiers' Home. The veterans themselves, many of them disabled and impoverished, funded the construction. Marion J. Dimmock, Sr., designed the Gothic Revival structure and Joseph F. Wingfield built it. The chapel was used regularly until the last resident veteran died in 1941. The home was then closed and the buildings were demolished, except for the chapel and the Robinson House, the superintendent's dwelling. The chapel was restored in 1960–1961.

SA-53 THE CARILLON

1300 Blanton Avenue, at Byrd Park. The Carillon, Virginia's War Memorial for World War I, was erected by the Commonwealth of Virginia to commemorate those who served. Designed by noted Boston architect Ralph Adams Cram, it is an interpretation of the Italian *campanile* in Georgian classicism. A commission was formed about 1922 to study a design and a site, but public campaigns altered the initial proposal and delayed construction until 1931. The tower was completed and dedicated on 15 October 1932. The Carillon reaches a height of 240 feet and its bells were originally intended to ring out patriotic concerts. The city of Richmond has maintained this structure since its construction.

SA-54 ENGINE COMPANY NO. 9 FIRE STATION

Southwest corner, 5th and Duval Streets. On 1 July 1950, the first professional Afro-

American firefighters in Virginia were hired and in September were stationed on the northeast corner of this intersection. These courageous pioneers created a loyalty and dedication to each other and their profession notwithstanding discriminatory practices. Harvey S. Hicks, among those first hired, became the city's first black fire captain in September 1961. On 14 June 1963, Hicks and firefighter Douglas P. Evans sacrificed their lives in a rescue attempt. The city integrated the fire department on 6 July 1963 and demolished the fire station in 1968.

SA-56 KAHAL KADOSH BETH SHALOME

14th Street, at East Franklin Street, at James Monroe Building. Jews have participated in Virginia's social and economic life from the colony's beginnings. Kahal Kadosh Beth Shalome (Holy Congregation House of Peace) was founded in Richmond in 1789, when the Jewish community grew large enough to establish the first Jewish congregation in Virginia and the sixth oldest in the United States. Temporary sites housed Beth Shalome until a permanent synagogue was built nearby and dedicated on 15 Sept. 1822. The modest one-story brick structure was sold in 1891 and demolished in 1934. Beth Shalome merged with Richmond's Beth Ahabah congregation in 1898.

SA-57 JOSEPH BRYAN PARK

Hermitage Road, at park. Before becoming a park, this property was part of the Young family's Westbrook estate in the 1700s and later Rosewood, home of the Mordecai family. It was a gathering place for participants in Gabriel's Rebellion in 1800. During the Civil War, Confederate troops camped here. Belle Stewart Bryan purchased this site in 1909 and donated it to the city of Richmond in memory of her husband, Richmond Times publisher Joseph Bryan. The park was designed in the English Naturalistic landscape tradition. It became an auto camp in the 1920s. Federal

relief programs in the 1930s resulted in further improvements. In 1952, the city's Parks Superintendent of Grounds and Structures Robert Harvey developed the 17-acre azalea garden, which became a popular tourist attraction.

SA-58 ALFRED D. "A.D." PRICE

212 East Leigh Street. Born into slavery in Hanover County in 1860, Alfred D. "A. D." Price moved to Richmond in the late 1870s. Soon after coming to Richmond, he set up a blacksmith shop, which expanded into a livery stable and the funeral home that stands here, now known as A. D. Price Funeral Establishment. In August 1894, Price became one of the first funeral directors in Virginia to receive a state embalming license. He served on the board of directors of a number of businesses and organizations, including the Southern Aid Society, a prominent insurance company. Price served as its president from 1905 until his death on 9 April 1921.

SA-60 FOREST HILL PARK

Forest Hill Avenue, at park. This 105-acre site was part of William Byrd III's vast 1700s holdings along the James River. In 1836, Holden Rhodes (1799–1857), noted jurist and early president of the Richmond and Petersburg Railroad Company, purchased the property, named it Boscobel, and built what is now known as the Stone House. In 1890, the Richmond & Manchester Railway Company established a trolley terminus and an amusement park here called Forest Hill Park. The amusement structures were dismantled in 1932 and the city of Richmond acquired the land in 1934. Depression-era Federal Emergency Relief Act funds paid for renovations to the Stone House and the construction of cobblestone walkways, picnic shelters, and landscape elements.

SA-61 JOHN MILLER HOUSE

Holly Street, near Belvidere Street (Rte. 1/301). John Miller, a free black cooper and minister, built this house about 1858. It is significant as a rare surviving antebellum house in Richmond constructed by and for a free African American family. More than two thousand free blacks lived in Richmond at the time of the Civil War; at least two hundred of them were homeowners. Miller was an influential member of the small free black community that existed in present-day Oregon Hill. Originally erected at 614 S. Laurel Street, the dwelling moved to its present location in 1917, two blocks to the west of here at 617 S. Cherry Street, by Richmond businessman Moses Nunnally.

SA-62 SAMUEL PLEASANTS PARSONS HOUSE

601 Spring Street, at Belvidere Street (Rte. 1/301). Completed in 1819, 601 Spring Street was the home of Samuel Pleasants Parsons (1783–1842). Parsons, a Quaker, was an early reform-minded superintendent (1816–1822, 1824–1832) of the Virginia State Penitentiary, formerly located across Belvidere Street. The Parsons family was part of a network of important Richmond Quaker families that were collectively involved in a series of abolition and prison reform activities. Parsons later served as a superintendent for the James River and Kanawha Company and was a founder of the Mechanicsville Turnpike. The house is a part of the Oregon Hill Historic District, listed on the National Register of Historic Places in 1991.

SA-63 JACOB HOUSE

619 West Cary Street. In 1817 George Winston built the Jacob House nearby, in the development known as Sydney. Winston (1759–1826), a Quaker who built the first Richmond Friends Meeting House at 19th and Cary Streets about 1798, employed a large number of free black apprentices. An important builder here during this period, Winston participated in the construction of the Virginia State Capitol and the Virginia

State Penitentiary. The Jacob House derives its name from John Jacob, an assistant superintendent at the Virginia State Penitentiary who bought the house in 1832. The building was moved to this site from 610 W. Cary Street in 1995.

SA-64 OAKWOOD CEMETERY, CONFEDERATE SECTION

Richmond Road, at Oakwood Cemetery. After the First Battle of Manassas, Richmond appropriated this approximately 7.5-acre lot on 12 Aug. 1861 for the burial of Confederate war dead. These soldiers from every Southern state either died in Richmond's military hospitals, such as Chimborazo, or were brought directly from local battlefields. Eventually they numbered about 17,200, including some 8,000 unknowns. The first recorded Memorial Day observance in Richmond occurred here on 10 May 1866, organized by the Ladies' Memorial Association for Confederate Dead in Oakwood Cemetery. Robert E. Lee, invited to speak, declined but wrote, "The graves of the Confederate dead will always be green in my memory, and their deeds be hallowed in my recollection."

SA-65 RICHMOND'S FIRST AFRICAN AMERICAN POLICE OFFICERS

Brook Avenue and Leigh Street, in Abner Clay Park. On 1 May 1946, Richmond's first professional African American police officers were hired and assigned to the First Precinct at Smith and Marshall Streets. They were Howard T. Braxton, Doctor P. Day, Frank S. Randolph, and John W. Vann. On 16 December 1949, Ruth B. Blair became the first professional African American female police officer hired and assigned to the Juvenile Division. On 18 July 1964, Sergeant Randolph was promoted to Detective Lieutenant. While challenged by segregated conditions and discriminatory practices, their perseverance created an inspiring legacy.

SA-66 EXECUTION OF GABRIEL

Broad Street, between North 16th Street and bridge over I-95. Near here is the early site of the Richmond gallows and "Burial Ground for Negroes." On 10 Oct. 1800, Gabriel, an enslaved blacksmith from Brookfield plantation in Henrico County, was executed there for attempting to lead a mass uprising against slavery on 30 Aug. 1800. A fierce rainstorm delayed the insurrection, which then was betrayed by two slaves. Gabriel escaped and eluded capture until 23 Sept., when he was arrested in Norfolk. He was returned to Richmond on 27 Sept. and incarcerated in the Virginia State Penitentiary. On 6 Oct. he stood trial and was condemned. At least 25 of his supporters were also put to death there or in other jurisdictions.

SA-67 MONROE PARK

Near North Laurel Street and South Cathedral Place, at park. In 1851 the City of Richmond planned a series of parks including Western Square now known as Monroe Park. In the 1850s it served as grounds for what became the state fair organized by the Virginia State Agricultural Society. During the Civil War it was the site of a Confederate instructional camp, and in 1864, a military hospital. In 1866, some of the city's earliest baseball games were played here. Its development as a park began in 1869 in one of Richmond's emerging fashionable neighborhoods. The park contains a pattern of walks radiating from an elaborate four-tiered, cast-iron fountain. A portion of it once was a playground and it has been the scene of political rallies, protest demonstrations, and concerts.

SA-68 BRANCH PUBLIC BATHS

1801 East Broad Street. John Patteson Branch (1830–1915), banker, philanthropist and community leader, erected Richmond's first public bath here in 1909 at 1801 East Broad Street as a gift to the city. In the late 19th and early 20th centuries, cities such as Baltimore, Philadelphia, and New York began operating municipally managed public baths that were open throughout the year to promote good public health. In 1913, Branch Public Bath No. 2 at 709 West Main Street was opened. At the peak in the early 1920s, more than 80,000 customers used the two facilities each year. The development of domestic indoor plumbing led to the closing of the two public baths in 1950.

SPOTSYLVANIA COUNTY

E-8 STUART

Rte. 1, 5.4 miles south of Falmouth. At this point J. E. B. Stuart had his headquarters and cavalry camp in December 1862.

E-30 TURN IN SHERIDAN'S RAID

Rte. 1, 1.8 miles south of Thornburg, near Spotsylvania/Caroline County line. At this point in his Richmond raid, Gen. Sheridan, after a fight with Confederate cavalry commanded by General Willians [Williams] C. Wickham, turned off the Telegraph Road to Beaver Dam, May 9, 1864. This change of route caused Sheridan to approach Richmond from the northwest instead of the north.

E-31 JERRELL'S MILL

Rte. 1, near Matta River, 1.1 miles south of Thornburg. Here, on May 9, 1864, Sheridan was attacked by Wickham's cavalry. Nearby, on May 22, 1864, Warren's (Fifth) Corps, moving to the North Anna, fought Rosser's cavalry.

E-32 MUD TAVERN

Rte. 1, Thornburg. Mud Tavern was the old name of this place. Six miles east, at Guinea Station, Stonewall Jackson died,

May 10, 1863. In the campaign of 1864, Ewell's and Longstreet's corps of Lee's army, coming from Spotsylvania Courthouse, here turned south, May 21, 1864. Lee fell back to the North Anna River as Grant swung around to the east.

E-33 FEDERAL RAID

Rte. 1, near Massaponax. On 5 Aug. 1862, two detachments of Union troops left Fredericksburg with the intention of damaging the Orange and Alexandria Railroad. Brig. Gen. John Gibbon led a brigade of some 2,000 men down Telegraph Road toward Hanover Junction, while Col. Lysander Cutler led a smaller force to Frederick's Hall via Spotsylvania Court House. Near Thornburg, Gibbon encountered Confederate cavalry and turned back. Cutler avoided the Confederates, however, and destroyed two miles of track before returning to Fredericksburg on 8 Aug. The Confederates quickly repaired the damage.

E-35 STANARD'S MILL

Rte. 1, north of Thornburg. Unable to defeat the Confederates at Spotsylvania Court House, on 21 May 1864 Lt. Gen. Ulysses S. Grant ordered the Army of the Potomac to march toward Bowling Green. Maj. Gen. Ambrose E. Burnside's Ninth Corps brought up the rear. Grant ordered Burnside to pursue the Confederates down Telegraph Road (present day U.S. Rte. 1), while the rest of the army struck at Robert E. Lee's troops from the east. Burnside encountered a small entrenched Confederate force at the Po River here at Stanard's Mill. Uncertain of the enemy's strength, he did not attempt to force a crossing, but instead reversed course, following the rest of the army to Guinea Station.

E-36 ROAD TO GUINEA STATION

Rte. 1, at Rte. 607. On 4 May 1863, the ambulance bearing wounded Confederate Maj. Gen. Thomas J. ("Stonewall") Jackson from the Chancellorsville battlefield turned east here en route to Guinea Station, where

he died on 10 May. A year later, Union troops of the Army of the Potomac followed the same route when marching from the Spotsylvania Court House battlefield south to Totopotomoy Creek in Hanover County. During this march, Union generals Grant and Meade stopped briefly at Massaponax Baptist Church, located two-thirds of a mile north of here.

E-38 LEE'S WINTER HEADQUARTERS

Rte. 636, near Rte. 2058. During the winter of 1862–1863, Confederate Gen. Robert E. Lee maintained his headquarters in a small clearing in the woods in this vicinity. The camp contained only a few tents and nothing but a flag to indicate it was Lee's headquarters. By mid-February the Army of Northern Virginia showed signs of scurvy and malnutrition, so Lee sent Lt. Gen. James Longstreet and a few other divisions to southeastern Virginia to gather supplies and counter Union forces. Lee remained at the site until late March 1863, when a serious throat infection forced him to take shelter at the nearby Thomas Yerby's house.

E-39 START OF SHERIDAN'S RAID

Rte. 1, 5.3 miles south of Falmouth. Here Sheridan, moving from camp, came into the Telegraph Road on his raid to Richmond, May 9, 1864, while Lee and Grant were fighting at Spotsylvania. The 10,000 Union cavalry filled the road for several miles. Turning from the road ten miles south, Sheridan came into it again at Yellow Tavern near Richmond May 11, 1864.

E-40 GRANT'S SUPPLY LINE

Rte. 208, near Rte. 639. The Fredericksburg Road, present-day Route 208, was the Army of the Potomac's supply line during the Battle of Spotsylvania Court House. For two weeks in May 1864, wagons shuttled back and forth along the road between the Union army and its supply base at Belle Plains on the Potomac River. Thousands of Confederate prisoners and wounded Union soldiers made their way to the rear along this road. As the Union army continued south toward Richmond, it shifted its supply base from Belle Plains to Port Royal, and abandoned the Fredericksburg Road about 21 May.

E-41 LONGSTREET'S WINTER HEADQUARTERS

Rte. 41, near Four Mile Fork. Following the Battle of Fredericksburg in Dec. 1862, Confederate Lt. Gen. James Longstreet established his headquarters in a tent near here. His command center was in close proximity to Generals Robert E. Lee and J. E. B. Stuart. Longstreet commanded the Army of Northern Virginia's First Corps, a force totaling approximately 40,000 men. In Feb. 1863 Longstreet left Fredericksburg with the divisions of Maj. Gens. George E. Pickett and John B. Hood to conduct an independent military operation near Suffolk. He rejoined the Army of Northern Virginia in May following the Battle of Chancellorsville.

E-42 COX HOUSE

Rte. 1, at Rte. 1228. Across the road to the northeast stood the Cox House, also known as the Wiatt House. In December 1862, Confederate Maj. Gen. Lafayette McLaws's division used it as a hospital, and there on 13 December, Brig. Gen. Thomas R. R. Cobb died from wounds received during the Battle of Fredericksburg. On 3 May 1863, during the Battle of Chancellorsville, Maj. Gen. Jubal A. Early rallied his Confederate troops at the Cox House after Union Maj. Gen. John Sedgwick drove them off Marye's Heights. Early later retook the heights and attacked Sedgwick's rear, while McLaws engaged him in battle near Salem Church.

E-46 COLONIAL FORT

Business Rte. 17/2, approximately 1 mile southeast of Rte. 638. The Virginia General Assembly authorized the construction of a fort built nearby along the Rappahannock River in 1676. It served as a defensive fortification for settlers of European descent on the frontier when periodic conflicts occurred between Virginia Indians and settlers. Maj. Lawrence Smith commanded the fort. Smith had patented 6,300 acres of property with Robert Taliaferro in the region in 1666. Smith later obtained more land nearby. The fort was abandoned about 1682, when the General Assembly ordered the dismantling of many of these structures.

E-78 MASSAPONAX BAPTIST CHURCH

Rte. 608, near Rte. 1. Massaponax Baptist Church, built in 1859, served a congregation founded in 1788. On 21 May 1864 Lt. Gen. Ulysses S. Grant and his commanders conferred on pews in the churchyard as the Union army marched from the Spotsylvania Court House battlefield to the North Anna River. Photographer Timothy O'Sullivan hauled his heavy stereo camera to the balcony of the church and recorded this conference in a unique series of candid images showing a war council in progress.

E-84 FORT HOOD

Business Rte. 17/2, at Rte. 608. In November 1862, Confederate forces under Maj. Gen. John Bell Hood constructed this fort a half mile northeast on the Rappahannock River in an effort to prevent Union gunboats from ascending the river toward Fredericksburg. Four rifled guns of Capt. H. M. Ross's Georgia Battery briefly occupied the work, but were withdrawn when the Union army crossed the river upstream from here on 11 December. Two days later, during the Battle of Fredericksburg, Union troops of the Iron Brigade captured the fort after a brief skirmish with the 13th Virginia Cavalry, which guarded this portion of the Confederate line.

E-113 JAMES FARMER, CIVIL RIGHTS LEADER

Rte. 1, north of Rte. 607. James Leonard Farmer was born in Texas on 12 Jan. 1920.

In 1942, he and other Civil Rights leaders founded the Congress of Racial Equality (CORE) in Chicago. CORE used Gandhi-inspired tactics of nonviolent civil disobedience to protest discriminatory practices against blacks. Under Farmer's leadership, in the spring of 1961, CORE organized "Freedom Riders" to desegregate interstate transportation in the Deep South. He was an assistant secretary in the U.S. Department of Health, Education and Welfare (1969–1970). Farmer taught at Mary Washington College (1985–1999) and received the Presidential Medal of Freedom in 1998. Farmer died on 9 July 1999. His house stands east of here.

E-118 The Chancellorsville Campaign

Rte. 1, near Four Mile Fork. While General Robert E. Lee engaged the Union army at Chancellorsville, Confederate Maj. Gen. Jubal A. Early confronted a smaller Union force led by Maj. Gen. John Sedgwick at Fredericksburg. On 3 May 1863, Sedgwick overran Early's lines at Marye's Heights, compelling Early to fall back to this point. When Sedgwick moved toward Chancellorsville, Early slipped in behind him, retaking Marye's Heights. Early and other Confederate troops then attacked Sedgwick on 4 May, forcing the Union general to retreat across the Rappahannock River at Scott's Ford.

E-127 Heth's Salient Battle Site

Bypass Rte. 208, just east of Heth's Salient battle site. After four days of probing attacks, Gen. Ulysses S. Grant ordered a frontal assault against the Confederate lines at Spotsylvania Court House on 12 May 1864. The focal point of the attack was the Muleshoe Salient, an outward bulge in the Confederate line. While the II and VI Corps struck the head of the salient, resulting in the struggle for the "Bloody Angle," Gen. Ambrose E. Burnside's IX Corps assaulted the Muleshoe's eastern face, known as Heth's Salient, located

nearby. Confederate defenders, ensconced behind log works, repulsed the early morning attacks and at 2 p.m. counterattacked through this area. During more than 20 hours of fighting the Federals lost some 9,000 killed, wounded, and captured. The Confederates lost an estimated 8,000 casualties.

E-128 Third Spotsylvania County Courthouse Site

Bypass Rte. 208, at third courthouse site. This site was the location of the third Spotsylvania courthouse. In 1722 the first county court session was held at Germanna (now in Orange County) and a courthouse was built soon after. The court was relocated to Fredericksburg in 1732. In 1778 the General Assembly permitted the county to move the courthouse again to a more central location. The first court session was held here in 1781. The County's courthouse, jail, pillory, stocks, and gallows were built, and a clerk's office and tavern were erected thereafter. A second courthouse, built in 1800, replaced the original. In 1837 it burned to the ground, and a replacement was built nearby at the present site of the Spotsylvania courthouse.

E-129 Penny's Tavern Site

Bypass Rte. 208, northwest of Rtes. 208 and 648. Nearby stood Penny's (Penney's) Tavern, named for Lincefield Penney who purchased the site in 1811. The tavern catered to travelers making their way to the old Spotsylvania courthouse site (1781–1837), located approximately one mile north of the tavern site across the Po River. After the Court House burned in 1837 and was moved to its present location, business greatly declined. By 1840 the property was sold to Mansfield Wigglesworth who operated a tavern there called Wigglesworth Tavern. The tavern was closed by the outbreak of the Civil War. The intersection where the tavern once stood was known as Penny's Crossroads into the twentieth century.

EH-8 ASBURY'S DEATHPLACE

Rte. 738, 5.5 miles south of Spotsylvania.
A short distance southeast is the site of
the George Arnold House where Bishop
Francis Asbury died, March 31, 1816.
Asbury, born in England in 1745, came to
America in 1771 and labored here until his
death. He was ordained one of the first two
bishops of the Methodist Episcopal Church
in America at the Baltimore Conference of
December, 1784.

EM-1 FREDERICKSVILLE FURNACE

Rte. 208, just southwest of furnace. Charles
Chiswell established the iron-making community of Fredericksville near this point
of Douglas Run, a tributary of the North
Anna River. The furnace had been in blast
for about five years when William Byrd
in 1732 toured the site in the company of
Chiswell and his iron-master, Robert Durham. An archaeological investigation of the
furnace was financed by Virginia Electric
and Power Company in 1970.

EM-2 ENGAGEMENT AT HARRIS FARM
(BLOOMSBURY)

Rte. 208, 0.25 miles west of Rte. 628. On 19
May 1864 Confederate forces commanded
by Lt. Gen. Richard S. Ewell attacked
Brig. Gen. Robert O. Tyler's heavy artillery
division on the Union right flank near the
Harris farm, Bloomsbury, about one-
quarter mile northwest. Newly arrived
from the forts protecting Washington,
D.C., the inexperienced "heavies" fought as
infantry and stubbornly held their ground.
At dark Ewell withdrew, ending the last
major engagement of the Battle of Spotsyl-
vania Court House. The Confederates suf-
fered 900 casualties at the Harris farm, the
Federals about 1,500. Two days later, the
Union army marched to the North Anna
River as Grant maneuvered south toward
Richmond.

J-37 JACKSON'S AMPUTATION

*Rte. 3, east of Rte. 20, east of Spotsylvania/
Orange County line.* Near here stood the

hospital tent to which the wounded "Stonewall" Jackson was brought during the
Battle of Chancellorsville. In that tent his
left arm was amputated on May 3, 1863. He
died seven days later at Guinea.

J-38 ELY'S FORD

*Rte. 610, 0.54 miles southeast of Spotsylvania/
Culpeper County line.* On this hill, May 3,
1863, Confederate General "J. E. B." Stuart
was notified that General "Stonewall" Jackson had been wounded at Chancellorsville
and that he was to take command of Jackson's Corps. Moments before, Stuart had
ordered his 1,000 men from North Carolina and Virginia to attack the 3,400 Penn-
sylvanians under General A. W. Averell at
Ely's Ford. After ordering three volleys of
musket fire at the Union troops below, Stuart cancelled the attack and left to assume
his command at Chancellorsville.

J-39 WOUNDING OF JACKSON

Rte. 3, west of Rte. 1792, near Chancellorsville.
Just 1.7 miles west, on this road (then the
Orange Plank Road), Lt. Gen. Thomas J.
"Stonewall" Jackson was wounded by
"friendly fire" about 9:30 P.M. on 2 May
1863 during the Battle of Chancellorsville.
Having brilliantly executed a flanking maneuver against the Federals, Jackson, with
eight aides, was returning from a reconnaissance between the lines. When skirmishing erupted, they were mistaken for
Federals in the darkness and fired on by the
18th N.C. Infantry, killing four and wounding Jackson. After a battlefield amputation
of his left arm, Jackson was taken 17 miles
southeast to Guinea Station, where he died
on 10 May from infection.

J-40 BATTLE OF CHANCELLORSVILLE

Rte. 610, near Rte. 3, Chancellorsville.
Hooker reached this point, April 30, 1863;
next day he entrenched, with his left wing
on the river and his right wing on this road
several miles west. That wing was surprised
by Jackson and driven back here, May 2.
The Confederates stormed the position

here, May 3. The Union army withdrew northward, May 5–6, 1863.

J-42 SPOTSWOOD'S FURNACE

Rte. 3, 3.29 miles west of Fredericksburg corporate limits. Four miles north, on this side road, is the site of an ancient iron furnace established about 1716 by Governor Alexander Spotswood, the first fully equipped iron furnace in the colonies. Iron was hauled along this road to the Rappahannock River for shipment. William Byrd visited the furnace in 1732 and described it.

JJ-25 GASPAR TOCHMAN

Rte. 621, 0.25 miles south of Rte. 611. A mile south is the unmarked grave of Gaspar Tochman (1797–1880), a major in the Polish army who participated in the failed 1830 revolt against Russia. Exiled, in 1837 he immigrated to the United States, where he practiced law, wrote, and lectured. During the Civil War he recruited the Polish Brigade (14th and 15th Louisiana regiments) of Jackson's Corps. A colonel in the Confederate army, he sought unsuccessfully the rank of brigadier general. Tochman settled here in 1866 and served as the European agent for the Virginia Board of Immigration.

N-3 THE GALLANT PELHAM

Business Rte. 17/2, 0.02 miles south of Rte. 608. Here Major John Pelham, commanding Stuart's Horse Artillery, executed a stunning flank attack on advancing Union troops during the Battle of Fredericksburg on 13 December 1862. Reduced to one cannon, the 24-year-old Pelham halted the Federals for almost two hours by employing the flying artillery tactics that he had perfected. Observing from a nearby hilltop, Lee exclaimed, "It is glorious to see such courage in one so young!" Lee's battle report commended "the gallant Pelham." The Alabamian was fatally wounded three months later at Kelly's Ford on the upper Rappahannock River.

N-10 COLONIAL POST OFFICE

Rte. 17, 0.4 miles northwest of New Post. Here was Newpost, headquarters of Alexander Spotswood (Governor of Virginia, 1710–22), deputy postmaster general for the colonies, 1730–39. Spotswood also had an iron furnace here.

WASHINGTON-ROCHAMBEAU ROUTE

Marker not erected. Original location: Business Rte. 17, 200 feet east of Rte. 1. Generals Washington and Rochambeau slept here the night of Sept. 12, 1781. Having learned that Admiral de Grasse had put to sea to fight the British fleet under Admiral Graves, Washington and Rochambeau with their staffs hastened to Williamsburg. *Note:* This is one of five unnumbered signs discussing aspects of the Washington-Rochambeau Route, which were a special gift from the French Government, Committee of the Bicentennial, to the Commonwealth of Virginia in 1976.

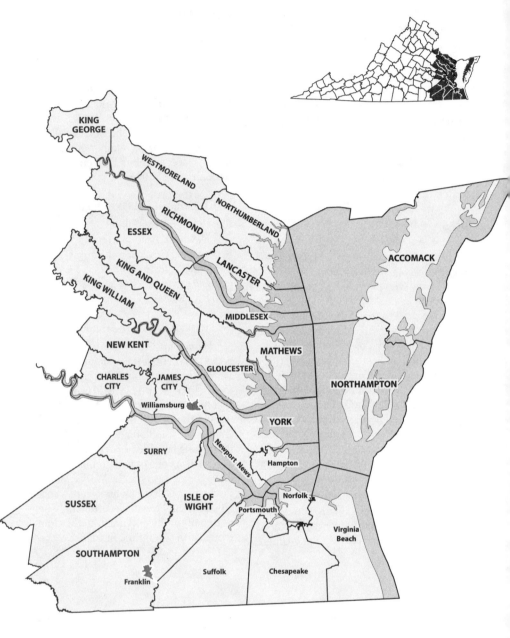

KING
GEORGE

WESTMORELAND

RICHMOND

NORTHUMBERLAND

ESSEX

LANCASTER

KING AND QUEEN

MIDDLESEX

KING WILLIAM

ACCOMACK

NEW KENT

MATHEWS

CHARLES
CITY

GLOUCESTER

JAMES
CITY

Williamsburg

NORTHAMPTON

SURRY

YORK

Newport News

Hampton

SUSSEX

ISLE OF
WIGHT

Norfolk

Portsmouth

Virginia
Beach

SOUTHAMPTON

Suffolk

Chesapeake

Franklin

MILES

0   10   25

Eastern Virginia

EASTERN VIRGINIA is bounded by the Potomac River to the north and North Carolina to the south, and includes the Chesapeake Bay and the state's eastern peninsula, comprising Accomack and Northampton Counties. The other counties in the region are Charles City, Essex, Gloucester, Isle of Wight, James City, King George, King and Queen, King William, Lancaster, Mathews, Middlesex, New Kent, Northumberland, Richmond, Southampton, Surry, Sussex, Westmoreland, and York. The major cities include Chesapeake, Franklin, Suffolk, Virginia Beach, and Williamsburg, and the ports of Hampton, Newport News, Norfolk, and Portsmouth.

Recent archaeological investigations have determined that people first inhabited present-day Virginia more than fifteen thousand years ago. By 1607, Wahunsunacok (better known as Powhatan) ruled as paramount chief over approximately thirty chiefdoms and most of eastern Virginia. This complex society existed when the English arrived at Jamestown that year. Periods of coexistence and hostility followed as Europeans expanded into Indian lands throughout the seventeenth century.

From Jamestown the European settlers established a number of communities along the region's navigable rivers. It was here that colonists combined the culture of tobacco with slavery to create a society that dominated the commonwealth well into the eighteenth century. Places such as Martin's Hundred, Bennett's Plantation, and Governor's Land are featured on historical markers in the region.

The first documented Africans in English America arrived at Jamestown in August 1619, the same year that the first English representative legislative body in North America met there. These Africans were indentured servants and were freed after their periods of servitude expired. Coexisting with indentured servitude was the institution of slavery, which evolved during the seventeenth century as Virginia colonists extended the length of service for Africans from a fixed term to life.

The College of William and Mary was established in 1693 as one of the earliest institutions of higher learning in the United States, and in 1699 Williamsburg became the capital of Colonial Virginia. Williamsburg was an important meeting place where leaders discussed and debated the issues that led to the outbreak of the American Revolution.

The last major battle of the Revolutionary War occurred at Yorktown in 1781, where the British surrendered to American and French forces. The route that George Washington and the comte de Rochambeau's troops and supplies took to Yorktown is documented on a number of historical markers. Several markers also describe the 1862 Peninsula campaign during the Civil War, when Union armies sought to lay siege to the Confederate capital of Richmond.

The Newport News–Hampton–Norfolk–Portsmouth area is the primary seaport of Virginia. The U.S. Navy and other federal government facilities based in the region, as well as the Newport News Shipbuilding and Dry Dock Company, have fueled its development and made it one of the most populated areas in the state. Meanwhile, interior portions of the Tidewater region remain heavily agricultural.

During the twentieth century, eastern Virginia witnessed numerous military and aviation milestones, including the first ship-to-shore flight, conducted by Eugene Ely in 1910; Brigadier General Billy Mitchell's successful bombing trials in 1921, which showed that air power could destroy battleships; and the training of America's first astronauts at Langley Field in the late 1950s and 1960s.

The state-recognized tribes of the Chickahominy, Eastern Chickahominy, Mattaponi, Nansemond, Pamunkey, Rappahannock, and Upper Mattaponi are located within this region. A few existing historical markers describe the important role that these tribes have played throughout the commonwealth; more are in process or planned to commemorate the history of Virginia Indians.

Markers dealing with African American history in eastern Virginia describe the development of segregated schools for and by blacks during the late nineteenth and early twentieth centuries, such as the Northern Neck Industrial Academy in Richmond County. Markers also highlight the contributions of African American leaders and politicians, such as the nineteenth-century state delegate and lawyer James Fields of Newport News, and document such important places as Little England Chapel in Hampton.

ACCOMACK COUNTY

EP-21 BIRTHPLACE OF GOVERNOR WISE

Business Rte. 13, Accomac. Here stood the birthplace of Henry Alexander Wise (1806–1876), Governor of Virginia (1856–1860) and General in the Confederate States Army. A talented orator and debator in an age of great orators, Wise was elected to six terms in Congress. He served as a delegate at the Virginia Conventions of 1850 and 1861, and as United States Minister to Brazil (1844–1847).

EP-22 MARY NOTTINGHAM SMITH HIGH SCHOOL

Business Rte. 13, 0.5 miles east of Rte. 13, Accomac. The first high school for blacks in Accomack County was dedicated on this site in 1932. It was named in honor of Mary Nottingham Smith (1892–1951), a black educator who dedicated her life to educating all young people. In 1956, the school was renamed for T. C. Walker, an attorney from Gloucester County. It was demolished in 1987. A second Mary N. Smith High School was built on another site in 1953.

Q-7-a TANGIER ISLAND

Tangier Island. The island was visited in 1608 by Captain John Smith, who gave it the name. A part was patented by Ambrose White in 1670. It was settled in 1686 by John Crockett and his sons' families. In 1814, it was the headquarters of a British fleet ravaging Chesapeake Bay. From here the fleet sailed to attack Fort McHenry near Baltimore. The Rev. Joshua Thomas, in a prayer, predicted the failure of the expedition. It was in this attack that the Star-Spangled Banner was written.

WY-12 PUNGOTEAGUE ENGAGEMENT

Rte. 626, approximately 0.25 miles from Rte. 13, Melfa. To the west, on 30 May 1814, during the War of 1812, Rear Admiral George Cockburn's British forces invaded Pungoteague Creek from the Chesapeake Bay. Early that morning, eleven barges and launches landed there with close to 500 soldiers. Maj. John Finney of the 2d Regiment of the local militia engaged the British forces. Forced back by an overwhelming number of enemy troops, Finney retreated to thickly wooded region. Finney's forces continued to engage the enemy until a bugle sounded on a barge and the British troops retreated to their landing vessels and sailed back to Tangier Island.

WY-13 OCCOHANNOCK INDIANS

Rte. 181, 0.125 miles from Rte. 12, Belle Haven. The Occohannock Indians, one of the important Virginia Indian groups on the Eastern Shore, were composed of several tribes including the Onancock, Machipongo, Metomkin, Chincoteague, Kegotank, Pungoteague, Chesconessex, and Nandua. Capt. John Smith visited them in 1608, but except for trading they had little contact with the English until the 1620s. The titular leader of the Occohannock and Accomac Indians in the 1620s was Esmy Shichans, also known as the "Laughing King." By the 1670s, the Occohannocks held only token areas in their former tribal territories. In the latter part of the 17th century, they moved back and forth between here and the large reservation of their linguistic relatives, the Pocomoke, in Maryland.

WY-14 ONANCOCK

Rtes. 13 and Rte. 179, Onley. Two miles west is Onancock, founded in 1680. A courthouse was then built and used for a few years. Militia barracks were there in the Revolution. From Onancock, Colonel John Cropper went to the aid of Commodore Whaley in the last naval action of the Revolution, November 30, 1782. Near by is Onley, home of Henry A. Wise, Governor of Virginia, 1856–60.

WY-15 FOUNDER OF PRESBYTERIANISM

Rte. 13, 7.5 miles south of the state line. Five miles west was the home of the Rev. Francis Makemie, founder of Presbyterianism in the United States. About 1684, Makemie established in Maryland the first Presbyterian church. Later he moved to Accomac and married. He died here in 1708.

WY-16 OAK GROVE METHODIST CHURCH

Rte. 13, Keller. Two miles east, on Rte. 600, meets what is possibly the nation's oldest continuous Sunday School. Begun by William Elliott in his home in 1785, it was moved in 1818 to Burton's Chapel and in 1870 to the present church.

WY-17 "THE BEAR AND THE CUB"

Rte. 13, Keller. This first play recorded in the United States was presented August 27,

1665. The Accomack County Court at Pungoteague heard charges against three men "For Acting a Play," ordered inspection of costumes and script, but found the men "Not Guilty."

WY-18 "THE BEAR AND THE CUB"

Rte. 178, 0.5 miles north of Pungoteague. Probable site of Fowkes' Tavern where this first recorded play in English America was performed August 27, 1665.

WY-19 DEBTORS PRISON

Rte. 764, Accomac. Built in 1783 in one corner of the jailyard to serve as residence for the jailer, the building served in this capacity for 41 years. Iron bars, oak batten doors and locks were added in 1842 when it was converted into a prison for debtors in Accomack County.

CHARLES CITY COUNTY

PA-250 BENJAMIN HARRISON

Rte. 5, 0.1 miles east of Rte. 156. Benjamin Harrison (1726–1791)—Virginia planter, politician, and signer of the Declaration of Independence—was born at nearby Berkeley plantation. He first served in the Virginia House of Burgesses in 1752, though elected in 1749, and remained in office until 1775. In 1774, the Virginia Revolutionary Convention sent Harrison to the Continental Congress, where he served through 1777. He was Speaker of the Virginia House of Delegates from 1778 to 1781 and governor of Virginia from 1781 to 1784. His son William Henry Harrison and great-grandson Benjamin Harrison were presidents of the United States.

PH-6 ACTION OF NANCE'S SHOP

Rte. 603, east of Rte. 106. In this vicinity the Union cavalryman, Gregg, guarding army trains moving to Petersburg, was attacked by Wade Hampton, June 24, 1864. Gregg was driven back toward Charles City

Courthouse, but the wagon trains crossed the James safely. This action closed the cavalry campaign that began at Trevillians, June 11–12, 1864.

V-6 SHIRLEY

Rte. 5, at Rte. 608, 17.1 miles southeast of Richmond. The house is a short distance south. Shirley was first occupied in 1613 and was known as West-and-Shirley Hundred. In 1664, Edward Hill patented the place, which was left by the third Edward Hill to his sister, Elizabeth Carter, in 1720. Here was born Anne Hill Carter, mother of Robert E. Lee, who often visited Shirley. The present house was built about 1740.

V-7 BERKELEY PLANTATION OR HARRISON'S LANDING

Rte. 5, at Herring Creek Road, west of Charles City. A short distance south. It was first settled in 1619, when the first Thanksgiving was held here. The present mansion, built in 1726, was the birthplace of Benjamin

Harrison, signer of the Declaration of Independence, and President William Henry Harrison. During July and August, 1862, it was the headquarters of General McClellan. The bugle call "Taps" was composed here then by General Butterfield.

V-8 WESTOVER

Rte. 5, at Herring Creek Road, west of Charles City. In 1619 the first settlement was made at Westover, about two miles southeast. Two settlers died in the Powhatan uprising of 1622. Theodorick Bland bought Westover in 1666; William Byrd I acquired it in 1688. About 1730 his son, Colonel William Byrd II, built the present house, which exemplifies the high level of architectural quality attained during the colonial era. In January 1781 the British army under General Charles Cornwallis crossed the James River at Westover in pursuit of the Marquis de Lafayette.

V-9 GRANT'S CROSSING

Rte. 5, at Rte. 618, 2.4 miles west of Charles City. In mid-June 1864, Grant abandoned his works at Cold Harbor and marched to Petersburg, a vital rail center. A mile south of here, at Wilcox Wharf (now Lawrence Lewis, Jr., Park), steamboats ferried the troops and wagons of two corps across the James River on 14–15 June. Three miles downstream, at Weyanoke Point, Union engineers built a 700-yard-long pontoon bridge in seven hours on 14 June. For three days parts of two corps, as well as supply, ammunition, and ambulance wagons, crossed the bridge in a column 50 miles long. Engineers then dismantled the bridge. Grant's attack on the Confederate lines at Petersburg failed, and the armies settled into a ten-month siege.

V-10 GREENWAY

Rte. 5, west of Charles City. This was the home of John Tyler, Governor of Virginia, 1808–1811. His son, John Tyler, President of the United States, was born here, March 29, 1790.

V-11 CHARLES CITY C. H.

Rte. 5, at Rte. 644, Charles City. In 1702 Charles City County, which then included both sides of James River, was divided; the courthouse here was built about 1730. Here Simcoe's British cavalry surprised a party of militia, January 8, 1781. Here Grant's army passed on its way to the river, June, 1864.

V-12 UPPER WEYANOKE

Rte. 5, at Rte. 619, east of Charles City. In 1617, Opechancanough, Chief Powhatan's younger brother, gave land to the south to future governor Capt. George Yeardley. Yeardley patented it and a portion became Upper Weyanoke, a James River plantation. Archaeological investigations there revealed an almost unbroken succession of settlements from the late 17th century to the late 19th century. On the grounds is a Greek Revival dwelling completed by 1859 for Robert Douthat. During the Civil War, about 14 June 1864 a pontoon bridge was constructed at Weyanoke Point across the James River for portions of Union Lt. Gen. Ulysses S. Grant's army. Upper Weyanoke was added to the Virginia Landmarks Register and the National Register of Historic Places in 1980.

V-13 SALEM CHURCH

Rte. 5, at Rte. 609, west of Charles City. This church, four miles north, was used as a field hospital, June, 1864, following the action at Nance's Shop, where the Union cavalryman Gregg, guarding a wagon train, was attacked by Wade Hampton. Gregg was driven from the field but saved the wagons. Wounded soldiers were brought to the church and some of the dead were buried there.

V-14 WESTOVER CHURCH

Rte. 5, 6.5 miles west of Charles City, at church. A short distance south is Westover Church. It was first built on the James River near Westover House early in the seventeenth century. About 1730 the site was changed and the present building erected. Defaced in the Campaign of 1862, the church was reopened for worship in 1867.

V-15 SCENE OF JEFFERSON'S WEDDING

Rte. 5, at Rt. 607, 15.1 miles southeast of Richmond. Two miles east is the site of "The Forest," home of Martha Wayles Skelton, widow of Bathurst Skelton. There she was married to Thomas Jefferson, January 1, 1772. The bridal couple drove in the snow to Jefferson's home, "Monticello."

V-21 PRESIDENT TYLER'S HOME

Rte. 5, 3.5 miles east of Charles City, at Sherwood Forest. Just to the south is Sherwood Forest, where President John Tyler lived after his retirement from the presidency until his death in 1862. He bought the place in 1842 and came to it as his home in March, 1845. Here Tyler, with his young second wife, entertained much and raised another large family. The house, well-furnished, was damaged in the war period, 1862–65.

V-22 EVELYNTON

Rte. 5, 4.73 miles west of Charles City, at Evelynton. Originally part of William Byrd's Westover, Evelynton has been occupied by the Ruffin family since 1847, when it was purchased by Edmund Ruffin, Jr. Fierce skirmishes took place on the property during the 1862 Peninsula Campaign. Confederate troops were led by generals J. E. B. Stuart and James Longstreet. The breastworks are still visible near the house. The dwelling and dependencies of the plantation were much damaged during the fighting. The Georgian-Revival house, built on the foundation of an earlier structure, was designed by noted architect, Duncan Lee, in 1935.

V-23 PINEY GROVE AND E. A. SAUNDERS

Rte. 5, 9.05 miles east of Charles City. Eight miles west on "The Old Main Road" is

Piney Grove. The original portion, built ca. 1800 on Southall's Plantation, is a rare survival of Tidewater log architecture. Edmund Archer Saunders, a successful Richmond businessman, operated a store at Piney Grove between 1857 and 1874 when he sold it to Thomas Harwood. Saunders later returned to Charles City County and purchased Upper Shirley and Weyanoke plantations. Harwood enlarged the building for his home in 1910.

V-24 NORTH BEND

Rte. 5, at Rte. 619, 1.27 miles east of Charles City. Three miles south is North Bend, a Greek Revival residence built in 1819. Sarah Minge, sister of President William Henry Harrison, and her husband, John, built the original portion of the house located on Kittiewan Creek. Thomas H. Wilcox greatly enlarged the dwelling in 1853. General Sheridan established his Union headquarters here while his 30,000 men crossed the James River on a pontoon bridge at Weyanoke.

V-27 LOTT CARY BIRTHPLACE

Rtes. 155 and 602. A mile and a half northwest, Lott Cary was born in slavery about 1780. In 1804 his owner, John Bowry, a Methodist minister, hired him out to a Richmond tobacco firm. Cary joined the First Baptist Church in 1807. He purchased his freedom and became a Baptist minister in 1813, then founded the African Missionary Society in 1815. Cary sailed for Africa in 1821 as the continent's first African-American missionary. He established Providence Baptist Church in Monrovia, Liberia, and several schools. As a political and military leader, Cary helped Liberia survive as a colony of free American blacks. He died there in November 1828.

V-34 FORT POCAHONTAS

Rte. 5, just east of Rte. 614, at turnout. South of here, on a bluff overlooking the James River, stands the half-mile-long Fort Pocahontas, built in the spring of 1864 by

Union soldiers during the Civil War. The fort protected Union vessels on the river and guarded the landing at Wilson's Wharf. Commanded by Brig. Gen. Edward A. Wild and manned by the 1st and 10th Regiments of U.S. Colored Troops and two guns of Battery M, 3d N.Y. Light Artillery, the 1,500-man garrison beat back assaults by 2,500 cavalrymen under Confederate Maj. Gen. Fitzhugh Lee on 24 May 1864. It was the only Civil War battle in Virginia in which nearly all the Union troops were black.

V-35 KENNON'S LANDING

Rte. 5, just east of Rte. 614, at turnout. Located 1½ miles south on the James River is Kennon's Landing. Richard Kennon married Anne Hunt about 1735 and lived there until his death in 1761. Anne Hunt's father was Captain William Hunt whose father William Hunt, a supporter of Nathaniel Bacon, is buried directly across the bay at Bachelor Point. The colonial government of Virginia opened a tobacco warehouse and inspection station at the landing in 1742. Hogsheads of tobacco were weighed, inspected for quality, and stored for shipment there. During the Revolutionary War, on 4 Jan. 1781, American-turned-British Gen. Benedict Arnold landed some of his troops at Kennon's and others at Westover, then marched to Richmond.

V-36 SHERWOOD FOREST—PRESIDENT JOHN TYLER'S HOME

Rte. 5, just east of Rte. 614, at turnout. John Tyler purchased this plantation one mile west in his native Charles City in 1842 while serving as tenth president of the United States, and made it his home from 1845 until his death in 1862. Tyler lengthened the wooden 18th-century house to over 300 feet long, thereby creating the longest frame house in America. Before becoming president, Tyler had served Virginia as congressman, governor, U.S. senator and vice-president. He served as president of the Washington Peace Conference in Feb. 1861; both sides occupied his Sherwood Forest property during the Civil War. Sherwood Forest, a National Historic Landmark, remains the home of Tyler's descendants.

V-38 PINEY GROVE AND SOUTHALLS

Rte. 615, 6 miles north of Rte. 5 from courthouse area. During the 18th century this property was established as a Southall family seat. Notable family members include James Barrett Southall, owner of Williamsburg's Raleigh Tavern, Turner Southall, member of the committee to build Thomas Jefferson's Virginia Capitol, and historian Douglas Southall Freeman. Furneau Southall constructed the original log part of the structure, later known as Piney Grove, about 1800 as a corncrib on his 300-acre plantation. "Southall's" was home to his family and 18 slaves. He was a grandson of family patriarch John Southall and served on the county Committee of Safety with John Tyler and Benjamin Harrison.

CITY OF CHESAPEAKE

K-262 CRANEY ISLAND

Rte. 17, at Churchland Bridge. This island in the Elizabeth River is about four miles northeast. British forces moving on Norfolk attacked American fortifications there June 22, 1813, but were repulsed. The Confederate Ironclad "Virginia" (MERRIMAC) was destroyed by her crew there May 11, 1862.

K-264 DALE POINT

3940 Airline Boulevard (Rte. 58). Just north is the birthplace of Commodore Richard Dale (6 Nov 1756–26 Feb 1826). He served on the United States brigantine Lexington. The British captured and wounded him several times during the Revolutionary War. Captain John Paul Jones chose him to be first lieutenant on the Bon Homme Richard. On 19 September 1779, the Bon Homme Richard defeated the British ship Serapis due largely to Dale's actions. He served as superintendent of the Norfolk Naval Yard in 1794. In 1801 he commanded a fleet of five vessels against the Barbary pirates. He later retired to Philadelphia.

K-265 FORT NELSON

Crawford Parkway, near Fort Nelson Towers. On the site of Portsmouth Naval Hospital stood Fort Nelson. There, Virginia's Revolutionary government late in 1776 constructed the fort of timber and rammed earth. Three years later, the British fleet commanded by Admiral Sir George Collier confiscated its artillery and supplies and destroyed most of the parapet. In 1779–1781, both Lord Cornwallis and General Benedict Arnold occupied the fort. It was reconstructed in 1799 of earth lined with brick, following a design by architect B. Henry Latrobe, and abandoned after the War of 1812. The Confederate government strengthened Fort Nelson, but on 10 May 1862 the Union army occupied Norfolk and Fort Nelson.

K-266 CRANEY ISLAND

Rte. 17, at Hodges Bridge. Seven miles northeast in the Elizabeth River is Craney Island, a landmark of two wars. During the War of 1812, the British attacked its fortifications on 22 June 1813, but were repulsed by its defenders including the Portsmouth artillery. During the Civil War, while abandoning Norfolk in April 1861, the Union forces scuttled the USS Merrimack. The Confederates refloated it and transformed it into their first ironclad, the CSS Virginia. Famous for its duel to a draw with the USS Monitor, the Virginia was scuttled at Craney Island on 11 May 1862, when the Confederates evacuated Norfolk.

K-275 BATTLE OF GREAT BRIDGE

Battlefield Boulevard and Cedar Road, at southwest corner. Nearby the first pitched battle of the American Revolution in Virginia was fought on 9 Dec. 1775 at the Great Bridge, a wooden causeway built across the marsh and open water of the Southern Branch of the Elizabeth River. Col. William Woodford of the Second Virginia Regiment had defensive works built at the southern end of the bridge. Lord Dunmore, the royal governor, sent a detachment of troops, to assault the works. The colonial forces easily withstood the attack and defeated Dunmore's troops. The governor's troops sustained a number of casualties, causing them to retreat to Norfolk. There Dunmore evacuated his forces to ships in the harbor.

KY-4 BATTLE OF GREAT BRIDGE

Just northeast of Rte. 168 Business and Intracoastal Waterway, at Great Bridge Battlefield Park. A short distance to the north stood a fort built by Lord Dunmore's troops in 1775. From there on 9 Dec. 1775 Dunmore attacked the Second Virginia Regiment over the Great Bridge, a wooden causeway across the marsh and open water of the Southern Branch of the Elizabeth River. Protecting their defensive works, the colonial forces, commanded by Col. William Woodford, easily defeated Dunmore's troop's detachment. This was the first pitched battle of the American Revolution in Virginia. The governor's troops sustained a large number of casualties, causing them to retreat to Norfolk, where they boarded ships in the harbor.

KY-5 BATTLE OF GREAT BRIDGE

Rte. 168, Great Bridge. In this vicinity, in 1775, was the southern end of a causeway, with bridges, by which the swamp and stream were crossed. Here William

Woodford's Virginia riflemen defended the passage. When Lord Dunmore's British regulars attempted to cross the swamp, on December 9, 1775, they were cut to pieces by the fire of the riflemen. This defeat forced Dunmore to evacuate Norfolk.

KY-6 NORFOLK COUNTY ALMSHOUSE

310 Shea Drive, at Chesapeake Municipal Center. During the colonial period, the established church cared for the poor as in Great Britain. Beginning in the late 18th century, local governments began to appoint overseers of the poor instead to support indigents with donated funds or house them in facilities built for the purpose. On 18 Dec. 1854, George A. Wilson donated 175 acres here to the Norfolk County overseers for an almshouse. The county cared for its indigent citizens here from 1855 to 1929, when the facility closed and the residents were moved to the Norfolk City Home. The City of Chesapeake Civic Center now stands on the site.

NW-15 DISMAL SWAMP CANAL

Rte. 17, 1 mile south of Rte. 104, Dismal Swamp. This canal, which connects Chesapeake Bay and Albemarle Sound, was chartered by Virginia in 1787 and North Carolina in 1790. It opened to traffic in 1805 and is now part of the Intracoastal Waterway. The area was visited by William Byrd II in 1728 when he surveyed the boundary between Virginia and North Carolina. In 1763, George Washington explored the area and organized the Dismal Swamp Land Company to drain it for farmland. The Great Dismal Swamp is now a National Wildlife Refuge.

WP-7 NORFOLK COUNTY COURTHOUSE

Rte. 168, Great Bridge. One-half mile west is the last courthouse of Norfolk County. It was built in 1962 and is now the Courthouse of the City of Chesapeake. Continuous court records beginning in 1637 are preserved here.

WP-10 ST. BRIDE'S CHURCH

Rte. 168, 4 miles north of state line. At this point stood St. Bride's Church, the Parish Church of St. Bride's Parish which was established in 1761. The church, sometimes known as Northwest Church, was built in 1762 and survived until 1853.

WP-11 HERRING (HERON) DITCH

Access road, near Rtes. 17 and 104. Herring Ditch was one of many ditches that connected with the Dismal Swamp Canal. Ditches were used to transport goods to the canal, allow access to swamp timber, and provide drainage. Walter Herron, a Dismal Swamp Canal Company stockholder, began the construction of Herring Ditch in the mid-1820s as a millrace that ran from the canal eastward three miles to present Shillelagh Road. It was later extended north to connect with the Southern Branch of the Elizabeth River providing a link between the Dismal Swamp and the Albemarle & Chesapeake Canals. The ditch also later linked the Lindsay Canal to the Dismal Swamp Canal. The ditch's access to the Dismal Swamp Canal was closed by the 1920s, when U.S. Route 17 was constructed.

WP-12 NORTH WEST CANAL

Rte. 17, at Great Dismal Swamp boat ramp. Approved by the Virginia General Assembly in 1818, the North West Canal was constructed by the Dismal Swamp Canal Company between 1828 and 1830. The canal was intended for carrying timber and farm products between the Dismal Swamp Canal and the Northwest River and as an alternate route to the Atlantic Ocean via the Currituck Inlet; however, the silting of the inlet in 1837 eliminated this latter use. The canal was about 24 feet wide and 4 feet deep and extended nearly 7 miles. It fell into disuse during the Civil War and by 1871 a drought necessitated the closing off of the canal to conserve water.

ESSEX COUNTY

N-9 EARLY SETTLEMENT

Rte. 17, 7 miles northwest of Caret. Two miles east near the river, Richard Coleman planted a frontier settlement and trading post in 1652. By 1660 a church was built, to which every man was required to come armed for protection against the Indians.

N-18 OLD RAPPAHANNOCK COURTHOUSE

Rte. 17, Caret. About half a mile northeast stood the old courthouse and clerk's office of Rappahannock County, 1665–1693. To this courthouse Thomas Goodrich and Benjamin Goodrich, ordered to appear with halters around their necks, came to express their penitence for taking part in Bacon's Rebellion in l676.

N-19 PORTOBACCO INDIANS

Rte. 17, at Rte. 641, 11.8 miles northwest of Caret. Along the Rappahannock River near here lived the Portobacco Indians, who may have been part of the Portobaccos of Maryland. After moving to Virginia in the 1650s, they lived here in peace with their Indian neighbors, who spoke a similar dialect and who also were farmers, fishermen, and hunters. In 1683–1684 they were joined by the Rappahannocks, creating an Indian "refuge area" on a frontier that was being attacked by the Senecas. The Portobaccos and the Rappahannocks occupied the reservation on the Portobacco Bay until about 1704, when English colonists claiming the land by patent drove them off.

N-20 FONTHILL

Rte. 17, at Rte. 631, 3 miles northwest of Caret, Champlain. A mile and a half west stands Fonthill, built in 1832 by Robert Mercer Taliaferro Hunter. He served variously as United States senator, Confederate secretary of state, Confederate States senator, and as a member of the peace commission that met with Union representatives near Fort Monroe in February 1865. Imprisoned briefly at the end of the war, Hunter soon resumed his public career, serving as treasurer of Virginia from 1874 to 1880.

N-21 HISTORIC TAPPAHANNOCK

Rte. 360, Tappahannock. The town was founded in 1680 under the name of Hobbs His Hole. In 1682, a port was established here and called New Plymouth. In 1808, the name was changed to Tappahannock. The British Admiral Cockburn shelled the town, December 1, 1814. An old customs house and a debtors' jail are here.

N-22 RITCHIE'S BIRTHPLACE

Cross Street, near Prince Street, Tappahannock. Here was born Thomas Ritchie, November 5, 1778. In 1804, he established the Richmond Enquirer, which ran until 1877, the most noted of Virginia newspapers. Ritchie was a political leader in Virginia and an editor of national fame. In 1845, he became editor of the Washington Union. He retired in 1851 and died, July 3, 1854.

N-23 VAUTER'S CHURCH

Rte. 17, 10.7 miles northwest of Caret, north of Champlain. This was the principal church of St. Anne's Parish, which was formed in 1704 from Sittenburne Parish and encompassed Essex County. According to tradition, part of the present church was built about 1719 with an addition constructed in 1731, but architectural evidence suggests that the church was built as a unit in 1731. After the American Revolution and the disestablishment of the Church of England, Vauter's Church passed out of service. In 1822 regular services resumed for the first time since 1776. The church was remodeled in 1827, when the box pews were reduced in height and the present two-deck pulpit replaced the colonial one of three decks.

N-24 FORT LOWRY—CAMP BYRON

Rte. 17, at Rte. 611, Dunnsville. Located
two miles N.E. on Rappahannock River at
Lowry's Point was a Confederate eight gun
"water battery" constructed in 1861. Here
at Dunnsville was located Camp Byron,
home of Company F (Essex Light Dragoons), Ninth Cavalry, C.S.A.; the company moved to Fort Lowry in October 1861
to assist in the fort's defense and to conduct
scouting missions.

N-25 TOPPAHANOCK INDIAN VILLAGE

*Rte. 17, approximately 0.87 miles north of
Tappahannock corporate limits.* In this
region near the Rappahannock River once
stood the Rappahannock Indian village of
Toppahanock. When John Smith explored
this region in 1607 and 1608, he found
fourteen Rappahannock villages along both
banks of the river. The river was the center
of the Rappahannocks' ancestral lands and
served as a food source and travel network.
The Rappahannock River was formerly
known as the Opiscatumek. Sometime
before 1607, the Rappahannock Indians
asserted themselves as the dominant group
on the river.

N-26 MANN MEETING HOUSE

Rte. 17, 12.4 miles southeast of Tappahannock.
Just to the east stood Mann Meeting
House, the first Methodist Episcopal
Church in this region. It was built before
1794 and abandoned about 1880. The site
is now occupied by the Macedonia Colored
Baptist Church.

N-27 GOULDBOROUGH PLANTATION
(LATER GOLDBERRY)

Rte. 17, 2.27 miles south of Caret. Just east
of here was the seat of the Waring family, members of which served the colony
and our fledgling nation in elected and
appointed offices and as officers in the
county militia and the Continental Line.
Thomas Waring II (ca. 1690–1754), Burgess 1736–1754, built a mansion here in
1733. His son Francis (1717–1771) Burgess
1758–1769, was an organizer of the Sons
of Liberty and a signer of the Leedstown
Resolves. The house, having survived three
wars, burned in the late 19th century.

N-28 RAPPAHANNOCK INDIAN MIGRATION

*Rte. 17, approximately 3.01 miles north of
Tappahannock corporate limits.* West of here,
on the ridge between the Mattaponi and
Rappahannock Rivers, the Rappahannock
Indians built a fort to defend themselves
from hostile settlers and other Indians
during Bacon's Rebellion in 1676. An order
of the colonial Virginia Council in 1682
granted 4,000 acres to the Rappahannocks
"about the town where they dwelt." In
1683, following increased attacks along the
Virginia frontiers by Iroquoian warriors,
the General Assembly ordered the Rappahannocks either to find a new home or
merge with the Nanzaticos. During January
and February 1684, the Rappahannocks
and their belongings were transported
35 miles up the Rappahannock River.

N-29 FORT LOWRY

Rte. 646, at fort site. Here in 1861 Confederates constructed an eight gun "water
battery" principally for the defense of
Fredericksburg. The guns were manned
by the 55th Infantry Regiment located
500 yards N.W. The cannons were moved
and the fort abandoned March 1862 after
Northern Neck troop withdrawal left unit
[*should read:* it] defenseless. On April 14,
1862, six Union gun boats bombarded and
burned the installation. Thereafter, the fort
functioned in limited capacity until the
war ended.

O-22 MATTAPONI INDIAN TOWN

*Rte. 360, at Essex/King and Queen County
line.* To the north, after the 1644–1646
conflict between colonists and groups still
loyal to the Powhatan chiefdom, the Mattaponi Indians found refuge on the headwaters of Piscataway Creek. Officers of then

Old Rappahannock County signed a treaty with the Mattaponi in 1656. By 1660, however, the Mattaponi's English neighbors were pressuring them to leave and in 1662 some colonists burned the chief's English-style house. The chief complained to the governor and an agreement was reached that three Englishmen would pay compensation and the tribe would relocate. By 1668, these Mattaponi had moved to the middle region of the Mattaponi River in King William County.

O-23 BACON'S NORTHERN FORCE

Rte. 360, Millers Tavern. At Piscataway, near here, the northern followers of Bacon the Rebel assembled in 1676. On July 10, 1676, an action was fought with Governor Berkeley's supporters, some of whom were killed and wounded. Several houses were burned. Passing here, the rebels marched south to the Pamunkey River, where they joined their leader, Bacon.

O-41 MT. ZION BAPTIST CHURCH (PISCATAWAY BAPTIST CHURCH)

Rte. 360, just west of Rte. 620, Millers Tavern. Founded nearby as Piscataway Baptist Church on 13 Mar. 1774, Mt. Zion Baptist Church was the first Baptist church in the region. Endeavoring to stop the spread of the Baptist movement, local authorities arrested Baptist ministers John Waller, John Shackleford, Robert Ware, and Ivison Lewis after the first church service for "preaching and expounding the Scriptures contrary to the law." In 1818 the church moved across the road from this site. The current brick building was constructed in 1854. In 1856 the congregation changed its name to Mt. Zion Baptist Church.

CITY OF FRANKLIN

U-126 FRANKLIN

Main Street, at South Street. Incorporated as a town in 1876, Franklin began as a Southampton County village in the 1830s. In October, 1862, during the Civil War, Union gunboats on the Blackwater River shelled the town and the railroad station. Several skirmishes occurred nearby in 1862 and 1863. A major fire destroyed 43 buildings in the town on February 26, 1881. The Camp Brothers' lumber mill and later their paper mill, as well as the peanut industry, helped Franklin prosper in this century. Franklin became an incorporated city in 1960.

U-131 CAMP FAMILY HOMESTEAD

221 Homestead Road. George Camp Jr (1793–1879) acquired this land in 1826. Several of his children incorporated the Camp Manufacturing Company in 1887 to operate sawmills. The company expanded into a wood product manufacturing company and later a paper mill. It became the largest employer in the region with operations in North Carolina, South Carolina, and Florida. In 1956, the company merged with Union Bag and Paper Company of New York, which became a part of International Paper in 1999. The Federal-style dwelling here was moved to this site early in the 1930s to replace the earlier family home that had burned in 1931.

UT-20 BLACKWATER LINE—FRANKLIN

2nd Avenue. A major Blackwater River crossing was located here at Franklin during the Civil War. Confederate forces guarded the crossing from 1862 to the end of the war as part of the Blackwater defensive line. Several skirmishes were fought around the pontoon bridge here in 1862 and 1863. During the morning of 11 April 1863, Confederate Maj. Gen. John Bell Hood's division crossed the river on the bridge on its way to aid Lt. Gen. James Longstreet's siege of Suffolk. Hood's division recrossed here on 4 May 1863 after the end of the siege.

GLOUCESTER COUNTY

M-66 MARLFIELD

Rte. 17, at Rte. 613, northwest of Gloucester.
A mile and a half west is the site of Marlfield, an eighteenth-century dwelling built
by the Buckner family. It was purchased in
1782 by William Jones, who gave the house
its name. Jones was among the first Virginia
planters to use marl in his agricultural practices. His descendants sold Marlfield in
1906 but retained ownership of the nearby
family cemetery. Marlfield had fallen into
ruins by the mid-twentieth century.

N-61 POPLAR SPRING CHURCH

Rte. 17, 5 miles northwest of Gloucester. This
is the site of Poplar Spring Church of
Petsworth Parish. In 1694, old Petsworth
Church was abandoned in favor of this
church. It was considered the finest church
of colonial Virginia. In 1676, the followers
of Bacon, the Rebel, interred here a casket
supposed to contain his remains, but in
reality filled with stones. The body was
buried secretly.

NA-1 GLOUCESTER COURTHOUSE

Rte. 17, Gloucester. The courthouse was
built in 1766. The debtors prison is also
old. A skirmish occurred near here between Confederate and Union cavalry,
January 29, 1864.

NA-2 WARE CHURCH

Business Rte. 17, at Rte. 3/14. A mile east is
Ware Church, built about 1693. Near by is
Church Hill, another relic of colonial days.
Not far distant is White Hall, a colonial
mansion built by the Willis family.

NA-3 TO GWYNN'S ISLAND

Business Rte. 17, at Rte. 3/14. Two miles east
is Toddsbury, home of the Todd family,
built in 1722. Farther east, in Mathews
County, are the old homes, Green Plains,
Auburn, and Midlothian. Some miles
beyond them is Gwynn's Island, where

General Andrew Lewis drove the last royal
governor, Lord Dunmore, from Virginia
soil, July, 1776.

NA-4 WARNER HALL

*Rte. 17, north of Gloucester Point, 4.2 miles
south of Gloucester.* Three miles east is Warner Hall. The estate was patented about
1650 by Augustine Warner, who built the
first house in 1674. Bacon, the Rebel, was
here for a time in 1676. The later house,
built about 1740 and burned in 1849, has
been beautifully restored.

NA-7 TARLETON'S LAST FIGHT

Rte. 1216, 2.1 miles north of Gloucester Point.
Here, at the Hook, Tarleton, commanding
the cavalry of Cornwallis's army, fought
an action with Choisy's French force and
Virginia militia, October 3, 1781. The Duke
de Lauzun's cavalry charged Tarleton, who
retired to Gloucester Point. There he was
blockaded by the French and by Virginia
militia.

NA-8 ROSEWELL AND WEROWOCOMOCO

Rte. 17, 5.3 miles south of Gloucester. Several
miles west is Rosewell, built about 1750,
home of the Page family, and the largest of
colonial Virginia houses. On York River,
probably at Purtan Bay some miles west of
Rosewell, was Werowocomoco, chief town
of the Indian ruler Powhatan in 1607.

NA-9 GLOUCESTER POINT

*Secondary road, off Rte. 17, at toll bridge,
Gloucester Point.* Known first as Tyndall's
Point. The colonists built a fort here in
1667. In 1676 Bacon led his rebels across
the river here. Tarleton and Dundas occupied the place in October, 1781, in the siege
of Yorktown. Cornwallis planned to break
through the blockade here, but a storm
kept him from crossing the river. The point
was fortified by the Confederates in 1861
and occupied by Union troops in 1862.

Powhatan ruled as paramount chief over approximately thirty chiefdoms by the arrival of the English in 1607. (Marker NA-8) (From a map of Virginia by John Smith, Library of Congress)

NW-5 Abingdon Church

Rte. 17, north of Gloucester Point, 6.2 miles south of Gloucester. This is the third church of Abingdon Parish and was erected in 1755 on the site of an earlier one. The parish, established between 1650 and 1655, had its first church near the river.

NW-6 Dr. Walter Reed's Birthplace

Rte. 17, 3.5 miles south of Gloucester. Dr. Walter Reed, U.S. Army medical officer and bacteriologist, was born on 13 Sept. 1851 in a nearby cottage at Belroi. He received medical degrees from the University of Virginia medical school and Bellevue Hospital College in New York City. In 1875 he joined the U.S. Army Medical Department. By 1890 Reed was spending most of his time conducting medical research. During the Spanish-American War, Reed served on the Typhoid Board that studied this disease. He was appointed in 1900 to head

the Yellow Fever Commission that proved the disease was transmitted by mosquitoes. This discovery led to its virtual eradication. Reed died on 23 Nov. 1902.

NW-10 Early Land Patent

Secondary road, off Rte. 17, at toll bridge, Gloucester Point. Argoll Yeardley patented 4000 acres of land, known as Tyndall's Neck, here on the north side of Charles (now York) River, October 12, 1640. This was one of the first land patents north of the York River.

NW-11 Thomas Calhoun Walker (1862–1953)

Business Rte. 17, 0.1 miles north of Rte. 3/14, Gloucester. Here lived Thomas Calhoun Walker, the first black to practice law in Gloucester County and a civil rights spokesman who vigorously advocated education and land ownership for blacks. Mr. Walker was elected for two terms to Gloucester's Board of Supervisors, serving from 1891 to 1895. President William McKinley appointed him the Commonwealth's first black collector of customs in 1893. He became the only black to hold statewide office in President Roosevelt's Works Project Administration when he was appointed Consultant and Advisor on Negro Affairs in 1934.

NW-12 Robert Russa Moton

Rte. 17, 0.04 miles south of Rte. 614, White Marsh. Robert Russa Moton was born in Amelia County, Virginia, on 26 August 1867, and was educated in a local freedman's school and at Hampton Institute (now Hampton University). He served as an administrator at the institute from 1890 to 1915, when he succeeded Booker T. Washington as president of Tuskegee Institute. There Moton led the school to full collegiate accreditation. An advisor to five U.S. presidents and a founder of the Urban League, he retired to Holly Knoll (10 miles northwest) in 1935. Moton died on 31 May 1940. Holly Knoll was designated a National Historic Landmark in 1981.

NW-13 UNITED NEGRO COLLEGE FUND

Rte. 17, 0.04 miles south of Rte. 614, White Marsh. Dr. Frederick D. Patterson founded the United Negro College Fund in 1944. He and the presidents of the member colleges of the Fund began meeting in 1946 at Holly Knoll, the retirement home of the late Robert Russa Moton. Patterson had established Holly Knoll Associates in 1945 to serve as a conference center for black educators. Their meetings contributed to the growth and reputation of the United Negro College Fund, which aids more than 40 historically black colleges, and provides student scholarships and faculty grants. The fund is known for its motto, "A mind is a terrible thing to waste."

NW-14 ROSEWELL

Rte. 17, approximately 0.25 miles south of Rte. 614, White Marsh. Three miles west, on Carter's Creek, stand the ruins of Rosewell, a grand mansion with the finest brickwork in the English colonies. Begun in 1725 by Mann Page I, and home to the Page family for more than one hundred years, Rosewell stood three stories tall. It was crowned with a parapet and twin octagonal cupolas and had two flanking dependencies on the north front that formed a forecourt. Rosewell contained fine paneling and wood carving. In 1916, fire swept the mansion, leaving a magnificent shell that is a testament to 18th-century craftsmanship.

NW-16 ZION POPLARS BAPTIST CHURCH

Rte. 17, approximately 0.8 miles south of Rte. 616. Zion Poplars Baptist Church houses one of the oldest independent African-American congregations in Gloucester County. It is named for seven united poplar trees under which the founding members first met for worship in 1866. The church was erected one and a half miles to the south in 1894 in the Gothic Revival architectural style, with both Victorian and classical detailing. During the 1930s the church was moved 110 feet because of road construction. The interior exhibits the creative craftsmanship of Frank Braxton, a former slave. The church was listed on the Virginia Landmarks Register and the National Register of Historic Places in 1999.

NW-17 ZION POPLARS BAPTIST CHURCH

Rte. 269, approximately 0.6 miles south of Business Rte. 17. Zion Poplars Baptist Church houses one of the oldest independent African-American congregations in Gloucester County. It is named for seven united poplar trees under which the founding members first met for worship in 1866. The church was erected here in 1894 in the Gothic Revival architectural style, with both Victorian and classical detailing. During the 1930s the church was moved 110 feet because of road construction. The interior exhibits the creative craftsmanship of Frank Braxton, a former slave. The church was listed on the Virginia Landmarks Register and the National Register of Historic Places in 1999.

NW-18 GLOUCESTER AGRICULTURAL AND INDUSTRIAL SCHOOL

Rte. 618, approximately 2 miles south of Rte. 614. On this site stood the Gloucester Agricultural and Industrial School, commonly known as Capahosic Academy, a private high school built for African Americans before public high schools were available to them. Founded in 1888 by local alumni of Hampton Institute (now Hampton University), it was taken over and funded by the American Missionary Association after 1891. William Gibbons Price (1868?–1941) was the principal from 1899 until it closed in 1933. Despite the school's name, graduates included not only well-trained farmers, but also many students who attended college and entered professions such as teaching. It was a cultural center of the local black community.

NW-19 GOVERNOR JOHN PAGE

Rte. 17, approximately 0.2 miles south of Rte. 628. John Page, planter, scholar, and Revolutionary patriot, was born in 1743 at Rosewell, three miles west of here. He attended the College of William and Mary with Thomas Jefferson. The two men developed a lifelong friendship and shared an interest in the natural sciences. Page served in the House of Burgesses and in the Virginia House of Delegates. He was a member of the United States House of Representatives (1789–1797), and was elected governor of Virginia by the Virginia General Assembly for three consecutive one-year terms (1802–1805). John Page died in Richmond in 1808 and is buried there at St. John's Church.

NW-20 BETHEL BAPTIST CHURCH

Rte. 614, at church. Bethel Baptist Church is one of the oldest African American congregations in Gloucester County. Founded nearby in 1867, it was originally known as the Old Sassafras Stage Church. Members of the congregation built a wooden structure here in 1889, which is the core of the present building. George W. Leigh and Thomas C. Walker, Sr., father of Thomas C. Walker, Jr., served as chairmen of the building committee. During the later years of the 19th century five other churches were organized from this congregation. Thomas C. Walker, Jr. (1862–1953), the first black lawyer in Gloucester County, is buried in the adjoining church cemetery.

NW-21 GLOUCESTER TRAINING SCHOOL

Rte. 629, east of Rte. 615. Built on this site in 1921 the Gloucester Training School became the first public high school for African Americans in Gloucester County. Thomas Calhoun Walker, Jr. and others constructed a wooden building with gifts from the Rosenwald Fund and other national and local donors. It offered African Americans an education beyond the elementary school level. A new brick structure replaced the original building by 1951 and was named for Walker in 1954. Following the integration of the county schools, the school in 1968 became Gloucester Intermediate School. The building became a middle school in 1975 and in 1986 it was named T. C. Walker Elementary School.

NW-22 FAIRFIELD

Rte. 17, south of Rte. 614, White Marsh. Two miles west stood Fairfield, also called Carter's Creek plantation, one of the most distinguished of Virginia's early brick homes. Built about 1694 for Lewis Burwell (ca. 1651–1710), the house was a grand T-shaped structure, with distinctive double and triple diagonally set chimney stacks joined at the caps, two separate vaulted cellars, and a large ballroom. The plantation also included a large formal garden, slave quarters, and other buildings necessary to operate a large plantation. The influential Burwell family lived here until about 1787, the house was destroyed by fire about 1897. The Fairfield site was listed in 1973 on the Virginia Landmarks Register and the National Register of Historic Places.

Q-10-a CAPPAHOSIC

Business Rte. 17, Gloucester. Seven and one-half miles southwest is Cappahosic, where a ferry was established early in the eighteenth century. On the old charts, this Indian district lay between Werowocomoco and Timberneck Creek. Powhatan is said to have offered it to Capt. John Smith for "two great guns and a grindstone." John Stubbs patented the Cappahosic tract in 1652 and 1702 and a few years later built "Cappahosic House," which has clipped gables and inside chimneys with eight unique corner fireplaces.

Q-10-b CAPPAHOSIC

Rte. 618, 7.5 miles southwest of Gloucester. Here is Cappahosic, where a ferry was established early in the eighteenth century. On the old charts, this Indian district lay between Werowocomoco and Timberneck

Creek. Powhatan is said to have offered it to Capt. John Smith for "two great guns and a grindstone". John Stubbs patented the Cappahosic tract in 1652 and 1702 and

a few years later built this the "Cappahosic House", which has clipped gables and inside chimneys with eight unique corner fireplaces.

CITY OF HAMPTON

S-28 John Baptist Pierce (1875–1942)

Rte. 60 (Settlers Landing Drive), near Tyler Street, at Hampton University. A Cooperative Extension Service pioneer, innovator, and educator, John Baptist Pierce was appointed in 1906 by Seaman Knapp and H. B. Frissell of Hampton Institute as the first Negro farm demonstration agent for Virginia. Pierce served for 35 years as district agent for Virginia and North Carolina and as the United States Department of Agriculture field agent for the upper southern states. Pierce's "Live-at-Home and Community Improvement Program" was a unique innovation which helped many rural Virginians raise their standards of living.

W-66 Battle of Big Bethel

Rte. 600 (Big Bethel Road), at Bethel Park. On 10 June 1861, the first land battle of the Civil War in present-day Virginia took place here at Big Bethel Church. Maj. Gen. Benjamin F. Butler, commanding at Fort Monroe, sent converging columns at night from Hampton and Newport News for a dawn attack against Confederate outposts there. The 1,408 Confederates, led by Cols. John B. Magruder and D. H. Hill, fell back to their entrenchments behind Brick Kiln Creek, near the church. Some 4,400 Federals under Brig. Gen. Ebenezer W. Pierce pursued, launched two disjointed attacks, and were repulsed. They then retreated to Fort Monroe, leaving the Confederates in control of most of the Peninsula.

W-75 Greenlawn Memorial Park

Marker not yet cast. Proposed location to be determined. Greenlawn Memorial Park, located on a part of the Montrose plantation,

has served as a cemetery for the Hampton and Newport News communities since 14 Feb. 1888. At the center of the cemetery is a 25-foot-high obelisk erected in 1900 to mark the mass grave of 163 reinterred Confederate prisoners of war. These soldiers died at the nearby Newport News prisoner-of-war camp between 27 Apr. and 5 July 1865. Several prominent individuals are buried here, including Raymond "Coca-Cola" Brown (1888–1979), who patented the stationary bottle opener. The cemetery was listed on the Virginia Landmarks Register in 1998 and the National Register of Historic Places in 1999.

W-84 First Battle of Ironclads

Chesapeake Avenue, between LaSalle and East Avenues. In Hampton Roads, southward and a mile or two offshore, the Virginia (Merrimac) and the Monitor fought their engagement, March 9, 1862. The day before the Virginia destroyed the Cumberland and Congress, wooden ships of the Union navy.

W-85 Wythe's Birthplace

Rte. 60, 0.5 miles west of Hampton. Eight miles north George Wythe, Revolutionary leader and Signer of the Declaration of Independence, was born, 1726.

W-86 Forts Henry and Charles

Veterans Administration Hospital, Strawberry Bank Boulevards. In 1610, after the expulsion of the Native American inhabitants of Kecoughtan, the English constructed two forts in the vicinity of the former Indian village. Forts Henry (1610) and Charles (1611) were built between the mouth of the Hampton River and Point Comfort primarily to defend Kecoughtan against the

Indians. Fort Henry was located on the east side of the Hampton River, Fort Charles on the west side. According to Don Diego de Molina, a Spaniard imprisoned in Virginia from 1611 to 1616, fifteen soldiers garrisoned each fort. Fort Henry was abandoned in 1637.

W-87 HISTORIC HAMPTON

Lincoln Street, at Hampton City Hall. The Native American village of Kecoughtan stood across the Hampton River in 1607. Soon after the English forcibly removed the inhabitants in 1610, the colonists settled there and the village grew. By the early eighteenth century, the royal customhouse, wharves, warehouses, and taverns were located in the bustling seaport town of Hampton. In an early Revolutionary War engagement, militiamen repulsed a British naval attack against Hampton on 24 Oct. 1775. During the Revolution, Hampton was the home port of the Virginia State Navy. On 25 June 1813, during the War of 1812, the British sacked the town. Confederates burned it in Aug. 1861 to prevent its use by Union troops and slaves.

W-88 LITTLE ENGLAND

4000 block, Victoria Boulevard. In 1634 Capps Point, later known as Little England, was patented by William Capps, a prominent planter who maintained a lucrative saltworks. He served as a burgess in the 1619 General Assembly, the first representative legislative body in the New World. On 25 June 1813, during the War of 1812, British Admiral George Cockburn sailed into the mouth of Hampton River and shelled Hampton. A complement of 450 Virginia militiamen tried in vain to hold the British at bay with several small cannons mounted in the fortification at Little England. Afterward the British occupied and plundered the town.

W-88 EMANCIPATION OAK

Settlers Landing Drive (Rte. 60), near ramp onto I-64 East. To the west, on the grounds of Hampton Institute, is the tree under which Mrs. Mary Peake, a Freedwoman, taught children of former slaves in 1861. Nearby stood the Butler School, a free school established in 1863 for colored children.

W-89 FORT ALGERNOURNE

Rte. 60, near Old Point Comfort, at Fort Monroe. Near here Captain John Ratcliffe built Fort Algernourne, 1609. In 1614, it was a stockade containing fifty people and seven cannon. In 1632, the fort was rebuilt. It was discontinued after 1667. In 1727, a new fort, Fort George, was ordered built here. This fort was destroyed by a hurricane in 1749.

W-90 FORT MONROE

Rte. 60, near Old Point Comfort, at Fort Monroe. The fort was begun in 1819 and named for President James Monroe. It remained in possession of the Union forces, 1861–65, and from it as a base McClellan began the Peninsular Campaign, 1862. Jefferson Davis was imprisoned here, 1865–67.

W-91 THE ZERO MILE POST

Rte. 258, at Fort Monroe. This zero mile post is a replica of the original post that stood here at the end of the track on the Chesapeake and Ohio Railway, from which point all main line distances have been measured for the 664.9 miles to Cincinnati, Ohio, since 1889. The Fort Monroe (Old Point Comfort) station located here ceased operation in December, 1939.

W-92 CONFINEMENT OF JEFFERSON DAVIS

Rte. 60, near Old Point Comfort, at Fort Monroe. In this casemate Jefferson Davis, President of the Confederate States, was confined, May 22–October 2, 1865. As his health suffered in the casemate, he was removed to Carroll Hall in the fortress, where he remained from October, 1865, until May, 1867, when he was released on bail. He was never brought to trial.

W-93 OLD POINT COMFORT LIGHT

Rte. 60, near Old Point Comfort, at Fort Monroe. The lighthouse, built in 1802, is the oldest standing structure at Fort Monroe. It remains an active navigational aid, the property of the U.S. Coast Guard. During the War of 1812, the tower was used as a lookout by a British invasion force while they attacked Washington. The adjacent house was the lightkeepers' quarters until the light was automated in 1973 when the house became Army property.

W-94 FREEDOM'S FORTRESS

Ruckman Road, at Fort Monroe. Fort Monroe was the site of Major General Benjamin F. Butler's decision in 1861 to accept escaping slaves as "contrabands of war." Thousands of former slaves who cast off their bondage and sought sanctuary here called this "The Freedom Fort." The First and Second Regiments of U.S. Colored Cavalry and Battery B, Second U.S. Colored Light Artillery, were raised here during the Civil War. In 1865 the Bureau for the Relief of Freedmen and Refugees ("Freedmen's Bureau") established its state headquarters here.

W-95 ABERDEEN GARDENS

1424 Aberdeen Road, at Aberdeen School. Built "by Negroes, for Negroes," Aberdeen Gardens began in 1934 as the model resettlement community for Negro families. It was the only such community in the United States designed by a Negro architect (Hilyard R. Robinson) and built by Negro contractors and laborers. Aberdeen Gardens is composed of 158 brick houses on large garden lots, a school, and a community store, all within a greenbelt. The streets, excepting Aberdeen Road, are named for prominent Negroes. Aberdeen Gardens offered home ownership and an improved quality of life in a rural setting. In 1994 this nationally significant neighborhood was listed as a Virginia landmark and in the National Register of Historic Places, through the efforts of former and current residents.

W-96 FIRST AFRICANS IN VIRGINIA

Marker not yet cast. Proposed location to be determined. The first documented Africans in Virginia arrived in August 1619 when a Dutch man-of-war landed here at Point Comfort. The Dutch captured the "twenty and odd" Africans from the Spanish, who had enslaved them, and traded them to the Virginia colonists in exchange for foodstuffs. Early Africans who lived here included Antony and Isabell, whose son, William Tucker, likely was the first black child born in present-day Hampton. The family served the household of Capt. William Tucker, commander at Point Comfort. Whether the early Africans were treated as indentured servants or as slaves is uncertain. The institution of slavery evolved during the 17th century as the term of service for Africans was extended for life. The United States abolished slavery in 1865.

W-97 MARY SMITH KELSEY PEAKE

Marker not yet erected. Proposed location: North King Street, at entrance to Elmenton Cemetery. Born a free person in Norfolk in 1823, Mary Peake devoted her life to the education and betterment of African Americans. About 1850, she founded the Daughters of Zion to aid the poor and the sick. A seamstress by day, Peake violated state law to teach her fellow blacks at night. During the Civil War, protected and encouraged by the occupying Union army and prominent local leaders, she taught openly in the shade of the Emancipation Oak in Hampton and at Fort Monroe. She founded the first black school in Hampton at Brown Cottage in September 1861 with the sponsorship of the American Missionary Association. Her school was a forerunner of Hampton University. Peake died on 22 February 1862.

W-98 EMANCIPATION OAK

East Tyler Street at I-64. To the west, on the grounds of Hampton University, stands the Emancipation Oak. Under its sheltering limbs, protected and encouraged by the occupying Union army and prominent local church leaders, Mary Smith Kelsey Peake (1823–22 Feb. 1862) taught her fellow African Americans to read and write as the Civil War began. She founded the first black school in Hampton at Brown Cottage in September 1861; it was a forerunner of Hampton University. In 1863, following the issuance of the Emancipation Proclamation by President Abraham Lincoln, Hampton residents gathered beneath the oak to hear the text read aloud.

W-99 WILLIAM CLAIBORNE

Carousel Park, on Settlers Landing Drive. Nearby, William Claiborne (1600–1677) built a warehouse about 1631 to support his trading post on Kent Island in Chesapeake Bay. When Maryland seized the island in 1632, Claiborne fought an unsuccessful "naval war." Born in Kent County, England, he had arrived in Virginia in 1621 as the colony's surveyor. He served on the governor's Council (1625–1638), as secretary of state (1626–1637, 1652–1660) and treasurer (1642–1677), as commander of military forces (1644–1645), and, during the Commonwealth period, as a parliamentary commissioner (1652) to secure the surrenders of Virginia and Maryland. In 1680, an act of assembly established Hampton on land he originally owned.

WY-87 BACK RIVER LIGHTHOUSE RUINS

Grand View Island, end of Beach Road. One mile north, the Back River Lighthouse and keeper's dwelling stood for 127 years. The lighthouse was built for $4,250 in 1829, automated in 1915, and decommissioned in 1936. A guide for watermen and a meeting place for the community, the "picturesque Grand View Light Station" also served as a "mecca for local and visiting artists" according to a 1950 local newspaper. The lighthouse was one of the oldest structures in the area until neglect, wind, and water took their toll. Hurricane Flossy completely destroyed it in 1956, leaving only a pile of stones in the surf to mark the remains of the thirty-foot tower.

WY-88 THIRD ELIZABETH CITY PARISH CHURCH

Pembroke Avenue and Parkdale Street. Here is the site of "the New Church of Kecoughtan," built before 1667 on Pembroke Farm as the third church of Elizabeth City Parish, established in 1610. It was a frame building and its brick foundation and some early colonial tombstones remain. When the town of Hampton was founded in 1691, this church lay outside it, and in 1727 was ordered to be replaced by a fourth parish church within the town, the existing St. John's Church, Hampton.

WY-89 SECOND CHURCH AT KECOUGHTAN

Tyler Street, at I-64, Exit 267. Nearby a monument marks the site of the second church at Kecoughtan (later Hampton), built in 1624 for Elizabeth City Parish, established 1610 and now the oldest Protestant parish in continuous existence in America. This building was replaced before 1667 by a third parish church west of the town and was pulled down in 1698.

WY-90 FIRST CHURCH AT KECOUGHTAN

LaSalle Avenue, at Kenmore Street. Near here on the church creek stood the first church at Kecoughtan (later Hampton). Built on the Parish Glebe Farm about 1616, as the first church of the oldest continuous settlement of English origin in America, William Mease was the first known minister of the Parish, from 1613 until about 1620.

WY-91 CAMP HAMILTON

College Place and East Queen Street. In this vicinity was situated Camp Hamilton, a large camp of Union troops first occupied in May, 1861. A great military hospital, Hampton Hospital, was here.

WY-92 BUCKROE

Atlantic Avenue and Mallo Street, at Buckroe Beach. In 1620, Frenchmen sent over to plant mulberry trees and grape vines settled here. The name was taken from a place in England.

WY-93 PHOEBUS

Mallory and Downes Streets. Settled as Mill Creek and Strawberry Banks by English Colonists, the Town of Phoebus was "Roseland Farm" until 1871 when it was divided into lots and became known as Chesapeake City. When the town was incorporated in 1900, it was named Phoebus in honor of its leading citizen, Harrison Phoebus.

WY-94 PHOEBUS

Near North County Street and Woodland Road. Settled as Mill Creek and Strawberry Banks by English Colonists, the Town of Phoebus was "Roseland Farm" until 1871 when it was divided into lots and became known as Chesapeake City. When the town was incorporated in 1900, it was named Phoebus in honor of its leading citizen, Harrison Phoebus.

WY-95 LITTLE ENGLAND CHAPEL

4100 Kecoughtan Road. Little England Chapel, originally known as the Ocean Cottage Sunday School, was built about 1879 on property provided by Daniel F. Cock. Hampton Institute students regularly offered Sunday school lessons here to the African American Newtown community from the early 1880s into the 20th century. By 1890 the chapel had become known for its sewing club. The Newtown Improvement and Civic Club also held meetings at the chapel and programs of worship, singing, and concerts took place here. The club acquired the property in 1954. The church was listed on the Virginia Landmarks Register in 1981 and the National Register of Historic Places in 1982.

WY-96 LANGLEY FIELD: CREATING AN AIR FORCE

Carousel Park, on Settler's Landing Drive. In Dec. 1916, the U.S. Army purchased land four miles north of here to build an airfield to use jointly with the National Advisory Committee for Aeronautics. During World War I, the Army trained aircrews and tested aircraft there. In 1921, Brig. Gen. William "Billy" Mitchell led bombing trials from Langley to demonstrate that air power could destroy battleships. On 1 March 1935, Air Corps combat units were realigned nationwide under the GHQ Air Force. Led from Langley by Maj. Gen. Frank Andrews, that combat air command was the forerunner of the Army Air Forces of World War II and marked the first real step toward the U.S. Air Force.

WY-97 LANGLEY FIELD: DISCOVERING AEROSPACE

Carousel Park, on Settler's Landing Drive. The National Advisory Committee for Aeronautics (NACA), created in 1915 to revitalize American aviation, was a pivotal force behind opening Langley Field in 1917 nearby to the north. It was named for the late Smithsonian Secretary Samuel P. Langley. The NACA's first research facility, Langley Memorial Aeronautical Laboratory, opened in 1918. Over the years it solved complex problems of atmospheric flight, yielding ongoing advances in aircraft design. After World War II, the laboratory also laid the foundation for space flight. When the National Aeronautics and Space Administration (NASA) emerged in 1958, Langley trained America's first astronauts.

ISLE OF WIGHT COUNTY

K-239 LAWNE'S CREEK

Rte. 10, 8.1 miles northwest of Smithfield.
Named for Christopher Lawne, who settled
at the mouth of the creek in 1619. In 1634
the plantations hereabouts became the
county of Warrascoyack. In 1637 the name
was changed to Isle of Wight.

K-240-b WRENN'S MILL

Rte. 10, 4.5 miles west of Smithfield. Wrenn's
Mill stood south of here on Pagan Creek.
A mill powered by water for grinding
grain existed there before 1685, when
Thomas Green bequeathed it to his wife.
The mill was referred to as Little Mill
and Green's Mill, before Charles Wrenn
obtained it in the 1820s. On 14 April
1864, members of the 23rd Massachusetts
Volunteers drove Confederates from their
position there, capturing a signal officer
and two privates of the 7th Confederate
Cavalry. The Union troops then fell back to
Fort Boykin. The mill was dismantled by
the early 1990s.

K-241 BENNETT'S PLANTATION

Business Rte. 10, at Hardy Elementary School.
By Nov. 1621, Edward Bennett had obtained a patent from the Virginia Company
to establish Bennett's Plantation, also
known as Warrascoyack and Bennett's Welcome. By Feb. 1622, the *Sea Flower* arrived
with the first residents and they began
settling the south bank of the James River
at the lower reaches of Burwell's Bay. On
22 Mar. 1622, the Powhatan-English War of
1622–1632 began with attacks coordinated
by Chief Opechancanough against many
English settlements including Bennett's
Plantation. More than 50 colonists died
there and the survivors were transported
to Jamestown. Bennett's Plantation was
reestablished by June 1623.

K-242 BASSE'S CHOICE

Business Rte. 10, at Hardy Elementary School.
In Nov. 1621, Capt. Nathaniel Basse received a grant of 300 acres of land, now
known as Basse's Choice, located nearby. It
was one of the first English settlements in
Isle of Wight County, though humans had
lived there more than 5000 years. On Mar.
1622, during the Powhatan-English War of
1622–1632, attacks coordinated by Chief
Opechancanough struck various English
settlements including Basse's Choice. Basse
was in England when this event occurred.
He resettled the region by 1624, when
twenty people lived there. Basse later
served in the House of Burgesses and was
appointed to the governor's council in Mar.
1630.

K-243 SMITHFIELD

*Business Rte. 10, east of Business Rte. 258,
Smithfield.* The town was established in
1752. The Masonic Hall was built in 1753.
Benedict Arnold occupied the town, January 15, 1781. At Cherry Grove Landing near
by, skirmishing took place on April 13–15,
1864, and the Confederates made a daring
capture of a Union vessel on December 5,
1864.

K-244 WARRASKOYACK INDIANS

*Rte. 665 (Smith's Neck Road), at Riverview
United Methodist Church.* Near here, where
the Pagan River empties into the James
River stood the small village of Mokete of
the Warraskoyack Indians. Another Warraskoyack village called Mathomank existed
on Burwell's Bay. The principal settlement
of Warraskoyack was located inland near
Smithfield. The Warraskoyacks occupied
the James River shoreline at the mouth of
the Pagan River and into the interior past
Smithfield. John Smith traded with the
Warraskoyacks as early as the fall of 1607,
obtaining corn for the colonists. By 1610,
however, hostilities had broken out with
the English attacking the Warraskoyack,
burning their homes, and destroying their
cornfields.

K-245 SAINT LUKE'S CHURCH

Rte. 10, near Benns Church, 4.25 miles south-east of Smithfield. St. Luke's Church, also known as "The Brick Church," and the Newport Parish Church, is likely America's purest expression of Gothic architecture. Its buttressed walls, lancet side windows, and traceried east windows link the building to the architecture of the Middle Ages. Although oral tradition dates the structure to 1632, architectural evidence suggests that the church with its tower was constructed during the last quarter of the 17th century. After the disestablishment of the Anglican Church in 1786, St. Luke's fell into disrepair and was more or less in ruins for most of the 19th century. A series of repairs began in the late 19th century and a thorough restoration was completed in 1957. (National Historic Landmark, 1960)

K-246 BENN'S CHURCH

Rte. 10, 4.2 miles southeast of Smithfield. This Methodist church was known in 1804 as Benn's Chapel. Bishop Asbury preached here in 1804.

K-247 JOSIAH PARKER (MACCLESFIELD)

Rte. 711. Col. Josiah Parker (1751–1810) served in the Revolutionary War in the 5th Virginia Regiment from Aug. 1776 until July 1778 when he resigned his commission. Parker distinguished himself at the Battle of Trenton (25–26 Dec. 1776), the Battle of Princeton (3 Jan. 1777), and the Battle of Brandywine (9–11 Sept. 1777), and was commended by Gen. George Washington. In 1781 Parker commanded the Virginia militia south of the James River. After the war, he served as a representative to Congress from 1789 to 1801. Nearby stood his home Macclesfield where he is buried.

K-260 BOYKIN'S TAVERN

Rte. 258, near Isle of Wight. Boykin's Tavern is a rare surviving example of the hostelries once common in Virginia courthouse complexes, where they offered food and accommodations for people attending court. The original structure was built in the late 18th century for Maj. Francis Boykin, a Revolutionary War officer who represented Isle of Wight County in the Virginia House of Delegates from 1787 to 1792 and served the county as a sheriff and a justice of the peace. Boykin donated two acres of adjoining land to the county in 1800 and erected several of the court buildings. Boykin's Tavern was listed on the Virginia Landmarks Register and National Register of Historic Places in 1974.

K-311 JAMES RIVER

Rte. 17, at southern end of James River Bridge. The James River flows about 340 miles from the junction of the Jackson and Cowpasture rivers in Botetourt County to Hampton Roads at the Chesapeake Bay. In 1607 the first permanent English settlement in the New World was established on its banks at Jamestown. The colonists used the river as a path for exploration. With modern cities and shipyards as well as ancient plantations lining its banks, the James River remains one of Virginia's most important natural resources.

K-316 OLD ISLE OF WIGHT COURTHOUSE

Business Rte. 258 (Main Street), near Business Rte. 10, Smithfield. Smithfield served as the county seat from 1752 to 1801. The Old Isle of Wight courthouse was built in 1752. Constructed by William Rand, it is one of Virginia's few surviving colonial court structures and is notable for having a semicircular apse with a conical roof, reflective of the Colonial Capitol in Williamsburg. Converted into a residence in 1812, the courthouse was acquired by the Association for the Preservation of Virginia Antiquities in 1938 and restored to its original appearance. A nearby house was converted into a tavern for the courthouse village by Rand around 1756; it was modified and enlarged over the years and is now known as the Smithfield Inn.

U-125 CAMP MANUFACTURING COMPANY

Business Rte. 58, near Blackwater River.
This industrial complex evolved from a sawmill that operated here prior to the Civil War. In 1887, three brothers, Paul D. Camp, James L. Camp, and Robert J. Camp, founded Camp Manufacturing Company, later Union Camp Corporation. The lumbering enterprise pioneered a program to purchase land as well as timber rights, allowing extensive reforestation efforts. The facility is a major producer of paper, paperboard, lumber, and particleboard. The Blackwater River and the railroads have traditionally provided transportation for raw materials and manufactured products for the western Virginia Tidewater area.

UT-19 SEVEN CONFEDERATE BROTHERS

Rte. 460, Windsor. On 22 Apr. 1861, at the beginning of the Civil War, six sons of Benjamin Mills Roberts and Mary Ann Wright Roberts enlisted in Co. D (Isle of Wight Rifle Grays), 16th Va. Inf. Regt. They were Mills W., John W., Sylvester J., Benjamin C., Francis C., and Nathaniel C. Roberts, who received a medical discharge. 1st Lt. Stephen W. Roberts, the seventh son, already had enlisted in the 11th N.C. Inf. All of the brothers were wounded while in service, and three surrendered at Appomattox Court House. Remarkably, all survived the war to return to the Windsor area.

JAMES CITY COUNTY

V-39 BATTLE OF GREEN SPRING

Rte. 614 (Green Spring Road), between Rte. 5 and Jamestown, at entrance to Mainland Farm. Nearby, late in the afternoon of 6 July 1781, Gen. Charles Cornwallis and cavalry commander Col. Banastre Tarleton with 5,000 British and Hessian troops clashed with 800 American troops commanded by Brig. Gen. "Mad" Anthony Wayne and the Marquis de Lafayette. Believing that the main British force was across the James River, and that he was attacking Cornwallis's rear guard, Wayne soon realized that he was facing far superior numbers. He startled the advancing British forces by charging them, exchanging volleys, and then withdrawing his troops from encirclement and certain defeat. Dusk prevented Cornwallis from pursuing the Americans.

V-41 GOVERNOR'S LAND

Rte. 614 (Green Spring Road), between Rte. 5 and Jamestown, at entrance to Mainland Farm. Situated near Jamestown, Governor's Land originally was a 3,000-acre tract encompassing open fields between the James River and Powhatan Creek. The Virginia Company of London set the parcel aside in 1618 to seat tenants who worked the land, giving half the profits to maintain the office of the governor. Deputy Governor Samuel Argall had already established the private settlement of Argall's Town in these environs in 1617. Virginia governors also leased the property to others. Colonial leaders including William Drummond, governor of the Carolina proprietary (1665–1667) and an insurgent in Bacon's Rebellion of 1676 held leaseholds here. Portions of tract provided income to Virginia governors into the 18th century.

V-42 GREEN SPRING ROAD

Rte. 614 (Green Spring Road), between Rte. 5 and Jamestown, at entrance to Mainland Farm. The 17th century road to Green Spring, home of Governor Sir William Berkeley, was the eastern part of the Great Road, the earliest-developed English thoroughfare in Virginia. The Great Road ran from Jamestown Island toward the falls of the James River. The road was an important thoroughfare used to transport goods and forward communications between settlements. Originally, the Green Spring Road followed close to the James River, linking Jamestown to Green Spring. On 6 July 1781, the Revolutionary War Battle of Green Spring was fought in the fields flanking this road. By this time, the lower portion of the road (a part of present day Rte. 614) had shifted eastward.

V-44 JAMESTOWN

Frontage road paralleling Rte. 31 (Jamestown Road), 0.2 miles north of Rte. 359. Nearby to the east is Jamestown, the original site of the first permanent English colony in North America. On 14 May 1607, a group of just over 100 men and boys recruited by the Virginia Company of London came ashore and established a settlement at Jamestown Island. They constructed a palisaded fort there within the territory of the Paspahegh Indians, who with other Virginia Indians had frequent contact with the English. In 1619 the first English representative legislative body in North America met there, and the first documented Africans arrived. Jamestown served as the capital of the Virginia colony from 1607 to 1699. Historic Jamestowne preserves this original site and the archaeological remains.

V-45 POCAHONTAS

Frontage road paralleling Rte. 31 (Jamestown Road), 0.2 miles north of Rte. 359. Matoaka, nicknamed Pocahontas ("mischievous one"), the daughter of Powhatan, was born about 1597. She served as an emissary for her father and came to Jamestown often in 1608. In 1613, Samuel Argall kidnapped Pocahontas while she visited the Patawomecks on the Potomac River. Argall hoped to exchange her for English prisoners and brought her to Jamestown. During lengthy negotiations, Pocahontas married John Rolfe in 1614, credited with developing Virginia's first marketable tobacco crop. Pocahontas took the baptismal name Rebecca. In 1616, she traveled with Rolfe and their son, Thomas, to England where King James I and Queen Anne received her. She died at Gravesend, England, in March 1617.

V-46 CHURCH ON THE MAIN

Rte. 614 (Green Spring Road), between Rte. 5 and Jamestown, at entrance to Mainland Farm. Less than one mile to the east is the site of the Church on the Main, a brick Anglican church built by the 1750s to serve James City Parish as replacement for the church on Jamestown Island, which had become difficult for communicants to reach. The Rev. James Madison (1749–1812) was its best-known rector, serving the church from about 1777 until it fell into disuse after the American Revolution and the disestablishment of the Anglican Church. Madison became president of the College of William and Mary (1777–1812) and Virginia's first Episcopal Bishop in 1790. By 1857 all aboveground traces of the church were gone.

V-47 HOT WATER/CENTERVILLE

Green Spring and Centerville Roads, at Freedom Park. Royal Governor William Berkeley, owner of nearby Green Spring plantation, purchased the land here by 1652, then known as Hot Water. After Berkeley's death, the Hot Water tract passed to the Ludwell and Lee families. William Ludwell Lee inherited the property in 1796 and died in 1803. Lee's will specified that his slaves be freed when they reached the age of 18. They were allowed to live on the property for ten years at no charge and "comfortable houses" were to be built upon the tract for them. Lee's philanthropy gave rise to one of Virginia's early free black settlements located at Centerville.

W-26 NEW KENT ROAD

Rte. 30, north of Rte. 60, south of I-64 interchange. By the 1720s, several taverns stood on New Kent Road (also called the Old Stage Road) between Williamsburg and New Kent Court House. During two wars, the road served opposing armies as well as travelers. In June 1781, near the end of the Revolution, British commander Gen. Charles Cornwallis marched his army from Richmond to Williamsburg on the road, with the Marquis de Lafayette and his army in cautious pursuit. During the Civil War, Gen. Joseph E. Johnston's Confederate army withdrew west on the road toward Richmond after the Battle of Williamsburg on 5 May 1862; Maj. Gen. George B. McClellan's Army of the Potomac slowly followed.

W-27 WHITE HALL TAVERN

Rte. 60, at Rte. 30, 1.3 miles northwest of Toano. This was a station on the old stage road between Williamsburg and Richmond, before 1860.

W-28 OLIVE BRANCH CHRISTIAN CHURCH

Rte. 60, at Rte. 602, east of Toano. In 1833 the founders of Olive Branch Christian Church (Disciples of Christ) met for worship at Hill Pleasant Farm. By 1835, the congregation had built a brick church on land donated by Dr. Charles M. Hubbard and Mary Henley. During the Civil War, Union soldiers occupied the church; they reportedly slept in the gallery and stabled their horses in the sanctuary. The congregation worshiped in the Farthing house until 1866, when the church was restored to usable condition. With that exception, Olive Branch Christian Church, one of the oldest churches of the Disciples of Christ in Virginia, has been in continuous use since its construction.

W-30 HICKORY NECK CHURCH

Rte. 60, 0.8 miles northwest of Toano, at church. Hickory Neck Church was built about 1740. Militia opposing the British camped here on April 21, 1781. A few miles north is the foundation of an ancient stone house, dating possibly from about 1650.

W-31 STATE SHIPYARD

Rte. 610, at Rte. 60, Toano. On this road five miles west was the State shipyard on

Chickahominy River, burned by the British General Phillips on April 21–22, 1781.

W-32 CHICKAHOMINY CHURCH

Rte. 60, Toano. Two miles south is the site of the colonial Chickahominy Church, now destroyed. Lafayette's forces camped there, July 6–8, 1781. The church was used as a hospital after the battle of Green Spring, July 6, 1781.

W-33 BURNT ORDINARY

Rte. 610, at Rte. 60, Toano. First called John Lewis's Ordinary and then Fox's, Burnt Ordinary received its name in Jan. 1780 when, according to the *Virginia Gazette,* Fox's Ordinary burned to the ground. Later, in Oct. 1781, when the French army's wagon train passed by, Alexander Berthier wrote that "two old chimneys" stood here in the fork of the road. Also in 1781, Samuel DeWitt, George Washington's cartographer, noted the site of the "Burnt Brick Ordinary" on one of his maps. Elements of Lafayette's army camped two miles south of here at Chickahominy Church after the Battle of Green Spring on 6 July 1781.

W-34 SIX-MILE ORDINARY

Rte. 60, at Rte. 614, Lightfoot. Six-Mile Ordinary, a popular 18th-century tavern also known as Allen's for its proprietor Isham Allen, stood six miles from Williamsburg. On 1 July 1774, a group of free holders congregated there and drafted the James City Resolves not to import British goods. Two years later, they gathered again to declare their support for American independence. On 21 April 1781, Col. James Innes notified the governor that 500 British infantrymen, 50 horses, and 4 pieces of artillery had come ashore at Burwell's Ferry. Because of this unexpected event, Innes and his troops retreated to Six-Mile Ordinary around midnight.

W-35 SPENCER'S ORDINARY

Rte. 60, at Rte. 614, Lightfoot. On this road, four miles south, the action of Spencer's

Ordinary was fought, June 24, 1781, between detachments from Lafayette's and Cornwallis's armies.

W-36 GREEN SPRING

Rte. 60, at Rte. 614, Lightfoot. On this road, five miles south, is Green Spring, home of Governor Sir William Berkeley. Bacon the Rebel occupied it in 1676. Cornwallis, after moving from Williamsburg by this road on July 4, 1781, was attacked by Lafayette near Green Spring on July 6, 1781. Anthony Wayne was the hero of this fight.

W-37 PENINSULAR CAMPAIGN

Rte. 60, at eastern entrance to Williamsburg. During the Peninsula Campaign of 1862, both Confederate Gen. Joseph E. Johnston and Union Maj. Gen. George B. McClellan led their armies west toward Richmond on this road. Johnston evacuated Yorktown on 3–4 May and withdrew up the Peninsula, with McClellan in pursuit. On 5 May, two Federal divisions clashed with the Confederate rear guard east of Williamsburg in a bloody but indecisive battle. Johnston's army continued its march west and on 6–7 May eluded McClellan's forces at Eltham's Landing on the York River opposite West Point. By mid-month the Confederates were secure behind the Richmond defenses.

W-38 JAMESTOWN ROAD

Rte. 31, north of Rte. 614, Jamestown. The ancient road that linked Jamestown, the original colonial capital, with Middle Plantation (later Williamsburg) followed a meandering course. It departed from Jamestown Island and then turned northeast, crossing Powhatan and Mill Creeks. As it approached Middle Plantation, it traversed a branch of College Creek that by the mid-17th century was dammed to form Rich Neck plantation's millpond, today's Lake Matoaka. Improvements to Jamestown Road, completed in time for the Jamestown Ter-Centennial Exposition, constituted the first project completed

with the assistance of the State Highway Commission, formed in 1906.

W-42 QUARTERPATH ROAD

Rte. 60, at eastern entrance to Williamsburg. James Bray owned land nearby in Middle Plantation by the 1650s, and Quarterpath Road probably began as a horse path to one of Bray's quarters or farm units. Over the years, the road was improved; it extended to Col. Lewis Burwell's landing on the James River by the early eighteenth century. As Williamsburg grew, Quarterpath Road became one of the principal routes by which travelers and trade goods were brought into the colonial capital.

W-43 BATTLE OF WILLIAMSBURG

Rte. 60, 0.3 miles southeast of Williamsburg. To the east of the road here, centering at Fort Magruder, was fought the battle of Williamsburg on May 5, 1862. The Union General McClellan was pursuing General Johnston's retiring army, the rearguard of which was commanded by General Longstreet. Johnston ordered Longstreet to hold off McClellan's attacking forces until the Confederate wagon trains, bogged down in mud, were out of danger. This mission was accomplished and Johnston continued his retirement.

W-44 MAGRUDER'S DEFENSES

Rte. 60, 0.3 miles southeast of Williamsburg. Here is a redoubt in the Line of Confederate defenses, built across the James-York peninsula in 1861–62 by General John B. Magruder.

W-47 KINGSMILL

Rte. 60, at Rte. 199, east of Williamsburg. Kingsmill Plantation, the home of Col. Lewis Burwell, was built in the mid-1730s and consisted of a mansion, outbuildings, garden, and 1,400 acres. The house burned in 1843. Only the office and the kitchen still stand; they are among the earliest brick dependencies in Virginia. Burwell, the naval officer (colonial customs inspector) for the upper James River, built his inspection station here at Burwell's Landing, which included a tavern, storehouse, warehouse, and ferry house. In Nov. 1775, American riflemen skirmished nearby with British naval vessels; later, the Americans built two earthen forts here that the British captured in 1781.

W-48   LITTLETOWN

1156 Jamestown Road, 200 feet northeast of Rte. 199. In the second quarter of the 17th-century, merchant George Menefie developed a 1,200-acre plantation just east of here he called Littletown. In March 1633, Dutch trader David DeVies observed that his two-acre garden was "full of Provence roses, apple, pear and cherry trees, . . . with different kinds of sweet-smelling herbs, such as rosemary, sage, marjoram, thyme." Richard Kemp later acquired the tract and called it Rich Neck. Rich Neck was home to three generations of the Ludwell family and Ludwell's Mill (at modern Lake Matoaka) was an important 18th-century landmark.

W-49   TREBELL'S LANDING

Rte. 60, 0.4 miles east of Carter's Grove main entrance. At Trebell's Landing on the James River, a mile southwest of here, the artillery and stores of the American and French armies were landed in September 1781. They were then conveyed overland some six miles to the siege lines at Yorktown. The troops disembarked at landings near Williamsburg. During the next few weeks, the allied armies under Gen. George Washington and the comte de Rochambeau besieged the British army commanded by Gen. Charles Cornwallis until he surrendered on 19 Oct. 1781, effectively ending the Revolutionary War.

W-50   CARTER'S GROVE

Rte. 60, 0.4 miles east of Carter's Grove main entrance. During the 17th century Carter's Grove was part of the Martin's Hundred Plantation. In the early 1720s, Robert "King" Carter purchased it and later named the tract Carter's Grove. Between 1750 and 1755 Carter Burwell, grandson of Robert "King" Carter, built the Carter's Grove mansion, a famous example of colonial Virginia plantation architecture. Burwell hired brickmason David Minitree to make and lay the brick; he brought Richard Baylis, an English joiner, to Virginia to execute the interior woodwork, some of the handsomest of the era. The house stood almost unaltered until 1928 when it was renovated and enlarged by the architect W. Duncan Lee.

W-51   MARTIN'S HUNDRED

Rte. 60, east of Carter's Grove, at James River Elementary School. This plantation was allocated to the London-based Society of Martin's Hundred by 1618 and was later assigned 21,500 acres. It was initially settled in 1620 around Wolstenholme Town, its administrative center, located near the James River. Archaeologists discovered the town site in 1977. They also located the graves of several people who died during the 22 March 1622 Indian attacks on English settlements coordinated by Chief Opechancanough, when 78 colonists here—half the plantation's population—were reported killed. These attacks were in response to English expansion into Indian lands. The area was soon resettled but the Society of Martin's Hundred's town was never rebuilt.

W-52   MARTIN'S HUNDRED CHURCH

Rte. 60, east of Carter's Grove, at James River Elementary School. The first Martin's Hundred Parish church was probably built at Wolstenholme Town, an early-17th-century settlement that was located a mile southeast of here. None of the structures excavated there has been identified as a church; it may have been in a portion of the town that has been lost to erosion. A second parish church was built about 1630. Martin's Hundred Parish was incorporated into Yorkhampton Parish in York County in 1712, and the Martin's Hundred Church may have been abandoned then. The cemetery there probably continued in use for some time afterward.

WT-1 First Africans in English America

Frontage road paralleling Rte. 31 (Jamestown Road), 0.2 miles north of Rte. 359. The first documented Africans in English America arrived at Jamestown in August 1619. A Dutch man-of-war captured them from the Spanish, who had enslaved them, and sold them to the Virginia colonists. The "twenty and odd" Africans, some of whom had been given Spanish names, may have been treated like indentured servants and later freed after their periods of servitude expired. From this beginning the institution of slavery evolved during the 17th century as the Virginia colonists extended the length of service for Africans from a fixed term to life. The United States abolished slavery in 1865.

WT-2 First Germans at Jamestown

Frontage road paralleling Rte. 31 (Jamestown Road), 0.2 miles north of Rte. 359. The first Germans to land in Jamestown, the first permanent English settlement in Virginia, arrived aboard the vessel *Mary and Margaret* about 1 October 1608. These Germans were glassmakers and carpenters. In 1620, German mineral specialists and sawmillwrights followed, to work and settle in the Virginia colony. These pioneers and skilled craftsmen were the forerunners of the many millions of Germans who settled in America and became the single largest national group to populate the United States.

KING AND QUEEN COUNTY

N-58 The Indentured Servants' Plot

Rte. 14, approximately 1 mile west of Rte. 17. During the summer of 1663, indentured servants (held for several years of service) in the Poropotank River and Purtan Bay region plotted an insurrection against their masters to occur on 13 Sept. 1663. It was prevented when John Berkenhead, servant of Maj. John Smith, of Gloucester County, informed the authorities of the planned uprising. For "his honest affection of the preservation of this Country" the Virginia House of Burgesses, on 16 Sept., granted Berkenhead his freedom and 5,000 pounds of tobacco. In addition, the Burgesses proclaimed that 13 Sept. would henceforth annually be "kept holy."

O-20 Clark Home

Rte. 360, at St. Stephens Church. About twelve miles east is the site of the original home of the family of George Rogers Clark, conqueror of the Northwest. The family moved from here to Albemarle County.

O-43 Mount Pleasant

Rte. 360, at Rte. 621. Near here stood the plantation and Thoroughbred stables of Col. John Hoskins (1751–1813), one of the foremost breeders in the country. In 1800 Col. Robert Sanders, of Scott Co., Ky., bought one of Hoskins's horses, Melzar, for ten times the usual price for stallions. Melzar was considered the best example in America of the bloodline of the Godolphin Arabian (one of the five Thoroughbred foundation sires), and improved Kentucky racehorses more than any other early sire. Hoskins, a Revolutionary War veteran of the Siege of Yorktown, served as a county justice and a commissioner in the Jefferson-Adams election of 1800. He also was the father-in-law of Spencer Roane, chief justice of the Virginia Supreme Court of Appeals.

OB-2 Bruington Church

Rte. 14, 6.2 miles northwest of Stevensville. This is Bruington Church, organized in

1790. Here Robert Semple, one of the most noted Baptist ministers in Virginia, long served and here he is buried.

OB-3 MATTAPONY CHURCH

Rte. 14, 4.1 miles northwest of King and Queen Court House. This is the ancient colonial Mattapony Church, used by the Baptists since 1824. Here are tombs of members of the family of Carter Braxton, signer of the Declaration of Independence.

OB-4 STATE FISH HATCHERY

Rte. 14, 1 mile northwest of Stevensville. Half a mile north. This fish cultural station was established in 1937 for hatching and rearing largemouth bass and other species of sunfish for the stocking of the public waters of Virginia.

OB-5 HILLSBORO

Rte. 14, 4.7 miles northwest of Stevensville. This house, four miles south, was built by Colonel Humphrey Hill about 1722. It is of quaint architecture having brick ends and frame front and rear. The place was raided by the British during the Revolution.

OB-6 WHERE DAHLGREN DIED

Rte. 631, 2.5 miles northwest of King and Queen Court House. Colonel Ulric Dahlgren, Federal officer, met death in the early morning, March 2, 1864, three hundred yards to the north. After the raid on Richmond, his force bivouaced [bivouacked] here and, in breaking camp he fell to the fire of Confederate detachments and Home Defense forces who had gathered during the night.

OB-8 PARK CHURCH

Rte. 721, at Rte. 625. Park Church was built in 1723 for the newly established Drysdale Parish. It stood on the west side of this road, two and one-half miles above Newtown. The brick church was cruciform in shape with arms approximately 75 feet long. It was known as Park Church because

of its proximity to Beverley Park, home of Robert Beverley, Jr., colonial historian of Virginia. The congregation declined in numbers when the Church of England was disestablished following the American Revolution. The church finally was abandoned in 1801.

OB-9 NEWTOWN

Rte. 721, at Rte. 625. Newtown began as a pre-Revolutionary tavern crossroads on the intercolonial King's Highway. The settlement prospered in the antebellum period, becoming King and Queen's largest post village and supporting several fine academies and schools. In June 1863 Newtown witnessed the last tactical action of General George Pickett's Division before its long march to Gettysburg.

OB-10 NEWINGTON

Rte. 14, 1 mile northwest of King and Queen Court House. A mile south on the Mattapony River is the site of Newington, birthplace of Carter Braxton (born September 10, 1736), signer of the Declaration of Independence. In earlier times, Colonel Jacob Lumpkin, supporter of Governor Berkeley in Bacon's Rebellion, 1676, lived there.

OB-11 APPLE TREE CHURCH

Rte. 360, 0.4 miles east of Rte. 14, St. Stephens Church. About two miles south stood the colonial church known as the Apple Tree Church or St. Clement's Church. First authorized by the House of Burgesses in 1710, it served as the upper church of St. Stephen's Parish until after the Revolution. It was then abandoned and later destroyed by fire.

OB-12 CORBIN'S CHURCH—THE NEW CHURCH

Rte. 14, 1 mile north of Rte. 33. The New Church, also known as Corbin's Church, stood to the east of this road. Councillor Richard Corbin, who also served as

Receiver-General of the colony, donated "Goliath's Old Field" for the church, which was completed in 1768 to replace two older Anglican churches in Stratton Major Parish. The New Church measured 50 by 80 feet and was 27 feet high with galleries. According to the parish vestry book, 275 persons were initially assigned pews in the church.

OB-16 LANEVILLE

Rte. 14, 10 miles southeast of King and Queen Court House. A mile and a half southwest stood Laneville, built by Richard Corbin, receiver general (treasurer) about 1760 on the site of an earlier house. There Patrick Henry sent, May 1775, to obtain money in payment for the colony's powder seized by Lord Dunmore. Laneville was one of the largest and finest houses in Virginia.

OB-18 COLONIAL CHURCH

Rte. 14, 8.5 miles southeast of King and Queen Court House. This church, the new church of Stratton Major Parish, was built in 1767. Rev. William Robinson, the Bishop of London's commissary, came to the parish in 1744 and was the first minister of the new church. It fell into disuse after the Revolution but later became a Methodist church.

OB-50 POROPOTANK CREEK

Rte. 14, near King and Queen/Gloucester County line. Land was patented on this creek as early as 1640. In 1653, John Lewis settled here. John Lewis, Jr., was living here in 1676 when Bacon's troops were encamped near by. He suffered from the depredations of the rebels.

KING GEORGE COUNTY

EP-7 HANOVER BAPTIST CHURCH

Rte. 301, approximately 0.4 miles north of Rte. 205. Hanover Baptist Church, the oldest Baptist church in King George County, was organized in 1789 with a 93-member congregation. The first meetinghouse was located at Shiloh, and Elder John Shackleford served as the first pastor. The first Sunday school was established in 1833. The second meetinghouse was located at Allnutt. In the early 1840s, during the Second Great Awakening, 1,025 new members were baptized. The third house of worship was built here after James F. Jones deeded the land to Hanover Baptist Church trustees William B. Coakley, William E. McClanahan, and John A. Peed in 1873.

EP-8 BIRTHPLACE OF MADISON

Rte. 301, at King George/Caroline County line. At this place, Port Conway, James Madison, Fourth President of the United States and Father of the Constitution, was born, March 16, 1751. His mother was staying at her paternal home, Belle Grove, 400 yards east, when her son was born. Madison's father, James Madison, Senior, lived in Orange County. The President had his home at Montpelier in that county.

EP-9 CLEYDAEL

Rte. 206, 1.35 miles south of Rte. 218. This T-shaped house was built in 1859 by Dr. Richard Stuart as a summer residence for his family. On Sunday afternoon, April 23, 1865, John Wilkes Booth and three companions came to this house seeking medical assistance from Dr. Stuart. Suspicious of his visitors and aware of Lincoln's assassination, Dr. Stuart refused to aid them and sent them away after dinner.

J-62 LAMB'S CREEK CHURCH

Rte. 3, 5.5 miles west of King George. This old church was probably built before 1750. The stepping stone at the door bears the date, 1782. Near here Kilpatrick's Union cavalry, on a raid to destroy gunboats at Port Conway, fought a skirmish, September 1, 1863.

J-63 MARMION

Rte. 3, 2.3 miles west of King George. Two miles north is Marmion, probably built by John Fitzhugh early in the eighteenth century and later named for Scott's poem. About 1785 it passed from Philip Fitzhugh to George Washington Lewis, Washington's favorite nephew, who died there. The place has come down in the Lewis family in direct line from him. The richly decorated interior is one of the best in Virginia.

J-65 ST. PAUL'S CHURCH

Rte. 3, at Rte. 206, 1.5 miles west of King George. Eight miles northeast is St. Paul's Church, built about 1766. The building was in a ruinous condition in 1812 but was repaired by the State and used both as a church and as a schoolhouse. About 1828 it once more became exclusively a church.

J-66 HISTORIC PORT CONWAY

Rte. 301, approximately 0.3 miles south of Rte. 3. The site of Port Conway is located five miles south on the Rappahannock River. Francis Conway laid out the town in 1783, and the next year the Virginia General Assembly passed an act establishing it. James Madison, Father of the Constitution and fourth president of the United States, was born at the Conway house on 16 March 1751. On 1 Sept. 1863 Brig. Gen. H. Judson Kilpatrick's Federal cavalry shelled two Union gunboats at Port Conway that had been captured by Confederates. John Wilkes Booth, the assassin of President Abraham Lincoln, fled across the river there on 24 Apr. 1865. Little remains of the town today.

KING WILLIAM COUNTY

O-16 RUMFORD ACADEMY

Rte. 360, at Rte. 30, Central Garage. Two miles east was Rumford Academy, established in 1804. It was one of the most noted Virginia schools of its time.

O-18 CAVALRY RAIDS

Rte. 360, Aylett. Kilpatrick, coming from the east, burned Confederate stores here, May 5, 1863. Dahlgren, coming from Richmond, crossed the Mattapony here March 2, 1864. Sheridan, returning from his Richmond raid, was here, May 22–23, 1864, and on his Trevilian raid passed here, June 7, 1864.

O-59 MONTVILLE

Rte. 360, approximately 1 mile west of Rte. 600, near Aylett. This property was home of Philip Aylett (1791–1848), for whom the village is named and who served in both the Virginia House and Senate. His son, William Roane Aylett (1833–1900), who rose to colonel in the Confederate army and later served as commonwealth's

attorney, also lived here. Until the early 20th century, two frame houses stood here side by side. The first incorporated an 1800 one-and-a-half story section with an 1830s two-story addition; this house was called Aylett's. The second house, the present Montville, dates to the mid-19th century and is a mirror image of the first, which burned in the early 1900s.

OC-14 PAMUNKEY INDIANS

Rte. 30, at Rte. 633. Eight miles south is the reservation on which the Pamunkey Indians live. The land has never been in non-Indian ownership and the Pamunkey live on it under a treaty made in 1677. In the early seventeenth century the Pamunkey were a chiefdom ruled by Opechancanough, brother and subject of the paramount chief Powhatan, the father of Pocahontas. Though they continually lost land to non-Indian settlers, they remained the most powerful chiefdom in eastern Virginia for as long as the traditional system lasted. Today the Pamunkey are governed by an elected chief, assistant chief, and council.

OC-15 MATTAPONI INDIANS

Rte. 30, at Rte. 640. Two miles east is the Mattaponi Indian reservation, home of descendants of the great chief Powhatan, father of Pocahontas. The reservation is situated on the Mattaponi River and is one of the oldest Indian reservations in the United States, existing since 1658. The Mattaponi tribe is governed by its chief and council and continues to exercise its laws and traditional customs.

OC-18 ST. JOHN'S CHURCH

Rte. 30, 8.9 miles northwest of West Point. This was the parish church of St. John's Parish, formed in 1680. It was built in 1734. Earlier churches stood at West Point and about one mile north of this site. Carter Braxton, Revolutionary Statesman, was a vestryman. Preserved by joint effort.

OC-20 MANGOHICK CHURCH

Rte. 30, near Rte. 671, Mangohick. Referred to by William Byrd in 1732 as the New Brick Church, Mangohick Church was built circa 1730 as a chapel of ease for those who lived in remote areas of St. Margaret's Parish. Distinguished by its fine Flemish bond brickwork, Mangohick became the Upper Church of St. David's when that parish was formed in 1774. It became a free church for use by any denomination following disestablishment of the Church of England in Virginia. It now serves the Mangohick Baptist congregation.

OC-22 CAMPAIGN OF 1781— LAFAYETTE'S ENCAMPMENT

Rte. 30, near Rte. 634. On 13 August 1781, the Marquis de Lafayette encamped his army in King William County. He placed his militia four miles east between the Pamunkey and Mattaponi Rivers and stationed his light infantry—commanded by Gen. John Peter Gabriel Muhlenburg and

Lt. Col. Christian Febiger—a mile south of here. From these positions Lafayette spied on the British army under Gen. Charles Cornwallis entrenching downriver at Yorktown, and prepared to block its escape routes. Early in September, Gen. George Washington and his army arrived from the north, accompanied by Rochambeau's French forces, to join Lafayette and begin the siege of Yorktown.

OC-25 CAMPAIGN OF 1781

Rte. 30, east of Rte. 635, northwest of West Point. About a mile to the east, August 13, 1781, Lafayette, then commanding American forces in Virginia, placed in camp his militia, consisting of Campbell's, Stevens' and Lawson's brigades. Wayne was at Westover; Muhlenberg and Febiger were in camp on the Pamunkey four miles northwest. The campaign of Yorktown was about to open; these troops were later engaged there.

OC-26 HOME OF SIGNER

Rte. 33, West Point. Carter Braxton, Signer of the Declaration of Independence, lived at West Point 1777–1786 after fire destroyed his plantation Chericoke, upriver on the Pamunkey. The Town House no longer stands. From West Point Braxton channeled war goods to Patriot Troops.

OC-27 KING WILLIAM COUNTY COURTHOUSE

Rte. 1301, just east of Rte. 619. The King William County courthouse, erected early in the second quarter of the 18th century, is one of the older courthouses still in use in the United States. This T-shaped building was constructed of brick laid in Flemish bond, with an arcade imitating the first capital in Williamsburg. One of the best preserved of Virginia's colonial courthouse buildings, it features fine Georgian brickwork. About 1840 the courthouse was enlarged with a unique stile and a brick wall was erected to enclose the court green. Its rural historic setting is a rare survival.

OC-28 SHARON INDIAN SCHOOL

Rte. 30, approximately 1.17 miles east of Rte. 360. Sharon Indian School served as a center of education for the Upper Mattaponi Tribe. In 1919, the King William County School Board built a one-room frame building and the students' families provided the furniture. The county replaced the original school with this brick structure in 1952. Before the integration of Virginia schools in the 1960s, Sharon provided a primary and limited secondary education. The students at Sharon Indian School had to attend other Native American, private, or public institutions, usually outside the Commonwealth, to obtain high school diplomas. Upper Mattaponi students—and children from the Rappahannock Tribe in the 1960s—attended school here until June 1965. It was one of the last Indian schools to operate in Virginia.

LANCASTER COUNTY

J-80 BIRTHPLACE OF WASHINGTON'S MOTHER

Rte. 3, 9.3 miles east of Farnham. Seven tenths mile west is Epping Forest. The land was patented by Colonel Joseph Ball, who died there in 1711. His daughter, Mary Ball, mother of George Washington, was born there in 1707/8. The house incorporates parts of the original structure.

J-81 BEWDLEY

Rte. 354, 2.13 miles east of Rte. 3. About three miles southeast, on the north bank of the Rappahannock River. Bewdley was one of the most unusual houses in Virginia, with two rows of dormer windows. It was built by Major James Ball, cousin of Washington's mother, about 1750. The first steamboat on the river touched at its warf [wharf]. The house burned in 1917; only one chimney remains.

J-82 ST. MARY'S WHITE CHAPEL

Rte. 3, Lively. Three miles southwest. A church was built there in 1669, and the tablets are of that date. The present church was built in 1741 and was later remodeled. St. Mary's White Chapel parish was united with Christ Church parish in 1752. The tombs of the Balls, ancestors and relatives of George Washington, are there.

J-83 WHITE MARSH CHURCH

Rte. 3, northwest of Kilmarnock. This church, founded in 1792, was the mother church of Methodism in the Northern Neck of Virginia. The first camp meeting in this section was held here. Bishops Enoch George and David S. Doggett were members of this church. Bishop Joshua Soule, author of the constitution of the General Conference of the American Methodist Church, preached at meetings here.

J-85 COROTOMAN

Rte. 646, 0.66 miles west of Rte. 3. This place was three miles south. Little remains of the house. John Carter obtained patents for a large grant here before 1654, but the place is better known as the home of his son, Robert ("King") Carter. In April, 1814, the British, raiding in the Chesapeake region, pillaged the plantation.

J-86 CHRIST CHURCH

Rte. 646, 0.66 miles west of Rte. 3. John Carter had the first church built on this site; it was completed in 1670 after his death. In 1730, his son Robert "King" Carter, colonial Virginia's most powerful planter, proposed to build a brick church here at his own expense, which the vestry of Christ Church Parish accepted. Finished in 1735, Christ Church is the best-preserved and most finely crafted of colonial

Erected early in the second quarter of the eighteenth century, King William County Courthouse is one of the oldest continuous-use courthouses in the United States today. A number of historical markers describe county courthouses throughout Virginia. (Marker OC-27) (Calder Loth, Virginia Department of Historic Resources)

Virginia's Anglican parish churches. The church's detailed brickwork, particularly the molded-brick doorways, distinguishes the exterior. The interior includes original high-backed pews, triple-decker pulpit, walnut altarpiece, and stone pavers. The elaborately carved tombs of Robert Carter and his two wives stand in the churchyard.

J-87 WINDMILL POINT

Rte. 695, approximately 6.5 miles east of Rte. 3. During the War of 1812, the British blockaded the Chesapeake Bay and sent raiding vessels up the rivers and creeks to plunder and destroy property. The lookout at Windmill Point (about a mile east) on Fleet's Island reported that on 23 April 1814, the enemy "landed near Windmill (Point) or North Point (about 2 miles northwest) and plundered a poor man . . . of a boat, everything he was worth." A detachment of the 92nd Regiment of Lancaster Militia posted in the vicinity fired across a creek nearby and drove the British back to their ship. This was the final raid of the War of 1812 in Lancaster County.

J-89 FIRST AMERICAN WOMAN MISSIONARY TO CHINA

Rte. 200, 0.8 miles north of Rte. 3, at Kilmarnock Baptist Church. Here was born, October 28, 1817, Henrietta Hall, (daughter of Colonel Addison Hall) first American woman missionary to China. She married

Rev. J. Lewis Shuck, and was sent with him to China by the Baptist Board of Foreign Missions, arriving there in September, 1836. She died at Hong Kong, November 27, 1844.

J-90 BARFORD

Rte. 604, at Rte. 611. Located one mile south on land lying between the eastern and western branches of the Corotoman River, is the site of Barford, the dwelling of Captain Thomas Carter who was living there by 1674. A gift from his father-in-law, Edward Dale, the property remained in the Carter family until 1782 when it was sold to Colonel James Gordon, Jr. by Edward Carter, great-grandson of Captain Thomas Carter.

J-91 A. T. WRIGHT HIGH SCHOOL

Rte. 637, 0.19 miles west of Rte. 3. Albert Terry Wright (1871–1944) was born in Hanover County, Virginia. He taught in the black schools of Richmond and, by 1908, at White Stone in Lancaster County. By 1921 Wright was principal of the county's first high school for blacks, which was constructed largely with funds raised by black residents. Named in his honor, A. T. Wright High School served black students until 1959, when the county opened Brookvale High School. The history of the man and his school exemplified the struggle for education by Virginia's rural blacks.

J-94 HENRY FLEETE AND FLEET'S ISLAND

End of Rte. 695, Windmill Point. Henry Fleete was born about 1602 in Kent, England, and moved to Jamestown, Virginia, in 1621. Fleete was seized by the Anacostan Indians during a trading expedition and held for five years. He learned their language and after his release in 1627 became a negotiator for the Virginia and Maryland colonies. Fleete helped establish Maryland in 1634 and served in its General Assembly from 1635 to 1638, and in the Virginia House of Burgesses from 1652 to 1661. He established the boundaries of Lancaster County when it was created in 1651. In May 1661, Fleete died and was buried at his home here on Fleet's Island.

J-96 QUEENSTOWN

Rte. 201, just east of Rte. 354. Seven miles southeast on Town Creek near the mouth of the Corrotoman River is the site of Queenstown. The town was created in 1692 in accordance with the Act of Ports passed that year by the Virginia General Assembly to establish in each county port towns to centralize trade and tax collection. Capt. David Fox and Robert "King" Carter served as town trustees and sold lots laid out on 50 acres of Capt. William Ball's land. Carter built the county courthouse and prison there about 1699. The town declined after his death in 1732, the county seat was moved to present-day Lancaster a decade later, and Queenstown slowly disappeared.

MATHEWS COUNTY

N-35 KINGSTON PARISH

Rte. 614, 0.25 miles east of Rte. 14. Kingston Parish was established about 1652. During colonial times, the Anglican parish administered the ecclesiastical and some civil affairs for the inhabitants of the area that later became Mathews County. The principal parish church is believed to have been located on this site since the early 18th century. In ruins by 1841, it was restored as Christ Church largely through the efforts of Elizabeth Tompkins, sister of Confederate Capt. Sally Tompkins. Both are buried here. After a fire in 1904, the church was rebuilt. Rev. Giles Buckner Cooke, former member of Gen. Robert E. Lee's staff during the Civil War, served as rector here from 1904 to 1915.

N-84 CAPTAIN SALLY L. TOMPKINS, C.S.A.—1833-1916

Rte. 611, 2 miles west of Mathews. Sally Tompkins, born at Poplar Grove 3 miles south of here, was the only woman granted a commission in the Army of the Confederacy. "Captain Sally" founded and directed Robertson Hospital in Richmond where over 1300 Confederate soldiers were cared for between 1861 and 1865. Her grave and monument are located in Christ Church Cemetery on Williams Wharf Road two miles to the south.

N-85 BATTLE OF CRICKET HILL

Rte. 223, 4 miles north of Mathews. On the shore here General Andrew Lewis, commanding the Virginia forces, erected a battery facing a stockaded camp on Gwynn's Island established by Governor Lord Dunmore, July, 1776. The fire from this point, Cricket Hill, damaged the camp and the British ships and forced the evacuation of the island. A little later Dunmore put out to sea.

N-86 FITCHETT'S WHARF

Rte. 642, northeast of Mathews, Moon. Fitchett's Wharf was a center of commercial activity for this area of Mathews County from 1845 until the early 20th century. It also served as a major port of call for vessels plying the Chesapeake Bay until 1932. An important shipyard, owned and operated by Lewis Hudgins, stood here until it was burned by Union forces in 1864. Several well-known brig and schooner class commercial ships were built here, including the *Victory* and the *Conquest*. The shipbuilder's house still stands nearby, and the wharf store has been restored as a residence.

N-87 KINGSTON PARISH GLEBE

Rte. 621, near Rte. 611, Mathews. Just south, between Put In Creek and Woodas Creek, lies the former glebe of Kingston Parish of the Church of England (now the Protestant Episcopal Church). In 1665 the parish acquired the first parcel (455 acres) of glebe land to support its minister. After the Revolution and subsequent disestablishment of the Church of England, parishes gradually relinquished their property. In 1802 the General Assembly ordered all glebes sold. Kingston Parish auctioned off its glebe in 1810 to help the poor.

N-88 MATHEWS COUNTY COURTHOUSE SQUARE

Rte. 611, 0.2 miles west of Rte. 14. Mathews County was formed in 1790 from Gloucester County and named for Thomas Mathews, of Norfolk, a soldier of the Revolution who was then Speaker of the Virginia House of Delegates. A local builder, Richard Billups, constructed the courthouse between 1792 and 1795. Other early buildings in the square include a jail (ca. 1795) and clerk's office (1859). The courthouse square is listed in the Virginia Landmarks Register and the National Register of Historic Places.

N-89 NEW POINT COMFORT LIGHTHOUSE

Rte. 600, just east of Rte. 14. Standing at the end of what was once the southernmost peninsula in Mathews County, now surrounded by water, the lighthouse marks the entrance to Mobjack Bay. Authorized by Congress in 1801, this 55-foot-high sandstone tower with its spiraling stone steps to the lighthouse cage, was built in 1805 by Elzy Burroughs, the first keeper. Except for a brief time during the Civil War, the light operated from 1806 until 1963. It is the third-oldest lighthouse still standing on Chesapeake Bay. A keeper's dwelling once stood next to the lighthouse on a five-acre tract.

NN-3 JOHN CLAYTON, BOTANIST

Rte. 3, 0.5 miles north of Rte. 14. One and a half miles north is the site of his home "Windsor" where he developed an excellent botanical garden. He was first president, Virginia Society for the Promotion of Useful Knowledge, and clerk of Gloucester County from 1722 until his death in 1773. His herbarium specimens, some still preserved in the British Museum, were the basis of "Flora Virginica," compiled by Gronovius with the collaboration of Linnaeus and originally published at Leyden in 1739.

MIDDLESEX COUNTY

N-40 GLEBE LANDING CHURCH

Rte. 17, at Rte. 606, 12.1 miles northwest of Saluda. This church was constituted in 1772 by the noted Baptist preacher, John Waller. The first building stood on the old glebe overlooking the Rappahannock River; hence the name Glebe Landing. The present building was erected in 1839.

N-45 HEWICK

Rte. 17, 3.1 miles northwest of Saluda, Warner. Three miles east is Hewick, built about 1678 by Christopher Robinson, clerk of Middlesex County. It was the birthplace of John Robinson, Speaker of the House of Burgesses and Treasurer of Virginia, 1738–1766, the leading man of the colony.

N-48 CHRIST CHURCH

Rte. 33, 2.4 miles south of Urbanna. Half a mile east is Christ Church, Middlesex. The first building was erected about 1666; the present one in 1712. About 1840 the church was restored. The colonial governor, Sir Henry Chicheley, is buried there.

N-49 TOMB OF PULLER

Rte. 33, 3 miles east of Saluda. In Christ Churchyard immediately to north lies buried Lt. Gen. Lewis Burwell Puller USMC. He led Marines in 19 campaigns from Haiti and Nicaragua through the Korean War receiving 53 decorations and the admiration and affection of those he led. He was a Marine's Marine and is a tradition of Virginia and our nation's history.

N-50 LOWER METHODIST CHURCH

Rte. 33, 9.3 miles southeast of Saluda. Built 1717, this was the second lower chapel of Christ Church Parish, Middlesex County. It occupies the site of the first lower chapel of this parish, built before 1661 as the church of Piankatank Parish. Bartholomew Yates was the first minister of the present church. After 1792 the church was unused, except by the Methodists or Baptists. In 1857 Robert Healy bought the church from the parish and gave it to the Methodists, who have worshiped here ever since.

N-77 STINGRAY POINT

Rte. 33, 8.6 miles west of Deltaville. Eight miles east, where the Rappahannock River joins Chesapeake Bay. Near there, in June, 1608, Captain John Smith, the explorer, was hurt by a stingray while fishing in the river. The point took its name from this incident.

OC-35 ROSEGILL

Rte. 227, 0.7 miles south of Urbanna. A short distance east is Rosegill. The house was built about 1650 by the first Ralph Wormeley; it became the summer home of the colonial governors, Sir Henry Chicheley and Lord Howard of Effingham. In 1776, the owner, the fifth Ralph Wormeley, was put under restraint as a Tory. In 1781, Rosegill was plundered by British privateersmen.

OC-36 CHRISTOPHER ROBINSON

Rte. 602, just north of Rte. 615, 0.5 miles west of Urbanna. In 1678, Christopher Robinson purchased 300 acres here that became Hewick, the Virginia seat of the Robinson family. Robinson's distinguished service to Virginia began as the clerk of Middlesex County Court from 1677 to 1688. He was elected to the House of Burgesses in 1691, and, in 1692, was appointed Councillor and Secretary of the Foreign Plantations by King William III of England. Robinson's final contribution to colonial Virginia came in 1693, when he served as a founding trustee of William and Mary College.

OC-40 URBANNA CREEK

Rte. 227, Urbanna. First known as Nimcock Creek, this creek was mentioned in a legislative act of 1680 as "Wormeley's Creek." After the town of Urbanna was named in 1705 for Queen Anne, the stream was given the same name. British privateersmen entered the creek, June 5, 1781, and pillaged Urbanna and Rosegill, the plantation of Sir Ralph Wormeley.

OC-41 OLD MIDDLESEX COUNTY COURTHOUSE

Rte. 227 (Virginia Street), at old courthouse, Urbanna. This building served as the Middlesex County courthouse from 1748 to 1852. Although much altered from its original appearance, it is one of Virginia's rare colonial courthouse buildings. During the American Revolution, the local Committee of Safety met here. According to tradition during the Civil War, it briefly housed Confederate troops. After use as the county courthouse, the building was remodeled and became a house of worship for several denominations. In 1948 Christ Church Parish transferred ownership to the Middlesex County Woman's Club, which once operated a community library here. The structure was listed on the Virginia Landmarks Register and the National Register of Historic Places in 1976.

WO-37 SCOTTISH FACTORS STORE

Rte. 33, 1.5 miles east of Saluda. Two miles to the north, in the colonial port of entry of Urbanna, is a restored eighteenth century storehouse. Scottish merchants became active commercial factors in the colony subsequent to the Act of Union of England and Scotland. Urbanna was established as a town in 1706.

NEW KENT COUNTY

E-12 CAPT. JOHN SMITH CAPTURED

Rte. 60, Bottoms Bridge. In Dec. 1607, while exploring the headwaters of the nearby Chickahominy River, Capt. John Smith and his party were captured by a hunting party consisting of members of the Paspaheghs, Chickahominies, Youghtanunds, Pamunkeys, Mattaponis, and Chiskiacks. Smith was taken to Rasaweck, a hunting camp and became friendly with Chief Powhatan's brother Opechancanough. During this time, Smith first met Chief Powhatan, the leader of the Virginia Indians of this region, at Werowocomoco, on the York River. A formal alliance was made between them. Smith returned to Jamestown early in Jan. 1608.

W-14 MCCLELLAN'S CROSSING

Rte. 60, Bottoms Bridge. Here a part of McClellan's army crossed the Chickahominy on May 23, 1862, advancing on Richmond. It was attacked by the Confederates at Seven Pines.

W-16 LAFAYETTE AND CORNWALLIS

Rte. 60, Bottoms Bridge. Lafayette camped near here, on May 4, 1781. On May 28, 1781, Cornwallis camped here in pursuit of Lafayette and camped here again on June 21, 1781, while retiring eastward before Lafayette and Wayne.

W-17 NEW KENT ROAD

Rte. 60, Bottoms Bridge. This was the main road to Williamsburg in early days. Cornwallis, retiring eastward, used this road in June, 1781. The Confederates, retreating westward, passed over it in May, 1862.

W-18 LONG BRIDGE

Rte. 60, at Rte. 106, 4.9 miles southeast of Bottoms Bridge. One mile south is Long Bridge over the Chickahominy River. Benedict Arnold sent Simcoe there in the British invasion of 1781. Longstreet crossed there in the Peninsular Campaign, May, 1862. Grant's Fifth and Second Corps crossed there, in June, 1864, on the way to Petersburg.

W-19 FORGE BRIDGE

Rte. 60, just east of Chickahominy River bridge, Providence Forge. The site of Forge Bridge over the Chickahominy River is located about a mile south of here. On 14 June 1862, Maj. Gen. J. E. B. Stuart and his cavalry brigade crossed there on their famous ride around Maj. Gen. George B. McClellan's Army of the Potomac. Because the bridge had been burned in May, Stuart's men first built a makeshift bridge of barn timbers to replace it. On 13–14 June 1864, the VI and IX Corps of Lt. Gen. Ulysses S. Grant's Army of the Potomac crossed the river there en route to Petersburg after the Battle of Cold Harbor.

W-20 PROVIDENCE FORGE

Rte. 60, just east of Chickahominy River bridge, Providence Forge. Here about 1770, Charles Jeffery Smith, a Presbyterian minister, settled and, with William Holt, built a forge for making farm implements.

Francis Jerdone became a partner in 1771. A militia camp was established here in 1781, and Lafayette was here in July and August, 1781.

W-21 STATE GAME FARM

Rte. 60, 2.8 miles southeast of Providence Forge. The Department of Game and Inland Fisheries established the first Virginia State Game Farm nearby in 1920. The state initially raised quail in captivity there to restock the birds throughout Virginia. The game farm was one of the earliest state facilities to breed quail in large numbers. Virginia's program attracted the attention of other states' game departments. In subsequent years the farm also bred wild turkeys for restocking. The site included a building for hatching eggs. In 1946 the farm's activities were transferred to the Cumberland Game Farm at the Cumberland State Forest in Cumberland County.

W-22 CHICKAHOMINY INDIANS

Rte. 60, 4.2 miles southeast of Providence Forge. One mile south is the home of descendants of the Chickahominy Indians, a powerful tribe at the time of the settlement of Jamestown. Chickahominies were among the Indians who took Captain John Smith prisoner in December 1607. Currently two state-recognized Chickahominy tribes reside in the area.

W-23 FORT JAMES

Rte. 60, near Rte. 627, Lanexa, 7.6 miles southeast of Providence Forge. A mile and a half south of here on the Chickahominy River stood Moysonec, an Indian village. Some of the Chickahominy Indians residing there captured Captain John Smith in 1607. In the wake of the 1644 Indian uprising, the colonists sought to control Native American access to the lower Peninsula. Thomas Rolfe, son of Pocahontas and John Rolfe, constructed Fort James at Moysonec in exchange for the land on which it stood. The colonists manned the fort for only three years.

W-24 DIASCUND BRIDGE

Rte. 60 at the New Kent/James City County line. As part of British Maj. Gen. William Phillips Apr. 1781 campaign in Virginia by the 21st he sent Lt. Col. Robert Abercrombie's Light Infantry from Barrett's Ferry, where it enters the James River, to destroy the state's naval docks, ships, warehouses, and numerous military stores along the Chickahominy River. Luckily for the Americans, most of Virginia's ships had been anchored in temporary safety up the James River at Osborne's in Chesterfield County. Abercrombie's troops accomplished the remainder of their mission including destroying naval stores held at Diascund Bridge during the night of 22 Apr., before meeting up with Phillips.

W-25 COOPER'S MILL

Rte. 60, just west of New Kent/James City County line. Half a mile north on Diascund Creek stood Cooper's Mill. On 23–24 June 1781, the British army commanded by Gen. Charles Cornwallis seized supplies there while en route to its camp at Williamsburg and Maj. John G. Simcoe's Rangers burned the bridge there. The small army under the Marquis de Lafayette pursued, but at a safe distance. In July, Cornwallis withdrew to Yorktown to await reinforcement or evacuation. The allied armies under Gen. George Washington and the Comte de Rochambeau besieged him there until he surrendered on 19 Oct. 1781, effectively ending the Revolutionary War.

W-29 TYREE'S PLANTATION

Rte. 60, just west of New Kent/James City County line. After a detachment of the Marquis de Lafayette's army defeated Maj. John G. Simcoe's cavalry at Spencer's Ordinary near Williamsburg on 26 June 1781, Lafayette shadowed the British army encamped at the colonial capital. He made his headquarters just north of here at Tyree's plantation, 28 June–5 July 1781, while he waited for the British commander, Gen. Charles Cornwallis, to tip his hand. Early in July, Maj. Gen. Henry Clinton, commander of British forces, ordered Cornwallis to send 3,000 of his men to New York. On 4 July, Cornwallis began marching to Portsmouth to embark, and Lafayette pursued him the next day.

W-39 LETITIA CHRISTIAN TYLER

Rte. 60, at Rte. 106, 4.9 miles southeast of Bottoms Bridge. Letitia Christian Tyler, wife of President John Tyler, is buried at Cedar Grove Cemetery a mile northeast. Born on 12 November 1790, a daughter of Robert and Mary Browne Christian, she married John Tyler at her home, Cedar Grove, on 29 March 1813. Her husband served as a congressman (1817–1821), governor of Virginia (1825–1827), senator (1827–1836), vice president (1841), and tenth president of the United States (1841–1845). Letitia Christian Tyler was the first First Lady to die in the White House when she succumbed on 10 September 1842 after a series of paralyzing strokes. Her body lay in state in the East Room of the White House, then was transported to her family home at Cedar Grove for interment.

W-74 LIBERTY BAPTIST CHURCH

Rte. 60, 0.10 miles west of New Kent/James City County line. Liberty Church was organized in 1830 with 25 members led by Elder Thomas S. Morris. In 1845, the Southern Baptist Convention appointed Samuel Cornelius Clopton, son of the second pastor, Elder James Clopton, as its first missionary. The third pastor, Elder John "Parson" Turner, served without pay, 1837–1867. During Maj. Gen. George B. McClellan's Peninsula Campaign of 1862, retreating Confederate soldiers destroyed the nearby bridge over Diascund Creek to slow the Federal advance on Richmond. Union forces rebuilt the bridge with floorboards and joists from the original church. For a century, church members were baptized in the creek. The present sanctuary was built in 1930.

WO-12 THE WHITE HOUSE

Rte. 249, just west of Rte. 106, Talleysville. This place, six miles northeast, was the home of Martha Custis. According to tradition, George Washington first met her at Poplar Grove, near by, in 1758. On January 6, 1759, Washington and Martha Custis were married, it is believed at the White House. The house was burned by Union troops when McClellan made the White House his base of operations in May, 1862.

WO-13 ST. PETER'S CHURCH

Rte. 249, just west of Rte. 106, Talleysville. Two miles northeast is St. Peter's Church, built in 1703 in English bond. David Mossom, rector there for forty years, was the minister who married George Washington. According to one tradition, the wedding took place at St. Peter's Church.

WO-14 STUART'S RIDE AROUND McCLELLAN

Rte. 249, just west of Rte. 106, Talleysville. J. E. B. Stuart, on his famous ride around McClellan's army, June 12–15, 1862, arrived here in the early night of June 13, coming from Hanover Courthouse. He rested here several hours and then pressed on to the Chickahominy River, rejoining Lee's army on June 15.

WO-16 NEW KENT COURTHOUSE

Rte. 249, at old courthouse, New Kent Courthouse. Lord Cornwallis's army was here, moving eastward, June 22, 1781; Lafayette, in pursuit, June 25; Washington, Rochambeau and Chastellux, on their way to Yorktown, September 14, 1781. A part of Joseph E. Johnston's army, retiring to Richmond, passed through, May, 1862.

WO-17 JAMES LAFAYETTE

Rte. 249, at old courthouse, New Kent Courthouse. James Lafayette was born in slavery about 1748 near here. His master William Armistead was commissary of military supplies when in the summer of 1781 the

Marquis de Lafayette recruited James as a spy. Posing as a double agent, forager, and servant at British headquarters, James moved freely between the lines with vital information on British troop movements for Lafayette. The Virginia General Assembly freed James in 1787 in recognition of his bravery and service, on the written recommendation of Lafayette, whose name he took for his own. He died in Baltimore on 9 Aug. 1830.

WO-18 Martha Washington's Birthplace

Rte. 249, at old courthouse, New Kent Courthouse. About two miles northeast stood Chestnut Grove, the plantation home of John and Frances Jones Dandridge, where Martha Dandridge, the eldest of eight children, was born on 2 June 1731. She lived there until 15 May 1750, when she married Daniel Parke Custis and moved to his plantation, White House, on the Pamunkey River. According to tradition, the wedding took place at Chestnut Grove. Custis died in 1757, and two years later Martha Custis married George Washington. Chestnut Grove, a two-story frame house with six rooms, burned in 1926.

WO-30 Eltham

Rte. 33, 1.9 miles west of West Point. Eltham, a mile north, was long the home of the Bassett family and one of the largest and finest colonial houses in Virginia. Burwell Bassett, the owner at the time of the Revolution, was a patriot leader. Washington was a frequent visitor at Eltham and was there in November, 1781, at the deathbed of his stepson, John Parke Custis, a soldier of Yorktown. The old house was burned in 1875; the foundation remains.

WO-31 Peninsular Campaign

Rte. 33, 1.9 miles west of West Point. A mile north, at Eltham Landing on the Pamunkey River, Franklin's division of McClellan's army disembarked on May 6, 1862. The next morning the Union troops came in contact with the Confederates retiring toward Richmond. The Confederate wagon trains were in danger; but Gustavus W. Smith drove Franklin back to the river. The action occurred in this vicinity, May 7, 1862.

WO-33 The Brick House

Rte. 33, 1.9 miles west of West Point. A short distance south stood the Brick House. In 1677, at the end of Bacon's Rebellion, the rebel leaders, Drummond and Lawrence, were at Brick House when West Point surrendered to Berkeley. They fled, Drummond to be caught and executed, Lawrence never to be heard of again. In August, 1716, Governor Alexander Spotswood crossed the river there on his western expedition.

CITY OF NEWPORT NEWS

W-54 Lee Hall

163 Yorktown Road. Lee Hall, a stately Italianate plantation dwelling, was built by 1859 for affluent planter Richard Decatur Lee. Confederate generals John Bankhead Magruder and Joseph Eggleston Johnston used the mansion as their headquarters during the April–May 1862 Warwick-Yorktown siege phase of the Peninsula Campaign. An earthen fort in the yard used to launch a Confederate hot-air balloon on 17 Apr. 1862 remains from the military occupation. A brief skirmish was fought here on 4 May 1862 during the Confederate retreat to Williamsburg. After the war, Lee strove to revitalize his farm but went bankrupt in 1870 and was foreclosed the next year.

W-56 Fort Eustis

Dozier Road and Warwick Boulevard. Fort Eustis, located half a mile south, is named for a native Virginian, Gen. Abraham

Eustis (1786–1843), a commander of Fort Monroe. In March 1918, the U.S. government established Camp Abraham Eustis as a coast artillery training center; it was designated a fort in 1923. It then served as a Federal Emergency Relief Administration transient camp during the Great Depression, an antiaircraft artillery training center, a prisoner of war camp during World War II, and the headquarters for the U.S. Army Transportation Corps. It later housed the Transportation Corps Regiment. The colonial-era Matthew Jones House and the remains of Fort Crawford, a Civil War site, survive on the post grounds.

W-57 MULBERRY POINT

Dozier Road and Warwick Boulevard. Mulberry Point is situated on the James River, on the grounds of present-day Fort Eustis. In 1609–1610, the harsh winter known as the "Starving Time" prompted the surviving colonists at Jamestown to abandon it. They and the recently arrived Lieutenant Governor Sir Thomas Gates sailed away on 7 June 1610, bound for Newfoundland and the English fishing fleet. The next day, about ten miles downstream at Mulberry Point, they encountered relief ships under the governor, Lord De La Warr, bearing new colonists and supplies, and turned back. This timely arrival saved Jamestown, which might have become England's second "lost colony."

W-58 LEE'S MILL

180 Rivers Ridge Circle, at Civil War Trail pull-off. Lee's Mill, a pre-war tide mill, formed part of Confederate Maj. Gen. John Bankhead Magruder's second Peninsula defensive line. When Union Gen. George B. McClellan began his Peninsula Campaign, his advance against Richmond was blocked here on 5 April 1862. Elements of the Union IV Corps led by Brig. Gen. William F. Smith skirmished with Confederates commanded by Brig. Gen. Lafayette McLaws at Lee's Mill. The Federals believed that the extensive defenses could only be taken with heavy casualties, and Union Maj. Gen. George B. McCellan [McClellan] besieged Yorktown from 3 April to 3 May 1862 rather than assault the fortifications.

W-60 WARWICK COURTHOUSE

14415 Old Courthouse Way (Rte. 60). The clerk's office was built in 1810, when Warwick Courthouse was moved here.

W-61 DENBIGH PLANTATION

Rte. 60, at Menchville Road, 2.2 miles southeast of Denbigh. Two miles to the southwest was Denbigh, plantation of Samuel Matthews, who came to Virginia in 1622 and was governor in 1658. A public storehouse was built there in 1633 and Warwick Courthouse in 1691.

W-62 PENINSULA CAMPAIGN— WARWICK RIVER

Constitution Way, at Discovery Center, in Newport News Park. Following the 10 June 1861 Battle of Big Bethel, Maj. Gen. John B. Magruder, commander of the Confederate Army of the Peninsula, organized the construction of three defensive lines of fortifications across the peninsula. The main line extended 12 miles from Yorktown to the Warwick River and downstream to Lee's Mill, then westward to Skiffes Creek, which flowed into the James River at the Mulberry Island Point battery. When Maj. Gen. George B. McClellan began his Peninsula Campaign to capture Richmond, the Warwick River fortifications blocked the progress of [the] Army of the Potomac on 5 April 1862. McClellan ordered a siege that lasted from 5 April to 4 May 1862.

W-63 YOUNG'S MILL

13035 Warwick Boulevard, near Oyster Point Road. Following the 10 June 1861 Battle of Big Bethel, Confederate Gen. John B. Magruder established a base at Young's Mill. This tide mill formed the right flank of Magruder's First Defensive Line, which reached across the Peninsula to Ship's Point on the York River. Extensive earthworks defended the crossing of the Warwick Road over Deep Creek. When Union Maj. Gen. George B. McClellan began his Peninsula Campaign on 4 April 1862 to capture Richmond, elements of Brig. Gen. Erasmus D. Keyes IV Corps led by Brig. Gen. William F. "Baldy" Smith advanced to Young's Mill. They skirmished with Confederate troops defending this mill dam crossing. The Confederates abandoned their position for a more determined stand on the Warwick River.

W-65 DENBIGH PARISH

Mitchell Point Road, near Oyster Point Road. Denbigh Parish was established about 1635 and took its name from the nearby Denbigh plantation. During colonial times, the Anglican parish administered ecclesiastical and some civil affairs for the upper portion of Elizabeth City Corporation, later Warwick County and present-day Newport News. Nearby on the banks of the Warwick River stood the first Denbigh Parish Church constructed before 1635. By 1686, a new structure near here replaced the former building. The Denbigh Parish and other local parishes in Warwick County were combined by 1725 to form Warwick Parish. A frame structure for Warwick Parish was built here about 1774 and the Baptists began using the site by 1834.

W-68 CAMP HILL AND CAMP ALEXANDER

Rte. 60 (Warwick Boulevard) and 69th Street. Camps Hill and Alexander were created when Newport News was designated a port of embarkation by the U.S. Army after the United States entered World War I in 1917. Camp Hill was established in Aug. 1917 and named for Confederate Lt. Gen. A. P. Hill. Besides processing men for overseas duty, it served as the port's animal embarkation area. Camp Alexander was established in 1918 and served as an embarkation and postwar debarkation camp for African

American troops. It was named for Lt. John Hank Alexander, one of the first African American graduates of West Point. After World War I, the camps were abandoned.

W-70 NEWPORT NEWS

Newport News city park visitor center, Constitution Way. The area was first referred to as "Newportes Newes" as early as 1619, and the first known English settler lived here in 1621. Several Civil War engagements took place here including the Battle of the Ironclads and the 1862 Peninsula Campaign. Newport News remained a small community until the late 19th century when it became the eastern terminus of the Chesapeake and Ohio Railway Co. The Newport News Shipbuilding and Dry Dock Co. was founded here in 1886. Newport News was established as a town in 1880 and became a city in 1896. It served as the headquarters of the Hampton Roads Port of Embarkation in World Wars I and II.

W-71 LEE'S MILL EARTHWORKS

Warwick Boulevard, at Lee's Mill Drive. These earthworks were part of General John B. Magruder's second line of defense. At this site on April 5, 1862, Confederate General Lafayette McLaw's four companies of the Tenth Georgia with Captain Joseph B. Cosnahan's two batteries stopped the advance of Union General William F. "Baldy" Smith's two divisions of the Fourth Army Corps and Captain Charles C. Wheeler's six batteries. Several skirmishes and engagements occurred here between April 5 and May 4, 1862 at which time the Confederate forces abandoned the earthworks and withdrew to Williamsburg.

W-73 PROVIDENCE MENNONITE CHURCH

13101 Warwick Boulevard (Rte. 60), at church. In 1897, a group of largely Midwestern Amish and Mennonite families, attracted by inexpensive farmland and rich timberland located near the growing urban center of Newport News, moved here to found the Mennonite Colony, an agrarian religious community. In 1900, David Z. Yoder, a minister and a founder of the colony, assisted several Amish families in establishing the Providence Amish Mennonite denomination here at Oyster Point. Christian K. Miller was the chief carpenter for the simple wood-frame church, which was built of locally harvested pine on land acquired from the Jones family. The church was moved and renovated in 1975 when Warwick Boulevard was widened.

W-76 NEWPORT NEWS

25th Street, at city hall. The area was first referred to as "Newportes Newes" as early as 1619, and the first known English settler lived here in 1621. Several Civil War engagements took place here including the Battle of the Ironclads and the 1862 Peninsula Campaign. Newport News remained a small community until the late 19th century when it became the eastern terminus of the Chesapeake and Ohio Railway Co. The Newport News Shipbuilding and Dry Dock Co. was founded here in 1886. Newport News was established as a town in 1880 and became a city in 1896. It served as the headquarters of the Hampton Roads Port of Embarkation in World Wars I and II.

W-77 JAMES A. FIELDS HOUSE

27th Street, at house. James A. Fields acquired this late-Victorian Italianate-style brick house in 1893. Fields, born into slavery in Hanover County, escaped in 1862 and became a contraband of war. He graduated in 1871 from what is now Hampton University and taught school. After receiving a law degree from Howard University in 1882, Fields served as the commonwealth's attorney for Warwick County in 1887 and represented the region in the House of Delegates (1889–1890). After Field's death in 1903, four doctors acquired the house in 1908 and it functioned as Newport News' first black hospital. Eventually the hospital became known as Whittaker Memorial Hospital at another site.

W-78 JESSIE MENIFIELD RATTLEY

2901 Jefferson Avenue. Educator, politician, and Civil Rights pioneer, Jessie Menifield Rattley (1929–2001) was born in Birmingham, Alabama. She graduated from Hampton University in 1951. Rattley founded the Peninsula Business College here in 1952. She was the first black woman elected to the Newport News City Council and served from 1970 until 1990. In 1986 she became the city's first black and female mayor. Rattley was the first black president of the Virginia Municipal League (1978–1979) and in 1979 was elected the first black woman president of the National League of Cities. Rattley also served on a number of commissions, delegations, and taskforces for the U.S. government and other organizations.

CITY OF NORFOLK

K-273 NEW TOWN

Princess Anne and Newtown Roads. New Town once stood to the south along the Eastern Branch of the Elizabeth River. The community was laid out in 1697 and General Assembly established it as a town in 1740. New Town served as county seat of Princess Anne County from about 1752 to 1778 and was an important port of entry until shortly after the Revolutionary War. During the siege and burning of Norfolk by colonial governor Lord Dunmore's troops begun on 1 Jan. 1776, many Norfolk residents fled to New Town for temporary shelter. By the early 19th century, like a number of often early colonial towns, New Town ceased to exist.

KN-1 HOSPITAL OF SAINT VINCENT DEPAUL

Kingsley Lane and Granby Street. Founded in 1855, the Hospital of Saint Vincent DePaul was Norfolk's first civilian hospital. Located two blocks south at the corner of Church and Wood streets, the hospital was opened in the home of Ann Plume Behan Herron by eight Daughters of Charity during a yellow fever epidemic. It was incorporated March 3, 1856, and later named DePaul Hospital when moved to its present site at Kingsley Lane and Granby Street.

KN-2 NORFOLK BOTANICAL GARDENS

Rte. 192, at entrance to gardens. These gardens were conceived by City Manager Thomas Thompson during the Great Depression. His idea was executed by city gardener Frederic Heutte; noted landscape architect Charles F. Gillette served as a consultant. In 1938 about 200 black women were paid with Works Progress Administration funds to clear and plant the first 25 acres. The first phase of the gardens, which now occupy 175 acres and include landscaped vistas, arboretums, and special display areas, were their creation.

KN-3 BANK STREET BAPTIST CHURCH

St. Paul's Boulevard and Charlotte Street. The Bank Street Baptist Church was built on this site in 1802 as a Presbyterian church. In 1840 it was purchased by a group of free blacks to serve them as a Baptist church. Because it had one of the first church bells in Norfolk, the building was known as the Bell Church. The church continued to serve the black community until its demolition in 1967 when the congregation moved to its new location on Chesapeake Boulevard.

KN-4 NORFOLK LIGHT ARTILLERY BLUES

Hampton Boulevard and 46th Street, at Old Dominion University. Here from 1914 to 1961 stood the third armory of the Norfolk Light Artillery Blues (Battery B, 111th Field Artillery, Virginia National Guard) formed in 1829, as well as the Headquarters Battery, Regimental Band, and the 104th Medical Corps Detachment. From here, the Blues were ordered abroad during three wars: the

1916 Mexican Punitive Expedition against Pancho Villa, the American Expedition to France in 1918 during World War I, and World War II. The Blues landed in the fifth wave on Omaha Beach in Normandy on D-Day, 6 June 1944, and fought in Europe for the remainder of the war. In 1961 the unit moved to a new armory near Broad Creek.

KV-1 FIRST FLIGHT SHIP TO SHORE

Fourth Street and I-64, at visitor's center. On 14 November, 1910, Eugene Ely in a Curtiss built "Hudson Flyer," utilizing a specially constructed platform with an uptilt at the end, took off from the cruiser Birmingham anchored off Fort Monroe and landed at Willoughby Spit, 2½ miles distant, thus completing the first flight from ship to shore and the first flight to utilize the "Ski Jump" deck. This was the birth of Naval aviation.

KV-2 NAVAL AVIATION DEPOT/ NORFOLK

Aircraft Tow Way, near Building V52, Naval Station Norfolk. The depot began in 1917 as part of the Naval Air Detachment of six canvas hangars servicing seven seaplanes. Before the depot closed in 1996, its name changed over time from Construction and Repair (1918), Assembly and Repair (1922), Overhaul and Repair (1948), and Naval Air Rework Facility (1967), to Naval Aviation Depot (1987). Reaching peak employment during WWII of more than 8,000, the facility later became Norfolk's largest employer. Through the decades, as naval aircraft advanced from seaplanes, to fighter jets, to air-to-air missiles, the master mechanics continued to play a leading role in advancing maintenance technology for the Navy, Air Force, and NATO forces.

KV-3 BIRTHPLACE OF NAVAL AVIATION

Vista Point, Massey Hughes Drive, Naval Station Norfolk. On 14 Nov. 1910, off Old Point Comfort across the harbor from here, the U.S. Navy demonstrated that airplanes could be launched from ships. Flying a

Curtiss biplane, Eugene Ely took off from a wooden ramp constructed atop the deck of the cruiser USS Birmingham. Aided by the five-degree slope of the ramp, a close-to-40-foot drop to the water, and an airplane engine that was powerful for the time, Ely gained enough speed to get the craft airborne and keep it aloft for the two-and-a-half-mile flight to Willoughby Spit. Ely's historic flight led to the founding of naval aviation in 1911.

KV-5 LANDING OF WOOL AND SURRENDER OF NORFOLK

Granby Street, at Sarah Constant Beach. Near here Major-General John E. Wool, on May 10, 1862, landed with 6000 Union troops. President Lincoln, Salmon P. Chase, Secretary of the Treasury, and Edwin M. Stanton, Secretary of War, watched the movement from a ship in Hampton Roads. As the Confederate troops had withdrawn, Wool marched to Norfolk, which was surrendered to him by Mayor W. W. Lamb that afternoon.

KV-6 *SUSAN CONSTANT* SHRINE

West Ocean View Avenue, near Fourth View Street. This shrine commemorates the *Susan Constant,* the flagship of the fleet that carried the first English settlers to Virginia in 1607. The *Susan Constant,* a 120-ton vessel, was built in 1605 and made one voyage to Spain before the Virginia Company of London chartered it. Captained by Christopher Newport, the *Susan Constant, Godspeed,* and *Discovery* sailed from London on 20 Dec. 1606 and arrived nearby off the Virginia capes on 26 Apr. 1607. The

colonists erected a cross claiming the land for England, explored the James River for a suitable settlement site, and planted the first permanent English colony at Jamestown on 14 May 1607.

KV-7 OPERATION TORCH, 1942

Ocean View Avenue (Rte. 60), just east of Tidewater Drive. The first major amphibious action of World War II was planned near here in the Nansemond Hotel, Hdq. of Amphibious Force U.S. Atlantic Fleet. An Army-Navy staff under Adm. H. K. Hewitt met with General G. S. Patton to plan the movement of Task Force "A" from Hampton Roads to North Africa.

KV-16 NAVY MESS ATTENDANT SCHOOL

Piersey Street and Maryland Avenue, Naval Station Norfolk. From 1933 to 1942, Navy recruits of African descent attended this school, located in barracks at Unit "K-West" and later at "B-East." Advancement opportunities for these sailors and counterparts of Asian-Pacific Island heritage were then limited to serving as officer's cooks or stewards. The school moved to Unit "X" in 1942 before training was relocated to Bainbridge, Maryland, and elsewhere. Though racial segregation continued, all job ratings were re-opened to qualified personnel in 1942. Mess attendants were re-designated "steward's mates" in 1943, and more than 1,100 members of the messman/steward branch were killed during World War II. Norfolk trainees decorated for heroism include Navy Cross recipients Doris Miller, William Pinckney, and Leonard Harmon.

NORTHAMPTON COUNTY

WY-2 SITE OF TIDEWATER INSTITUTE

Rte. 636, 0.75 miles east of Rte. 13. Tidewater Institute was incorporated in 1903 with the stated purpose of establishing an industrial, academic, collegiate, and seminary boarding school for the education of black

youth. Founded by the Rev. George E. Reid, and supported by the Northampton/Accomack Baptist Association, the institute attracted students from both Virginia and other Atlantic seaboard states. For twenty-eight years, the school was dedicated to the education and molding of lives of young black men and women of Virginia's Eastern Shore.

WY-3 SALEM METHODIST CHURCH

Rte. 13, at Rte. 636. 1.8 miles east of here stood Salem Methodist Church (1836–1918), scene of the initial violence resulting from the schism between northern and southern Methodists in 1846. A northern circuit preacher was dragged from the pulpit by members of the congregation. The building burned in 1870 and was replaced. Salem was the mother church of congregations at Cheriton and Oyster and five Eastern Shore Methodist ministers.

WY-4 CAPE CHARLES

Rte. 13, near Rte. 184. Two miles west of here, the town of Cape Charles was founded in 1884 as the Eastern Shore terminus of the New York, Philadelphia, and Norfolk Railroad, connecting the northeast with Norfolk by car float. Enjoying rapid growth, the planned community established itself as the commercial and residential center of Northampton County. No longer a railroad center, the business district and many of the railroad-era residences are listed on the Virginia Landmarks Register and the National Register of Historic Places.

WY-5 ARLINGTON

Rte. 13, south of Cape Charles. Two miles west stood Arlington, original home of the Custis Family, built by John Custis. The family tombs are still preserved there. Governor Wm. Berkeley made his headquarters there during Bacon's Rebellion in 1676. Arlington on the Potomac was named for this Arlington.

WY-6 STRATTON MANOR

Rte. 13, 3 miles north of Cape Charles. Benjamin Stratton, a member of the family that had owned the land since 1636, constructed this finely crafted house

nearby about 1764, according to dated chimney bricks. Perhaps built on the site of an earlier Stratton dwelling, the house exemplifies the 18th-century vernacular architecture typical of Virginia's Eastern Shore. Among the features of the regional form are frame construction, Flemish-bond brick ends, chevron patterns in the gables, exterior chimneys with steeply sloping weatherings, and paneled chimney walls inside. Stratton was a chairmaker as well as a farmer, giving the house significance as an artisan's dwelling of the Revolutionary era.

WY-7 TOWNE FIELDS

Rte. 13, at Business Rte. 13, Cheriton. This site, two and a half miles west, was the first seat of local government on the Eastern Shore. Francis Bolton preached there in 1623, and the first church was built before 1632. The oldest continuous county records in the English Colonies began there in 1632. The first courthouse (built for that purpose) on the Eastern Shore was erected in 1664 and used until Court moved to the Eastville area in 1677.

WY-8 HOME OF THE FIRST SETTLER

Rte. 13, south of Eastville. Thomas Savage, a lad of thirteen, arrived at Jamestown on 2 Jan. 1608 with Capt. Christopher Newport on the ship John and Francis. John Smith later wrote, "The next day Newport came a shore. . . . A boy named Thomas Savage (whom Newport called son) was then given unto Powhatan." Savage resided several years with the Indians, growing up in association with Pocahontas. He became proficient in the Indian languages and later served as an interpreter. Savage settled on the Eastern Shore by 1619. There Debedeavon, the "Laughing King," gave him a large tract of land, perhaps 9,000 acres for increasing trade with the Indians.

WY-9 GINGASKIN INDIAN RESERVATION

Rte. 13, 1 mile south of Eastville. The Gingaskin Indian Reservation was located nearby from 1640 to 1813 and was created from a land patent in 1640 that set aside land for the Accomac Indians. When the Accomacs moved there, they became known as the Gingaskins. They continued to practice their traditional economy of farming, hunting, and fishing. By the 1760s, portions of the reservation had been leased to outside groups to help support the Gingaskins, who were suffering from a decreased population and pressures from their white neighbors. The legal termination of the tribe began in 1813, essentially against the Gingaskins' will, when their land was divided into plots and deeded to surviving members.

WY-10 OLD COURTHOUSE

Rte. 13, Eastville. The courthouse was moved to Eastville in 1677, and court has been held here ever since. The old courthouse was built about 1731; from its door the Declaration of Independence was read, August 13, 1776. Militia Barracks were here during the Revolution. Just behind the courthouse is the debtors' prison.

WY-11 THREE NORTHAMPTON LANDMARKS

Rte. 13, 2.8 miles south of Nassawadox. Three miles west stands the third church of Hungars Parish, begun in 1742 and completed by 1751, one of two colonial churches remaining on Virginia's Eastern Shore. The parish built the glebe house or minister's residence, 5.5 miles west, about 1745. Ordered by the state to sell it after disestablishment of the English Church in 1786, the vestry protested and retained custody until 1859. Vaucluse, named for a region of southern France and long the seat of the Upshur family, stands 4.5 miles south of the glebe. Abel Parker Upshur, born there in 1799, served President John Tyler as secretary of state from 1843 until 1844 when a cannon explosion aboard USS Princeton killed him and other officials.

NORTHUMBERLAND COUNTY

J-88 DITCHLEY AND COBBS

Rte. 200, 1.4 miles north of Kilmarnock. Ditchley, five miles northeast, was patented in 1651 by Colonel Richard Lee. The first house dated from 1687, the present house was built by Kendall Lee in 1752. Cobbs Hall, near by, was acquired by Richard Lee, probably before 1651. A house was built there by Charles Lee in 1720; the present house is modern.

JT-9 BRITISH RAIDS ON THE COAN RIVER

Rte. 360 (Northumberland Highway), east of Rte. 612 (Forest Landing Road). During the War of 1812, on 7 Aug. 1814 ten British ships and smaller vessels appeared on the Coan River, which flows into the Potomac. The invaders sent three barges to capture three American schooners situated within two miles of Northumberland Court House. The Lancaster County militia repulsed the attack until British reinforcements arrived. Before leaving, the British seized the schooners and destroyed property at Northumberland Court House. On 4 Oct. 1814, two British detachments of 3,000 infantry invaded Northumberland County from the Coan River. After initially resisting, the outnumbered militia retreated. The British captured ammunition, arms, and personal property before debarking.

JT-12 NORTHUMBERLAND HOUSE AND MANTUA

Rte. 360, 1 mile east of Heathsville. Five miles northeast is the site of Northumberland House, built by the third Peter Presley, who was murdered in 1750. He was the last male descendant of the first William Presley, who settled there and who was a burgess as early as 1647. Mantua, near by, was built by James Smith, who died in 1832. It is a good house of the old Virginia type.

JX-5 MORATTICO BAPTIST CHURCH

Rte. 200, 1.6 miles south of Rte. 679. On the hill is Morattico church, organized in 1778, the mother Baptist Church of the Northern Neck. The present building was erected in 1856. Lewis Lunsford, first pastor, is buried here.

O-48 HOLLEY GRADED SCHOOL

Rte. 360, approximately 0.35 miles east of Rte. 626. In 1868, Caroline Putnam (1826–1917) established a school for the children of former slaves here. In 1869, her lifelong friend, Sallie Holley (1818–1893) of N.Y., abolitionist and suffragette, purchased this two-acre site. Holley was an agent of the American Anti-Slavery Society from 1851 to 1870. In 1917 this site was deeded to a board of eleven local black trustees. The third school built here was begun in 1914 and completed in 1933 with funds raised solely within the black community. The four-room structure was the largest black elementary school in Northumberland County. Since 1917 Holley Graded School has remained under the trustees' control.

O-49 ST. STEPHEN'S PARISH

Rte. 360, Heathsville. Formed in 1653 as Chickacone Parish and renamed Fairfield in 1664. The upper part was known locally as Bowtracy Parish. When St. Stephen's Parish was formed in 1698, Fairfield became its lower part and Bowtracy its upper part.

O-51 REEDVILLE

Rte. 360, at Rte. 726. Elijah W. Reed, a New England ship captain, established the town in 1874 after building a factory here to process menhaden, a small bony fish rich in oil. Reedville soon became the center of the industry and home port to the Atlantic menhaden fleet. By the early 20th century the town, which resembled a New England fishing village, reputedly had one of the highest per capita incomes in the country. Its historic district contains early fishermen's houses and Victorian mansions. The oldest dwelling is the Walker House (1875).

O-53 CHERRY POINT AND COWART'S WHARF

Rte. 360, at Rte. 624. Settled by Englishmen about 1640, Cherry Point was later a childhood home of Mary Ball, the mother of George Washington. In August 1814 American militia repulsed a British force there. From the early 1800s to the 1940s, steamboats plied the waters of Chesapeake Bay and its tributaries, and linked Baltimore with such Northern Neck ports of call as Cowart's Wharf. There, by the late 19th century, Slater ("Bump") Cowart had established a general store, seafood factory, and other businesses. From about 1920 to 1946, Samuel and Giles Headley built skipjacks, the preferred vessel of bay fishermen, at their nearby boatyard on Cherry Point.

O-54 CHAMBERS STAMP FACTORY

Rte. 360, 0.4 miles west of Rte. 202, Callao. Two miles northeast, at Lodge, stood the Chambers Stamp Factory, owned by the same family for four generations. Founded in Washington, D.C., about 1830 by Benjamin Chambers, Sr., an engraver and inventor of a breech-loading cannon, the company specialized in postmark and cancellation stamps. From 1867 to 1931 the company was the sole supplier for the U.S. Post Office Department. Benjamin Chambers, Jr., moved the factory to Lodge in 1877. After his death in 1908, his son Henry B. Chambers, Sr., assumed direction of the company until he died in 1927. Henry B. Chambers, Jr., succeeded him. In July 1931 the postal department awarded the contract to Pitney Bowes and the Chambers Stamp Company closed the next year.

O-56 COAN BAPTIST CHURCH

Rte. 360, at Rte. 612. One mile west stands Coan Baptist Church. The congregation, first known as Wicomico Baptist Church, was organized on 17 November 1804. The members worshiped in each other's houses until a frame building, Coan Meeting House, was moved to this site in 1811. In the 1830s, under its pastor, Jeremiah Bell

Jeter, the congregation grew, necessitating a larger building. On 3 October 1847, pastor Addison Hall dedicated the present church, built of locally fired bricks. The stone steps were transported from Baltimore on a sailing vessel to Barnes's Wharf (Nokomis) and from there on ox-drawn carts to the church. The church exhibits two architectural styles, Federal outside and Greek Revival inside.

O-60 RICE'S HOTEL/HUGHLETT'S TERN

Rte. 360, just east of Rte. 1003. Originally known as Hughlett's Tavern, this building, located behind the courthouse, served visitors to court for more than 150 years. John Hughlett erected the original portion of the tavern before 1795. Griffin H. Foushee, who purchased it in 1824, significantly enlarged it. John Rice bought it in 1866 and the Rice family enlarged the building and operated it as a hotel until the 1920s when they converted it to apartments. Donated to the Northumberland County Historical Society by the Rice family in 1990, Rice's Hotel/Hughlett's Tavern is one of the few surviving structures of its type in Virginia.

O-61 JULIUS ROSENWALD HIGH SCHOOL

Rte. 360, just west of Rte. 726. Originally known as Northumberland County Training School, this institution opened in 1917, under principal John M. Ellison. Local African Americans raised more than $7,000 to build the school and received additional funding from the Rosenwald Fund. Julius Rosenwald, chairman of the board of directors of Sears Roebuck and Co., created this fund in 1917 to finance the building of rural southern schools for blacks. Some 5,000 Rosenwald schools were built in 15 states, including 308 in Virginia. On 12 Nov. 1932, under its principal the Reverend Dr. Henry M. Ruffin, the school was renamed the Julius Rosenwald High School. It closed in 1958.

O-65 JOHN HEATH

Rte. 360, just west of Rte. 601. John Heath was born on 8 May 1758 in Northumberland County. He attended William & Mary College and on 5 Dec. 1776, he and four of his classmates founded Phi Beta Kappa, a prestigious undergraduate honors organization. He became its first president. Heath served in the Revolutionary War and practiced law here and in Richmond. He was Northumberland County's commonwealth's attorney (1781–1784, 1787–1793) and a member of the U.S. House of Representatives (1793–1797). Heath also served on the Council of State, that advised the governor, from 1803 to his death on 13 Oct. 1810 in Richmond.

O-66 NORTHUMBERLAND ACADEMY

Rte. 360, just west of Rte. 636. The Virginia General Assembly incorporated the Northumberland Academy in 1818. The school provided a classical education for male students to prepare them for college or positions of leadership in the community. Because universal state funded public education did not commence in Virginia until 1870, this was an important regional educational facility. Between 30 to 70 students studied at the academy and a three story educational building stood on a 125-acre tract near here. The trustees sold the school in 1853 and R. S. Lawrence, then Robert Hall, and finally William P. Hudgins operated it privately, until it burned late in 1864 or early in 1865.

CITY OF PORTSMOUTH

Q-8-a TRINITY CHURCH

Court Street, near High Street. Built in 1762 as the parish church of Portsmouth parish, established in 1761. Later named Trinity; enlarged in 1829; remodeled in 1893. Colonel William Crawford, founder of Portsmouth in 1752, was a member of the first vestry. Buried here is Commodore James Barron, commander of the U.S. frigate Chesapeake when attacked by H.M.S. Leopard in 1807; the result was his celebrated duel with Stephen Decatur in 1820. The graves of many Revolutionary patriots are here.

Q-8-b MONUMENTAL METHODIST CHURCH

Dinwiddie Street, near High Street. This church, founded 1772, is one of the oldest Methodist churches in Virginia. The first building was erected, 1775, at South and Effingham streets. The church was moved to Glasgow Street near Court in 1792. It established the first Sunday School in Portsmouth in 1818. Monumental was moved to this site, Dinwiddie Street, in 1831.

Q-8-c WATTS HOUSE

517 North Street. Built by Colonel Dempsey Watts in 1799 and inherited by his son, Captain Samuel Watts, who lived here until his death in 1878. Here Chief Black Hawk, of the Black Hawk Indian War, was entertained in 1820, and Henry Clay in 1844.

Q-8-d BALL HOUSE

213 Middle Street. Built about 1784 by John Nivison at the corner of Crawford and Glasgow streets and moved to this site in 1869. It served as a barracks in the War of 1812. Lafayette was entertained here in 1824 and President Andrew Jackson in 1833. The Ball family acquired the property in 1870.

Q-8-e BENEDICT ARNOLD AT PORTSMOUTH

Bayview and Maryland Avenues. Arnold, after going over to the British, was sent to Virginia to make war on the state. He reached Hampton Roads in December, 1780, raided to Richmond and came to Portsmouth, January 19, 1781. Establishing his headquarters in Patrick Robinson's house, and using the old sugar house on

Crawford Street as a prison and barracks, Arnold remained here until spring. Then again he went up the James to open the fateful campaign of 1781 that won the war for America.

Q-8-f CORNWALLIS AT PORTSMOUTH

Crawford Parkway, east of Court Street. Lord Cornwallis, commanding the British troops in the South, reached Portsmouth, July, 1781. He prepared to send a portion of his force to New York. Before the movement was made, orders came for him to take up a position at Old Point. Cornwallis selected Yorktown, however, and Portsmouth was abandoned.

Q-8-g COLLIER'S RAID

Washington Street and Crawford Parkway. A British fleet under Commodore Sir George Collier sailed up the Elizabeth River and shelled Fort Nelson in May 1779, during the Revolutionary War. A landing force of 1,800 infantrymen led by Brig. Gen. Edward Mathew captured the fort on 10 May after a brief resistance. The British occupied Portsmouth, Gosport, and Norfolk, and burned Suffolk and the Gosport shipyard. Collier also captured or burned 137 vessels in Hampton Roads and dismantled Fort Nelson. The British force then embarked and sailed to New York.

Q-8-h PORTSMOUTH NAVAL HOSPITAL

Affington and Crawford Streets. This was begun in 1827 and opened in 1830. The hospital was taxed to its capacity in the great yellow fever epidemic of 1855 which decimated Portsmouth and Norfolk. This hospital has cared for the sick and wounded of the Navy in all wars of the United States since its establishment. It is the oldest hospital of the Navy.

Q-8-k ELIZABETH RIVER

Crawford Parkway, at Court Street. The Elizabeth River, explored by Captain John Smith in 1608, was named for Princess Elizabeth. Shipbuilding activity began in 1620 when

John Wood, a shipbuilder, requested a land grant. Many historic ships were built at the naval shipyard here, including the USS Delaware, first ship dry-docked in America, and CCS Virginia, (Ex-Merrimac), first ironclad to engage in battle.

Q-8-l CITY OF PORTSMOUTH

Academy Avenue and Western Branch Boulevard. The site of this city was patented in 1659 by Captain William Carver. Established as a town in 1752 and named by its founder, Lt. Col. William Crawford. Chartered as a city in 1858, it has the country's oldest naval shipyard, established in 1767, the nation's oldest naval hospital, commenced in 1827, and is the birthplace of the world's largest naval installation.

Q-8-m CRAWFORD HOUSE

Crawford and Queen Streets. Erected 1835 by J. W. Collins, Portsmouth's first five-story building and for many years a leading hotel. Presidents Van Buren, Tyler, and Fillmore were entertained here.

Q-8-n NORFOLK COUNTY COURT HOUSE, 1845–1962

High and Court Streets. Begun 1845, occupied 20 July 1846. The architect, William R. Singleton, a Portsmouth native, also designed the old Norfolk City Court House. This building stands on one of the four corners dedicated for public use in 1752 by Lt. Col. William Crawford, founder of Portsmouth. The site was formerly occupied by the clerk's office when an earlier court house, occupied in 1803, stood on the northeast corner, opposite.

Q-8-o ARNOLD'S BRITISH DEFENSE, 1781

Washington and King Streets. This marks a line of British redoubts erected in March 1781 by order of Brigadier General Benedict Arnold who, under Major William Phillips, commanded British troops occupying Portsmouth. The line of fortifications extended in an arc along Washington Street

from the northern waterfront to Gosport Creek and defended Portsmouth from American attack from the west.

Q-8-p ARNOLD'S BRITISH DEFENSES, 1781

Crawford Parkway, at Court Street. This marks the Northern limit of a line of British redoubts erected in March 1781 by order of Brigadier General Benedict Arnold who, under Major General William Phillips, commanded British troops occupying Portsmouth. This line of fortifications extended in an arc south along Dinwiddie and Washington Streets to Gosport Creek and defended Portsmouth from American attack from the West.

Q-8-q ARNOLD'S BRITISH DEFENSES, 1781

Crawford Street, near Harbor Court Road. This position is near the southern limit of the line of British redoubts erected during the Revolutionary War in March 1781 by order of Brig. Gen. Benedict Arnold, who commanded the British troops that occupied Portsmouth. This line of fortifications, then located west of the town, extended north in an arc along present-day Washington Street to the waterfront near Court Street. Arnold, who had burned Richmond in Jan. 1781, had retreated to Portsmouth to evade capture by the French fleet and the Marquis de Lafayette's army. After Maj. Gen. William Phillips arrived in March with a replacement garrison, Arnold led his force against Petersburg.

Q-8-r NORFOLK NAVAL SHIPYARD

Lincoln Street, at Quarters A. Norfolk Naval Shipyard, the nation's first government-owned yard, was privately founded here as Gosport Shipyard on 1 Nov. 1767. Virginia seized it in 1776, and it served the state navy during the American Revolution. The U.S. Navy leased it in 1794 and bought it in 1801. Drydock One, started in 1827, opened on 17 June 1833. Construction began in 1837 on the central brick portion of Quarters A, the residence of shipyard commanders. Frame wings were added in 1890 and 1910. Quarters B and C (north) date from 1837 to 1842. All four structures are listed in the National Register of Historic Places.

Q-8-s JOHN LUKE PORTER—(19 SEPT. 1813–14 DEC. 1893)

Water and High Streets. John Luke Porter, first president of the Portsmouth common council, was born just two blocks south of here. An accomplished naval constructor, commissioned first by the United States and later by the Confederacy, Porter supervised, at the Norfolk Navy Yard, the conversion of the frigate Merrimac to the ironclad CSS Virginia. On 8 March 1862, the Virginia rammed and sank USS Cumberland and destroyed USS Congress at Newport News. The next day Virginia fought a historic but inconclusive battle with USS Monitor in nearby Hampton Roads, in the world's first naval combat between ironclads. Porter later became chief naval constructor for the Confederacy, designing 21 ironclads. He died in Portsmouth.

Q-8-t EMANUEL A.M.E. CHURCH

Green and North Streets. Emanuel A.M.E. Church is rooted in the African Methodist Society that was formed soon after the founding in 1772 of the Methodist Society in Portsmouth. The African Society met independently until Nat Turner's Insurrection in 1831, worshiped with white Methodists for three years, then met under white supervision until 1864. The members occupied a Methodist church on Glasgow Street until the building burned in 1856. Slaves and free blacks provided most of the funds and labor to construct North Street Methodist Church in 1857. In 1871, the congregation adopted the name Emanuel ("God with us") and became part of the African Methodist Episcopal movement.

Q-8-v ST. PAUL'S ROMAN CATHOLIC CHURCH

High and Washington Streets, at church. St. Paul's Roman Catholic Church was first built by French and Irish immigrants between 1811 and 1815 and was the first Catholic congregation established in Portsmouth. Increasing membership necessitated the building of new structures in 1831 and 1851. Fire destroyed the third building in 1859; that same year the congregation began constructing a fourth structure, completed in 1868. It burned in 1897. The current Gothic Revival church here, noted for its stained glass windows, was designed by John Kevan Peebles and dedicated in 1905. It was listed on the Virginia Landmarks Register and the National Register of Historic Places in 2002.

RICHMOND COUNTY

J-73 MENOKIN

Rte. 690, Menokin. Near here is Menokin, home of Francis Lightfoot Lee, signer of the Declaration of Independence. Lee was a member of the Continental Congress from 1775 to 1779 and died at Menokin in 1797.

J-77 NORTH FARNHAM CHURCH

Rte. 692, Farnham. This is the church of North Farnham Parish, built about 1737. In 1814, a skirmish was fought here between raiders from Admiral Cockburn's British fleet and Virginia militia; bullet holes are still visible in the walls. The church was used as a stable by Union soldiers, 1863–65. It was restored in 1872, damaged by fire in 1887 and restored again in 1924.

J-78 CYRUS GRIFFIN'S BIRTHPLACE

Rte. 3, slightly more than 1 mile east of Rte. 687. Four and a half miles southwest was born Cyrus Griffin, July 16, 1748. Educated in England, he served in the Virginia House of Delegates, 1777–8, 1786–7. He was a member of the Continental Congress, 1787–1788, in which last year he was president of the body. Griffin was president of the court of admiralty, commissioner to the Creeks, 1789, and a United States district judge. He died at Yorktown, December 14, 1810.

J-99 NORTHERN NECK INDUSTRIAL ACADEMY

Rte. 3, slightly more than 1 mile east of Rte. 687. The Northern Neck Baptist Association established the Northern Neck Industrial Academy in 1898 through financial contributions from local black Baptist churches. The academy opened approximately three miles to the west on Route 608 at Oak Hill Farm in Oct. 1901 as the first high school for blacks in Richmond County. Students from Lancaster, Northumberland, Westmoreland, King

George, and Essex Counties also attended the academy, often living in on-site dormitories. Sunday school and church services took place here as well. The establishment of public county high schools in the early 20th century resulted in its closure by 1938. The property was eventually sold and the main buildings are no longer standing.

O-46 WARSAW

Rte. 360, at Rte. 3, Warsaw. When Richmond County was formed in 1692, this place became the county seat and was known as Richmond (County) Courthouse. The present courthouse building was erected in 1748–49. The village was renamed Warsaw about 1846 in sympathy with the Polish struggle for liberty. It was the home of Congressman William A. Jones, advocate of Philippine independence.

SOUTHAMPTON COUNTY

U-102 TARLETON'S MOVEMENTS

Rte. 58, 8.2 miles east of Emporia. Near this point Tarleton, the British cavalryman, entered the road from the south and moved westward to clear the fords for Cornwallis's army, May 14, 1781. Cornwallis was moving north on Petersburg.

U-105 JOHN Y. MASON'S HOME

Rte. 58, 8.2 miles east of Emporia. Four miles west stood the home of John Y. Mason, statesman. Mason was a member of the House of Representatives; United States district judge; twice Secretary of the Navy; United States Attorney General, and Minister to France. He took part in the famous "Ostend Manifesto," 1854. Mason died in Paris, October 3, 1859.

U-115 BUCKHORN QUARTERS

Rte. 58, 4.5 miles west of Courtland. One mile north was the estate of Major Thomas Ridley. In the servile insurrection of August, 1831, the houses were fortified by faithful slaves and made a place of refuge for fugi-

tive whites. In this vicinity Nat Turner, the leader of the insurrection, spent the night after his defeat near Courtland, August 23, 1831.

U-119 MARLE HILL

Business Rte. 58, Franklin. Birthplace of Colgate Whitehead Darden, Jr.
1897–1981
Soldier–Educator–Statesman
Veteran, World War I
Member of the General Assembly of Virginia
Member of the United States Congress
Governor of Virginia
President of the University of Virginia
Delegate to the United Nations

U-120 GENERAL THOMAS' BIRTHPLACE

Rte. 58, 1.7 miles southeast of Courtland. General George H. Thomas, "The Rock of Chickamauga," was born on July 31, 1816, about five miles to the south. A graduate of West Point, Thomas sided with the Union during the Civil War and won distinction in the campaigns in Tennessee.

U-122 NAT TURNER'S INSURRECTION

Rte. 35, near Rte. 665. On the night of 21–22 August 1831, Nat Turner, a slave preacher, began an insurrection some seven miles west with a band that grew to about 70. They moved northeast toward the South-ampton County seat, Jerusalem (now Courtland), killing about 60 whites. After two days militiamen and armed civilians quelled the revolt. Turner was captured on 30 October, tried and convicted, and hanged on 11 November; some 30 blacks were hanged or expelled from Virginia. In response to the revolt, the General Assem-bly passed harsher slave laws and censored abolitionists.

U-123 MAJOR JOSEPH E. GILLETTE

Rte. 58, 0.9 miles west of Franklin. The "Southampton Cavalry" was formed just north of this site in May, 1861 at what was the Gillette Farm, Cedar Lawn. Joseph E. Gillette was elected captain. The Company eventually became Company A of the 13th Virginia Cavalry. Gillette was promoted to major in the regiment. He died here Novem-ber 1, 1863, after being wounded at Brandy Station. The company served gallantly until the end of the Civil War as part of General J. E. B. Stuart's cavalry in General Robert E. Lee's Army of Northern Virginia.

U-124 NOTTOWAY INDIANS

Rte. 58, at Southampton High School. The Nottoways' first recorded contact with the English colonists occurred in 1650 in pres-ent-day Sussex County. By 1694, due to hostile Indian attacks and encroaching set-tlers, the Nottoways had moved their main settlement to the mouth of Assamoosick Swamp in Southampton County. The Nottoway were farmers and hunters and their language was related to that of the Iroquois. By 1713, the House of Burgesses set the boundaries for the Nottoway Indian reservation. Over time, due to a decreasing

population and white settlers' claims, Nottoway land was sold to outsiders. The legal termination of the Nottoway Indian reservation began in 1824 and by 1878 the last parcels of land had been divided among the surviving Nottoways.

US-3 WILLIAM MAHONE'S BIRTHPLACE

Rte. 258, 2.2 miles south of Franklin. Three and a half miles southwest, at Monroe, Major-General William Mahone was born, December 1, 1826. He served brilliantly in the Confederate army throughout the war, and won the title, "Hero of the Crater," at Petersburg, July 30, 1864. He was United States Senator, 1881–1887. Mahone died in Washington, October 8, 1895.

US-6 SOUTH QUAY

Rte. 189, between Rtes. 690 and 747. Nearby along the eastern bank of the Blackwater River once existed the community of South Quay, also sometimes called South Key, Old Quay, or Old South Quay. Founded by 1657, South Quay by 1701 had become the site of a landing and trading post. A customs house for international trade had been built at South Quay by 1776. Dur-ing the Revolutionary War, supplies from overseas arrived there for the colonial army and at least two ships were built there. South Quay was destroyed by fire by Brit-ish troops on 16 July 1781. The port was rebuilt, but its prominence diminished by the end of the 18th century, and eventually the community disappeared.

UT-21 BLACKWATER LINE— BLACKWATER BRIDGE

Rte. 603, at boat ramp. During the Civil War, Confederate forces guarded this Blackwater River crossing as a part of the Blackwater defensive line. On 14 Nov. 1862, Col. Charles C. Dodge, 1st Battalion New York Mounted Rifles, led his troops in a skirmish against elements of W. C. Claiborne's Confederate cavalry. The Feder-als drove the Confederates away from the bridge and captured their supplies, but left the bridge standing. The same forces fought another skirmish on 9 March 1863 that resulted in the same outcome. In addition, the Federals captured four Confederates.

UT-22 BLACKWATER LINE—JOYNER'S FORD

Rte. 611, south of bridge. Confederate forces guarded this Blackwater River crossing from 1862 to the end of the Civil War. On 12 Dec. 1862, Capt. J. H. Sikes and soldiers of Company D, 7th Confederate Cavalry, were captured during a dismounted skirmish with elements of the 13th Indiana Regiment. More than 50 soldiers were reported killed or wounded during this engagement. On 22 Dec. 1862, Union Lt. Col. George Stetzel, 11th Pennsylvania Cavalry Regiment, reconnoitered with four companies to Joyner's Ford. Encountering

Confederate soldiers across the river, the Federals captured four pickets and a horse.

UT-23 BLACKWATER LINE—NEW SOUTH QUAY

Rtes. 189 and 714. Several skirmishes were fought at the South Quay crossing over the Blackwater River between 1862 and the end of the Civil War. On 3 Oct. 1862, Union gunboats on their way to attack Franklin exchanged fire with Confederate infantry and artillery lining the banks of the river. Early in the morning of 9 Dec. 1862, Union artillery shelled the Confederate camp on the west side of the river nearby. Confederate divisions commanded by Gens. Micah Jenkins and George E. Pickett crossed here on a pontoon bridge on 11 April 1863 to aid Lt. Gen. James Longstreet's siege of Suffolk. They recrossed here on 4 May 1863 at the end of the siege.

CITY OF SUFFOLK

K-248 CHUCKATUCK

Rte. 10, 9.2 miles northwest of Suffolk proper. A colonial church is here. In July, 1781, the British cavalryman Tarleton was at Chuckatuck. On May 3, 1863, a skirmish took place here between Union and Confederate forces as Longstreet withdrew from the siege of Suffolk.

K-249 DUMPLING ISLAND

Rte. 10, 6 miles northwest of Suffolk proper. The ceremonial heart of the Nansemond Indian district stood a mile east on Dumpling Island in the Nansemond River. In 1608, Capt. John Smith led colonists upriver to obtain corn from the Nansemonds, who attacked but were defeated and forced to feed them. The next summer, anticipating what was later called the "starving time" Smith transferred Capt. John Martin and 60 of the Jamestown colonists to the island. After his advance party disappeared, Martin attacked the Nansemonds, looted and burned their houses

and temples, despoiled their dead, and seized their corn. The Indians soon counterattacked, driving the colonists back to Jamestown.

K-250 NANSEMOND INDIAN VILLAGES

Rte. 10, 5.5 miles northwest of Suffolk proper. The principal villages of the Nansemond Indians stood just east of here on the Nansemond River. The Nansemonds fought frequently with the English colonists who arrived in 1607 as the Indians resisted the newcomers' attempts to occupy their villages and seize their corn. Two major periods of hostility occurred in 1609 and again after Opechancanough's coordinated assault on the English settlements on 22 Mar. 1622 that began the Powhatan-English War of 1622–1632. Sir George Yeardley retaliated for the assault by burning the Nansemond villages and destroying their cornfields. The surviving Nansemonds scattered, their power broken.

K-251 EARLY HISTORY OF SUFFOLK

North Main Street, just south of Nansemond River. A community developed here in the 1720s around John Constant's wharf, dwelling, and tobacco warehouse. The Virginia House of Burgesses chartered the town of Suffolk in 1742. It was incorporated as a town in 1808 and as a city in 1910; in 1974 it merged with Nansemond County. American troops occupied Suffolk during the Revolutionary War and a British force burned it on 13 May 1779. The Marquis de Lafayette visited the town in February 1825 during his American tour. Union forces held Suffolk for most of the Civil War. The town suffered disastrous fires in 1837, 1885, and 1888 but was quickly rebuilt each time.

K-252 SIEGE OF SUFFOLK

Rte. 460, 0.5 miles west of old city limits. The town was occupied by Union Troops from May, 1862, until the end of the Civil War. Confederate forces under Longstreet unsuccessfully besieged Suffolk, from April 11, to May 3, 1863, when they withdrew across the James on Lee's orders.

K-253 THE GREAT DISMAL SWAMP

Business Rte. 58, near Rte. 337. William Byrd II visited the swamp, just to the south, in 1728 while he was surveying the boundary line between Virginia and North Carolina. Byrd, and later George Washington, advocated the construction of a canal through the swamp. Washington and his partners purchased some 50,000 acres, began to log them, and built a ditch to transport the timber. The Dismal Swamp Canal Company, formed in 1787 to connect the Chesapeake Bay with Albemarle Sound, began construction in 1793 and completed the canal in 1805. In 1974, the U.S. Congress created the Great Dismal Swamp National Wildlife Refuge to protect the swamp's fragile ecosystem.

K-254 REVOLUTIONARY CAMP

Rte. 337, near Wilroy Road. On 10 May 1779, during the Revolutionary War, a British expeditionary force commanded by Gen. Edward Matthews disembarked in Portsmouth to capture the major Tidewater Virginia towns. About 200 Nansemond County militia under Col. Willis Riddick immediately assembled in Suffolk and marched toward Portsmouth. The soldiers camped here in a field in front of Capt. James Murdaugh's house on the night of 11 May, while several officers slept in nearby dwellings. A British advance party surprised two captains at Hargrove's Tavern a mile east, killing one. The militia retreated to Suffolk and later dispersed as the enemy approached. The British burned Suffolk on 13 May.

K-255 YEATES SCHOOL

Rte. 337, Driver. Before 1731 John Yeates established two free schools in this neighborhood, one on each side of Bennett's Creek. By his will, September 18, 1731, he left his property for the use of these schools. They continued until 1861 and were sold in 1866 under an act of legislature.

K-256 SLEEPY HOLE FERRY

Rte. 337, Driver. Three miles east. Benedict Arnold, returning from his Richmond raid, crossed the river there, January 16, 1781; Cornwallis, going to Portsmouth, crossed there in July, 1781.

K-257 BENNETT'S HOME

Rte. 337, across from Glebe Church. On this stream, Bennett's Creek, stood the home of Richard Bennett. He was one of the commissioners to "reduce" Virginia after the victory of Parliament in the civil war in England, 1651, and the first governor under the Cromwellian domination, 1652–1655.

K-258 GLEBE CHURCH

Rte. 337, at church. Built in 1738. In 1775 the parish minister, Parson Agnew, was driven from the church for preaching loyalty to the king. The building was repaired in 1854.

K-259 SIEGE OF SUFFOLK

Rte. 10, 1.5 miles northwest of Suffolk proper. Across the road here ran the main line of Confederate works, built by Longstreet besieging Suffolk, April, 1863. He abandoned the siege and rejoined Lee at Fredericksburg.

K-261 PIG POINT BATTERY

Rte. 58, near Rte. 672. In June 1861, Union Maj. Gen. Benjamin F. Butler, in order to clear a route for the capture of Suffolk, sought to neutralize the Confederate battery at Pig Point three miles north on the James River at the mouth of the Nansemond River. At 9:00 A.M. on 5 June, the steamer USS *Harriet Lane* shelled the battery. The Portsmouth Rifles, manning the guns there, returned fire and struck the vessel twice. One shot hit a tub of musket balls; the flying balls wounded six men. No Confederates were injured in the engagement, which ended after twenty minutes when the *Harriet Lane* withdrew.

K-270 HARGROVE'S TAVERN

Rte. 337, at Glebe Church. On 10 May 1779, during the Revolutionary War, a British expeditionary force commanded by Gen. Edward Matthews disembarked in Portsmouth to capture the major Tidewater Virginia towns. About 200 Nansemond County militia under Col. Willis Riddick immediately assembled in Suffolk and marched toward Portsmouth. While the main body camped about a mile west on the night of 11 May, Capt. King and Capt. Davis came here to Hargrove's Tavern. After a British advance party surprised them and killed Davis, King hastened to warn the Virginia camp. The militia retreated to Suffolk and later dispersed as the enemy approached. The British burned Suffolk on 13 May.

K-271 FLORENCE GRADED SCHOOL

4540 Nansemond Parkway. Florence Graded School was named for Florence Bowser, a noted educator who taught here and was instrumental in having the school constructed. It was built in 1920 with state and local funds and a grant from the Julius Rosenwald Fund, which had been created about 1912 to finance elementary schools for rural southern African Americans. Some 5,000 Rosenwald schools were built in 15 states, including 308 in Virginia; 9 were in Suffolk (then Nansemond County). Elements of the original frame building survive in the present brick structure. The adjoining Florence Bowser Elementary School was completed in 1963.

K-310 JAMES BOWSER, REVOLUTIONARY SOLDIER

Rte. 629 and Driver Lane. James Bowser, a free African American born in Nansemond County about 1763, was one of many black Virginians who served in the army or navy of the United States during the Revolutionary War. He enlisted in the 1st Virginia Regiment of the Continental Line under Col. William Davies on 1 Jan. 1782 in Shenandoah County for the duration of the war. After the war ended in 1783, he returned to Nansemond County, where he lived nearby, married, and reared a large family of freeborn citizens. For his service to his country, Bowser's heirs were granted a bounty land warrant in 1834.

K-322 AFRICAN AMERICAN OYSTERMEN

8300 Crittenden Road. Hobson is an example of an African American oystering village that developed during the last quarter of the 19th century on the James River, the Chesapeake Bay and their tributaries. As in other watermen communities, people also farmed and worked at nearby shucking houses and canning facilities. Hobson's black oystermen worked oyster beds in the James and Nansemond Rivers and Chuckatuck Creek that were leased primarily from the state. Bay region oyster beds were once among the richest in the world. Starting in the late 1950s Virginia's oyster production declined because of pollution, such as the chemical kepone, oyster diseases, weather, and overharvesting, which caused many of the oystermen to leave in the search of other employment.

KO-1 ST. JOHN'S CHURCH

Rte. 125, 1 mile east of Chuckatuck. Founded about 1643 and formerly known as Chuckatuck Church. The present building, the third on or near the site, was built in 1755 and is the second oldest church building in Nansemond County. Renamed St. John's Church in 1828.

KO-2 NANSEMOND COLLEGIATE INSTITUTE

East Washington Street, near 5th Street. Here stood the Nansemond Collegiate Institute, founded in 1890 as the Nansemond Industrial Institute by Rev. William W. Gaines to provide local black children with an education, because free public schools were closed to them. Eventually the institute offered elementary, secondary, and normal school courses of instruction. In 1927 a public school for black students was opened; competition for students and a series of disastrous fires forced the institute to close in 1939.

QB-1 FIRST SUFFOLK CHURCH

Western Avenue, west of Church Street. Here stood the Colonial Suffolk Church, a large, cross-shaped, brick building, erected in 1753 as the second parish church of Upper Parish, Nansemond County, and the first house of worship in the town of Suffolk. It survived the burning of Suffolk by the British in 1779 but fell to ruin and was torn down by 1802.

U-127 FIRST RURITAN CLUB

Business Rtes. 58 and 189, Holland. The first Ruritan Club was founded here in Holland, Va., on May 21, 1928. Ruritan is an organization of rural leaders striving through community service, fellowship and good will to make the rural community a better place in which to live.

U-130 DISMAL SWAMP

Rte. 58, 4.7 miles east of Suffolk. This swamp was visited by William Byrd in 1728. In 1763, George Washington made explorations in it and organized a company to drain it for farm land. Lake Drummond is in its midst.

UT-28 CIVIL WAR CAVALRY SKIRMISH

Rtes. 604 and 460. Federal forces occupied Suffolk on 12 May 1862 and built earthworks around the town; Brig. Gen. John J. Peck took command in October. Cavalry vedettes, or mounted pickets, were posted some distance outside the fortifications to warn of Confederate attacks. During the winter of 1862–1863, small detachments of Federal and Confederate troops harassed each other west of Suffolk. Near here, about 4:00 P.M. on 28 Dec. 1862, Confederate cavalrymen attacked Union vedettes at Providence Church and drove them back toward Suffolk. Federal reserves repulsed the attack and forced the Confederates west several miles to their main body of cavalry.

SURRY COUNTY

K-137 QUIYOUGHCOHANNOCK INDIANS

Rte. 10 (Colonial Trail East), near Highgate Road, at Mount Nebo Baptist Church. The Quiyoughcohannocks were one of the first Virginia Indian groups the English encountered in 1607 after landing at Jamestown. Situated primarily in present-day Surry County, the Quiyoughcohannocks had four villages in the region likely east of Upper Chippokes Creek. The Quiyoughcohannocks in 1608/1609 escorted Nathaniel Powell and Anas Todkill southward in an unsuccessful attempt to locate survivors of the Roanoke Colony. The English observed a part of a ritual initiation into manhood, the huskanaw, at a Quiyoughcohannock village in 1608.

K-222 CABIN POINT

Rte. 10, at Rte. 613, Cabin Point. Beginning about 1689, a village known as Cabin Point stood here. It was a tobacco shipping port in the 18th century. Colonial troops were stationed here during the American Revolution in 1780 and 1781. By 16 Jan. 1781 Maj. Gen. Friedrich Wilhelm von Steuben arrived at Cabin Point with 700 additional soldiers to resist a further invasion of British forces led by Brig. Gen. Benedict Arnold. Soon after British forces set up camp in Portsmouth on 19 Jan., Steuben put Brig. Gen. Peter Muhlenberg in charge of the troops here and left to obtain supplies. Cabin Point remained a commercial center in the 19th century for plantations south of the James River.

K-223 FLYING POINT

Rte. 10, 4 miles northwest of Spring Grove. This is six miles north. William Rookings patented land there in 1636. His son, William Rookings, was one of the leaders in Bacon's Rebellion, 1676.

K-224 PACE'S PAINES

Rte. 10, at Rte. 618, 3.5 miles west of Surry. Nearby to the north, Richard Pace and his family received a land patent in Dec. 1620 establishing Pace's Paines plantation. In response to English expansion into Indian lands, such as occurred at Pace's Paines and elsewhere, Chief Opechancanough planned a 22 Mar. 1622 coordinated offensive on English settlements. Prior to the event, Pace learned about the impending affair from a Virginia Indian living with him. Pace rowed a boat across the James River to Jamestown and told Gov. Sir Francis Wyatt of the danger. Jamestown was not attacked, but many residents of outlying plantations died in the conflict.

K-225 CLAREMONT

Rte. 613, Claremont. The Quiyoughcohannock Indian village nearby was first visited by English settlers in May, 1607. The first land patent at Claremont was 200 acres granted to George Harrison in 1621. Arthur Allen, who built the house now known as Bacon's Castle, first purchased land here in 1656. The estate was called "Cleremont" by William Allen by 1793, and Claremont Manor was probably built by him after 1754. Situated on land that had been part of the Allen estate, the town of Claremont was incorporated in 1886.

K-226 WAKEFIELD AND PIPSICO

Rte. 10, at Rte. 40, Spring Grove. Located five miles to the north is Wakefield. Benjamin Harrison patented this land about 1637. His descendents became major landowners and were influential in Virginia and United States politics. Governor Benjamin Harrison was a signer of the Declaration of Independence and William Henry Harrison served as president of the United States. Harrison family members owned portions of Wakefield until approximately the end of the 18th century. Seven miles to the northeast is the property known as Pipsico that was first patented by Henry Browne about 1637. Pipsico was named for the Quiyoughcohannock Indian chief that lived in Surry County and assisted the early settlers.

K-227 PLEASANT POINT

Rte. 10, 1.3 miles southeast of Surry. Four miles north is Pleasant Point on James River. William Edwards patented land there in 1657; the house is ancient. Edwards was clerk of the general court and a member of the House of Burgesses.

K-228 GLEBE HOUSE OF SOUTHWARK PARISH

Rte. 10, approximately 0.25 miles east of glebe house, west of Surry. Nearby stands the glebe house of the formerly Anglican Southwark Parish that was built soon after

1724. A glebe was a parcel of land owned by a colonial church and farmed to pay the minister's expenses. This glebe house was used as a parish rectory and is one in a rare surviving group in Virginia. The first to live here was the Reverend John Cargill, a leading colonial cleric. The disestablishment of the Anglican church resulted in the property's sale into private ownership in 1802. Exterior chimneys were added and the gable roof was rebuilt as a gambrel. The property was listed on the Virginia Landmarks Register in 1975 and the National Register of Historic Places in 1976.

K-229 SOUTHWARK PARISH CHURCHES

Rte. 10, at Rte. 618. Southwark Parish was established in 1647. To the northeast stood the second Southwark church built by 1673 and abandoned shortly after the American Revolution. To the east, near Bacon's Castle, Southwark Parish vestry completed the Lower Southwark Church in 1754. It too fell into disuse after the American Revolution and the disestablishment of the Anglican Church, but other denominations occasionally held services there. Episcopalians settled a mission at the church in 1847, but were forced by the other groups using the building to erect their own church nearby. Fire gutted the building in 1868, but some brick ruins remain.

K-231 SWANN'S POINT

Rte. 10, Spring Grove. Ten miles northeast is Swann's Point on James River. In 1635 William Swann patented land there. The English commissioners investigating Bacon's Rebellion met at Swann's Point in 1677. William Swann's tomb, dated 1680, is there.

K-232 CYPRESS CHURCH

Rtes. 31 and 618. Nearby to the southeast once stood Cypress Church. It was established by order of the Southwark Parish vestry on 5 April 1743. The rectangular brick building, about 60 by 27 feet in size, was completed by Feb. 1745. After the disestablishment of the Anglican Church following the American Revolution, Cypress Church's membership declined, but it remained an Episcopal church until about 1837. The building then was used by local Baptist and Methodist congregations and sold to a local Methodist congregation in 1877. The roof collapsed in 1919, but portions of the building remained until the late 1920s.

K-233 SMITH'S FORT PLANTATION

Rte. 10/31, in courthouse parking lot, Surry. Captain John Smith began Smith's Fort in 1609, two years after the first permanent English colony in the New World was established at Jamestown. The remains of the fort, a two-foot-high earthwork, constitute the oldest extant structure of English origin in Virginia. The fort stands on a high bluff overlooking Gray's Creek and encloses a triangle of about two hundred feet on each side. Thomas Rolfe, the only child of John Rolfe and Pocahontas, probably owned this tract. The house is a mid-18th-century Tidewater plantation dwelling likely built for Jacob Faulcon, Surry County clerk, from 1781 to 1801.

K-234 HISTORY ON CROUCH'S CREEK

Rte. 10, at Rte. 634. Originally called Tappahannock Creek by the English, Crouch's Creek flowed through a number of early English settlements. By 1625 George Sandys had holdings in Surry County, known as Treasurer's Plantation, east of the creek. Sandys was a poet, a member of the Council of State, and treasurer of the Virginia Company. Returning to England by the late 1620s, he published an English translation of Ovid's *Metamorphoses*. Thomas Crouch patented land on the creek in 1638 and eventually the creek took his name. By 1702, a ferry operated between Jamestown and Crouch's Creek.

K-235 BACON'S CASTLE

Rte. 10, at Rte. 617, Bacon's Castle. This house, just to the north, was built by

Arthur Allen in 1655. In Bacon's Rebellion, 1676, the house was seized by a party of rebels and fortified. On December 29, 1676, it was captured by sailors from a ship in James River who were engaged in putting down the rebellion.

K-236 ORGANIZATION OF THE CHRISTIAN CHURCH

Rte. 10, 1.5 miles west of Surry. At "Old Lebanon Church" here, the Christian Church was established under the leadership of James O'Kelly, August, 1794. O'Kelly had withdrawn from the Methodist Church, 1792.

K-237 HOG ISLAND

Rte. 10, Bacon's Castle. On this point, in James River nine miles northeast, the settlers kept their hogs in 1608. When abandoning Jamestown in June, 1610, they stopped at the island for a night. The next morning, proceeding down the river, they met a messenger from Governor Lord Delaware, who had just arrived, and returned to Jamestown.

K-279 CHIPPOKES PLANTATION

Rte. 10, 1.3 miles southeast of Surry. This plantation, four miles to the northeast, was established in 1619 by Captain William Powell of Jamestown. Structures and artifacts on the property reflect plantation life from the early 17th century to the present. Donated to the Commonwealth by Mrs. Victor Stewart in 1967 for use as a state park, Chippokes is noted for its 350 years of continuous agricultural production and its modern recreational facilities.

K-300 LAWNES CREEK CHURCH

Rte. 10, at Rte. 650, east of Bacon's Castle. Approximately six miles to the north, near Hog Island Creek, is the site of Lawne's Creek Church. Authorized in 1629 as a "chapel of ease" for the settlers in the area by the Council and General Court of Colonial Virginia, the church was the site of a meeting in 1673 to protest unjust taxation and government without representation and to manifest a spirit of religious independence.

K-301 JAMESTOWN FERRY

Rte. 31, at ferry, Scotland. Near this site on February 26, 1925, the ferry *Captain John Smith* began the first automobile ferry service crossing the James River. Captain Albert F. Jester was the inaugurator and owner/operator until it was sold to the Commonwealth of Virginia in 1945. This ferry system provided an important link for the Maine-to-Florida traveler through Surry County to Jamestown Island, the site of the first permanent English settlement in America.

K-312 CARSLEY UNITED METHODIST CHURCH

Rte. 615, at Rte. 612. On 23 November 1811 William Carsley sold an acre of land here to trustees of the Methodist Episcopal Church. The first Methodist church built in Surry County was constructed here soon thereafter. During the 19th century it was replaced by a second plain structure, which like the first faced the "rolling road" to the south. In 1897 the present sanctuary was built. Ramey's Store, constructed across the road soon after the Civil War, was moved to its present location in 1990 to function as the fellowship hall. Carsley United Methodist Church serves the oldest continuously active congregation in Surry County.

K-319 ENGLISH SETTLEMENT ON GRAY'S CREEK

Rte. 10, at Rte. 618, west of Surry. English settlement along Gray's Creek began by 1609 when Capt. John Smith ordered a defensive fortification built on the tidal creek opposite Jamestown. Though the English did not finish constructing the fort (known as Smith's Fort) and soon abandoned it, an earthwork remains on a high bluff overlooking Gray's Creek. It is believed that Thomas Rolfe, the only child of John Rolfe and Pocahontas, inherited his father's patent along this creek. The stream was named Smith's Fort Creek and then Rolfe's Creek. By 1648 it became known as Gray's Creek for Thomas Gray, who had patented land at the mouth of the creek.

K-320 JERUSALEM BAPTIST CHURCH

5007 Carsley Road, Waverly. Jerusalem Baptist Church was organized as Mt. Joy Baptist Church in 1867 at the nearby home of Mondoza Bailey, community leader and carpenter. Amelia "Mother" Howard assisted in the organization of this and six other churches. Sent by the United States Freedmen's Bureau, Howard, a teacher from Pennsylvania, helped to establish African American schools and churches in the region. Bailey led church members in the construction of a wooden building. Nancy Ellis James, born a free African American woman, and her family provided the land here for the church. The current brick structure was built in 1993.

SUSSEX COUNTY

K-230 COLONEL MICHAEL BLOW

Rte. 460, at Rte. 628, Wakefield. One mile south on Seacock Swamp stood the home of Col. Michael Blow. He was the first Chairman of the Committee of Safety of Sussex County, member of the House of Burgesses, member of the First Virginia Convention (1774), County Justice, and colonel in the Revolutionary Army.

K-306 EARLY PEANUT CROP

Rte. 460, north of Wakefield. One mile northwest Dr. Matthew Harris grew the first commercial crop of peanuts in the United States, according to tradition, in or soon after 1842.

K-308 MILES B. CARPENTER

Rte. 460, 0.11 miles north of Rte. 40, Waverly. Miles B. Carpenter (1889–1985) moved to a Sussex County peanut farm from Pennsylvania in 1902. He entered the lumber business in 1912 with a planing mill and sawmill. When business slowed during World War II, he whittled figures but did not carve in earnest until the 1960s, when his watermelons, peanut men, and whimsical monsters earned him a national reputation as a folk artist. Carpenter's woodcarvings reflected the influence of Sussex County's two major industries: lumber and peanuts.

K-309 COPPAHAUNK SPRINGS

Rtes. 9403 and 1018, off Rte. 40, Waverly. A Nottoway Indian town was located two miles south at the springs when the English settlement was established at Jamestown in 1607. The Nottoways gave the three springs the name, Coppahaunk, meaning "good health or healing waters." About 1825, Coppahaunk Tavern was built; a post office opened in 1835. Before the Civil War, a spa resort operated here. Afterward, a private boy's academy opened in the former tavern, and girls were later admitted. From the turn of the century until the Great Depression, spring water was bottled and sold, and during the late 1920s the water was used in the production of ginger ale.

K-314 ELLIS PREACHING HOUSE

Rte. 460, at bark plant, north of Wakefield. Nearby to the northeast stood Ellis Preaching House, an early Methodist meetingplace in Sussex County. Francis Asbury, a pioneering Methodist leader and circuit rider, first visited the Ellis family in 1775 and later conducted services at the preaching house on numerous occasions. The Ellis Preaching House, built by 1782, received its name because it was constructed on property owned by William Ellis. Annual conference meetings were held there in April 1782, May 1783, and April 1784. After the 1784 meeting, Methodists convened in Baltimore, Maryland, and formed the Methodist Episcopal Church. The preaching house was still standing in the 1820s.

UM-12 JARRATT'S STATION

Rte. 139, Jarratt. On 8 May 1864 Jarratt's Station, a nearby depot on the Petersburg Railroad, was the subject of a Union cavalry raid. Brig. Gen. August V. Kautz led his division on a series of raids in early May to cut the railroad from Petersburg to Weldon, North Carolina. Kautz's cavalry tore up the road in several locations, destroyed bridges, and burned the depot at Jarratt's Station on 8 May. The raids slowed the flow of supplies to Lee's army in Richmond and Petersburg.

UM-14 OLD HALIFAX ROAD

Rte. 301, Jarratt. Here the highway merges with the Halifax Road, the ancient road from Petersburg to Halifax, North Carolina. Over this road Cornwallis marched in May, 1781, from Halifax to Petersburg in his invasion of Virginia. Over this road the Confederates hauled supplies during the siege of Petersburg, 1864–65, and over it parts of the Union and Confederate armies constantly passed.

UM-16 NOTTOWAY RIVER CROSSINGS

Rte. 301, 3.4 miles south of Stony Creek. Several important river crossings took place over the Nottoway River during two wars. Revolutionary War cavalry commander Lt. Col. John Graves Simcoe led British forces across the river in this area on 11 May 1781, as he rode south to join Gen. Charles Cornwallis. In mid May, Cornwallis marched north from North Carolina, crossed the Nottoway River nearby, and reached Petersburg on 20 May. During the Civil War,

at the end of Gen. James H. Wilson's and Brig. Gen. August V. Kautz's railroad raids, a portion of Gen. Wilson's forces crossed the river nearby on 28 June 1864, on their way back to Union lines near Petersburg.

UM-18 HISTORY AT STONY CREEK

Rte. 301, Stony Creek. In 1864, supplies for Lee's army were carted from the Weldon railroad here to Petersburg. Here the Union cavalryman, Wilson, returning from his raid to Burkeville, fought an action with Lee's cavalry, June 28–29, 1864. The place was raided by the Union cavalryman, Gregg, on December 1, 1864.

UO-5 THE CATTLE (BEEFSTEAK) RAID

Rtes. 35 and 626. One mile southwest, on September 16, 1864, General Wade Hampton's Confederate Cavalry herded about 2500 head of captured cattle across the Nottoway River, while two miles northwest, at Belsches' Mill, Federal troops sent to recapture the cattle were intercepted and repulsed.

UO-6 ANTIOCH BAPTIST CHURCH

Rte. 735, at Rte. 631. Antioch Baptist Church was the first of its denomination in Sussex County and one of the earliest in Virginia. It was formed on 13 June 1772 with 87 members, the result of effective preaching by Elder John Meglamre, of Kehukee Baptist Church in Halifax, North Carolina. In 1777 the reformed Kehukee Association of 19 Baptist churches in Virginia and North Carolina held its organizational meeting here. Known as Raccoon Swamp Meetinghouse until 1852, Antioch was the mother church of six congregations located in four counties. The present sanctuary was built in 1839.

CITY OF VIRGINIA BEACH

K-272 KEMPSVILLE

5200 block, Princess Anne Road, west of Witchduck Road. Originally known as

Kemp's Landing, Kempsville is located at the head of the eastern branch of the Elizabeth River. By the middle 1700s, it had become an important port community. Colonial Governor Lord Dunmore's forces fought the Princess Anne County militia at Kemp's landing on 14/15 Nov. 1775 for possession of the strategically important bridge there. After a brief engagement, the militia retreated. Established as a town in 1783, Kempsville served as the county seat of Princess Anne County from 1778 to about 1823. Princess Anne County was consolidated with the City of Virginia Beach in 1963 and the town became part of the city.

K-274 PRINCESS ANNE COUNTY TRAINING SCHOOL/UNION KEMPSVILLE HIGH SCHOOL

Near 213 North Witchduck Road, between Virginia Beach Boulevard and Cleveland Street. This is the site of the former Princess Anne County Training School/Union Kempsville High School that served African American children in the former Princess Anne County from 1938 to 1969. To give them a clean, safe environment for learning, the Princess Anne County Training Association, which was composed of African American parents, community leaders, and citizens, raised money to purchase property and to support the construction of the school. The last class graduated in 1969.

K-276 THE TESTING OF GRACE SHERWOOD

Independence Boulevard, north of Witchduck Road. The witchcraft case of Grace Sherwood is one of the best known in Virginia. She was accused of bewitching a neighbor's crop in 1698. Allegations grew over time until the Princess Anne County government and her accusers decided she would be tested by ducking, since water was considered pure and would not permit a witch to sink into its depths. Sherwood's accusers on 10 July 1706 tied her hands to her feet and dropped her into the Western Branch of the Lynnhaven River near what is now known as Witch Duck Point. Sherwood floated, a sign of guilt. She was

imprisoned, but was eventually released. Sherwood lived the rest of her life quietly and died by 1740.

K-277 EASTERN SHORE CHAPEL

Oceana Boulevard, near POW/MIA Park. Originally named for its proximity to the eastern shore of the Lynnhaven River, the first Eastern Shore Chapel was built elsewhere by 1689. The vestry of Lynnhaven Parish commissioned the building of the third Eastern Shore Chapel in 1754. This brick structure located north of here on the site of the second chapel (circa 1730), had a gable roof skirted by modillion cornices, typical of Virginia's simpler colonial churches. Because of the expansion of Naval Air Station Oceana, this chapel was dismantled in 1952. Built to the northwest of here, the current church was completed in 1954 and took selected remnants of the interior fabric, including the gallery steps and pews from the 1754 building.

K-280 OLD DONATION CHURCH

Independence Boulevard, just north of Witchduck Road. Just east stands Old Donation Episcopal Church, built in 1736. It is the third building to serve the colonial era Lynnhaven Parish, established by 1642. The second church, once adjacent to the current building, was converted into a school in 1737. The church received its present name in the early 19th century likely in commemoration of a gift of land. An 1882 fire left only portions of its brick walls standing. The building was restored in 1916 and was listed on the National Register of Historic Places in 1972.

KV-4 SEASHORE STATE PARK

Rte. 60, 1 mile east of Rte. 615. This park was developed by the National Park Service, Interior Department, through the Civilian Conservation Corps, in conjunction with the Virginia Conservation Commission. It covers 3400 acres and was opened, June 15, 1936. Two miles west is Lynnhaven Bay, in or near which there were naval actions in 1672 and 1700, and naval movements in 1781 and 1813.

KV-15 First Landing

Rte. 60, Cape Henry. Near here the first permanent English settlers in North America first landed on American soil, April 26, 1607. From here they went on to make the settlement at Jamestown. The brick lighthouse was built in 1791.

KW-16 Adam Thoroughgood House

Near house at 1136 Parish Road. This dwelling illustrates the transition from Virginia's temporary frontier structures of the early 17th century to the more permanent, gentry houses of the 18th century. It stands on land obtained in 1636 by Adam Thoroughgood, who came to the colony as an indentured servant and gained prominence as a landowner and Burgess. Constructed about 1680 by a relative of Thoroughgood, the exterior and part of the interior were returned to its original appearance during restoration initiated in 1957 after the Adam Thoroughgood House Foundation acquired the property. The building was listed on the National Register of Historic Places in 1966 and the Virginia Landmarks Register in 1969.

WESTMORELAND COUNTY

J-64 Bristol Iron Works

Rte. 3, 2.6 miles west of Oak Grove. On the river a short distance south is the site of the Bristol Iron Works, which were projected by John King and Company of Bristol, England, and established in 1721 by John Tayloe, John Lomax and associates. The works, which were on the Foxhall's Mill property owned in 1670 by Major Underwood, were in operation in 1729 and later.

J-67 History at Oak Grove

Rte. 3, Oak Grove. Here George Washington, while living at Wakefield with a brother, went to school, 1744–1746. Here Union cavalry came on a raid through the Northern Neck, May 1863. Several miles north of this place, James Monroe, fifth President of the United States, was born, 1758.

J-68 Westmoreland Association

Rte. 3, Oak Grove. At Leedstown, seven miles south, an association was formed to resist the enforcement of the Stamp Act, February 27, 1766. The resolutions, drafted by the Revolutionary leader, Richard Henry Lee, were one of the first protests against the Stamp Act and influenced public opinion in all the Colonies.

J-69 George Washington's Birthplace (Wakefield)

Rtes. 3 and 204, Popes Creek. George Washington's birthplace is two miles north, on Pope's Creek, just off the Potomac River. He was born on 22 Feb. 1732 and lived there only for three years. Washington's father, Augustine, purchased the land in 1718 and built the house by 1726. President Washington's half-brother Augustine, Jr., inherited the property after his father's death in 1743. The dwelling, a U-shaped timber-frame house, burned on Christmas Day 1779. The present Memorial House, erected in 1930–31 is a Colonial Revival–style version of a medium-size planter's house. Originally known as Pope's Creek, the property was renamed Wakefield about 1770 by George Washington's half-nephew William Augustine Washington.

J-69-a Popes Creek Episcopal Church

Rte. 3, west of Westmoreland State Park, 4.8 miles southeast of Oak Grove. On this site, a part of "Longwood," stood Popes Creek Episcopal Church, built about 1744 on land given by the McCarty family. The Lees and Washingtons worshiped here. About 1826 it fell into disuse and was burned as being unsafe.

J-71 OLD WESTMORELAND COURTHOUSE

Rte. 3, at courthouse, Montross. At a public meeting here, on June 22, 1774, resolutions of Richard Henry Lee offering aid to Boston, whose port had been closed by the British government, were adopted. Here, on May 23, 1775, the Westmoreland Committee of Safety passed resolutions denouncing the royal governor, Lord Dunmore, for seizing the colony's powder supply at Williamsburg.

J-72 NOMINI HALL

Rte. 202, just east of Rte. 626. The house was built about 1730 and burned in 1850. It was not rebuilt. Only some poplar trees remain. A fine colonial mansion, it was the home of the celebrated "Councillor" Robert Carter. Philip Fithian, tutor at Nomini Hall, 1773–74, wrote his well-known "Journal" there.

J-75 WESTMORELAND STATE PARK

Rte. 3, at entrance to park, 4.7 miles northwest of Montross. This park was developed by the National Park Service, Interior Department, through the Civilian Conservation Corps, in conjunction with the Virginia Conservation Commission. It covers 1300 acres and was opened, June 15, 1936. It was originally included in "Clifts Plantation," patented by Nathaniel Pope about 1650, and became a part of Stratford estate when purchased by Thomas Lee in 1716.

J-76 STRATFORD AND CHANTILLY

Rte. 3, 4 miles northwest of Montross. Two miles east of Stratford, built about 1725 by Thomas Lee (1690–1750), President of the Virginia Council and father of Richard Henry Lee and Francis Lightfoot Lee, both signers of the Declaration of Independence. Here also was born Robert Edward Lee (1807–1870). Three miles east of Stratford stood Chantilly the home of Richard Henry Lee in his later years.

J-79 NOMINI BAPTIST CHURCH

Rte. 3, at Rte. 202, Templeman. Nomini Baptist Church was established on 29 April 1786 with 17 members. By 1809 it was reputedly the largest Baptist church in Virginia with 875 members. The original meetinghouse, built nearby in 1790 on land donated by a charter member, Captain Joseph Pierce, was replaced in 1858–59 by the present brick church. During the past two centuries Nomini Baptist Church has had 27 ministers, beginning with Elder Henry Toler, and is considered the mother church of ten congregations in three counties.

J-84 NOMINI BAPTIST MEETINGHOUSE

Rte. 690, near Templeman. Nearby stood the original "Nomony" (early variant spelling) Meetinghouse. On 29 Apr. 1786, 17 members established Nomini Baptist Church. Until 1790, when the meetinghouse was built on land donated by charter member Joseph Peirce, the congregation met in the homes of Peirce, Samuel Templeman, and Elizabeth Steptoe. With 875 members by 1809, Nomini was the largest Baptist church in Virginia. The meetinghouse served the congregation for almost three-quarters of a century until replaced in 1858–59 by the present brick structure located at Templeman's Crossroads nearby. Nomini Baptist Church is the mother church of ten congregations in three counties.

J-98 PISSASECK INDIANS

Rte. 637, Leedstown. The Pissaseck Indians lived along the Rappahannock River, here at Leedstown and in a few other villages in Westmoreland County. They spoke a language derived from the Virginia Algonquian family and were hunters and farmers. The Pissasecks were tributaries of Chief Powhatan, who ruled a political configuration of Indian groups that occupied the coastal plain of Virginia from the James River to the Potomac River. English Capt. John Smith featured the Pissaseck Indians on his Virginia map published in 1612.

JP-6 BIRTHPLACE OF MONROE

Rte. 205, 1.8 miles south of Colonial Beach. In this vicinity stood the Monroe home where James Monroe, fifth President of the United States, was born, April 28, 1758. His father was Spence Monroe and his mother, Elizabeth Jones. He left home at the age of sixteen to enter William and Mary College and left college to enter the army.

JT-2 NOMINY CHURCH

Rte. 202, 3.7 miles east of Templeman. One of the two churches of Cople Parish. It was built in 1704 on land given by Youell Watkins, and was replaced in 1755 by a brick church on the same site. George Washington attended services here twice in 1768. The last colonial church was burned (1814) by the British Admiral Cockburn, who carried off the church silver. The present building was erected about 1852. The first Nominy Church of 1655 stood on the north side of the river opposite this place.

JT-3 THE GLEBE

Rte. 202, 4.4 miles east of Templeman. Five miles north is the home of the rectors of Cople Parish, one of whom, Walter Jones, married Washington's parents, March 6, 1731. Here lived Thomas Smith, rector of the parish, 1764–1799, and chairman of the county Committee of Safety, 1775. He entertained Washington, May 25, 1771. The house is possibly the oldest in the Northern Neck.

JT-4 WASHINGTON'S MOTHER

Rte. 202, 4.8 miles northwest of Callao. At Sandy Point, seven and a half miles east, Mary Ball, Washington's mother, spent her youth in the home of her guardian, George Eskridge. There she was married to Augustine Washington, March, 1731. She is supposed to have named her eldest son for George Eskridge.

JT-5 BUSHFIELD

Rte. 202, 4.4 miles east of Templeman. A mile and a half east. This was the home of John Augustine Washington, younger brother of George Washington, who visited here. Here was born, in 1762, Bushrod Washington, who became a justice of the United States Supreme Court in 1798, and died in 1829. He inherited Mount Vernon.

JT-6 RICHARD HENRY LEE'S GRAVE

Rte. 202, 8.8 miles southeast of Templeman. A mile and a half north, in the Lee burying ground, is the grave of Richard Henry Lee, who died, June 19, 1794. Lee was one of the first leaders of the American Revolution. On June 7, 1776, he introduced a resolution in the Continental Congress for a declaration of independence, and argued for it, June 7–10. The declaration was signed, July 4, 1776.

JT-7 YEOCOMICO CHURCH

Rte. 202, 8.1 miles northwest of Callao. Two miles east. Built in 1655 of oak timbers sheathed with clapboards. Rebuilt of brick in 1706. In this vicinity Mary Ball lived under the tutelage of Colonel George Eskridge, of Sandy Point, from 1721 until her marriage to Augustine Washington in 1730, and attended church here. In 1906 an association was formed to preserve the church.

JT-8 KINSALE

Rte. 202, 4.8 miles northwest of Callao. Two miles east, on picturesque Yeocomico River, is Kinsale, the founding of which the Assembly ordered in 1705. The town was established in 1784. Near by at the old home of the Bailey family, "The Great House," is the tomb of Midshipman James B. Sigourney, who in command of the sloop "Asp" fell in an engagement with the British in Yeocomico River, June 14, 1813.

JT-15 LEEDSTOWN

Rte. 637, Leedstown. Here at the then thriving port of Leedstown on February 27, 1766, ten years before the Declaration of Independence, the Leedstown Resolutions (or Westmoreland Association) were drawn. This association, a protest against the Stamp Act and a pledge of mutual aid in event of its execution, was signed by 115 men from Westmoreland and surrounding counties.

JT-16 SANDY POINT

Rte. 604, Sandy Point. Here at Sandy Point, Mary Ball, George Washington's Mother, spent her youth in the home of her Guardian, Colonel George Eskridge. Here she married Augustine Washington in March 1731. She is supposed to have named her eldest son, George, for Colonel Eskridge.

JT-17 PRIVATE TATE—BUFFALO SOLDIER

Rte. 645, 2 miles north of Rte. 3. Walter Tate was born nearby in 1854. He enlisted as a private on 6 May 1879 at Fort Concho (present-day San Angelo), Texas, in Company M, 10th Regiment, U.S. Cavalry. Tate and those who served with him on the western frontier defended settlements, livestock, the U.S. mail, and stage routes from bandits, cattle thieves, and Mexican revolutionaries. The Indians called Tate and other soldiers of color "Buffalo Soldiers" because of their dark curly hair, endurance, and strength, claiming that these attributes reminded them of their much-prized buffaloes. Tate was discharged on 5 May 1884. This buffalo soldier died in Westmoreland County in 1933.

JT-18 ZION BAPTIST CHURCH

Rte. 202, just west of Rte. 611. Zion Baptist Church is home to one of the oldest African American congregations in Westmoreland County. Before slavery ended, according to local tradition, services were first held under a dogwood bush arbor on Gawen's Farm, near Tucker Hill, approximately one and a half miles north of here. The members had most likely worshiped at the nearby white Machodoc (Sandy Valley) Baptist Church. Zion Baptist Church was formally organized in 1867, when the congregation constructed a log building. During the latter half of the 1800s, a fire and expanding membership required the construction of two other buildings. The present church was erected in 1932.

JT-19 ARMSTEAD TASKER JOHNSON SCHOOL

Rte. 3, Templeman. The A. T. Johnson High School was built in 1937 in the Colonial Revival style as the first public high school constructed for African Americans in Westmoreland County. The new school was named for Armstead Tasker Johnson (1857–1944), a black educator and community leader of the grassroots effort for its construction. Local African Americans raised money to build the school. Additional financing came from the federal Works Progress Administration, the Jeanes and Slater black education funds, and the Westmoreland County School Board. The school was converted to a junior high school in Sept. 1970 and served as a middle school from Sept. 1990 to June 1998. It was listed on the Virginia Landmarks Register and the National Register of Historic Places in 1998.

JT-20 McCOY REVOLUTIONARY WAR SOLDIERS

Rte. 604, just west of Rte. 202. Bennett and James McCoy, free men (probably brothers) from Westmoreland County, were among the many African Americans who served in the Virginia militia and the United States Army or Navy during the Revolutionary War. Bennett McCoy served for three years starting in 1777, participated in several major battles, and reenlisted with the 15th Virginia Regiment until the end of the war. James McCoy rendered guard service on the Potomac River from 1777 to 1778. In 1781, he was drafted and

British forces surrendered to the American and French forces at Yorktown in October 1781, as depicted in this drawing by François Godefroy, ca. 1784. Historical markers in the region describe the troop movements and skirmishes leading up to this climactic event, which led to the end of the Revolutionary War. (Washington-Rochambeau Route [York County] marker) (Library of Congress)

stationed on the York River at Yorktown and acted as a bowman to assist "his captain" in navigating the river. Each of the McCoys received a pension for his service.

CITY OF WILLIAMSBURG

W-40 FIRST BALLOON FLIGHT IN VIRGINIA

Richmond Road and Stadium Drive, on the College of William and Mary campus. On May 7, 1801, J. S. Watson, a student at William and Mary, wrote a letter detailing attempts at flying hot air balloons on the Court House Green. The third balloon, decorated with sixteen stars, one for each of the existing states, and fueled with spirits of wine, was successful. Watson wrote, "I never saw so great and so universal delight as it gave to the spectators." This is the earliest recorded evidence of aeronautics in the commonwealth.

WASHINGTON-ROCHAMBEAU ROUTE

2150 Richmond Road (Rte. 60). Generals Washington and Rochambeau and their staffs arrived in Williamsburg on September 14, 1781. Here they gathered their troops and supplies prior to laying siege to Cornwallis at Yorktown 12 miles away on September 28, 1781. *Note:* This is of five unnumbered signs discussing aspects of the Washington-Rochambeau Route, which were a special gift from the French Government, Committee of the Bicentennial, to the Commonwealth of Virginia in 1976.

YORK COUNTY

NP-1 CHARLES CHURCH

Rtes. 134 and 17, Tabb. About one mile east, on north (lefthand) side of road (see stone marker and old foundations) stood the last colonial church of Charles Parish, built about 1708 and burned a century later, on the site of two earlier churches of the parish, built about 1636 and 1682. This parish was first known as New Poquoson Parish in 1635 and was renamed Charles Parish in 1692.

NP-3 SEAFORD

Rte. 622, Seaford. Settlement began here in 1636, when John Chisman patented 600 acres on Crab Neck, a peninsula bounded by Chisman Creek and Back Creek, a tributary of York River. The neck then lay in Charles River Parish in York County, one of the eight original shires created in 1634. A Confederate fortification stood near the narrowest part of the neck in 1862, and during the Civil War Union troops destroyed Zion Methodist Church here. Crab Neck post office was established in 1889; its name was changed to Seaford in 1910.

NP-12   GOODWIN NECK

Rte. 173, 3.5 miles east of Rte. 17. This area, locally known as Dandy, was part of the land granted to John Chew July 6, 1636, and was sold by his heirs to James Goodwin, a member of the House of Burgesses from Jamestown, August 27, 1668. The area was strategically important both to British General Charles Cornwallis and to Confederate General John B. Magruder, who erected earth redoubts at the heads of several creeks on Goodwin Neck.

W-41   PATRICK NAPIER, COLONIAL SURGEON

Rte. 143, 0.23 miles east of Rte. 132, near Camp Perry. Nearby lived "Patrick Napier of Queenes Creek in the County of Yorke chirurgeon," one of the earliest surgeons of Scottish descent in Virginia. Born about 1634, and apprenticed to the surgeon general of the Scottish army defeated by Cromwell in 1650, Patrick Napier arrived here before 1655. He married Elizabeth, a daughter of Robert Booth, clerk of the York County Court and a member of the House of Burgesses. By horse and boat, Napier attended the sick, performed surgery, bled his patients, and dispensed various remedies consistent with the practice of medicine in the mid-17th century. He died in 1669. He was the progenitor of most of the Napiers in America.

W-45   WHITAKER'S HOUSE

Rte. 60, southeast of Rte. 199. A mile north of the road is Whitaker's House, headquarters of General W. F. Smith, battle of Williamsburg, May 5, 1862.

W-46   VINEYARD TRACT

Secondary road off Rte. 641, 1.4 miles east of Williamsburg. One mile north of the highway, an experimental farm for the culture of grapes was established by the Virginia government in 1769. On this tract stood a hospital of the French-American army, 1781.

WASHINGTON-ROCHAMBEAU ROUTE

Rte. 1020 and Colonial Parkway, Yorktown. General Washington and the French troops under General Rochambeau began the siege of Great Britain's General Cornwallis at Yorktown on September 28, 1781. Cornwallis surrendered his army on October 19 after a siege of 21 days. *Note:* This is one of five unnumbered signs discussing aspects of the Washington-Rochambeau Route, which were a special gift from the French Government, Committee of the Bicentennial, to the Commonwealth of Virginia in 1976.

Southern Piedmont and Blue Ridge

THE SOUTHERN PIEDMONT and Blue Ridge region of this guidebook encompasses the counties of Amherst, Appomattox, Bedford, Brunswick, Buckingham, Campbell, Charlotte, Cumberland, Franklin, Greensville, Halifax, Henry, Lunenburg, Mecklenburg, Nelson, Nottoway, Pittsylvania, and·Prince Edward, the town of South Boston, and the cities of Bedford, Danville, Emporia, Lynchburg, and Martinsville.

By the early eighteenth century, Europeans slowly began to move into this area. Siouan-speaking tribes inhabited the region at the time of contact. A few historical markers provide a glimpse of the interaction various native groups had with these early European settlers. The state-recognized Monacan Indian Nation is still based in Amherst County.

Considerable European settlement in the region began in the 1740s. Roughly the eastern and central portions became tobacco-growing areas, while more varied farms dominated the western part.

In February 1781, General Nathanael Greene's forces successfully eluded British troops led by Lord Cornwallis and crossed the Dan River into Halifax County from North Carolina. The "Race to the Dan" shifted the British away from their main supply line in Charleston, South Carolina, and allowed American forces to regroup and gather reinforcements.

The Civil War also left its mark on the region. Several historical markers discuss the battle of Lynchburg and the various defenses that were built around the city. The Confederate army withstood a number of assaults during this June, 1864, engagement.

After four years of fighting, Confederate General Robert E. Lee and Union General Ulysses S. Grant met at Appomattox Court House on April 9, 1865, to arrange for the surrender of the Army of Northern Virginia, an event that led to the end of the war.

In the years following, parts of the region—especially around the hubs of Lynchburg, Danville, and Martinsville—experienced economic growth from industry based on tobacco, timber, and textiles. Today, changing economics have led to the loss of much of this industry.

A number of markers in the area showcase contributions that local individuals made to society. Signs in Lynchburg recognize Harlem Renaissance poet Anne Spencer (1882–1975) and Pearl S. Buck (1892–1973),

NELSON

AMHERST

BUCKINGHAM

CUMBERLAND

C Dillwyn

Lynchburg

Bedford

BEDFORD

CAMPBELL

APPOMATTOX

PRINCE
EDWARD

NOTTOWAY

FRANKLIN

CHARLOTTE

LUNENBURG

HENRY

PITTSYLVANIA

HALIFAX

South
Hill

BRUNSWICK

Emporia

Danville

South
Boston O

MECKLENBURG

GREENSVILLE

MILES

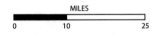

0   10   25

the internationally known author who wrote *The Good Earth*. A marker in Danville commemorates the career of Nancy Langhorne, Lady Astor (1879–1964), who was born there. She became internationally renowned for her advocacy for women's rights and served in the British House of Commons. Two markers are devoted to Dr. Carter G. Woodson (1875–1950), who was born in Buckingham County. Woodson became a noted teacher, educator, and historian and established the *Journal of Negro History* and Negro History Week, the forerunner of Black History Month.

Important events in the struggle for civil rights also occurred in this region. The Robert Russa Moton High School marker, in Farmville, commemorates the start of the April 23, 1951, strike by the students of this African American school to protest inadequate and unequal facilities. The result was the case of *Davis v. County School Board of Prince Edward County*, which was later combined with several others and ultimately addressed by the U.S. Supreme Court in *Brown v. Board of Education*. This landmark 1954 decision struck down the "separate but equal" doctrine governing public education.

AMHERST COUNTY

I-5 CENTRAL VIRGINIA TRAINING CENTER

Rte. 210, at center. Established in 1910 as the Virginia State Epileptic Colony, the center admitted its first patients in May 1911. The facility originally served persons with epilepsy and began accepting individuals with mental retardation in 1913. Due to the new national emphasis in the mid-1950s on mental retardation, a number of new training and developmental programs for individuals with mental retardation were developed here. The facility has undergone several name changes, and became known as the Central Virginia Training Center in 1983. The campus also contains a cemetery and a number of early twentieth-century Colonial Revival buildings.

K-148 BUFFALO LICK PLANTATION

Rte. 672, at end of road. Patented in 1742 by John Bolling, Jr., the 2,735-acre Buffalo Lick Plantation tract along the James River includes three notable historic sites. One mile southeast stand the ruins of Mount Athos, the home of William J. Lewis, an officer in the American Revolution and member of Congress (1817–1819). The house burned in 1876. The Southside Railroad constructed the Six Mile Bridge here six miles east of Lynchburg in 1854. Confederate Fort Riverview was built nearby during the Civil War to guard this strategic structure. Southern Maj. Gen. Lunsford L. Lomax ordered the bridge destroyed near the end of the war; it was rebuilt soon after.

R-4 LYNCHBURG DEFENSES

Rte. 210, at Main Street and Colony Road, north of Lynchburg. During the Civil War, a line of trenches and fortified artillery positions extending past here were built late in 1863 to defend Lynchburg against attack from the north. Brig. Gen. Francis T. Nicholls was responsible for ensuring that the local militia, invalids, and convales-cents properly manned the fortifications. On 12 June 1864, Nicholls ordered the local militia and invalids into these lines to repel a possible advance by Federal cavalry commanded by Brig. Gen. Alfred Duffié, but the Federals altered their course to Lexington. Soon after, the Confederates moved into defense works south of the city to face Maj. Gen. David Hunter's assault on 17–18 June 1864.

R-20 SWEET BRIAR COLLEGE CHARTERED 1901

Rte. 29, 2 miles south of Amherst. This Liberal Arts College for women, opened in 1906, granted its first Bachelor of Arts Degrees in 1910. Established under the will of Indiana Fletcher Williams as a memorial to her only daughter, Daisy, the College is located on a 2800-acre tract of land acquired by Elijah Fletcher before 1830. The eighteenth-century homestead, remodeled and named "Sweet Briar House" by the Fletchers, is set in a boxwood garden.

R-21 RUCKER'S CHAPEL

Rte. 29, at Rte. 661, north of Madison Heights. Nearby stood Rucker's Chapel, one of the first Anglican (present-day Episcopal) churches in Amherst County. Also known as Harris Creek Church and later as St. Matthew's, the church was founded by Col. Ambrose Rucker before 1751. It stood on part of a 5,850-acre tract his father, John Rucker, patented in 1745. The church served its congregation until 1847, when the members moved to Ascension Church, in Amherst. Logs from the chapel were later used to construct a corncrib at Sweet Briar College, two miles north.

R-22 JAMES RIVER BATTEAU

Rte. 29, at Rte. 661, north of Madison Heights. Near here lived Anthony and Benjamin Rucker, inventors of the James River batteau, which superseded the double dugout canoe and rolling road for transporting tobacco hogsheads. These long (about 50 or 60 feet), double-ended vessels dominated the commercial traffic on the James River and other Southern upland waterways between the 1770s and 1840s. A dispute arose in 1821 when the Rucker brothers' heirs sought to patent the design. A letter from Thomas Jefferson testifying to his presence at the first batteau's launch resolved the matter in the Ruckers's [Ruckers'] favor.

R-59 CONSTITUTION FOREST

Rte. 60, at the Amherst/Rockbridge County line. In 1938, in celebration of the 150th anniversary of the United States Constitution, the Virginia Daughters of the American Revolution sponsored the planting of Constitution Forest in this area. With the help of the Civilian Conservation Corps and the United States Forest Service, the memorial forest commemorates the Virginia framers of the Constitution. In 1987, the 45 acres of red and white pine seedlings have matured to a forest that provides protection for birds and other wildlife as well as for the watershed of the James River.

R-60 GRAVE OF PATRICK HENRY'S MOTHER

Rte. 151, just south of Clifford. In the grove of trees some hundreds of yards to the west is the grave of Sarah Winston (Henry), mother of Patrick Henry, who died in November, 1784.

R-61 ACTION AT TYE RIVER

Rte. 29, at Tye River, at Amherst/Nelson County line. On 11 June 1864, about 800 yards east, the Botetourt Battery prevented the destruction of the Orange and Alexandria Railroad bridge across the Tye River. This bridge was an important part of the Confederate railroad network for the movement of troops and supplies throughout Virginia. Confederate pickets of the Botetourt Battery, deployed as infantry and commanded by Capt. Henry C. Douthat, kept the Federal cavalry from destroying the bridge. This enabled Lt. Gen. Jubal A. Early and the 2d Corps of Lee's Army of Northern Virginia to reach Lynchburg by train, to prevent its capture by Union Maj. Gen. David Hunter.

APPOMATTOX COUNTY

K-152 CONCORD DEPOT

Rte. 460, at Campbell/Appomattox County line, Concord. The South Side Railroad provided service at Concord in 1854 when the track was completed from Petersburg to Lynchburg. During the Civil War, these rail lines were important for transporting troops and supplies. On 11 June, seven days before the Battle of Lynchburg, Union army forces were dispatched from Brig. Gen. William W. Averell's Second Cavalry Division to destroy rail and telegraph lines in the region. On 14 June the Federals burned the Concord Depot, a train, a portion of the track, and other railroad structures, and severed telegraph lines. They then marched towards Rustburg.

K-156 THE LAST FIGHT

Rte. 460, at Rte. 131, west of Appomattox corporate limits. Two miles north, at sunrise of April 9, 1865, Fitz Lee and Gordon, moving westward, attacked Sheridan's position. The attack was repulsed, but a part of the Confederate cavalry under Munford and Rosser broke through the Union line and escaped. This was the last action between the Army of Northern Virginia and the Army of the Potomac.

K-157 SURRENDER AT APPOMATTOX

Rte. 460, at Rte. 131, west of Appomattox corporate limits. At the McLean house at Appomattox, two miles north, took place the meeting between Lee and Grant to arrange terms for the surrender of the Army of Northern Virginia. This was at 1:30 P.M. on Sunday, April 9, 1865.

K-158 APPOMATTOX COURT HOUSE—NEW AND OLD

Rte. 131 (Main Street), at courthouse. This building, erected in 1892 when the county seat was moved to this location, should not be mistaken for the original, built in 1846 and destroyed by fire in 1892. Three miles northeast is Old Appomattox Court House and the McLean House where Lee surrendered to Grant on April 9, 1865, thus ending the War Between the States. The village of Old Appomattox Court House is now preserved as a national shrine by the Federal Government.

K-159 BATTLE OF APPOMATTOX STATION—1865

Rte. 131 (Main Street), at train station. Near this building stood the station of the South Side Railroad where, on April 8, 1865, three trains unloading supplies for the Army of Northern Virginia were captured by units of Sheridan's Union Cavalry under Gen. Geo. Custer. Significant for its relationship to the surrender by Gen. Robert E. Lee at Appomattox Court House, this action also marked the last strategic use of rail by Confederate forces.

M-65 ELDON

Rte. 24, northeast of Appomattox. Three miles north is Eldon, birthplace and home of Henry D. "Hal" Flood (2 Sept.1865–8 Dec.1921). A member of the Virginia House of Delegates (1887–1891) and Senate (1891–1900), Flood also served in the U.S. Congress from 1901 to 1921. He served from 4 March 1901 until his death as the chairman of the House Committee on Foreign Affairs. As chairman, in 1917, he wrote the resolution declaring that a state of war existed between the United States and the German and Austro-Hungarian Empires. This marked the entry of the U.S. into World War I. Flood died in Washington.

M-66 ELDON

Route 26, 0.1 miles west of Appomattox Bypass. Three miles north is Eldon, birthplace and home of Henry D. "Hal" Flood (1865–1921). A member of the United States House of Representatives (1901–1921), and Chairman of the Committee on Foreign Affairs (1913–1919), he drafted the Resolution declaring war on Germany and Austria, April 6, 1917.

M-67 CLAY SMOKING PIPES

Rte. 460, Pamplin. According to local tradition, residents of this region were making clay smoking pipes here by the mid-eighteenth century. By 1879 the Pamplin Pipe Factory was in operation. Machines there were used to mold clay into pipes, which were then allowed to dry. After drying, the pipes were fired in a kiln, cooled, and shipped in barrels throughout the world. By 1919 the clay pipe industry had peaked, but the factory supplied a national and international market well into the 1930s. The factory may have produced one million pipes a month at the height of its output. The factory closed by 1952.

M-68 POPULARIZER OF THE BANJO

Rte. 24, 3.2 miles east of Appomattox. Nearby is buried Joel Walker Sweeney (ca. 1810–1860), the musician who redesigned this African instrument into the modern five-string banjo that is known today. Although slaves apparently added the fifth string to what had been a four-string instrument, Sweeney popularized the new form on the minstrel circuit. He toured with his two brothers, Sam and Dick, in minstrel shows from 1831 until his death in 1860. During the Civil War, Sam Sweeney served as Maj. Gen. J. E. B. Stuart's personal banjo picker until Sweeney's death in the winter of 1863–1864.

MG-1 APPOMATTOX COURT HOUSE CONFEDERATE CEMETERY

Rte. 24, 0.2 miles east of Appomattox. Here were buried eighteen Confederate soldiers who died April 8 and 9, 1865 in the closing days of the War Between the States. The remains of one unknown Union soldier found some years after the war are interred beside the Confederate dead. About 500 yards east of this cemetery is the McLean House where Lee and Grant signed the surrender terms.

MG-2 THE LAST POSITIONS

Rte. 24, northeast of Appomattox, south of Vera. On 8 Apr. 1865, Gen. Robert E. Lee and his Army of Northern Virginia, retreating from Petersburg toward Pittsylvania County, reached the hills to the northeast. Gen. Ulysses S. Grant and his Federal army, pursuing Lee to the south, blocked him here. At dawn on 9 April, Palm Sunday, Maj. Gen. John B. Gordon's corps, with Maj. Gen. Fitzhugh Lee's cavalry, assaulted the Union line. Initially successful, the attempted breakout failed when additional Union infantry arrived on the field. That afternoon, Lee rode through the lines here to surrender his army.

MG-3 THOMAS S. BOCOCK

Rte. 24, Vera. Thomas S. Bocock, lawyer and politician, was born in present-day Appomattox Co. (then part of Buckingham Co.) on 18 May 1815. In 1846, he was elected to the U.S. House of Representatives and served there until 1861. In 1859, Bocock was nominated for Speaker of the House, but withdrew after eight weeks of debate and multiple ballots failed to elect a speaker. He served in the unicameral Provisional Confederate Congress (July 1861–Feb. 1862) and as the only Speaker of the Confederate House of Representatives (Feb. 1862–Mar. 1865). After the Civil War, Bocock resumed his law practice and remained active in politics. He died at his nearby home, Wildway, on 5 Aug. 1891 and was buried in the family cemetery there.

CITY OF BEDFORD

K-132 HOME OF JOHN GOODE

Rte. 221, 0.5 miles north of Rte. 43. Here is the home of John Goode, political leader, born 1829, died, 1909. Goode was a member of the secession convention of 1861; of the Confederate Congress and of the United States Congress; Solicitor General of the United States; president of the Virginia constitutional convention of 1901.

K-133 RANDOLPH-MACON ACADEMY— LIBERTY ACADEMY

College Street, near Rte. 43. Randolph-Macon Academy, a Methodist preparatory school for boys, occupied a building on this site from 1890 until 1934 when the school was consolidated with the Randolph-Macon Academy at Front Royal. In 1936, the property was purchased by Bedford County. Liberty Academy, a public and consolidated elementary school, occupied the building until 1964. The large and imposing Romanesque-style structure designed by W. M. Poindexter of Washington, D.C., was later demolished.

K-134 BEDFORD

Business Rte. 460, at courthouse. This place became the county seat of Bedford when it was moved from New London in 1782. First called Liberty (incorporated in 1839), the town changed its name to Bedford City in 1890 and to Bedford in 1912. A third courthouse, built in 1834, was replaced by the present building in 1930. The Union General Hunter, with his army, passed here in June, 1864, on his way to Lynchburg, and repassed on his retreat.

K-136 PEAKS OF OTTER ROAD

Rte. 221, at Rte. 43. This road was followed by General Hunter when he crossed the Blue Ridge at the Peaks of Otter and came to Bedford en route to Lynchburg, June 16, 1864.

BEDFORD COUNTY

K-121 COLONIAL FORT

Rte. 460, approximately 12 miles west of Bedford. Near here stood a fortified dwelling used for shelter during periods of warfare between European colonists and Native Americans. To this fort in 1756 came Mary Draper Ingles (Mrs. William Ingles) for protection following her escape from captivity by the Shawnee Indians. She was taken prisoner on 30 July 1755 following an attack on the Draper's Meadows settlement in Montgomery County near present-day Blacksburg. The story of her forced march to the Ohio Indian towns, her subsequent escape, and her long trek back home is part of the folklore of frontier Virginia. During the French and Indian War (1754–1763), many settlers abandoned this area and fled eastward.

K-130 HUNTER'S BIVOUAC

Rte. 460, approximately 5 miles west of Bedford. Near here General Hunter, on his retreat from Lynchburg, halted for the night of June 18, 1864. He resumed his retreat early in the morning of June 19.

K-131 LYNCHBURG AND SALEM TURNPIKE

Rte. 460, approximately 7.5 miles west of Bedford/Campbell County line. The Lynchburg and Salem Turnpike Co. was incorporated in 1818 to build a turnpike from Lynchburg west to Salem. The road reached Liberty (now Bedford) in 1828 and was completed to Salem in 1836. In Bedford County, covered bridges spanned the Big Otter and Little Otter rivers. The latter bridge remained until 1947. This turnpike, with five tollgates, served as the main thoroughfare in the region until the Virginia & Tennessee Railroad was built in the 1850s. In 1854, the company abandoned responsibility for the road between New London and Liberty and the county took control.

K-135 CALLAWAY-STEPTOE CEMETERY

Rte. 460, 0.2 miles west of Lynchburg city limits. Nearby are buried several prominent area settlers and their descendants. Col. William Callaway, in 1755 one of the first two members of the Virginia House of Burgesses from Bedford County, donated the hundred acres of land on which the town of New London was built. His son Col. James Callaway served as county lieutenant (commander in chief) of the Bedford County militia during the Revolutionary War. James Callaway's son-in-law James Steptoe was a close personal friend of Thomas Jefferson and served for 54 years as the first clerk of Bedford County. Steptoe's home, Federal Hill, stands nearby.

K-138 POPLAR FOREST

Rte. 221, approximately 3 miles west of Lynchburg. A mile and a half south is Poplar Forest, Thomas Jefferson's Bedford estate. He came here in June, 1781, after his term as governor expired, and while here was thrown from a horse and injured. During his recovery he wrote his "Notes on Virginia."

K-140 ST. STEPHEN'S CHURCH

Rte. 221, 5 miles west of Lynchburg. Half a mile north, is St. Stephen's Church, built about 1825 under Rev. Nicholas Cobb, later Bishop of Alabama. In the old cemetery here many members of early families of the community are buried.

K-141 NEW LONDON ACADEMY

Rte. 460, at academy. Chartered by the state in 1795, this is the oldest secondary school in Virginia in continuous operation under its own charter. Conducted for many years as a private school for boys, it began to receive public funds in 1884. It now operates as a public school.

KM-5 Quaker Baptist Church

Rte. 24, at Rte. 722, approximately 3 miles east of Rte. 122. A Quaker meeting was established on Goose Creek in 1757, and a meeting house built. Fear of Indians caused most of the Quakers to move elsewhere though some of them returned. Unsuc-cessful attempts were made to re-establish the Goose Creek meeting. Before 1824 a church was established near here, known as Difficult Creek Baptist Church. The present Church (Quaker Baptist), built in 1898, stands near the site of the old building.

BRUNSWICK COUNTY

S-57 Birch's Bridge

Rte. 1, south of Birch's Bridge, 2.8 miles south of McKenney, at Brunswick/Dinwiddie County line. At Birch's Bridge (very near this bridge) the second William Byrd and his party crossed the river, in September, 1733, on their way to inspect Byrd's land holdings in North Carolina. Byrd wrote an account of this trip which he called "A Journey to the Land of Eden." On his return [*should read:* On his way], he "laid the foundation" of Richmond and Petersburg.

S-58 Ebenezer Academy

Rte. 1, 6.8 miles north of Cochran. A few hundred yards east is the site of Ebenezer Academy, founded in 1793 by Bishop Asbury, the first Methodist school established in Virginia. It passed out of the hands of the church but remained a noted school for many years.

S-60 Sturgeon Creek

Rte. 1, 5.7 miles north of Cochran. A branch of the Nottoway, named for the huge fish once caught in it. William Byrd, returning from the expedition to survey the Virginia–North Carolina boundary line, camped on this stream in November, 1729.

S-65 Old Brunswick Courthouse

Rte. 1, Cochran. Here the first courthouse of Brunswick County was built about 1732. In 1746, when the county was divided, the county seat was moved east near Thomasburg. In 1783, after Greensville County had been formed, the courthouse was moved to Lawrenceville.

S-66 Fort Christanna

Rte. 1, Cochran. Nearby to the south stood Fort Christanna, a wooden structure built in 1714 under the auspices of Alexander Spotswood and the Virginia Indian Company. Members of the Meiponsky, Occaneechi, Saponi, Stuckenock, and Tutelo Indian tribes lived within the fort and built a nearby settlement. The fort included a frontier trading post and the English operated a school to educate and convert the Indians to Christianity there. The Virginia Indian Company was dissolved in 1717; funding for the garrison ceased the next year. By 1740 the Indian groups no longer lived at the fort but had migrated to other areas nearby in the region.

S-67 Brunswick County, Virginia— "The Original Home of Brunswick Stew"

Rte. 1, at Brunswick/Mecklenburg County line. According to local tradition, while Dr. Creed Haskins and several friends were on a hunting trip in Brunswick County in 1828, his camp cook, Jimmy Matthews, hunted squirrels for a stew. Matthews simmered the squirrels with butter, onions, stale bread, and seasoning, thus creating the dish known as Brunswick stew. Recipes for Brunswick stew have changed over time as chicken has replaced squirrel and vegetables have been added, but the stew remains thick and rich. Other states have made similar claims but Virginia's is the first.

S-68 Brunswick County, Virginia—"The Original Home of Brunswick Stew"

Rte. 1, at Rte. 712 and Brunswick/Dinwiddie County line. According to local tradition, while Dr. Creed Haskins and several friends were on a hunting trip in Brunswick County in 1828, his camp cook, Jimmy Matthews, hunted squirrels for a stew. Matthews simmered the squirrels with butter, onions, stale bread, and seasoning, thus creating the dish known as Brunswick stew. Recipes for Brunswick stew have changed over time as chicken has replaced squirrel and vegetables have been added, but the stew remains thick and rich. Other states have made similar claims but Virginia's is the first.

S-72 Meherrin Indians

Rte. 58, at Brunswick/Greenville County line. The Meherrin Indians lived in the coastal plain of Virginia and North Carolina along the Meherrin River. They farmed and hunted and spoke a language, Meherrin, that belonged to the Iroquoian language family. The Meherrin remained relatively undisturbed by the English settlements, until about 1650 when trading in furs increased their contact with settlers. By 1680 the Meherrin had become official tribute-paying subjects of the Virginia colony that temporarily gave them a protected land base around their villages. By the early 18th century members of the Meherrin had migrated along the Meherrin River to near the fork where it joins the Chowan River in North Carolina.

S-74 Staunton River Raid

Rte. 1, at Rte. 637, 7.3 miles south of Cochran. The Union General Wilson, returning to Grant's army from a raid to Staunton River, crossed the road near here, June, 1864.

SN-58 Brunswick County, Virginia—"The Original Home of Brunswick Stew"

Rte. 46, just north of state line. According to local tradition, while Dr. Creed Haskins and several friends were on a hunting trip in Brunswick County in 1828, his camp cook, Jimmy Matthews, hunted squirrels for a stew. Matthews simmered the squirrels with butter, onions, stale bread, and seasoning, thus creating the dish known as Brunswick stew. Recipes for Brunswick stew have changed over time as chicken has replaced squirrel and vegetables have been added, but the stew remains thick and rich. Other states have made similar claims but Virginia's is the first.

SN-59 Brunswick County, Virginia—"The Original Home of Brunswick Stew"

Rte. 46, south of bridge, at Brunswick/Nottoway County line. According to local tradition, while Dr. Creed Haskins and several friends were on a hunting trip in Brunswick County in 1828, his camp cook, Jimmy Matthews, hunted squirrels for a stew. Matthews simmered the squirrels with butter, onions, stale bread, and seasoning, thus creating the dish known as Brunswick stew. Recipes for Brunswick stew have changed over time as chicken has replaced squirrel and vegetables have been added, but the stew remains thick and rich. Other states have made similar claims but Virginia's is the first.

SN-60 Mason's Chapel

Rte. 46, 14.5 miles south of Rte. 58. Near here stood Mason's Chapel, one of the earliest Methodist churches in southern Virginia. The first Virginia conference, May, 1785, was held here or nearby; Bishop Asbury presided. The conference of 1801 was held here. The present Olive Branch church is four miles west.

SN-61 SMOKY ORDINARY

Rte. 712, 4.2 miles north of Rte. 58. The ordinary that stood on this site catered to travelers on the north-south stage road as early as 1750. During the American Revolution local warehouses were burned by British Colonel Tarleton, and legend says that it was from that occurrence that the ordinary derived its name. During the Civil War the post office (1832–1964) and inn were spared when a Union officer recognized the inn's owner, Dr. George M. Raney, as being a former classmate at the University of Pennsylvania.

SN-63 ST. PAUL'S COLLEGE

Rte. 46, at college, Lawrenceville. Saint Paul's College was established in 1883 by the Venerable James Solomon Russell (1857–1935) as an Episcopal mission school to serve the black community of Southside Virginia. Born into slavery in Mecklenburg County, Russell was educated at Hampton Institute and trained for the clergy at Bishop Payne Divinity School in Petersburg. His school was chartered in 1888 and incorporated as Saint Paul's Normal and Industrial School in 1890. Classes were held in the three-room Saul Building on the campus. The charter was amended in 1941, changing the school to a four-year, degree-granting college. Its name was changed to Saint Paul's College in 1957.

U-90 FORT CHRISTANNA

Rte. 46, 1 mile south of Rte. 58. Nearby to the south stood Fort Christanna, a wooden structure built in 1714 under the auspices of Alexander Spotswood and the Virginia Indian Company. Members of the Meiponsky, Occaneechi, Saponi, Stuckenock, and Tutelo Indian tribes lived within the fort and built a nearby settlement. The fort included a frontier trading post and the English operated a school to educate and convert the Indians to Christianity there. The Virginia Indian Company was dissolved in 1717; funding for the garrison ceased the next year. By 1740 the Indian groups no longer lived at the fort but had migrated to other areas nearby in the region.

U-91 BRUNSWICK COUNTY, VIRGINIA—"THE ORIGINAL HOME OF BRUNSWICK STEW"

Rte. 58, just west of Brunswick/Greensville County line. According to local tradition, while Dr. Creed Haskins and several friends were on a hunting trip in Brunswick County in 1828, his camp cook, Jimmy Matthews, hunted squirrels for a stew. Matthews simmered the squirrels with butter, onions, stale bread, and seasoning, thus creating the dish known as Brunswick stew. Recipes for Brunswick stew have changed over time as chicken has replaced squirrel and vegetables have been added, but the stew remains thick and rich. Other states have made similar claims but Virginia's is the first.

U-92 BRUNSWICK COUNTY, VIRGINIA—"THE ORIGINAL HOME OF BRUNSWICK STEW"

Rte. 58, at Rte. 659, east of Brodnax Fire Station. According to local tradition, while Dr. Creed Haskins and several friends were on a hunting trip in Brunswick County in 1828, his camp cook, Jimmy Matthews, hunted squirrels for a stew. Matthews simmered the squirrels with butter, onions, stale bread, and seasoning, thus creating the dish known as Brunswick stew. Recipes for Brunswick stew have changed over time as chicken has replaced squirrel and vegetables have been added, but the stew remains thick and rich. Other states have made similar claims but Virginia's is the first.

BUCKINGHAM COUNTY

F-53 CARTER G. WOODSON—1875–1950

Rte. 15, 10 miles north of Dillwyn. Three miles east is the birthplace of the noted teacher, educator and historian, Dr. Carter G. Woodson. He was the founder of the Association for the Study of Negro Life and History, Journal of Negro History, originated Negro History Week and authored more than a dozen important works dealing with his race in the United States.

F-54 FEMALE COLLEGIATE INSTITUTE

Rte. 15, at Rte. 617, 5 miles north of Dillwyn. Two miles east is the site of the first college for women in Virginia, the Female Collegiate Institute. Opened in 1837, it failed in 1843. Reopened in 1848, it survived until 1863. The school building has been destroyed but the "President's Cottage" still stands.

F-55 GOLD MINES

Rte. 15, Dillwyn. This was the most notable gold-mining region in the country before the California gold rush in 1849. The Morrow Mine here, opened before 1835, was one of the earliest gold mines in which underground mining was employed. Profitably worked for a number of years, it was finally closed. Many other unworked mines are near by.

F-56 OLD BUCKINGHAM CHURCH

Rte. 15, 0.75 miles southwest of Rte. 610, north of Dillwyn. The original or southwest wing was erected about 1758 as a church for the newly-formed Tillotson Parish. It was abandoned following the Disestablishment of the Anglican Church in Virginia in 1784, and thereafter wwas acquired by the Buckingham Baptist Congregation, organized in 1771. It continues in use as the meeting house of Buckingham Baptist Church.

F-57 CARTER G. WOODSON BIRTHPLACE

Rte. 15, at Rte. 670. Carter Godwin Woodson was born about three miles east on 19 December 1875. As a youth he mined coal near Huntington, W.Va. He earned degrees at Berea College (B.L., 1903), University of Chicago (B.A. and M.A., 1908), and Harvard (Ph.D., 1912)—one of the first blacks awarded a doctorate by Harvard. In 1915 he organized the Association for the Study of Negro Life and History and in 1916 established the *Journal of Negro History*. Known as the Father of Afro-American History, Woodson founded Negro History Week—now Afro-American History Month—in 1926. He died in Washington, D.C., on 3 April 1950.

F-59 MARCH TO APPOMATTOX

Rte. 15, 8.8 miles south of Sprouses Corner, Curdsville. Part of Lee's army passed here retreating westward, April 8, 1865. The Sixth (Wright's) Corps of Grant's army passed here, in pursuit, in the afternoon of the same day, moving on toward Appomattox.

F-60 EVE OF APPOMATTOX

Rte. 15, at Rte. 636, 11.3 miles south of Sprouses Corner, Sheppards. Part of Lee's army passed here, April 8, 1865, retreating westward. The Second (Humphrey's) Corps of Grant's army passed, in pursuit, in the afternoon of the same day. Grant spent the night here, receiving early in the morning of April 9 a note from Lee in regard to surrender. He sent a reply and then went on to Appomattox.

F-61 NEW STORE VILLAGE

Rte. 15, 11.3 miles south of Sprouses Corner, Sheppards. Four miles west is the site of New Store Village, in early times an important stop on the Stage Coach Road between Richmond and Lynchburg. Philip Watkins McKinney, Governor of Virginia

1890–1894, was born here in 1832. Peter Francisco, Revolutionary War hero, grew to maturity at nearby Hunting Towers, home of Judge Anthony Winston, an uncle of Patrick Henry.

F-62 BUCKINGHAM TRAINING SCHOOL

Rte. 15, at Rte. 20, Dillwyn. One mile southeast stood Buckingham Training School, the first high school in the county for African American students. In 1919 the Rev. Stephen J. Ellis organized the County-Wide League for School Improvement to persuade the Buckingham County School Board to build a secondary school for black students. When this effort failed, Ellis and his supporters raised $3,000 to match a grant from the Julius Rosenwald Fund, established in 1917 to build schools for black students in the rural South. The four-room high school opened in 1924 with Thomas L. Dabney as principal and served the community until it closed in 1953.

F-63 CIVILIAN CONSERVATION CORPS— CAMP P-56, COMPANY 1367

Rte. 15, south of Dillwyn. On this site in July 1933, CCC Camp P-56, Company 1367, opened with an enrollment of 192 Virginia men. The camp, which was organized as one of President Franklin Delano Roosevelt's New Deal employment programs, consisted of 52 small barracks, a large dining hall, two garages, and many other buildings. While at this camp, the men constructed 275 miles of forest roads, several bridges, three lookout towers, and numerous recreation buildings. The CCC also provided opportunities for the young men to further their education. In December 1937 "the camp" closed and all the buildings soon were demolished.

F-64 ARVONIA

Rte. 15, north of Dillwyn. The name Arvonia was derived from Caernarvon, Wales, home to the Welsh quarrymen who settled the area in the mid-19th century. Arvonia is known for the long-lasting and unfading blue-black Buckingham slate that adorns many of Virginia's historic buildings including Berkeley and the Executive Mansion, as well as Colonial Revival dwellings across the nation. Most Arvonia houses, and other buildings, are ornamented with slate; it is also used for tombstones in local cemeteries. Buckingham slate earned gold medals at the Philadelphia Exposition in 1876, the 1893 World's Columbia Exposition, and the Louisiana Purchase Exposition at the 1904 Saint Louis World's Fair.

O-38 MILLBROOK—HOME OF JOHN WAYLES EPPES

Rte. 15, 6.5 miles south of Rte. 60, south of Dillwyn. Approximately 2 miles east stood Millbrook (1811–1866), home of U.S. Senator John Wayles Eppes (1772–1823). He attended the University of Pennsylvania, was graduated from Hampden-Sydney College, and was admitted to the Bar in 1794. He married Maria, daughter of Thomas Jefferson, in 1797. His second wife was Martha Burke Jones. Eppes served in the Virginia House of Delegates and the Congress of the United States. It is believed that Jefferson advised Eppes on the design and landscaping of Millbrook. The house burned in 1866.

O-39 GEOGRAPHICAL CENTER OF VIRGINIA

Rtes. 60 and 24, Mount Rush. About two miles south and one-half mile west is the geographical center of the state. Latitude: 37° 30.6′ north Longitude: 78° 37.5′ west

O-42 AFTER APPOMATTOX

Rte. 60, 1.1 miles east of Buckingham, at Robert E. Lee wayside. Just to the south a monument marks the spot where the tent of Robert E. Lee stood the night of April 12–13, 1865.

CAMPBELL COUNTY

FR-16 Hat Creek Church

Rte. 40, 2.1 miles east of Brookneal. Four and a half miles north stands Hat Creek Presbyterian Church, founded by John Irvin and associates (first settlers) about 1742. William Irvin, son of John, and the noted blind preacher, James Waddel, were among its pastors. The first log building was replaced in 1788, and two other churches have been since built on the original site.

FR-25 Patrick Henry's Grave

Rte. 40, 2.5 miles east of Brookneal. Five miles southeast is Red Hill, the last home and burial place of Patrick Henry, governor of Virginia and the great orator of the American Revolution. Henry is especially famous for his "Liberty or Death" speech made in 1775 in Saint John's Church in Richmond. Henry purchased Red Hill in 1794 and died there on 6 June 1799. To the east of the reconstructed house site are the graves of Patrick Henry and his second wife, Dorothea Dandridge. Although the main house was destroyed by fire in 1919 and later reconstructed above the original foundation, Henry's law office survives and has been restored.

FR-27 Birthplace of General Pick

Rte. 40, Brookneal. Lt. Gen. Lewis Andrew Pick was born here on November 18, 1890. Educated at Rustburg and at VPI, (where he was a member of the Corps of Cadets), General Pick served in two world wars and in the Korean conflict. Best known as the builder of the 1,030-mile long Ledo Road, used to supply American and Chinese troops in the China-Burma-India Theatre during World War II, Pick also served as chief of the Army Corps of Engineers before his death in 1956.

K-139 New London

Rte. 858, 4 miles west of Lynchburg. [*Obverse*] At New London, Patrick Henry made one of his most famous speeches. John Hook, a Tory, brought suit for two steers impressed for the American army in 1781. Henry, the opposing counsel, so pictured the sufferings of the patriots in that critical year and their joy at Cornwallis's surrender, and so ridiculed Hook, that the case was laughed out of court. [*Reverse*] This place, on the old stage road, was the first county seat of Bedford; the first courthouse, built in 1755, was standing until 1856. In 1781, New London was raided by the British cavalryman, Tarleton, seeking military stores. It came into Campbell County in 1782. An arsenal here was afterward removed to Harper's Ferry.

K-149 Mount Athos

Rte. 460, 6 miles east of Lynchburg. Two miles north stand massive sandstone walls and four chimneys, the ruins of Mount Athos, overlooking a bend of the James River. The house was built about 1800 for William J. Lewis (1766–1828) on land that had been patented in 1742 by John Bolling and called Buffalo Lick Plantation. Lewis, who bought the land from Bolling's heirs in 1796, had commanded riflemen at Yorktown in 1781. He served in the Virginia House of Delegates (1810–1811; 1814–1817) and the U.S. Congress (1817–1819). Mount Athos stood one story high on a raised basement, with a portico on the north front and two octagonal projections on the south. It burned in 1876.

K-150 Oxford Furnace

Rte. 460, east of Lynchburg. Just south across Little Beaver Creek stand the ruins of the last of three Oxford Iron Works furnaces built in the vicinity. Virginia and Pennsylvania investors began the ironworks nearby between 1768 and 1772 as a small bloomery forge. According to local tradition, James Callaway built the first blast furnace a mile south before the Revolutionary War. David Ross, a Petersburg entrepreneur, bought the property and built the second furnace on another branch of the creek by late 1776. Thomas Jefferson praised Oxford iron for its high quality. William Ross, an heir of David Ross, and his partners operated the third furnace from about 1836 to 1875.

K-318 COL. VINCENT W. "SQUEEK" BURNETT

Rte. 24, 3.5 miles east of Rustburg. Born in Lynchburg in 1913, Col. Vincent W. "Squeek" Burnett learned to fly at age 16. By the mid-1930s, he was one of America's renowned aerobatic pilots and a member of the Flying Aces Air Circus. He performed such signature maneuvers as the Square Loop, Beer Bottle Loop, and Inverted Ribbon Cut. During World War II, Burnett served as technical advisor to Brig. Gen. James H. Doolittle and a demonstration pilot of the difficult to fly Martin B-26 Marauder bomber, nicknamed the "Widow-Maker." He successfully taught pilots to fly the B-26, which played an important role in America's World War II air effort. Burnett later retired to his nearby Lakemont farm and died in 1989.

L-12 SHADY GROVE

Rte. 501, near Rte. 652. Two miles east is Shady Grove, which was built in 1825 by Dr. George Cabell, of Point of Honor in Lynchburg, for his daughter Paulina and her husband Alexander Spotswood Henry, son of Patrick Henry. Shady Grove is a handsomely proportioned and detailed Federal farmhouse constructed on a raised basement. It contains highly sophisticated and academic architectural embellishments by country craftsmen. The interior features an elaborate carved mantel based on one at Point of Honor, Paulina Henry's childhood home. The family cemetery is across the road and contains the Henry family graves.

L-30 ORIGIN OF LYNCH LAW

Business Rte. 29, at northern entrance to Altavista. During the Revolutionary War, loyalists in the Virginia backcountry periodically conspired against the Revolutionary authorities. Colonels Charles Lynch, James Callaway, and other militia officers and county justices formed extralegal courts to punish them, which were "not strictly warranted by law." "Lynch's Law," or lynching, as such punishment has been called, did not at first include hanging. According to local tradition, accused loyalists were tied to a large black walnut tree here at Lynch's home, Green Level, and whipped, not hanged. In contrast with the lynchings that began the next century, legally appointed officials meted out "Lynch's law" mostly with fines and jail terms. Later, the Virginia General Assembly passed acts protecting Lynch and his associates from prosecution for their activities.

R-15 PATRICK HENRY'S GRAVE

Main Street, Brookneal. Five miles east is Red Hill, the last home and gravesite of Patrick Henry, the great orator of the Revolution. Henry is especially famous for his "Liberty or Death" speech made in 1775 in St. John's Church in Richmond. Henry moved to Red Hill in 1796 and died there on 6 June 1799. To the southeast of the house is a walled enclosure containing the graves of Patrick Henry and his second wife, Dorothea Dandridge. Although the main house was destroyed by fire in 1919 and later reconstructed above the original foundation, the law office, Henry's last, survives and has been restored.

R-62 OLD RUSTBURG

Rte. 24, just west of Rte. 838. Rustburg was named after Jeremiah Rust, who patented land here in 1780. Rust donated 50 acres of land, known as Rust Meadows, in 1784, for the county seat of Campbell County. A temporary courthouse and other public buildings were constructed starting in 1783 and a village grew around them. A new Classical Revival courthouse was built about 1848. In 1786, Henry Finch started an inn at his nearby home that evolved into the Fountain Hotel about 1795. It became a favorite stopping and meeting place that operated into the 20th century.

CHARLOTTE COUNTY

F-75 OLD BRIERY CHURCH

Rte. 15, 2.4 miles north of Keysville, at Charlotte/Prince Edward County line. Just to the north stands Briery Church, organized in 1755 following the missionary work of Presbyterian Minister Samuel Davies. The first church was built about 1760 and was replaced in 1824. The present Gothic Revival church was built about 1855 to designs of Robert Lewis Dabney.

F-77 EARLY EXPLORATION

Rte. 15, 0.2 miles north of Keysville. Batts, Fallam and Thomas Wood, sent by Abraham Wood to explore Western Virginia, passed near here, September, 1671.

F-78 CAMPAIGN OF 1781

Business Rte. 15, at south entrance to Keysville. Tarleton, British cavalryman, returning from his raid to Bedford, passed near here, July, 1781.

F-80 ROANOKE PLANTATION

Rte. 15, Wylliesburg. Nine miles west is Roanoke, home of John Randolph, a member of the House of Representatives for many years, and Senator. Randolph at first was Jefferson's lieutenant and later on an opponent and critic, but he never lost the love of his constituents. He died in Philadelphia, May 24, 1833, and was buried here; later his remains were removed to Richmond.

F-82 STAUNTON BRIDGE ACTION

Rte. 15, Wylliesburg. The railroad bridge over Staunton River, nine miles west, was held by a body of Confederate reserves and citizens from Halifax, Charlotte and Mecklenburg counties against Union cavalry raiding to destroy railroads, June 25, 1864. When the Unionists attempted to burn the bridge, they were repulsed. Meanwhile Confederate cavalry attacked from the rear. Thereupon the raiders retreated to Grant's army at Petersburg.

FR-3 RED HOUSE

Rte. 727, Red House. This old tavern was built by Martin Hancock about 1813 on the site of his earlier cabin. It was a noted stopping place and trade center on the old south road to the West.

FR-6 EDGEHILL

Rte. 40, 2 miles east of Charlotte Court House. Three miles north is Edgehill, home of Clement Carrington. He ran away from Hampden-Sydney College to join the Revolutionary army, served in Lee's Legion, 1780–81, and was wounded at Eutaw Springs, September 8, 1781.

FR-7 GREENFIELD

Rte. 40, 2 miles east of Charlotte Court House. Half a mile north is Greenfield, built in 1771 by Isaac Read. Read was a member of the House of Burgesses, 1769–1771, and of the Virginia conventions of 1774 and 1775. He served as an officer in the Revolutionary War, dying of wounds in 1777.

FR-8 JOSEPH MORTON

Rte. 15, north of Keysville, at Charlotte/Prince Edward County line. Seven miles west stood Roanoke Bridge, the colonial homestead of Joseph Morton, who patented land nearby in the 1740s. He was an elder of Briery Presbyterian Church on its founding in Prince Edward County in 1755, and later a trustee. He served as a justice from the formation of Charlotte County on 4 March 1765 until his death in 1784. In 1775, at the beginning of the American Revolution, he became a member of the county's committee of correspondence. About that time, he built Roanoke Bridge, a frame dwelling later called Hillandale. The house served as a post office from 1885 to 1904, and burned in the mid-20th century.

FR-9 CHARLOTTE COURT HOUSE HISTORIC DISTRICT

Rte. 40, at Rte. 47. The historic district, a rare example of a 19th-century rural courthouse town, is concentrated on two main streets. Begun as Dalstonburg in 1755 during the French and Indian War, and later called Marysville and Smithville, the town was named Charlotte Court House in 1901. The court square contains an 1823 courthouse designed by Thomas Jefferson, an 1830 records office, a 1900 clerk's office, and a 1936 jail. The district also includes antebellum houses, commercial buildings, churches, and a brick tavern. Ambassador David K. E. Bruce donated the library, library garden, and other county office buildings in the 1930s.

FR-10 HENRY AND RANDOLPH'S DEBATE

Rte. 40, Charlotte Court House. Here, in March, 1799, took place the noted debate between Patrick Henry and John Randolph of Roanoke on the question of States' Rights. Henry denied the right of a state to oppose oppressive Federal laws. Randolph affirmed that right. This was Henry's last speech and Randolph's first. Henry died three months later.

FR-12 CAMPAIGN OF 1781

Rte. 40, Charlotte Court House. At Cole's Ferry on Staunton River, twelve miles southwest, Steuben halted his southward march, June 10, 1781.

FR-14 CUB CREEK CHURCH

Rte. 40, 2 miles east of Phenix. Six miles south is Cub Creek Presbyterian Church, the oldest church in this section. The neighborhood was known as the Caldwell Settlement for John Caldwell, grandfather of John C. Calhoun of South Carolina. About 1738 he brought here a colony of Scotch-Irish and obtained permission to establish a church.

FR-15 ROUGH CREEK CHURCH

Rte. 727, north of Phenix. A chapel was built here in 1765–1769 by order of the vestry of Cornwall Parrish. Following the disestablishment and a brief period of irregular use, the property passed to the Republican Methodists, a denomination then active in the South. It was received under the care of Hanover Presbytery in 1822, and the present building was erected in 1838 on the original site. Rough Creek is the mother church of Madisonville, Oak View, and Phenix Presbyterian churches organized 1907–1914.

M-9 PAUL CARRINGTON

Rte. 15 at Rte. 607, Wylliesburg. Member of House of Burgesses, 1765–1775, of Virginia conventions, 1774–1788, including Constitutional Conventions, of first Supreme Court of Appeals of Virginia. A founder of Hampden-Sydney College. Lived and is buried at Mulberry Hill nearby.

CUMBERLAND COUNTY

JE-35 LEE'S STOPPING PLACE

Rte. 690, at Rte. 612, 8.8 miles south of Columbia. Here at Flannagan's (Trice's) Mill, Robert E. Lee spent the night of April 13–14, 1865, on his journey from Appomattox to Richmond.

JE-36 CLIFTON

Rte. 690, at Rte. 605, 11 miles south of Columbia. One mile north; home of Carter Henry Harrison, land patented, 1723. Harrison, as a member of the Cumberland Committee of Safety, wrote the instructions for independence (adopted April 22) presented by the county delegates to the Virginia convention of May, 1776. Apparently this was the first of such declarations publicly approved. The convention declared for independence.

MJ-2 NEEDHAM LAW SCHOOL

Rte. 45, at Farmville corporate limits. Just east of here is Needham, location of Virginia's first proprietary law school and home of founder Judge Creed Taylor (1766–1836), politician, jurist, and legal educator. Taylor's law school at Needham, which opened in 1821 and closed by 1840, was Virginia's second law school and among the earliest in the United States. He trained more than 300 men for the law, including President John Tyler, Jr., several congressmen, and other prominent officials. Taylor was one of the first to use the moot court as a primary system of instruction. He is buried south of Needham in an unmarked grave.

O-44 CAMPAIGN OF 1781

Rte. 60, at Rte. 45, 1.8 miles west of Cumberland. Steuben, both on his retreat from Simcoe and on his return north to join Lafayette, passed near here, June, 1781.

O-49 CUMBERLAND COUNTY COURT HOUSE

Rte. 60, Cumberland. In 1749 the Virginia House of Burgesses divided Goochland County to establish Cumberland County. William A. Howard, an associate of Thomas Jefferson's master builder, Dabney Cosby, built the present Cumberland County courthouse (1818–1821). The unusual temple-form, Jeffersonian-Classical building has a finely executed Tuscan portico on the long side instead of the end and stands only one story high. Howard also designed the diminutive brick clerk's office to the east that was completed in 1821. Today, the two buildings stand near the center of the village with a jail (ca. 1823), a 19th-century well, and a 1901 Civil War monument.

O-52 ENGAGEMENT AT CUMBERLAND PRESBYTERIAN CHURCH, 7 APRIL 1865

Rte. 45, approximately 2 miles north of Farmville. After successfully crossing the Appomattox River at nearby High Bridge, Maj. Gen. Andrew A. Humphreys' II Corps attacked Confederate forces under Maj. Gen. William Mahone that were entrenched on the high ground around Cumberland Presbyterian Church. Protecting Lee's flank and wagons, Mahone held off two Union assaults until darkness allowed him to withdraw from the battlefield. Near the church, Mahone's headquarters, Lee received the first message from Grant suggesting the surrender of the Army of Northern Virginia. The army continued its march west, finally surrendering on 9 April at Appomattox Court House.

O-55 JAMES F. LIPSCOMB

Rte. 45, approximately 3 miles north of Farmville. James F. Lipscomb was born a free black on 4 December 1830 in Cumberland County. He worked first as a farm laborer, then as a carriage driver in Richmond. In 1867 he returned to Cumberland County, where he accumulated more than 500 acres of land. Lipscomb served in the House of Delegates between 1869 and 1877, one of 87 African-Americans elected to the General Assembly in the late 19th century. In 1871 he opened a general store in his home, part of which stands nearby, and operated it until his death on 10 August 1893. His grandson and granddaughter-in-law, John and Romaine Lipscomb, moved it into a new building on this site in 1921. The Lipscomb store, a community institution and social center, was closed in 1971 and demolished in 1987.

O-57 CIVILIAN CONSERVATION CORPS COMPANY 2354

Marker missing. Original location: Rte. 60, at Rte. 13. On the north side of this road, Civilian Conservation Corps Company 2354 built and occupied Camp P-89 from Aug. 1935 until about 5 Dec. 1941. During its years of operation, unemployed youths found useful work here. They cut fire trails, made passable roads, built a fire tower, and planted trees. They also built two pavilions in present-day Bear Creek Lake State Park and reforested abandoned farmland in what became Cumberland State Forest, illustrating soil conservation techniques. During World War II, the Signal Corps trained here, and in 1945 the camp held German prisoners of war.

ON-5 CAMPAIGN OF 1781

Rte. 45, Cartersville. Early in June 1781, Maj. Gen. Friedrich Wilhelm von Steuben saved some military stores at Point of Fork from

British troops and then retreated south to Staunton River before being called to join Lafayette's forces. On 16 June Steuben crossed to the north bank of the James River at Carter's Ferry, and joined Lafayette in Hanover County three days later. Lafayette and the colonial forces continued to follow the British as they moved east, but Steuben soon took leave of the army because of illness.

ON-7 CAMPAIGN OF 1781

Rte. 45, 1.8 miles south of Cartersville. Two miles north, near the mouth of Willis River, Steuben camped, June 5–6, 1781, when driven from Point of Fork by Simcoe.

CITY OF DANVILLE

L-53 SAPONI RELIGIOUS BELIEFS EXPLAINED

Rte. 29, at state line. On 12–15 October 1728, Col. William Byrd II and his party camped just west of here while surveying the Virginia–North Carolina boundary. Bearskin, Byrd's Saponi guide, described his tribe's religious beliefs, which, wrote Byrd in his diary, contained "the three Great Articles of Natural Religion: the Belief of a God; the Moral Distinction betwixt Good and Evil; and the Expectation of Rewards and Punishments in another World." Bearskin's religion also included a Hindu-like belief in reincarnation.

Q-5-a LAST CONFEDERATE CAPITOL

Main Street, between Sutherlin and Holbrook Avenues. This, the former home of Major W. T. Sutherlin, is regarded as the last capitol of the Confederacy, April 3–10, 1865. Here President Davis stayed and here was held the last full cabinet meeting, Breckinridge alone being absent. The establishment of the Confederate government in Danville ended when the news of Lee's surrender arrived on April 10.

Q-5-b WRECK OF THE OLD 97

Rte. 58, between Pickett and Farrar Streets. Here, on September 27, 1903, occurred the railroad wreck that inspired the popular ballad, "The Wreck of the Old 97." The southbound mail express train on the Southern Railroad left the tracks on a trestle and plunged into the ravine below. Nine persons were killed and seven injured, one of the worst train wrecks in Virginia history.

Q-5-c THE GIBSON GIRL/LADY ASTOR

Main and Broad Streets.
[*Obverse*] Lady Astor
Here stood the residence in which Nancy Langhorne, Viscountess Astor, 1879–1964, was born. Lady Astor, noted for her wit, advocacy of Women's Rights, strong views on temperance, and articulate affection for her native state, was the first woman to sit, 1919–1945, in the British House of Commons.
[*Reverse*] The Gibson Girl
Here stood the residence in which Irene Langhorne Gibson, 1873–1956 was born. Her beauty, charm, and vivacity captivated the artist Charles Dana Gibson who, following their marriage in 1895, cast his

celebrated, style-setting "Gibson Girl" illustrations in her image.

Q-5-c LOYAL BAPTIST CHURCH

400 block, Loyal Street. The Loyal Street Baptist Church congregation, which was organized between 1865 and 1866 on Old Hospital–Dance Hill by former slaves, built its church here in 1870. Worship continued at this site until 1924 when the congregation moved to Holbrook Street. The name was then changed to Loyal Baptist Church.

Q-5-d DANVILLE SYSTEM

Patton Street. On this site stood Neal's Warehouse where the "Danville System" of selling tobacco began in 1858. Previously tobacco had been sold by sample from hogsheads, but under the new system it was sold at auction in open, loose piles so buyers could examine the whole lot. It is in general use today.

Q-5-e STRATFORD COLLEGE

1125 West Main Street. Stratford College (1930–1974) and its constituent preparatory school, Stratford Hall (1930–1954), maintained the tradition of liberal arts education for women begun in 1854 at the Danville Female College. Main hall was built in 1883 to house the Danville College for Young Ladies (1883–1897) and is a landmark also of its successors, Randolph-Macon Institute (1897–1930) and Stratford.

Q-5-f CALVARY UNITED METHODIST CHURCH

Marker no longer erected; church no longer exists. Original location: 293 Main Street. An outgrowth of the mother church on Lynn Street in Danville, the North Danville Methodist Episcopal Church, South, was founded by 47 devoted members at the corner of Church and Keen Streets on November 14, 1879. This was the first organized religious group in North Danville. On November 14, 1887, a new sanctuary on this site was dedicated and known as Calvary Methodist Episcopal Church, South. In 1968 the name was changed to Calvary United Methodist Church.

Q-5-g FREDERICK DELIUS— (1862–1934)

North Main Street, at Keen Street. One block west on Church Street is the site of the Henry P. Richardson house where Frederick Delius lived while teaching music at Roanoke Female College, now Averett. An unsuccessful orange grower in Florida, the Britisher Delius worked in Danville in 1885–1886 to earn return passage to Europe where he pursued a musical career, becoming an internationally acclaimed composer.

Q-5-h CONFEDERATE PRISON NO. 6

Loyal Street, at Lynn Street. Constructed in 1855 as a tobacco factory by Major William T. Sutherlin, this renovated structure housed Union prisoners during the Civil War, 1861–1865. It was one of six Danville Confederate prisons in which as many as 7000 Union soldiers were confined.

Q-5-k SCHOOLFIELD

West Main Street, at Baltimore Avenue. Schoolfield, established in 1903 as a textile mill village, was named for three brothers who founded Riverside Cotton Mills, later Dan River Mills. By the 1920s, this company town—complete with a school, churches, stores, a theatre, and other recreational facilities—was home to over 4,500 residents, mostly mill employees and their families, living in some 800 rental houses. A strike in 1930–31 ended a decade of employer/employee cooperation known as "Industrial Democracy," yet the community's tradition of neighborhood and family life continued to flourish. Danville annexed Schoolfield in 1951.

Q-7-d HOLBROOK-ROSS HISTORIC DISTRICT

Holbrook and Ross Streets, near 900 block, Main Street. The Holbrook-Ross Historic District, named for two major streets, is significant as the first neighborhood in Danville for African American professionals. Lawyers, ministers, dentists and physicians, as well as, business owners, insurance agents, postal clerks, and skilled craftsmen, made it their home in the late 19th century. It grew rapidly during the 1880s following the construction of the Danville School, the city's public school for blacks. By the turn of the 20th century, Holbrook Street had become Danville's foremost black residential address. The district is listed on the National Register of Historic Places and the Virginia Landmarks Register.

Q-7-e 750 MAIN STREET—DANVILLE

750 Main Street. On this site stood the residence of James E. Schoolfield. In the parlor of his house were held the meetings to organize both Dan River, Inc. on July 20, 1882 and the Young Women's Christian Association of Danville on December 19, 1904.

U-39 DIX'S FERRY

Rte. 58 East, near Danville Airport. In 1766 John Dix established his ferry approximately three miles south of here on the Dan River. During the American Revolution, in February 1781, the ferry was a strategic site in Gen. Nathanael Greene's "race to the Dan," the pursuit of Greene to the Dan River in Virginia by British Gen. Charles Cornwallis. The ferry also transported troops and supplies for Greene's

Tobacco was an important cash crop in Southside Virginia. Here, tobacco farmers and buyers review a warehouse full of carefully sorted and displayed leaves. (Marker Q-5-d) (The Library of Virginia)

army in his actions against the Cornwallis [*should read:* actions against Cornwallis] at the Battle of Guilford Courthouse. In 1791

President George Washington crossed the Dan River on the ferry as he returned from his 1,887-mile southern tour.

CITY OF EMPORIA

UM-38 GRAVE OF GEN. JOHN R. CHAMBLISS, JR.

Rte. 301 (South Main Street), just south of Brunswick Avenue. Brig. Gen. John Randolph Chambliss, Jr., C.S.A., is buried just west of here. Born in Hicksford (present-day Emporia) on 23 January 1833, Chambliss graduated from the U.S. Military Academy at West Point in 1853. During the Civil War, he commanded the 41st Virginia Infantry Regiment in the Seven Days' campaign. He next led the 13th Virginia Cavalry and served under J. E. B. Stuart. Chambliss was killed in an engagement on the Charles City Road east of Richmond on 16 August 1864. His former West Point schoolmate, Union Brig. Gen. David M. Gregg, took charge of the body and sent it home.

UM-39 BENJAMIN D. TILLAR, JR.

Rte. 301 (Main Street), at Battery Street. Benjamin Donaldson Tillar, Jr. (1853–1887), a Greensville County native, president of the Atlantic and Danville Railroad, and member of the House of Delegates, is known as "the man who named Emporia." Two villages, Hicksford and Belfield, merged in 1887 to form the town. Tillar named the town after Emporia, Kansas, the hometown of his friend, United States Senator Preston B. Plumb. Emporia comes from the Latin word meaning a place of plenty where business is transacted. The town became a city in 1967.

UM-42 VILLAGE VIEW

Rte. 301 (Main Street), at Jefferson Street. Village View, a stately Federal-style mansion, was built about 1795 by James Wall and remodeled in 1823 by Nathaniel Land. It is notable for its elaborate scrollwork in the fanlight and sidelights around the front door, ornately carved mantels, decorative interior moldings, and massive hewn beams. During Civil War engagements at Hicksford, 7–12 December 1864, Confederate major generals W. H. F. "Rooney" Lee and Wade Hampton, attended by Village View owner Capt. William H. Briggs, met at the house. After the war, Briggs conducted the Briggs Academy, a private school for boys, in a small dwelling on the east lawn. Village View is listed in the Virginia Landmarks Register and the National Register of Historic Places.

UM-43 BISHOP WILLIAM MCKENDREE

500 block, South Main Street (Rte. 301), at Greensville Avenue. William McKendree was born in King William County in 1757. He soon moved with his family to present-day Greensville County, and later served in the Revolutionary War. In 1786, the county licensed him to keep a tavern at his house (12 miles south). The next year, transformed by the Second Great Awakening, McKendree entered the Methodist ministry as a circuit rider. In 1790, Francis Asbury ordained him Deacon. McKendree became presiding elder in the Western Conference extending from western Virginia to Illinois in 1800. In 1808, he became the first native-born American elected Bishop of the Methodist Episcopal (now United Methodist) Church. He died on 5 March 1835.

UM-44 EMPORIA RAILROAD HISTORY

Halifax and Baker Streets. The Petersburg Railroad was constructed in the early 1830s between Petersburg, Virginia, and Weldon, North Carolina, through the towns of Belfield and Hicksford (present-day Emporia). It is considered the first railroad in the South built in a north–south direction. During the Civil War, the railroad carried food and equipment to Gen. Robert E. Lee's Army of Northern Virginia. A skirmish on 8 December 1864 destroyed the tracks here and temporarily disrupted Lee's supply route. The Atlantic Coast Line Railroad bought the Petersburg Railroad in 1893. In 1967 it was renamed the Seaboard Coast Line and in 1985 the CSX Railroad.

UM-45 GORDON LINWOOD VINCENT (1867–1926)

Rte. 301 (Main Street), at Main Street Baptist Church. Here lived Gordon L. Vincent, who represented Greensville and Sussex counties in the 1901–1902 Virginia Constitutional Convention. A successful and respected business leader, Vincent headed the Emporia Manufacturing Company, then one of the largest lumber companies in Southside Virginia. He also was president of the Emporia Machine Company, the Emporia Ice Company, and the Emporia Cotton Seed Oil Company, and vice president of the Citizens National Bank. He served as a member of the Greensville County School Board and the Emporia Town Council. His death on 18 July 1926 ended a notable business career.

UM-46 HICKSFORD RAID

Rte. 301 (Main Street), at Meherrin River Park. On 7 Dec. 1864, Union Maj. Gen. Gouverneur K. Warren led 28,000 men south from Petersburg to destroy the Petersburg Railroad between Stony Creek and the Meherrin River railroad bridge at Hicksford, thereby severing the Confederate supply line. Two days later, here at Hicksford, a Confederate force under Maj. Gen. Wade Hampton and Maj. Gen. W. H. Fitzhugh Lee confronted him. To avert the capture of the railroad bridge, Hampton and Lee ordered it burned, but Union gunfire drove off the firing party. On 10 Dec., Warren withdrew and the Confederates quickly repaired 17 miles of the railroad.

UM-47 EARLY MASONIC LODGES

Rte. 301 (South Main Street), at Masonic Temple. Hicksford Lodge No. 37, the first in Greensville County, was chartered in 1793. It became dormant by 1829, but several former members, with new recruits from Southampton County, formed Widow's Son Lodge No. 150, Ancient Free and Accepted Masons of the Grand Lodge of Virginia. The new lodge first met on 7 June 1829 (Anno Lucie 5829) at the home of William Fennell near Haley's Bridge in southeastern Greensville County. The lodge moved to the courthouse in Hicksford in 1840, then in 1905 to this Classical Revival–style temple. The following year, the Royal Arch Chapter was formed and met here as well.

UM-48 JOHN DAY

Rte. 301 (Main Street), between municipal building and post office. John Day, a free African American cabinetmaker and brother of Thomas Day, cabinetmaker and builder, was born in Hicksford (present-day Emporia) on 18 Feb. 1797. Licensed in 1821 as a Baptist minister, he sailed in December 1830 to Liberia, where in 1853 he became pastor of Providence Church in Monrovia, the capital. In 1854 he established Day's Hope High School. He was a delegate to Liberia's constitutional convention, a signer of its constitution and its Declaration of Independence in 1847, and the second chief justice of its supreme court. Day died in Monrovia on 15 Feb. 1859.

UM-49 ROBERT HICKS

Rte. 301 (South Main Street), municipal building and courthouse. Robert Hicks was born about 1658. By the 1690s he lived at Fort Henry near Petersburg and led traders to the Indians on the southern frontier. About 1709 he moved here to the future site of Hicksford (present-day Emporia) and became captain of the Surry County Rangers, a frontier militia unit. He commanded Fort Christanna from about 1714 to 1718. In 1722 he helped Virginia Lt. Gov.

Alexander Spotswood conclude a peace treaty with the Iroquois in Albany, New York. He briefly joined William Byrd II and his crew surveying the Virginia–North Carolina boundary line in 1728. Hicks died nearby before 7 Feb. 1739/40.

UM-50 CHAPLAIN THOMAS M. BULLA

Spring and Main Streets. Thomas McNeill Bulla was born in North Carolina on 4 Jan. 1881. Ordained a Presbyterian minister, he was called here to the First Presbyterian Church of Emporia in 1911. In April 1917, he became chaplain of the 116th Infantry Regiment, 29th Infantry Division, and in June 1918 sailed to France. There he joined the troops in the trenches, often venturing into no-man's-land to rescue wounded soldiers. On 15 Oct. 1918, during the Battle of the Meuse, he was himself wounded. He died two days later, the only chaplain of a Virginia regiment to lose his life in the war.

UM-51 BUTTS TAVERN

Intersection of Virginia Avenue and North Main Street (Rte. 301). According to local tradition, the first court meeting for newly formed Greensville County occurred in Butts Tavern two blocks east on 22 Feb. 1781. Built about 1770 at the intersection of Fort Christianna and Halifax Roads for William Edwards, the tavern was named for John Butts, who owned it early in the 19th century. By midcentury, the tavern was either remodeled or enlarged to become a Greek Revival–style frame dwelling. After the Civil War, Sallie W. Reese operated the Belfield Seminary for Young Ladies and Children there between 1877 and 1891. While undergoing restoration, the building was damaged by fire on 10 Feb. 1965. The ruins were demolished in 1968.

UM-53 GENERAL EDWARD E. GOODWYN

Rte. 301, across from Church Street. Edward Everard Goodwyn was born in Greensville Co. on 26 Sept. 1874. An Emporia businessman and civic leader, he also commanded the Virginia American Legion (1922–1923) and was a member of its National Executive Committee (1923–1925). Goodwyn served in the Fourth Virginia Regiment of the Virginia Volunteers reaching the rank of colonel. During World War I, he was stationed in France. In 1940, Gov. James H. Price appointed him brigadier general of the Virginia Protective Force, a post he held throughout World War II. He was a member of the Senate of Virginia from 1946 to 1947. Goodwyn died on 29 April 1961 and is buried northwest of here.

FRANKLIN COUNTY

A-60 ROCKY MOUNT

Business Rte. 220, at courthouse, Rocky Mount. This place was established as the county seat when Franklin County was formed. The first court was held in March, 1786. The first (log) courthouse was replaced in 1831. In 1836 the town consisted of 30 dwellings and a number of business houses. General Jubal A. Early practiced law here. The town was incorporated in 1873. The present courthouse was built in 1909.

A-93 FORT BLACKWATER

Rte. 220, north of Rocky Mount, at Blackwater River Wayside. Near here stood a stockade erected by Capt. Nathaniel Terry and garrisoned by men under his command. Washington made "Terry's Fort" a link in his chain of forts and inspected it in the fall of 1756.

A-95 BIRTHPLACE OF GENERAL JUBAL EARLY

Rte. 116, 5.2 miles west of Rte. 122. Near this place, on land occupied since the 1780s by the Early family, Confederate General Jubal

Early was born in 1816. The General practiced law in Franklin County and served in the Mexican War before the Civil War. Early fought in more battles than any other Confederate general and came closest to capturing Washington. Because of his undying devotion to the southern cause, he became known as "The Unreconstructed Rebel."

A-96 CAROLINA ROAD

Rte. 220, 0.7 miles south of Franklin/Roanoke County line. Here through the Maggoty Gap, the Great Wagon Road from Philadelphia to Georgia, known locally as the Carolina Road, passes through the Blue Ridge. Originating as the Great Warrior Path of the Iroquois centuries before, the path was frequently used by the Iroquois before being ceded to the whites in 1744 to become one of the most heavily traveled roads in all Colonial America.

A-97 WASHINGTON IRON WORKS

Business Rte. 220, 0.5 miles south of courthouse, Rocky Mount. Here stands the furnace and ironmaster's house of the Washington Iron Works, Franklin County's first industry. Originally established in 1773 by Col. John Donelson, father-in-law of President Andrew Jackson, the iron plantation was acquired in 1779 by Col. James Callaway and Jeremiah Early and expanded to 18,000 acres to become one of the last great iron plantations in Virginia. The

Saunders family continued the operation until 1850, supplying iron locally and as far south as Georgia.

A-98 TAYLOR'S STORE

Rte. 122, 1.6 miles north of Rte. 116. Here stood Taylor's Store, established in 1799 by Skelton Taylor, a lieutenant in the Bedford County militia during the Revolutionary War. After Franklin County was formed, he became a militia captain and overseer of the poor. His store and ordinary served travelers along the nearby Warwick Road, which linked the Southside Piedmont counties with Richmond. The store became the hub of a community known as Taylor's Store and functioned as a post office between 1818 and 1933. It was dismantled ca. 1970.

KP-14 BOOKER T. WASHINGTON BIRTHPLACE

Rte. 122, just north of Hales Ford Church. Booker T. Washington was born a slave on the nearby Burroughs plantation on April 5, 1856. He was graduated from Hampton Institute in 1875 where he became an instructor. Because of his achievements as an educator, he was selected to establish a normal school for blacks in Alabama which later became the Tuskegee Institute. Recognized as an orator and author of *Up From Slavery,* he exerted great influence both in the Republican party and as a humanitarian for the benefit of his fellow blacks. He died November 14, 1915.

GREENSVILLE COUNTY

UM-40 TARLETON'S MOVEMENTS

Rte. 301, Emporia. At this point Tarleton, the British cavalryman, crossed the Meherrin River, May 14, 1781. Sent ahead of Cornwallis's army, he had raided through Southampton and Greensville counties.

UM-41 SITE OF HOMESTEAD

Rte. 58, 0.125 miles east of Chapman's Ford Road. Near here stood Homestead, the

plantation of James Mason (1744–1784), a captain in the 15th Virginia Regiment from 1776 to 1778 and a colonel in the Brunswick County militia during the Revolutionary War. It was also the home of his son Edmunds Mason (1770–1849), member of the Virginia General Assembly (1802–1805) and county clerk (1807–1834), and birthplace of his grandchildren John Y. Mason (1799–1859), member of

Congress (1831–1837) and U.S. attorney general (1845–1846), and Dr. George Mason (1809–1895). Before the Civil War, Dr. Mason and his mother-in-law, Mary A. Jones, operated a school at Homestead that had opened at nearby West View about 1840.

UM-52 Mabry's Chapel

Rte. 58, near Rte. 607 (Westward Road). Eight miles northeast stood Mabry's Chapel, the fourth Methodist house of worship built in Virginia. It was constructed in 1780, five years after the congregation first met at John Mabry's dwelling. By 1804, a new, larger church was built; it included a balcony for black worshipers. Bishop Francis Asbury, Thomas Rankin, and Devereux Jarratt preached here in 1775. Two sessions of the Virginia Annual Conference, the 11th in Nov. 1794 and the 13th in Nov. 1796, met at Mabry's Chapel with Asbury presiding. The congregation relocated to a church on Allen's Road in 1847.

HALIFAX COUNTY

R-77 History of Halifax

Rte. 501, Halifax. The town of Halifax has been the county seat of Halifax County since 1777. It is named for George Montague, the second Earl of Halifax, an English statesman. Previously this community had been called Banister, Houston, and Halifax Court House. Portions of Gen. Nathanael Greene's troops were here in Feb. 1781. George Washington was in the region on 4 June 1791. During the spring of 1827, John Randolph of Roanoke spoke here to a large gathering of people. The present courthouse is a Classical Revival structure built in 1839, constructed by Dabney Cosby, Sr., one of Thomas Jefferson's master builders. Union Gen. George Custer camped in the region in Apr. 1865.

R-78 Halifax Church

Rte. 624, at Rte. 623. Halifax Church is the oldest Presbyterian church in Halifax County. The Congregation was formed in June, 1830, from Cub Creek Church in Charlotte County. The organizational group included the Reverend Clement Read of Cub Creek and twenty-six local communicants including sixteen black members, mostly slaves. Visiting ministers preached occasionally at the church until June, 1831, when the Reverend Thomas A. Ogden began four years of service as the congregation's first pastor. The building was restored in 1983 and placed on the Virginia Landmarks Register in 1987.

R-79 Green's Folly

Rte. 501, 2 miles south of Halifax. Built about 1789 by Captain Berryman Green, a quartermaster in Washington's army at Valley Forge and later a deputy clerk of Halifax County.

R-80 Minister Who Married Lincoln

Rte. 501, 2 miles south of Halifax. Here lived Rev. Charles A. Dresser, rector of Antrim Parish and builder of St. Mark's Church, 1828. Dresser left this parish in 1835 for Peoria, Illinois, whence he moved to Springfield. There he married Abraham Lincoln to Mary Todd, November 4, 1842.

U-47 Carter's Tavern

Rte. 659, approximately 3.3 miles east of Halifax/Pittsylvania County line. Joseph Dodson, Sr., built the smaller section of Carter's Tavern as his dwelling before 1773. His younger son, Joseph Dodson, Jr., operated it as an ordinary early in the 19th century here on River Road, then the principal highway between Halifax Court House and Danville and part of the main state road between New York and New Orleans. Samuel Carter bought the tavern in 1807, enlarged it with a two-story addition, and managed it until his death in 1836. His widow, Elizabeth Carter, operated it until she died in 1843; the tavern then closed. Restored in the 1970s, Carter's Tavern is a rare example of a once-common Virginia institution.

U-48 STAUNTON RIVER STATE PARK

Rte. 360, 7.1 miles east of Halifax. This park was developed by the National Park Service, Interior Department, through the Civilian Conservation Corps, in conjunction with the Virginia Conservation Commission. It covers 1200 acres and was opened, June 15, 1936. Near by is Occaneechee Island where Nathaniel Bacon defeated the Indians in 1676.

U-50 NATHANIEL TERRY'S GRAVE

Rte. 360, just north of Rte. 613. A short distance south is the grave of Nathaniel Terry, colonial soldier and statesman. Terry served as sheriff of Halifax County, 1752, and captain of Rangers, 1755. He

was a member of the House of Burgesses, 1755–1765, 1771–1775, and also sat in the convention of 1776 that framed the Constitution of Virginia. Terry died in 1780.

U-51 WILLIAM MUNFORD TUCK (1896–1983)

Rte. 58, at Rte. 601. William M. Tuck was born near High Hill, Halifax County, Virginia. After service in the U.S. Marine Corps in World War I, he attended the College of William and Mary and earned a law degree from Washington and Lee University. Governor Tuck served three terms in the Virginia House of Delegates, followed by service in the Virginia Senate (1932–1942) and as Lieutenant Governor (1942–1946). As Governor of Virginia (1946–1950), Governor Tuck worked for passage of Virginia's Right-to-Work Act. Tuck served in the United States House of Representatives from 1953–1969. He died in South Boston, June 9, 1983.

HENRY COUNTY

A-54 FORT TRIAL

Rte. 220, just north of Bypass Rte. 220, north of Martinsville. Fort Trial, constructed in 1756, once stood nearby overlooking the Smith River. It was one in a series of forts authorized by the General Assembly to be built on the frontier to protect settlers from Indians during the French and Indian War. The square fort was made of twenty-foot split timbers erected close together. Four feet of timber were buried in the earth and the walls were about sixteen feet high. George Washington visited Fort Trial in 1756. It was abandoned near the end of the eighteenth century when hostilities between colonists and Indians had subsided.

A-57 WILLIAM BYRD'S CAMP

Rte. 220, 3.5 miles south of Ridgeway, just north of state line. Near here, on Matrimony Creek, William Byrd pitched his camp,

November, 1728, while determining the Virginia–North Carolina boundary line.

A-135 BELLEVIEW

Rte. 220, at Rte. 685, 4 miles south of Martinsville. Three miles southwest is Belleview, home of Major John Redd, a pioneer in this section. Redd served in the Indian wars and in the Revolution, being present at the siege of Yorktown in 1781.

U-40 PATRICK HENRY'S LEATHERWOOD HOME

Rte. 58, approximately 0.08 miles west of Rte. 1095, east of Martinsville. Once located to the south was Leatherwood, the plantation of Patrick Henry, governor of Virginia and great orator of the American Revolution. Henry is especially famous for his "Liberty or Death" speech made in 1775 in Saint John's Church in Richmond. Henry initially purchased ten thousand acres of land lying on Leatherwood Creek, built a house, and lived there from 1779 to 1784. While residing there, Henry served in the Virginia General Assembly (1780–1784). He was elected governor of Virginia in November 1784 and moved to Chesterfield County that same year.

LUNENBURG COUNTY

SN-45 CRAIG'S MILL

Rte. 40, 0.3 miles north of Kenbridge. Two miles south of Kenbridge stood Craig's Mill on Flat Rock Creek. There flour was ground and supplies were stored for the Revolutionary army. Tarleton, the British cavalryman, burned the mill in July, 1781, when raiding through the Southside. Rev. James Craig, the owner, is said to have been forced to help kill hogs for the troopers.

SN-62 HOME OF THE REVEREND JAMES CRAIG

Rte. 40, 2.3 miles west of Kenbridge. To the south is the site of the late-18th-century home of the Reverend James Craig, minister of Cumberland Parish (1759–1795), physician, and Revolutionary patriot. During the Revolutionary War his nearby mill was burned by Colonel Banastre Tarleton, and Craig was taken prisoner and paroled. John Orgain, Jr. married Reverend Craig's granddaughter. A member of the House of Delegates (1838–1840; 1859–1863), and county judge (1850), he operated a school, the Flat Rock Female Seminary, on the property from 1834 until his death in 1871.

SN-64 TOWN OF VICTORIA

Rte. 40 East, 1.3 miles east of Victoria. The town of Victoria, located halfway between Roanoke and Norfolk, was conceived in 1906 when the Virginian Railway was built to transport coal from Southwest Virginia to Tidewater. Henry H. Rogers, builder of the Virginian Railway, probably named the town after Queen Victoria. The town grew up around the railroad shops, and was built on farmlands and forests. The shops remained in Victoria until 1959, when the railroad merged with the present-day Norfolk Southern. Victoria was incorporated by the Lunenburg County Circuit Court in April 1909, and later by the General Assembly on 11 March 1916.

SN-65 TOWN OF KENBRIDGE

Rte. 40 (South Boston Street), Kenbridge. Kenbridge was settled during the late nineteenth century as a farming community. It was originally named Tinkling for a post office that was established here in Feb. 1890. The Virginia Railway laid its track through the community by 1907 and a telegraph station was established by 1909. On 14 March 1908 the Virginia General Assembly incorporated the town of Kenbridge, which took its name from the last names of local citizens William F. Kennedy and Lewis Bridgforth. By 1910, the first tobacco warehouses had been constructed, which with the railroad helped Kenbridge to become an important tobacco market and a business center for the region.

CITY OF LYNCHBURG

K-142 JOHN DANIEL'S HOME

720 Court Street. This Federal-style mansion was built by John Marshall Warwick in 1826. It was the birthplace of John Warwick Daniel, grandson of the builder, whose father was Judge William Daniel, resident of nearby Point of Honor. John W. Daniel was known as the "Lame Lion of Lynchburg" due to extensive wounds suffered in the Civil War. He later served in the Virginia Assembly as both delegate and senator and for sixteen years in the United States Congress as congressman and senator.

K-146 Chestnut Hill

Business Rte. 501. Nearby stood Chestnut Hill, the home of Charles Lynch, Sr. He was the father of John Lynch, the founder of Lynchburg, and of Charles Lynch, Jr., a Revolutionary officer. Charles Lynch, Sr., died in 1753 and is believed to be buried at Chestnut Hill. The wooden house was later owned by Judge Edmond Winston and then by Henry Langhorne, during whose occupancy it burned. Members of the Lynch family were among the first Quaker settlers in the area.

L-20 Quaker Meeting House

5810 Fort Avenue, at Quaker Parkway. In the mid-18th century, members of the Religious Society of Friends (Quakers) settled in the Lynchburg area, initially worshiping in one another's houses. According to local tradition, the first meetinghouse was constructed here of logs in 1757 and enlarged in 1763. In 1768 it burned and the next year a frame church was built. It stood until 1792, when construction began on a stone meetinghouse completed in 1798. It deteriorated after 1835 as many Quakers, who opposed slavery, emigrated from Lynchburg and Virginia to free states. The meetinghouse was restored in the 20th century as the Quaker Memorial Presbyterian Church. John Lynch, the founder of Lynchburg, and his mother, Sarah Lynch, are buried in the adjacent cemetery.

L-21 Montview

University Boulevard, at entrance to Liberty University. Montview was constructed in 1923 as the home of Senator and former Secretary of the U.S. Treasury, Carter Glass. Glass served in the House of Representatives and Senate from 1902 to 1946 and was known as the "Father of the Federal Reserve System" in recognition of which his likeness appears on the $50,000 Treasury note. Glass was a co-sponsor of the Glass-Steagall Act of 1933. In 1941, he was sworn in as President Pro-Tem of the U.S. Senate on the sun porch of Montview.

L-22 Sandusky

5810 Fort Avenue, at Quaker Parkway. To the northwest is Sandusky, built by Charles Johnston about 1808. He named it after a place in Ohio where Indians had held him prisoner in 1790. The two-story structure was one of the Lynchburg area's first houses to display the details and refinement of high-style Federal architecture. In 1864, during the Battle of Lynchburg, Sandusky served as headquarters for Union Maj. Gen. David Hunter. Future presidents Rutherford B. Hayes and William McKinley served on Hunter's staff. Hunter had been a West Point classmate of Confederate Maj. George C. Hutter, who owned Sandusky at the time of the Union occupation.

M-60 Lynchburg Defenses

Rte. 501, at eastern entrance to Lynchburg. The earthwork on the hilltop, two hundred yards to the east, was thrown up as a part of the system of defenses for Lynchburg, 1861–65. The city was an important supply base and railroad center.

Q-6-1 Fort Early

Fort Avenue, near Early Monument. Named for Confederate Lt. Gen. Jubal A. Early, this roughly square earthen redoubt served as a part of the outer line of defense for Lynchburg in June 1864. Fort Early and the outer fortifications were constructed to provide additional protection for the vital railroad facilities in Lynchburg threatened by Union Maj. Gen. David Hunter's troops after Early arrived on 17 June. On 18 June, Hunter advanced his troops towards Confederate positions, while Union artillery bombarded Fort Early and other Confederate fortifications. After a number of unsuccessful assaults during the day, Hunter ordered a retreat that night. His troops withdrew to the southwest toward present-day Roanoke.

Q-6-2 FORT McCAUSLAND

Business Rte. 501 (Langhorne Road), just west of Clifton Street. The fort on the hill here was constructed by General J. A. Early to protect the approach to Lynchburg from the west. Union cavalry skirmished with the Confederates along the road immediately west of the fort. The Unionists, driven back by General McCausland, were unable to enter the city from this direction.

Q-6-3 INNER DEFENSES 1864

12th Street, between Fillmore and Floyd Streets. Here ran the inner line of Lynchburg defenses thrown up by General D. H. Hill in June, 1864. General John C. Breckinridge, confronting General Hunter in the Shenandoah Valley, made a forced march to forestall Hunter. Hill constructed a shallow line of trenches, occupied by Breckinridge, and hospital convalescents and home guards. It became a reserve line when General Early arrived.

Q-6-4 INNER DEFENSES

Bedford Avenue and Monsview Place. A line of shallow Civil War entrenchments extended across Bedford Avenue near this spot to connect with other trenches crossing the present-day railroad tracks. These works were constructed to protect Lynchburg from attack by way of the Lexington Turnpike (now Hollins Mill Road) and were a portion of Lynchburg's inner defense lines manned by Confederate Maj. Gen. John C. Breckinridge's troops in June 1864. Lt. Gen. Jubal A. Early arrived in the city on 17 June and oversaw the hasty construction of a second line of defenses. The outer defenses paralleled the first line about a mile and half to the west and successfully withstood the Union attack during the 18 June Battle of Lynchburg.

Q-6-5 DEFENSE WORKS

Rivermont Avenue and Langhorne Road (Business Rte. 501). On the crest of the hill just to the south was a redoubt forming part of the defenses thrown up by General D. H. Hill, June, 1864. These works were held by General Imboden's cavalry. A military road was constructed to connect this point with Fort McCausland. Signs of this road may still be seen in old Rivermont Park.

Q-6-6 MUSTERED AND DISBANDED 1861–1865

Park Avenue, near Park Lane. At this point the Second Virginia Cavalry was mustered into service, May 10, 1861. At the same place the remnant of this regiment was disbanded, April 10, 1865, completing a service of four years lacking one month. The regiment participated in many campaigns and engagements.

Q-6-7 INNER DEFENSES 1864

Rivermont Avenue and Byrd Street. A line of shallow entrenchments extended from near this point along the crest of the hill to the east. These works were occupied by the cadets of the Virginia Military Institute, who had marched here with General Breckinridge after the Institute at Lexington was burned by General Hunter.

Q-6-8 INNER DEFENSES

Park and Floyd Avenues. Here, facing west, ran the inner defenses of the city, located by General D. H. Hill. They were constructed by convalescents and home guards. General Early, after an inspection of the system, moved most of the men to the outer works well to the westward.

Q-6-9 INNER DEFENCES [DEFENSES]

5th and Wise Streets. Near here ran the line of inner defences [defenses] located by Gen. D. H. Hill, June, 1864. He had been sent from Petersburg by Gen. Beauregard to assist Gen. Breckinridge then in command. On Gen. Early's arrival, troops were moved to the outer works.

Q-6-10 Miller-Claytor House

Rivermont Avenue and Treasure Island Road. This building formerly stood at Eighth and Church streets. It now stands one block north. It was built by John Miller about 1791. Thomas Wiatt bought the house, long known as the "Mansion House." Samuel Claytor purchased it in 1825. For many years doctors' offices were here. For ninety years the house was owned by the Page family. The Lynchburg Historical Society moved and restored it.

Q-6-11 Lynchburg

9th and Church Streets. [*Obverse*] In 1757 John Lynch opened a ferry here; in 1765 a church was built. In 1786 Lynchburg was established by act of assembly; in 1791 the first tobacco warehouse was built. Lynchburg was incorporated as a town in 1805. In 1840 the James River and Kanawha Canal, from Richmond to Lynchburg, was opened; the section to Buchanan, in 1851. Lynchburg became a city in 1852. [*Reverse*] Trains began running on the first railroad, the Virginia and Tennessee, in 1852. Lynchburg was a main military supply center, 1862–65. Here the Confederates under General Early defeated the Union General Hunter, June 18, 1864. In 1893 Randolph-Macon Woman's College opened; in 1903, Lynchburg College. In 1920 the council manager form of government was adopted.

Q-6-12 Carter Glass

829 Church Street. Born January 4, 1858, in a house which stood on this site. Newspaper publisher; member of the State Senate and Delegate to the State Constitutional Convention of 1901–1902; member of the United States House of Representatives, 1902–1918, and principal author of the Federal Reserve Act; Secretary of the Treasury, 1918–1920; member of the United States Senate from 1920 until his death in 1946.

Q-6-13 Lynchburg College

Lakeside Drive (Rte. 221), at entrance to college. Lynchburg College was founded in 1903 as Virginia Christian College by Dr. Josephus Hopwood and a group of Christian Church (Disciples of Christ) clergymen and lay leaders. It is one of the earliest colleges in Virginia to be founded as a coeducational institution. Its name was changed to Lynchburg College in 1919. The former Westover Hotel served as the college's original building. Renamed Westover Hall, it was dismantled in 1970. Hopwood Hall, designed in the Classical Revival style by architect Edward G. Frye and completed in 1909, is the oldest classroom building on campus and is still in use.

Q-6-14 Randolph-Macon Woman's College

Rivermont Avenue and Princeton Circle. Founded by Dr. William Waugh Smith in 1891 and opened in 1893 as a member of the Randolph-Macon System of Educational Institutions, this Liberal Arts College has been recognized from its opening year for its high standards of scholarship. The scenic campus of 100 acres extends to the James River.

Q-6-15 Virginia University of Lynchburg

Dewitt Street and Garfield Avenue. In 1886 the Virginia Baptist State Convention founded the Lynchburg Baptist Seminary as an institution of "self-reliance," "racial pride," and "faith". It first offered classes in 1890 as the renamed Virginia Seminary. Under the direction of Gregory Willis Hayes, the second president of the college who served from 1891 to 1906, the school became a pioneer in the field of African American education. In 1900 the school was reincorporated as the Virginia Theological Seminary and College and in 1962 became the Virginia Seminary and College. The college was renamed and incorporated as Virginia University of

Lynchburg in 1996. Among its graduates was the poet Anne Spencer.

Q-6-16 ALLEN WEIR FREEMAN, M.D.—7 JAN. 1881–3 JULY 1954

Rivermont Avenue, at 400 Main Street, at southern end of Rivermont Bridge. Born at 416 Main Street, Allen W. Freeman, brother of editor and historian Douglas Southall Freeman, was a pioneer in public health administration and education. He was educated at the University of Richmond and the Johns Hopkins University School of Medicine in Baltimore, Md. He served as medical inspector of the Richmond City Health Department; first assistant commissioner of health for Virginia; epidemiologist, U.S. Public Health Service; commissioner of health for Ohio; professor and dean, Johns Hopkins University School of Hygiene and Public Health; president, American Public Health Association; and consultant to several foreign governments in developing public health programs.

Q-6-17 DOUGLAS SOUTHALL FREEMAN

Rivermont Avenue, at 400 Main Street, at southern end of Rivermont Bridge. Born at 416 Main Street on 16 May 1886, the son of a Confederate veteran, Douglas Southall Freeman moved with his family to Richmond three years later. He graduated from the University of Richmond in 1904 and earned a doctorate from Johns Hopkins University in 1908. Freeman subsequently held several posts as an educator and editor, but he is best known as the editor of the *Richmond News Leader* (1915–1949) and as the author of Pulitzer Prize–winning biographies of Robert E. Lee and George Washington. Freeman died in Richmond on 13 June 1953.

Q-6-18 SAMUEL D. ROCKENBACH— 1869–1952—BRIGADIER GENERAL, U.S. ARMY CAVALRY

8th and Court Streets. Nearby at 805 Madison Street is the birthplace of General Rockenbach, "Father of the U.S. Army Tank Corps." He began his education in Lynchburg schools and was an honor graduate of Virginia Military Institute in 1889. As first chief of the Army's tank corps in 1917, he pioneered training schools and field organization for tank warfare in World War I.

Q-6-20 THE ANNE SPENCER HOUSE— 1313 PIERCE STREET

1313 Pierce Street. This was the home of Edward Alexander and Anne Bannister Spencer from 1903 until her death on July 25, 1975. Born on February 6, 1882, in Henry County, Va. Anne Spencer was to receive national and international recognition as a poet. Published extensively between 1920 and 1935, she belonged to the Harlem Renaissance school of writers.

Q-6-21 LUKE JORDAN, BLUES PIONEER

Jefferson Street. Singer-guitarist Luke Jordan (1892–1952) was a familiar presence on the streets of Lynchburg from the 1920s until World War II. Jordan and other African American musicians in the Southeast merged blues with an existing repertoire of ballads, ragtime, and tent-show songs, creating a syncopated and upbeat style now called Piedmont or East Coast Blues. The Victor Record Company, seeking blues artists to satisfy popular demand, recorded Jordan in 1927 and 1929, issuing classics such as "Church Bell Blues" and "Pick Poor Robin Clean." The Great Depression hurt sales and ended Jordan's career, but he remained an important and widely imitated Virginia blues musician.

Q-6-22 PEARL S. BUCK

2615 Rivermont Avenue, at Randolph-Macon Woman's College. Internationally known author and humanitarian Pearl Sydenstricker Buck (1892–1973) graduated in 1914 from Randolph-Macon Woman's College, where she wrote for the college's literary magazine. She was the author of more than 70 books, many of which were best sellers. In 1932, Buck received the Pulitzer Prize for the widely read novel *The Good*

Earth. In 1938 she became the first United States woman to receive the Nobel Prize for literature. At the time of Buck's death, she was one of the most widely translated United States writers. In 1941, Buck was a founder of the East and West Association, dedicated to cultural exchange between the United States and Asia.

Q-6-23 CHAUNCEY E. SPENCER, SR.

1306 Pierce Street. Chauncey E. Spencer, Sr., aviation pioneer and Civil Rights activist was born in Lynchburg on 5 Nov. 1906, the son of poet Anne Spencer. He moved to Chicago and by 1934 began pursuing his pilot's license. As a charter member of the National Airmen's Association of America, he and Dale L. White in 1939 made an aeronautical tour from Chicago to Washington, D.C., to lobby for the inclusion of African Americans in the Army Air Corps. This included meeting Senator Harry S Truman. Spencer also worked for the U.S. Air Force and was a public servant in Michigan and California. He lived here from 1977 until his death on 21 Aug. 2002.

Q-13 JACOB E. YODER

Jackson Street. Jacob Eschbach Yoder (22 Feb. 1838–15 Apr. 1905), reared a Mennonite in Pennsylvania, came to Lynch-burg after the Civil War to teach former slaves in the Freedmen's Bureau's Camp Davis School. Following Reconstruction, Yoder served as supervising principal of Lynchburg's African American schools for more than 25 years and helped start the College Hill Baptist Church Sunday school. When he died, black teachers declared that "he had devoted his life unselfishly, and unstintingly to our race, and wore himself out in service to us." In 1911, the Lynch-burg School Board named the new Yoder School for blacks, which stood here, after this public school pioneer.

Q-18 COURT STREET BAPTIST CHURCH

Court Street. The congregation was organized in 1843, when Lynchburg's African American Baptists were separated from First Baptist Church. The new African Baptist Church of Lynchburg met in a converted theater. It was demolished in 1879, after the deaths of eight people during a panic caused by fear of structural collapse. Church members provided all the money to buy land at Sixth and Court Street for a new building. Local architect Robert C. Burk-holder designed the church, combining the Romanesque Revival and Second Empire styles. It was the largest church building with the tallest spire in the city in 1880.

CITY OF MARTINSVILLE

A-94 MARTINSVILLE

West Main Street, at Jones and Bridge Streets. Named for Joseph Martin, pioneer, who settled here in 1773. In 1793 the courthouse of Henry County was moved here and the town was established. Patrick Henry, for whom the county was named, lived near here once. In 1865, Stoneman, moving south to join Sherman, captured Martins-ville. It was incorporated as a town in 1873 and as a city in 1929.

MECKLENBURG COUNTY

F-89 SGT. EARLE D. GREGORY

Rte. 49/92, at Boyd Street, Chase City. Born in Powhatan County on 18 Oct. 1897, Earle D. Gregory enlisted in 1914 at Chase City in the Virginia Volunteers (Virginia National Guard). He served in the 116th Inf. Regt., 29th Inf. Div., in WWI. On the first day of combat near Verdun, France, on 8 Oct. 1918, heavy German machine-gun fire stalled the division's attack. Saying, "I will get them," Gregory seized a rifle and trench-mortar shell, moved ahead of his platoon, and singlehandedly captured a machine gun, a howitzer, and 22 Germans. He became the only Virginian awarded the Medal of Honor during WWI. Gregory died in Tuscaloosa, Ala., on 6 Jan. 1972.

F-95 PRESTWOULD PLANTATION

Rte. 15, at Rte. 1601, north of Rte. 58, near Clarksville. The second William Byrd obtained land here about 1730 and named the place "Blue Stone Castle." The estate extended ten miles along Roanoke River. Before the Revolution Sir Peyton Skipwith came into possession and built the present house, which he named Prestwould.

F-98 OCCANEECHI INDIANS

Rte. 15, near state line. The Occaneechi Indians once lived nearby on an island in the Roanoke River. Well known for trading goods with other Indians [Indian] nations and colonists, the Occaneechi resided close to several Indian paths. They also hunted, fished, and raised crops that included corn, beans, and tobacco. In May 1676, Nathaniel Bacon enlisted the Occaneechi to help defeat Susquehannocks and then turned on the Occaneechi and attacked them. The Occaneechi left Virginia with their neighbors the Saponis and Toteros soon afterward. By 1701, the Occaneechi were living on the Eno River in North Carolina.

S-70 SALEM CHAPEL

Rte. 1/58 (West Danville Street), near Goodes Ferry Road, South Hill. A mile south is the site of Salem Chapel, one of the pioneer Methodist churches of the state. Of it Francis Asbury wrote, "the best house we have in the country part of Virginia." There he held four sessions of the Virginia Annual conference: November, 1795; April, 1798; March, 1802; April, 1804. The building was burned about 1870.

U-60 OCCANEECHI INDIANS

Rte. 58 and Occoneechee Road, east of Clarksville. The Occaneechi Indians once lived nearby on an island in the Roanoke River. Well known for trading goods with other Indians [Indian] nations and colonists, the Occaneechi resided close to several Indian paths. They also hunted, fished, and raised crops that included corn, beans, and tobacco. In May 1676, Nathaniel Bacon enlisted the Occaneechi to help defeat Susquehannocks and then turned on the Occaneechi and attacked them. The Occaneechi left Virginia with their neighbors the Saponis and Toteros soon afterward. By 1701, the Occaneechi were living on the Eno River in North Carolina.

U-61 TOWN OF LA CROSSE

Rte. 621, just south of Rte. 58, La Crosse. La Crosse became the junction of the Atlantic and Danville Railway and the Seaboard Air Line Railway in 1900. Surveyed as early as 1748, the area was known as Piney Pond by 1767, for a body of water that no longer exists. When a post office was established here in 1890, the region was known as La Crosse. The Virginia General Assembly incorporated the town of La Crosse on 15 February 1901. Around the railroad tracks, a business district, which included two depots, a bank, and several stores then prospered. The rail tracks were removed by 1990.

U-80 A REVOLUTIONARY SOLDIER

Rte. 58, 0.3 miles west of Boydton. Richard Kennon of Mecklenburg served as an officer in the 5th Virginia Regiment, 1776–1778 and later in the State Militia. He served in both houses of the General Assembly and was Presiding Officer of the Senate, 1800–1802. He died in 1805.

U-81 THYNE INSTITUTE

Rte. 47, 0.1 miles north of Chase City town limits. In 1876 the United Presbyterian Church and the Rev. J. J. Ashenhurst, first principal, formed Thyne Institute, the only facility in Mecklenburg County offering courses for blacks until 1923. Two years after opening in a small building that had been used for curing tobacco, the school moved to a new building that John Thyne, for whom the school was named, had erected on five acres of land. The Institute grew in time into a boarding school and later into a four-year high school. Purchased by the Mecklenburg County School Board in 1946, the site presently serves as Chase City Elementary School.

UL-4 OLD RANDOLPH-MACON COLLEGE

Rte. 58, 0.3 miles west of Boydton. This is the original campus of Randolph-Macon College, the oldest Methodist-affiliated college still operating in the United States. Chartered by the Virginia General Assembly in 1830 and named for Congressmen John Randolph of Roanoke, Charlotte County, Virginia, and Nathaniel Macon, of Warren County, North Carolina, the college opened on 9 October 1832. Dabney Cosby, a builder employed by Thomas Jefferson at the University of Virginia, was a contractor. In 1868, largely due to economic difficulties caused by the Civil War, the college was moved to Ashland, where it continues in operation. The vacated buildings later housed a freedmen's school, as well as the

Boydton Academic and Bible Institute, which operated until the mid-1930s.

UL-5 TAYLOR'S FERRY

Rte. 58, 0.3 miles west of Boydton. Seven miles south. There a detachment of Virginia militia crossed the Roanoke River in February, 1781, on the way to join Greene in North Carolina. There Baron Steuben, commanding the forces in Virginia, had a depot of supplies.

UL-6 BOYDTON AND PETERSBURG PLANK ROAD

Rte. 58, 0.3 miles west of Boydton. The Boydton and Petersburg Plank Road was built between 1851 and 1853 and was funded by stock bought by the state as well as the public. The all-weather toll road increased the transportation of crops to market and also carried stagecoach traffic between Boydton and Petersburg. The road was constructed of pine and oak planks eight feet long, one foot wide, and three to four inches thick laid across parallel beams, slanted slightly to improve drainage. A ten-foot-wide shoulder let vehicles pass each other. By 1860 the road, except for an 1856 extension to Clarksville, was declared unsafe, due to heavy wear, poorly suited untreated lumber, and the collapse of the Meherrin River Bridge.

NELSON COUNTY

OQ-4 THOMAS MASSIE

Rtes. 56 and 666, Massie's Mill. One mile from here is "Level Green," the home of Major Thomas Massie (1747–1834). Commander of the Sixth Virginia Regiment of Infantry, later Aide to Governor Thomas Nelson at the siege of Yorktown, and one of the first magistrates of Nelson County when it was formed in 1807.

OQ-5 WILLIAM CABELL

Rte. 56, at Nelson/Buckingham County line, Wingina. Three miles southwest is Union Hill, home of William Cabell. He was born, March 30, 1730. Cabell was a burgess, signer of the Articles of Association, member of the Revolutionary conventions and of the ratifying convention of 1788. He died, March 23, 1798.

OQ-6 PETER CARTWRIGHT—(1 SEPT. 1785–25 SEPT. 1872)

Rte. 56, east of Shipman. Known for helping to develop Methodism as a circuit rider in Kentucky, Tennessee, Indiana, Ohio, and Illinois, Peter Cartwright was born three miles southeast. His library, which he carried in his saddlebag, included a Bible, a hymnal, and *The Book of Discipline*. Lacking formal education himself he encouraged it in others; several Midwestern colleges count him as a founder. In 1828 he was elected to the Illinois General Assembly. In 1832, he was one of four candidates elected in a field of thirteen; Abraham Lincoln ran eighth and lost. In 1846, Lincoln defeated Cartwright for Congress.

R-50 BOYHOOD HOME OF COLONEL JOHN MOSBY

Rte. 6, 3 miles north of Woods Mill. Confederate Col. John Singleton Mosby was born in Powhatan County on 6 Dec. 1833. Nearby stood the early childhood home in which Mosby lived from soon after his birth until his family moved to Charlottesville by 1841. Before the Civil War, Mosby was a lawyer in Bristol, Va. During the war, Mosby and his Partisan Rangers (43d Battalion, Virginia Cavalry) used guerilla tactics to raid Union outposts, communications, and supply lines in Northern Virginia. On 21 Apr. 1865, Mosby disbanded his rangers in Salem (present-day Marshall, Fauquier Co.), after learning of Confederate Gen. Joseph E. Johnston's surrender. After the war, Mosby practiced law and was U.S. consul to Hong Kong (1879–1885). He died on 30 May 1916.

R-51 HURRICANE CAMILLE

Rte. 29, near Woods Mill, at Nelson County Wayside. On August 20, 1969, torrential rains, following remnants of Hurricane Camille, devastated this area. A rainfall in excess of 25 inches largely within a 5-hour period, swept away or buried many miles of roads, over 100 bridges, and over 900 buildings. 114 people died and 37 remain missing. The damage totalled more than $100,000,000 and Virginia was declared a disaster area.

R-56 LOVINGSTON

Business Rte. 29, Lovingston. This place became the county seat of Nelson when it was formed from Amherst in 1807. It was named for James Loving, Jr., who gave the land for the courthouse, built in 1808–09. The town was incorporated in 1807 and again in 1871, and deincorporated in 1938.

R-57 OAK RIDGE ESTATE

Rte. 29, at Rte. 653 (Oak Ridge Road), 4 miles south of Lovingston. About two miles east is Oak Ridge, a 4,800-acre estate first patented in the 1730s. Robert Rives (1764–1845), a tobacco planter and international trader, built his house there in 1802. In 1867, William Porcher Miles (1822–1899), a former Confederate congressman, acquired the plantation. Nelson County native and Wall Street financier Thomas Fortune Ryan (1851–1928) purchased Oak Ridge in 1901 and transformed it into a country estate. He remodeled Rives's Federal farmhouse into a Colonial Revival mansion and built some 80 structures, including schools, a telephone company building, a movie theater, and stables for Ryan's 200 Thoroughbreds. A Crystal Palace–style greenhouse, a racetrack, and a private railroad station are among 50 surviving structures.

R-58 BIRTHPLACE OF RIVES

Rte. 29, at Rte. 653 (Oak Ridge Road), 4 miles south of Lovingston. Two miles east, at Oak Ridge, was born William Cabell Rives, May 4, 1792. He was minister to France, 1829–32 and 1849–53; United States Senator, 1832–45; member of the Peace convention of 1861 and of the Confederate Congress. He died, April 25, 1868. Later, Oak Ridge was owned by Thomas Fortune Ryan.

R-81 CABELLSVILLE

Rte. 29, near Rte. 855. In 1803, the Virginia General Assembly established Cabellsville one mile west of here on the Old Stage Road, on 25 acres owned by Congressman

Samuel Jordan Cabell. The village was platted before Nelson County was formed from Amherst County in 1807, and the new community developed around the first Amherst County courthouse constructed after that county was created in 1761. After the formation of Nelson County, its justices continued to meet periodically in the old building in Cabellsville until a new courthouse was erected on land that James Loving donated in Lovingston.

RA-4 ROCKFISH CHURCH

Rte. 151, 10.5 miles south of Afton. The Rockfish meetinghouse was established here by 1746, making it one of the oldest Presbyterian churches in the region. James McCann conveyed land for a church and school. Samuel Black became the first pastor of the church in 1747. Thomas Mason built a new frame structure for the congregation about 1771. The present Greek Revival brick structure was constructed by 1854. Further modifications have been made to the building and grounds since that time, including an addition completed in 1995.

RA-6 WILLIAM H. CRAWFORD

Rte. 151, 12.7 miles south of Afton, Nellysford. William Harris Crawford was born in this vicinity, February 24, 1772. Early in life he was taken to Georgia and became a leading politician of the era. He was United States Senator; Minister to France; Secretary of War and of the Treasury; candidate, 1824, for the Presidency, which was decided by the House of Representatives.

W-218 ROCKFISH GAP MEETING

I-64 East, on Afton Mountain, at first scenic overlook. The commission appointed to select a site for the University of Virginia met 1–4 August 1818 in the tavern that stood nearby. Among the 21 members present were former presidents Thomas Jefferson and James Madison, as well as judges Spencer Roane, Archibald Stuart, and Creed Taylor. The commissioners chose Charlottesville over Lexington and Staunton for the site of the university. The tavern at which they met was owned by Samuel Leake (1790–1858) and Walter Leake (1792–1859). Enlarged later, as part of the Mountain Top Hotel and Springs, the popular tavern burned in 1909.

W-219 FLIGHT OF RICHARD C. duPONT

I-64 East, on Afton Mountain, at first scenic overlook. Near this site on September 21, 1933, Richard C. duPont was launched from Afton Mountain in his Bowlus sailplane, Albatross. Four hours and fifty minutes later he landed at Frederick, Maryland, establishing a United States distance record for sail planing of 121.6 miles, almost double the previous U.S. Record of 66 miles.

NOTTOWAY COUNTY

K-170 NOTTOWAY COURTHOUSE

Rte. 460, 0.2 miles west of Nottoway. Near here on 23 June 1864, Confederate Maj. Gen. W. H. F. "Rooney" Lee positioned his cavalrymen between those of Union generals August V. Kautz and James H. Wilson, who were riding toward Burkeville. The resulting engagement, according to Wilson, was one of the hottest of the war. Gen. U. S. Grant passed by here on 5 April 1865 with part of his army, in pursuit of Gen. Robert E. Lee's Army of Northern Virginia. Here Grant received word that Lt. Gen. Philip H. Sheridan was at Jetersville, blocking Lee's line of retreat southward and forcing him west toward Farmville and then Appomattox Court House.

K-172 BLACKSTONE

Rte. 460/40, Blackstone. Blackstone was first known as Blacks and Whites, after two rival late 18th-century taverns. One of these taverns, Schwartz (Blacks) Tavern, listed on the National Register of Historic Places, still stands. The town was renamed for the English jurist Sir William Blackstone and incorporated in 1888. The Battle of the Grove, a Civil War cavalry action, was fought just west of here on 23 June 1864. The United Methodist Assembly Center, formerly the Blackstone College for Girls, is located here. At the turn of the 20th century, the town was a prosperous manufacturing, tobacco, and educational center in Southside Virginia. Nearby Fort Pickett was built in 1942.

K-173 Fort Pickett

Business Rte. 460, at entrance to fort. Named in honor of Confederate Maj. Gen. George Edward Pickett upon its creation in 1942, Camp Pickett was dedicated to the cause of a "reunited nation at war." Established as a 46,000-acre World War II Army installation, Camp Pickett was home to eight combat divisions, seven infantry divisions, and one armored division, during both the European and the Pacific campaigns. The famed "Cross of Lorraine" 79th Infantry Division trained here before the invasion at Normandy. The post was redesignated Fort Pickett and became a full-time training facility in 1974.

K-174 Blackstone College

Rte. 40, Blackstone. Three blocks south is the campus of the former Blackstone Female Institute, after 1915 Blackstone College for Girls, a teacher-training school that opened in 1894 with some 75 students including 29 boarders. James Cannon Jr., a controversial Methodist bishop and prohibitionist, twice served as chief administrator (1894–1911, 1914–1918). In 1906, U.S. Steel magnate Andrew Carnegie donated money to expand the main building. The Beaux-Arts president's home, called The Gables, was built in 1915. Enrollment neared 500 before fires in 1920 and 1922 destroyed the classroom and dormitory buildings. Rebuilt on a smaller scale, the

college operated until 1950. It became the Virginia Methodist Assembly Center in 1955.

K-175 Creation of Camp Pickett

Off Rte. 460, at main entrance to Fort Pickett. Late in 1941, the U.S. government began the condemnation of some 46,000 acres near Blackstone to establish Camp Pickett and train troops for World War II. The action forced 263 families (totaling 1,181 individuals) from their farms early in 1942. Many relocated to other farms but some had to abandon the only way of life they had known. Within months, their homes were demolished, the graves of their ancestors moved elsewhere, and the camp erected. Because of the sacrifices of these citizens, more than one million men trained at Camp Pickett and fought bravely on battlefields around the world.

K-315 Nottoway Training School

Epes and Irvin Streets, Blackstone. On this site stood the Nottoway Training School, the first public school to provide secondary education for African Americans in Nottoway County. In 1909, public appeals to raise funds led to the establishment of the school by 1913, making it one of the first training schools for African Americans opened in the Commonwealth. The John F. Slater Fund helped finance teachers' salaries. County training schools were built to provide rural students vocational and agricultural education, as well as to prepare them for teaching careers or college. Nottoway Training School became an accredited high school in 1931. It closed in 1950 when the Luther H. Foster High School opened.

M-16 Lee's Retreat

Rte. 360, Burkeville. The Union General Ord reached this place in the night of April 5, 1865, to head off Lee. On April 6, Ord sent a cavalry force from here to burn the bridges near Farmville and then moved westward with the Twenty-fourth Corps.

New Deal–era Civilian Conservation Corp camps were situated throughout Virginia during the Great Depression. CCC workers were responsible for a number of federally sponsored projects in the commonwealth, including the construction of Skyline Drive, shown here. (Marker M-21) (Shenandoah National Park Archives)

M-17 HISTORIC BURKEVILLE

Rte. 360, Burkeville. Tarleton's British cavalry, raiding west, stopped here in July, 1781. When railroads were built, the place was known as Burke's Junction. The Union cavalryman Kautz destroyed the railways here in June, 1864. Jefferson Davis passed through Burkeville, going south, April 3, 1865. Grant's headquarters were here, April 6, 1865.

M-18 FRANCISCO'S FIGHT

Rte. 360, 6 miles northeast of Burkeville. American Revolutionary soldier Peter Francisco in July 1781 encountered about nine of British Lt. Gen. Banastre Tarleton's dragoons to the east at Ward's Tavern. Using his legendary strength and cunning, Francisco single-handedly bested his enemies, sending them in retreat, and allowing him to capture a number of their horses. Standing more than 6 feet tall and weighing about 260 pounds, Francisco was celebrated for his feats of strength and bravery, attributes featured in a number of period drawings and paintings. He served as the Sergeant-at-Arms for the Virginia House of Delegates from the late 1820s to his death in Jan. 1831 and is buried in Shockoe Hill Cemetery in Richmond.

M-20 T. O. SANDY

Rte. 460, 2.1 miles east of Burkeville. First Farm Demonstration Agent in Virginia

lived one mile south. Appointed State Agent in 1907. Under his able leadership programs in Farm and Home Demonstration work, Boys Corn Clubs and Girls Canning Clubs were developed. In 1914 the Agency was transferred to the Virginia Polytechnic Institute and became the Extension Service now embracing mens and womens [men's and women's] work and 4-H clubs.

M-21 CIVILIAN CONSERVATION CORPS COMPANY 1370

Rte. 460, at Crewe eastern corporate limits. Near here is the site of CCC Company 1370 from 1935–1940. Among the most popular New Deal programs, the CCC was designed to encourage conservation of natural resources and employment training during the Great Depression. CCC 1370 enrollees were actively involved in soil erosion control and extensive reforestation efforts in this county.

M-22 ROGER ATKINSON PRYOR— (19 JULY 1828–14 MAR. 1919)

Rte. 460, at Meade Railroad Park. Roger A. Pryor was reared at Old Place near present-day Crewe. A lawyer and newspaper editor, he won election to the House of Representatives in 1859 and resigned in 1861. He agitated for secession in Charleston, S.C., and before the attack on Fort Sumter declined the opportunity to fire the first shot. Elected to the Provisional Confederate Congress, he resigned to command the 3d Va. Infantry, and was promoted to brigadier general in 1862. When his brigade was dismantled in 1863, he served as a scout until captured in 1864. After the war he moved to New York and in 1896 was appointed a justice on the New York Supreme Court.

SM-2 LOTTIE MOON—(1840–1912)

Rte. 49, 0.4 miles south of Crewe. Lottie Moon, a native of Charlottesville, was appointed by the Southern Baptist Foreign Mission Board as a missionary to China in 1873 where she served for forty years. She died on her trip home in Kobe, Japan, on Christmas Eve, 1912, and her ashes were buried in her brother's plot in the Crewe Cemetery in 1913. The Lottie Moon Christmas offering is the largest mission offer-ing taken during the year in all Southern Baptist churches.

SM-2 UNION ACADEMY

Rte. 40, at southern entrance to Blackstone. Near here stood Union Academy, conducted by Hardy and Crenshaw from 1861 to about 1869. Dr. Walter Reed, who discovered the carrier of yellow fever, and Dr. Robert E. Blackwell, long President of Randolph-Macon College, attended school here. Nearby was an iron foundry, established in 1855 by Captain Richard Irby.

UK-4 OLD NOTTOWAY MEETING HOUSE

Rte. 723, 2.5 miles south of Burkeville. This is the site of the Old Nottoway Meeting House, built in 1769, the second Baptist church established south of James River. Jeremiah Walker was the first minister.

PITTSYLVANIA COUNTY

KG-23 PITTSYLVANIA COURT HOUSE

Business Rte. 29, at courthouse, Chatham. This Greek Revival building was erected in 1853 as the third Court House of Pittsylvania County. The county, formed in 1767, and the Town of Chatham were named for William Pitt, First Earl of Chatham. The present Court House replaced a structure built in 1783 one block west where the old office of the clerk still stands. The court was removed to this locality from Callands in 1777.

L-32 CLEMENT HILL

Business Rte. 29, Hurt. The house on the hill three hundred yards to the west was the home of Captain Benjamin Clement, who was one of the first makers of gunpowder in Virginia, 1775. The land grant was made in 1741.

L-48 WHITMELL P. TUNSTALL

Rte. 29, at Rte. 703, south of Chatham. One mile east stands Belle Grove, the home of Whitmell Pugh Tunstall (1810–1854). Educated at Danville Academy and the University of North Carolina, Tunstall was admitted to the bar in 1832. He served in the House of Delegates (1836–1841; 1845–1848) and the Senate of Virginia (1841–1842). As a delegate representing Pittsylvania County, he fought for a decade to charter the Richmond and Danville Railroad (part of the present-day Norfolk Southern Railway). He served as the company's first president from 1847 until his death. Tunstall is buried at Belle Grove.

L-49 CLAUDE A. SWANSON

Rte. 29, 0.5 miles north of Business Rte. 29, north of Chatham. A native of Pittsylvania County, Claude Augustus Swanson (1862–1939), practiced law in Chatham until he won election to Congress in 1892. He served seven terms in the House of Representatives (1893–1906); was governor of Virginia (1906–1910) and United States senator (1910–1933); and served as secretary of the navy under President Franklin D. Roosevelt (1933–1939). As governor, Swanson persuaded the General Assembly to reform the public school system, improve rural roads, and create the position of state health commissioner. His last home in the county was at nearby Eldon.

L-50 PEYTONSBURG

Rte. 29, near Rte. 685, Chatham. Nearby to the east once stood the community of Peytonsburg, a part of Halifax County when the county was formed in 1752. Peytonsburg was incorporated as a town in 1759 by the Virginia General Assembly and became part of Pittsylvania County in 1766. During the Revolutionary War, by the late 1770s, Peytonsburg was serving as a supply depot for southern colonial troops. Horseshoes and wooden canteens were made there for colonial troops. During the 1780s, Peytonsburg was a terminus of a mail route that ran from the town to Richmond. The inhabitants gradually left the town during the 19th century, and the buildings gradually disappeared.

L-52 MARKHAM

Rte. 29, near Rte. 685, Chatham. Some miles northeast is the site of Markham, where was born Rachel Donelson, wife of President Andrew Jackson, 1767. Her father, John Donelson, leaving Virginia, became one of the first settlers of Tennessee. Fort Donelson was named for him.

L-61 BEAVERS TAVERN

Business Rte. 29, 5 miles north of Danville. The house to the east was Beavers Tavern, 1800–1840. This was the muster ground of the county militia and a popular stage station. John C. Calhoun was a frequent visitor here.

L-62 RAWLEY WHITE MARTIN RESIDENCE

Business Rte. 29, Chatham. Here stands Morea, the home of Lt. Col. Rawley W.

Martin (1835–1912), a physician who served with Pittsylvania County soldiers during the Civil War in the 53d Virginia Infantry Regiment of Brig. Gen. Lewis A. Armistead's brigade. At Gettysburg, Pa., on 3 July 1863, Martin led the regiment in the Confederate attack known as Pickett's Charge, and was wounded and captured. After the war, Martin resumed his practice here and, in 1873, bought this ca. 1840 house. He later served on the University of Virginia Board of Visitors, and as president of the state Board of Health, the Board of Medical Examiners, and the Medical Society of Virginia.

LT-1 CALLANDS

Rte. 57, at Rte. 969, Callands. Pittsylvania was cut off from Halifax in 1767 and the courthouse built here. In 1769 a town named Chatham was established here on land of James Roberts. A few years later Samuel Calland opened a store and the town took his name. In 1777 Henry County was cut off from Pittsylvania, and the county seat moved to Competition, more centrally located. The name Competition became Chatham in 1874.

Q-12-a CLERK'S OFFICE

Rte. 969, 0.05 miles north of Rte. 57, Callands. Site of first county seat of Pittsylvania County. The building that served as the debtor's prison, 1767–1771, and later as the clerk's office, 1771–1777, remains. Nearby stands the debtor's gaol, built in 1773. It later served as Samuel Calland's store and in 1803 became the post office for Callands.

RG-5 JOHN WEATHERFORD'S GRAVE

Rte. 640, south of Rte. 57, at Shockoe Baptist Church. One half mile west is the grave of Elder John Weatherford (1740?–1833) Baptist preacher for 70 years and early advocate of religious liberty. Jailed five months in Chesterfield in 1773 for unlicensed preaching, his release was secured by Patrick Henry.

U-38 WHITMELL SCHOOL

Rte. 750, Whitmell. Founded in 1878 as
a two-room school and named for state
senator Whitmell P. Tunstall, in 1918 the
Whitmell Farm-Life School became the
first rural consolidated school in Pittsylvania County. Sarah Archie Swanson Beverley, who between 1916 and 1951 taught
here and served as principal, believed that
"the country school must be the center of
community life." Under her leadership,
Whitmell School attained that goal as a
model progressive school. In 1920, the
national Conference on Rural Education
and Country Life was held here, followed
in 1923 by the Virginia Rural Life Conference, which Gov. E. Lee Trinkle and U.S.
Sen. Carter Glass addressed.

U-40 BERRY HILL

Rte. 58, just west of Danville corporate limits.
Berry Hill is situated 5½ miles to the south
on the Dan River. The original portion of
the main house was built in 1745 and there
have been several additions. The property
was used as a hospital for General Nathanael Greene's army during the spring of
1781, following the battle of Guilford Court
House.

PRINCE EDWARD COUNTY

F-65 OLD WORSHAM

*Rte. 15, 5.6 miles south of Farmville, Wor-
sham.* A short distance south stands the
colonial jail of Prince Edward County, built
about 1755; the courthouse was near by.
The British cavalryman, Tarleton, raided
here in July, 1781. Here Patrick Henry
made a great speech against the ratification
of the United States Constitution, 1788.
Washington was here on his southern tour,
June 7, 1791.

F-66 SLATE HILL PLANTATION

*Rte. 15, 6.5 miles south of Farmville, south
of Worsham.* To the west is the estate of
Nathaniel Venable (1733–1804), Slate Hill
Plantation. He was a prominent citizen
of Prince Edward County, serving in the
Virginia House of Burgesses from 1766
to 1768. During the Revolutionary War,
he was a member of the Prince Edward
County Committee of Safety and represented his community in the Senate of
Virginia from 1780 to 1782. Members of
the Hanover Presbytery met at Slate Hill
on 1–2 Feb. 1775 and formed the Prince
Edward Academy, which in 1776 was
named Hampden-Sydney College. Venable
became one of the charter trustees of the
institution.

F-69 RANDOLPH-MACON MEDICAL SCHOOL

Rte. 15, 5 miles south of Farmville. Just to
the west was the medical school of John
Peter Mettauer, which became a branch of
Randolph-Macon College in 1847. It was
discontinued, probably in 1861. Dr. Mettauer, one of the leading surgeons of the
day, practiced until his death in 1875.

F-70 KINGSVILLE

*Rte. 15, at Rte. 133, 4.5 miles south of Farm-
ville.* Here, before the Revolution, stood
King's Tavern. The British cavalryman,
Tarleton, raiding, camped here in 1781.
In the same year sick and wounded French
soldiers were brought to this place from
Yorktown; seventy of them are buried
here. Nearby is the site of the colonial
church of which Archibald McRoberts
was minister.

F-71 PROVIDENCE

Rte. 5, 5.6 miles south of Farmville, Worsham.
Two miles east is the glebe house where the
Rev. Archibald McRoberts lived during the
Revolution. Tarleton, raiding through this
section in July, 1781, set fire to the house,
but a timely rain put out the flames. Accordingly, the place was named "Providence."

F-72 CAMPAIGN OF 1781

Rte. 15, 5.6 miles south of Farmville, Wor-sham. Tarleton, sent by Cornwallis to destroy supplies at Bedford, passed here going west, July, 1781.

F-73 HIGH BRIDGE

Rte. 460, just west of Rte. 640. One mile north stood the Southside Railroad Bridge, spanning the 75-foot-wide Appomattox River. On 6 April, 1865, nine hundred Union soldiers attempting to burn the 2500-foot-long, 126-foot-high structure were captured by Confederate cavalry. Crossing on 7 April, retreating Confederates burned four spans but failed to destroy the lower wagon bridge thus allowing Union soldiers to cross and attack at Cumberland Church north of Farmville.

I-9 HAMPDEN-SYDNEY COLLEGE

Rte. 692, at college. Hampden-Sydney College, in continuous operation since 10 Nov. 1775, was established "to form good men and good Citizens." It was named for John Hampden (1594–1643) and Algernon Sydney (1622–1683), champions of parliamentary rule in England. Patrick Henry and James Madison were early trustees, and President William Henry Harrison was a member of the class of 1791. Student companies were formed in the Revolutionary War and the Civil War. It is affiliated with the Presbyterian Church. The campus includes a distinguished collection of 19th-century buildings that were listed on the Virginia Landmarks Register in 1969 and the National Register of Historic Places in 1970.

I-14 FOUR SORORITIES FOUNDED

High Street, at Longwood University, Farmville. Longwood College, formerly known as the State Female Normal School, is the only U.S. school where four national sororities were founded. Kappa Delta, founded on 23 Oct. 1897, was the first sorority organized in Virginia. The sorority with the longest continuous presence at Longwood College, Sigma Sigma Sigma, was founded on 20 Apr. 1898. Zeta Tau Alpha, established on 15 Oct. 1898, is the only sorority in Virginia to be granted a charter by a special act of the General Assembly. The Prince Edward County Circuit Court granted Alpha Sigma Alpha its charter on 15 Nov. 1901. All four sororities are members of the National Panhellenic Conference, which was organized in 1902.

I-15 LONGWOOD COLLEGE

Business Rte. 15, at entrance to Longwood University, Farmville. The college opened here in October 1884 as a "State Female Normal School". In 1914 the name was changed to "State Normal School for Women at Farmville"; in 1924 to "State Teachers College at Farmville"; in 1949 to "Longwood College". Conferring the B.S. degree was authorized in 1916, and later the B.A. degree. William H. Ruffner, first State Superintendent of Public Instruction, was the first president. The fourth, J. L. Jarman, served from 1902 to 1946.

I-15-a LONGWOOD UNIVERSITY

Rte. 15, at entrance to university, Farmville. Longwood University is a state-supported institution developed from the privately owned Farmville Female Seminary that was incorporated in 1839. In 1884, it became a public institution when the Commonwealth acquired the property and renamed it the State Female Normal School at Farmville. It was the first state institution of higher learning for women in Virginia. Former Virginia superintendent of public instruction, William H. Ruffner, was its first president, serving from 1884 to 1887. The school has undergone a number of name changes and became Longwood College in 1949 and Longwood University in 2002. The university became coeducational in 1976.

I-19 PRESBYTERIAN SEMINARY

Rte. 1001, off Rte. 692, on Hampden-Sydney College campus. The first Presbyterian seminary in the South was established here in 1812 as the Theology Department of Hampden-Sydney College. It became independent of the college in 1822. After the synods of Virginia and North Carolina assumed joint ownership in 1827, it was called Union Theological Seminary; several of its buildings still stand. When the seminary moved to Richmond in 1898, its property on the south side of this road was purchased by Maj. Richard M. Venable, of Baltimore, and donated to the college.

M-1 ROBERT RUSSA MOTON HIGH SCHOOL

Business Rte. 15, south of Longwood University, Farmville. On this site 4-23-51, the students staged a strike protesting inadequate school facilities. Led by Rev. L. Francis Griffin, these students' actions became a part of the 1954 U.S. Supreme Court's Brown v. Board of Education decision, which ruled racial segregation in public schools unconstitutional. To avoid desegregation, the Prince Edward County public schools were closed until 9-2-64.

M-23 PRINCE EDWARD STATE PARK FOR NEGROES

Rte. 360, at Rte. 621. Prince Edward State Park for Negroes was established in 1950 one mile west on the site of the former Prince Edward Lake Recreation Area for Negroes. Maceo C. Martin, an African American from Danville, sued the state when he was denied access to Staunton River State Park. Governor William M. Tuck funded the new park to provide "similar and equal" facilities in lieu of access. The park, with a black superintendent, was operated separately from neighboring Goodwin Lake Recreation Area until the passage of the Civil Rights Act of 1964. The two parks merged in 1986 to form Twin Lakes State Park.

M-24 LEE'S RETREAT

Rte. 307, 3 miles east of Rice. Two miles north are the battlefields of Sailor's Creek, April 6, 1865. There Grant captured more men than were captured in any other one day's field engagement of the war.

M-25 BATTLE OF SAILOR'S CREEK

Rte. 460, at Rte. 307, Rice. Six miles north took place the battle of Sailor's Creek, April 6, 1865. Lee's army, retreating westward from Amelia Courthouse to Farmville by way of Deatonsville, was attacked by Sheridan, who surrounded Ewell's Corps. After a fierce action the Confederates were overpowered. Ewell, other generals, and several thousand men were captured. This was the last major engagement between Lee's and Grant's armies.

M-27 VERNON JOHNS

Rte. 665, at Rte. 666, approximately 8 miles southeast of Farmville. Rev. Dr. Vernon Johns was born here in Darlington Heights

On April 23, 1951, students at Robert Russa Moton High School in Farmville began a strike to protest inadequate and unequal school facilities. The result was the case of Davis v. County School Board of Prince Edward County, which was later combined with similar suits on its way to the U.S. Supreme Court as Brown v. Board of Education. (Marker M-1) (Calder Loth, Virginia Department of Historic Resources)

on 22 April 1892. A graduate of Oberlin College, Johns was an orator of great renown and the first African-American minister included in *Best Sermons of the Year* (1926), an international publication. He was pastor of Court Street Baptist Church (1920–1926; 1941–1943) and president of Virginia Theological Seminary and College (1929–1934), both in Lynchburg. Later he was pastor of Dexter Avenue Baptist Church in Montgomery, Alabama (1948–1952). A blunt-spoken opponent of racial segregation and a champion of civil rights, Johns exhorted his congregations to resist the laws that constricted their lives. He died in Washington, D.C., on 10 June 1965, and is buried just north of here.

M-29 CCC COMPANY 1390— CAMP GALLION

Rte. 360, near Rte. 623. A short distance west is the site of Camp Gallion, home from 1933 to 1941 of Civilian Conservation Corps Company 1390. This all–African American company performed extensive work in the present-day Prince Edward–Gallion State Forest. Company 1390 built five forest-fire lookout towers, 94 miles of forest-fire lanes, 62 miles of truck trails, 33 bridges, and both Goodwin and Prince Edward Lakes, now the centerpieces of Twin Lakes State Park. The men also thinned 500 acres of forest, planted 4,500 trees, and performed 3,142 hours of fire-fighting duty. In addition, the company conducted an education program to reduce illiteracy among its members.

M-30 SULPHUR SPRING BAPTIST CHURCH

Rte. 657, just east of Rte. 615. According to local tradition, the Sulphur Spring Baptist Church was founded in 1867, when services were held in a brush arbor. During the Reconstruction period, formerly enslaved African Americans formed congregations throughout the South similar to this

church. By 1876 a log structure had been built and in that year the congregation purchased the one-acre tract of land on which it stood. The founding members of the church included Phillip Harris, William Wright, Alex Scott, William Green, and Daniel Carter. The first frame structure was built in 1900 and used until 1914 when the original part of the current church was constructed.

M-32 ACTION AT HIGH BRIDGE

Rte. 460, at Rte. 307. During the night of 6–7 April 1865, part of Gen. Robert E. Lee's Army of Northern Virginia crossed the South Side Railroad's High Bridge three miles north of here as Union armies under Lt. Gen. Ulysses S. Grant pursued closely. After the last Confederate units crossed, elements of Maj. Gen. William Mahone's division set fire to the bridge, as well as the small wagon bridge downstream. About 7 A.M. on 7 April, Union Brig. Gen. Francis C. Barlow's 19th Maine Infantry arrived at the wagon bridge and extinguished the flames with their canteens and tents despite Confederate gunfire. Part of High Bridge burned and collapsed.

M-33 LONGWOOD ESTATE

Johnston Drive and main entrance to Longwood University, Farmville. Peter Johnston (1763–1831)—jurist, Speaker of the House of Delegates (1805–1807), and father of Confederate Gen. Joseph E. Johnston—inherited Longwood estate from his father. He sold the property after he became a judge on the General Court of Virginia in Washington County in 1811. State delegate and businessman Nathaniel E. Venable inherited the property from his relative Samuel Woodson Venable and built a house there about 1815, soon after a fire destroyed an earlier structure. The State Teachers College at Farmville, now Longwood University, obtained the house in 1929. In 1949, the college incorporated Longwood in its name.

M-34 SHARON BAPTIST CHURCH

10293 Green Bay Road, Rice, at church.
On this site prior to 1745 the Church of England's Raleigh Parish established Sandy River Chapel. Construction was completed on a new wooden church by 1765, some of which is believed to survive within the present building. In 1782 several different denominations began using it as a meeting-house. It became Sharon Baptist Church in Oct. 1827 with the Rev. Daniel Witt as its first minister. Witt and his boyhood friend Jeremiah Jeter were the first missionaries for the Baptist General Association of Virginia, conducting preaching tours in eastern and western Virginia in 1823. Witt served as pastor here until his death in 1871 and is buried here.

MJ-1 BIZARRE

Rte. 45, near Farmville northern corporate limits. Near here is the site of Bizarre, owned in 1742 by Richard Randolph of Curles. In 1781, his grandson, John Randolph of Roanoke, took refuge at Bizarre with his mother on account of Arnold's invasion. John Randolph lived here until 1810, when he moved to Roanoke in Charlotte County.

TOWN OF SOUTH BOSTON

UL-2 CAMPAIGN OF 1781

Rte. 501, near Rte. 304. Boyd's and Irwin's ferries to the west were used by Nathanael Greene in his passage of Dan River, in mid-February, 1781, while Cornwallis was in close pursuit. Edward Carrington collected the boats for the crossing.

Southwest Virginia

SOUTHWEST VIRGINIA encompasses the region extending from Roanoke
County in the northeast to Cumberland Gap in the southwest tip of the state,
and includes the Blue Ridge Mountains to the east. The area is bounded
by four states—West Virginia and Kentucky to the west, and Tennessee
and North Carolina to the south—and comprises the counties of Bland,
Buchanan, Carroll, Dickenson, Floyd, Giles, Grayson, Lee, Montgomery, Patrick, Pulaski, Roanoke, Russell, Scott, Smyth, Tazewell, Washington, Wise,
and Wythe; its cities include Bristol, Galax, Radford, Roanoke, and Salem.
Mountains, valleys, ridges, and plateaus define the region.

Archaeological evidence indicates that humans have lived in southwest
Virginia for at least ten thousand years. The Cherokee consider the area
to be part of their ancestral territory. Although there was some European
settlement by the 1740s, the region was more commonly used as a migratory
route: the Wilderness Road led from the Valley of Virginia to Cumberland
Gap and Kentucky. Both the British and the French sought allies among the
Native American nations, leading to multiple conflicts during the period of
the Seven Years' (1754–63) and the Revolutionary (1775–83) Wars.

By the beginning of the Revolutionary War, colonial settlers had built
a series of fortifications throughout the area, some of which were briefly
commanded by Daniel Boone. Many of these forts are featured on highway
markers.

Several communities had been settled by the middle of the nineteenth
century, including Abingdon, Big Lick (present-day Roanoke), Goodson
(present-day Bristol), and Salem. Between 1862 and 1865, Civil War battles,
raids, and skirmishes occurred at such places as Saltville, Marion, and Jonesville, each of which is featured on a marker.

Virginia Polytechnic Institute and State University was founded in 1872
as a land-grant college, marking the beginning of scientific agricultural and
industrial instruction in the commonwealth.

In the 1850s, railroad companies began building lines in southwest Virginia, often using slave and immigrant labor. The railroads spurred development in the region after the Civil War. Roanoke emerged as a rail center
during the 1880s, with the Norfolk and Western headquarters and numerous
other operations located there.

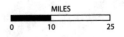

MILES

0   10   25

Railroad construction continued throughout the region into the twenti-eth century. One marker describes the "Virginia Creeper," which started in Washington County and wound through the mountains of Grayson County and into North Carolina.

This activity allowed for and promoted development of the timber and coal industries in southwest Virginia. Coal company towns arose throughout the region, while small farmsteads remained isolated in mountain hollows. Many workers found jobs in textile and garment mills that opened in such places as Grayson County, Galax, and Hillsville during the early part of the century.

One of southwest Virginia's lasting and influential legacies is its music. Noted twentieth-century musicians, including the legendary Carter family, Henry Whitter, Ernest Stoneman, and Carl Martin, are featured on histori-cal markers. Also highlighted is the Barter Theatre in Abingdon, which is the State Theatre of Virginia.

BLAND COUNTY

KC-1 BLAND

Rte. 52, near I-77. The community center was first known as Crab Orchard. The place became the county seat of Bland County when it was formed in 1861 under the name of Seddon, which was later changed to that of the county. At Rocky Gap a skirmish was fought in Crook's raid against the Virginia and Tennessee Railroad, May, 1864.

KC-2 A NOTED PREACHER

Rtes. 606 and 52, off I-77, Exit 62. William Elbert Munsey was born a few miles east in the mountains of Giles (present-day Bland) County on 13 July 1833. Despite little formal schooling, Munsey possessed an insatiable appetite for knowledge. He entered the ministry of the Methodist Church in 1855, preached his first sermon near here, and extended his ministry to several states. Regarded by many who heard him as the greatest Methodist preacher of his day, Munsey was poetic by nature, and his unrivaled word pictures held large audiences spellbound. His kindness extended to giving his own shoes and coat to a Confederate soldier who had none. Munsey died on 23 Oct. 1877.

KC-3 ONE OF THE "BIG FOUR"

Rte. 52, 7 miles south of Bland. Here is the home of S. H. Newberry, who, with three others, composed the "Big Four" in the Virginia Senate. These four men united to defeat objectionable measures of the Readjuster movement.

KC-5 HENRY C. GROSECLOSE

Rtes. 42 and 625, Ceres. Henry Casper Groseclose (1892–1950), a native of Ceres, was one of the founders of Future Farmers of Virginia (FFV). While teaching agricultural education at Virginia Polytechnic Institute, Groseclose, Walter Newman, Edmund Magill, and Harry Sanders in September 1925 established the FFV. Groseclose named the organization and wrote its constitution and bylaws. FFV developed as a statewide association for boys enrolled in high school vocational agriculture and was a model for establishing the Future Farmers of America in 1928. Groseclose, called by some the father of the Future Farmers of America for his role in its formation, served as its executive secretary (1928–1930) and treasurer (1930–1941).

CITY OF BRISTOL

K-42 BRISTOL, VIRGINIA

Rte. 11, at northern corporate limits. The Sapling Grove tract (Bristol) was surveyed for John Tayloe, 1749. It was owned by Isaac Baker and Evan Shelby, who built a post about 1770. The Virginia tract was bought by John Goodson, whose son founded the town of Goodson, incorporated in 1856. In 1863 and 1865 it was raided by Unionists and partly burned. In 1890 it was named Bristol when incorporated as a city.

K-43 HISTORIC BRISTOL

Randall Expressway and State Street, at train station. Evan Shelby, noted Indian fighter, settled here about 1765 on a tract called "Sapling Grove." His home was a neighborhood fort, the refuge of settlers in Indian attacks. Bristol grew around this place and became an early railroad center.

BUCHANAN COUNTY

XB-25 GRUNDY

Main Street, at courthouse. This place became the county seat when Buchanan County was formed, in 1858, and was probably named for Felix Grundy of Tennessee, statesman. In October, 1864, the Union General Burbridge passed through Grundy on his raid to Saltville. The town was incorporated in 1876.

CARROLL COUNTY

KD-12 HILLSVILLE

Rte. 52, at old courthouse, Hillsville. This place became the county seat when Carroll County was formed. The first court was held here, 1842; A. W. C. Nowlin was the first judge. The courthouse, built in 1872, was remodeled some years ago. The town was incorporated in 1900 and rechartered in 1940.

U-27 JOHN CARROLL

Rte. 58, approximately 1 mile east of Hillsville. During the 1842 session of the Virginia General Assembly, despite opposition, John Carroll successfully sponsored a bill partitioning Grayson County and forming a new county, thus fulfilling his campaign pledge. Local tradition holds that the controversy over the new county's name was resolved when there was agreement to honor Charles Carroll of Carrollton in Maryland, the last surviving signer of the Declaration of Independence. John Carroll's last residence, located nearby, was a plain two-story frame house with a gable roof. Carroll, born in Ireland in 1801, died in 1860 and is buried in Wytheville.

DICKENSON COUNTY

XB-10 OLD BUFFALO SCHOOL

Rte. 63, Nora. Established in 1875 on land given by Simpson Dyer, the Old Buffalo School became the first free school of Dickenson County in 1880. Alexander Johnson Skeen served as first teacher. The school remained in operation for twenty-five years, during which time it educated many future leaders in the area.

XB-11 CLINTWOOD

Rte. 83, Clintwood. The name originally was Holly Creek. In 1882 the county seat of Dickenson County was moved from Ervington to this place, which was named Clintwood for Major Henry Clinton Wood. The town was incorporated in 1894. With the coming of the railroad to the county in 1915, the population rapidly increased as the mineral and timber resources were opened.

XB-12 EARLY SETTLER

Rte. 83, Clintwood. Near here, on Holly Creek, John Mullins settled in 1829; becoming the second settler in this county. The county seat was moved from Nora to Clintwood in 1882.

XB-13 JOHN MULLINS

Rte. T-1009, at Rte. 83, Clintwood. Near here on Holly Creek, John Mullins settled in 1829, becoming the second settler in Dickenson County. His father John Mullins, the only known Revolutionary War soldier resting in this county, spent his last years here with his son. He died in 1849 and is buried nearby.

XB-23 INDIAN AND SETTLER CONFLICT

Rte. 80/83, Haysi. In August 1792, during a period of frontier unrest, Indians attacked the home of David Musick and his wife,

Annie, near Honaker in Russell County. They killed Musick and captured his wife and their five children, Abraham, Elijah, Samuel, Elexius, and Phoebe. The prisoners were marched to present-day Dickenson County at the junction of Russell Fork and Russell Prater Creek. Nearby a company of militiamen attacked the Indians and the surviving Musick family members escaped.

During the skirmish one Indian was killed and another was wounded. The remainder retreated westward.

XB-24 COLLEY'S CABIN

Rte. 80, 3 miles south of Haysi. Near here stood the cabin of Richard "Fighting Dick" Colley who was one of the earliest settlers in what is now Dickenson County.

FLOYD COUNTY

KG-5 FLOYD

Rte. 8, at courthouse, Floyd. This place became the county seat when Floyd County was formed in 1831. First called Jacksonville for Andrew Jackson, its name was changed to that of the county. The court-

house was built on land given by the Phlegar family. The town was incorporated in 1892 and rechartered in 1936. Here was born Admiral Robley D. Evans, hero of the Spanish-American War.

CITY OF GALAX

U-26 GALAX

Rte. 89 (Main Street), at park. The town is on the dividing line between Grayson and Carroll counties. Its original name was Bonaparte, which was changed to Galax,

the name of a mountain shrub abundant in the vicinity. In 1904 a spur of the Norfolk and Western Railroad came here, bringing the town into existence. It was incorporated in 1906.

GILES COUNTY

KB-56 EGGLESTON'S SPRINGS

Rte. 730, at Rte. 813, Eggleston. Near here Adam Harmon, probably in 1750, established what is believed to be the first settlement in Giles County. Here, in 1755, he found Mary Ingles as she was making her way back to Draper's Meadows after her escape from the Indians.

KG-14 CAMP JOHN J. PERSHING— CIVILIAN CONSERVATION CORPS— COMPANY 1370–2386

Rte. 460, at Rte. 1404, Pembroke. Near here is the original site of C.C.C. Company 1370–2386, known as Camp John J. Pershing, from 1933 to 1935, when it was moved to Nottoway County. Among the most popular New Deal programs, the

Civilian Conservation Corps was designed to encourage conservation of natural resources and employment training during the Great Depression. C.C.C. Company 1370–2386 built roads, fire trails, and fire towers, and carried out extensive reforestation efforts in this county.

KG-15 MOUNTAIN EVANGELIST

Rtes. 750 and 730. The Reverend Robert Sayers Sheffey (1820–1902), although one of a kind as to style and personality, was a Methodist Circuit Rider in the classic frontier tradition. Celebrated for the intensity of his faith and prayer, as well as for his eccentricities, Sheffey's authority was recognized throughout this region. He is buried nearby, in Wesley Chapel Cemetery, beside his second wife, Elizabeth Stafford Sheffey.

KG-16 OLD-FASHIONED CAMP MEETING

Rte. 100, 3.1 miles south of Giles/Pulaski County line. Adjacent to and named for this stream, Wabash Campground was exemplary of a religious and social institution, indeed of a way of life, which flourished during the 19th century. Hundreds of families would camp for two weeks or more while attending the revival meetings first held here in 1834. The campground functioned until the early 1900's, when the large shed used during worship and many family shelters were destroyed by fire.

KG-17 SNIDOW'S FERRY

Rte. 460, at New River bridge, 3 miles east of Pearisburg. In this vicinity Christian Snidow, pioneer, established a ferry over the river in 1786, and built a house in 1793.

KG-19 NEW RIVER

Rte. 460, at state boat ramp, approximately 2 miles west of Narrows corporate limits, Rich Creek. The New River is estimated to be more than 100 million years old, making it one of the oldest rivers in the world. It is a remnant of the prehistoric Teays River. The first written documentation of the New River was by explorers Thomas Batte and Robert Hallom. A Totera Indian guide led them there on 13 Sept. 1671. First called Wood's River, most likely for Abraham Wood, who launched the expedition, it became known as the New River by the middle of the 18th century. The New River is known for its treacherous current and stretches more than 300 miles through Virginia, North Carolina, and West Virginia.

KG-20 FIRST COURT OF GILES COUNTY

Rte. 460, just west of Rte. 640, Bluff City. Giles County was formed from Montgomery, Monroe (now in West Virginia), and Tazewell Counties in 1806. It was named for William Branch Giles, United States senator from Virginia and later governor. North of here, the first court of Giles County was held on 13 May 1806 at the house of George Pearis. The new county seat, Pearisburg, was established in 1808. Pearis donated 53 acres of land for the town. A temporary log structure was built by 1807 to house the court until a permanent stone courthouse was built around 1810. It was replaced by the current courthouse that was erected in 1836.

KG-21 PEARISBURG

Business Rte. 460, at courthouse, Pearisburg. The town was laid off in 1806 when Giles County was formed, and named for Captain George Pearis, early settler. Established in 1808, it was first incorporated in 1835, and reincorporated in 1914. Here, in May 1862, Union troops under Colonel Rutherford B. Hayes were defeated by Confederates under General Henry Heth. The present courthouse was erected in 1836.

KG-22 NARROWS

Rte. 61, Narrows. Named for the narrows in New River. The place was occupied by Confederate troops under French and Jackson in May, 1864. Combining with McCausland, they forced the Union General Crook to evacuate Blacksburg. Crook passed here on his way to West Virginia. The Norfolk and Western Railroad came in 1884; the Virginian in 1910. The town was incorporated in 1904.

GRAYSON COUNTY

KC-10 CATY SAGE

Rte. 21, 4 miles south of Grayson/Wythe County line. Nearby was the home of James and Lovice Sage, whose five-year-old daughter Caty was abducted in 1792. Fifty-six years later her brother Charles located her in eastern Kansas after a Wyandot Indian told him that a woman, named Yourowquains, with similar features to his lived with the Wyandots. Another brother, Samuel, investigated and confirmed that she was their sister. Through an interpreter, Yourowquains told them that a "white man" abducted her. She lived with the Cherokee, before they gave her as a present to the Wyandots, who adopted her. She had three Wyandot husbands and died in Jan. 1853.

U-22 INDEPENDENCE

Rtes. 58 and 21, Independence. This place became the county seat of Grayson County in 1850; the first case was tried in the newly erected courthouse in 1851. The present courthouse was built in 1908. Independence was incorporated in 1934.

U-23 PEYTON GUYN HALE

Rte. 21, at Elk Creek. Born in Elk Creek, Virginia, June 29, 1821, Member of the House of Delegates, 1874–1877. Member State Senate, 1879–1882. One of the "Big Four," a group which resisted many of the proposals of the Readjusters. Died in Elk Creek, December 25, 1885.

U-25 FIRST COUNTY SEAT

Rte. 640, near Galax. Here at Old Town, in 1794, was built the first courthouse of Grayson County. The land was donated by Flower Swift. A second courthouse was built in 1838. The county seat was removed to Independence about 1850.

UE-2 FRIES

Rte. 94, at Fries southern corporate limits. Fries is named for Colonel Francis H. Fries, of North Carolina, founder of the Washington Mills Company. By 1900, Fries and his associates had determined that the New River could power a textile mill. The town was incorporated in 1902, and by the following year a dam, a textile mill, and 300 houses had been built. The town of Fries is also known for its early influence on country music. Henry Whitter, a local employee at the textile mill, traveled to New York City in Dec. 1923 and recorded the "Wreck on the Southern Old 97" and "Lonesome Road Blues." Inspired by Whitter, local musicians Kelly Harrell and Ernest Stoneman also recorded songs.

UE-5 FIRST COURT OF GRAYSON COUNTY

Rte. 805, 5 miles southwest of Fries. Near here, in the barn of William Bourne, was held the first court of this county, May 21, 1793.

UE-6 FRIES—CENTER OF EARLY RECORDED COUNTRY MUSIC

Rte. 94, Fries. On 10 Dec. 1923, millhand Henry Whitter of Fries, Virginia, recorded nine songs in New York City for OKeh Records. Released early in 1924, the coupling of "Wreck on the Southern Old 97" and "Lonesome Road Blues" became one of the first successful country recordings. Whitter recorded more than 100 songs from 1923 to 1930. Whitter's success inspired others who had worked with him at the Fries Textile Plant to travel to New York and audition. Ernest V. "Pop" Stoneman made his first recordings in Sept. 1924, eventually exceeding Whitter's output. Likewise, Kelly Harrell traveled north in 1925 and continued to record throughout the 1920s.

UE-7 "NEW RIVER TRAIN" SONG

Rte. 94, at Rte. 1001, Fries. The original "New River Train" song was claimed by the Ward family of Galax as part of their repertoire as early as 1895. The song was believed to refer to the train that ran on the New River Line in 1883 as part of the Norfolk and Western system serving the town of Fries until 1985. It was first recorded in December 1923 by Henry Whitter. It has since been recorded by a number of artists, including local residents Kelly Harrell in 1925 and E. V. "Pop" Stoneman in 1928.

UE-8 MOUNT ROGERS

Rte. 600, 2 miles north of Mount Rogers fire station. Mount Rogers is the highest mountain peak in Virginia, and once was called Balsam Mountain likely for its large number of Fraser firs (*Abies fraseri*) then referred to as "Balsam" trees. It was named for William Barton Rogers (1804–1882), Virginia's state geologist from 1835 to 1842. During his tenure, he and his assistants inventoried natural resources throughout the state. He later founded the Massachusetts Institute of Technology, which admitted its first students in 1865, and served as its first president. Mount Rogers is located in the Mount Rogers National Recreation Area, which was created by the U.S. Congress in 1966.

UE-9 WHITE TOP FOLK FESTIVAL

Rte. 600, at National Forest Road. The White Top Folk Festival was held annually from 1931 to 1939 (except 1937) on Whitetop Mountain—the second highest peak in Virginia. Annabel Morris Buchanan, John Powell, and John A. Blakemore organized the event that featured banjo players, fiddlers, string bands, and ballad singers, as well as storytelling, clog dancing, morris and sword dancing, and theatrical presentations. Thousands of people attended the festival each year, including nationally known academic folklorists, art critics, composers, and in 1933 First Lady Eleanor Roosevelt. The festival was cancelled in 1940 because of heavy rains and floods and never resumed.

UE-10 "VIRGINIA CREEPER" RAILROAD

Rtes. 755 and 726, at former train station, Whitetop. The Abingdon Branch of the Norfolk & Western Railway was nicknamed the "Virginia Creeper," likely for the train's slow speed through this mountainous region. Initially chartered by the Abingdon Coal & Iron Railroad in 1887, little construction occurred until it was reorganized into the Virginia-Carolina Railway in 1898. By 1901 the railroad began providing passenger and freight service from Abingdon to Damascus and by 1913 reached Whitetop Station. By 1915 service was extended to present-day Todd, North Carolina. The line merged into the Norfolk & Western Railway in 1919. The last train ran in 1977. In the 1980s a portion of the old railroad bed was converted into the Virginia Creeper National Recreation Trail.

LEE COUNTY

K-1 CUMBERLAND GAP

Rte. 58, at Cumberland Gap Park. This pass was long the gateway to the West. On April 13, 1750, Dr. Thomas Walker reached the gap, which he named for the Duke of Cumberland, son of George II. A few years later Daniel Boone and numberless pioneers passed through it on the way to Kentucky. In August, 1863, Cumberland Gap was captured by a Union army under General Ambrose E. Burnside.

K-3 INDIAN MOUND

Rte. 58, 2 miles west of Rose Hill. A short distance north is the Ely Mound, the best-preserved Indian mound in Virginia. It dates to the Late Woodland–Mississippian Period (AD 1200–1650), during which more complex societies and practices evolved, including chiefdoms and religious ceremonies. Often, temples, elite residences, and council buildings stood atop substructure or townhouse mounds such as Ely Mound. Lucien Carr, assistant curator of the Peabody Museum in Boston, led an excavation here in 1877. By proving the connection between this mound and present-day Indians, Carr refuted the then-popular "lost race" hypothesis for Mound Builders in eastern North America.

K-4 MARTIN'S STATION

Old Rte. 58, Rose Hill. In March 1769 Joseph Martin led a party of men to the Powell

Valley, and attempted to establish a settlement nearby. By that fall they abandoned the site after conflicting with Native Americans. Martin returned here with a party of men in early 1775 and built a fort, known as Martin's Station on the north side of Martin's Creek. The wooden fort contained between five and six cabins built about 30 feet apart with stockades between each building. This site was abandoned in June 1776 during further regional conflicts between settlers and Native Americans.

K-5 FANNY DICKENSON SCOTT JOHNSON

Rte. 58, near Stickleyville Elementary School. In this valley in June 1785, Fanny Dickenson Scott's husband, Archibald Scott, their four children and a young male member of the nearby Ball family were killed by members of four different Indian tribes. The rest of the Ball family escaped, but Fanny Scott was taken prisoner. She later was able to flee her captors. After evading Indians and enduring many hardships, she reached the New Garden settlement in present day Russell County by 11 August. Newspapers as far as away as Philadelphia reported her ordeal. She later married Thomas Johnson for whom Johnson County, Tennessee is named. She died in May 1796 in Russell County.

K-6 THOMPSON SETTLEMENT CHURCH

Rte. 758, 10.2 miles southwest of Jonesville. This Baptist church, a mile southeast, is the oldest church in Lee County. It was organized in 1800; the original site was on Powell's River, a short distance west. James Kinney was the first pastor. The church was removed to the present site in 1822.

K-7 WHITE ROCKS

Rte. 58, 0.25 miles west of Ewing. The cliffs to the north were a familiar landmark along the Wilderness road which was blazed by Daniel Boone in March, 1775, and which was the principal route from Virginia to Kentucky. They are part of the Cumberland Mountains.

K-8 DOCTOR STILL'S BIRTHPLACE

Rte. 58, at Rte. 662, Jonesville. Andrew Taylor Still, physician and founder of osteopathy, was born two miles southwest, near the Natural Bridge of Lee County, August 6, 1828. Dr. Still served in the War between the States. He established the first American school of osteopathy in 1892 at Kirksville, Missouri. He died there, December 12, 1917.

K-9 JONESVILLE METHODIST CAMP GROUND

Rte. 58, 1 mile west of Jonesville. This Camp Ground was established in 1810 as a place for religious services for the Methodists of Lee County on lands given by Elkanah Wynn. In June 1827, Rev. Abraham Still, Daniel Dickenson, George Morris, Evans Peery, Henry Thompson, Elkanah Wynn and James Woodward were appointed trustees; the present auditorium was built in 1827–28. The massive oak columns were hewn by Henry Woodward, David Orr, Robert Wynn and Rev. Joseph Haskew.

K-10 JONESVILLE

Rte. 58, Jonesville. This town was established in 1794 as the county seat of Lee County and was named for Frederick Jones. Here on January 3, 1864, General William E. Jones, assisted by Colonel A. L. Pridemore, defeated a Union force, capturing the battalion. Union troops burned the courthouse in 1864. The present courthouse was erected in 1933. The town was incorporated in 1834, and reincorporated in 1901.

K-32 DEATH OF BOONE'S SON

Rte. 58, near Stickleyville Elementary School. In this valley, on 10 Oct. 1773, Delaware, Shawnee, and Cherokee Indians killed Daniel Boone's eldest son, James, and five others in their group of eight settlers en route to Kentucky. Separated from Daniel Boone's main party, the men had set up camp near Wallen's Creek. At dawn the Indians attacked and killed James Boone, Henry Russell, John and Richard Mendenhall (brothers), a youth whose last name was Drake, and Charles (one of two slaves in the party). Isaac Crabtree and Adam, a slave, escaped. This event prompted Boone and his party to abandon their first attempt to settle Kentucky.

KA-8 Donelson's Indian Line

Rte. 23, 5 miles south of Big Stone Gap. John Donelson's line, surveyed after the treaty of Lochaber with the Indians, 1770, crossed the road here. This line separated Indian territory from land open to settlement. Violations of the line by settlers contributed to Dunmore's War, 1774.

X-24 Seminary United Methodist Church

Rte. 58, a few miles south of Big Stone Gap. The Seminary United Methodist Church was established in 1851 in Turkey Cove. Over the years this structure has served as a church, a school, and a Masonic Lodge. Its first board of trustees included W. N. G. Barron, James F. Jones, Henry C. Slemp, John W. Slemp, and John Snodgrass. W. W. Farthing was the first circuit rider. The building, made of local brick, originally had a wooden second story. It was damaged by fire in the 1860s; only the brick walls

remained. A committee was appointed in 1873 to rebuild the structure. Heavy winds about 1923 caused further damage. When repairs were made, memorial stained glass windows were installed.

X-26 Members of Congress

Rte. 58, a few miles south of Big Stone Gap. Three men who served in Congress were born within a one-mile radius of this point. James B. Richmond (1842–1910) was a member of the House of Representatives from 1879 to 1881 as a Democrat. Campbell Slemp (1839–1907), a Republican, was elected to the House of Representatives in 1902 and served until his death on 13 Oct. 1907. His son, Campbell Bascom Slemp (1870–1943), replaced him in the House in 1907 and was reelected to seven consecutive terms until he retired in 1922. The next year, he was appointed President Calvin Coolidge's secretary and served until 1925.

X-30 Pennington Gap

Rte. 58, Pennington Gap. Pennington Gap is a mountain pass named for an early settler. The town came into existence with the extension of the Louisville and Nashville Railroad, 1890. It was incorporated in 1891. Standing on a short-cut highway to eastern Kentucky, it is a center for an extensive coal-mining region.

MONTGOMERY COUNTY

I-2-a Virginia Polytechnic Institute and State University

Rte. 460, just west of Rte. 777, Christiansburg. Five miles south lies the main campus of Virginia Polytechnic Institute and State University, founded in 1872 as a land-grant college specializing in agriculture and mechanical arts. The land-grant college system initiated scientific agricultural and industrial instruction in the Commonwealth. Over the next century, Virginia Tech became nationally recognized as a

comprehensive research university with a broad range of scientific, technological, business, and liberal arts instruction. The 3,000-acre campus includes the site of Draper's Meadow, where Shawnee Indians attacked settlers on 30 July 1755 at the beginning of the French and Indian War.

I-2-b Virginia Polytechnic Institute

Rte. 11, at western entrance to Christiansburg. Nine miles north is the Virginia Polytechnic

Institute, a state college of agriculture, engineering and business, established in 1872, as a land-grant college, on the site of the Draper's Meadows massacre of 1755. Its founding marked the beginning of scientific agricultural and industrial instruction in Virginia. The college includes agricultural and engineering experiment stations.

I-2-c VIRGINIA POLYTECHNIC INSTITUTE

Rte. 460, Blacksburg. A state college of agriculture, engineering and business, established in 1872, as a land-grant college, on the site of the Draper's Meadows massacre of 1755. Its founding marked the beginning of scientific agricultural and industrial instruction in Virginia. The college includes agricultural and engineering experiment stations.

I-2-d VIRGINIA POLYTECHNIC INSTITUTE AND STATE UNIVERSITY

Business Rte. 460, Blacksburg. Virginia Polytechnic Institute and State University was founded in 1872 as a land-grant college specializing in agriculture and mechanics. The land-grant college system marked the beginning of scientific agricultural and industrial instruction in the Commonwealth. Over the next century Virginia Tech became nationally recognized as a comprehensive research university with a broad range of scientific, technological, business, and liberal arts instruction. The 3,000-acre main campus includes the site of Drapers Meadow where settlers were killed and captured on 8 July 1755 by Ohio-based Shawnee Indians at the beginning of the French and Indian War.

I-2-e VIRGINIA POLYTECHNIC INSTITUTE AND STATE UNIVERSITY

Rte. 314, 0.25 miles east of Bypass Rte. 460, at Southgate Drive information center, Blacksburg. Virginia Polytechnic Institute and State University was founded in 1872 as a land-grant college specializing in agricul-

ture and mechanics. The land-grant college system marked the beginning of scientific agricultural and industrial instruction in the Commonwealth. Over the next century Virginia Tech became nationally recognized as a comprehensive research university with a broad range of scientific, technological, business, and liberal arts instruction. The 3,000-acre main campus includes the site of Drapers Meadow where settlers were killed and captured on 8 July 1755 by Ohio-based Shawnee Indians at the beginning of the French and Indian War.

I-20 SOLITUDE

Rte. 314 (West Campus Drive), at Virginia Polytechnic Institute, Blacksburg. The earliest portion of Solitude was constructed about 1801 on land owned by Philip Barger, who sold the property in 1803 to James Patton Preston, governor of Virginia (1816–1819). Governor John Floyd (1830–1834), Preston's brother-in-law, lived at Solitude about 1814–1815. Preston's son, Col. Robert Preston, enlarged the house from a simple log dwelling to a central-passage-plan, Greek Revival–style house about 1851. Col. Preston sold Solitude in 1872 to secure the location of Virginia's first land-grant university, Virginia Polytechnic Institute and State University.

K-64 FOUNDING OF THE FUTURE FARMERS OF VIRGINIA

Rte. 314, 0.25 miles east of Bypass Rte. 460, at Southgate Drive information center, Blacksburg. The Future Farmers of Virginia (FFV) was founded on the campus of Virginia Polytechnic Institute by four members of the Agricultural Education Department in September, 1925. Developed as a statewide organization for boys enrolled in high school vocational agriculture, the FFV was used as a model for establishing the Future Farmers of America. The four founders were Walter Newman, Henry Groseclose, Edmund Magill, and Harry Sanders.

K-67 FOTHERINGAY

Rte. 11, 2 miles south of Elliston, 4.5 miles west of Montgomery/Roanoke County line. Fotheringay was the home of George Hancock (1754–1820), a colonel in the Virginia Line during the Revolutionary War and aide-de-camp to Count Casimir Pulaski. He later served in both the Virginia House of Delegates and in the U.S. Congress, and was the father-in-law of explorer William Clark. Fotheringay, an elegant expression of the Federal style, was built about 1796 with a steep mountain as a dramatic backdrop. Fotheringay's interior woodwork, particularly its chimneypieces and doorways, features delicately carved motifs copied from the pattern books of English architect William Pain.

K-68 CHRISTIANSBURG INDUSTRIAL INSTITUTE

Business Rte. 460, 1 mile west of Rte. 11, Christiansburg. In 1866, Captain Charles S. Schaeffer, a Freedmen's Bureau agent, organized a school for blacks on the hill just to the southeast. Charles L. Marshall of Tuskeegee [Tuskegee] Institute became principal of the school in 1896. Under his guidance and with support from Philadelphia Quakers, a library, dormitories, classrooms, shops, and barns were constructed. Both academic and industrial classes were offered at the institute until 1947 when it became a public high school. In 1966, the institute graduated its last class, and its property was sold at public auction.

K-71 LEWIS-MCHENRY DUEL

Rte. 11, at courthouse, Christiansburg. In this town occurred the duel between Thomas Lewis and John McHenry in May, 1808. This was the first duel with rifles known to have taken place in Virginia. It resulted in the death of both men. Dr. John Floyd, later Governor of Virginia and member of Congress, was the attending surgeon. This affair contributed to the passage in January, 1810, of the Barbour Bill outlawing dueling in Virginia.

K-72 CHRISTIANSBURG

Business Rte. 11/460, east of Rte. 111, Christiansburg. Christiansburg, originally known as "Hans' Meadows," was established in 1792 and named for Colonel William Christian noted Colonial and Revolutionary Indian fighter. It became an important place on the route to the West. On May 10, 1864, Averell raided the town on an expedition into southwest Virginia. On April 5, Stoneman raided it while destroying railroads.

K-73 FORT VAUSE

Rte. 753 (Old Rte. 11), approximately 0.75 miles from Rte. 11, Shawsville. Ephraim Vause was appointed Captain of Horse in 1753 and was considered a man of considerable influence. For the protection of his family and his neighbors he built a simple palisaded fort nearby on his farm. In June 1756, during the French and Indian War, Indians attacked and burned the fort; a relief party led by Maj. Andrew Lewis arrived too late to save most of the occupants. Capt. Peter Hogg quickly rebuilt the fort, as a composite earth-and-palisade structure. George Washington inspected Fort Vause in October 1756 during his tour of Virginia's frontier defenses.

KG-8 COLONEL WILLIAM PRESTON

Business Rte. 460, Blacksburg. One mile west is "Smithfield", old home of Col. Wm. Preston, who materially guided the destiny of the Virginia frontier from the French and Indian War through the Revolution. On this estate two Virginia governors were born: James P. Preston, 1816–19; John B. Floyd, 1849–52. The latter was the son of another Virginia governor, John Floyd, 1830–34, who while in office advocated before the legislature abolition of slavery in Virginia.

KG-9 SMITHFIELD

Rte. 314, 0.25 miles east of Bypass Rte. 460, at Southgate Drive information center, Blacksburg. Smithfield, visible to the northeast, was the last home of Col. William Preston, a noted surveyor who fostered the settlement of western lands. Preston was also a Revolutionary officer, Indian fighter, and member of the House of Burgesses. Built soon after 1773, Smithfield is one of the earliest surviving houses in southwestern Virginia. The house is a remarkable expression of architectural sophistication in what only a generation before had been the edge of the frontier. Smithfield remained in the possession of Preston descendants for almost two hundred years.

KG-10 MARY DRAPER INGLES

West Campus Drive, at Duck Pond Drive, at Virginia Polytechnic Institute, Blacksburg. On 30 July 1755, during the French and Indian War, Shawnee Indians attacked the Draper's Meadow settlement nearby. They killed Col. James Patton, Casper Barger, Mrs. George Draper, and a Draper child, wounded James Cull, and captured Mary Draper Ingles, her two sons, Mrs. John Draper, and Henry Leonard. The Indians took their captives to Ohio. After several months, Ingles escaped and wandered some 800 miles to return home, a legendary feat. She and her husband, William, moved near Radford and operated a New River ferry. She died and was buried there in 1815, aged 83.

KG-12 MONTGOMERY WHITE SULPHUR SPRINGS

I-81 North, 0.75 miles north of Exit 128, at Ironto rest area. Near here stood Montgomery White Sulphur Springs, popular resort area of 19th century America. During the Civil War the resort was converted into a military hospital staffed by Catholic nuns. Several hundred victims of smallpox including nurses and soldiers are buried nearby. The Southern Historical Society was reorganized here in August, 1873, when Jefferson Davis delivered the principal address.

KG-24 WILLIAM BLACK

Business Rte. 460 (Main Street), near Jackson Street, Blacksburg. Just northeast stood the home of William Black, the founder of Blacksburg. In 1797, he laid out a 16-block grid and petitioned the Virginia General Assembly to incorporate a town here; the legislature approved his petition on 13 January 1798. On 4 August 1798, he deeded the 38¾-acre site to the town's trustees, who included his brother and himself. Black served as a justice of the peace before moving to Ohio. He died there in 1850 at the age of 84 and he was buried in Pike Township, Clark County.

KG-25 PRICE'S FORK

Price's Fork Road, Blacksburg. Price's Fork is within the area often referred to as the German New River Settlement. Before 1745, German immigrants moved from Pennsylvania and began settling in this region within the Price's Fork–Tom's Creek area near and along the horseshoe bottoms of the New River. They were among the earliest settlers of European descent in the western section of present-day Virginia. Price's Fork received its name from the Price (Preisch) family, early German settlers here, whose land bordered both sides of the road. Price's Fork evolved into a village during the mid-19th century. Portions of the community's buildings are within the Prices Fork Historic District on the National Register of Historic Places.

PATRICK COUNTY

AS-1 FAIRY STONE STATE PARK

Rte. 623, near park. Roanoke newspaper publisher Junius B. Fishburn donated the land to create Fairy Stone State Park. It is named for the cross-shaped crystals found in the region, which according to legend were formed from the tears of fairies. The National Park Service and the Civilian Conservation Corps, in conjunction with the Virginia Conservation Commission, developed the park. Construction began in 1933 and the park was opened on 15 June 1936. It was one of the first six state parks opened in Virginia, covering close to 5,000 acres, and is one of the largest.

HD-1 COLONEL ABRAM PENN

Rte. 626, 8.6 miles north of Rte. 58. 200 yards south is "Poplar Grove," Penn's old home and burial place. At age 21, he "won his spurs," leading a company under General Lewis at Point Pleasant. During 1780–81 he organized the first Revolutionary troops from Henry and adjoining counties, and led his regiment to aid General Greene in the battles of Guilford Court House and Eutaw Springs. He helped organize Patrick County.

KG-2 STUART'S BIRTHPLACE

Rte. 773, off Rte. 103. To the west stood Laurel Hill (built about 1830), where Confederate Maj. Gen. James Ewell Brown "Jeb" Stuart was born on 6 Feb. 1833 to Archibald Stuart, a lawyer and politician, and Elizabeth Letcher Pannill Stuart. The house burned in the winter of 1847–1848. After graduation from the U.S. Military Academy at West Point in 1854, Stuart served as a U.S. Army officer until May 1861 when he joined the Confederate army. In 1862, he became cavalry commander of the Army of Northern Virginia, and his fame is a part of the history of that army. Wounded while defending Richmond on 11 May 1864, Stuart died there the next day. He is buried at Hollywood Cemetery in Richmond.

U-28 BLUE RIDGE MISSION SCHOOL

Rte. 8, at Rte. 613. The Blue Ridge Mission School was established by the Virginia Baptist General Convention in 1916 at a site just to the southeast. It provided general education and religious training, on both the elementary and secondary level, to day and boarding students. Its program was increasingly coordinated with, and in 1941 superseded by, that of the newly-developed public school system.

U-30 STUART

Rte. 58, at courthouse, Stuart. This place, first known as Taylorsville for George Taylor, early settler, was established in 1792 after the formation of Patrick County. In 1849 it contained about fifty dwellings. The name was changed to Stuart for General J. E. B. Stuart, C.S.A., who was born in the county. The courthouse was built in 1852 and remodeled in 1928.

U-32 FRONTIER FORT

Rte. 58, 14 miles east of Stuart. About three miles north stood Fort Mayo, commanded by Captain Samuel Harris in 1756 and visited in that year by Washington. This fort was the southernmost of the line of stockade forts built from the Potomac River to North Carolina as a frontier defense in the French and Indian War.

U-34 REYNOLDS HOMESTEAD

Rte. 58, at Rte. 626, Critz. Four miles to the north is Rock Spring Plantation, the boyhood home of Industrialist R. J. Reynolds. The land was settled in 1814 by Abram Reynolds and his wife Mary Harbour. About 1843 their son Hardin William Reynolds built the present brick house for his bride Nancy Jane Cox. The couple had 16 children, including Richard Joshua Reynolds, who founded R. J. Reynolds Tobacco Company. In 1970 the house was restored by Hardin's granddaughter, Nancy Susan Reynolds.

U-36 WILLIAM BYRD'S SURVEY OF 1728

Rte. 660, 4 miles south of Rte. 8, at state line. This was the westernmost point of the survey of the Virginia–North Carolina border run in 1728 by a Joint Commission from both colonies led by Col. William

Byrd II of Westover. The exact end of the line was marked on October 16, 1728, by a blazed red oak tree on the east bank of Peter's Creek.

PULASKI COUNTY

K-25 THE NEW RIVER

Rte. 11, at New River bridge, near Pulaski/ Montgomery County line. Not "new" at all, the New River, the second oldest in the world, is more than 320 million years old. Only the Nile is older. The river received its original English name, Wood's River, perhaps from Colonel Abraham Wood who explored the area in 1654, from the 1671 expedition on which he sent Thomas Batte and Robert Hallom, or from Thomas Wood (possibly his son) who died on the 1671 trip. The name New derives from New Brittaine or New Virginia, for the western territory of the Carolinas and Virginia where the river begins, as mentioned after 1651 in official London reports.

K-29 FIRST SETTLEMENT

Rte. 11, 1.9 miles south of Radford. About five miles southwest is Dunkard Bottom, where Dr. Thomas Walker found [founded] a settlement in 1750. The fort there was built about 1756 and was the first fort in Virginia west of New River. The first store and first mill were also there.

K-38 BATTLE OF CLOYD'S MOUNTAIN

Rte. 100, 1.4 miles north of Rte. 627, north of Dublin. In April 1864 Grant ordered Brig. Gen. George Crook to cut the Virginia & Tennessee RR in Southwest Virginia. Near Cloyd's Mountain, five miles north of Dublin, on 9 May Crook battled Confederate defenders commanded by Brig. Gen. Albert G. Jenkins. Attacking Jenkins's right flank, Crook drove him from his earthworks after a sharp engagement with heavy casualties on both sides. Jenkins was mortally wounded and lost 538 of 2,400 men (23 percent). Crook severed the railroad at Dublin and withdrew on 11 May.

K-40 DRAPER'S VALLEY

Rte. 11, 1.9 miles south of Pulaski. John Draper's wife, Bettie Robertson Draper, was captured by the Shawnee at Draper's Meadow (Blacksburg) in 1755. Mrs. Draper was carried into the Ohio country along with her sister-in-law Mary Draper Ingles and five others. Six years later John Draper found his wife living in the family of an Indian chief. After paying for her return, the Drapers went home to the New River Valley. About 1765 they moved into a log cabin in the area still known as Draper's Valley—just to the south and west.

K-41 PULASKI

Rte. 11, Pulaski. The town sprang up at the coming of the railroad and was first known as Martin's Tank. Governor John Floyd lived near by. The county seat was moved here from Newburn in 1894. The town, like the county, was named for Count Casimir Pulaski, killed in the siege of Savannah, 1779. It was incorporated in 1886. Zinc and iron were early industries.

K-45 PAGE'S MEETING HOUSE

Rte. 11, 1.5 miles south of Radford. One mile to the north stood this Methodist Chapel, an early one in the New River area. It was built on land given in 1795 by Alexander Page. Bishop Francis Asbury preached in the Chapel in 1802 and again in 1806.

KE-5 BATTLE OF CLOYD'S MOUNTAIN

Rte. 100, 5 miles north of Dublin, at Clebourne Wayside. Just to the west took place the battle of Cloyd's Mountain, May 9, 1864. The Union General Crook, raiding to destroy the Virginia and Tennessee Railroad (N.&W.), met and repulsed General A. G. Jenkins, who was mortally wounded.

CITY OF RADFORD

K-65 RADFORD

Rte. 11, just north of Rte. 177, at Radford University,. It originated as a railroad town in 1856 and was known as Central. In 1862–65 this section was in the range of Union raids; Confederates burned the bridge at Ingles Ferry to retard raiders. Incorporated in 1887 as a town, the place was incorporated as a city in 1892 and named Radford, for Dr. John B. Radford, prominent citizen. Radford State Teachers College was established here, 1913.

K-66 STATE TEACHERS COLLEGE AT RADFORD

Marker missing. Original location: Rte. 11, at Radford University. A state college for women established in 1910. Opened 1913. Empowered by legislature in 1916 to grant degrees in education and in the arts and sciences. Present name authorized in 1924. The John Preston McConnell Library,

named for the first president of the college, contains a valuable collection on the history of Southwest Virginia.

K-70 INGLES FERRY ROAD

Rte. 11, just west of Rte. 177. As the population in the New River valley increased in the 18th century, the western branch of the Great Wagon Road from Philadelphia to the backcountry of the Carolinas and Georgia crossed the region. The branch became known as the Wilderness Road. After Daniel Boone and others improved it about 1775, it was the main route of migration to Kentucky and the West through Cumberland Gap. This segment of the Wilderness Road ascended the Allegheny Mountains at Christiansburg, crossed the New River at Ingles Ferry, then continued west. In the 19th century, the Ingles Ferry Road was incorporated into the South Western Turnpike.

CITY OF ROANOKE

K-76 OLD LUTHERAN CHURCH

Rte. 11 (Brandon Avenue). Tradition has it that the church near by was built where Moravian and Lutheran missionaries preached soon after the Revolution. Here, in 1796, Lutherans held services and, a little later, organized their first congregation in this section. In 1828, the Lutheran synod of North Carolina met here and consecrated the church.

K-95 ROANOKE

Rte. 221, at Jefferson Street and Day Avenue, at library. [*Obverse*] The first village here, at Pate's Mill and Tavern on Evans' Mill Creek, was called Big Lick for nearby salt marshes. In 1839 it was laid off as the town of Gainesborough. After the coming of the Virginia and Tennessee Railroad (later N.&W.) in 1852, another village sprang up about the old Stover House that was also

named Big Lick. Gainesborough became known as Old Lick. [*Reverse*] In June, 1864, General Hunter passed here retreating from Lynchburg. In 1874 Big Lick was incorporated. In 1881, with the junction of the new Shenandoah Valley Railroad with the N.&W., rapid growth began. In 1882 the name was changed to Roanoke; in 1884 it was incorporated as a city. In 1909 the Virginian Railroad operated its first train. In recent years Roanoke became the third city of Virginia.

K-96 ROANOKE CITY MARKET

Campbell Avenue and Market Street, at Center in the Square. The Roanoke farmers' market is one of the oldest such markets in continuous use in Virginia. In 1882, licenses were issued to twenty-five hucksters. The City of Roanoke's first charter formally authorized a municipally owned market in 1884, and

In 1892, the Norfolk and Western Railroad built the Hotel Roanoke, pictured here in 1931. The hotel is an important landmark in Roanoke and is listed on the National Register of Historic Places. (Markers K-98-a and K-98-b) (Virginia Department of Historic Resources)

the first permanent market building was completed in 1886. This formed the core of a continuing curb market in and around the Market Square. The present market building was erected in 1922 to replace the original market structure.

K-98-a HOTEL ROANOKE

Wells Avenue, at tunnel walkway, Hotel Roanoke Conference Center. The Hotel Roanoke was built in 1892 by the Norfolk and Western Railroad. Over the next century, despite fire and depression, it became the city's social center. The Tudor Revival building became a beloved landmark for thousands of visitors. Its original 34 rooms had grown to 384 rooms when, in 1989, the N&W donated it to Virginia Polytechnic Institute and State University. After a major renovation and the addition of a conference center, it reopened in 1995. The Hotel Roanoke was listed on the Virginia Landmarks Register in 1995 and the National Register of Historic Places in 1996.

K-98-b HOTEL ROANOKE

Wells Avenue, at entrance, Hotel Roanoke Conference Center. The Hotel Roanoke was built in 1892 by the Norfolk and Western Railroad. Over the next century, despite fire and depression, it became the city's social center. The Tudor Revival building

became a beloved landmark for thousands of visitors. Its original 34 rooms had grown to 384 rooms when, in 1989, the N&W donated it to Virginia Polytechnic Institute and State University. After a major renovation and the addition of a conference center, it reopened in 1995. The Hotel Roanoke was listed on the Virginia Landmarks Register in 1995 and the National Register of Historic Places in 1996.

K-99 MOUNT MORIAH BAPTIST CHURCH

Rte. 460, 0.14 miles east of King Avenue, at church. The members of Mount Moriah Baptist Church belong to one of the region's earliest African American congregations, originating in a Sunday school for slaves established in the mid-1800s by Dr. Charles L. Cocke, founder of Hollins College. The group gained permission in 1858 to build its first church. The present church, the congregation's third, was built about 1908. It was added to the National Register of Historic Places and the Virginia Landmarks Register in 1994. The nearby cemetery was expanded from a former slave burial ground.

K-100 FIRST TRAIN TO BIG LICK

Marker not yet cast. Proposed location to be determined. Nearby, on 1 Nov. 1852 the first

Virginia & Tennessee Railroad train arrived in Big Lick (now Roanoke), three years after the company had been incorporated. The track from Lynchburg to Bristol, Tennessee, built largely using slave and Irish immigrant labor, was completed in 1856. In 1870, the railroad combined with the Southside and the Norfolk & Petersburg Railroads to form the Atlantic, Mississippi & Ohio Railroad, which became the Norfolk & Western Railroad in 1881. During the 1880s, Roanoke became a rail center. Numerous railroad facilities were located here including locomotive and railcar manufacturing plants, roundhouses, a large freight yard, a passenger station, and the headquarters of Norfolk & Western (1881–1982).

K-116 A COLONIAL FORD

Business Rte. 220, near Wiley Drive. The Great Wagon Road from Philadelphia to the backcountry of the Carolinas crossed the Roanoke River here at Tosh's Ford, named for Thomas Tosh, in the eighteenth century. Nearby stood Daniel Evans's mill,

another landmark on the road. A group of Moravians, among the many thousands of settlers who passed this way, crossed the ford at dawn on 2 Nov. 1783 en route from Bethlehem, Pa., to Bethabara, N.C. One wrote in his diary of the ford's "slippery stones" and reported that "a quarter of a mile beyond we came to Even's mill." Mill Mountain is named for Evans's mill.

K-117 BUZZARD ROCK NATIVE AMERICAN SETTLEMENT

13th Street, north of Tayloe Street. The archaeological sites on the extensive floodplain nearby represent at least ten thousand years of periodic use by Native Americans. The artifacts and evidence from one site suggests that separate villages were occupied there some six hundred to one thousand years ago. The site is believed to have been inhabited by ancestors of a Siouan-speaking community, such as the Totero Indians, who were allied with the Monacan Indians and other communities of central and western Virginia.

ROANOKE COUNTY

A-79 HOLLINS COLLEGE

Rte. 11, 5.8 miles north of Roanoke, at college. First chartered college for women in Virginia, established 1842. The estate was the pioneer home of William Carvin, who settled here before 1746.

I-4 CATAWBA SANATORIUM

Rte. 311, near Rte. 779, Catawba. This institution, one mile northeast, stands on the site of the old Roanoke Red Sulphur Springs, which by 1859 was a noted summer resort. The sanatorium was established by the General Assembly of Virginia in 1908 for the treatment of persons suffering with incipient tuberculosis. It opened its doors on July 30, 1909. The location was selected for its bracing and healthy climate.

K-74 COLONIAL MANSION SITE

Rte. 11, 0.5 miles west of Salem city limits. The home of James Campbell, a leading colonial pioneer, who settled here in 1742, stood on this site. On his land Fort Lewis was built in 1756.

KH-7 HANGING ROCK

Rte. 419, near I-81, north of Salem, Hanging Rock. On June 31, 1864 General Hunter, retreating from defeat at Lynchburg by General Early, met Confederate forces led by General John McCausland. After losing some of his artillery here, Hunter continued his withdrawal northwest through New Castle to Lewisburg.

RUSSELL COUNTY

KA-13 DORTON'S FORT

Rte. 71, approximately 2 miles from Rtes. 71 and 58. William Dorton Sr and his family settled near here by 1773 and built a fort, one of several defensive structures built by settlers of European descent on the Virginia frontier. Dorton's sons William Jr, Moses, and Edward fought in the Revolutionary War. Edward and at least one of the two other brothers served at the Battle of King's Mountain on 7 Oct. 1780. During this period, conflicts occurred between early settlers and Native Americans in this region, resulting in the death of a fourth son, name unknown, in 1777. Capt. William Dorton Jr served in the Washington and Russell County militias and died in 1826. He is buried just southwest of here.

X-3 FRANCES DICKENSON SCOTT JOHNSON

Rtes. 80 and 619, 3.8 miles east of Rte. 19/460. Near this site is the grave of Frances Dickenson Scott Johnson (died 1796), sister of Henry Dickenson who was the first clerk of Russell County. In 1785, while living in Powell's Valley in Scott County, her first husband, Archibald Scott, and their four children were murdered by Indians, and she was taken captive. She ultimately escaped, and after wandering in the rugged mountains of Kentucky for nearly a month, made her way back to Russell County. She later married Thomas Johnson.

X-4 OLD RUSSELL COUNTY COURTHOUSE

Rte. 19, 0.5 miles east of Rte. 71, Lebanon. This building, erected in 1799, served as the second courthouse of Russell County and is one of the earliest public buildings still standing in Southwest Virginia. Russell County was formed in 1786 from Washington County and originally encompassed the greater part of what is now Lee, Scott, Wise, Dickenson, Buchanan, and Tazewell counties. The county sold the building when the county seat was moved to the town of Lebanon in 1818.

X-5 EARLY SETTLERS IN RUSSELL COUNTY

Rte. 71, at Grassy Creek Church. In 1787, Isaiah Salyer (1752–1818), son of Zachariah Salyer (1730–1789) of North Carolina, settled on Copper Creek, two miles southeast of here. Isaiah's brothers John Benjamin, and Zachariah, and sisters Sarah, wife of Solomon Saylor, and Rebecca, wife of Stephen Kilgore, settled on nearby land. The Salyer land was officially surveyed in 1790. The Salyers intermarried with other Virginia pioneer families—Castle, Isaacs, Nickels, Stapleton, Vicars, and Byerley.

X-6 RUSSELL COURTHOUSE

Rte. 19, Lebanon. The county government was organized at Russell's Fort, May 9, 1786, with the following officers: Alexander Barnett, County Lieutenant; David Ward, Sheriff; Henry Dickenson, Clerk. Justices: Alexander Barnett, Thomas Carter, Henry Smith, Henry Dickenson, David Ward, John Thompson, Samuel Ritchie. The present courthouse was built in 1874.

X-7 RUSSELL'S FORT

Rte. 615, Castlewood. On the hill to the north stood Russell's Fort, an important link in the chain of forts built to protect settlers on Clinch River in the Indian War of 1774. William Russell, who established it, was a prominent soldier of the Revolution.

X-8 GLADE HOLLOW FORT

Rte. 71, 1 mile west of Lebanon. A short distance south stood Glade Hollow Fort, garrisoned by twenty-one men in 1774. From Witten's to Blackmore's these Clinch Valley forts were the frontier defenses in Dunmore's War, 1774.

X-9 ELK GARDEN FORT

Rte. 19, 8 miles east of Lebanon. This fort was one of a string of defensive posts and protective forts that served the community of Elk Garden and isolated homes in the Clinch Valley in the 18th century. There is no known date of construction, but it is believed to have been a large and well-stockaded fort. An important outpost during the Indian wars of the frontier period, it was garrisoned by 1774 under the command of Captain John Kinkead. The site was later the homestead of Governor Henry Carter Stuart (1914–1918).

X-18 MOORE'S FORT

Rte. 65, Mew. Moore's Fort, also referred to as Byrd's Fort, stood nearby close to the Clinch River. Built by 1774 and likely named for the owners of the property, the wooden structure served as defensive fortification for settlers of European descent on the frontier. Daniel Boone commanded this fort and Blackmore's and Cowan's forts on the Clinch River during Lord Dunmore's War in 1774. During that war and the American Revolution (1775–1783), periodic conflicts between Native Americans and settlers occurred there, in part, because of increased settlement.

XY-17 SMITH'S FORT

Rte. 19, 17.5 miles east of Lebanon. Near here, in 1774, stood Daniel Smith's Fort, also known as Fort Christian. The fort was named for Smith, who was a surveyor and captain of the military company on upper Clinch River.

CITY OF SALEM

I-11-b ROANOKE COLLEGE

Rte. 112, 0.5 miles north of Rte. 11/460. At Salem is a liberal arts institution for men and women. Founded in Augusta County in 1842 as Virginia Institute, it was chartered in 1845 as Virginia Collegiate Institute; moved to Salem in 1847; chartered as Roanoke College in 1853, and was in operation throughout 1861–65. The students formed a company in the Confederate Army, Virginia Reserves, September 1, 1864.

K-75 GENERAL ANDREW LEWIS

Boulevard, 0.25 miles southeast of Alternate Rte. 11/460, at entrance to Salem Civic Center. Andrew Lewis was born on 9 Oct. 1720 in Ireland, and his family immigrated to Virginia by 1732. He attained prominence as a frontier soldier during Dunmore's War when on 10 Oct. 1774 his troops defeated Indians led by Shawnee Chief Cornstalk, at Point Pleasant in present-day West Virginia. As a brigadier general in the Revolutionary army, his troops drove Lord Dunmore from Virginia in July 1776, but he resigned his commission in 1777. Lewis also served in the House of Burgesses, participated in the Virginia's Revolutionary Conventions, and served on the Virginia's Executive Council from 1780 until his death 26 Sept. 1781. Nearby stood his home Richfield.

K-77 ANDREW LEWIS' GRAVE

Rte. 460, Main Street and Park Avenue, at East Hill Cemetery. This famous pioneer, patriot, statesman, and soldier, is buried here on part of his 625 acre estate. Member of House of Burgesses, 1772–1775; defeated Indians at battle of Point Pleasant 1774; drove Lord Dunmore from Virginia 1776. Died 1781.

K-78 SGT. JAMES WALTON—SALEM FLYING ARTILLERY, C.S.A.

Rte. 460, Main Street and Park Avenue, at East Hill Cemetery. Here at East Hill Cemetery is buried Sgt. James Walton (1838–1875). A gunner in Capt. Charles B. Griffin's Battery (Salem Flying Artillery), Walton fired one of the last artillery shots by Gen. Robert E. Lee's Army of Northern

Virginia at Appomattox Court House. Stationed in the yard of the George Peers house at the northeastern end of the village, Griffin's battery fired at Union cavalry until ordered to stop. Walton had just loaded powder into a gun when the order arrived; he discharged the cannon to clear it and saved the primer as a souvenir.

K-79 LYNCHBURG AND SALEM TURNPIKE

Lynchburg Turnpike, near Idaho Street. The Lynchburg and Salem Turnpike Co. was incorporated in 1818 to construct a turnpike from Lynchburg west to Salem "to establish a communication between Lynchburg [to Salem] and the western part of Virginia." It was funded by stock bought by the state as well as the public. The road reached Liberty (now Bedford) in 1828 and was completed to Salem in 1836. This turnpike, with five tollgates, served as the main thoroughfare in the region until the Virginia & Tennessee Railroad was built in the 1850s. In Sept. 1873, the commonwealth sold its shares of the turnpike stock at auction.

K-88 OLD SALEM INNS

Rte. 112, 0.1 miles north of Rte. 11/460. Salem, founded in 1803, was a notable stopping place on the route to the West. The inns located near this spot were the Bull's Eye, Ye Olde Time Tavern, the Globe, the Indian Queen, and the Mermaid.

SCOTT COUNTY

K-11 GATE CITY

Business Rte. 23, Gate City. The town was laid off in 1815 as the county seat of Scott County. The original name of Winfield, for General Winfield Scott, was changed to Estillville for Judge Benjamin Estill. In 1886, the name was changed to Gate City because of its situation in Moccasin Gap, through which the old Wilderness Road to the West passed. It was incorporated, 1892.

K-12 FARIS (FERRIS) STATION

Business Rte. 23, Gate City. About two miles east of Moccasin Gap, Elisha Faris (Ferris) in 1787 obtained 116 acres on both sides of the Moccasin Creek. He and his family settled in the area about 1782 and their home became a stop on the Wilderness Road. On 26 Aug. 1791, Bob Benge, also known as "Chief Benge" and "Capt. Bench," and other Native Americans raided the Faris property and killed, Elisha Faris, his wife, and a couple other family members. Benge conducted raids in the region and other neighboring states during an extended period of conflict in response to attacks on Cherokee communities in the South.

K-13 BLACKMORE'S FORT

Business Rte. 23, Gate City. Blackmore's Fort stood to the northeast on the Clinch River near the mouth of Stony Creek. John Blackmore and others likely constructed the fort by 1774. It served as a defensive fortification for settlers of European descent on the frontier. During Dunmore's War in 1774, Daniel Boone commanded Blackmore's Fort as well as Moore's and Cowan's Forts on the Clinch River. During that war and the American Revolution (1775–1783), periodic conflicts between Native Americans and settlers occurred there, in part because of increased settlement. In the nearby cemetery are buried some of the early settlers to the area.

K-14 McCONNELL'S BIRTHPLACE

Rtes. 23 and 58, Weber City. Four miles south was born John Preston McConnell, noted educator. He taught in Milligan College, the University of Virginia and Emory and Henry College. He was president of the Radford State Teachers' College, 1913–1937. Dr. McConnell was president of Southwestern Virginia, Incorporated, and was associated with many cultural agencies. He was active in every phase of educational work, writing several books and many articles.

K-15 BIG MOCCASIN GAP

Rtes. 23 and 58, Weber City. In March, 1775, Daniel Boone made a road through this gap to Boonesboro, Kentucky. It followed the original Indian path and was known as the Wilderness Road. For a long time it was the main route to Kentucky from the East.

K-16 DONELSON'S INDIAN LINE

Rtes. 23 and 58, Weber City. John Donelson's line, surveyed after the treaty of Lochaber with the Indians, 1770, crossed the road here. This line separated Indian territory from land open to settlement. Violations of the line by settlers contributed to Dunmore's War, 1774.

K-17 HOUSTON'S FORT

Rte. 613, 6.8 miles south of Rte. 71. The first known settler of European descent in Scott County, Thomas McCullough, moved here in 1769 and lived on Big Moccasin Creek until about 1771. Houston's Fort, built by William Houston and other settlers about 1774, stood near McCullough's property on Big Moccasin Creek. The fort served as a defensive fortification for settlers on the frontier. During the American Revolution (1775–1783), periodic conflicts between Native Americans and settlers occurred there, in part because of increased settlement. In 1776, while riding home to his family, Samuel Cowan was wounded nearby during a Cherokee Indian attack. He died soon after at Fort Houston.

K-18 PATRICK PORTER (1737–1805)

Rte. 65, 0.5 miles east of Rte. 72, in Dungannon. Patrick Porter was among the early pioneer settlers in present Scott County. Nearby on Fall Creek is the site of Porter's Mill, built by Porter in 1774, the earliest licensed mill on waters of the Clinch River.

Porter is also credited with the erection of a fort house in the same year to protect residents from Indian attacks. His son Samuel travelled with Daniel Boone to Kentucky in 1773 and in 1778 answered Boone's request for assistance in defending Boonesborough.

KA-7 CARTER'S FORT

Rte. 23, 0.5 miles west of Rte. 871. Near here stood a fort first known as Crissman's Fort, and later as Carter's or Rye Cove Fort, and by militia officers as Fort Lee. Built by Isaac Crissman, Sr. in 1774, it was acquired by Thomas Carter (1731–1803) after Crissman's death at the hands of Indians in 1776. The fort was rebuilt in 1777 by Col. Joseph Martin and his militia troops who occupied it until at least 1794. The fort was under the command of Captain Andrew Lewis, Jr. from 1792 to 1794.

KA-9 KILGORE FORT HOUSE

Rte. 71, 1.2 miles west of Nickelsville. The Kilgore Fort House was built in 1786 by Robert Kilgore whose family were early settlers in this area. It was one of the twelve forts between Castlewood and Cumberland Gap providing ready refuge for settlers from Indian attacks in the late 18th century. Kilgore later was a preacher in the Primitive Baptist Church, often holding religious services at the Fort House. He married Jane Porter Green, daughter of Patrick Porter who built Porter's Fort on Fall Creek.

KA-10 CARTER'S FORT

Rte. 871, 1 mile east of Sunbright. Three miles east, in Rye Cove, stood Carter's Fort, built by Thomas Carter in 1784. It was a station on the old Wilderness Road from North Carolina to Kentucky.

KA-15 FIRST COURT OF SCOTT COUNTY

Rte. 23, just west of Rte. 58, Moccasin Gap. The monument in the field to the west marks the site of Benjamin T. Hollins's home, in which was held the first court of this county, February 14, 1815.

Hailing from southwest Virginia and known as the "First Family of Country Music," A. P. Carter, Sara E. Dougherty Carter, and Maybelle Addington Carter were popular musicians of their era who recorded more than 250 songs from 1927 to 1943. (Marker KA-18) (Carter Family Museum, Hiltons, Virginia)

KA-16 PATRICK HAGAN AND DUNGANNON

Rte. 65, Dungannon. Patrick Hagan (1828–1917) emigrated from Dungannon, Ireland,

about 1844 and joined his uncle, Joseph Hagan, in Scott County. He read law, was admitted to the bar, and became one of the state's foremost land lawyers. Hagan amassed large holdings of coal and timber lands, including Osborne's Ford, as it had been called since 1786 when Stephen Osborne obtained a land grant. The community, which Hagan renamed for his birthplace, grew rapidly after the Clinchfield Railroad built a depot in 1912. Hagan also designed the town plan, and Dungannon was incorporated in 1918.

KA-18 CARTER MUSICAL FAMILY

Rte. 23, Moccasin Gap. The Carter Family of Scott County, the "First Family of Country Music," consisted of Alvin Pleasant "A. P." Carter (1891–1960) who sang and composed; Sara E. Dougherty Carter (1898–1979), who sang lead and played the guitar and autoharp; and Maybelle Addington Carter (1909–1978) who sang and played the guitar and autoharp. After their first recording session in Bristol for the Victor Talking Machine Company in 1927, the trio enjoyed tremendous popularity, appearing on the radio, and recording more than 250 songs until 1943. The Carter Family incorporated unique harmony vocals into traditional tunes and original material. A. P. and Sara Carter are buried in Maces Springs, Va., near Hiltons. Maybelle Carter is buried in Hendersonville, Tenn.

SMYTH COUNTY

K-19 SEVEN MILE FORD

Rte. 11, 2.9 miles east of Chilhowie. The place takes its name from the highway ford on the Holston, seven miles west of Royal Oak. The land here belonged to General William Campbell, hero of King's Mountain, 1780. It descended to the wife of John

M. Preston. The town originated as a railroad station. It was occupied in Stoneman's raid of December, 1864.

K-20 WILLIAM CAMPBELL'S GRAVE

Rte. 11, 2 miles east of Chilhowie. The nearby Aspenvale Cemetery contains the grave of

Brig. Gen. William Campbell, Revolutionary War soldier, militia commander, and regional political leader. Campbell was born in Augusta County, Virginia, in 1745, and by 1768 he had moved to present-day Smyth County. During the Revolutionary War, Campbell led his soldiers to victory at the Battle of King's Mountain in North Carolina on 7 Oct. 1780. In Jun. 1781, Campbell joined the Marquis de Lafayette in eastern Virginia until Campbell's death on 22 Aug. 1781. He was buried at Rocky Mills in Hanover County. By 1832, his remains were reinterred at the Aspenvale Cemetery.

K-21 FARTHEST WEST, 1750.

Rte. 11, Chilhowie. Near here, in 1750, Dr. Thomas Walker, on his first journey southwest, assisted Samuel Stalnaker in building his cabin. At that time this was the farthest west settlement.

K-22 CHILHOWIE

Rte. 11, Chilhowie. About 1748, Col. James Patton patented land here and reportedly hoped this site would one day become a town. The region became known as Town House for a house known by this name that stood nearby. By the Revolutionary War, a settlement of the same name began to develop around the house. In 1856, the Virginia and Tennessee Railroad arrived and the settlement was renamed Greever's Switch for a local resident. The community's name was changed to Chilhowie in the late 1880s at the suggestion of George Palmer. Chilhowie is believed to be an Indian word meaning either "home of many deer" or "valley of many deer." The town was incorporated in 1913.

K-24 ROYAL OAK PRESBYTERIAN CHURCH

Highland Drive (parallel to Rte. 11), Marion. According to tradition, the Upper Holston congregation of the Presbyterian Church was organized in 1776 on John Campbell's land at Royal Oak and built a log structure there. This was one of the first denominations to organize in present-day Smyth County. Eventually it was named the Royal Oak Presbyterian Church; a nearby cemetery plot still exists. The congregation moved to a brick building in Marion in 1853, and in 1885 a new structure was constructed on the current site of the church. In 1923, the 1885 structure was torn down and a Late Gothic Revival–style church was built.

K-26 BATTLE OF MARION

Rte. 11, at Marion eastern corporate limits. Here, on December 17–18, 1864, General Stoneman, raiding to Saltville, fought an engagement with John C. Breckinridge, Confederate commander in southwest Virginia.

K-27 SITE OF COLONIAL HOME

Rte. 11, at Rte. 16, Marion. Royal Oak, home of Arthur Campbell, Indian fighter and Revolutionary leader, who settled here in 1769, stood three hundred yards south. The house was a neighborhood fort and in it, in 1832, the first court of Smyth County was held.

K-28 SALTVILLE HISTORY

Rte. 107, 1 mile south of Saltville. William King built salt works there in 1795. In October, 1864, Union troops, raiding Saltville, were driven off; but in December 1864 the works were destroyed by General Stoneman.

K-30 EARLY SETTLERS

Rte. 11, 8.5 miles east of Marion. Stephen Holstein (Holston), coming here before 1748, gave his name to the river and valley. James Davis settled on this place, "Davis' Fancy," in 1748 and his home became a neighborhood fort.

K-33 HUNGRY MOTHER STATE PARK

Rtes. 16 and 348, at entrance to park. In 1933 local residents assisted in the creation and donated 2,000 acres of land to Virginia for the establishment of a state park in Smyth County along Hungry Mother Creek. The unusual name comes from the legend of a nearby Indian-settler conflict that resulted in Molly Marley and her child being captured. They later escaped but Marley died. When a search party found the toddler who [*should read:* found the toddler, it] could only utter the words "Hungry Mother." The National Park Service and the Civilian Conservation Corps, in conjunction with the Virginia Conservation Commission, developed the park as a New Deal project. It opened on 15 June 1936 and was one of the first six state parks established in Virginia.

K-34 MARION

Rte. 11, Marion. The community center here was known as Royal Oak, home of Arthur Campbell, frontiersman. The place became the county seat when Smyth County was formed and was named for Francis Marion, Revolutionary hero. It was incorporated in 1832; the courthouse was built in 1834; the railroad came in 1856. A cavalry action was fought here, December 1864, in Stoneman's raid.

K-46 SHERWOOD ANDERSON

Rte. 11, near Marion eastern corporate limits. Renowned author Sherwood Anderson's works influenced Faulkner, Hemingway, and other 20th century writers. Anderson was born in Camden, Ohio, on 13 Sept.

1876, moved to this area in 1926, and lived here until his death. He built his home, Ripshin, near Troutdale, and was for a time owner and publisher of two Smyth County weekly newspapers. He was best known for his book of short stories, *Winesburg, Ohio.* En route to begin a research tour of labor conditions in South America, with his fourth wife Eleanor Copenhaver of Marion, Anderson died on 8 Mar. 1941 in Colón, Panama. He is buried at Round Hill Cemetery.

KB-6 SALTVILLE

Rte. 91, Saltville. Saltville is named for the vast salt deposits that exist under this valley. The commercial salt industry began developing here in the 1780s. During the Civil War, Saltville played a vital role in providing salt for the Confederacy. On 2 Oct. 1864 Confederate forces defeated Federal troops, while on 20 Dec. 1864 Union forces led by Maj. Gen. George Stoneman damaged the saltworks operation. The Mathieson Alkali Works opened here in 1892 and produced a variety of products using salt and other mineral resources from the area. The General Assembly officially incorporated Saltville as a town in 1896.

UC-5 STATE FISH HATCHERY

Rte. 16, 5 miles southeast of Marion. This fish cultural station was established in 1930 for hatching and rearing trout for the trout waters of Virginia.

TAZEWELL COUNTY

X-10 WILLIAM WYNNE'S FORT

Business Rte. 19, Tazewell. On the hillside to the north stood Wynne's Fort. A settlement was made here as early as 1752. Some years later William Wynne obtained land here and built a neighborhood fort. After 1776 the State government built a fort and garrisoned it.

X-11 TAZEWELL

Business Rte. 19, Tazewell. The town was laid off as the county seat, in 1800, when Tazewell County was formed, on land given by William Peery and Samuel Ferguson. First known as Jeffersonville, the name was changed to Tazewell, for Senator Henry Tazewell. Averell was here in May, 1864, and the town was occupied in other raids. It was incorporated in 1866.

X-12 BURKE'S GARDEN

Rte. 61, 1.8 miles east of Tazewell. Eight miles east is Burke's Garden, discovered by James Burke in 1749. Major Lewis's expedition against the Indians, 1756, camped there, and Burke's fort was there in 1774. In 1781 Indians raided into Burke's Garden, carrying off the wife and children of Thomas Ingles.

X-12-a BURKE'S GARDEN

Rtes. 666 and 623. Known for its fertility and great natural beauty, the bowl-shaped Burke's Garden is the highest valley in Virginia. James Burke discovered it during the 1740s while hunting and settled here about 1754. After four years Burke and his family moved to North Carolina, where he died in 1783. The threat of Indian attack and the remoteness of the area discouraged permanent white settlment [settlement] until the early 19th century.

X-15 BLUEFIELD VIRGINIA

Rte. 19, at western entrance to Bluefield. The place was first known as "Pin Hook." In 1883 the New River branch of the N. & W. Railroad was completed here and the first coal shipped from the Pocahontas mines. The town of Graham was incorporated in 1884 and named for Thomas Graham of Philadelphia. The town was reincorporated and the name changed to Bluefield, 1924, to conform to its sister city.

X-16 INDIAN-SETTLER CONFLICTS

Business Rte. 19, 2 miles west of Tazewell. During Dunmore's War (1774) and the Revolutionary War (1775–1783) conflicts between Indians and colonists often intensified as European powers encouraged Indians from the Ohio region to attack frontier settlers. Tensions also sometimes increased when settlers moved into lands that were once Indian territory. Nearby to the south, an early conflict occurred in the upper Clinch River Valley, when Indians attacked and killed John Henry, his wife and

their children on 8 Sept. 1774. Additional conflicts took place during this period, including a March 1782, Indian attack on the house of James Maxwell that killed two of his daughters.

X-25 PISGAH UNITED METHODIST CHURCH

Rte. 19/460 and Business Rte. 19. The Reverend John Kobler preached the first sermon by a Methodist in Tazewell County here in 1793 and received eleven members into the church. The church building, constructed on a parcel of land donated by Thomas Peery, was the first church of any denomination in the county. The construction of the Clinch Valley Railroad in 1889 necessitated the relocation of the church to its present site. Pisgah is the mother church of numerous Methodist and later United Methodist congregations and ministers.

X-27 MATHIAS HARMAN, SR.

Rte. 637, 7 miles north of Rte. 460. Just east of here is the last home site and grave of Mathias Harman, Sr. (1736–1832), early explorer, hunter and Revolutionary War veteran. Harman helped establish the first permanent English settlement in eastern Kentucky in 1755. In 1789 he founded Harman's Station on the Levisa River near John's Creek in present-day Johnson County. He and his wife, Lydia, settled in this area in 1803.

X-28 FIRST COURT FOR TAZEWELL COUNTY

Business Rtes. 19 and 460, Tazewell. The first Court for Tazewell County was held June 1800 at the residence of Henry Harman, Jr. The house site is located two tenths of a mile to the northeast. Harman's grave is to the north. In the same burying ground is the marked grave of his brother Daniel Harman who was killed by Indians in 1791.

X-29 ROARK'S GAP INCIDENT

Rtes. 631 and 637, near Gap Store. During the French and Indian War (1754–1763) and the American Revolution (1775–1783), European powers encouraged their Indian allies to attack frontier settlers. Such conflicts took place as settlers moved into lands that once were Indian territory. During the winter of 1780, a food shortage caused hardship for people and animals. While James Roark, an early settler of this region, and two of his sons went on a hunting trip, Indians attacked his home, on 18 Mar. 1780. The Indians, alleged to be Shawnee, killed Roark's wife and seven of their children. This event was unanticipated by the settlers because snow covered the ground.

X-31 BLUEFIELD COLLEGE

Rte. 102, at college. Bluefield College was chartered in May 1920 as "an institution of learning for the instruction of boys and young men in the various branches of science, literature, philosophy, and the liberal and useful arts." With strong support from the Baptist General Association of Virginia and citizens of the area, it opened as a junior college with three buildings in 1922. Women attended as day students from 1922; the school became fully coeducational in 1951. Bluefield College was accredited by the Southern Association of Colleges and Schools as a four-year institution in 1977.

XH-1 MOLLY TYNES'S RIDE

Rte. 61, 1.35 miles east of Tazewell corporate limits. To the north stood Rocky Dell, the home of Samuel Tynes. In July 1863, during the Civil War, Union Col. John T. Toland led a cavalry expedition from West Virginia to destroy the Virginia & Tennessee R.R. at Wytheville. The Federals camped nearby on 17 July, and when Tynes discovered their objective he sent his twenty-six-year-old daughter Mary (Molly) Elizabeth Tynes to alert the town's defenders. She rode all night, a distance of some forty miles. Confederate reinforcements arrived in time to stiffen resistance, and the Federals inflicted little damage; Toland himself was killed in the fight.

XH-2 SHAWVER MILL

Rte. 61, at Rte. 614. The Shawver Mill community grew up here around the gristmill that George Shawver built before 1860. William Leffel and Adam Britts soon built sawmills, and the community developed like many in Virginia during the 19th century. By 1911 it sustained a general store, Odd Fellows hall, post office, cemetery, two churches, and a baseball team. The end of milling operations in 1947, together with new road construction, diminished the community. By 1992 only the mill dam, the cemetery on the hill, and Chestnut Grove Church survived.

XL-4 RICHLANDS

Rte. 460, Richlands. This fertile region was known as Richlands from an early period. In 1782 and later Richlands was a militia station for frontier defense. The town was laid off in 1890, with the coming of the Norfolk and Western Railroad, and was incorporated in 1891. It is the center of an agricultural section.

XL-5 SITE OF JAMES BURKE'S GARDEN

Rte. 623, Burke's Garden. Burke's Garden is named for James Burke who surveyed the region with James Patton by 1750. According to tradition, Burke buried some potato peelings in the region's fertile soil during a survey expedition. Sometime later another group camped at the same site and discovered the potatoes, resulting in the area becoming known as Burke's Garden. Burke built a cabin nearby and lived here from about 1753 until 1756 when hostilities began during the French and Indian War. Burke's Garden is a topographically rare elongated basin rimmed entirely by the Garden Mountain.

XP-4 POCAHONTAS

Rte. 102, just east of Pocahontas. This region was visited by the explorer, Dr. Thomas Walker, in 1750. Following a report by Captain I. A. Welch in 1873, the first coal mine was opened here in 1882. Shipment of coal followed in 1883, when the Norfolk and Western Railroad reached this point from Radford. First known as "Powell's Bottom", the town was incorporated in 1884 and named for the Indian princess Pocahontas.

XP-5 ABB'S VALLEY

Rte. 102, just east of Pocahontas. Five miles southwest is Abb's Valley, discovered by Absalom Looney. James Moore and Robert Poage were the first settlers, about 1770. In July, 1786, Shawnee Indians raided the valley, killing or carrying into captivity the Moore family. Mary (Polly) Moore, Martha Evans and James Moore (captured earlier) finally returned. They are known as "The Captives of Abb's Valley."

XP-6 ENGAGEMENT AT FALLS MILLS

Rte. 102, at Rte. 643. Here at dawn on 20 July 1863 the Confederate cavalry of Maj. Andrew J. May surprised a Union raiding party led by Lt. Col. Freeman E. Franklin. Aroused from its bivouac in Brown's Meadow, where it was preparing to burn the Falls Mill, the Union cavalry fled north toward Abb's Valley. Brig. Gen. John S. Williams's Confederate cavalry struck the raiders as they withdrew up the valley, compelling them to abandon captured livestock and contraband slaves.

XY-13 MAIDEN SPRINGS FORT

Rte. 91, 12 miles southwest of Tazewell. On the hillside to the west stood Maiden Springs Fort, also known as Reese Bowen's Fort. It was garrisoned in Dunmore's War, 1774. Reese Bowen, the founder, fought at Point Pleasant, 1774, and was killed at King's Mountain, 1780.

XY-14 BIG CRAB ORCHARD OR WITTEN'S FORT

Rte. 19/460 and Business Rte. 19, Tazewell. On the hillside to the south stood Big Crab Orchard Fort, also known as Witten's Fort. Thomas Witten obtained land here in 1771 and built the fort as a neighborhood place of refuge. It was garrisoned in Dunmore's War, 1774.

WASHINGTON COUNTY

I-7 EMORY AND HENRY COLLEGE

Rte. 11, 8.3 miles east of Abingdon. One mile north is Emory and Henry College, founded in 1836, the first institution of higher learning in Southwest Virginia. It was named for Bishop John Emory of the Methodist Church and Patrick Henry, the orator of the Revolution. Four bishops of the Methodist Church, three governors, and one United States Senator are among its alumni.

K-47 KING'S MOUNTAIN MEN

Rte. 11, at western entrance to Abingdon. From this vicinity went forth a force of Virginians, under the command of Colonel William Campbell, to fight against the British in the Carolinas, 1780. The Virginia troops played an important part in the victory of King's Mountain, South Carolina, won by the Americans over Patrick Ferguson, October 7, 1780.

K-48 SITE OF BLACK'S FORT

Rte. 11 and Raven Street, Abingdon. The fort, built in 1776, stood a short distance to the south. Here the first court of Washington County was held, January 28, 1777.

K-49 ABINGDON

Rte. 11, at Martha Washington Inn, Abingdon. First known as Wolf Hills, land was patented here by Dr. Thomas Walker in 1750. Black's Fort was built, 1776. The town of Abingdon was established in 1778 as the county seat of Washington County. A courthouse, built about 1800, was replaced in 1850. In 1862 the church bells were melted for cannon. In Stoneman's raid, December, 1864, the town was partly burned. A new courthouse was built, 1869.

K-50 BOYHOOD HOME OF GEN. JOSEPH E. JOHNSTON

0.02 miles west of Rtes. 11 and 75, Abingdon. Born in Prince Edward Co. on 3 Feb. 1807, Joseph Eggleston Johnston, the son of Judge Peter Johnston, moved a mile north of here with his family in 1811. He attended Abingdon Male Academy and graduated from the U.S. Military Academy at West Point in 1829 with fellow Virginian Robert E. Lee. During the Civil War, he was the only officer to command both of the major Confederate armies, the Army of the Potomac (later Army of Northern Virginia) in 1861–62 and the Army of Tennessee in 1863–65; he surrendered at present-day Durham, N.C., on 26 Apr. 1865. He died on 21 March 1891 in Washington, D.C., and is buried in Green Mount Cemetery, Baltimore, Md.

K-51 BRIG. GEN. WILLIAM E. "GRUMBLE" JONES, C.S.A.

Rte. 11 (Main Street), near Martha Washington Inn, Abingdon. Brig. Gen. William Edmondson "Grumble" Jones was born nearby on 9 May 1824. Educated at Emory and Henry College and the U.S. Military Academy at West Point, Jones served on the frontier from 1848 until he resigned in 1857. He organized the Washington Mounted Rifles as its captain when Virginia seceded in 1861, became colonel of the 1st and then the 7th Virginia Cavalry, and was promoted to brigadier general in Sept. 1862. Jones later served under Maj. Gen. J. E. B. Stuart, with whom he disagreed. Commanding the Dept. of Southwest Virginia, Jones was killed at the Battle of Piedmont on 5 June 1864 and bur-

ied here in Old Glade Spring Presbyterian Cemetery.

K-52 SINKING SPRING CEMETERY

Alternate Rte. 58, Abingdon. In 1773, the Rev. Charles Cummings became the first minister of the Sinking Spring Presbyterian congregation, among the earliest in Southwest Virginia, and the first meetinghouse was soon constructed here of logs. The earliest marked grave in the cemetery is dated 1776. Buried here are pioneers; veterans of the Revolutionary War, the War of 1812, and the Civil War; and two antebellum Virginia governors (David Campbell and John B. Floyd, who also served as President James Buchanan's secretary of war). Cummings's log manse, among the oldest east of the Mississippi River, was moved here in 1971 from its original site two miles north.

K-53 BARTER THEATRE

Rte. 11 (West Main Street), at theatre, Abingdon. The Barter Theatre building was constructed about 1830 as a church, which was remodeled several times. Among the oldest theaters in America, the building hosted its first performance in 1876. During the Great Depression of the 1930s, Robert Porterfield, an enterprising actor and Washington County native, created the Barter Theatre and proposed exchanging "ham for Hamlet." The theater opened its doors on 10 June 1933; admission was "35 cents or the equivalent in victuals" to feed the actors. Many stage and screen actors, designers, and playwrights have polished their craft here. In 1946, the Barter Theatre was designated the State Theatre of Virginia.

K-54 STONEWALL JACKSON FEMALE INSTITUTE

Rte. 11, at Barter Theatre, Abingdon. Sinking Spring Presbyterian Church established the institute in 1868 for the education of young women. As a tribute, it was named for Confederate Lt. Gen. Thomas J. "Stonewall" Jackson. The Floyd family property was purchased in Feb. 1868 to house the school. Classes began on 15 Sept. 1868, when boarding and day students as young as seven enrolled. It was renamed the Stonewall Jackson College in 1914 when the Montgomery Presbytery assumed joint ownership. On 24 Nov. 1914, the main buildings were destroyed by fire. The college continued to operate until 1930 when it closed because of mounting debts.

K-55 WASHINGTON COUNTY COURTHOUSE

Rte. 11, at courthouse, Abingdon. Three earlier courthouses stood on this site, the first constructed about 1800. The present Washington County courthouse was completed in 1868, replacing the 1850 building burned by a Union soldier in Dec. 1864. The only new courthouse built in Virginia during Reconstruction, it features four Greek Doric columns and an Italianate cornice and tower. A Civil War monument located in the courtyard was unveiled on 10 May 1907 to commemorate the men who served from Washington County. Dedicated on 4 July 1919, a Tiffany stained-glass window above the courthouse entranceway honors those who served in World War I.

K-56 MARTHA WASHINGTON COLLEGE

Rte. 11, at Martha Washington Inn, Abingdon. The McCabe Lodge No. 56, Independent Order of Odd Fellows decided in 1853 to establish a women's college named after Martha Washington. The Holston Conference of the Methodist Church assumed control of the project by 1858. That same year the conference purchased the Gen. Francis Preston House (ca. 1832) to house the college. In 1860, the first classes were held at Martha Washington College. Several additions were made to the college's main building over the next 70 years. The school merged with nearby Emory & Henry College in 1918. In 1921 Martha Washington became a junior college but closed in 1931. In 1937, the former main

college building was converted into the Martha Washington Inn.

K-57 GREEN SPRING PRESBYTERIAN CHURCH

Rtes. 75 and 670, Abingdon. Green Spring Presbyterian Church was organized by 1784 and met in a log structure that stood east of here. The present church location has been in use since about 1794 when James Montgomery deeded the property to the congregation as long as its minister adhered "to the West Minster confession of faith" and the Catechism was taught here. The original log church was replaced by a frame structure in 1884. A fire destroyed this building on 9 Oct. 1921. The first services were held in the current brick building in 1925. The church cemetery dates to the early 19th century.

K-58 GOVERNOR DAVID CAMPBELL

Cummings Street, at entrance to Mont Calm, Abingdon. David Campbell was born in Aug. 1779 at Royal Oak in Washington County (present-day Smyth County), Virginia. His family eventually moved to Hall's Bottom outside Abingdon. Campbell served in the infantry during the War of 1812 and was promoted to lieutenant colonel of the 20th Regiment in March 1813. He also served in the Senate of the Virginia [*should read:* Senate of Virginia] (1820–1824) and as Washington County Court clerk. During this time Campbell's federal style home, Mont Calm was completed. Elected governor in 1837, Campbell served until 1840. He died on 19 March 1859 and was buried in Sinking Spring Cemetery.

K-59 GOVERNOR JOHN B. FLOYD

Rte. 11 (Main Street), near Martha Washington Inn, Abingdon. John Buchanan Floyd, son of Governor John Floyd (1738–1837), was born in Montgomery County on 1 June 1806. He represented Washington County in the Virginia House of Delegates (1847–1849) and served as governor of Virginia (1849–1852). Floyd was appointed

U.S. Secretary of War in 1857. He resigned in Dec. 1860 and became a Confederate brigadier general in Mar. 1861. Floyd was relieved of duty in Mar. 1862 over controversies surrounding his command of Fort Donelson, Tenn., but was soon commissioned a major general in the Virginia militia. He died nearby on 26 Aug. 1863.

K-60 REVOLUTIONARY WAR MUSTER GROUND

Colonial Road, approximately 0.2 miles from Rte. 11. To the south at Craig's (Dunn's) Meadow, is the likely site of the Washington County militia's muster ground for the Revolutionary War's Kings Mountain Campaign. In Sept. 1780, under the command of Col. William Campbell the militiamen left for Sycamore Shoals, near Elizabethton, Tenn. By 25 Sept., the militia rendezvoused with additional Washington County militiamen and forces from present-day Tennessee and North Carolina and then headed south. On 7 Oct. 1780 these forces with additional troops from South Carolina and Georgia defeated British Maj. Patrick Ferguson's soldiers at the Battle of Kings Mountain in South Carolina. The nearby muster site is certified as part of the Overmountain Victory National Historic Trail.

WISE COUNTY

I-2 SOUTHWEST VIRGINIA MUSEUM

Alternate Rte. 58, Big Stone Gap. This museum is located in a mansion built by lawyer and industrialist Rufus Ayers, Virginia attorney general in the 1880s. Janie Slemp Newman and her brother, C. Bascom Slemp, a former U.S. congressman and private secretary to President Calvin Coolidge, assembled the initial collection of artifacts on display. Slemp bequeathed the collection to the Commonwealth of Virginia in 1946 and the Southwest Virginia Museum opened to the public in 1948. The museum chronicles the development of Southwest Virginia and presents a picture of life in the past.

KA-11 BIG STONE GAP

Business Rte. 23, Big Stone Gap. Big Stone Gap, originally known as Three Forks, received its charter, February 23, 1888. A postoffice was established April 12, 1856. In the early nineties it became the center of iron and coal development. It was the home and workshop of John Fox, Jr., novelist, and author of "Trail of the Lonesome Pine."

KA-12 ORIGINS OF BIG STONE GAP

Rte. 610 (Wood Street) and Jermone Street, Big Stone Gap. This was the site of the Gilley family farm, settled by John and Mary Barger Gilley about 1790. The family cemetery was located just south, at the end of Graveyard Alley. Named Imboden after Confederate Brig. Gen. John D. Imboden when it was laid out on parts of the Gilley, Horton, and Flanary farms, the town was incorporated on 7 Apr. 1882 as Mineral City. Its name was changed to Big Stone Gap on 23 Feb. 1888, when the town boundaries were enlarged. Soon, as several railroads converged here, the town grew due to the importance of the iron and coal-mining industries.

KA-14 NAPOLEON HILL

Rte. 23, 0.45 miles north of southern intersection of Business Rte. 23, Wise. Napoleon Hill was born nearby on 26 Oct. 1883. At age 13, he became a "mountain reporter" for small-town newspapers. He left Southwest Virginia in 1908 to write magazine profiles of such business leaders as Andrew Carnegie, Henry Ford, and Thomas Edison. Hill virtually invented the gospel of personal achievement by distilling their principles of financial success into several motivational books. He published *Think and Grow Rich,* the century's most popular such book, in 1937. Hill lectured widely and served as an advisor to presidents Woodrow Wilson and Franklin D. Roosevelt. He died in Greenville, S.C., on 7 Nov. 1970.

KA-17 CARL MARTIN—EARLY MUSICAL PIONEER

East 3rd Street North and Shawnee Avenue, Big Stone Gap. Carl Martin was born in Big Stone Gap in April 1906. He grew up in Southwest Virginia and moved to Knoxville, Tenn., in 1918. He performed regionally on the guitar, mandolin, bass, and violin at coal camps, dances, and in traveling shows. In 1930, Martin's string band recorded two instrumentals for Vocalion, released under the band name "Tennessee Chocolate Drops" for a black audience and the "Tennessee Trio" in the white old-time music series. Martin moved to Chicago in the 1930s, recording blues and performing with such artists as Big Bill Broonzy and Tampa Red until serving in World War II. The 1960s folk revival brought Martin before new audiences. He died in Detroit on 10 May 1979.

KA-19 THE UNIVERSITY OF VIRGINIA'S COLLEGE AT WISE

Corner of Thomas Jefferson and Smiddy Drives, at Smiddy Hall, on campus. The college was founded in 1954 as Clinch Valley College of the University of Virginia, through the efforts of local citizens and University of Virginia officials including President Colgate W. Darden, Jr.; Samuel R. Crockett, extension services director in Southwest Virginia; and George Zehmer, director of the extension division. Located on the former Wise County Poor Farm, the college began as a two-year co-educational branch of the University of Virginia. In 1970, Clinch Valley College awarded its first bachelor's degrees. In 1999, it became The University of Virginia's College at Wise. It is a nationally recognized, public, liberal arts college.

X-20 COEBURN

Rte. 58, at Rte. 72, Coeburn. The town stands on the site of one of Christopher Gist's camps when he was returning from his exploration of the Ohio Valley about 1750. Big Tom and Little Tom creeks are named for him and his son. The name of the town comes from W. W. Coe, chief engineer of the N. & W. Railroad, and Judge W. E. Burns of Lebanon. Coeburn was incorporated in 1894.

X-21 NORTON

Business Rte. 23, Norton. As early as 1750 Christopher Gist explored in this vicinity. The first house here was built about 1785 by William Prince, for whom the settlement was called Prince's Flat. It was later named Norton for Eckstein Norton, president of the Louisville and Nashville Railroad, and was incorporated in 1894. Norton is the center of a bituminous coal region. High Knob, National Forest area, is nearby.

X-22 BENGE'S GAP

Rte. 23, at Powell Valley Overlook. Beginning in 1774, Chief Benge led a part of the Shawnee from the Ohio River on raids along the frontier. Benge, who was part white and part Cherokee, frequently captured slaves and then resold them; he also seized white women and children who were then adopted by various Indian groups. On 6 Apr. 1794, Benge attacked the Henry and Peter Livingston farm on the Holston River, took several residents prisoner, and marched them northeast. Three days later, when they entered the Powell Mountain gap just south, Lt. Vincent Hobbs and eleven Lee County militiamen ambushed them, killed Benge with the first volley, and freed the captives.

X-23 APPALACHIA

Rte. 78 and Business Rte. 23, Appalachia. The town sprang up after the Louisville and Nashville Railroad and Southern Railroad made a junction here in 1890. Named for the Appalachian Mountains, in the heart of which it stands, it was incorporated in

1906; the streets were laid out in 1907. Appalachia, in the Jefferson National Forest area, is the trading center of the Wise coal fields.

XB-4 Wise

Main Street, Wise. The town of Wise was known as Big Glades when a post office was established here in 1850. Before being incorporated as Wise in 1924, it was also called Gladeville and Wise Court House. Since the creation in 1856 of Wise County, named for Henry Alexander Wise, governor of Virginia (1856–1860), the town has served as the county seat. During the Civil War, a skirmish was fought here between Union and Confederate troops on 7 July 1863. After the Civil War the town grew because of the expansion of the railroads and the increased mining of coal in the region. The current county courthouse was completed in 1896.

XB-7 Pound Gap

Rte. 23, 0.14 miles from state line. Pound Gap probably was named for a nearby grain-pounding mill. Christopher Gist, returning from the Ohio River where he surveyed land for the Ohio Company, crossed the gap in 1751. During the Civil War, Pound Gap gained strategic importance as a gateway between Virginia and Kentucky. Union Col. James A. Garfield (later president) and his brigade forced the gap from the Kentucky side on 16 March 1862 after a skirmish with Confederate forces under Brig. Gen. Humphrey Marshall. On 1 June 1864, Confederate Brig. Gen. John Hunt Morgan forced it from the Virginia side, capturing and destroying property in Kentucky.

WYTHE COUNTY

FR-26 St. John's Lutheran Church

Rte. 52, near Rte. 21. German settlers formed a congregation here that was a center of Lutheranism in Virginia throughout the 19th century. The church built around 1800 was replaced by the present structure in 1854. The cemetery has distinctive stones dating from 1804 to the present. St. John's became a part of Holy Trinity, Wytheville, in 1924.

K-23 Walter Crockett

Rte. 11, at eastern entrance to Wytheville. Walter Crockett was born in the 1730s. By 1760, he had joined the Augusta County militia. Rising to the rank of lieutenant colonel, he subsequently served in the militias for Botetourt, Fincastle, and then Montgomery Counties, beginning in 1769. He participated in the Point Pleasant expedition of 1774 during Dunmore's War, and in Revolutionary War activities in southwestern Virginia in 1779 and 1780. He represented Montgomery County in the Virginia House of Delegates (1777–1779 and 1789) and at Virginia's convention to ratify the U.S. Constitution in 1788. Crockett became the clerk of the court of Wythe County in 1790. He died in 1811.

K-31 Site of Mount Airy

Rte. 11, 12.9 miles west of Wytheville. In 1811, Martin Staley transferred land here to his son Valentine. A year later, his son formed the town of Mount (Mt.) Airy, sometimes referred to as Staleytown. The tract was divided into about 72 lots, including Main Street, Cross Street, and a public square. Following Valentine Staley's death in 1817, his wife and children successfully petitioned the General Assembly to sell more lots. With the establishment of a nearby railroad center at what became Rural Retreat and an attack on Mount Airy by Federal troops during the Civil War, Mount Airy ceased to exist about 1875.

K-35 Wytheville

Rte. 11, Wytheville. When Wythe County was formed, this place became the county

*While the commonwealth's colo-
nial-era history is evident in the
eastern parts of the state, markers
such as this one featuring the lead
mines in Wythe County, shown here
circa the 1930s, remind Virginians
that the western part also played a
significant role during the Colonial
and Revolutionary eras. (Marker
K-39) (The Library of Virginia)*

seat under the name of Evansham. It was
incorporated in 1839 as Wytheville. The
old Wilderness Road to Cumberland Gap
passed here. In July, 1863, Toland's raiders
captured the town. In May, 1864, Averell
passed here on a raid; the town was again
occupied by Union troops in December,
1864, and April, 1865.

K-36 ANCHOR AND HOPE PLANTATION

Rte. 52, Fort Chiswell. One mile north is a
plantation that was surveyed in March,
1748, and patented, in June, 1753, by Colonel John Buchanan and named by him
"Anchor and Hope." There in 1792 an academy was established to teach oratory. The
pioneer educator, Thomas E. Birch, was
instructor and minister for the settlement.

K-37 ROBERT ENOCH WITHERS

Rte. 11, at eastern entrance to Wytheville.
Robert Enoch Withers was born in Campbell County on 18 Sept. 1821. After gradu-

ation from the medical department at the
University of Virginia in 1841, he practiced
medicine in Campbell County and Danville
until 1861. During the Civil War Withers
achieved the rank of colonel in the Confederate army. He served as the lieutenant
governor of Virginia from 1874 to 1875 and
in the United States Senate from 1875 to
1881. Withers was the U.S. Consul at Hong
Kong from 1885 to 1889 and he died nearby
at his home, Ingleside, on 21 Sept. 1907.

K-39 LEAD MINES

Rte. 52, Fort Chiswell. Nine miles south on
New River. Discovered in 1756 by Colonel
John Chiswell, these mines supplied lead
for the patriots in the Revolutionary War.
Tories attempted to seize them in 1780 but
were suppressed.

KC-4 TOLAND'S RAID

Rte. 52, at Wythe/Bland County line. Col.
John T. Toland of the 34th Regiment

Mounted Ohio Volunteer Infantry leading Federal cavalrymen, marched from Tazewell County, and raided Wytheville during the evening of 18 July 1863. Confederate troops under Maj. Thomas M. Bowyer and local citizens fortified in buildings at first withstood the attack, killing Toland. After the Confederates withdrew, Federal forces burned several buildings. After learning that Confederate troops were situated at present day Rural Retreat, the federals left Wytheville early the next morning initially headed north towards Walker Mountain.

KD-5 FINCASTLE COUNTY

Rte. 52, 5.5 miles southeast of Fort Chiswell. Fincastle County, established in 1772, was formed from Botetourt County. The Fincastle County seat was located opposite the lead mines on the north side of the New River in the western end of present day Austinville. In 1775, the Fincastle County Committee of Safety filed its resolutions with the Continental Congress supporting other American colonies' efforts for self-determination. The resolutions suggested the citizens were supportive of King George III, but they were not willing to be subjected to the possible loss of liberty and property. The county became extinct in 1776 when it was split into Montgomery, Washington, and Kentucky (now the state of Kentucky) Counties.

KD-6 JACKSON'S FERRY AND SHOT TOWER

Rte. 52, 7.7 miles southeast of Fort Chiswell. By 1770 Capt. William Herbert had established a ferry across the nearby New River that became known as Jackson's Ferry. Thomas Jackson erected the 75-foot shot tower in the early 1800s to manufacture shot for firearms. The Austinville mines supplied lead for this business. Molten lead was dripped though a sieve from the top of the tower, then fell through the structure and an additional 75-foot shaft beneath the building into a kettle of water. While falling, the lead cooled and developed into

shot pellets; the water cushioned the fall. The shaft was connected to the riverbank by a tunnel though which the shot was carried and then loaded onto boats.

KD-8 AUSTIN'S BIRTHPLACE

Rte. 52, Poplar Camp. Near Austinville, five miles west, was born Stephen F. Austin, "Father of Texas," November, 1793. He began his colonization work in 1821.

KD-9 CROCKETT'S COVE

Rtes. 600 and 603. Crockett's Cove has been home to the Crockett family for two centuries. It was named for Lt. John Crockett, Sr. (1737–1799), son of Samuel and Esther Thompson Crockett, a Revolutionary War veteran buried in the family cemetery a mile east. His half-brother Lt. Col. Robert Sayers (1754–1826), buried on a hill near him, also served in the war and later became a justice of the peace and a member of the Virginia General Assembly. On 10 May 1864 during the Civil War, just east of the Allen Crockett house here, occurred a cavalry engagement between the brigades of Union Brig. Gen. William W. Averell and Confederate Brig. Gen. William E. "Grumble" Jones.

KD-10 WYTHE COUNTY POORHOUSE FARM

Rte. 610, approximately 2 miles east of I-77. The 340-acre Wythe County Poorhouse Farm was established in 1858 for the care of the elderly, disabled, and impoverished people of Wythe County. It was governed by the Wythe County Board of Supervisors and owned by the county until 1957 when the poorhouse farm was sold at public auction. An administrator known as the overseer of the poor was appointed and paid by the county to operate the facility. The property included eight pauper houses, the overseer's residence, and supporting farm structures. It was listed on the Virginia Landmarks Register in 1999 and the National Register of Historic Places in 2000.

Z Marker List

Historical markers with a Z followed by a number at the top are placed at county and state lines. One side of the marker includes facts about the jurisdiction the traveler is entering, and the other includes information about the jurisdiction the traveler is leaving.

Z-1	Accomack/Northampton Counties; Rte. 13	Z-19	Rockbridge/Amherst Counties; Rte. 501
Z-2	Richmond/Northumberland Counties; Rte. 360	Z-20	Nelson/Albemarle Counties; Rte. 250
Z-3	Richmond/Lancaster Counties; Rte. 3	Z-21	Albemarle/Nelson Counties; Rte. 29
Z-4	Westmoreland/Northumberland Counties; Rte. 202	Z-22	Buckingham/Fluvanna Counties; Rte. 15
Z-5	Westmoreland/Richmond Counties; Rte. 3	Z-23	Louisa/Fluvanna Counties; Rte. 15
Z-6	King George/Westmoreland Counties; Rte. 3	Z-24	Prince Edward/Appomattox Counties; Business Rte. 460
Z-7	Stafford/King George Counties; Rte. 3	Z-25	Fluvanna/Goochland Counties; Rte. 250
Z-8	Gloucester/Mathews Counties; Rte. 14	Z-26	King William/King and Queen Counties; Rte. 33
Z-9	King and Queen/Gloucester Counties; Rte. 33	Z-27	Goochland/Henrico Counties; Rte. 6
Z-10	King and Queen/Gloucester Counties; Rte. 14	Z-28	Goochland/Henrico Counties; Rte. 250
Z-11	Rappahannock/Madison Counties; Rte. 231	Z-30	Southampton/Isle of Wight Counties; Rte. 58
Z-12	Madison/Orange Counties; Rte. 15	Z-31	Sussex/Southampton Counties; Rte. 35
Z-13	Madison/Greene Counties; Rte. 29		
Z-14	Orange/Greene Counties; Rte. 33	Z-32	Greensville/Southampton Counties; Rte. 58
Z-15	Albemarle/Greene Counties; Rte. 29	Z-33	Sussex/Greensville Counties; Rte. 301
Z-16	Rockingham/Greene Counties; Rte. 33	Z-34	Prince George/Sussex Counties; Rte. 35
Z-17	Amherst/Campbell Counties; Business Rte. 29	Z-35	Dinwiddie/Sussex Counties; Rte. 40
Z-18	Nelson/Amherst Counties; Rte. 151		

Z-36	Brunswick/Greensville Counties; Rte. 58	Z-62	Pittsylvania/Halifax Counties; Rte. 360
Z-37	Dinwiddie/Brunswick Counties; Rte. 1	Z-63	Halifax/Charlotte Counties; Rte. 92
Z-38	Mecklenburg/Brunswick Counties; Rte. 58	Z-64	Campbell/Charlotte Counties; Rte. 40
Z-39	Nottoway/Dinwiddie Counties; Rte. 460	Z-65	Campbell/Halifax Counties; Rte. 501
Z-40	Lunenburg/Brunswick Counties; Rte. 137	Z-66	Amherst/Bedford Counties; Rte. 501
Z-41	Lunenburg/Mecklenburg Counties; Rte. 49	Z-67	Bedford/Campbell Counties; Rte. 43
Z-42	Lunenburg/Mecklenburg Counties; Off Rte. 138	Z-68	Botetourt/Bedford Counties; Rte. 460
Z-43	Charlotte/Mecklenburg Counties; Rte. 92	Z-69	Roanoke/Franklin Counties; Rte. 220
Z-44	Charlotte/Mecklenburg Counties; Rte. 15	Z-70	Craig/Roanoke Counties; Rte. 311
Z-45	Lunenburg/Nottoway Counties; Rte. 40	Z-71	Henry/Pittsylvania Counties; Rte. 58
Z-46	Charlotte/Lunenburg Counties; Rte. 40	Z-72	Henry/Patrick Counties; Rte. 58
Z-47	Amelia/Chesterfield Counties; Rte. 360	Z-73	Henry/Franklin Counties; Rte. 220
Z-48	Nottoway/Amelia Counties; Rte. 360	Z-74	Floyd/Patrick Counties; Rte. 8
Z-50	Cumberland/Powhatan Counties; Rte. 13	Z-75	Floyd/Patrick Counties; Rte. 58
		Z-76	Alleghany/Botetourt Counties; Rte. 220
Z-51	Prince Edward/Charlotte Counties; Rte. 15	Z-77	Alleghany/Rockbridge Counties; Rte. 850
Z-52	Charlotte/Prince Edward Counties; Rte. 360	Z-78	Bath/Alleghany Counties; Rte. 220
Z-53	Prince Edward/Nottoway Counties; Rte. 460	Z-79	Bath/Alleghany Counties; Rte. 42
Z-54	Nottoway/Prince Edward Counties; Rte. 360	Z-80	Montgomery/Pulaski Counties; *Missing* (was on Rte. 11)
Z-55	Cumberland/Prince Edward Counties; Rte. 45	Z-81	Montgomery/Floyd Counties; Rte. 8
Z-56	Appomattox/Prince Edward Counties; Rte. 460	Z-82	Carroll/Floyd Counties; Rte. 58
Z-57	Appomattox/Buckingham Counties; Rte. 60	Z-83	Giles/Montgomery Counties; Rte. 460
Z-58	Campbell/Appomattox Counties; Rte. 460	Z-84	Bland/Wythe Counties; Rte. 21
		Z-85	Smyth/Grayson Counties; Rte. 16
Z-59	Buckingham/Prince Edward Counties; Rte. 15	Z-86	Grayson/Carroll Counties; Rte. 58
		Z-86	Grayson/Carroll Counties; Rte. 221
Z-60	Pittsylvania/Campbell Counties; Business Rte. 29	Z-88	Wythe/Grayson Counties; Rte. 21
		Z-89	Carroll/Wythe Counties; Rte. 52
Z-61	Pittsylvania/Halifax Counties; Rte. 40	Z-91	Washington/Russell Counties; Rte. 19
		Z-92	Dickenson/Russell Counties; Rte. 63
		Z-93	Buchanan/Russell Counties; Rte. 80
		Z-94	Wise/Russell Counties; Alt. Rte. 58

Z-95   Scott/Washington Counties;
       Rte. 58
Z-96   Wise/Lee Counties; Rte. 58
Z-97   Lee/Scott Counties; Rte. 58
Z-99   Middlesex/Gloucester Counties;
       Rte. 17
Z-100 Pulaski/Wythe Counties; Old Rte.
       11/F-044
Z-101 Tazewell/Smyth Counties; Rte. 91
Z-102 Wythe/Smyth Counties; Rte. 11
Z-103 Wythe/Carroll Counties; Rte. 52
Z-104 Carroll/Grayson Counties; Rte. 94
Z-105 Roanoke/Montgomery Counties;
       Rte. 11/460
Z-106 Botetourt/Roanoke Counties;
       Rte. 11
Z-106 Botetourt/Roanoke Counties;
       Rte. 11
Z-107 Franklin/Pittsylvania Counties;
       Rte. 40
Z-108 Augusta/Rockbridge Counties;
       Rte. 42
Z-109 Augusta/Rockbridge Counties;
       Rte. 11
Z-110 Augusta/Highland Counties;
       Rte. 250
Z-111 Augusta/Nelson Counties; Rte. 250
Z-114 Appomattox/Charlotte Counties;
       Rte. 26
Z-115 Prince George/Surry Counties;
       Rte. 10
Z-116 Amelia/Dinwiddie Counties;
       Rte. 33
Z-117 Bedford/Campbell Counties;
       Rte. 221
Z-118 Bedford/Franklin Counties;
       Rte. 122
Z-120 Clark/Fauquier Counties; Rte. 50
Z-121 Clark/Frederick Counties; Rte. 50
Z-122 Frederick/Clark Counties; Rte. 7
Z-123 Frederick/Clark Counties; Rte. 340
Z-124 Rappahannock/Culpeper Counties;
       Rte. 211
Z-125 Shenandoah/Page Counties;
       Rte. 211
Z-126 Clark/Warren Counties; Rte. 12
Z-128 Tennessee/Lee County; Rte. 70
Z-129 Rockbridge/Botetourt Counties;
       Rte. 11
Z-130 Lee County/Tennessee; Rte. 58

Z-131 Buchanan County/West Virginia;
       Rte. 83
Z-132 Smyth/Washington Counties;
       Rte. 91
Z-133 Wise/Dickenson Counties; Rte. 83
Z-134 Lee/Scott Counties; Rte. 23
Z-135 Rockbridge/Bath Counties;
       Rte. 42/39
Z-136 Nelson/Appomattox Counties;
       Rte. 60
Z-137 Amherst/Nelson Counties; Rte. 60
Z-138 Rockbridge/Amherst Counties;
       Rte. 60
Z-139 Pittsylvania/Halifax Counties;
       Rte. 58
Z-140 Halifax County/North Carolina
       Rte. 501
Z-141 Page/Rockingham Counties;
       Rte. 340
Z-142 Buckingham/Cumberland Coun-
       ties; Rte. 60
Z-143 Loudoun/Fairfax Counties; Rte. 7
Z-144 Fairfax/Prince William Counties;
       Rte. 1
Z-145 New Kent/James City Counties;
       Rte. 30
Z-146 Albemarle/Fluvanna Counties;
       Rte. 250
Z-147 Henrico/Hanover Counties;
       Rte. 360
Z-148 Caroline/Hanover Counties; Rte. 2
Z-149 Spotsylvania/Caroline Counties;
       Rte. 2
Z-150 Nelson/Amherst Counties; Rte. 29
Z-151 Albemarle/Louisa Counties;
       Rte. 22
Z-153 Henrico/Charles City Counties;
       Rte. 5
Z-154 Hanover/Henrico Counties; Rte. 1
Z-155 Caroline/Hanover Counties; Rte. 1
Z-156 Spotsylvania/Caroline Counties;
       Rte. 1
Z-157 Culpeper/Madison Counties;
       Rte. 29
Z-158 Stafford/Prince William Counties;
       Rte. 1
Z-160 Hanover/King William Counties;
       Rte. 211
Z-162 New Kent/James City Counties;
       Rte. 60

Z-163   Henrico/New Kent Counties; Rte. 60

Z-164   Caroline/Essex Counties; Rte. 17

Z-165   Essex/Middlesex Counties; Rte. 17

Z-166   King and Queen/Essex Counties; Rte. 360

Z-167   Orange/Spotsylvania Counties; Rte. 20/3

Z-168   Loudoun/Fairfax Counties; Rte. 50

Z-169   Prince William/Fairfax Counties; Rte. 29

Z-170   Fauquier/Prince William Counties; Rte. 28

Z-171   Rockingham/Augusta Counties; Rte. 11

Z-173   Warren/Rappahannock Counties; Rte. 522

Z-174   Page/Rappahannock Counties; Rte. 211

Z-175   Rappahannock/Culpeper Counties; Rte. 522

Z-176   Culpeper/Orange Counties; Rte. 3

Z-178   Shenandoah/Rockingham Counties; Rte. 11

Z-179   Frederick/Shenandoah Counties; Rte. 11

Z-180   Clark/Loudoun Counties; Rte. 7

Z-181   Fauquier/Loudoun Counties; Rte. 626

Z-182   Rockingham/Augusta Counties; Rte. 42

Z-183   Dickenson/Buchanan Counties; Rte. 83

Z-184   Buchanan/Tazewell Counties; Rte. 460

Z-185   Appomattox/Buckingham Counties; Rte. 24

Z-186   Floyd/Roanoke Counties; Rte. 221

Z-187   Fauquier/Culpeper Counties; Rte. 15/29

Z-188   Culpeper/Madison Counties; Rte. 15

Z-189   Lee/Wise Counties; Alt. Rte. 58

Z-190   West Virginia/Tazewell County; Rte. 16

Z-191   Southampton/Isle of Wight Counties; Rte. 460

Z-192   Dickenson/Wise Counties; Rte. 60

Z-193   Louisa/Hanover Counties; *Missing* (was on Rte. 33)

Z-193   Henrico/Hanover Counties; Rte. 33

Z-194   Alleghany County/West Virginia; Rte. 311

Z-195   Wise/Scott Counties; Rte. 72

Z-196   Mecklenburg/Brunswick Counties; Rte. 1

Z-197   Cumberland/Powhatan Counties; Rte. 60

Z-198   Halifax/Mecklenburg Counties; Rte. 58

Z-199   Highland/Bath Counties; Rte. 220

Z-200   Spotsylvania/Caroline Counties; Rte. 17

Z-201   Rockingham/Augusta Counties; Rte. 340

Z-202   Craig/Giles Counties; Rte. 42

Z-203   North Carolina/Grayson County; Rte. 221/21

Z-204   Carroll/Floyd Counties; Rte. 221

Z-205   Maryland/Accomack County; Rte. 13

Z-206   Loudoun County/Maryland; Rte. 15

Z-207   Pittsylvania County/North Carolina; Rte. 29

Z-208   Pittsylvania County/North Carolina; Rte. 62

Z-209   Craig County/West Virginia; Rte. 311

Z-210   West Virginia/Clark County; Rte. 340

Z-211   West Virginia/Giles County; Rte. 460

Z-212   West Virginia/Highland County; Rte. 84

Z-213   Rockingham County/West Virginia; Rte. 33

Z-214   West Virginia/Bland County; Rte. 52

Z-215   West Virginia/Frederick County; Rte. 522

Z-216   Roanoke/Botetourt Counties; Rte. 460

Z-217   West Virginia/Frederick County; Rte. 50

Z-218   Mecklenburg County/North Carolina; Rte. 1

Z-219   Mecklenburg County/North Carolina; Rte. 15

Z-220   Henry County/North Carolina; Rte. 220

Z-221   Washington County/Tennessee; Rte. 75

Z-222   Tazewell County/West Virginia; Rte. 19

Z-223   West Virginia/Alleghany County; Rte. 311

Z-224   Greensville County/North Carolina; Rte. 301

Z-225   Norfolk County/North Carolina; Rte. 17

Z-226   Kentucky/Lee County; Rte. 58

Z-227   Carroll County/North Carolina; Rte. 52

Z-228   Kentucky/Wise County; Rte. 23

Z-229   Kentucky/Wise County; Rte. 160

Z-230   Scott County/Tennessee; Rte. 23

Z-231   Southampton County/North Carolina; Rte. 255

Z-232   Patrick County/North Carolina; Rte. 8

Z-233   West Virginia/Highland County; Rte. 220

Z-236   Prince George/Sussex Counties; Rte. 301

Z-237   Nottoway/Lunenburg Counties; *Missing* (was on Rte. 45)

Z-238   Nottoway/Dinwiddie Counties; Rte. 40

Z-240   Prince George/Sussex Counties; Rte. 460

Z-241   Henry County/North Carolina; Rte. 87

Z-242   Surry/Isle of Wight Counties; Rte. 10

Z-244   Smyth/Washington Counties; Rte. 11

Z-245   Washington County/Tennessee; Rte. 91

Z-246   Caroline/King William Counties; Rte. 30

Z-247   Shenandoah/Warren Counties; Rte. 55

Z-248   Warren/Page Counties; Rte. 340

Z-249   West Virginia/Frederick County; Rte. 55

Z-250   Grayson County/North Carolina; Rte. 89

Z-251   Kentucky/Lee County; Rte. 42

Z-252   Gloucester/Mathews Counties; Rte. 198

Z-253   King George/Caroline Counties; Rte. 301

Z-254   Roanoke/Bedford Counties; Rte. 24

Z-255   Bedford/Campbell Counties; Rte. 460

Z-256   Wythe/Carroll Counties; Rte. 100

Z-257   Henry/Franklin Counties; Rte. 108

Z-258   Giles/Pulaski Counties; Rte. 100

Z-259   Giles/Bland Counties; Rte. 42

Z-260   North Carolina/Patrick County; Rte. 773

Z-261   Montgomery/Pulaski Counties; Rte. 114

Z-262   North Carolina/Patrick County; Rte. 103

Z-263   Pulaski/Wythe Counties; Rte. 100

Z-266   James City/York Counties; Rte. F-137

Z-268   Sussex/Southampton Counties; Rte. 460

Z-277   Orange/Louisa Counties; Rte. 231

Z-277A Louisa/Orange Counties; Rte. 33/15

Z-278   Culpeper/Fauquier Counties; Rte. 211

Z-279   Culpeper/Orange Counties; Rte. 522

Z-280   Fauquier/Warren Counties; Rte. 55

Z-281   Loudoun/Prince William Counties; Rte. 15

Z-282   Nelson/Buckingham Counties; Rte. 56

Z-283   Frederick/Shenandoah Counties; Rte. 55

Z-284   Nottoway/Amelia Counties; Rte. 40

Z-285   Prince Edward/Nottoway Counties; Rte. 307

Z-286   West Virginia/Alleghany County; I-64 East rest area, in Alleghany County

Z-287   Tennessee/Washington County; Rtes. 421 and 75

Z-288 Kentucky/Buchanan County;
Rte. 460

Z-289 West Virginia/Giles County;
Rte. 219

Z-290 West Virginia/Highland County;
Rte. 250

Z-291 West Virginia/Frederick County;
Rte. 11

Marker Name Index

Marker Number Index

Subject Indexes

TRANSPORTATION AND COMMUNICATION